INSIDERS

INSIDERS' GUIDE® TO CINCINNATI

SEVENTH EDITION

FELIX WINTERNITZ AND
SACHA DEVROOMEN BELLMAN

INSIDERS' GUIDE®

GUILFORD, CONNECTICUT
AN IMPRINT OF THE GLOBE PEQUOT PRESS

The prices and rates in this guidebook were confirmed at press time. We recommend, however, that you call establishments before traveling to obtain current information.

To buy books in quantity for corporate use or incentives, call **(800) 962–0973, ext. 4551,** or e-mail **premiums@GlobePequot.com.**

INSIDERS' GUIDE®

Previous editions of this book were published by Falcon Publishing Inc. in 1998 and 2000.

Lyrics on page 174 by Zak Morgan
Text design by LeAnna Weller Smith
Maps by XNR Productions Inc. © Morris Book Publishing, LLC

ISSN 1527-1188
ISBN-13: 978-0-7627-4180-9
ISBN-10: 0-7627-4180-5

Manufactured in the United States of America
Seventh Edition/First Printing

CONTENTS

Directory of Maps

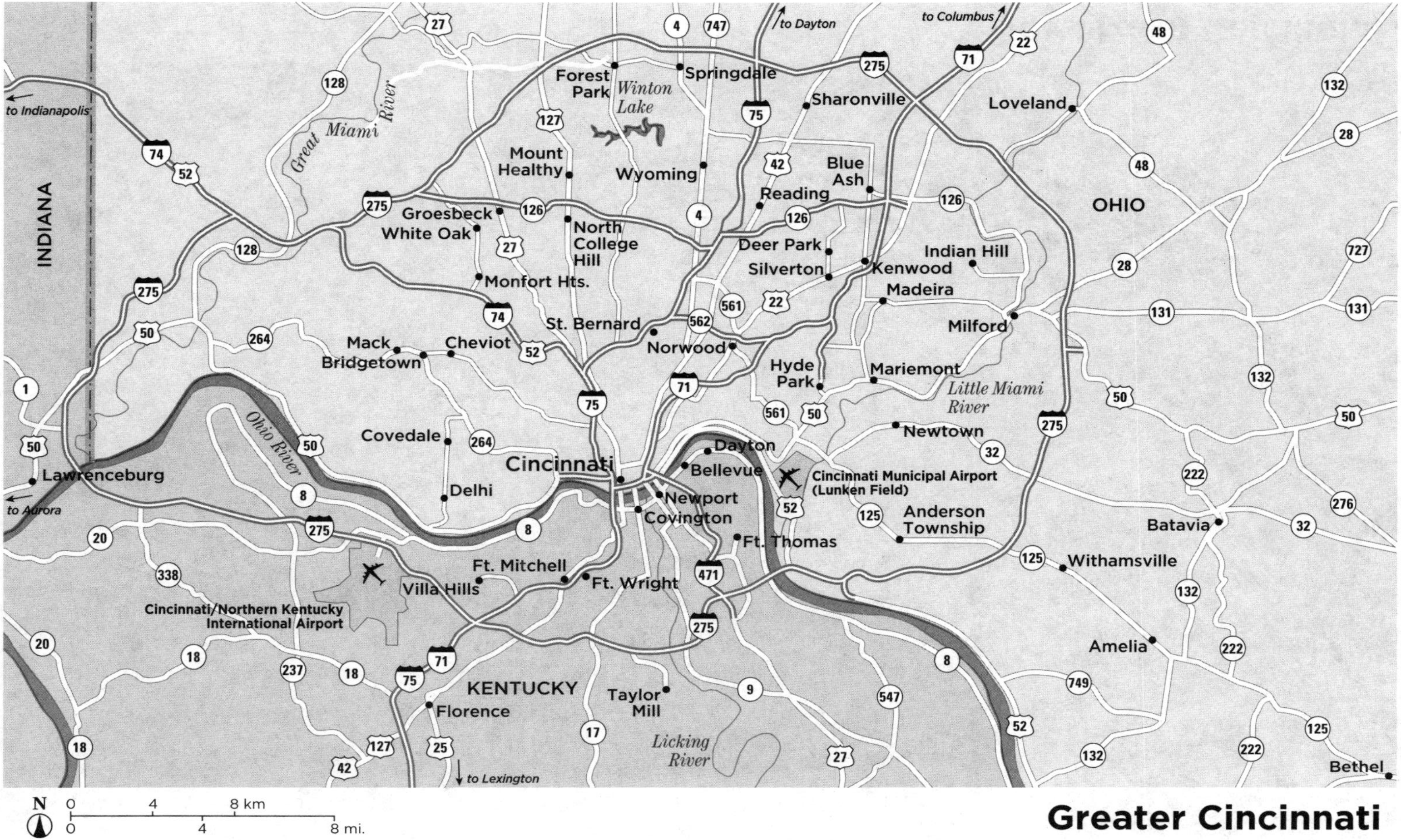

Greater Cincinnati

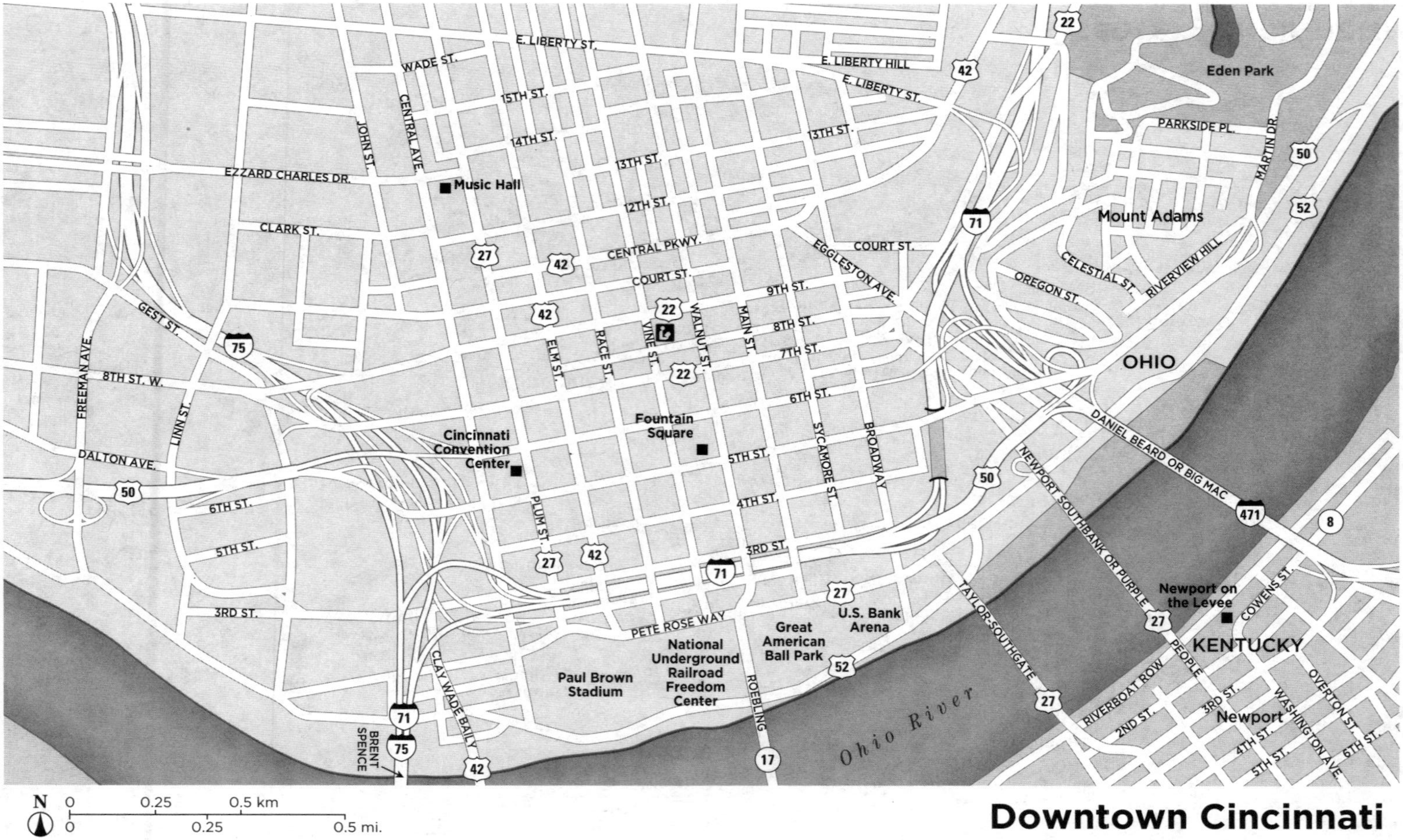

Downtown Cincinnati

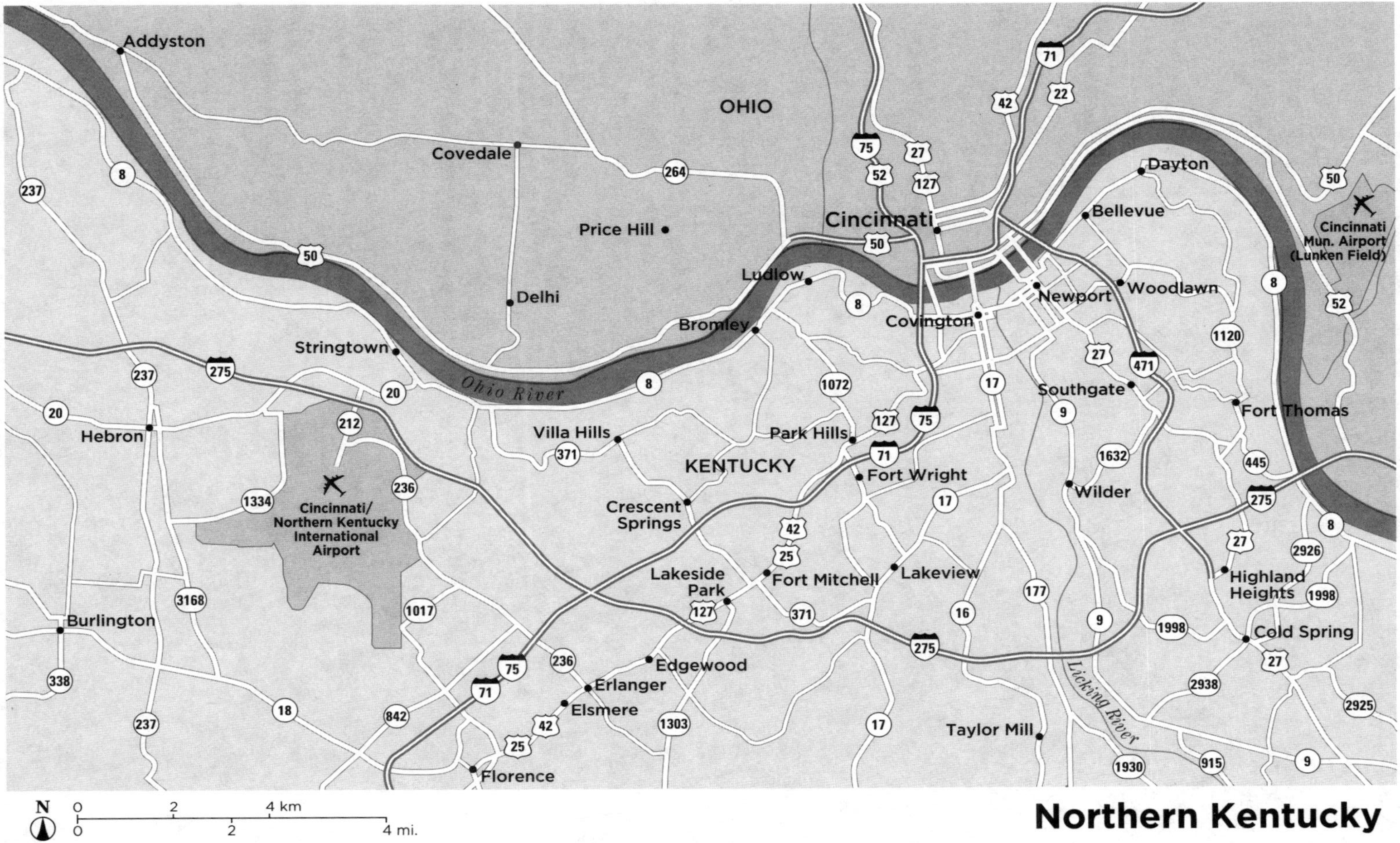
Northern Kentucky
OHIO
KENTUCKY
Ohio River
Licking River
Addyston
Covedale
Price Hill
Delhi
Cincinnati
Ludlow
Bromley
Stringtown
Covington
Newport
Bellevue
Dayton
Woodlawn
Southgate
Fort Thomas
Wilder
Cincinnati Mun. Airport (Lunken Field)
Highland Heights
Cold Spring
Taylor Mill
Park Hills
Fort Wright
Villa Hills
Crescent Springs
Lakeside Park
Fort Mitchell
Lakeview
Edgewood
Erlanger
Elsmere
Florence
Hebron
Burlington
Cincinnati/ Northern Kentucky International Airport
N
0 2 4 km
0 2 4 mi.

PREFACE

If you haven't seen Greater Cincinnati in, say, the past 15 years, you wouldn't recognize the place.

The downtown is in the midst of a retail and lively arts renaissance, with a new department store, the downtown Tower Place mall, a new Tiffany's, and the Aronoff Center for the Arts, a mighty state-funded theatrical complex that brings a taste of Broadway to the city. The Backstage area sprouting up around the Aronoff features shops and restaurants open late into the night, defying the city's long-standing reputation as a place that rolls up the sidewalks at 7:00 P.M. And there's the Lois & Richard Rosenthal Center for Contemporary Art, a $34 million high-rise museum. Architect Zaha Hadid's design has been praised by no less than the *New York Times* for its innovation.

Down on the riverfront, there's the recently opened National Underground Railroad Freedom Center and the Great American Ball Park for the Cincinnati Reds. Paul Brown Stadium and development of "the Banks"—an engaging concept of restaurants, theaters, and condos—add to the mix. Fort Washington Way along the river has been reconfigured to accommodate all these, the largest public works project in the history of Cincinnati.

Look across the river, where hotels are sprouting up in reaction to the Northern Kentucky Convention Center and the Newport Aquarium. Other hot spots on the "south side of Cincinnati," as Northern Kentucky labels itself in this era of regional cooperation, are the Newport on the Levee entertainment, restaurant, and retail complex, as well as the Kentucky Speedway.

The Cincinnati/Northern Kentucky International Airport, for its part, is now one of the busiest in the country. The corporate relocation of Ashland Inc. to Northern Kentucky, as well as the opening of Toyota's massive Midwest Parts Center, is a significant achievement and solidifies Northern Kentucky's reputation as a medium for economic growth. To the west, meanwhile, the powerhouse presence of resort casinos is changing the face of rustic Indiana river towns and bringing millions more travelers to the region.

The biggest recent event was the opening of the National Underground Railroad Freedom Center. The $110 million museum commemorates the Underground Railroad network that helped slaves escape from the South during the 1800s.

The Freedom Center is built on the banks of the Ohio River along the Cincinnati shoreline. (The Ohio River was known by escaping slaves as the "River Jordan.") Three pavilions represent freedom, courage, and the cooperation needed to support the 19th-century freedom movement. Glass passageways link the pavilions, which feature undulating walls and roofs.

The region is growing—and fast. Greater Cincinnati's population shattered the two million mark in 2000, reports the U.S. Census Bureau. And if growth in the northern suburbs continues, experts predict that "Cin-Day" is soon coming—an eventual merger of the metropolitan areas of Cincinnati and Dayton.

Of course, with prosperity comes change—and confusion. That's where the *Insiders' Guide to Cincinnati* comes in. We approached this book as if we were putting an arm around our visiting uncle or aunt's shoulder, whispering inside information, and offering advice about this river city that only a local could possibly know.

Greater Cincinnati is a city of neighborhoods. That's the first thing you should learn if you're a newcomer, especially if you hail from a city that's one great metro government such as Columbus, Indianapolis, or the like. Greater Cincinnati crosses the borders of three states and is composed of some 200 distinct villages, townships, hamlets, boroughs, towns, and cities individual in character and in content.

Even the city of Cincinnati proper is split into dozens of urban neighborhoods, and believe us, residents know *exactly* where the borders are. Don't confuse Mount Adams with Mount Airy, or you'll appear the dunce. Such urban neighborhoods as Price Hill, Avondale, Walnut Hills, the East End, Hyde Park, and Mount Lookout have distinct cultures and quasi-governmental councils. You'll be amazed to find families who have been born, lived, and died in the same neighborhood for generations.

If you've just moved to Cincinnati—or even if you're visiting—be careful. You may just get stuck here for the rest of your life because you'll never want to leave. This happens to unsuspecting folks who think they've been transferred to some backwater burg only to find that the burg has just about everything they like about bigger cities, such as premier arts institutions and terrific restaurants, without so many of the things they don't like, such as rampant crime and other pronounced forms of urban decay.

Cincinnati is a great place to rear a family. It offers many choices of safe neighborhoods and schools, both urban and suburban. It's also a beautiful city with a varied collection of grand mansions and vintage buildings because it was the second-biggest city this side of the Alleghenies in the mid-1800s. Thanks to the handiwork of Ice Age glaciers, Cincinnati also offers a variety of stunning views atop its seven hills. Cincinnati, in fact, spends more money on hillside reclamation and erosion control than any city in America, including San Francisco.

If you're a tourist, you are not alone. Nearly 6 million convention delegates and other visitors traveled to downtown Cincinnati recently, pumping $3 billion into the local economy. Outlying tourism attractions thrived, as well. Some 6 million people visited the Argosy Riverboat Casino; 5 million hit the Grand Victoria Casino; 4 million flocked to Paramount's Kings Island amusement park; 2 million headed to Reds games; 13 million visited the Cincinnati Zoo; 1 million flowed through Museum Center; and another nearly 3 million tourists divided up their visits between the Bengals, Renaissance Festival, the Beach Waterpark, Riverbend Music Center, Turfway Park, and Coney Island.

If you're moving to town, welcome to perhaps the happiest city in Ohio. Headlines have announced "Region's Colleges Calculate Economic Impact: $1.3 Billion a Year," "Children's Hospital Plans Expansion: $128 Million Project Rivals New Bengals and Reds Stadiums," "Major Crimes Keep Going Down: Violent Cases Fall 16.9 Percent," and "Cincinnati a Biotech Business Hub: City No. 4 in Nation for Emerging Firms." At least a half-dozen corporations are committed to major expansions.

Property values in Hamilton County ballooned by $6 billion in the new century. Residential and commercial properties in the county gained value so fast that they outpaced the gross domestic products of Cuba, El Salvador, Nicaragua, and the Bahamas all put together. With all this economic vitality, it's an exciting time to be living and working in Greater Cincinnati.

The *Insiders' Guide to Cincinnati* is written by two writers who moved to Cincinnati years ago, fell in love with the city, and stayed. What follows is an attempt to give newcomers a guide to this unique place. So kick up your feet, lean back, and give us a read. Then come and enjoy this fabulous city of ours—who knows, maybe you too will end up making it your city.

ACKNOWLEDGMENTS

On my first day in Cincinnati, oh those many years ago, I landed at the airport, strolled off the jet, and was shocked to discover I'd somehow wound up in the wrong state. The greeting signs welcomed me to Kentucky. I panicked until a fellow passenger informed me that, strange as it may seem, Greater Cincinnati's international airport isn't even located in the state of Ohio but in Kentucky.

This, I discovered, is quintessential Cincinnati. Confused and perplexed. In desperate need of a guidebook. Here it is.

Thanks go to the dozens of writers and journalists I've worked with along the way since that first day, people who've taught me more about Greater Cincinnati than is imaginable: Mark Bowen, Linda Cagnetti, Toni Cashnelli, Jim DeBrosse, Jim Delaney, John Fox, Patricia Gallagher Newberry, Jon C. Hughes, Sean Hughes, Jim Knippenberg, Gail Madden, Lisa Mauch, Mary McCarty, Dale Parry, Laura Pulfer, Larry Thomas, and many more. To Jerry Grove and Dottie Scott at the Anderson Area Chamber of Commerce for allowing me to tap their considerable knowledge and resources. To Beth Charlton of the Fine Arts Institute, who was always armed with the correct answer. To Janice Forte and Dr. Don Walker at the Cincinnati Historical Society. To Jimmy Gherardi, surely the most plugged-in man in Cincinnati. To Jay and Judy Yeager for all your support and love. To Bernard Adelsberger, Mike Brehm, Doug Scott, and Paul Suszynski for 30 years of friendship. To Roger and Nancy Hopkins-Greene and the entire fellowship at St. Timothy's Episcopal Church. And to the memory of my late mother, Josephine, the wittiest woman I've ever known.

Thanks to my coauthor, Sacha DeVroomen Bellman, and to the folks at The Globe Pequot Press for making this book a reality. And to my predecessors in previous editions, Skip Tate and Jack Neff, who laid much of the groundwork in these pages.

Special thanks go to my wife, Connie Yeager, and our daughters, Kathryn Ann and Abigail Grace. They lived this project as much as I did and aided at every turn. (Well, except the day Abby chewed two pages of a chapter.) I won't thank the cats. Fiddler and Whistler already know they did their part, purring on my lap at every midnight deadline.

—Felix Winternitz

When my family moved to the United States almost 30 years ago, I had never even heard of Cincinnati. My family was moving to Northern Kentucky to a 160-acre horse farm, and I wasn't even aware of what the nearest "big" city was.

But throughout my teenage years and college, I learned a lot about Cincinnati because that's where we went for things to do. I attended concerts and went to nightclubs, sporting events, and restaurants. And when I moved back to the area in 1988, I really learned more about not only the "fun" things but also what it was like to live in Greater Cincinnati.

I was surprised, however, how much information this guidebook has gathered in its various editions. I learned a lot about my city, and in updating it have added my two cents' worth whenever I could.

But I must acknowledge that I wouldn't have been able to do my job without my predecessor, Skip Tate, who was the first author of the *Insiders' Guide to Cincinnati.*

And from the very beginning of this project, my coauthor Felix Winternitz also was there for me, guiding me along the planning process, feeding me information, and being all-around supportive. Thanks, Felix.

I also appreciate the work of my editors for their editing and organizational skills and for the suggestions to make the book better to read and more interesting.

Thanks also to my former colleagues at the *Kentucky Post* and *Community Press* and my students at Miami University for teaching me about all the different places and people in the Greater Cincinnati area. The years I spent at each organization prepared me in many ways for this project. Also thanks to my fellow journalists in the Queen City Chapter of the Society of Professional Journalists for keeping me focused on the profession and its mission to provide information to the public.

More personal thanks go to the many friends and relatives who supported me in this project. First of all, to my husband and partner, Tom Bellman, for all of his love and support. He somehow survived the project and the many days I needed his help in watching the boys because I had a deadline.

My two sons, Brett and Alex Bellman, inspired me to provide a most accurate view of their hometown that they can look back to when they are adults. I appreciated their support throughout the project, which took the form of being quiet when mommy was on the phone.

My mother, Netty DeVroomen, and in-laws, Pat and Larry Bellman, as well as other relatives, provided moral support and always came through when I needed some extra help. Also thanks to Leah Rupp for helping with my research.

I also want to pay tribute to my father, who had the courage and foresight to move to Greater Cincinnati in 1978 to provide a better future for us kids in a fast-growing area of the United States. He lived the American dream for 10 years before he died in 1988. But I'd like to think he's smiling down today on how his youngest daughter is living that same dream in the 21st century.

—Sacha DeVroomen Bellman

HOW TO USE THIS BOOK ?

Unlike some aspects of Greater Cincinnati, there is a logical order to this book. A method to its madness, if you will. Because the book deals with so many topics and each topic covers three states, eight counties, and numerous independent cities, we had no choice but to put some order to it—if not for you, at least for ourselves.

As you work your way through, you may begin to notice some of the patterns and tendencies we've employed. Some are fairly obvious; others are more subtle. They all have their reason for being and their importance, except perhaps for chapter order. We arranged the chapters so that each one has some connection with the chapter before and the chapter after, kind of like the JCPenney catalog. Truly, though, it makes absolutely no difference in what order you read this book. It isn't a novel. Start in the front, in the back, in the middle, with Attractions, with Restaurants, with History, or even with the Insiders' tips (indicated by **i**). If you happen to read it in order, we hope the order will make the trip smoother.

Otherwise, to help you along, here's what we've done:

Many chapters are organized geographically. On a large scale, they begin with the city of Cincinnati and Ohio counties, then head to Northern Kentucky and then Southeastern Indiana. Within the boundaries of Cincinnati and the Ohio counties, we generally subdivided it this way: First, the city, which is the heart of the area, including downtown; then the central suburbs, which are the communities squeezed between Interstates 75, 71, and 275; then the east, west, and north. The east comprises those communities east of I-71, the west those west of I-75, and the north those north of I-275. Some references may be made to northeastern suburbs, an area that is rapidly expanding and developing its own unique characteristics. This area is generally east of I-71 and north of I-275. In listing addresses assume the city is Cincinnati and the state is Ohio unless otherwise stated.

Some chapters, for logical reasons, are arranged in categories, such as types of food or attractions. No matter how the chapters are arranged, the listings in each section are arranged alphabetically.

A word about area codes, however, and that word is "confusion." Ma Bell now assigns no fewer than five area codes to Greater Cincinnati. In southern Ohio, it's either 513 or 937 (with a third designation threatened soon). Sometimes, but not always, you can't connect to a 937 number from the 513 area without having the operator direct dial the number for you. And it's quite possible to be within the 513 area code and still have to dial 513 to reach your number, especially in the far-flung northern towns such as Oxford. That's the Ohio side of things. In Southeastern Indiana, there's yet another area code, 812.

Wait, things get even better. In Northern Kentucky, the area code is either 859 or 606. To simply dial across the Ohio River from Cincinnati to, say, Covington, you have to use the 859 prefix. But don't dial a "1" in front of that prefix, because it's not technically a long-distance call. If you do dial a "1," you get a "sorry, we can't connect, please check your number" recording. There's no rhyme or reason to this. It's the phone company. Just because.

We hope this guide will help you newcomers feel at home and you natives discover something you may have missed.

Although we have made every effort to ensure accuracy and to include all the best of Cincinnati, we're only human. We update this guide every two years, so if you find a mistake, if you disagree with something we've written, or if you'd like to see additions or changes in future editions, please take the time to let us know.

We'd love to hear any suggestions or comments that will help us improve our effort to make the most of your time in Cincinnati. Write to us in care of Insiders' Guides, The Globe Pequot Press, P.O. Box 480, Guilford, CT 06437. Or log on to www.GlobePequot.com—and give us your feedback electronically.

AREA OVERVIEW

Picture Cincinnati in your mind and you think of its beautiful skyline. The scenic Ohio River twisting between the hilly banks. The riverfront, the high-rise office buildings, and downtown, surrounded by neighborhoods seeping into the hills all around the city.

It is very scenic with some prominent landmarks.

You'll see the Carew Tower, Cincinnati's tallest building, which was built in less than a year during the height of the Great Depression by hundreds of hands eager for the work. You'll also see most of the high-rises that have been built since, with new ones going up on both sides of the river on a yearly basis.

It's appropriate that the center of the city is near the riverfront. After all, it is the Ohio River that gave birth to the city and made Cincinnati at one time the second-largest city west of the Alleghenies and the sixth-largest city in the nation. The river continues to be one of the things that draw people downtown. There are some beautiful parks and restaurants that flank both sides of the river.

The skyline changed again with the addition of two sports facilities that have taken the place of Cinergy Field, which used to be known as Riverfront Stadium. More development planned along the river will make the city even more fun to visit.

But the skyline doesn't show you why Partners for Livable Communities named Cincinnati its Most Livable City in 2004.

It's the people. It's like a big city with small-town people. You can ask people on the street for the time of day and they will give it to you. People enjoy spending their lunchtime on Fountain Square along the Tyler Davidson Fountain, talking to each other and watching the world go by.

Many of the first settlers of the city were German, bringing along with them the root of the conservative, hardworking philosophy still evident in many of the city's residents. In the last few decades, the city has become more diverse, with people coming in from all over the world to work at companies in the tristate area. However, the tristate remains very conservative, both politically and socially.

But there are other reasons. Low crime rates, for one—the sixth lowest among major U.S. cities. The area also has some of the lowest unemployment figures and has affordable housing.

In 1993 Cincinnati was rated as America's Most Livable City by *Places Rated Almanac.* Although the city has dropped in the almanac listing since then, it remained in the top 5 percent through five consecutive editions. Its millennium edition rated Cincinnati eleventh.

The city has received other commendations. *Employment Review* also rated Cincinnati in 1996 as one of the 20 best cities in the country in which to live and work, and *Fortune* magazine ranked it seventh among cities balancing business and quality of life. In 1996 *Entrepreneur* magazine ranked Cincinnati seventh on its list of the 30 best cities for small-business development, citing its diverse economy, new zoning laws for home-based businesses, and eager-to-lend banks. In 2004 *Esquire* magazine rated Cincinnati in its top-10 Cities That Rock. And *American Style* magazine rated the Queen City the No. 5 arts destination.

That's plenty of proof for some people that Cincinnati is truly a special place to live. It has the amenities of a big city, they will point out, without most of the urban problems. Others, though, will argue that new ideas are met with cynicism, that the city is so conservative and set in its ways that it can easily be described as dull. Mark Twain, who lived in Cincinnati for six months and left unimpressed, wrote, "If

Greater Cincinnati is made up of about 200 different cities, villages, and townships, but dialing 911 will get you through to the police, fire department, or life squad no matter where you are.

the world would end, I would come to Cincinnati, for everything happens here 10 years later."

Mostly, though, the city is typical. Psychographically, *American Demographics* ranks the area as the ninth most typical metro area in the United States, as measured by a number of attitudinal issues. It is also the eleventh most typical city demographically and one of only four cities nationwide to rank in the top 25 in both categories. A strong showing overall—that's typical of Cincinnati.

Demographically the city of Cincinnati squeezes 331,000 people into just 77.62 square miles. Geographically it is at the midpoint of the 981-mile-long Ohio River and sits 540 feet above sea level. The Cincinnati area is more than just the city, though. It is a region that encompasses portions of three states, eight counties, and dozens of smaller cities, unincorporated townships, incorporated villages, and tiny one-horse towns. Collectively, the area is better known as the tristate or Greater Cincinnati.

Put it on a map and Greater Cincinnati engulfs the southwesternmost portion of Ohio, the northernmost portion of Kentucky, and the southeasternmost portion of Indiana. As a whole, this tristate region takes up 3,810 square miles and includes two million people, making it the second-largest city in Ohio and the 23rd largest in the country.

Despite its size, the area is easily accessible. Even the most distant suburbs are reachable within 30 minutes, affording residents the opportunity to live fairly deep in the country yet still within easy driving distance of downtown. And despite the city's efforts to develop more housing downtown, most of the area's residents live in the suburbs.

NEIGHBORHOODS AT A GLANCE

Greater Cincinnati can be divided into seven geographic areas: the city, central suburbs, East Side, West Side, northern suburbs, Northern Kentucky, and Southeastern Indiana. Ask someone where they live, though, and most won't answer with a geographic area but with a very specific community because even within each region, the communities are very different.

Where you live in Cincinnati automatically brings with it an unspoken commentary about who you are. The *Cincinnati Enquirer* editorial cartoonist Jim Borgman once poked fun at the vast differences between the East Side and the West Side, for instance, equating Vine Street (the dividing point) with the Berlin Wall. On the western side were blue-collar people with bowling balls and kegs of Hudepohl beer, listening to the Reds game on the radio while flipping burgers on the grill. On the East Side were white-collar sorts, playing tennis, drinking Perrier, walking poodles, and shopping at Kenwood Towne Centre. "Gorbachev would have less of an identity crisis settling in California than most of us would have moving across town," Borgman jokes.

There is a big difference between the West Side and East Side, although the lines have gotten blurry the more you move north. Closest to the Ohio River in such communities as Mount Lookout, Mount Adams, Hyde Park, and Oakley, the people are typical of the East Siders described above. On the West Side, places such as Delhi, Cheviot, Price Hill, and Westwood do have a lot of longtime residents whose roots trace the blue-collar people who founded the area. But as soon as you get north of Interstate 74 and the Norwood Lateral, it tends to be more of a mixed bag. Although there are still lots of longtime residents in those areas, the growth of the area has been tremendous, and more "outsiders" have moved in.

The City

Downtown, which is in the river valley and is wrapped on three sides by steep hills, is the anchor of the city. It's been said that Cincinnati is built on seven hills, like Rome, but no two Cincinnatians agree on which seven hills. Cincinnati has 15 "Hill" communities (Bond Hill, College Hill, Crestview Hills, Greenhills, Indian Hill, North College Hill, Oak Hills, Paddock Hills, Park Hills, Price Hill, Seven Hills, Villa Hills, Walnut Hills, Western Hills, and Winton Hills) and nine "Mount" communities (Mount Adams, Mount Airy, Mount Auburn, Mount Carmel, Mount Healthy, Mount Lookout, Mount Repose, Mount Washington, and Mount Zion). Many of the hills and mounts make for wonderful vistas of the city.

City leaders are trying to attract more residents to the city by building affordable dwellings around downtown. Mostly, though, those who live in the city can either afford to live in one of the few upscale developments or can't afford to move. The city also includes the low-income Over-the-Rhine district and Laurel Homes, one of the nation's largest public-housing projects.

Central Suburbs

The central suburbs encompass the greatest array of neighborhoods, from low-income areas such as Lincoln Heights to wealthy communities such as Glendale and Amberley Village. And many of the communities, despite their economic differences, exist side by side. Most of these neighborhoods are well established, and little new development occurs. The central suburbs include Norwood, which is a separate city surrounded on all sides by the city of Cincinnati, and Blue Ash, which was listed in *Places Rated Almanac* as one of the best places in the country to raise a family. The central suburbs offer the best access to all parts of Greater Cincinnati, with Interstate 71, Interstate 75, Ronald Reagan Highway (formerly known as the Cross County Highway), and the Norwood Lateral (Ohio Highway 562) within easy reach.

East Side

The East Side contains the largest collection of affluent neighborhoods in Greater Cincinnati, including Anderson, Mariemont, Hyde Park, Mount Lookout, Madeira, and Greater Cincinnati's most luxurious neighborhood, Indian Hill. Much of the East Side's affluence is the result of the population explosion of young, dual-income families looking for nice places to live. Previously undeveloped farmlands are sprouting new subdivisions, and the outlying edges of what once defined the East Side are now spilling over into bustling Clermont County.

Most of the business activity on the East Side is retail, with many small, quaint, upscale shopping districts such as Hyde Park Square and Mount Lookout Square, in addition to some large malls, such as Anderson Towne Center, Eastgate Mall, Rookwood Pavilion, and the most popular mall in the area, Kenwood Towne Centre. Thousands of stores also line popular roadways such as Beechmont Avenue and Montgomery Road. Interstates 275 and 71 are the two main access routes for the East Side and become crowded during rush hours.

West Side

Older, well-cared-for homes make up most of the West Side. In Cincinnati's early years, when the affluent first headed for the hills to escape the smoke and pollution of the industrial valley that is now downtown, they moved to the West Side. Many of their homes still exist. Most of the homes on the West Side are one-timer homes—lived in by the same family for generations. Homes feature front porches and small yards, and neighborhoods have a Catholic church every few blocks and a small tavern on just about every corner. A few upscale subdivisions are being built on the West Side, some with fantastic river views. The West Side also has some of the area's nicest parks, including Mount Echo Park and Mount Airy Forest.

Northern Suburbs

Residential growth has boomed here, with large, upscale homes built on what only a few years ago were large farm fields. The area includes West Chester, Fairfield, Mason, Landen, and Symmes. Growth in this area is so great that the school districts are being forced to create makeshift classrooms in trailers or, in several instances, build more schools. Lakota School District in West Chester had to close its high school, build two new ones, and split up its students. The area is close to three major shopping malls—Tri-County, Northgate, and Cincinnati Mills—and hundreds of stores along Colerain Avenue and Ohio Highway 4 (commonly called Route 4 or Dixie Highway) but is only about a 30-minute drive from downtown on I-75.

A large number of businesses are also located along the I-75 corridor in the Mason area. The area's annual Homearama event, in which home builders and designers build dream homes and show off their most outrageous ideas, is frequently held on farmland in the northern suburbs. Kings Island, the Beach Waterpark, and the ATP tennis tournament facilities are nearby.

Northern Kentucky

Northern Kentucky likes to call itself the southern side of Cincinnati. It is the area's largest suburb, and growing. To a certain extent, residents (at least longtime residents) still feel a loyalty to one side of the river or the other. Kentucky, to some, is another world. Newcomers, though, usually don't care—what they find so attractive about this area is a lot of affordable homes, including many large Victorian-era homes that are still in good condition, as well as newly built homes on the Bluegrass State's rolling hillsides.

When *Cincinnati Magazine* conducted a study of the area's top neighborhoods, the top three were in Northern Kentucky. Villa Hills was named the most livable neighborhood in Greater Cincinnati by *Cincinnati Magazine* in 1994.

However, Northern Kentucky is a vast area, so it cannot be lumped into one package. It includes everything from the very rural to the very upscale urban. Access to the western half is limited to the always-clogged I-75/I-71. The eastern half is accessible from Interstate 471, with I-275 cutting through the southern portion.

Southeastern Indiana

Many of Cincinnati's workers live in Southeastern Indiana and endure the 30- to 45-minute commute into downtown for one main reason: to take advantage of the rural setting and vast acres available for those who prefer to get away from the city. The homes in areas such as Hidden Valley Lake are large and secluded on wooded tracts.

This area has seen more development, since riverboat gambling was legalized and casinos have opened in Lawrenceburg and Rising Sun, both off U.S. Highway 50 in Southeastern Indiana.

ECONOMY AND GOVERNMENT

Economically, living in Greater Cincinnati is a blessing. The median price of a house in the area is 14 percent cheaper than the U.S. average. A home that costs $345,000 in Boston or $483,000 in San Francisco is only $142,500 here.

Recessions tend to have less of an impact on the area too because of the diversity of local businesses. No single company employs more than 3 percent of the area's population, helping unemployment stay between 3 and 4 percent.

The environment for business has attracted many companies to Greater Cincinnati, and especially Northern Kentucky because of its tax incentives. Look around and you'll see the headquarters of many famous businesses that moved here: Chiquita, Kroger, Federated Department Stores, and Scripps-Howard. Toyota Motor Manufacturing of North America moved its headquarters to Northern Kentucky, and Ashland Inc. left its headquarters in Ashland for riverfront offices in Covington.

Major employers in the area are Kroger, which has 14,000 employees, the federal government with 16,000 employees, Procter & Gamble with 12,000 employees, University of Cincinnati with 15,400 employees, and Health Alliance with 13,000 employees.

And there are plenty of other good numbers to make for a good economy in Greater Cincinnati. The average household income in Greater Cincinnati was $72,041 in 2000, with more than one-third of the households making more than that.

Although people always grumble about paying taxes on that income, Cincinnatians must like government at least a little because we sure have a lot of it, and it can be a confusing mess.

Laws and politics don't cross the borders as easily as workers do. The Greater Cincinnati area has nearly 200 local political jurisdictions, including cities, villages, townships, and counties, and what holds true for one may not hold true for another. And this patchwork of local government can become downright absurd at times. Columbia Township in Hamilton County, for instance, is split by municipal boundaries into several noncontiguous parcels—"God's little half acres," as a township trustee once wryly put it.

Not surprisingly, many longtime residents don't even know which local government they belong to. The city of Cincinnati gets a small windfall each year from suburbanites who think they live in the city limits and thus send the local portion of their license tag fees downtown.

Once in a while some ambitious civic leader, politician, or other sort of do-gooder talks about consolidating some of these governments for the sake of efficiency or sanity. One need only look toward nearby Indianapolis or Lexington to see the benefits of metro government. But such talk is generally short lived in Cincinnati. Don't look for local governments from Madeira or Delhi to willingly surrender power to anyone downtown anytime soon. Even in Northern Kentucky, where the cities are numerous and not as established, metro government has failed to get beyond the talking stage.

The voters in the city of Cincinnati elected their first "strong mayor" in 2001. The city had long been run by a city manager, and the top vote getter in the city council race won the seat of mayor.

Ohio and Indiana counties operate with a three-member commission and a county administrator. In Kentucky the highest elected county official is the judge executive, who oversees the Fiscal Court. An Ohio-Kentucky-Indiana Regional Government also exists for problems that overlap the three states.

No discussion of government in Cincinnati would be complete without mentioning the Cincinnati Business Committee. This is a group of top executives from the major public and private companies in the city that takes an active advocacy—and in many cases advisory—role in government affairs. It is the unofficial fourth branch of Cincinnati government, and some might say more than that.

The Cincinnati City Council and the Cincinnati School Board often have called on the business community for answers to troublesome situations. City council asked former Procter & Gamble chairman and CBC member John Smale

CLOSE-UP

Third-Party Candidates for More Than 80 Years

It's not just the Republicans and Democrats duking it out when it's time for Cincinnati City Council elections. There is a third party alive and well in Cincinnati.

The Charter Committee (dubbed the Charter Party by locals) generally has several candidates running and has been very successful getting them elected, even if they are not well known. The current vice-mayor Jim Tarbell is one of theirs.

"It's the oldest third party in the nation that has continually elected officials to office," observes committee board president Michael Goldman.

It's been almost 80 years since the Charter Committee launched itself with the intent to reinvent local government—and eliminate the corruption of the Boss Cox era—by reforming the city charter.

"Murray Seasongood is the famous name in that first slate of council candidates," notes Goldman, who says he can't even count the number of Charter wins that have come over the decades since. "A lot of council candidates, certainly. And a lot of mayors, most recently Bobbie Sterne and Arn Bortz."

The Charter Party differs from the two major parties because it functions strictly at a local level. "Our candidates are only interested in serving in local government, as citizens, and generally don't have higher office in the back of their minds," Goldman says.

The Charter board of directors is all volunteer: "They are people who are setting aside their national party affiliations to focus on nonpartisan good government at a local level. We have Democrats and Republicans on our board."

Currently, another Charterite on council besides Tarbell is Chris Bortz, a nephew of Arn Bortz.

to lead a study of the city's infrastructure needs in the 1980s, so he did. When Cincinnati's public schools faced a financial crisis in the early 1990s, they turned to the CBC for help, and many of the recommended ways to improve school efficiency and performance were ultimately implemented.

City council also turned to CBC members and other business leaders to help create a development plan for downtown. The downtown reform project, which includes two new sports stadiums, is still under way and is one of the most debated subjects regionally. Efforts are being made to add to the shopping, cultural, residential, and entertainment aspects of downtown.

Greater Cincinnati Vital Statistics

Size: Metropolitan area, which includes counties in Ohio, Kentucky, and Indiana, is 3,810 square miles.

Population: 2 million.

Visitors: 5 million annually.

Airport: Cincinnati/Northern Kentucky International Airport in Boone County, Kentucky.

Sales tax: Ranges from 5 percent in Indiana to 6.25 percent in Adams County, Ohio. Most of the area, including downtown and Northern Kentucky, has a 6 percent sales tax.

Room tax: 10.5 percent downtown.

Median price of home: $142,500.

Average income: $72,041.

Climate: Average annual temperature: 53 degrees; average temperature in January: 31 degrees; average temperature in July: 76 degrees.

Annual precipitation: 41.33 inches.

Percentage of sunny days: 49 percent.

Major attractions: Cincinnati Zoo and Botanical Gardens; Paramount's Kings Island; Newport Aquarium; and riverfront area.

Major sports: Major League Cincinnati Reds baseball and National Football League Cincinnati Bengals.

Major universities: University of Cincinnati, Xavier University.

Major employers: Kroger Company, U.S. Government, Procter & Gamble, University of Cincinnati, and Health Alliance.

Major interstates: Interstates 75, 71, 74, 275, and 471.

Daily newspapers: *Cincinnati Enquirer* and *Cincinnati Post.*

Chamber of commerce and visitor centers: Greater Cincinnati Convention and Visitors Bureau, 300 West Sixth Street, Cincinnati 45202, (513) 621-2142; Northern Cincinnati Convention and Visitors Bureau, 11641 Chester Road, Sharonville 45246, (513) 771-5353; Northern Kentucky Convention and Visitors Bureau, 50 East RiverCenter Boulevard, Suite 100, Covington, Kentucky 41011, (800) 447-8489; Clermont County Convention and Visitors Bureau, 410 East Main Street, Batavia, Ohio 45103, (513) 732-3600; Greater Cincinnati Chamber of Commerce, 441 Vine Street, Suite 300, Cincinnati 45202, (513) 579-3111.

Important dates in Cincinnati's history

October 27, 1811: The very first riverboat, *Orleans,* steams into town, changing everything. A settlement becomes a city in short order.

October 31, 1837: Candle maker William Procter and soap maker James Gamble first formulate plans for starting a soap business together.

December 31, 1866: The Roebling Suspension Bridge opens, providing a much-needed overland link between Kentucky and Ohio.

March 15, 1867: An ordinance is passed by Cincinnati City Council accepting the gift of a public fountain, to be located between Vine and Walnut Streets. The fountain will later grace Fountain Square.

April 5, 1870: Louis Graeter sells his first ice cream from a Court Street market stand. A chip off the old block.

November 7, 1874: The "Tanyard Murder" case unfolds, turning *Cincinnati Enquirer* reporter Lafcadio Hearn into a national figure.

July 1, 1883: Barney Kroger opens a storefront grocery at 66 East Pearl Street on the waterfront. Let's go Krogering.

March 29, 1884: Some 10,000 people riot, burning the Hamilton County Courthouse and killing 56 people. Marchers are upset over the light sentence handed a confessed murderer. The Ohio National Guard is called to quell this, the bloodiest of Cincinnati's 16 major riots to date.

March 21, 1921: Powel Crosley Jr. buys his first radio set and quickly decides to start his own radio manufacturing business. Crackle—the Reds, Crosley cars, WLW radio, and more, are on the horizon.

October 9, 1923: Murray Seasongood, vowing to "starve" out the Boss Cox political machine, launches the Charter Reform Party. The Boss and the "strong mayor" form of government are toast.

March 31, 1933: Work is completed on the city's new transit central, Union Terminal rail station. The cost is $41 million (less than the estimated value of the Rookwood tile in the building today).

January 24, 1937: "Black Sunday" and the Great Ohio River Flood. Glub.

June 10, 1944: A 15-year-old named Joe Nuxhall pitches a Reds game and becomes history's youngest-ever Major Leaguer.

September 9, 1947: The *Island Queen* riverboat burns, essentially ending the steamboat era in Cincinnati. Sniffle.

June 22, 1949: Cincinnati's Ezzard Charles becomes the heavyweight champion of the world. For a half century Charles is the defining athletic figure and role model for Cincinnati kids.

October 8, 1949: Nicholas Lambrinides opens a restaurant in Price Hill, naming it Skyline Chili in honor of the panoramic view. Burp.

April 24, 1960: "Sabin Sunday." Nearly 200,000 Cincinnati schoolchildren are the first of their generation to be inoculated with a new polio vaccine developed by a Children's Hospital physician named Albert B. Sabin.

August 21, 1966: The Beatles play the Cincinnati Gardens. Yeah, yeah, yeah.

June 11, 1967: A black man is arrested for "loitering" near the statue of Abraham Lincoln on Reading Road, prompting more than 400 to riot in Avondale, Bond Hill, Winton Terrace, Walnut Hills, and the West End. The mayor calls out the Ohio National Guard. One person is killed, 63 are injured, and 404 are arrested.

September 16, 1967: Michael Xanadu signs on the air with the *Jelly Pudding Show.* The station is WEBN, and Xanadu is Frank "Bo" Wood. "The Frog" is born.

December 3, 1967: Paul Brown wins the AFL franchise for Cincinnati.

April 4, 1968: Dr. Martin Luther King Jr. is assassinated. Some 260 are arrested in the Cincinnati protests that follow Dr. King's death. Two are killed, 220 are injured.

October 9, 1969: A virtual unknown named George "Sparky" Anderson is hired as the new Cincinnati Reds manager. The headlines decry "Sparky Who?" but the seed of the Big Red Machine is planted.

June 24, 1970: The last game is played at Crosley Field.

June 30, 1970: The first game at Riverfront Stadium.

September 6, 1971: Coney Island closes as a full-scale amusement park. Kings Island is born.

October 28, 1972: Amtrak's "George Washington" leaves Union Terminal, the last train. The rail terminal is closed.

September 8, 1974: A new manuever saves a choking victim. The method was developed by Cincinnati's Dr. Henry Heimlich.

September 17, 1974: The Albee, the last of downtown's grand movie theaters, shuts its doors.

October 22, 1975: Game 7, the World Series. The first of two back-to-back series wins.

January 18, 1977: The Blizzard of '77. At 25 degrees below zero, the Ohio River freezes. Thousands take the opportunity to stroll across the frozen river.

May 28, 1977: The Beverly Hills Supper Club in Southgate, Kentucky, burns, killing 165 people.

October 12, 1977: Sheriff Simon Leis takes on both *Oh! Calcutta* at Music Hall and, in the same month, *Hustler*'s Larry Flynt.

December 1, 1977: Jerry Springer, 33, is sworn in as the city's youngest mayor.

January 11, 1978: The Blizzard of '78. The wind chill reaches 52 degrees below zero, with 50 inches of snow and yet another frozen Ohio River.

September 18, 1978: *WKRP in Cincinnati* premieres on CBS.

November 27, 1978: In Room 1118 of the Los Angeles Airport Marriott, general manager Dick Wagner fires Reds coach Sparky Anderson in a power play.

December 3, 1979: The Who concert at Riverfront Coliseum. Eleven people die, changing the way Cincinnati handles concerts.

June 2, 1984: An Air Canada DC-9 burns on the runway at Greater Cincinnati International, killing 25 passengers.

December 22, 1984: A local car dealer, Marge Schott, announces she is buying the Reds.

September 11, 1985: Peter Edward Rose steps to the plate at Riverfront Stadium. Hit 4,192 surpasses the record set by Ty Cobb.

June 23, 1987: Channel 9 anchor Pat Minarcin airs his investigation, a report that, for the first time, links male nurse Donald Harvey to 40 murders at Drake Hospital.

August 26, 1987: GM shuts its auto plant in Norwood, a 65-year-old institution.

October 14, 1988: The first Tall Stacks opens, the crown of the city's bicentennial celebration.

August 24, 1989: The baseball commissioner bans Pete Rose from the game for life.

April 6, 1990: Mapplethorpe: The Perfect Moment opens at the Contemporary Arts Center (CAC).

October 5, 1990: A jury clears the CAC and its director, Dennis Barrie, of any wrongdoing in showing the Mapplethorpe exhibit.

October 12, 1990: Coach Lou Piniella and his Reds win the World Series, a sweep against Oakland after a wire-to-wire season.

November 3, 1990: Museum Center opens inside the shuttered Union Terminal.

December 24, 1991: Bengals coach Sam Wyche is canned and is replaced by Dave Shula.

May 3, 1998: The *Enquirer* publishes a major series on Chiquita. By the time all the dust settles from the botched investigation, the editor is canned, the reporters are gone, Chiquita is $14 million richer, and American journalism is changed for the worse.

June 10, 2000: The Big Pig Gig kicks off.

August 19, 2000: The first game at Paul Brown Stadium, the taxpayer-funded project to end all public projects.

April 10, 2001: After an unarmed African-American youth is shot and killed by police, rioting breaks out. Eight hundred are arrested in the civil violence that follows, and the city is put under a strict curfew.

November 6, 2001: Cincinnati's first "strong mayor" in nearly a century, Charlie Luken, is elected.

March 25, 2002: The Big Flower Power Gig kicks off. More than 200 lavishly decorated pots overflowing with flowers brighten up downtown Cincinnati and Northern Kentucky.

January 14, 2003: Marvin Lewis is hired as coach of the Cincinnati Bengals and quickly turns around what had been a losing team under Bruce Coslet and Dave Shula.

March 28, 2003: The new Great American Ball Park opens for business on the Cincinnati riverfront.

April 26, 2003: The giant Purple People Bridge opens, offering a new way to cross the Ohio River. The former L&N Railroad Bridge, painted in glorious neon purple, begins a new life as a pedestrian walkway spanning the waters between the Cincinnati shorefront and Newport on the Levee mall in Newport, Kentucky.

May 17, 2003: The Cincinnati Art Museum unveils its new, $10 million wing, while at the same time instituting its "no charge" admission policy. The new wing includes 15 galleries with some 18,000 square feet of exhibit space.

May 31, 2003: The Lois & Richard Rosenthal Center for Contemporary Art opens. The six-floor high-rise is touted by the *New York Times* as a "breakthrough design in the use of space to punch up contemporary art" and by *Newsweek* as "perfect . . . for a museum devoted to the 'art of the last 10 minutes.'"

September 5, 2003: Bats Incredible, a whimsical public art project created in the spirit of the Big Pig Gig from a few summers previous, rolls out sculptures constructed with

Louisville Slugger baseball bats, a nod to Cincinnati's Major League heritage and its new ballpark for the Cincinnati Reds.

May 15, 2004: The Taft Museum of Art reopens, more than two years after it closed for a major renovation. The $23 million facelift includes a new wing, gardens, a performance facility, and a 70-car parking garage.

May 21, 2004: Those demonic, locustlike creatures, the cicadas, return in full force after a 17-year sleep.

May 29, 2004: Boomerang Bay, the giant new water-park resort at Paramount's Kings Island, opens for the first time.

August 21, 2004: The $100 million National Underground Railroad Freedom Center opens. The center commemorates the Underground Railroad network that helped slaves escape from the South during the 1800s as well as all freedom seekers across the world.

July 25, 2005: The Maisonette, the restaurant that has spent more consecutive years on the *Mobil Guide* five-star list than any other culinary institution in America, closes.

August 24, 2005: In an amazing power play, University of Cincinnati Bearcats basketball coach Bob Huggins is forced out by new university president Nancy Zimpher.

November 8, 2005: Ohio state senator Mark Mallory is elected mayor of Cincinnati. He is the first mayor in 70 years who had never served on city council.

Famous folks call Greater Cincinnati "home"

Greater Cincinnati is the home of—or the place once called home by—many of the nation's most famous citizens, from five presidents to stars of the silver screen to great sports legends to corporate leaders. We've compiled a list of some of the better-known citizens we claim as our own. Some of them, we must admit, we claim begrudgingly. Even the sun has its dark spots.

Leaders and Scientists

Neil Armstrong, the first man on the moon.

John James Audubon, naturalist.

Daniel Carter Beard, Boy Scouts founder.

Cardinal Joseph Bernardin, archbishop of Cincinnati.

Jim Bunning, U.S. senator from Northern Kentucky, baseball Hall of Fame pitcher.

Salmon P. Chase, chief justice of the United States.

Powel Crosley Jr., inventor, radio pioneer.

Thomas Edison, inventor.

Ulysses S. Grant, U.S. president.

Benjamin Harrison, U.S. president.

William Henry Harrison, U.S. president.

Rutherford B. Hayes, U.S. president.

Dr. Henry Heimlich, inventor of the Heimlich maneuver.

Charles Keating, lawyer/banker, convicted of fraud in savings and loan scandal.

Kenesaw Mountain Landis, hard-line judge, baseball commissioner.

Charles Manson, convicted murderer.

Adolph Ochs, *New York Times* publisher.

Norman Vincent Peale, clergyman, author of *The Power of Positive Thinking.*

Jerry Rubin, 1960s activist.

Dr. Albert B. Sabin, inventor of oral polio vaccine.

Potter Stewart, U.S. Supreme Court justice.

Robert Taft, U.S. senator.

William Howard Taft, U.S. president.

Ted Turner, businessman.

Artists and Authors

John Alexander, opera star.

Babyface, song producer.

Robert S. Duncanson, painter.

Frank Duveneck, painter.

Henry Farney, painter.

Stephen Foster, composer.

Haven Gillespie, songwriter.

Nikki Giovanni, Pulitzer Prize–winning poet.

Earl Hamner, author.

Erich Kunzel, conductor.

James Levine, Metropolitan Opera musical director.

William Holmes McGuffey, author, *McGuffey Readers.*

Lee Roy Reams, dancer.

John Ruthven, painter.

Thomas Schippers, conductor.

Leopold Stokowski, conductor.

Harriet Beecher Stowe, author.

Mark Twain, author.

Bill Watterson, cartoonist (*Calvin & Hobbes*).

Athletes

Eddie Arcaro, jockey.

Johnny Bench, Hall of Fame catcher for the Reds.

Paul Brown, legendary football coach.

Steve Cauthen, Triple Crown–winning jockey.

Ezzard Charles, former heavyweight boxing champion.

Dave Cowens, basketball Hall of Famer.

Buck Ewing, baseball Hall of Fame catcher.

Ken Griffey, Cincinnati Reds outfielder.

Ken Griffey Jr., Cincinnati Reds outfielder.

David Justice, baseball player.

Barry Larkin, baseball player.

Anthony Munoz, NFL Hall of Fame tackle.

Jim O'Brien, football player.

Darrell Pace, Olympic gold-medal archer.

Aaron Pryor, "The Hawk," former middleweight boxing champion.

Jack "Hacksaw" Reynolds, football player.

Oscar Robertson, the "Big O," arguably the greatest basketball player ever.

Pete Rose, Cincinnati Reds great.

Bud Smith, former lightweight boxing champion.

Roger Staubach, football star.

Bill Talbert, tennis star.

Tony Trabert, tennis star.

Jack Twyman, NBA Hall of Famer.

John Wooden, UCLA's legendary basketball coach.

Entertainers

Theda Bara, silent screen actress.

David Canary, soap star.

Rocky Carroll, actor.

George Clooney, actor.

Nick Clooney, former host of *American Movie Classics,* father of George Clooney, brother of Rosemary.

Rosemary Clooney, singer.

Bootsy Collins, funky 1970s rocker.

Ray Combs, comedian, *Family Feud* host.

Doris Day, actress.

Jimmy Dodd, head Mouseketeer.

Carmen Electra, actress.

Lilias Folan, television yoga instructor (*Lilias, Yoga and You*).

Peter Frampton, 1970s British rock 'n' roll star.

Woody Harrelson, actor.

Libby Holman, singer.

Durward Kirby, TV personality.

Drew Lachey, singer, entertainer.

Nick Lachey, singer, actor

Vicki Lewis, actress.

Annie Oakley, sharpshooter and entertainer.

Hugh O'Brien, actor.

Sarah Jessica Parker, actress.

Tyrone Power, actor.

Edward G. Robinson, actor.

Roy Rogers, singer/cowboy.

Nipsy Russell, rhyming comedian.

Rod Serling, *Twilight Zone* creator.

Red Skelton, comedian.

Steven Spielberg, movie producer.

Ben Turpin, silent screen actor.

Andy Williams, singer.

And ...

Jerry Springer, news anchor, TV personality, radio host, and onetime Cincinnati mayor.

ARTS AND CULTURE

The $82 million Aronoff Center for the Arts, opened in 1995, showcases Broadway Series performances, the Cincinnati Ballet, the Cincinnati Opera, and dozens of smaller productions.

Dozens of small theaters also stage regular performances, including Taft Theater, Showboat Majestic, Playhouse in the Park, University of Cincinnati College-Conservatory of Music, and, of course, Music Hall.

Individuals with a good set of vocal cords can be part of the May Festival Chorus, the oldest chorus in the country (see the Arts chapter). Annual auditions are held for the chorus's 200 spots. Those with an attraction to the silver screen can also find themselves in the movies locally, as filmmakers regularly flock to Cincinnati with cameras in hand and hire extras by the score.

Several top-notch museums cater to lovers of the visual arts. These include the Cincinnati Art Museum, Contemporary Arts Center, and Taft Museum. The area has more than 100 art galleries and annually stages several outdoor arts exhibitions downtown. (See the Arts chapter for lots of information on museums and art galleries.)

For those who prefer cuisine with their culture, 2 blocks west of the Aronoff is the prestigious Palace restaurant in the luxurious Cincinnatian Hotel. Greater Cincinnati has more top-rated restaurants than any other city its size (see the Restaurants chapter).

If you have a taste for something different, Cincinnati chili is an area favorite. The chili is sweet, not hot like Texas chili, and is served over a plate of spaghetti or a hot dog and smothered in cheese.

At one time, one-quarter of the area's population was German immigrants. Although Greater Cincinnati's heritage remains primarily European, there is some ethnic diversity among area residents: 85 percent are white, 13 percent are African-American, and 2 percent are Asian or Hispanic. The median age is 35 years.

Greater Cincinnati's strong German background is still evident, though, in the odd usage of the word "please." When Greater Cincinnatians say "please?" they really mean "pardon me?" "come again," or "what?" This linguistic quirk dates to those German settlers who would say "bitte?"—German for "please?"—when they didn't get your drift. The direct English translation became everyday parlance for most residents. Today you can still identify lifelong Cincinnatians by their use of the word "please?" The usage gets rarer the farther you get from the city and is virtually unheard outside of the eight-county area.

Another local cultural oddity is Parrothead frenzy. Each year when singer Jimmy Buffett performs at Riverbend Music Center, the town becomes crazed, wearing bright flowered shirts, grass skirts, and funky hats decorated with parrots, cheeseburgers, sharks, margarita glasses, salt shakers, and anything else associated with one of Buffett's songs. Cincinnati is where the singer began calling his fans Parrotheads, and the area is perversely proud of that fact.

Otherwise, musical preferences are varied. Country music and hip-hop are just as popular as rock music. Numerous musical groups bring their tours through Greater Cincinnati each year, playing at Riverbend Music Center, U.S. Bank Arena, Great American Ball Park, or even smaller venues such as Bogart's and Paramount's Kings Island.

The Cincinnati Zoo and Botanical Garden is world-renowned as "the sexiest zoo in the country," according to *Newsweek* magazine, because of its successful breeding of wild animals. You'll see plenty of wildlife outside of the zoo too, particularly in area parks. Bald eagles occupy some Hamilton County parks. Hawks, falcons, blue herons, and pheasants are spotted frequently. And the 800-acre Cincinnati Nature Center is a 30-minute drive from downtown. The area has 16,700 acres of parkland, including several city parks that offer an escape from the concrete jungle so typical of most downtowns.

Greater Cincinnati has more than 60 public golf courses and 34 private clubs and plenty of other sporting activities too—most notably Reds baseball and Bengals football. The University of Cincinnati and Xavier University basketball teams are nationally ranked. The ATP tennis tour stops in Greater Cincinnati each year. Two major horse-racing tracks are in the area, and the Kentucky Derby and Indianapolis 500 are both about two hours away. Other annual events such as the World Figure Skating Championships and the NCAA basketball tournament are frequently held here.

For those whose favorite sport is shopping, Greater Cincinnati has more malls than other areas its size, plus smaller shopping centers and traditional retail storefronts.

The Public Library of Cincinnati and Hamilton County has 40 branch libraries and has the second-highest per capita circulation figures in the nation. Surrounding counties have a total of 29 additional libraries.

A few cultural attractions won't be found in Cincinnati, though. There are no strictly adult bookstores (with the glaring exception of Larry Flynt's Hustler bookstores in nearby Monroe and downtown), no peep shows, and no red-light districts.

The establishment of several exotic dance businesses in the area set the vice squad scurrying.

A First Amendment controversy remains in the court system. It involves the Internet; a regional task force raided several local bulletin-board operators and seized their computer equipment because they were allegedly providing access to pornographic material. Even before that, the vice squad invaded the Contemporary Arts Center and charged its director with pandering obscenity for showing a traveling exhibit of photographs by Robert Mapplethorpe. The charges were dropped, but that effort earned Cincinnati the nickname "Town Without Pity," thanks to an article in *GQ* magazine. The whole issue left a scar on the city, and it remains a touchy subject with the citizens, who are split on whether all this censorship is good or bad.

GETTING HERE, GETTING AROUND

Greater Cincinnati is at the crossroads of the country. Although it is considered the Midwest by some around the country, it's kind of in between all the major regions. But that's part of its beauty. It is in the heart of the country with easy access to major points all around. Within a five- to six-hour drive are some major cities including Cleveland, Chicago, and Detroit.

It has five major highways and an airport with a Delta hub, and a river runs through it with eight bridges tying the area together. Besides the main transportation methods, the area also has buses and boats, limos and taxis, river ferries and horse-drawn carriages.

Two major highways run through the Queen City, meeting up downtown to cross the Ohio River together. Interstate 71 runs from Cleveland to Louisville. Interstate 75 runs from Detroit to Miami. It's great to have such major interstates nearby when you're traveling, but when you're driving locally, it oftentimes means those roads are busy.

Every weekend many holiday travelers pass through the Greater Cincinnati area either heading south for vacation or on their way back to Michigan and Ontario. For that reason, Friday night rush hours are a nightmare and Sunday afternoons also can bring traffic jams at the I-75 bridge downtown. But that's the price we must pay for having major interstates.

People who live on the west side of town often have to also deal with the sun—making for interesting traffic reports that mention "sun delays." People who live on the west side of town (off Interstate 74) used to be the blue-collar workers who got to work downtown before the sun was up. They also generally got home before the sun set in the west. So sun was not a problem for them. But now that the workers are more white collar, they end up with the sun in their eyes on the way to and from work during rush hour.

But overall the city is not hard to get around in. The two major highways are well connected with other highways and state routes that will quickly take you to wherever you need to go.

You can make it from one part of the metropolitan area to another in about half an hour—if traffic is moving. The eight bridges across the Ohio River tie all the interstates and areas together. So aside from rush hour and the vacationer traffic jams mentioned above, traffic generally moves pretty well.

Regardless of the multitude of highways, governmental agencies are always looking to the future with talk of broadening our horizons in this area. For several years, there has been discussion of light-rail that would run from Kings Island north of the city to the Cincinnati/Northern Kentucky International Airport southwest of the city.

The city has train service a few times a week to Chicago and Washington, D.C.

There also is quite a lot of competition for airplane dollars. Because Cincinnati/Northern Kentucky International Airport is a Delta hub, there is little airline competition, which makes flights out of that airport expensive. Many of us have discovered that you can find cheaper fares with just a short drive to Louisville, Kentucky; Columbus, Ohio; Dayton, Ohio; or Indianapolis. In recent years airlines that offer cheaper rates have moved in and out of the airport as well.

ROADWAYS AND CROSSINGS

Highways and Interstates

Five major interstate highways—I-75, I-71, I-471, I-275, and I-74—run through the area, creating a maze of roads. Two crosstown arteries—the Norwood Lateral and the Ronald Reagan Highway—add to the jumbled picture along with U.S. Highways 22, 27, 42, 50, 52, and 127 in Ohio and 25 in Northern Kentucky.

I-75 runs north and south from Detroit to Miami and right through the heart of Greater Cincinnati. It's as wide as five lanes through part of the area and is still constantly busy, especially during rush hour and the aforementioned vacation rush. I-75 serves as the main thoroughfare for people living in West Chester and the northern suburbs. Just across the river in Northern Kentucky, the road includes "Death Hill." It got the name from a number of fatal accidents over the years when trucks would come barrelling down the steep slope at high speeds. A truck limit has been in place on the northbound lanes for many years, and the state also has straightened out the curve that added to the problem. The only problem that remains on the hill is that the trucks going south on Death Hill still have a hard time making it up the steep section of road. A tip would be to stay out of the two right lanes so you don't get stuck behind the slow-moving 18-wheelers.

I-71 runs northeast and southwest from Cleveland to Louisville and actually merges with I-75 around downtown before splitting again 20 miles to the south in Northern Kentucky. The highway is the primary access for commuters working in Blue Ash, the area's second-largest business district, as well as for residents of Landen, Loveland, and other northeastern suburbs. It also is tied in with I-471 and Columbia Parkway downtown.

I-275 is the beltway that encircles the area, running through six counties in Cincinnati, Northern Kentucky, and Southeastern Indiana. It is one of the the longest full-circumferential beltways in the nation, at 83 miles long. The northern section from Tri-County Mall all the way to I-71 and the eastern section between I-71 and I-471 are the busiest on a daily basis. The airport also is along this highway in Northern Kentucky; the west loop goes about 3 miles through Indiana. Trucks that don't have business in the area are supposed to take this loop, although many don't as it does add a little time to the trip.

I-471 runs from the eastern part of I-275 in Northern Kentucky to downtown. The highway is only about 5 miles long, ending at the entrance to Northern Kentucky University in Highland Heights. But it is highly traveled by downtown commuters from Northern Kentucky and eastern Cincinnati.

I-74 begins at I-75 just northwest of downtown, runs west through Indianapolis, and ends in Iowa's Quad Cities. The highway serves the western suburbs and Southeastern Indiana and is usually busy during rush hours as well leading to and from downtown.

The **AA Highway** (Alexandria, Kentucky, to Ashland, Kentucky) connects Greater Cincinnati with Interstate 64 in eastern Kentucky, which stretches southeast to Norfolk, Virginia.

The **Norwood Lateral** (aka Ohio Highway 562) and **Ronald Reagan Highway** (Ohio Highway 126; formerly the Cross County Highway) provide crosstown shortcuts, running east-west inside of the I-275 beltway. The Norwood Lateral runs between I-71 and I-75. It should be noted,

Listen to WLW radio (700 AM) for traffic reports every 10 minutes during rush hours. The reports tell where the problems are, suggests alternate routes, and verbally chastises people who unnecessarily cause traffic problems.

Getting Out of Town

City	Miles	Drive Time	Flight Time
Atlanta	373	9 hours	1:09
Boston	752	17 hours	1:52
Chicago	265	6 hours	1:02
Cleveland	221	5 hours	:50
Columbus	116	2 hours	:36
Detroit	230	5 hours	:51
Indianapolis	98	2 hours	:32
New York	589	13 hours	1:34
Philadelphia	507	11 hours	1:24
Washington, D.C.	411	10 hours	1:04

however, that there are no signs in the city that say "Norwood Lateral." It's just a given name, and everyone assumes everyone else knows what it is. The signs actually say NORWOOD and OHIO 562. Ask someone, though, what Ohio 562 is and they probably won't know.

The Norwood Lateral's crosstown companion, the Ronald Reagan Highway runs from I-275 in western Hamilton County to Montgomery Road in Montgomery on the east side of town.

Bridges

One big aspect of transportation around this river town are the eight bridges that connect Cincinnati to Northern Kentucky, the names of which are often mentioned in directions and on the radio as the cause of traffic backups. With the exception of the Roebling Suspension Bridge, named after builder John Roebling, almost all the bridges carry the names of famous Kentuckians because most of the Ohio River is under Kentucky's jurisdiction. Several of the bridges are better known by nicknames, though. We'll list both here from east to west.

The **Combs-Hehl Bridge,** named for a former governor and a former Campbell County judge, is on the eastern half of the I-275 loop and connects the eastern portions of Cincinnati and Northern Kentucky. Many travelers from the eastern half of Cincinnati cross the bridge and jump onto I-471 to get into downtown.

The **Daniel Beard Bridge** is named in honor of the founder of the Boy Scouts. It is better known as the "471 bridge" because it's on I-471, or the "Big Mac bridge" because of its yellow arches. The bridge connects I-471 in Northern Kentucky with Columbia Parkway, Fort Washington Way, Sixth Street downtown, or I-71 in Cincinnati.

The new **Newport Southbank Bridge/Purple People Bridge** is the former L&N Railroad Bridge. Painted in glorious neon purple, it is a pedestrian walkway spanning the waters between the Cincinnati shorefront and Newport on the Levee mall in Newport, Kentucky. The bridge makes it possible for U.S. Bank Arena concert-goers or Reds fans at Great American Ball Park to grab a quick bite at one of the Levee's many restaurants without ever getting into their cars. (Reds fans take note: You can also park at the

Levee's five-story garage and hoof over to the ballpark, a half-mile stroll that avoids ballpark traffic congestion.)

The **Taylor-Southgate Bridge** is the light gray bridge next to U.S. Bank Arena that connects downtown with Newport, Kentucky.

The **John Roebling Suspension Bridge** is right next to Great American Ball Park and connects downtown with Covington, Kentucky. This two-lane bridge is instantly recognizable for its stone piers, gold crowns, and the lights tracing its blue suspension cables. Pedestrian walkways flank each side of the bridge. The bridge has a distinct sound because the roadway is not made out of concrete but rather has a metal grid floor. You might remember seeing and hearing the bridge in the movie *Rain Man*.

The **Clay Wade Baily Bridge** is named after a noted *Kentucky Post* political reporter. The underused bridge connects western downtown at Third Street with Covington, Kentucky.

The **Brent Spence Bridge** is named for a well-known Kentucky congressman. It is also known as the "I-75 bridge" or the "Car-Strangled Spanner." I-71 connects with I-75 just before the bridge on the Cincinnati side and creates monumental traffic jams during rush hours. The bridge is a double-decker, with northern traffic moving under southern traffic.

The **Carroll Lee Cropper Bridge** is on I-275 west and connects Southeastern Indiana with Northern Kentucky. This bridge isn't mentioned very often by name and it even took some research by Kentucky Transportation officials to come up with Cropper's name. He was a judge in Boone County. Locals call it "the I-275 bridge to Indiana."

Ferries

Bridges aren't the only way of getting a car across the river. Two ferries operate in the area, taking cars back and forth the old-fashioned way. The **Anderson Ferry** has been transporting cars and people since 1817. It operates an eight-car ferryboat between Boone County, Kentucky, and Delhi on the western side of Cincinnati. The boat lands on the Kentucky side just north of the airport and is a more scenic and historic way of getting across the river. The cost is $3.00 per car. Its hours are 6:00 A.M. to 8:00 P.M. Monday through Friday, 7:00 A.M. to 8:00 P.M. on Saturday and holidays, and 11:00 A.M. to 8:00 P.M. Sunday. The ferry is open till 9:30 P.M. between May and October.

The smaller **Augusta Ferry** runs cars from US 52 on the Ohio side to Augusta, Kentucky (about 50 miles upriver from Cincinnati). Ferry hours are 8:00 A.M. to 8:00 P.M. and the cost is $5.00 per car (see the River Fun chapter).

Tips to Make the Drive Easier, Safer, and Legal

In comparison to other large cities, the rush hour in Cincinnati isn't that bad, except when construction or accidents throw a wrench in the works.

And that happens more here than in other Ohio cities, according to the Ohio Department of Public Safety. Cincinnati has the most accident-prone drivers in Ohio with 53 crashes for every 1,000 residents (the state average is 35).

But without accidents and stalled cars messing up the daily commute, the normal traffic jams are generally predictable and not very serious.

Driving sometimes gets erratic between 7:00 and 9:00 A.M. and 4:00 to 6:00 P.M.—people often cut in at the last minute if you leave just a little too much room between you and the guy in front of you or squeeze in even if you didn't leave enough room. Overall, though, it is not near as bad as most big cities and that's probably because most people are friendly and the traffic is not very heavy.

However, all bets on the great traffic situation we just outlined are off when there is either rain or snow. People tend to slow down even for the rain because of sloping roadways, particularly in Northern Kentucky and the areas closer to the river and downtown.

When snow or ice hits, this area goes into a state of panic. Meteorologists on television will tell people not to go out unless they have to, and many of the schools will close. The problem is that Cincinnati is right on that line between being a northern and southern state. There are mild winters with very little snow, but sometimes winters have several severe storms. So it's hard for the municipalities to justify buying a lot of the equipment needed to remove snow. Cincinnati tends to be a little better about snow removal than Kentucky mostly because we have more equipment.

And when we say snow removal, we really mean salt trucks. The trucks often don't even use their snow blades to plow the roads. Oftentimes they rely on cars driving the roads to help clear the roads, which means the main roads are in better shape, mostly because they get more traffic.

Kentucky really never seems prepared for snowstorms. It is hilly and takes more time to clear off the roads, so you'll hear more often about closed roads; schools can be closed for a week after a snowstorm until everything is melted.

When the snow does melt, there are new problems, namely dodging the potholes. It's so bad that television stations have reports on huge potholes and ask people to report the potholes in their neighborhoods.

A unique springtime sickness known as the Orange Barrel Blues also inflicts area drivers. Every spring, some portion of one of the major interstates or driving routes undergoes minor repair, and traffic flow becomes restricted by the placement of orange barrels. It's as inevitable as death and taxes. The best tool any driver can have is a radio or cellular phone. Most of the radio stations have traffic reports to keep listeners up to date about any traffic tie-ups or accidents that may delay you.

To help move the rush hour traffic, several of the major routes to and from downtown also have middle lanes whose direction is dictated by the time of day. Sometimes referred to as "chicken lanes" or "suicide lanes," they are used for traffic heading toward downtown in the morning and away from downtown in the afternoons. Lights above the lanes—green arrows or red Xs—will alert drivers as to which way the traffic is currently heading.

ARTIMIS (Advanced Regional Traffic Interactive Management and Information System) is a $37 million regional traffic manager center that includes an electronic "smart highway" messaging system. It monitors 88 miles of the busiest highways around Cincinnati with 1,100 pavement sensors, more than 60 television cameras, and radar units mounted on poles. The information is relayed to a central operator, who dispatches information to 40 electronic message boards that hang over the highways, informing drivers about conditions ahead.

SmarTraveler traffic service is part of ARTIMIS and provides up-to-the-minute traffic information for eight specific roadways in the area, along with a direct link to TANK, Metro (see Public Transportation later in the chapter), JetPort Express (see the Airports section in this chapter), RideShare, and details on transportation to special events. It also now includes information about road construction in the area.

For information about a specific highway, call 511 and then push the highway number and the star button. For instance, to get information on I-275, call 511 and push 275*. For the Ronald Reagan Highway, push 126*. For the Norwood Lateral, push 562*. For information about downtown, push 1. For downtown Covington and Newport, including the riverfront, dial 2. For Transit info, dial 3; JetPort Express is 96*, RideShare 95*.

There are alternatives to driving to work downtown. **RideShare,** (513) 241-

For traffic information that's updated every 10 minutes, call 511 on your cellular phone to reach ARTIMIS, a regional traffic manager center. Once the automated service answers, dial the highway number followed by the star button. (dial 1 for downtown). The service tells you about accidents, construction, and other traffic problems.

RIDE, or **Van Ohio,** (800) VAN-RIDE, arrange for car- or vanpooling from outlying communities. But it doesn't get you there quicker. The area highways do not offer special lanes just for carpoolers.

There also are 21 park-and-ride locations in Cincinnati and another 18 in Northern Kentucky. You can park your car there and take the bus downtown. More on the bus services later.

Other pieces of information about driving in Greater Cincinnati:

- New residents have 15 days to get new license plates in Kentucky, 30 days in Ohio, and 60 days in Indiana.
- The speed limit on most interstate roads that go through Greater Cincinnati is generally 65 mph, although there are sections on each highway in which the speed limit will suddenly drop to 55 for no apparent reason, so pay attention to the signs.
- You can turn right on red unless otherwise posted. And a left turn on red is permissible from a one-way street onto another one-way street.
- Although motorcycle drivers are not required to wear helmets, all motorcycle passengers are.
- A child age three or younger, under 40 pounds, or less than 40 inches tall must be strapped into a child safety seat.
- Seat belts are required to be worn in all the tristate communities.

GETTING AROUND DOWNTOWN

By car or on foot, getting around downtown is easy. The streets running east-west are numbered, starting at the river (Second Street, though, was renamed Pete Rose Way). The streets running north-south have your typical downtown street names—(in order, from east to west) Broadway, Sycamore, Main, Walnut, Vine, Race, Elm, Plum, and Central Parkway. A silly saying that uses the first letter of the street names helps people remember the order: Big Strong Men Will Very Rarely Eat Pork Chops. Vine Street is the dividing point between east and west addresses.

Cincinnati's downtown isn't so big that it can't be walked from one end to the other. With the reconstruction of Fort Washington Way, pedestrian traffic between downtown and the river has improved. New pedestrian bridges were constructed to make the area more pedestrian friendly.

Parking is one of the big problems for drivers downtown. Plenty of lots and garages are available, but many are full or costly on weekdays. A number of larger lots exist on the perimeter of downtown but require a several-block walk to get into the heart of downtown. Some downtown parking lots offer three hours for $1.00 to get more people to go shopping downtown. While you're shopping downtown, you can get Park-and-Save coupons with your purchases, which cut down or eliminate the cost of parking.

PUBLIC TRANSPORTATION

Greater Cincinnati's public transportation system is divided between the Metro, a bus line serving Hamilton County and parts of Clermont, Warren, and Butler Counties, and the Transit Authority of Northern Kentucky, known as TANK.

Metro
120 East Fourth Street
(513) 621-4455
www.sorta.com
Metro (no clever acronym) has five local bus and commuter express routes into downtown daily. Metro runs express routes to Bengals games and special events such as Riverfest and Oktoberfest.

Rates for riding the Metro differ depending on the region of your trip. Fares are $1.00 in the city. A 50-cent charge is added to the fare if the bus changes zones. A fare of $2.00 to $2.25 is charged on routes in suburban areas.

Metro has three zones: 1) within the city, 2) outside of the city but still in Hamilton County, and 3) into surrounding counties. Exact change is required for all Metro rides.

Children under 45 inches on Metro and transfer riders from TANK to Metro pay only 50 cents. Bus riders who are age 65 or older, are on Medicare, or have a disability also receive Fare Deal discounts, in which rides are 50 cents. Many Metro routes feature buses equipped with a wheelchair lift. For those with a more severe disability who cannot ride Metro buses, Metro offers the curb-to-curb Access Shuttle within the I-275 beltway. Monthly passes on Metro are $40 for one zone, $60 for two zones, and $80 for all zones. A pass that is good on both Metro and TANK is $70 a month.

Most Metro routes culminate at Government Square, on Fifth Street between Walnut and Main Streets downtown. For more information, call the number above between 6:30 A.M. and 6:00 P.M. Monday through Friday, 8:00 A.M. to 4:00 P.M. on Saturday, or check Metro's Web site.

TANK
3375 Madison Pike, Fort Wright, KY
(859) 331-8265
TANK operates as far south as the Kentucky towns of Florence, Grants Lick, and Independence, with many routes leading to Fourth and Main Streets in downtown Cincinnati.

Fares for all TANK trips within its service area are $1.25, although children shorter than 45 inches ride for free, students ride for 75 cents between 6:00 A.M. and 6:00 P.M., and senior citizens and those with disabilities ride for 50 cents if they have a photo ID. Exact change is required, and transfers are free. Unlimited-ride monthly passes cost $45.00; unlimited rides on TANK and Metro cost $70.00; weekly ticket books for 10 rides cost $11.25.

TANK offers a Regional Area Mobility Program, or RAMP, for eligible riders.

TANK started a riverfront entertainment shuttle that runs through Covington, Newport, and Cincinnati's riverfronts. Cost is $1.00 per ride; it runs every 20 minutes from 6:00 A.M. to 10:00 P.M. Monday through Thursday and every 15 minutes from 6:00 A.M. to midnight on Friday, from 10:00 A.M. to midnight on Saturday, and Sunday 10:00 A.M. to 10:00 P.M.

TANK has shuttles from various park-and-ride lots to Bengals and Reds games as well as Tall Stacks. Call the information line for details.

TAXIS AND LIMOUSINES

More than 20 taxi companies operate in Greater Cincinnati. Taxis aren't used in the area as widely as they are in, say, New York, but they can easily be found lined up on downtown streets, in front of hotels, at the airport, or spread throughout the suburbs. Cabs cost $2.60 for the drop of the flag and $1.60 per mile.

To make sure you have a cab waiting for you, call **Yellow Cab,** (513) 241-2100 or check the Yellow Pages.

For something with a little more style, there are a number of limousine companies in Cincinnati. Most offer the traditional six-seat stretch or 10-seat ultrastretch limousines that include a color TV, VCR, stereo, cellular phone, and a wet bar. Use of the phone is an extra cost, and Ohio law prohibits stocking a limo's bar with alcohol. Ultrastretch limos seating up to 10 rent for

CLOSE-UP

Underground Cincinnati

One of Cincinnati's most notable transit legacies is rarely seen because it's hidden underground; even many longtime locals don't know it still exists.

We're talking the Cincinnati Subway, the long-abandoned 2 miles of rail lines and platforms that snake beneath the downtown and Over-the-Rhine. The subway was never completed, a victim of the Great Depression. But it's there, kept in pristine condition by the city engineer's office. The Cincinnati Historical Society has opened the tunnels to public tours, and we were lucky enough to be invited on one of the first trial tours of this transportation landmark.

Our tour begins at the Central & Vine subway station. Well, not a station in the formal sense of the word as there are no ticket booths or even much in the way of lights. But there is no mistaking it, as you enter from the median on Central Parkway right across from the AAA headquarters building. Descend the stairway and you've entered another world, a subterranean concrete cavern with high ceilings, a passenger platform, and two rail lines.

Our hosts, the good folks from the Historical Society's Heritage Program and the city engineer's office, have graciously invited us on a preliminary walk-through of the tunnels. Along for the meandering stroll are safety engineers and architectural experts.

As we stroll the underground, we see that graffiti lines the walls. GRAND CENTRAL '38 reads one huge painted phrase. Here, even the graffiti comes with its own sense of history.

We come across rusting 17-gallon drinking-water barrels marked OFFICE OF CIVIL DEFENSE. We're told the subway was designated in the 1950s as the fallout shelter for the Cincinnati mayor and other key officials in the event of a nuclear attack.

Someone on the walk mentions how the University of Cincinnati once considered this landmark for a wind tunnel. Somebody else mentions that it was once considered as a site for an atomic super collider. The subway's history as a fallout shelter is duly observed, as is its central role in the Jim DeBrosse mystery novel, *Hidden City.*

Somebody suggests that a Subway sandwich shop could open a franchise outlet down here for the tourists. Another gamely suggests marketing T-shirts that sport the motto, "I Survived the Cincinnati Subway."

We finally ascend to daylight. The musty odor is all that suggests this incredible city resource had sat unused for a half century. The Cincinnati Subway lives on. Some have called it a boondoggle; we call it an opportunity.

The Cincinnati Historical Society's Heritage Program offers annual tours for $50 per person. Call (513) 287-7031 to make reservations.

around $75 to $95 an hour with a three-hour minimum. SUV limos, seating 12 to 14, cost $125 to $145 with a four-hour minimum. A Hummer stretch costs $195 to $225 with a four-hour minimum. One of the most popular limousine companies is **M & M Limousine,** (513) 598-5530.

Schworer's **Beverly Hills Limousine Service,** (859) 356-6255, www.classicrolls limo.biz, rents a 1964 Rolls Royce Silver Cloud III, which is identical to the cars used in the Grey Poupon commercials. But of course. The car has a large moonroof, leather seats, a cellular phone, a television, and wooden tables that unfold from the backs of the front seats. The Rolls rents for $450 for three hours and $150 per hour thereafter.

For a listing of various limo companies, check www.limoraces.com.

Car Rentals

Greater Cincinnati has more than 25 car-rental agencies spread throughout the area. Those at the Cincinnati/Northern Kentucky International Airport include **Alamo,** (800) 327-9633; **Avis,** (859) 767-3773; **Budget,** (800) 527-7000; **Dollar,** (866) 434-2226; **Hertz,** (859) 767-3535; and **National,** (859) 767-3655. For something a little less expensive, try **Rent-A-Heap Cheap,** (513) 631-0099.

Carriage Rides

Horse-drawn carriage rides through downtown are available all year, although during the summer there seems to be a carriage at every turn. The rides offer a good way to tour downtown, and the drivers are usually knowledgeable about different aspects of the area and generally love to answer questions. Several carriage companies operate downtown and are very competitive.

You can privately rent a horse-drawn carriage. Prices vary a lot depending on the type of carriage. But basic prices for a single-horse carriage are $30 for a 20-minute ride from Fountain Square, and prices increase from that point. Some operators require a deposit of as much as 50 percent at the time reservations are made. Carriage companies include **Cincinnati Carriage,** (513) 941-4474, and **Elegant Carriages,** (859) 491-7655.

The suspension bridge between Cincinnati and Covington was built by John Roebling and was the prototype for the Brooklyn Bridge, which he built 17 years later. It took 10 years and $1.5 million to build and, when completed in 1866, the 2,252-foot bridge was the world's longest. On its second day 120,000 people—half the city's population—walked across the bridge.

RIVER TRAVEL

The Ohio River gets crowded once the weather turns nice. Water-skiers, Jet Skiers, boaters, barges, and bridges all compete for space, and the river becomes very congested, particularly around downtown. A piece of advice: Keep an eye out for bridges and barges. Barges take a mile or more to stop, always have the right of way, and can sink a boat in seconds. So can bridge piers. It sounds like common sense, but every year a boater hits one or the other and always loses.

There is a "no wake" rule on the Ohio River between the Brent Spence Bridge (I-75 bridge) and the Daniel Beard Bridge (Big Mac bridge at 471). That doesn't mean you can't wake people up; it means boats have to go slowly enough to not create a wake in the water.

You can set sail on the river in one of two ways: Unhitch a trailered boat at a launch ramp or rent a slip at a local marina. Cincinnati has three main public launch ramps. On the East Side, the ramp is at Schmidt Playfields along Eastern Avenue in the East End, about 4 miles from downtown. On the West Side, the ramp is in Riverside on Southside Avenue, also about 4 miles from downtown. And downtown, the ramps are at the Public Landing. A small fee is charged for launchings from Schmidt Playfields.

The area offers 12 local marinas for docking. Many of the marinas offer winter storage areas. Most restaurants along the riverfront also offer piers for boat docking.

Most of the river is under the control and responsibility of Kentucky, according to a U.S. Supreme Court decision, but both states as well as the Coast Guard patrol the river and enforce boating laws.

And if a boating excursion takes you more than 35 miles in either direction of downtown, be prepared to get in line with barges and every other boat for a trip through a set of dam locks.

For non-boat owners looking for river excursions, many local charter companies offer trip packages (see the River Fun chapter). The boats feature indoor or outdoor seating, catering, wet bars, and even gambling—well, pretend gambling, since it's still illegal in Ohio and Kentucky. For the real thing, you'll have to go to Southeastern Indiana (see the River Fun chapter). The trips are popular for office parties and weddings. The largest charter company is **BB Riverboats,** (859) 261-8500, located at 101 Riverboat Row near Newport on the Levee, with boats that can hold from 20 to 900 people. Several luxury yachts that ply the river are also available for rent. For several other smaller charter companies, check the River Fun chapter.

AIRPORTS

Cincinnati/Northern Kentucky International Airport
Interstate 275 and Kentucky Highway 212, Hebron, KY
(859) 767-3151
www.cvgairport.com

It's puzzling to many passengers flying into Greater Cincinnati for the first time when they realize the airport isn't in Cincinnati or even Ohio, but Kentucky. The Cincinnati/Northern Kentucky International Airport is a prime example of how the area overcomes state boundaries and works together to form a cohesive region.

Since the federal government deeded it to the Kenton County Airport Board in 1945, the airport has proved to be the ideal location for the region's air transportation. The rural setting, about 12 miles south of downtown Cincinnati, allows the airport to acquire space and slowly grow to meet the area's changing transportation needs without butting heads with residential expansion. Its rural setting also keeps it away from the bulk of the daily traffic, so travelers don't have to mix with commuters in the fight to make a flight.

This is one of the nation's fastest-growing airports. About 500 flights depart daily to 122 cities nonstop. More than 20 million passengers fly out of the airport annually. The airport is also a key international location, with nonstop flights taking off daily to Amsterdam, Frankfurt, London, Montreal, Paris, Rome, Toronto and, during certain parts of the year, to Nassau in the Bahamas.

And it's a key business location, situated within an hour's flight of 50 percent of the nation's population and 50 percent of its manufacturing facilities. Numerous businesses relocating to the area from other parts of the country cite the airport as a primary factor in their decision. Cincinnati's airport is within a 90-minute flight of 14 of the 20 top cities in the United States.

The airport is also one of the most vital players in the region's economic picture. Every time a plane takes off from the airport, almost $16,000 is contributed to the local economy through direct and indirect expenditures, for a daily average of $8.7 million and an annual impact of $3.9 billion.

A $500 million expansion completed in 1994 added a terminal, a new road system, a new control tower, an automated baggage system that carries 21,000 bags an hour, an underground train that carries passengers to the terminal, and two new concourses. The airport now has all of the major conveniences of a small city—a wide variety of stores and bars, a barbershop, a chapel, two banks, and its own police station, fire department, and post office.

Because of the increase in flights, nearby residents continually sound off about the nonstop noise. The airport board is buying as many nearby houses as it can, sound-insulating others, and trying to route its planes over less-populated areas. It still continues as a battle between progress and people, though.

But although it is nice to have an airport with so many connections nearby, it is not always the cheapest place to catch a flight. Delta is able to set the prices since it has a hub here. As a result, competition is weak and the rates are high. If money outweighs time as a factor, you can more than likely find cheaper flights in Columbus, Dayton, Louisville, or Indianapolis. All four airports are about a two-hour drive from Cincinnati.

However, the Cincinnati/Northern Kentucky airport is convenient, and getting from the airport to downtown is easy. Cabs are available with a set fee of $26 for taking one to four passengers downtown. Direct phone lines for all major car-rental agencies are located in the baggage claim areas of each terminal, and buses go directly from outside these areas to the on-site rental companies.

Airlines operating from the airport are Air France, American, American Eagle, Comair, Continental, Delta, Northwest/KLM, Skyway, United, and USAir Express.

Lunken Airport
Kellogg and Wilmer Avenues
(513) 321-4132

The city of Cincinnati owns and operates Lunken, which was the area's primary airport in the early days of aviation. The airport is in the Little Miami River valley, about 15 minutes east of downtown.

If your car breaks down on one of the major interstates during rush hour, a good Samaritan will help. Five CVS/Samaritan vans patrol the highways within the I-275 loop on both sides of the river. Certified auto mechanics, who are also emergency medical technicians, staff the vans from 6:30 to 9:30 A.M. and from 3:00 to 6:00 P.M. each weekday.

Because of its positioning in the valley, the airport often became enshrouded in fog or flooded during the spring thaw and earned the nickname Sunken Lunken. As airplanes became bigger, the landlocked airport became too small, and Sunken Lunken also became Shrunken Lunken. It now serves private, corporate, and air cargo commercial planes. Flight schools, hangars, major and minor maintenance, and tie-downs are available here. Also, several fixed-base operations, executive jet management, and jet charter companies operate out of the airport. Car rentals are available.

Blue Ash Airport
Plainfield and Glendale-Milford Roads, Blue Ash
(513) 791-8500

The Blue Ash Airport, about 15 miles north of downtown, is operated by the city of Cincinnati. It is adjacent to a 500-acre industrial park and near the area's second-largest business district, making it convenient for corporate planes. Executive Aviation has several World War II vintage military planes, known as the War Birds, at the airport. Tours of the planes are free.

Clermont County Airport
Old Ohio Highway 74, Batavia
(513) 735-9500

The Clermont County Airport is a small airport serving mostly private planes, about 30 miles east of downtown. It is also the home of Sporty's, which operates a well-known international retail and cata-

Roads and bridges in Cincinnati are generally known by nicknames, but very often the road signs don't show those nicknames. The Cross County Highway's real name is Ronald Reagan Highway. The Norwood Lateral is really Highway 562 on signs. The Big Mac bridge is also known as the bridge at I-471. The newest name is the Purple People Bridge, whose real name is Newport Southbank Bridge.

log merchandise business aimed at the aviation industry. The airport is privately owned and managed by Eastern Cincinnati Aviation.

Hamilton/Fairfield Airport
Bobmeyer Road on borderline of Hamilton and Fairfield
(513) 896-9999
The Hamilton/Fairfield airport is owned and operated by the Butler County Airport Authority. It is about 25 miles north of downtown and about 4 miles southeast of Hamilton. The airport is served by Pro Aero, which provides flight lessons. It is home to planes ranging from single engine to corporate jets. This airport is similar to Lunken but serves the northern tristate area.

BUS SERVICE

Greyhound
1005 Gilbert Avenue
(513) 352-6012
(800) 231-2222, route information
Greyhound operates a modern bus station on Gilbert Avenue on the northeastern edge of downtown. The station offers regular daily departures to cities across the country in addition to package express and charter services. Trailways charter services shares space at the station.

TRAINS

For years trains were the main purpose of **Union Terminal** at 1301 Western Avenue. **Amtrak** keeps part of the legacy alive by operating a limited service there. Three trains a week depart from the station heading east to New York or Washington, D.C. Eastbound trains depart at 5:04 A.M. on Sunday, Wednesday, and Friday. Westbound trains heading to Chicago depart at 3:05 A.M. on Monday, Thursday, and Saturday. Call (800) 872-7245 for information and reservations or (513) 651-3337 to reach the station directly. Or check www.amtrak.com.

HISTORY

It's hard to believe, but Cincinnati—firmly entrenched in the Midwest—once sat in the heart of the Northwest Territory. In the 1700s this area was the wilds, the untamed and unknown frontier. British policy up through the Revolutionary War, when we were nothing more than "the colonies" to the crown, was to leave the area to the Indians, who were already angry about being pushed from their eastern territories.

Native Americans were prominent here, and their influence is seen in many of the names and historic sites found in the area. Native American artifacts, in fact, are still being discovered during excavations for new buildings. Burial grounds and serpent-shaped mounds are scattered throughout the region. While digging to expand a runway at the Cincinnati/Northern Kentucky International Airport, workers unearthed a 2,700-year-old Indian site and 7,000 artifacts.

Shortly after the Revolutionary War, the newly victorious American government declared the territory available for settlement. Ohio and all points west had nothing more to offer settlers than opportunity, although that was plenty to entice explorers, range rovers, and wide-eyed gamblers looking for a chance to strike it rich in real estate.

The westward movement began, and it didn't take long for people to find the area that would become Cincinnati. Because of its rich soil and abundance of rivers, which were vital to the transportation and livelihood of the day, settlers started arriving as early as 1788. Most of the city's early settlers arrived by putting several weeks' worth of food and their life's possessions on a flatboat—basically a small log cabin sitting on a modified Huck Finn–style raft—and drifting down the Ohio River. The current was their source of power, and travel was slower than on an L.A. freeway during rush hour.

John Filson, one of the area's first settlers, originally named the area Losantiville, a compilation of Latin, Greek, French, and Delaware Indian meaning "town opposite the mouth of the Licking River." Shortly after coming up with the name, Filson wandered into the nearby woods and was never heard from again.

As a base for Northwest Territory exploration and a defense against Indian attacks, Fort Washington was built in 1789. The fort, demolished in 1808, was located on what is now Third Street, on a hill just above the river basin. A small park near the intersection of Third and Broadway marks the site. A plaque on a nearby parking garage on Broadway notes the site of the fort's powder magazine. The five-sided, 15-foot-deep magazine was discovered when the garage was being built in 1952.

The name Losantiville lasted about as long as Filson in the woods. In 1790, two days after Gen. Arthur St. Clair arrived to assume command of Fort Washington and the Northwest Territory, he invoked his newly given powers and renamed the area Cincinnati in honor of the Society of Cincinnati, an organization of Revolutionary War officers to which he belonged. The society drew its name from Lucius Quintus Cincinnatus, a farmer who rescued the Roman army after it became trapped by the Aequi during the early period of the Roman Empire. After Cincinnatus saved the army (and possibly the Roman Empire), he decided he didn't like military life and returned to farming.

General St. Clair didn't have as much success militarily as Cincinnatus, however. After recruiting a militia in Pittsburgh, he set out to take on the Indians. Desertion and illness depleted St. Clair's army, and the Miami Indians, led by Chief Little Turtle, whupped him, inflicting upon the U.S. Army its worst defeat ever. The boys in Washington summoned "Mad" Anthony

The bridges along the Ohio River have become part of the city's ambience, particularly the Roebling Suspension Bridge. The city of Covington made the area even more interesting by adding several murals along the flood walls near the bridge. The murals depict what the area might have looked like at various stages in history.

Wayne in relief, and he eventually defeated the Indians.

STEAMBOATIN' AND PORK PACKIN'

Meanwhile, settlers kept flowing into the area. When the *Orleans* steamed into port on October 27, 1811, though, the city became more than just a flotation destination. The steamboat changed Cincinnatians' lifestyle almost as much as the apple changed Adam's. People were shocked and mystified by the fact that it took the *Orleans* just 45 hours to make the 180-mile trip upriver—against the current—from Louisville.

The steamboat not only made trade and transportation upriver easy for the farmers plowing the area's rich soil, it gave Cincinnati a new industry. The area produced more than a quarter of all steamboats built in the United States during the next decade, about 30 a year.

On the other side of the Ohio River, Northern Kentucky got its start when three Cincinnatians—John and Richard Gano and Thomas Carneal—crossed the river and plotted the city of Covington in 1814. Neighboring Newport was recognized as a city in 1834.

Inland transportation was still rough and slow, however, and in order to expand the city's commerce center, the Miami-Erie Canal was conceived and built, connecting the Ohio River with the Great Lakes. The section between Cincinnati and Dayton opened in 1829.

With more and more immigrants coming to America and better transportation methods getting them off the East Coast, Cincinnati boomed. Between 1830 and 1850 the city's population grew by 40 percent, faster than that of any other city in the country. It became known as the Queen City of the West, developing into the country's sixth-largest city and its third-largest manufacturing center.

Cincinnati's major industries during this period included metalworking, woodworking, and, most importantly, pork packing. Ummm, good eats. By 1835 the city was the nation's chief pork-packing center and would later become the largest such center in the world. Slaughterhouses were in such abundance that the city was given the moniker Porkopolis. Pigs were herded through the streets hundreds at a time on their way to the slaughterhouses. Small companies sprang up to process pork by-products such as lard, which was turned into soap and candles. One of these companies, started in 1837, was called Procter & Gamble.

Residents fully expected Cincinnati to become the largest city in the country. However, city leaders failed to plan adequately for the introduction of the railroad. When river transportation was replaced, Cincinnati quickly found itself being bypassed for cities such as St. Louis and Chicago.

RHINELAND REVISITED

Perhaps because the area reminded them of their homeland, German immigrants flocked to Cincinnati, forming communities such as Over-the-Rhine and building breweries and beer gardens by the dozens. Cincinnati's German population more than doubled between 1840 and 1850, eventually comprising 25 percent of the city's population. German language classes were taught in city schools. Four German newspapers were published. And the strong, no-nonsense work ethic the Germans brought with them formed a foundation for what is to this day the area's employment philosophy.

The potato famine in Ireland brought thousands of Irish immigrants and greater ethnic diversity to Cincinnati. Racial diversity was more limited, as few free blacks chose to live so close to the Mason-Dixon Line. Thousands of blacks passed through the area, however, because Greater Cincinnati played a major part in the Underground Railroad, providing a crucial path for escaped slaves to reach freedom. Homes and businesses with hidden rooms can still be found on both sides of the river. The city also played an important role in the antislavery movement; Harriet Beecher Stowe penned *Uncle Tom's Cabin* based on her Cincinnati experiences.

Although Cincinnati was a border city during the Civil War, it wasn't as affected by the war as other cities in nearby Pennsylvania, West Virginia, and Kentucky. Only once was the city in grave danger of a Confederate invasion, and then Gen. Lew Wallace, better known for writing *Ben Hur,* rallied 72,000 squirrel hunters and ordinary citizens to its defense.

UPWARD AND ONWARD

The 4 square miles of the river valley (surrounded by hills on three sides and the river on the fourth) that is now downtown Cincinnati were becoming increasingly crowded, with as many as 30,000 people living in each square mile. It was like New York City without the attitude. The solution to the problem came in 1872 with the opening of the Mount Auburn incline, which used steam-powered motors and cables to raise and lower platforms carrying people, horses, wagons, and, later, electric street trolleys to the nearby hills. By 1876 inclines encircled the basin like giant escalators.

As soon as they could, the more affluent residents of the city fled to the hills, placing themselves above the smoky industrial valley—and the less affluent.

They moved first to the West Side, upwind from the smoke. (Many Victorian homes from this period are now being restored.) The middle class followed shortly, moving farther away from the basin and creating new communities and early versions of the suburbs. The last incline closed in 1948.

It was during this period that many of the historic landmarks that define Cincinnati today were developed: Findlay Market in 1852, the Roebling Suspension Bridge and Isaac Wise Temple in 1866, the Tyler Davidson Fountain in 1871, Hebrew Union College in 1875, the Cincinnati Zoo in 1875, Music Hall in 1878, the Rookwood Pottery in 1880, the art museum in 1886, and Cincinnati City Hall in 1893.

Cincinnati's most famous landmark, the Tyler Davidson Fountain, was a gift from businessman Henry Probasco in honor of his deceased brother-in-law. Probasco toured several foundries in Europe to find the fountain's statue. The city tore down a market house in the center of Fifth Street to make way for the fountain, which, 100 years later, was moved to what is now Fountain Square.

THE INDUSTRIAL REVOLUTION

Industrial areas began developing outside of the basin as the city of Cincinnati expanded its borders through annexation. Avondale, Norwood, and the Millcreek Valley blossomed with industrial businesses, forcing the basin to become less industrialized and more focused on retail, banking, and other services.

Up on the hills or down in the basin,

i

Some frontier history has been preserved in Anderson Township. The Miller-Leuser Log Cabin, a 200-year-old log cabin that has not been rebuilt, is used as a teaching tool for more than 6,000 schoolchildren each year. It's located at 6540 Clough Pike.

the manufacturing and service industries that now form the core of Cincinnati's business community were founded during this time: Cincinnati Gas & Electric in 1843, Fifth Third Bank in 1858, U.S. Playing Card Co. in 1867, the Cincinnati Reds in 1869, Cincinnati Bell in 1873, Kroger Co. in 1883, Children's Hospital in 1883, Cincinnati Milacron in 1884, LeBlond-Makino Machine Tool Co. in 1887, Western and Southern Life Insurance Co. in 1888, the Christ Hospital in 1888, and Bartlett & Co. in 1898.

The rapid changes brought about by the Industrial Revolution and general labor conditions, however, were unsettling to many workers. In May 1886 their unrest peaked and laborers organized a strike. In early May, 12,000 workers walked off their jobs. By the end of the month, 20,000 more had joined them. Businesses, hit hard by the lack of employees, eventually agreed to their demands, including limiting workdays to just eight hours.

ROLLING ON THE RIVER, RIOTING IN THE STREETS

Cincinnati had a rough year in 1884. In February the Ohio overflowed its banks and didn't stop until it crested at 71.9 feet, flooding much of the downtown basin and not receding for two weeks. A few weeks later, when a local resident was murdered, the city's temper got almost as high as the river. When the killer was found guilty only of manslaughter, people began venting their anger.

A crowd of 20,000 gathered, threw stones, called for a lynching, and twice rushed the jail, which at the time was attached to the courthouse. Unable to find the murderer, they then rushed the courthouse, claiming injustice and setting the courthouse afire. The Ohio National Guard was called in to clear the streets. By the end of the riot, almost 60 people had died and more than 200 were injured.

With the courthouse in ashes and the jail ransacked, city leaders laid plans for better protection against such acts. They hired architect Samuel Hannaford to design a municipal building/jail that was riot- and fireproof. His work is now Cincinnati City Hall, with its steep slate roof and stone exterior.

BOSS COX

As in many other cities across the country, a single, strong political voice dictated the operations of Cincinnati in the late 1800s. That voice belonged to George B. Cox, a hard-drinking, rough businessman better known as Boss Cox. He sat on the city council for just a few years, but he virtually controlled the political scene for 30 years from his office above a saloon. Cox helped hold together and build certain parts of the city—albeit mostly for self-serving purposes—until 1910, when he "retired" shortly before the election of reformer Henry Hunt as mayor.

During Cox's "tenure," the city's debt was among the country's highest, taxes were outrageous, and *McClure's* magazine found Cincinnati to be the worst-governed city in America. Hunt offered a reasonable alternative to Cox's measures; however, Hunt's plans were costly, and the people hated expense more than they hated inefficiency. Hunt wasn't reelected and, fuming with frustration, he left the city and returned only once. Cox died of a stroke in 1916. Reform was under way, though, and in 1956 Cincinnati was called the best-run big city in America by *Fortune* magazine.

WAR AT HOME

The onset of World War I was a major story in Cincinnati, even more so than in other cities because of its huge German population. At the start of World War I, the city still published German newspapers, taught German in schools, and was decidedly populated with German immigrants, who defended their native country and published attacks on America's position on the war.

By the time America joined the war in 1917, anti-German sentiment had become so intense that the city changed the German names of streets, banned German books from the library, required German newspapers to be censored, and eliminated the teaching of German in city schools. It wasn't until 1996 that the city got over this, adding secondary signs to the renamed streets noting their original German names.

ROARING '20s, DEPRESSING '30s

The Roaring '20s hit hard at one of the cornerstones of Cincinnati's foundation: beer. At one time, 32 breweries operated in Cincinnati. It was a drunkard's dream. Prohibition forced the closing of more than two dozen local breweries and hundreds of pubs.

The 1930s didn't bring much more good news, as the Great Depression hit and the city's worst flood ever struck in 1937. The river rose to 79.9 feet, more than 25 feet above flood stage. Forty-five square miles of the city were under water. The waterworks and electric generators were put out of commission. More than 60,000 people were left homeless. The suspension bridge was the only bridge open along the entire Ohio River. Even Crosley Field, which sat several miles outside of downtown, was under 20 feet of water. Some jocular fans circled the bases in rowboats. The city remained flooded for 19 days.

The second great wave of development occurred during this time, though, and many of the landmarks that define how Cincinnati looks today came about: the Dixie Terminal in 1921, the Doctor's building in 1923, the Cincinnati Club in 1924, the Queen City Club building in 1927, the Masonic Temple in 1928, the CG&E building in 1929, the Carew Tower in 1930, the Cincinnati Bell Telephone building in 1931, the *Times-Star* building in 1933, and Union Terminal in 1933.

If you're a history buff, you may want to partake in some of the Cincinnati Historical Society Heritage Program tours and presentations. Each year the programs focus on various parts of the Cincinnati community, including Union Terminal and other tristate landmarks. Call (513) 287-7056 to get a brochure of scheduled events or for more information.

As a result of the construction, much of which was privately financed, Cincinnati was cushioned, temporarily at least, from the impact of the Great Depression. At one point in 1933, however, the economy caught up with the city and only half of the city's workforce was employed full-time.

BACK AT WAR

Even before the United States entered World War II, Cincinnati was involved in the war effort. The city converted its abundance of manufacturing businesses into production facilities for military supplies. Procter & Gamble, LeBlond-Makino Machine Tool Co., Cincinnati Milacron, even the U.S. Playing Card Co. shifted gears to stock the troops. Although it was top secret at the time, U.S. Playing Card hid maps of Germany in packs of its cards, which were then distributed to prisoners of war to help with escapes.

After the war Union Terminal was the country's main transfer station for soldiers heading to their homes in the West. And as part of the country's effort to clean out its war chest, the federal government deeded its aircraft training centers in Boone County, Kentucky, to the neighboring Kenton County Airport Board, which turned them into what is now the Cincinnati/Northern Kentucky International Airport.

CLOSE-UP

Ohio: The Haunt of It All

With every bit of history, there are inevitably a few ghosts to go along with it.

Take the symphony's Music Hall, for instance, where spirits and macabre doings are nearly legend. And the venerable Cincinnati Art Museum, where the collection of apparitions and weirdness is perhaps one too many collections for curators there. And how 'bout the historical Northern Kentucky bed-and-breakfast—which we won't name here because the proprietor is scared stiff of losing business—where a ghostly apparition sometimes appears on the staircase? "You get this weird feeling that something weird just happened. A little breeze," says the shaky owner.

Yeah, we've got ghosts. Isn't this, after all, the city where Rod Serling launched his *Twilight Zone* career? The Cincinnati Historical Society's Don Walker leads an annual tour of local hauntings and can refer you to numerous books on the topic—call the historical society's Heritage Program project at (513) 287-7031 for more information. (See also the listing for Heritage Programs in the Kidstuff chapter for more about other tours and happenings.)

Meanwhile, enjoy our phantasmic tour of local haunts below. Just remember, in the words of the *X-Files:* The truth is out there.

The Mirror Lake Gazebo's Specter
Numerous joggers and strollers have reported seeing a spirit here in the early dawn hours, and local legend has it that the Mount Adams gazebo is haunted by the specter of Imogene Remus, decked out in all her finery—including a wide-brim Paris hat and black silk dress. Her bootlegger husband, George, killed her in the gazebo in 1927 and got away scot-free with the murder. Her petulant spirit has haunted the gazebo ever since. Hey, we'd be petulant too.

The Cincinnati Art Museum's Howls 'n' Haunts
Must be something in the air in Mount Adams, because the art museum is just crawling with spirits too. Chief curator Anita Ellis reports two close encounters herself, and hears of many more. "All kinds of ghost stories are floating around here," says Ellis. "One night we were working late installing a show, and the tall case grandfather's clock in the period room started to chime. We knew this was impossible. The weights had been taken out so it wouldn't make noise in the museum. We immediately packed up and left." Another time, Ellis recounts, she was working late, heard someone at the door of a gallery, and, as she reached for the doorknob, the door jerked open and dragged her with it into

the adjoining room. However, there was nobody there. "I made haste," she says, "with dignity."

Music Hall's Bones and Shivers

Any huge hall can be creepy, but Music Hall carries demonic baggage all its own. Built on the site of a pauper's field, the construction site in 1876 was a gruesome mass of skeletons and caskets. Workers were still finding old bones as late as 1988, when the drilling of an elevator shaft unearthed 200 pounds of bones and 19 skulls. It's not just the subbasement that can give you the shivers, however. Doors open and close in the ballroom, with nobody nearby. Night watchmen report startling screams and moans. And inhumane screeching is heard onstage . . . oh, wait, that's opera.

The Reuben Resor House's Spirit

The Gothic-Italianate mansion (at 3517 Cornell Place in Clifton) was once home to a school for young ladies but closed after one of the girls died in the house during the 1919 flu epidemic. Her restless spirit still haunts the halls of this place, now an apartment building. Experts from the University of Cincinnati have even visited but left unable to explain mysterious cries, knocks, footsteps, and smells.

The Ghost of Bobby Mackey's

A century-old murder case, called the crime of the century, amounts to Greater Cincinnati's own version of the Nicole Simpson murder. In 1896 the headless body of 22-year-old Pearl Bryan was discovered across the river. It has since been the topic of a dozen books and numerous ballads and, at the University of Texas, it's even included in an American folklore course. Pearl's spirit is said to haunt everything from Bobby Mackey's Nightclub in Wilder to a home near the Highland Country Club. Sensationalism reigned during the investigation of the crime as well as the subsequent trial and hanging of a dental student, especially when trial goers learned Pearl was alive during the head severing. To this day, it's traditional for people who visit Pearl's grave in Fort Mitchell, Kentucky, to leave pennies Lincoln side up, so she'll have her head.

The *Delta Queen*'s Prohibitionist

Captain Mary Greene died aboard the *Delta Queen* riverboat in 1950, at the age of 83, but still likes to take the odd trip aboard the paddle wheeler. According to reports, Captain Greene is most likely to visit the Texas deck and shatter glasses at the bar. You see, when Captain Greene commanded, the bar was the ship's library and drinking most definitely wasn't allowed aboard the *Queen.*

MODERN TIMES

Following World War II and into the 1950s, area residents once again fled to the outskirts of the area, creating newer suburbs. As automobiles became more affordable, people didn't need to live as close to where they worked.

As in the rest of the country, the 1960s brought strife and unrest to the Cincinnati area. A weeklong race riot, in fact, broke out in the suburb of Avondale in 1967, prompting the calling in of the National Guard.

On the brighter side, that same year the city was awarded a professional football team, the Bengals, who began playing in 1968 under the guidance of the legendary Paul Brown. Three years later the team made the playoffs. Another 1960s sports milestone occurred in the city: Pete Rose played in his first game as a Red in 1963.

Very little downtown development took place between the 1930s and the 1960s, but in the 1970s a third major development phase occurred. Riverfront Stadium, later Cinergy Field, was built, opening in 1970. Fountain Square was built and dedicated in 1971, 100 years and 10 days after the fountain was originally dedicated. The first segment of the skywalk system opened—a second-story elevated sidewalk that wove through part of downtown until it was removed in 2006. Riverfront Coliseum, now U.S. Bank Arena, opened in 1975. The Serpentine Wall was completed in 1976. This concrete riser at the base of the downtown area is actually a flood wall, but it also has steps down to the river and serves as a place to sit and watch the activity on the river. The serpentine design makes it architecturally interesting. Throughout the 1980s and early 1990s, more modern skyscrapers were built as the real estate market boomed, creating much of the familiar skyline the city has today.

To make room for the new buildings, many old, historic, architecturally rich buildings were destroyed, despite the efforts of many angry citizens to save them. Even recently the Aronoff Center for the Arts met with resistance because of the destruction of historic buildings on the site. Cincinnatians hate change, especially when old, architecturally interesting buildings are replaced with bland structures that lack personality.

The area had the pleasure—and, oh, was it a pleasure!—of recording another piece of history in the 1970s: snow and cold. The mercury dipped to an area record of 25 degrees below zero on January 18, 1977. A year later a blizzard hit, dumping more than 50 inches of snow and completely freezing the river, sinking boats and allowing Cincinnatians to walk across to Kentucky. As they walked, they later said they could hear the ice cracking and feel the river flowing beneath the ice.

The Big Red Machine (the Cincinnati Reds, to the uninitiated) dominated baseball in the 1970s and is still considered by real fans to be the greatest team ever. Another notable date in Reds history occurred on September 11, 1985, when Pete Rose got his 4,192nd hit, becoming baseball's all-time hits leader.

Also in 1985 Cincinnati opened the floodgates for what would become the nation's savings-and-loan disaster. Depositors made a rush to withdraw their savings from Home State Savings after learning of the bank's bad investments. State officials later closed the bank and 70 others for three days to stop the onslaught of withdrawals.

In 1988 the city celebrated its 200th anniversary and dedicated the $15 million, 22-acre Bicentennial Commons park along the riverfront. The park reflects upon much of Cincinnati's past. Winged pigs on top of smokestacks at the entrance speak of the steamboats and slaughterhouses. A 100-foot-high pole notes the heights of the city's worst floods. A portion of the old stone waterworks building was turned into an amphitheater. And Cincinnatus, now bronzed and 10 feet tall, stands in Yeatman's Cove, where the first settlers landed, welcoming you to his city.

In 2001 Cincinnati made the national news with its race riots. The riots happened after a white police officer shot an unarmed black man who was wanted on 14 outstanding misdemeanor warrants. The Ohio National Guard was called in to help and a curfew was imposed in the city for several days. The police officer was later acquitted of the criminal charges filed after the shooting. Race relations continue to be strained, although the mayor has appointed a commission to work on the issue.

RESTAURANTS

Cincinnati's dining scene is rife with baffling contradictions. We're far from the Texas border but known worldwide for our chili. We're populated largely by settlers of German extract but claim relatively few German restaurants. We've hardly any settlers from France but boast top-rated French restaurants.

These contradictions are in perfect keeping with Cincinnati, a city of delightful discrepancies. The only constant on the town's dining scene is that Cincinnati restaurants, whether they serve haute cuisine or eclectic eats, are a solid value. Cincinnatians are noted penny-pinchers, and they tolerate neither fools nor pricey food gladly. This is terrific news for the visitor or newcomer, who will find that the area abounds in tasteful, comfortable, delicious eateries, nearly all reasonably priced.

If you are the kind of diner who likes to immediately sample the regional cuisine and scenery, head first to any Skyline Chili outlet for Cincinnati chili, slightly sweet rather than spicy (some say the secret ingredient is cinnamon or cocoa) and served atop spaghetti. The other lunch landmark you shouldn't miss is Arnold's, the city's oldest bar and grill—it fairly drips with the essential flavors of Cincinnati. Come dinner choose Jean-Robert at Pigall's for a formal continental meal. And for a late dessert or snack, indulge in raspberry chocolate chip at any Graeter's ice-cream parlor.

Cincinnati's trendy dining scene is generally centralized into two areas: Riverboat Row and the Backstage entertainment district. Here's a brief overview of the two:

Riverboat Row: This refers to the lineup of floating and stationary restaurants that dot the Newport and Covington shoreline of the Ohio River, immediately across from downtown Cincinnati—all claim to offer the most fantastic view of the city skyline, and many charge dearly for the privilege. As a general rule, Riverboat Row restaurants are packed on days when the Reds are playing at home. In no particular order, these barge bistros include Hooter's, Mike Fink, the Waterfront complex (which includes South Beach Grill), and BB Riverboats (offering dinner cruises). There are also landbound restaurants along Riverboat Row, such as Don Pablo's, Joe's Crab Shack, and the Embassy Grille. There is no corresponding Riverboat Row on the Ohio side of the river because, of course, dining patrons want to look at the city skyline, not be a part of it. The only downtown restaurant on the Ohio riverfront, in fact, is the Montgomery Inn Boathouse.

Backstage district: This refers to the restaurants that have sprouted around the gigantic Aronoff Center for the Arts, the city's venue for traveling Broadway productions and mainstream pop music acts. If Riverboat Row's general theme is seafood, the Backstage district's motif is ethnic fare. There's Akash for Indian food, Nicholson's for Scottish fare, Bella for seafood, Trattoria Roma for Italian, plus more typical American provisions at Jeff Ruby's Steakhouse, Rock Bottom Brewery, Pizzeria Uno's, and First Watch.

Beyond the two dining districts, there are selected streets with a high density of diverse restaurants per block. They include Ludlow Avenue in Clifton, St. Gregory Street in Mount Adams, Mount Lookout Square in Mount Lookout, Fourth Street downtown, Madison Road in O'Bryonville, Sixth Street inside MainStrasse Village in Covington, and Vine Street in Corryville.

This isn't to say you can sample the full flavor of Cincinnati by simply visiting this handful of neighborhoods. At last count, there were some 700 nonchain restaurants in the region. You could dine out for a full year and not savor the entire range of Queen City fare.

You'll find that most restaurants in Greater Cincinnati are fairly kid friendly. You probably won't want to take kids to the Palace or other fine downtown restaurants, but there are few other places where bringing a child would be inappropriate.

City of Cincinnati law requires restaurants to provide a nonsmoking section. Outside the city limits, nonsmokers aren't quite as lucky, and your chance of finding a smoke-free restaurant decreases mightily if you drive south into Kentucky, a big-time tobacco farm state. We've noted those restaurants that don't have a nonsmoking section in the listings. Greater Cincinnati does offer 350 smoke-free restaurants, by last count. The local American Lung Association will happily mail you a list of them—call (513) 985-3990.

We chose to organize this chapter alphabetically by culinary categories rather than by neighborhood or other geographical listing. And while we generally don't list neighborhoods in our addresses if those neighborhoods are within Cincinnati city limits, we thought it would be helpful to do so in the restaurant chapter because so many newcomers and tourists seek out restaurants. If there's just a street address, it's downtown Cincinnati.

We offer a mix of the venerable establishments and the newest trendsetting bistros. If you truly want to dazzle your guests, then check out our listings for the Palace, the Restaurant at the Phoenix, Palm Court, or the Golden Lamb (all under American Traditional); Palomino Euro Bistro or South Beach Grill (under American Contemporary); the Celestial or Jean-Robert at Pigall's (under French); or the Precinct or Jeff Ruby's (under Steak Houses).

As a rule, we don't list chain restaurants unless they offer something unique or exceptional from what you can expect to find at the chain's other outlets elsewhere in the country.

Want to bite into a slice of local history? Dish up some Queen City legend and folklore? Cincinnati restaurants aren't just places to eat. Many are historical treasures, and while the wrecking ball seems to destroy a few more each year, Cincinnati still preserves more than most. We've included some of our most notable century-old institutions in this chapter, including Arnold's, Mecklenburg Gardens, the Golden Lamb, Scotti's, Century Inn, and Palm Court.

If you want an unrestricted view of the world, know that the Radisson Hotel Riverview is the area's revolving restaurant. In the mood for a magnificent Sunday buffet? Among the undisputed champs around here are the Albee, Palm Court, Michael G's, Geoffrey's Bar and Grille, Iron Horse Inn, Grand Finale, and Sturkey's.

Here are a few other tips about how to use this chapter and on dining in general in Greater Cincinnati: Dress in Cincinnati restaurants is usually casual, even more so the farther you get from downtown. But as a rule, don't wear jeans, shorts, or tennis shoes to restaurants with a $$$ or above rating. Restaurants with dress codes are noted, as are those that are particularly kid friendly or that confound expectations one way or the other.

Unless otherwise noted, assume the restaurants listed here accept major credit cards. Even so, check before you order if you don't have the cash. And unless otherwise noted, all restaurants are open daily and serve both lunch and dinner. Restaurants that serve breakfast or brunch are so noted.

Finally, please remember that it's impossible for even us to go everywhere in one year. Cincinnati just has too many terrific restaurants. So if you don't see your favorite place listed below, stay tuned for future editions.

PRICE CODE

The following ratings are based on the average price of two entrees, excluding tax, tip, appetizers, desserts, and beverages.

$	Less than $20
$$	$20 to $35
$$$	$36 to $50
$$$$	$51 and more

AMERICAN CONTEMPORARY AND ECLECTIC

This is, granted, an arbitrary category. Presumably all restaurants located within the borders of the United States could be labeled "American." And you could drive a semi through the hole left by the description of "contemporary" and "eclectic." Suffice to say we've included trendy bistros, lively dining spots, and establishments that are, in one way or another, uniquely Cincinnati.

Allyn's Cafe **$$-$$$**
3538 Columbia Parkway
Columbia-Tusculum
(513) 871-5779

You'll find little to sing the blues about at Allyn's Cafe. Enter this bustling blues-and-jazz bar and everybody seems to know each other, but they happily make room for strangers too. Pictures of carousing customers line the wall. The beer list is extensive—regulars recommend the Pilsner Urquell from the Czech Republic, first brewed in 1292. The menu is generally divided into categories of Cajun, Mexican, Nex Mex (a low-fat selection of Mexican), L'il Italy, and Blackened Thangs. Try Al's Cajun Seafood Platter, with its incredible variety of blackened catfish, popcorn shrimp, jerk scallops, hush puppies, and Cajun rice. For the daring there's the Shrimp & Gator, served Creole style with red pepper and garlic linguini. Allyn's Cafe is, of course, as much about music as food. Locals such as Brian Lovely, the Goshorn Bros., and the Bluebirds Big Band are regularly featured acts.

Anchor Grill **$-$$**
438 West Pike Street, Covington, KY
(859) 431-9498

This Greater Cincinnati institution is famous for never closing, a 24-hour-a-day operation except for Christmas Day. Goetta-and-cheese omelet ("the big seller"), steaks, and cheeseburgers are among the entrees at this folksy, down-home eatery.

Arnold's Bar and Grill **$-$$**
210 East Eighth Street
(513) 421-6234
www.arnoldsbarandgrill.com

Time for only one quick meal in Cincinnati? To soak up as much local color as possible, head immediately downtown to Arnold's, the oldest tavern in town (established 1861). The cost of beer and sarsaparilla may have changed, but not the ambience. Prohibition finally forced Arnold's into the restaurant business, but the bathtub (for brewing illegal gin) remains. "The upstairs has never been remodeled," says Arnold's official historian and one-time proprietor, Jim Tarbell. "It represents late-19th-century decor, fireplaces and all." Arnold's is where the town's politicos and newspaper types, as well as local law enforcement, judges, radio DJs—you name it—hang out. Just sit at the long bar and you'll get a crash course in "Cincy speak." Tarbell, who's now a city councilman after all those years of serving brews to same, handed over the reins to two of his former employees. They've sworn to keep the place as is. The house specialty is Greek Spaghetti Deluxe, bathed in olive oil, butter, and garlic sauce, then topped with sautéed olives, bacon, and vegetables. The enclosed courtyard offers outdoor dining, and some of the town's finest Celtic, folk, and bluegrass musicians appear on stage. Arnold's is closed on Sunday (except for brunch). No lunch Saturday. Bar service only Monday night.

Behle Street Cafe **$$-$$$**
50 East RiverCenter Boulevard, Covington, KY
(859) 291-4100
Settle down to comfort foods, including pork chops and the town's tastiest shepherd's pie, in a casual setting. The servings, especially the cheeseburgers, are huge. The decor includes Hollywood celebrity still photos.

Bella **$$-$$$**
600 Walnut Street
(513) 721-7100
www.bellacincinnati.com
Bella was named Best New Restaurant by the readers of *Cincinnati CityBeat,* and little wonder. Executive chef Allen Stickell hopped over from the Jump Cafe to create a menu here that includes Unorthodox Shrimp Spring Rolls in a Thai vinaigrette; smoked jalapeño BBQ chicken quesadilla; sautéed Brie with sun-dried cranberry salsa; Bella crab cakes in a hot pepper and avocado relish; ginger and orange glazed portobello mushroom salad with lemon shallot vinaigrette; the Bella salad with blackened tuna, raisins, Gorgonzola, and hearts of palm; Asian chicken salad with baby spinach, pears, and soba noodles in a peanut dressing; the Ultimate Fish Sandwich (cod encrusted in cornmeal and topped with cheddar cheese); and our favorite, Pasta Frutti di Mare, with saffron pasta, rock shrimp, lump crab, and roasted peppers. Bella is located directly next door to the Aronoff Center for the Arts, making it an ideal stop on the way to the theater. No lunch on Saturday, brunch on Sunday.

Bistro 151 **$$-$$$**
151 Goodman Avenue, Avondale
(513) 481-3544
www.marriott.com
Parents who are visiting offspring at the University of Cincinnati, please take note: While most of the fare found on the campus proper leans toward soggy pizza, fast food, and vendo machines, Bistro 151—located in the university's impressive Kingsgate Conference Center—provides such fascinating entrees as barley-and-mushroom risotto, smoked pork chop with napa cabbage, and half chicken simmering in a cilantro lime and tequila marinade. So if Johnny Jr. tries to get away with taking you to the campus Mickey D's, just say no.

Brontë Bistro **$-$$**
2692 Madison Road, Norwood
(513) 731-7770
www.josephbeth.com
You'd think that when a business tries to be a bookstore, music store, toy store, and restaurant all at the same time, it wouldn't do a good job at any of them. Guess again. The cafe at this popular Joseph-Beth bookstore is terrific, offering everything from a tasty blue-cheese-and-mushroom polenta to spicy shrimp and olive pasta. Lunch and dinner are served daily, and there's a Sunday brunch. Buy the latest issue of your favorite magazine and lounge around here.

Brown Dog Cafe **$$$-$$$$**
5893 Pfeiffer Road, Blue Ash
(513) 794-1610
www.browndogcafe.com
The Brown Dog Cafe offers up American cuisine, including crab in butter sauce, tuna crusted with sesame seeds, pan-roasted sea bass, and venison loin. The Brown Dog does not serve lunch on Saturday; it's closed Sunday.

Cabana on the River **$**
7445 Forbes Road, Sayler Park
(513) 941-7442
If you're looking for casual on the river, this is the place to go on the West Side. Down the river from downtown, this summertime restaurant is relaxing, for you can eat while watching the boats go by. The place boasts a huge deck with a view of the river and casual food—Cabana's bluefin tuna dinners, burgers, and hoagies are well known in the area. This restaurant is right down from where the Fore and Aft used to be.

One of the best Sunday buffet deals in town comes courtesy of the Hamilton County Park District—but only in the winter. The rangers open up the Sweetwine Lodge at Woodland Mound in Anderson for a 40-item all-you-can-eat smorgasbord (juice and coffee are included) for $10.80 per person; $5.40 for children age 10 and under. No tips accepted. Call (513) 474-3008.

Clough Crossings $$
6892 Clough Pike, Anderson
(513) 624-7800

Housed in a striking building that once was a schoolhouse, Clough (pronounced Cluff) Crossings presents a varied menu of Cajun seafood fettuccine, chicken quesadillas, and Bird of Paradise salad. The tournedos of beef are particularly notable: two filet medallions served two different ways—one is blackened, the other is topped with a mushroom demi-glace. All the seafood arrives fresh daily from Keegan's Seafood, one of the most sumptuous fish shops in the area (see our listing in the Shopping chapter). There's an outdoor patio here sheltered by trees, and an impressive mahogany bar. It's closed Sunday. Lunch is served Tuesday through Friday only.

Coco's $$
322 Greenup Street, Covington, KY
(859) 491-1369

This intimate neighborhood spot with exposed brick walls and southwestern accents is the kind of place you'd expect to find in Mount Adams, only it's in the increasingly rejuvenated Covington. Popular fare includes crab cakes, baked Brie with fresh fruit, and a focaccia pizza with prosciutto, roasted asparagus, and arugula pesto.

Daveed's at 934 $$$-$$$$
934 Hatch Street, Mount Adams
(513) 721-2665

There's all sorts of culinary excitement going on at Daveed's at 934, found high atop Mount Adams in the heart of this neighborhood's trendy shopping and dining district. It's here you'll find such unusual menu items as maple cumin-lacquered quail, free-range veal medallions with mushroom and currants, applewood smoked bacon compote, seared Hudson Valley foie gras, and grilled balsamic-marinated flank steak with potato rutabaga puree, haricot verts, orange reduction, and veal demi-glace. Desserts include Tropical Oasis (phyllo with mango pastry creme and lemongrass syrup). Closed Sunday and Monday.

Dee Felice Cafe $$$-$$$$
529 Main Street, Covington, KY
(859) 261-2365
www.deefelice.com

A Cajun restaurant playing Dixieland jazz may be a little incongruous with surrounding MainStrasse Village, but never mind the culture clash. Superb gumbo and jambalaya combined with Dixieland and classic jazz seven nights a week make this one of the top restaurants and nicest low-key nightspots south of the river. It's also a popular place for lunch away from the hustle and bustle, though it does not serve lunch on Saturday. Open for Sunday brunch.

deSha's American Tavern $$$-$$$$
11320 Montgomery Road, Symmes
(513) 247-9933
www.deshas.com

This restaurant at the Shops of Harper's Point shopping center is among the best midrange restaurants around, with well-prepared dishes such as cranberry apricot pork loin, London broil, whiskey-barbecued rib-eye steak, and oven-roasted halibut. Don't miss the house corn bread. No smoking.

First Watch $-$$
700 Walnut Street
(513) 721-4744

2692 Madison Road, Norwood
(513) 531-7430

8118 Montgomery Road, Kenwood
(513) 891-0088

11031 Montgomery Road, Symmes
(513) 489-6849

9233 Floer Drive, West Chester
(513) 942-5100
www.firstwatch.com
If the business breakfast meeting hadn't already become a staple by the time First Watch opened, it would have had to be invented. These restaurants are the breakfast destination of choice for many Cincinnatians who live on the Interstate 71 corridor from Hyde Park to Symmes—and a good ways beyond. They're always delectable, always reasonably priced, and always packed. Specialties include the Bacado (our favorite, it's an omelet stuffed with avocado and bacon), the turkey dill "crepegg," and great pancakes. Breakfast is served all day, but the restaurant also has a lunch menu, a selection of light fare and salads. First Watch does not serve dinner.

Floyd's **$**
127 Calhoun Street, Clifton Heights
(513) 221-2434
Floyd's serves some excellent roasted chicken marinated in Mediterranean spices, in addition to dolmas, falafel, hummus, tabbouleh, and other well-prepared Middle Eastern staples. Extremely reasonable prices make this one of the better deals on the university-area strip or anywhere in town. Floyd's is open Tuesday through Friday only. No credit cards.

Geoffrey's Bar and Grille **$-$$**
5880 Cheviot Road, White Oak
(513) 385-9999
Yet another West Side institution, this is much more than the name implies. Geoffrey's serves grilled food, yes, but daily specials include entrees that remind you of home, such as beef stew, potato soup, steaks, pork chops, hamburgers, and salads. Very popular with those people who live in the area, Geoffrey's is even crowded on a weeknight. Closed Monday.

Grand Finale **$$-$$$**
3 East Sharon Avenue, Glendale
(513) 771-5925
Set in a century-old Victorian tavern, this is the perfect place to bring your visiting parents or that hard-to-please maiden aunt. The house specialty is Chicken Ginger marinated in soy, sherry, and honey, then grilled with ginger and walnuts. You also can't go wrong with the crabmeat crepes in butter cream sauce at Grand Finale. There are a half-dozen crepe options on the menu, including Crêpes Champignon (mushrooms laced with a blend of melted cheeses) and spinach crepes. Not exactly finger food. At meal's end, try one of the four flaming desserts. The Sunday brunch here is awesome, with fascinating items such as poached eggs on artichoke hearts. This restaurant is closed on Monday.

Habanero **$**
358 Ludlow Avenue, Clifton
(513) 961-6800
Former Palomino Euro Bistro chef Max Monks opened this casual counter-service restaurant that features Latin fare with a trendy twist. Pork, fish, and steak wraps are prepared with stimulating ingredients such as roasted pumpkin, cinnamon, grilled apple, and pineapple almond salsa.

The Iron Horse **$$-$$$$**
40 Village Square, Glendale
(513) 771-4787
This restaurant has garnered wide attention chiefly due to chef Ron Wise's daring menu. Begin with duck sausage in a cabernet demi-glace, then proceed to the sea bass with garlic mayo or filet mignon topped with smoked duck breast and Gorgonzola. No lunch Saturday, closed Sunday.

CLOSE-UP

Counter Intelligence

Cincinnatians literally eat up nostalgia, be it through '50s-style lunch counters, drive-ins, root beer stands, luncheonettes, or creamy whips. Perhaps, it's because all these remnants of another era beckon back to a more innocent time, or perhaps it's just because of our penny-pinching ways. At a lunch counter, for instance, you're not paying for fancy decor or table-side service—just for good eats like mom used to make. You should assume that none of the places listed below take a credit card—what luncheonette or creamy whip would?

A few of the local favorites:

Something of a Cincinnati landmark, **Camp Washington Chili** opened back in 1940 (serving a dozen cheese Coneys for a buck). The counter is genuine Formica, the padded stainless-steel stools are comfy, and wall jukeboxes add to the atmosphere. In the early mornings, the blue-and-white tile floor is lit up with a fluorescent glow from the CHILI sign outside. The 4:00 A.M. crowd includes University of Cincinnati students battling hangovers (Cincinnati chili after a bender is a coming-of-age rite around here). A regular breakfast menu is also offered, however, for the sane and sober. In addition to chili, the double-deckers are terrific. You can find Camp Washington Chili at 3005 Hopple Street in Camp Washington, (513) 541-0061. It's closed Sunday.

"We've got *the* old-time lunch counter," says one employee of the **Echo,** 3510 Edwards Road, Hyde Park, (513) 321-2816—and indeed, this institution just off Hyde Park Square always does a bustling lunchtime trade. The menu roams from blueberry hotcakes to Swiss steak.

The grande dame of luncheonettes, **Hathaway's,** in the Carew Tower Arcade, (513) 621-1332, is the kind of place where the waitresses (who've been working here forever) learn customers' first names—or, in a pinch, just call you "hon." The lunch counter is vintage 1930s. Order up a chocolate ice-cream soda from the old-time soda fountain and enjoy. The fish sandwich here can't be beat. Hathaway's is closed on Sunday.

Johnny Rockets is the place for a burger with pickles and a chocolate malted. The nostalgia is a bit forced (with '50s posters adorning every inch of wall space), but the eats are excellent and the service friendly. The waitress even hands you a coin for the jukebox. Johnny Rockets is at 7800 Montgomery

Road in Kenwood, (513) 791-5606, and at Newport on the Levee in Newport, KY.

And then there's **Newtown Creamy Whip,** at the corner of U.S. Highway 32 and Newtown Road in Newtown (no phone). Isn't there a shack like this in everybody's summer? In the East, they might call the specialty of the house "frozen custard." But here, it's just plain creamy whip, softee, or soft serve. Folks line up with their kids, and sometimes their dogs (who don't hesitate to partake in the melted vanilla and chocolate drippings!). Located directly in downtown Newtown, which is only about a block long, so it's hard to miss. Closed in the winter.

Sure, **Skyline Chili** is everywhere. But the very first Skyline opened in 1949 at 3822 Glenway Avenue in Price Hill. Although the original one closed in 2002, there are many others still outfitted with a lunch counter, stools, the works. Order up a sloppy five-way. After all, at a lunch counter, nobody can spot the chili stains on your tie.

In a city full of places such as the Cone, Dari Crest, and Tummy Treats, **Putz's** stands above. Any place with its own street named after it has to be an institution. The white shack at 2673 Putz Place in Westwood, (513) 681-8668, is a West Side favorite, offering soft serves, metts, and more. Why go to Dairy Queen ever again? Closed in the winter.

The Root Beer Stand at 11566 Reading Road in Sharonville, (513) 769-4349, is a local classic. The root beer is made on-site using well water and is served in a frosty mug. The eats are pretty good too, especially the foot-long hot dogs. Closed in the winter.

It's 1958 again at the **Sonic Drive-in,** 3105 West U.S. Highway 22 in Landen, (513) 583-1854. Ritchie Valens is belting out "La Bamba" on the intercom, classic cars line up in the parking spots, carhops scurry to take orders. Corn dogs, Sonic burgers, cherry limeades, and onion rings adorn the menu. You'll feel like you've died and gone to 1950s heaven.

The **Starlite Drive-In,** 2255 Ohio Pike, Amelia, (513) 734-4001, is the destination on any warm summer night, though the place is filled up as often with carloads of nostalgic adults as carloads of kids. Crack open a Coke, scarf down a hot dog with mustard relish, and relive your teen years. Closed in the winter.

Cincinnati is known for any number of culinary innovations, beyond its unique cinnamon chili spaghetti. Due largely to the city's pork-packaging and brewing heritage, Cincinnati is the home of "city chicken" (pork cubes on a sticks), "Cincinnati oysters" (a slang term for pickled pig's feet), and a "Cinci," which is 1880s slang for a short glass of beer.

LeBoxx Cafe **$**
819 Vine Street
(513) 721-5638
www.leboxx.com
This downtown cafe's peculiar name is a reminder that it delivers boxed lunches to those hardworking, chained-to-the-desk types downtown, but it's a cut above your usual we-deliver deli. LeBoxx seems to be thriving in a spot where others have failed by offering creative touches on old favorites. Some of the best dishes include the Jack and Coke burger and the buffalo chicken wrap. LeBoxx serves lunch only, Monday through Friday.

The Melting Pot **$$$$**
11023 Montgomery Road, Milford
(513) 530-5501
www.meltingpot.com
If you didn't get enough fondue during the '70s, this is the place for you. We'll break the chain rule here because this Florida-based chain has sites mainly in the Southeast and some people may not be familiar with it. It has fondue everything, from filet mignon to dessert. It's open for dinner only.

Newport Syndicate **$$$-$$$$**
18 East Fifth Street, Newport, KY
(859) 491-8000
www.newportsyndicate.com
This restaurant features a Florida art deco theme and ballroom entertainment. Very classy. Very expensive. There's a full range of steak, seafood, chicken, and pasta dishes as well as a terrific house salad. The surf and turf is one of the most popular entrees. Dinner only. Closed Sunday and Monday.

Palomino **$$$-$$$$**
505 Vine Street
(513) 381-1300
www.palomino.com
With its wood-fired Mediterranean cuisine, this visually impressive restaurant—with lots of Matisse reproductions and a salmon-burgundy color scheme—overlooks Fountain Square and is a destination dining spot for downtowners and tourists alike. With neighbors such as Tiffany's and Brooks Brothers, this is not the place to go to slug down a couple of brewskies after a Reds game. Specialties include apricot cilantro chicken and lobster ravioli. Even the desserts come out of the wood-fired ovens, including the roasted pear bread pudding with bourbon sauce. Brunch is served on Saturday and Sunday.

The Quarter Bistro **$$-$$$$**
6904 Wooster Pike, Mariemont
(513) 271-5400
Restaurateur Elliot Jablonsky brings a little bit of Havana to Mariemont Square with this Cuban eatery. Specials of the house include the Cuban sandwich (thin-sliced pork, chihuahua cheese, and pickles on focaccia), shrimp scallop tamales, grilled pork chops, and Caribbean barbecue wings (served with plantain chips and lemon cream). Dinner only.

Redfish **$$-$$$**
Seventh and Race Streets
(513) 929-4700
The place to get gumbo in Cincinnati (granted, the Cajun options are limited 'round here). Try the seafood gumbo, stocked with crawfish tails and oysters, or the chicken and Andouille sausage gumbo. Redfish's mashed potatoes side dish, blended with cheddar cheese, garlic, and Andouille sausage, is a meal in itself.

Shadowbox Cabaret **$$$**
1 Levee Way, Newport on the Levee, Newport, KY
(859) 957-7625
www.shadowboxcabaret.com
A combination theater/comedy club and eatery, this nightclub boasts a full-service bar as well as an appetizing menu. Your waiter, as it happens, is a member of the theatrical troupe. Shows, which lean toward skits reminiscent of the Capitol Steps or *Saturday Night Live*, are Wednesday through Saturday. Raucous rock music is also on the agenda. Bring earplugs.

Sky Galley **$$-$$$**
262 Wilmer Avenue, Mount Washington
(513) 871-7400
The unpretentious bar and grill is more notable for its locale than its food. Located inside Lunken Airport, the city's original air terminal, Sky Galley is a terrific place for bringing the kids to watch the Cessnas take off and land. Order up a sandwich by the window and enjoy the show. Next door is a gift shop with model jets and those old-time balsa wood airplanes we all flew as children. It all makes for a fun, educational outing. (When the Goodyear blimp is in town for a Bengals game, by the way, it docks right here at Lunken—yet another kid pleaser.)

South Beach Grill **$$$-$$$$**
14 Pete Rose Pier, Covington, KY
(859) 581-1414
www.jeffruby.com
This is Cincinnati's all-around glitziest restaurant, a place for special occasions and a regular hangout for athletes and other celebrities, some of whom are part owners (including former Bengals Cris Collinsworth and Boomer Esiason and some guy named Pete Rose, along with restaurateur-to-the-stars Jeff Ruby). In addition to the same selection of steaks (and to a large extent, clientele) you'll find at Ruby's the Precinct in Columbia-Tusculum, this riverfront institution offers seafood and other entrees. Don't leave without trying the escargot. Chef Jeff Leopard serves up a double mustard salmon and wonderful PB&J pork chops (employing spicy peanut, cucumber, and currant demi).

Other specialties include the Chilled Lobster Martini, a one-pound lobster piled into a martini glass and topped with a mango remoulade, and the flaming Brazilian Sabers (shish kebabs done one better, with the meats skewered on stainless-steel swords and set flaming tableside).

Sturkey's **$$$-$$$$**
400 Wyoming Avenue, Wyoming
(513) 821-9200
www.sturkeys.com
Chef Paul Sturkey was already well known to radio listeners in town for his daily *Everybody's Cooking* show. Now he's opened his own restaurant, with a menu ranging from seared artic char to roasted duck breast. For dessert, try pastry chef Pam Sturkey's fried chocolate truffles (crunchy balls with molten bittersweet chocolate inside). Only dinner is served Saturday and Sunday.

Through the Garden **$$-$$$**
10738 Kenwood Road, Blue Ash
(513) 791-2199
Through the Garden is a thoroughly American bistro that offers one of the most delectable stir-fries in town. Loaded with fresh vegetables, your pick of chicken, beef, or shrimp, plus three tangy sauces to choose from. We recommend the Jamaican spicy oriental glaze or the fruity olive oil. Take a wok on the wild side.

Tinks **$$-$$$**
3410 Telford Avenue, Clifton
(513) 961-6500
Located inside a converted Clifton Gaslight District establishment, just off busy Ludlow Avenue, Tinks boasts a varied and eclectic menu that includes grilled eggplant brochettes, crab cakes with remoulade, grilled lemon chicken over spinach, and lamb with tabbouleh. Its signature chocolate fondue was named Best

Dessert by the urban weekly *CityBeat*, and indeed, it's an evil temptation to which we happily succumb. Chunks of kiwi, pineapple, strawberry, and starfruit are provided for dipping. Hey, that makes it health food, doesn't it? No lunch Sunday.

Trio **$$-$$$$**
7565 Kenwood Road, Kenwood
(513) 984-1905
www.triobistro.com
When Gregg Pancero opened Trio a few years back, he brought a cultured pedigree to the operation as a member of Chaîn des Rôtisseurs and L'Ordre Mondial Gourmets Dégustateurs. Pancero has managed to earn high marks from his patrons—and what patrons they are. Much of the traffic hauls in from nearby (and very posh) Indian Hill, the third richest zip code in Ohio. Indeed, one of the restaurant's claims to fame is that it's a favorite of billionaire Carl Lindner (look for his Rolls in the parking lot). Pancero's varied entrees hint at many cuisines: Californian, Cajun, Greek, Asian . . . even of the Deep South. The menu features hoisin BBQ glazed chicken with wasabi mashed potatoes; seared salmon cake with whole-grain mustard dill sauce; pecan tilapia with curried rice and spicy mango sauce; and mushroom fettuccine, a sauté of wild mushrooms, sun-dried tomatoes, and roasted garlic oil. One of the restaurant's most popular items is the Santa Fe salad, mixed greens with cilantro and lemon-marinated chicken, grilled in mesquite and accompanied by black bean salsa, tortilla strips, and a zingy jalapeño citrus dressing.

Tropicana **$$-$$$$**
1 Levee Way, Newport on the Levee, Newport, KY
(859) 491-8900
www.jeffruby.com
If you like corned-beef sandwiches, come to Tropicana. The corned beef is hard to beat (if you're willing to pay the price), flown in directly from the Carnegie Deli in New York City. At better than $10 a sandwich, though, we presume these suckers are flown into town first-class, sipping their martinis while watching the in-flight movie. Dinner only. Closed Sunday.

Vineyard Cafe **$$-$$$**
2653 Erie Avenue, Hyde Park
(513) 871-6167
At the Vineyard Cafe on Hyde Park Square, chef/owner Elliot Jablonsky has created a unique kitchen with no range hoods. This means no grilling, no frying, no sautéeing—everything's oven-baked or roasted. The menu includes Asian crab cakes with yaki soba noodles and Thai chili sauce, roasted tuna, spanakopita, roasted portobella bruschetta, a chicken and Brie quesadilla, penne Firenze, smoked salmon pizza, and other trendy California-style fare.

What's for Dinner? **$-$$**
3009 O'Bryon Road, O'Bryonville
(513) 321-4404
Tucked just off the main drag (Madison Road) of O'Bryonville, this restaurant answers its own question astutely. Try the grilled crostini bread with sun-dried-tomato tapenade or stick to traditional meat loaf. Whatever you do, save room for a Carmellita, a rich and gooey treat that is well worth the assault it will make on your arteries and waistline. Sunday brunch is served.

York Street Cafe **$$**
738 York Street, Newport, KY
(859) 261-9675
A genteel little cafe, York Street Cafe has the look and feel of a Victorian parlor, complete with sofas where you can eat your meal over coffee tables. Bookcases line the walls. Reasonably priced dishes include a wide selection of tasty sandwiches and focaccia creations. York Street's "Conversational Platters" are an inexpensive way to feed an entire group. Vietnamese noodle salad comes with spicy shrimp and cilantro-mint dressing, while the ever-popular Mediterranean Board is filled with hummus, tabbouleh, baba ghannoush, Greek salad, and pita bread.

Zebo's Bistro **$$$$**
Cincinnati Marriott at RiverCenter,
10 RiverCenter Boulevard
Covington, KY
(859) 392-3750
This way-above-average Marriott dining room shows off entrees such as grilled Cincinnati pork chop with garlic mashed potatoes, caramelized apple and sweet potato pancake, fresh fish, local Amish chicken, and hand-cut steaks. Breakfast is also served. The Covington lunch crowd has discovered the restaurant's offbeat sandwiches, which include creations such as lobster strudel.

AMERICAN TRADITIONAL

These are the mainstays of the Cincinnati dining experience, the places frequented by locals and admired by out of towners. The food is hearty and midwestern—lots of steaks, fowl, and pork (appropriately enough for the town once nicknamed "Porkopolis").

The Albee **$$-$$$**
21 East Fifth Street
(513) 852-2740
Overlooking Fountain Square in the Westin Hotel downtown, the Albee boasts a tremendous view of the square and the horse-drawn carriages that come and go all evening. Built on the site of the old Albee movie theater, silver-screen memorabilia lines the restaurant walls. Fare includes pan-seared Amish chicken breast, orzo pasta with lemon basil sauce, cheese-stuffed meat loaf, grilled apricot pork loin, veal stuffed with Brie cheese, and roasted swordfish. The Albee Bar serves hors d'oeuvres.

The Golden Lamb **$$-$$$**
27 South Broadway, Lebanon
(513) 932-5065
www.goldenlamb.com
Talk about staying power, the Golden Lamb's been here for 200 years and still packs 'em in. Under the ownership of the Comisar family, the tradition rests in good hands. The Golden Lamb is to traditional American cuisine what Pigall's is to French cuisine. Some specialties here include the roast leg of lamb (natch), roast Indiana duckling, and chicken Oscar. Rooms are named after famous guests, such as Charles Dickens and Mark Twain. Greater Cincinnati's top antiques stores are located nearby, so make a day of shopping and fine dining. Lunch is not served on Sunday. Open holidays, except Christmas Day.

National Exemplar **$$$-$$$$**
6880 Wooster Pike, Mariemont
(513) 271-2103
www.nationalexemplar.com
This spot, operated by the same folks who run the wildly popular local chain of First Watch restaurants, is renowned for great breakfasts that feature giant omelets, gourmet pancakes, frittatas, and crepes. But they want you to know they also serve lunch and dinner—notably, Nova Scotia salmon, veal Suzanne, and steak KP—at this beautifully appointed restaurant at the Best Western Mariemont Inn.

The Palace **$$$$**
601 Vine Street
(513) 381-6006
www.cincinnatianhotel.com
The Palace restaurant, located just off the lobby of the century-old Cincinnatian Hotel (originally the Palace), has all the trappings of its rank: mahogany paneling, fresh flowers, sterling silver trays, serving domes, and formally attired servers. The Palace whips up specialties that include Caribbean bouillabaise, Wagyu beef filet, and roasted Baramundi (a bean dish). While you're waiting for a table, you can take a seat in the Cricket Lounge, where Cincinnatian Hotel guests such as Billy Joel and Stevie Nicks have taken a turn at the piano. There is no smoking allowed at the Palace—another notch in its favor, as far as we're concerned. Dinner dress code calls for men to wear jackets (ties optional). Reservations are a must. Lunch is not served on weekends.

Orchids at Palm Court **$$$-$$$$**
35 West Fifth Street
(513) 564-6465
www.hilton.com
This restaurant is inside the Hilton Netherland Hotel in the Carew Tower. Check out the intricately carved moldings and unusual art deco accents throughout this downtown institution, which opened in 1931 and is a National Historic Landmark. A variety of well-prepared regional American cuisine makes this historic restaurant a great place for a special occasion. It has what is probably the city's most extensive wine list. No lunch served.

Parkers Blue Ash Grille **$$-$$$$**
4200 Cooper Road, Blue Ash
(513) 891-8300
If you like history dished up with your food, Parkers is the place. Lots of fireplaces and a cozy atmosphere make for a relaxing dining experience. Fare includes hearth-roasted cedar-planked salmon, roasted prime rib, peppercorn filet mignon, and a standout brûlée cheesecake. No lunch Saturday. Sunday brunch served.

Radisson Hotel Riverview **$$$-$$$$**
668 Fifth Street, Covington, KY
(859) 491-1200
www.radisson.com
For some, a culinary tour of any city must include a visit to a revolving restaurant. So be it. Riverview is our choice, not only because it offers a splendid panorama of the skyline and environs, but because the menu would move you even if the floor didn't. Particularly worth sampling are the lamb chops, seafood medley, and—unusual for staid Cincinnati—filet of ostrich served with shallot mustard sauce.

The Restaurant at the Phoenix **$$$-$$$$**
812 Race Street
(513) 721-8901
www.thephx.com
This highly rated restaurant is a landmark and one of the most beautiful places to eat downtown. It's a good, slightly out-of-the-way place to impress out-of-town friends or business associates without taking them to the Palace. Entrees include filet mignon, veal chop, rack of lamb, and sea bass. The Restaurant at the Phoenix serves dinner only and is closed Sunday, Monday, and Tuesday.

Symphony Hotel **$$-$$$**
210 West 14th Street, Over-the-Rhine
(513) 721-3353
Opened in the former Clyde Hotel, a gracious Victorian stone mansion, this is a distinctly upscale establishment that offers five-course meals. Hours are odd—dinner is only offered on nights when there is a performance at nearby Music Hall.

The White House Inn **$$-$$$**
4940 Muhlhauser Road, West Chester
(513) 860-1110
A huge restored farmhouse with fireplaces and a gazebo, the inn is surrounded by herb gardens and outdoor patios. The house specialty is steak Lynchburg, a strip steak studded with peppercorns and bathed in Jack Daniel's sauce. Also excellent is the Farmhouse Duck in peach-and-cherry sauce.

ASIAN

What happened? This is Cincinnati, Ohio, as typical a midwestern burg as you could ever find. Yet we've got this incredibly diverse and delightful assortment of Chinese, Japanese, Indian, Thai, Korean, Vietnamese, and even Sri Lankan eateries. Enough to satisfy the yen of any occidental tourist.

Akash India **$$**
24 East Sixth Street
(513) 723-1300
One of the city's newest Indian restaurants is Akash, which translates as "blue sky." This is where downtown's power elite go to, ahem, curry favor with local politicos. Seriously, the curries here are terrific, as is

the service. Try the shrimp Biryani (tossed with nuts and raisins) or the tangy chicken vindaloo. Order up a Mango Lassi (a mango and yogurt concoction) to cool your taste buds. The restaurant sits directly next to Ruth Lyons Alley (for the uninitiated, Ruth Lyons was the Erma Bombeck of Cincinnati's airwaves).

Ambar India **$-$$**
350 Ludlow Avenue, Clifton
(513) 281-7000
www.ambarindia.com
Ambar India is a perennial winner as best Indian restaurant in the seemingly endless restaurant polls conducted by the city's newspapers and magazines. The title, however, is well deserved. Vegetarians flock to this Ludlow Avenue haunt, long known for its northern India oven dishes and exotic curries. Meat lovers will find plenty of choices too, from a savory lamb and shrimp curry to chicken tandoori.

Beluga **$$-$$$**
3520 Edwards Road, Hyde Park
(513) 533-4444
Safe to say, this is the only sushi restaurant along Hyde Park Square, Cincinnati's most yupscale shopping district. But there's actually a little bit of Asian to suit every taste: egg rolls stuffed with duck confit, Asian vegetables and pickled ginger served with mango chutney, Japanese tempura and teriyaki. The varied menu also includes a caviar course (hence the restaurant's moniker), jumbo Cape Cod lobster, blackened lobster pasta, Colorado lamb, and veal chops. Fusion cuisine, the melding of two or more distinct geographical eats, is definitely the approach here. Dinner only. Closed Sunday.

Chung Kiwha
Korean Barbecue **$$$-$$$$**
7800 Commerce Drive, Florence, KY
(859) 525-9978
Fans of Mongolian barbecue or the melting pot style of cooking your meal yourself will like Chung Kiwha Korean

Hungry at 3:00 A.M.? Twenty-four-hour restaurants in the region include Anchor Grill, Camp Washington Chili, Chili Company, Chili Time, Pepper Pod, and selected Perkin's. And there's a Skyline Chili outlet near the University of Cincinnati campus that stays open until 3:00 A.M. Shanghai Mama's, a downtown Chinese eatery, keeps its carryout open till 3:00 A.M. on Friday and Saturday.

Barbecue. You grab a dish, pile on from the buffet of raw ingredients, then prepare them at your table's private charcoal grill. The sushi bar is a la carte.

Doodles **$-$$**
3431 Edwards Road, Hyde Park
(513) 871-7388
A trendy storefront dining nook just off Hyde Park Square, Doodles offers a different take on traditional Chinese. Sample Ming's moo shu pork, for instance, light and delicate Chinese vegetables that are stir-fried with tender pork and egg, then wrapped in a Mandarin pancake and served with elegant plum sauce. The Chinese chicken taco is an example of the enterprising ethnic fusion occurring at this eatery; the taco fixings are enfolded into a huge iceberg lettuce leaf. Don't leave without a scallion pancake.

JoAn **$-$$$**
3940 Olympic Boulevard, Erlanger, KY
(859) 746-2634
JoAn—specializing in Japanese cuisine—is strategically located across the way from Toyota's Northern Kentucky headquarters. No question, Kotaro Nakamura's restaurant serves up the tristate's most authentic Japanese food, including egg custard with shrimp, herring roe in miso, and the ever-popular sea eel.

Lemon Grass **$-$$**
2666 Madison Road, Hyde Park
(513) 321-2882
Named favorite restaurant by the readers

of *CityBeat* alternative newspaper, this Thai find serves up a spicy Panang chicken curry and other fare. Emphasis is on the attractive display of dishes as well as taste. Lunch is served on weekdays only.

LuLu's Asian Diner **$**
135 West Kemper Road, Springdale
(513) 671-4949
LuLu's occupies an unpretentious storefront in a shopping strip, but it's gaining critical acclaim. Noodle bowls generously overflow with plump shrimp or chicken and exotic Asian vegetables. It's closed on Sunday. No credit cards.

The Pacific Moon Cafe **$$-$$$**
1 Levee Way, Newport, KY
(859) 957-7625
Be sure to allow ample time to peruse the voluminous menu, which includes dishes from throughout the Pacific Rim. Chef Alex Chin has long been producing some of the city's finest Asian fare. Some of his specialties include ginger scallops (delivered tableside in a sizzling wok) and a steamed pike that's out of this world.

Riverside Korean Restaurant **$$-$$$**
512 Madison Avenue, Covington, KY
(859) 291-1484
For the adventurous only. The menu includes Bin Dae Duk, a pancake mixed with ground beans and vegetables; Dolsot Bimbahp, mixed rice with vegetables and beef; and O Jing Uh Bokum, a stir-fried squid with vegetables. Sides include pickled bean sprouts, seasoned small intestines, and bean jelly. Lunch served Tuesday through Friday only. Closed Monday.

Shanghai Mama's **$-$$**
216 East Sixth Street
(513) 241-7777
A rice and noodle shop, themed to circa 1920s Shanghai, this brainchild of chef Alex Chin prepares anything from crabmeat and shrimp wrapped around sugarcane, to crabmeat cannoli, bamboo cocktail, warm duck salad, and Mama's Big Bowl Noodle Soup (full of ribs, mushrooms, and more). The prices are exceedingly reasonable, topping out at $9.95. Carryout is open till 3:00 A.M. on Friday and Saturday. Closed Sunday.

Sushi Ray **$-$$**
1018 Delta Avenue, Mount Lookout
(513) 533-9218
The owners are from south Florida, but this hip sushi spot is all Japanese. Take your choice by the piece or in combinations. A variety of rolls include such fixin's as barbecued eel, cucumber with smoked salmon, crab and cream cheese with avocado, and more. Don't pass up the Sumo Maki, a jumbo roll of tuna, yellowtail, salmon, avocado, and caviar. This is one place where, no matter what you choose, you're guaranteed a raw deal.

Ta Han Mongolian Bar-B-Q **$$**
11483 Chester Road, Sharonville
(513) 772-5855
They call the fare authentic Mongolian cuisine. And you almost can picture Ghengis and the boys, after a hard day of terrorizing Eurasia, filing out of their yurts, filling up their plates with chopped meat, veggies, and Ta Han's combination of nine sauces, and then gathering around the 48-inch-diameter steel conical woks as they share ribald tales of conquest. OK, not quite. But the food is superb, and the self-serve stir-fry concept is a winner. Ta Han is closed on Sunday.

Tandoor India Restaurant **$$-$$$**
8702 Market Place Lane, Montgomery
(513) 793-7484
This casual, brightly decorated spot in a somewhat out-of-the-way retail strip specializes in northern Indian cuisine, which is creamier and milder than dishes from the south side of the continent. Some of the best bets from an abundant menu include the dal and mulligatawny soup, the shish kebab, and the tandoori mixed grill. A lunch buffet—always a good bet with relatively unfamiliar ethnic foods—is available. Tandoor is closed on Sunday.

Teak Thai Cuisine **$$-$$$**
1049 St. Gregory Street, Mount Adams
(513) 665-9800
Just when you thought Mount Adams didn't really need another great restaurant, another one comes along. The decor, including a giant mural, and the inventiveness of the dishes have quickly made Teak one of the most popular Asian restaurants in town. Among the specialties are crab spring rolls and Thai sweet-and-sour pork.

BARBECUE JOINTS

Hey, come on, this isn't Memphis. That said, there are unique barbecue joints in town, some that even feature blues music. Here are some favorites.

The Boathouse **$$$**
925 Riverside Drive
(513) 721-7427
Before his death, owner Ted Gregory was the undisputed Ribs King of Cincinnati. Indeed, comedian Bob Hope used to have a slab of Gregory's pork loin ribs flown to his California estate on a weekly basis, along with the special barbecue sauce. The Boathouse is our favorite of the Montgomery Inn ribs outlets (see the Montgomery Inn listing below) because of its striking view of the river, colorful sports memorabilia, and nearby Bicentennial Commons riverfront park. The restaurant is bright with plenty of wide windows. The hustle and bustle, however, may discourage large groups or those with young kids. For dessert, indulge in another Cincinnati culinary tradition: Graeter's black raspberry chip ice cream. On your way out, purchase a bottle of the barbecue sauce at the gift shop to take home. No lunch on weekends.

Burbank's Real Bar-B-Q **$-$$$**
11167 Dowlin Drive, Sharonville
(513) 771-1440
Burbank's would be worth a visit if only to take in a little of the shtick of Cincinnati's most popular radio personality, Gary Burbank. Here's where you can buy the voluminous collections of annual Burbank tapes, featuring such popular characters as Earl Pitts and Gilbert G-N-A-R-L-E-Y. The menus are newspapers featuring Burbankesque humor. You can even catch Burbank's routines playing on the sound system in the bathroom. But don't overlook the food, which is still the main attraction. Besides ribs, other specialties include the pulled (shredded) pork platter and sandwich, smashed potatoes (with the skins), and supersweet corn bread and sweet potatoes. The barbecue sauces also tend to the sweet side, harkening to Burbank's Memphis roots. They come in three levels of hotness, from mild to "911," which isn't really unbearably hot. Doc Wolfe, Burbank's radio sidekick and now a successful cookbook author, concocted all the sauces.

Kenning's Circle K **$-$$$**
6616 Bridgetown Road, Mack
(513) 574-5613
Ribs are the specialty at Kenning's Circle K—besides the friendly service, that is. A very unpretentious restaurant that has been on the West Side for a quarter century, Kenning's Circle K also does a lot of carryout business.

Montgomery Inn **$$-$$$**
9440 Montgomery Road, Montgomery
(513) 791-3482
This is Cincinnati's most popular rib joint and must be counted among the area's culinary institutions. The late Ribs King Ted Gregory only let the Ribs Queen know the secret recipe of the sauce, lest it slip into enemy hands. The sauce (also available in grocery stores throughout the region) is a somewhat less-sweet recipe that Cincinnatians simply love. The uncompromising quality of the ribs themselves also keeps 'em coming back. Other specialties include Saratoga chips (extra-thick potato chips with barbecue sauce on the side for dipping) and Pigs in a Pocket (rib meat with sauce in pita

One of Cincinnati's more fascinating culinary contributions to the national dining scene is the McDonald's Filet-O-Fish sandwich. Way back in 1963, a Mickey D franchisee named Lou Groen created the sandwich at his Monfort Heights golden arches, satisfying an overwhelming demand from his Catholic customers during Lent. The rest, as they say, is McHistory.

bread). You can also find Montgomery Inn ribs and sauce at such diverse locations as the Boathouse, Paramount's Kings Island, and Coney Island.

Porkopolis **$-$$$**
1077 Celestial Avenue, Mount Adams
(513) 721-5456
This restaurant in a historic former pottery sits high atop Mount Adams. Housed in a Tudor-style structure, the giant kilns are still here, but now they've got tables and chairs in them. Insiders know to specifically ask to be seated in one of them. The menu features all versions of BBQ pork.

BURGER JOINTS

Sure, you can head to a Fuddrucker's or some other national chain eatery for your burger fix. We say been there, bun that. We prefer the hometown burger joints listed below. That said, however, it's hard to ignore White Castle, the "hamburger specialists since 1921." The regional chain got its start in Columbus and immediately flourished due to the popularity of its "sliders," best described as miniature square cheeseburgers with pickles and chopped onion folded in. Residents literally buy 'em by the sack. Outlets are open 24 hours a day, another reason for White Castle's incessant popularity.

Century Inn **$-$$**
10675 Springfield Pike, Woodlawn
(513) 771-4816
If you're a history buff, know that the oldest existing restaurant in Hamilton County is the Century Inn in Woodlawn, built in 1806. "We've reached 200," says partner Jack Jett gleefully of his bicentennial celebration. A full selection of sandwiches and burgers is served.

Choo Choo's **$-$$**
7701 Railroad Avenue, Madeira
(513) 272-2466
Located inside Madeira's former train depot, Choo Choo's is famous for its Angus beef burgers. Also on the menu: meat loaf, pot roast, pan-fried trout, and delicious pies. If you're here for the breakfast, head straight for the French toast: Dipped in vanilla and cinnamon egg batter, it's served with three pieces of bacon and real maple syrup. Open for breakfast as well as lunch and dinner.

City View Tavern **$**
403 Oregon Street, Mount Adams
(513) 241-8439
Finally, a place that lives up to its name. The City View Tavern has one of the finest views of the city anywhere, yet prices are dirt cheap. This no-frills Mount Adams bar and grill (the proprietors prefer the term "dive") serves burgers as well as Myrt's Wurst (a hot quarter-pound mett—a local delicacy, like a bratwurst—with horseradish, onion, and mustard, guaranteed to help relieve "the Cincinnati sinus"). We've whiled away many an hour on the breezy patio. The "dive" is hard to find, so call for directions first. Hours vary by the season. No credit cards.

Quatman Cafe **$**
2434 Quatman Avenue, Norwood
(513) 731-4370
There's nothing the least bit fancy about this place. Just hefty—and cheap—half-pound hamburgers and quick service. The crowd of "regulars" is sometimes a little cool to tourists—so be it. Closed Sunday. No credit cards.

Salem Gardens $
6396 Salem Road, Mount Washington
(513) 231-9666
Everybody, even the authors of a travel guide, has to have a favorite dive. This is it. Perhaps it's the Formica tables that remind us of favorite burger shacks while growing up. Perhaps it's the friendly bartenders and wait staff here. Certainly the cheeseburger itself, adorned with the freshest tomato, lettuce, and onion available and served with hot dripping fries, can claim some of the credit. Mount Washington families have been coming here for generations. In fact, this classic neighborhood bar and grill has been around since 1926, plenty of time to perfect the art of grilling a cheeseburger in paradise. And despite the fact it's a tavern, Salem Gardens is incredibly kid friendly (the dining area is separate from the liquor facilities).

Zip's Cafe $
1036 Delta Avenue, Mount Lookout
(513) 871-9876
An insider hesitates even to mention Zip's because this place needs another customer like the Cincinnati city council needs another publicity hound. Every additional person who finds out about this local favorite burger joint is an additional person ahead of us in line. Alas, sense of duty prevails. Zip's offers some of the juiciest hamburgers this side of your backyard grill at reasonable prices in a cozy, quaint neighborhood diner. You can entertain yourself while you wait by watching sports on TV and entertain the little ones with the electric train that runs nonstop along the wall near the ceiling. This is no place for an intimate conversation, though. The booths and tables are crammed together.

CELTIC

Cincinnati claims one of the larger St. Patrick's Day celebrations in the country, and rightly so. Yes, this town's Germanic heritage is indisputable, but the city's Celtic roots also run deep, influencing a variety of ethnic fare straight from the British Isles.

Claddagh Irish Pub $$
1 Levee Way, Newport on the Levee, Newport, KY
(859) 581-8888
A meal at Claddagh Irish Pub is nearly always memorable, though perhaps not for the reasons you'd expect. Yes, the barkeep will draw your "pint of plain" in the time-honored manner of the old sod; the Guinness is tapped using the two-part pour method to assure a perfect head. And yes, the fish-and-chips here are the real deal, a heaping platter of cod fillets coated in a Bass ale batter, all served with a dry cabbage slaw (no sugar, no mayo as in its American cousin, cole slaw). But what distinguishes Claddagh from its Celtic brethren in town is the speed of service. Be it for a Bushmill's and a pound of steamed black mussels or a pint and the pub's hearty shepherd's pie, you'll be in and out in 45 minutes.

Jack Quinn's Irish Ale House & Pub $$-$$$
112 East Fourth Street, Covington, KY
(859) 491-6699
Best known for its Breakfast Boxty (potato pancake filled with eggs, bacon, ham, tomato, and cheese, served with country gravy), Jack Quinn's also serves Irish stew, shepherd's pie, corned beef, fish-and-chips, and the restaurant's signature Ring of Kerry appetizer. There's an ample selection of beers and ales on draft. The restaurant has attracted some national, and even international, Celtic music acts. Breakfast is served daily.

Nicholson's Tavern & Pub $$-$$$
625 Walnut Street
(513) 564-9111

One of the restaurants anchoring the so-called Backstage district near the Aronoff Center for the Arts, this Scottish pub features appetizers such as wood-smoked mussels and Scotch eggs. The hearty entrees include fish pie, wood-roasted chicken, pork, Scottish salmon, bangers and mash, and the ploughman's lunch (roast beef, Scottish bacon, liver terrine, and pickled vegetables). Hoot man, it's delectable. Some say this place has the widest selection of single malts and draft ales in town. This tavern fills to the brim with theatergoers, and even actors and stagehands, on nights when the Aronoff is lit. And if the Chieftains are playing the theater, well, forget it. Lunch is served Monday through Saturday.

CINCINNATI CHILI

If a Cincinnatian offers to take you out for a three-way, he's not making an improper suggestion. A three-way is Cincinnati chili in its most basic form—spaghetti below, grated cheddar cheese above, and the chili in the middle. A four-way adds chopped onions on top. A five-way mixes in kidney beans. Insiders know to order their Cincinnati chili "dry"—that is, requiring the cook to drain the spaghetti of water before the chili and cheese is added. Otherwise, the dish is messier than need be. (And don't turn down the offer of the plastic bib. Everybody here uses one.) The most popular local chain is Skyline Chili, but there's also Cincinnati Chili, Dixie Chili, Empress Chili, Gold Star Chili, and other chains to choose from.

Blue Ash Chili $
9565 Kenwood Road, Blue Ash
(513) 984-6107
Get a glimpse of Blue Ash from before the days of sprawling, shimmering glass office buildings at this down-home chili and sandwich parlor. The restaurant is known for its huge double- and triple-deckers and a good rendition of Cincinnati-style chili. No credit cards.

Skyline Chili $
Seventh and Vine Streets
(513) 241-2020

290 Ludlow Avenue, Clifton
(513) 221-2142
There are 101 Skylines, but we've listed two of the most popular locations. We recommend Skyline over such other chains as Gold Star and Empress. Why? By popular consensus, it's the winner, selling some 3,800 tons of the stuff a year. The recipe is still a closely guarded secret, but locals suspect cinnamon or cocoa gives the recipe its slightly sweet tinge. Skyline is a mandatory stop for campaigning presidential candidates as well as tourists; every four years, the Secret Service calls and asks to scout locations. Be aware: The original ambience has given way to yuppified decor in the new Skylines.

COFFEEHOUSES

Coffeehouses are a Cincinnati staple and were so long before the invasion of the Starbucks. The franchises aside, there are some unique, locally owned coffeehouses worth your time. And isn't unique what a coffeehouse is supposed to be all about?

Highland Coffeehouse $
2839 Highland Avenue, Corryville
(513) 861-4151
The granddaddy of Cincinnati coffeehouses, Highland Coffeehouse serves deli-style sandwiches and the much-loved peanut butter, honey, and banana sandwich. It accepts cash only and is open all day, though there's a limited menu at lunch. No credit cards.

Sitwell's Coffee House $
324 Ludlow Avenue, Clifton
(513) 281-7487
We particularly crave the offbeat sandwiches here, including the salami, cream cheese, and cucumber sandwich (with ranch dressing and dill) and the Gouda-and-guacamole melt. For dessert try the

Milky Way Malt (a shake made with fudge ice cream, hazelnut syrup, and nutmeg).

FRENCH

Continental fare thrives in this town, due in no small part to the existence of Jean-Robert at Pigall's but aided and abetted by other cafes and restaurants.

Brandywine Inn **$$$**
204 South Main Street, Monroe
(513) 539-8911
The Brandywine Inn is an unusual alternative in that it offers a fixed-price menu: $22.95 per person for the night's entree, appetizer, and dessert. The inn has been serving multicourse continental meals for two decades and claims never to have repeated a meal exactly. Request the month's printed schedule in advance of making reservations (which are required), so you're not stuck with an entree you don't like. Seatings are exactly at 7:00 P.M. on Thursday, Friday, and Saturday, so plan to arrive promptly.

The Celestial **$$$$**
1071 Celestial Street, Mount Adams
(513) 241-4455
The menu's in French, the cuisine is continental European with some American twists, and the atmosphere is formal—jacket and tie required for men at dinner, no jeans or shorts anytime. The Celestial offers one of the best views from any restaurant in Greater Cincinnati. Favorite dishes include Colorado rack of lamb, fresh Dover sole, Hawaiian ahi tuna, and foie gras. Dinner only.

JeanRo Bistro **$$**
413 Vine Street
(513) 621-1465
JeanRo Bistro is another entry from gourmet chef Jean-Robert de Cavel, this one a casual cafe instead of a fancy nightspot (see Jean-Robert at Pigall's, below). *"Si vous êtes satisfaits dites-le à vos amis,"* reads the menu. (Translated: "If you're satisfied, tell your friends.") The decor is a lively scheme of French posters and odd knickknacks on the walls. The menu features Perona Farm smoked salmon with egg mimosa; country terrine with onion marmalade; rabbit, mushroom and blue cheese quiche; fish soup Marseillaise style, vichyssoise; mussels Marinière with *pommes frites;* roasted salmon with sauce *moutarde* and capers; sautéed haddock with almondine butter; chicken coq au vin in red wine sauce; and pork loin with roasted cabbage and curry sauce.

As scrapple is to Philadelphia, goetta is to Cincinnati. For the uninitiated, the German meat product (pronounced "get-uh") is a combination of steel-cut pinhead oatmeal, pork, beef, and seasonings. The large influx of German immigrants who swarmed here in the 19th century introduced the fare, and we've been hooked ever since. It's on many menus as standard fare, and the only goetta-packing plant in North America is located right here as well.

Jean-Robert at Pigall's **$$$$**
127 West Fourth Street
(513) 721-1345
Jean-Robert at Pigall's is the most talked-about restaurant in Cincinnati, as well as the most expensive eatery in town. Chef Jean-Robert de Cavel serves a fixed-price menu set at $75 for three courses (including tax and tip). *Wine Spectator* magazine recently called this one of the three most exciting new restaurants in the Midwest. Dinner only. Closed Monday and Sunday. Business and elegant attire recommended.

GERMAN

Cincinnati boasts surprisingly few authentic German restaurants, given its ancestry. Still, the ones we've got are standouts, from the schnitzel at Mecklenburg Gardens to the sauerbraten at Iron Skillet. We also choose to list Izzy's here, which is no one's idea of a traditional German restaurant but which does offer its own unique spin on Reubens and other ethnic fare.

Hofbrauhaus **$-$$$**
200 East Third Street, Newport, KY
(859) 491-7200
If you've ever wanted to visit the famed Hofbrauhaus brewery and restaurant in Munich but couldn't afford the overseas airfare, here's your opportunity. Because of its heavy Germanic population, Greater Cincinnati was chosen as home to the first-ever Hofbrauhaus to be sanctioned outside the Bavarian borders. The gigantic beer hall, which serves 700 at a clip, is more of a Teutonic entertainment event than mere dining experience. The 13,000-square-foot Hofbrauhaus—located, appropriately enough, in the former Dennert Beer Co. warehouse—offers communal dining at large tables with wooden benches (all the wood and stained glass is imported from Germany). Live bands entertain and lead sing-alongs as you munch on *weisswurst, kasseler rippchen,* sauerbraten, *wurstlteller, shmankeriplatte,* Wiener schnitzel, and *Munchener schweinhaxe* (the eatery's signature shank-of-pork dish). Original recipe beers (brewed on-site using sanctioned Munich methods) include the Helles-style lager—the standard beer of Germany, Dunkel caramel dark lager, Weissbier Bavarian wheat ale, and seasonal specialties.

Iron Skillet **$-$$**
6900 Valley Road, Newtown
(513) 561-6776
Head here if you're on the east side of town and hungering for Hungarian or German fare. Try the sauerbraten, schnitzels, Hungarian goulash, and, for dessert, the wonderful Gundel crepes (creamy walnut filling, topped with warm chocolate sauce). It's closed Monday and does not serve lunch on Sunday.

Izzy's **$**
800 Elm Street
(513) 721-4241
This Cincinnati culinary institution is famous for its kosher sandwiches piled high with corned beef, pastrami, and other meats. It's also known for the large, thick, and delectable potato pancakes that come with every sandwich, great fresh kosher dill pickle slices and sauerkraut condiments, and its lively kitchen banter. "You're only a stranger once" is one of the late Izzy Kadetz's mottos. And even strangers get treated pretty well. Payment is on the honor system, so you just tell the cashier what you ate and pay for it. Izzy's is closed Sunday.

Mecklenburg Gardens **$-$$**
302 East University Avenue, Corryville
(513) 221-5353
The rebirth of this once-great restaurant, which closed in the 1980s, marks a welcome comeback to what had become a rundown corner of Corryville. The German-influenced cuisine, including tasty chicken and pork schnitzel, is rife with creative touches, from creamy Gorgonzola salad dressings on way-above-average garden salads to the citrus cheesecake or Black Forest cake for dessert. Mecklenburg is a culinary reminder of this town's Germanic roots and the Rhineland restaurants that once thrived here. No lunch on weekends.

Wertheim's **$-$$**
514 West Sixth Street, Covington, KY
(859) 261-1233
Located in MainStrasse Village, Covington's shopping-and-dining mecca, Wertheim's is (surprisingly) one of the few places in the village where you can order authentic German fare. They've also got one of the best Reubens in town. The restaurant sits in the shadow of the impressive Carroll Chimes Bell Tower—don't miss its hourly automaton puppet show.

ITALIAN

Traditional Italian fare isn't a Cincinnati staple (Scotti's Italian Restaurant excepted), if only because our grandparents and great-grandparents tended to hail from Germany or Ireland, not Italy. That said, there is Italian food to be found, usually with a distinct American twist. A word on pizza, and that word is "LaRosa's." Buddy LaRosa began his giant chain with a single outlet on the West Side; now, his name is synonymous with fast-food pizza in Greater Cincinnati. True, there are better pizzas to be found at gourmet pizzerias such as Dewey's. But if you need a pizza quick and find yourself picking up the phone—shudder—to call a Pizza Hut or Domino's, dial (513) 347-1111 instead (that's Buddy's centralized computer number, which can automatically route your order to the LaRosa's nearest you).

Dewey's Pizza $$-$$$
1 Levee Way, Newport on the Levee, Newport, KY
(859) 431-9700

3014 Madison Road, Oakley
(513) 731-7755

11338 Montgomery Road, Harper's Point, Symmes
(513) 247-9955

This is no mere neighborhood pizza joint. Gourmet pizzas are topped with fresh tomatoes and parsley after baking; the fresh ingredients include Gorgonzola, roasted garlic, and sun-dried tomatoes. A full selection of wine and beer is also available. The Oakley and Symmes outlets are not open for lunch Sunday.

Indigo Casual Gourmet Cafe $-$$
2637 Erie Avenue, Hyde Park
(513) 321-9952

2053 Dixie Highway, Fort Mitchell, KY
(859) 331-4339

One of our all-time favorite Italian restaurants in the area, Indigo Casual Gourmet Cafe cooks up a terrific stromboli, not to mention delicious calzones, pizzas, and pastas. We lean toward the sun-dried cranberry-zucchini-thyme butter pasta, the Cuban black-bean pizza, and the Heimlich Kashi Salad with soy-ginger dressing (named after famous local vegetarians Jane and Henry Heimlich, he of Heimlich maneuver fame).

Pomodori's Pizzeria and Trattoria $-$$
121 West McMillan Street, Clifton Heights
(513) 861-0080

Fans come from far and wide to sample the delectable wood-fired pizzas, especially the leeks pancetta and goat cheese, the Gorgonzola-walnut, and Pomodori's famous apple pizza. There's also a Pomodori's outlet in Montgomery, but this one is the original and still champ. The brick-and-copper decor and unusual offerings make this pizzeria several cuts above your typical college pizza joint.

Pompilio's $-$$
600 Washington Street, Newport, KY
(859) 581-3065

Dustin Hoffman, Tom Cruise, and the gang from *Rain Man* made this Newport institution famous, but it should have been anyway. The now-named Rain Man Sampler, which includes spaghetti, lasagna, and eggplant Parmesan, was a favorite of the movie crew, and it's still a good choice for an overview of the delicious, reasonably priced Italian fare. An intricately carved wooden bar and large circular mirrors make the decor a throwback to many periods past. You can also play boccie ball (Italian lawn bowling) out back.

Primavista $$$-$$$$
810 Matson Place, Price Hill
(513) 251-6467

Primavista offers one of the most striking views of downtown of any restaurant in Cincinnati, and fantastic northern Italian cuisine as well. The menu features sautéed sea bass topped with lobster butter sauce, osso buco, Costolette DiVitello Discepoli (veal chop topped with shrimp, artichoke hearts, capers, and mushrooms in a sherry sauce), *pollo* Gorgonzola, *salmone in sacco* (salmon in parchment paper), seafood, poultry, and lamb. Primavista serves dinner only.

Scotti's Italian Restaurant **$$-$$$**
919 Vine Street
(513) 721-9484
Scotti's has been owned and operated by Guido DiMarco and his family since 1912 and claims on its menu to be "Cincinnati's oldest existing restaurant." (That's technically true, since Arnold's—the other contender—was more of a tavern than restaurant until Prohibition.) Scotti's menu is written in Italian, the place oozes history, and you'll feel as if you've been invited into the dining room of an Italian immigrant fresh from Sicily. Are all the veal dishes politically incorrect? Of course. Is the wait staff rude? Of course. Get over it—history beckons. Scotti's is closed on Sunday and Monday.

MEXICAN AND TEX-MEX

Cactus Pear **$-$$**
3215 Jefferson Avenue, Corryville
(513) 961-7400
They may be short on Tex-Mex authenticity, but they're long on imagination at this popular university-area restaurant. Don't miss the chunky salsa. Other specialties include the fajitas, red pepper noodles with pasta, and grilled chicken with vegetables. Lunch is served on weekdays.

El Coyote **$$-$$$**
7404 State Road, Anderson
(513) 232-5757
One of three El Coyotes in the region, but this one is the original. Nothing beats their pork tenderloin fajitas, though the empanada—a baked pastry pie stuffed with shredded beef, cheese, and onions—is a close second. No lunch is served during the week.

Javier's Mexican Restaurant **$**
39 East Court Street
(513) 381-EATS
Javier's is where many downtown office workers indulge in quick Mexican lunches. The place is definitely no-frills, a narrow space crammed with tables and chairs. The menu promises fusion-Mexican cuisine: corn tortillas with chicken and mole (chocolate) sauce, Mexican lasagna, pork *carnitas* with avocado, tostada salad, and burritos. Lunch only Monday through Friday.

La Mexicana **$-$$**
642 Monmouth Street, Newport, KY
(859) 291-3520
La Mexicana is just about as Mexican as Cincinnati is going to get. From *birria* (seasoned goat meat) to tequila lollipops, this place oozes authenticity. The bottles of Coke are labeled as bottled in Mexico. Even the jukebox is the real thing: Every song is a Latin American hit or standard.

Margarita's Mexican Cantina **$-$$**
214 East Sixth Street
(513) 241-1223

3218 Dixie Highway, Erlanger, KY
(859) 426-9792

8600 Beechmont Avenue, Anderson
(513) 474-4154
This is no upscale Taco Bell but the real thing. No timid Americanized Mexican fare here—just lots of fajitas, chimichangas, tamales, and enchiladas served just as you'd expect them south of the border. The *ceviche* is an authentic specialty, shrimp marinated in pure lime juice, then served with mild peppers, avocado, and cilantro. The shrimp chimichanga is unbeatable, as are the fajitas Cozumel (pineapple and chorizo sausage). The bar is stocked with Dos Equis (on tap, yet), every brand of tequila imaginable, and if you're an especially good gringo, the bartender will whip up his killer Mexican iced tea for you. Downtown location is closed Sunday.

MICROBREWERIES

Rock Bottom Brewery **$$**
10 Fountain Square
(513) 621-1588
The Rock Bottom Brewery features terrific salads and pizzas. Five microbrews are made on-site, but only one is pure Cincinnati—the malty Crosley Field Pale Ale. We also like the alder-smoked fish-and-chips, a beer-battered cold smoked salmon.

Teller's of Hyde Park **$$**
2710 Erie Avenue, Hyde Park
(513) 321-4721
This trendy Hyde Park Square establishment opened inside a savings-and-loan bank building, and it even uses old safe-deposit-box drawers as centerpieces. You'll find plenty of real bankers to go with the theme. Teller's serves up tasty yuppie chow, such as gourmet portobello pizza and grilled tuna, along with plenty of handcrafted microbrews.

Watson Bros. Bistro and Brewery **$$**
4785 Lake Forest Drive, Blue Ash
(513) 563-9797
As you enter Watson Bros., you pass the brewing tanks, all quite massive and imposing. The booths are roomy cherrywood, and the benches comfortably padded. Probably most unusual among the entrees here is shepherd's pie—in the Watson Bros. incarnation, this English treat is jazzed up to include ground lamb, veal, and beef, all sunk in a broth of mushrooms, zucchini, carrots, and peas, finally topped by the house garlic mashed potatoes. Order it with the Steamboat Stout, a full-bodied creamy blend with a hint of dark chocolate. Practically any other brew would be overwhelmed by the dish. The salmon in champagne dressing with crab is a seafarer's delight, accompanied by a mélange of cauliflower, broccoli, and carrots all perfectly steamed.

SEAFOOD

For being a thousand miles from the nearest ocean, Cincinnati has an ongoing love affair with fresh seafood. Perhaps it's because we are a thousand miles from the beach.

Embassy Grille **$$-$$$$**
10 East RiverCenter Boulevard, Covington, KY
(859) 261-8400
The Embassy Grille at the Embassy Suites Hotel is our favorite hotel restaurant for two reasons: It's reasonably priced—for what you get and considering the terrific river view—and it hasn't been discovered yet by locals, so there's rarely a crowd. Top-notch seafood includes the blackened salmon fillet with five-onion sour cream.

Four Seasons Restaurant **$$-$$$$**
4609 Kellogg Avenue, Columbia-Tusculum
(513) 871-1820
Stroll into the Four Seasons and you'll think you've somehow been transplanted to a seafaring eatery at some West Coast marina. Indeed, this floating seafood spot is located near the city neighborhood of California, among the many seafood shanties and marinas that line the Ohio River here. Decor is lots of portholes, low ceilings, and nautical stuff. (This isn't just for show. Peek out any porthole and you'll see yachts docked just a few paces away.) The restaurant is actually quite cozy, seating just a

i

Cincinnati has a (burp) history as a brewing town, but relatively few beers are still produced here. The most popular? You'll hear insiders tell of the joys of swigging down Hudy Delight, a light beer, and Little Kings, a cream ale. The best of the bunch? Christian Moerlein, a premium beer that sells for a premium price.

On one of the last Sundays in October, the Sacred Heart Church Ravioli Dinner, a favorite since 1910, is held. Folks travel from as far as Michigan to grab one of the 200,000 dinners served. Insiders know to bring their own Tupperware containers if they're planning to buy in bulk. The price tag: $7.00 per dinner.

hundred or so, making reservations a necessity. The seafood buffet, served in the fall and winter, is a popular attraction: all-you-can-eat lobster, shrimp, mussels, crawfish, Alaskan crab legs, and oyster for $30 per person. Closed Monday and during periods of high water. Open Wednesday through Sunday during the winter season.

The Green Derby **$-$$**
846 York Street, Newport, KY
(859) 431-8740
The Green Derby is known for serving its "filet mignon of the sea"—Icelandic halibut, cut from the fletch. Awarded "Best Fish Sandwich" in more taste tests and "Best of" competitions than we could possibly count, the fish sandwich here is indeed dreamy. It's encased in a light, crunchy breading, then draped with Boston lettuce and homemade pickle/onion tartar sauce—all folded into dark rye. There's also catfish, cod, orange roughy, fillet of sole, and jack salmon on the menu. In this heavily Catholic town, expect to encounter a lot of white-collar workers here. (White collar as in priests, that is.) The rest of the congregation shows up on Fridays during Lent, when the place packs up like a Planet Hollywood.

Jag's Steak and Seafood **$$$-$$$$**
5980 West Chester Boulevard
West Chester
(513) 860-5353
West Chester is Ohio's second-richest zip code (beating even Indian Hill in the last U.S. Census) and requires a pricey hangout. This is it. A couple of the steak and seafood entrees run $49 here. The lowest-priced dinner entree is the Parmesan-encrusted chicken breast with garlic linguini and tomato cream, priced at $19. There's a classy piano lounge here too. Dinner only. Closed Sunday.

Michael G's **$$$-$$$$**
Anderson Towne Center,
7578 Beechmont Avenue, Anderson
(513) 533-3131
This seafood delight recently moved from Rivertowne Marina. The smoked Norwegian salmon appetizer is a terrific way to start. Entrees include mussels and clams bathed in a white wine/garlic butter sauce and swordfish Oscar, topped with crabmeat, asparagus, and béarnaise. The menu features a full selection of fresh fillets: Chilean sea bass, tilapia, Georges Bank sole, and yellowfin tuna, among others. The Friday night lobster special is tossed in a red chili pepper glaze—no, this is not your father's Red Lobster. Live jazz Friday and Saturday. Sunday brunch is served, but no lunch on Saturday. Closed Monday.

Mitchell's Fish Market **$$$-$$$$**
1 Levee Way, Newport on the Levee,
Newport, KY
(859) 291-7454
Mitchell's is right next door to the Newport Aquarium, ironically enough, and is a favorite seafood stop for both natives and tourists. All fish can be served "Shang Hai style," steamed with ginger, scallions, and soy rice wine sauce over spinach and sticky rice. The menu includes cedar plank salmon, hoisin-glazed yellowfin tuna, New Orleans seafood stew, Florida grouper, filet mignon Oscar, and surf and turf.

Mt. Adams Fish House **$$$-$$$$**
940 Pavilion Street, Mount Adams
(513) 421-3250
The Mt. Adams Fish House has rapidly gained a reputation as one of the city's most experimental seafood houses. On any given day you'll find salmon, mahimahi, tilapia, and other ocean favorites prepared in innovative presentations. The way to go

here, in our humble opinion, is to order the Lemon Peppered Izumi Dai, a pan-seared red snapper in a lemon beurre blanc sauce. It's one of the least expensive items on the menu ($19) and yet one of the tastiest. No lunch on Saturday and Sunday.

Pelican's Reef **$**
7261 Beechmont Avenue, Anderson
(513) 232-CLAM
A delight you'd never expect to find in a strip mall, Pelican's Reef is more reminiscent of those friendly little fish 'n' beer shacks you find along Florida's coast. A sea motif and casual atmosphere (no napkins, just rolls of paper towels at each table) make this a nifty place. The calamari is consistently voted best in town by local restaurant polls, but we like the grilled halibut. The prices can't be beat either.

STEAK HOUSES

Cincinnati has the full complement and ever-growing number of chain steak houses, including Morton's of Chicago, Mountain Jack's, Longhorn, Lone Star, Outback Steakhouses, and so on. But we also have a few homegrown steak houses, which we've listed here.

Carlo & Johnny's **$$$-$$$$**
9769 Montgomery Road, Montgomery
(513) 936-8600
This "mob-style restaurant" created quite, um, a stink from day one: Invitations to the premiere featured a dead fish wrapped in newspaper, with a ransom note. The place has been busy ever since, though, gently poking fun at its own crime boss theme (billing itself as a Chicago steak joint with "gangster flavor"). There's a full menu that includes a raw bar, seafood, and steak. Dinner only. Closed Sunday.

Jeff Ruby's Steakhouse **$$$$**
700 Walnut Street
(513) 784-1200
www.jeffruby.com
Jeff Ruby's is a sophisticated 1940s-style steak house anchoring the downtown Backstage entertainment district next door to the Aronoff Center for the Arts. The ebullient proprietor (not surprisingly, a guy named Jeff Ruby) was well known in town already for his legendary Precinct and South Beach Grill restaurants. Ruby presents a varied and exciting menu that make this a must destination for any carnivore: dry-aged porterhouse and New York strip steaks, braised pork osso buco, jumbo lobster tail, and Dover sole. Dessert includes Chocolate Vesuvius, a warm molten-chocolate-center cake. No lunch served. Closed Sunday.

Jimmy D's **$$$-$$$$**
7791 Cooper Road, Montgomery
(513) 984-2914
Restaurateur Jimmy Duane opened this steak house to much acclaim. The menu showcases dry-aged Kansas City strip; carpaccio (tenderloin beef thinly sliced and served with watercress and avocado); Colorado rack of lamb; and a delicious pecan, pear, and poppy-seed salad, sprinkled with bacon and blue cheese. Dinner only. Closed Sunday.

Maury's Tiny Cove **$$$**
3908 Harrison Avenue, Cheviot
(513) 662-2683
A well-known West Side establishment in an inconspicuous spot along Harrison Avenue, Maury's Tiny Cove has thrived for more than a half century. The atmosphere reminds one of those dark Chicago clubs with smoke all around and where *cocktails* isn't a dirty word. Maury's is best known for its martinis and manhattans and, of course, its steak. No lunch Saturday and Sunday.

The Precinct **$$$$**
311 Delta Avenue, Columbia-Tusculum
(513) 321-5454
Located in a converted police precinct house, the Precinct is Cincinnati's most prestigious—and priciest—steak house. Steaks are named after local sports celebs, and you're as likely to see those

same sports celebs dining at the next table as not. A popular entree is the Steak Collinsworth, a filet crowned with crabmeat and béarnaise sauce. Heaven. The lowest-priced dinner entree is the wood-grilled pork chops in a mushroom/apple/fig sauce, priced at $24. Open for dinner only.

ICE-CREAM PARLORS

So they're not exactly restaurants—we didn't want you to miss them!

Aglamesis Brothers **$**
3046 Madison Road, Oakley
(513) 531-5196

9887 Montgomery Road, Montgomery
(513) 791-7082

Here's the inside scoop: The vintage Aglamesis Brothers ice-cream parlor first opened in Oakley Square in 1913 and has the reputation as Cincinnati's oldest operating authentic soda fountain. Two Greek immigrants, Thomas and Nicholas Aglamesis (pronounced Ag-lu-me-sis), began dishing up their unique mix of high egg yolk content paired with honey as a sweetener, and the rest is good-humored history.

The parlor's trademark flavors are French vanilla and chocolate and mocha chips. Other flavors range from Dutch Holland chocolate to fresh banana, rum raisin to pistachio, Oreo to spumoni. The most expensive treat on the menu? The $16.95 French Quarter, featuring eight scoops, bananas, strawberries, and various drizzled sauces.

The soda fountain itself is vintage Americana, hailed by no less than *Bon Appétit* magazine as one of the nation's great ice-cream parlors. Built with marble imported from Italy and outfitted with Tiffany lamps and intricately designed tile flooring, the pink and white palace has changed little since the doors opened nearly a century ago.

Graeter's **$**
2704 Erie Avenue, Hyde Park Square, Hyde Park
(513) 321-6221

332 Ludlow Avenue, Clifton
(513) 281-4749

6918 Wooster Pike, Mariemont
(513) 272-0859

Multiple additional locations

When Cincinnati's Louis Graeter began concocting ice cream way back in 1870, he could never have imagined that one day, Oprah Winfrey would crown Graeter's as her very favorite brand on *Oprah* nationwide.

The phone lines haven't stopped ringing since.

In Graeter Cincinnati everyone—it seems—has a favorite parlor in the chain. Some lean toward the shop located on the village square in Mariemont, others prefer the downtown branch. But for an all-around original experience, the parlor in Hyde Park Square is hard to whip. This parlor, which opened some 80 years ago, is laden with vintage flavor. There's a nod to modern with the neon ice-cream cones glowing on the wall, but the tin ceiling and nostalgic atmosphere are a trip back in time. On a summer's eve many patrons choose to stroll Hyde Park Square with their delectable creations in hand. Call it the Cone Zone.

Graeter's makes ice cream in a French pot, an old-world technique, according to Graeter family members such as Rich and Chip (seriously, those are their names). The French pots are vertical-batch freezers that press the air out of the mixture (some commercial brands actually *add* air to fluff up their products). The ice cream is lovingly paddled by hand in two-gallon batches.

Another unique aspect of Graeter's is that the chip flavors (including the perennially popular black raspberry chip) aren't chocolate chips at all, but are more like chunks. July's flavor of the month, one of the best sellers among the monthly choices, is peach; the Graeter family credits its use of fresh peaches, not canned, for the flavor's peachy success.

United Dairy Farmers **$**
1124 St. Gregory Street, Mount Adams
(513) 723-1900

Multiple additional locations

United Dairy Farmers, UDF for short, is a Cincinnati staple. The convenience stores are found on practically every block, but the ice-cream parlors within are particularly notable. Try a cone with the UDF brand's signature cookies 'n cream first.

Although there are a hundred UDFs spread around the area, we've listed one that sparkles like new with all the yupscale amenities. If you go to another location for a milkshake, however, be aware that not every UDF has a soda fountain.

NIGHTLIFE

Greater Cincinnati has an abundance of nightlife. There's something for everybody, regardless of musical preference, age, or social status. You can boot scoot, disco, line dance, slam dance, sumo wrestle, arm wrestle, rub elbows with celebrities, watch five games at once, drink alcohol, drink Perrier, play pinball, play volleyball, sing along, sail, laugh, cry, or even do your laundry all in the name of nightlife.

And like other vibrant metropolitan areas, the segments of nightlife seem to be congregated into certain areas. We've organized certain of our listings by those areas.

With the construction of the stadiums downtown, the nightlife in the city has moved away from the river onto Main Street and to Newport on the Levee. In Kentucky other riverfront establishments continue to draw people of all ages, especially during the summer months.

It would be impractical, however, to list in this chapter all the bars, nightclubs, and other such entertainment establishments in the area. There are simply too many, and they change too fast. So rather than list every joint, we just mention those institutions that are a tried-and-true part of the area's social scene.

And it should be duly noted that there's more to nightlife than just bellying up to a bar. This chapter examines some different nocturnal options as well. Other types of nightlife, though, may be in other chapters in this book. Concerts by the Cincinnati Symphony Orchestra or Pops, for instance, are listed in the Arts chapter. Sports events are in the Spectator Sports chapter. Restaurants often feature bands and other types of entertainment. (Conversely, if a nightspot listed in this chapter serves food, chances are you'll find a write-up about it in the Restaurants chapter.) We encourage you to check out these other chapters as well.

You will find that most of the nightspots listed in this chapter have a cover charge, particularly those that have live bands performing. Most cover charges will be a minimum of $3.00, although they can get as high as $15.00 for some national acts, so be prepared. Also be prepared to be carded no matter where you go. The legal drinking age in Ohio, Kentucky, and Indiana is 21, and many bars won't let anyone in—even adults with graying hair who haven't been younger than 21 in many years—without some sort of identification. And even though some bars cater to those 18 and older, that doesn't necessarily mean they serve liquor to those customers. Most of the bars shut down at 2:00 A.M., and it is illegal to drink and drive anything—including boats and bicycles—with a blood-alcohol level of more than 0.10.

One final note about one form of nightlife that the local law enforcement agencies aren't crazy about, especially in the city of Cincinnati. There are some clubs with dancing that is frowned upon by some Cincinnatians. Most are near the river in Northern Kentucky or on the northern fringes of Cincinnati in Butler, Warren, and Clermont Counties. If you're interested you can find them easily enough without our help.

ADULT GAMES

There is one "adult game" entertainment place to tell you about. Part of a trend to allow us to act like kids without a backward glance, this establishment quickly became popular in Greater Cincinnati.

Dave & Buster's
11775 Commons Drive, Springdale
(513) 671-5501
www.daveandbusters.com
This "adult playground" has 65,000 square feet of space and offers a little bit of everything: play-for-fun blackjack casino, a grand dining room, four bowling lanes, four bars, a party room, custom-made billiard tables, a golf simulator, a 130-seat special-event theater, shuffleboard, and an arcade room with more than 150 games and simulators, including virtual-reality games. It's located just off Interstate 275 at Ohio Highway 747.

In the arcade room, rather than plug coins into the machines, you purchase credit on a special card that slides into the machines. Food from the restaurant can be ordered at the pool tables or Midway Bar. And while it sounds like some sort of carnival arcade that's going to be overrun by kids, anyone under the age of 21 must be accompanied by a legal guardian and must stay with an adult age 25 or older. Only two kids per guardian are allowed.

CINEMAS

If you want to catch a movie, Greater Cincinnati has nearly 20 multiscreen megaplex theaters that feature first- and second-run films, in addition to a couple of drive-ins and numerous smaller cinemas that feature foreign, art, classic, or cult films. There also is an OMNIMAX theater at the Museum Center, which is listed in the Kidstuff chapter.

Discount Cinemas

Danbarry Dollar Saver Cinema
5190 Glencrossing Way, Western Hills
(513) 451-2300
Seats at Danbarry's 12-screen cinema are $2.50 at most times. All of the movies are either blockbusters at the tail end of their showings or lesser-known titles. Matinees are shown daily and late shows are offered Friday and Saturday nights.

Midway Theater
210 West Plane Street, Bethel
(513) 734-2278
The Midway Theater is a discount cinema in price only, as it somehow manages to offer first-run blockbuster movies for only $4.00. Matinees are $3.50. It's not well advertised outside of Bethel, but it's worth the effort to find out what's showing and make the drive.

Turfway Park 10
7650 Turfway Road, Florence, KY
(859) 647-2828
Turfway Park 10 offers three blockbuster first-run movies at discount prices. All shows are $2.50. On Tuesday seats are $1.75

Walnut Theater
352 Walnut Street, Lawrenceburg, IN
(812) 537-0460
A one-screen theater that has first-run movies. There are 300 seats in the old-time theater, which was restored in 1987. Admission is $4.00, $3.00 for matinees.

Alternative Film Theaters

Cincinnati Art Museum
953 Eden Park Drive
(513) 251-6060
www.cincinnatiartmuseum.org
The Cincinnati Film Society has screenings in the museum's auditorium.

i

A new area to hang out in the evenings is Newport on the Levee. Not only does it have a 20-screen theater complex, it also has a comedy club, cabaret, and plenty of restaurants and bars. Don't forget about the Hofbrauhaus across the street, which offers great German food and a beer garden.

CLOSE-UP

Drive-in Fun

There are more drive-in theaters in Ohio than in any other state except California.

Think about this slice of trivia for just a moment. The residents of Ohio passionately love their drive-in theaters—obviously—or we wouldn't lead the nation in this uniquely American cinematic experience.

"We're quite lucky. Cincinnati alone has three drive-ins," says Larry Thomas, former owner of the Movies repertory cinema downtown and one of the area's foremost film experts. "I'm a fan of drive-in movie theaters and have been for years. Some towns our size have *no* drive-ins—Louisville and Lexington, for instance. We have one east of town, one west of town, and one north of town. We could use one south of town in Kentucky, but we're still a pretty fair drive-in town."

Sure, time and the changing expectations of moviergoers have whittled away at the number of existing drive-ins over the decades. But you can still experience the nostalgic retro feel of munching popcorn while watching the latest summer action flick seated comfortably in your own front (or back) seat at these three Greater Cincinnati venues. All three show first-run films at second-run prices, making them a must for bargain hunters.

Start first at the **Starlite Drive-In,** located at 2255 Ohio Pike in Amelia. (Call 513-734-4001 for movie times.) The vintage Starlite is Clermont County's only drive-in, offering first-run movies every night at dusk during warm weather. It's a tremendous venue easily overlooked by even drive-in diehards. No pets are allowed, however. The movie's sound is

Cost is $6.00 for the general public and $4.00 for society members and CAM Members.

Esquire Theatre
320 Ludlow Avenue
(513) 281-8750
The Esquire is a six-screen theater that offers art and alternative films. It was, for instance, the only place in Greater Cincinnati to show the Academy Award–winning *Shine*. The theater is a bit of a throwback in that it sits in the heart of the quaint Clifton business district, just as it did in the 1940s. Its location allows moviegoers a great variety of after-movie dessert, coffee, and drink options. Matinees are shown daily, and Tuesdays are Bargain Days, with movies $5.50 all day and night. Matinees cost $6.00 and regular price is $8.00. The theater will validate parking up to two hours.

Mariemont Theatre
6906 Wooster Pike, Mariemont
(513) 272-2002
www.mariemonttheatre.com
The Mariemont Theatre is a sister theater to the Esquire and also offers alternative movies. Like the Esquire, it has matinees daily and Bargain Tuesday with films all day for $5.50. Tickets are

broadcast over an FM radio frequency, so make sure your car radio works or you'll be in for the silent treatment. Cost is $5.00 for adults, $2.00 for children under age 12. Tuesday night is $10 per carload, so cram your cruiser with friends and save. Take the I-275 Amelia/Beechmont exit and head toward Amelia. A side note: Starlite's "Trail of Terror" is perhaps Ohio's only haunted house at a drive-in; the movie theater screens various horror films throughout the month of October.

Closer to the center of Cincinnati is the **Oakley Drive-In,** located at 5033 Madison Road. (Call 513-271-4600 for movie times.) On balmy summer eves, this place fills up fast, so be forewarned. On Friday and Saturday only, the first feature is repeated at 1:15 A.M. The theater is open seven nights a week. Admission is $6.75 per person, children age 11 and under $2.75. Take the Fairfax/Red Bank Road exit off Interstate 71 and head to Madison Road; turn right and you're there. As with the Starlite, the movie's sound is broadcast over an FM radio frequency, so make sure your car radio works or, as an alternative, bring a portable radio.

The **Holiday Auto Theatre** is found on Ohio Highway 130 (Old Oxford Highway) in Hanover Township. (Call 513-929-2999 or consult www.holidayautotheatre.com for movie times.) This classic, fully restored auto theater boasts the area's largest and brightest screen. The motto of the Holiday is that it's found "on the hilltop, under the stars." It's open every night, all year. A classic cartoon accompanies the double feature. The soundtrack is broadcast on "Super FM StereoSound," and a pleasant bonus is the new refreshment concession stand. Cost is $7.00 for adults, $3.00 for children ages 4 to 11; children under age 4 are free. Take I-275 to Northgate, then jump onto U.S. Highway 27 north to OH 130, then turn right.

$8.00 in evenings, matinees are $6.00, and seniors are $6.00 all the time. The theater, which dates from 1938, sits in the middle of the upscale Mariemont Square, a replica of an English Tudor village with shops, restaurants, and plenty of after-movie options.

Cinema Grill

Mt. Lookout Cinema Grill
3187 Linwood Avenue
(513) 321-3211
The owners of Mt. Lookout Cinema Grill took out the traditional movie seats from the old theater on Mount Lookout Square and replaced them with tables and chairs where moviegoers can sit and be served dinner while watching a movie. It is a nonsmoking facility, but beer, wine, and cocktails are served. Tickets are $4.00, $2.50 for matinees, plus you pay for whatever you decide to eat. No one under age 18 is admitted without a guardian.

COMEDY CLUBS

The Funny Bone
Newport on the Levee, Newport, KY
(859) 957-2000
www.funnyboneonthelevee.com

Part of one of the busiest areas for nighttime activities, the Funny Bone has national acts as well as a restaurant. Admission varies depending on the act at the club. Shows are at 7:30 P.M. from Tuesday through Thursday, 8:00 and 10:30 P.M. Friday, 7:00 and 10:30 P.M. Saturday, and 7:00 P.M. Sunday. The early shows on Friday and Saturday and the Sunday show are nonsmoking. Smoking is otherwise permitted.

Go Bananas
8410 Market Place, Montgomery
(513) 984-9288
www.gobananascomedy.com
Go Bananas features top-of-the-line comics from around the country, many of whom are regularly seen on HBO or Showtime. Generally, you can find out who is performing by listening to local radio stations—the comics get on the morning shows and rattle off a few gags in hopes of boosting attendance. Call for reservations and show times.

CONCERT VENUES

Bogart's
2621 Vine Street
(513) 281-8400
Bogart's, which is located near the University of Cincinnati, brings in many smaller national acts to its 1,300-seat venue but occasionally has a major act that's looking for a cozier setting. A second-floor balcony gives you an excellent view of the shows. Bogart's likes to bill itself as one of the Midwest's premier rock halls, and that's not far from the truth. B. B. King, George Thorogood, Megadeath, Johnny Land, the late Warren Zevon, and Carly Simon have performed here. The telephone number above is a 24-hour concert line.

i

Ticketmaster is the only game in town when it comes to ordering tickets by phone. But Ticketmaster slaps a $6.45 service charge plus a $3.50 per order handling fee. And if you use credit cards, there is an additional 35-cent fee (to offset the higher charges the credit card firms charge the ticket broker). That's 10 bucks on top of the ticket price. You'll do better to drive over to your nearest Ticketmaster kiosk (at selected Kroger grocery stores). Buying in person, with cash only, adds only $5.50 to your entire ticket order.

Riverbend Music Center
Interstate 275 and
Kellogg Avenue, Anderson
(513) 232-6220
Riverbend is the primary site of Greater Cincinnati's musical mania each year. This outdoor amphitheater seats roughly 6,000 in its covered pavilion and another 10,000-plus on its sloping grass lawn area.

Every major musical act eventually performs here. There's some kind of concert on virtually every night during the spring, summer, and early fall—when the river allows. Riverbend, as its name suggests, sits along a bend in the Ohio River. Each spring when April showers are bringing May flowers, the river tends to overflow its banks and put the stage and half the pavilion seats under water. So if you're planning to attend a concert in the spring, don't be surprised if it's canceled and rescheduled for a date later in the summer.

The venue, which shares space with Coney Island, Sunlite Pool, and River Downs racetrack, has two 10-by-14 video screens at the back of the pavilion structure and turns a camera on the stage, so those with lawn seats can get a close-up of the performers. It's a nice addition. Riverbend also just began letting kids age four and younger sit on the lawn for free with an adult who has a lawn ticket.

Riverbend does have its drawbacks. Because of a lawsuit a few years ago, it now lets cars park for "free" in the parking lot, but adds a $2.50 surcharge for parking to each ticket, so it doesn't pay to carpool because you're paying for parking whether you drive or not. Also, because shows are held rain or shine, the lawn tends to get torn up during the spring rains and has a hard time recovering during the rest of the summer. As a result, it can sometimes become quite muddy, despite efforts to keep it repaired.

For some concerts, lawn chairs are allowed. If the lawn is packed, though, and those in chairs block the view of those behind them, forget it. Generally, blankets are recommended for all shows. Also, umbrellas are not allowed, nor are bottles, cans, alcohol, or drinks of any kind. Bringing your own food, though, is allowed but not in coolers. A stack of forbidden goodies is usually piled outside the entrances, where people drop them rather than haul them back to their cars.

Timberwolf Amphitheater
Paramount's Kings Island, Mason
(513) 754-5700
http://pki.com

The 10,000-seat Timberwolf Amphitheater is another concert venue. The theater is part of the amusement park and a concert ticket can be bought in combination with a ticket to get into the park. The screams from the riders on the nearby roller coasters make an interesting backdrop for shows. This facility used to bring in a variety of national music acts, but in recent years most of the concerts have been part of a Christian concert series.

U.S. Bank Arena
Broadway and Pete Rose Way
(513) 421-4111

During the winter, concerts head indoors, and the major shows are held at the 16,000-seat U.S. Bank Arena. Formerly Firstar Center and Riverfront Coliseum, U.S. Bank Arena was purchased in 1996 and underwent extensive renovation. The facility is now much cleaner and has plush seats and additional concession stands, including some where you can buy microbrewed beer made in vats in the arena's lower level. And some really good news for female concertgoers: The number of women's restrooms was doubled. The new owners also brought in the Michigan-based Nederlander Group to manage the facility. Nederlander, owned by SFX Entertainment, books major concerts throughout the country, including those at Riverbend during the summer months.

The facility has about 15 concerts between October and April. As a concert facility, the U.S. Bank Arena is generally like any other indoor arena, with the stage at one end of an oval and concertgoers wrapped around the stage, though for some acts, the stage is arranged in the middle, so that the audience is on all sides.

ENTERTAINMENT DISTRICTS

Corryville/Clifton

The Corryville/Clifton entertainment district is populated mostly by college students from the nearby University of Cincinnati, and as a result the clubs tend to be geared toward the interests of today's twenty-something crowd. Alternative, punk, and hard rock music are popular, along with moshing, black clothes, boots, body piercing, and tattoos, although that is not the limit of the nightspots in Corryville.

Corinthian Restaurant & Lounge
3253 Jefferson Avenue
(513) 961-0013

Although the name conjures up Greek images, Corinthian is a popular place on Friday and Saturday nights, when it has Latino nights. Patrons jam the club, with its abundance of tropical plants spread about, including a canopy of plants hanging from the ceiling, and dance to the sounds of Latino music. Another great benefit is that the restaurant, which offers Greek, Italian, and American food, doesn't close until 10:00 P.M. on the Latino nights.

Fries Cafe
3247 Jefferson Avenue
(513) 281-9002
Fries is two and sometimes three bars in one. Its first-floor bar is as basic as it gets, with tables and a bar for sitting and a jukebox, foosball, and shuffleboard tables as entertainment. Upstairs is a pool lounge with nothing but pool tables and dartboards. The basement also has more pool tables. During the warm months, an outdoor patio makes a third bar, with two boccie ball courts and an outdoor grill.

Mad Frog
1 East McMillan Street
(513) 784-9119
Mad Frog is located at the corner of East McMillan and Vine Streets, where Cory's used to be. Mad Frog is two bars in one—a front bar section that is a traditional bar, and a larger, more open back room with a stage on one side of the room and a second bar on the other. Mad Frog has live music every night. Monday night is Latin night, Tuesday night is house music, Wednesday night is new music by young bands, Thursday night is funk, Friday and Saturday nights are regional music bands, and on Sunday there are jam bands. And for a long evening, the pool table is free from 4:00 to 8:00 P.M. before the bands start playing.

Mecklenburg Gardens
303 East University Avenue
(513) 221-5353
Mecklenburg Gardens, located at the corner of East University and Highland Avenues, is a 130-year-old German biergarten that served German immigrants in the late 19th and early 20th centuries. Mecklenburg has opened and closed twice, but this time it is placing a stronger emphasis on the beer part, with 60 different beers in bottles and 16 on tap. It also has a selection of wines. It is a bit too far off the beaten path for university students to cram into, which offers a respite from the rowdiness. Its patio is open year-round, weather permitting, and is built around trees covered with vines.

Murphy's Pub
2329 West Clifton Avenue
(513) 721-6148
Darts is the king of the bar games at Murphy's, which offers two pool tables, several video games, and five dartboards. At different times of the year, the pub holds tournaments and leagues for those with enough skill to hit the bull's eye. The bar, which opened in 1970, offers a wide selection of draft beers inside and has a small courtyard outside that is open during the warmer months. Cookouts are common in the courtyard.

Perhaps its most distinguishing characteristic is its "Wall of Shame," a space reserved for embarrassing moments in the lives of bar patrons captured on film by one of the bar's employees. It costs a donation to a cystic fibrosis foundation to get the picture down.

Sudsy Malone's Rock & Roll Laundry and Bar
2626 Vine Street
(513) 751-2300
www.sudys.com
Sudsy's is one of the most unusual nightspots in town, giving people a chance to down some suds while cleaning their duds. The laundry/bar has live rock and alternative music almost every night, 365 days a year, and it offers an instant solution to spilling your beer down the front of your shirt. But it isn't just the uniqueness of the concept that makes Sudsy's so popular, it's the quality of the bands it brings in. Sudsy's has turned into one of the area's top destinations for small regional and national acts. Besides washers and dryers, the bar has video games if you need more than a drink to entertain you during the spin cycle.

Top Cat's
2820 Vine Street
(513) 281-2005

Top Cat's can be found in University Village and is one of the most popular bars for University of Cincinnati students, in part because it welcomes those age 18 and older. The club has live alternative rock Tuesday through Saturday nights. Downstairs at Fat Cat's, which is 21 and over, there is a large number of dartboards, pool tables, and pinball machines. The bar also claims to have the largest patio, spanning a city block; it's open when the weather permits.

Downtown

The city is trying to revive nightlife downtown the hard and expensive way—by forcing it. It upgraded the area around the new Aronoff Center for the Arts by tearing up streets and sidewalks and replacing the concrete with brick pavers. It is offering incentives to entrepreneurs to buy old buildings, sweep out the old tenants, rip down or repair the structures, and bring in new, upscale, glitzy occupants. It may work; the jury is still out. The area that is being called the Backstage entertainment district is off to a good start, though.

All of the hotels downtown, of course, offer entertainment venues, and a few other notable nightspots are located downtown.

Arnold's Bar and Grill
210 East Eighth Street
(513) 421-6234
Arnold's is the oldest bar in town, dating from 1861 and doing quite well. Once the restaurant crowd clears out, traditional jazz, blues, folk, and other types of acoustic music fill the air. Arnold's is relatively small but offers one of the quaintest patios in the city, where you can escape from the crowd on nice evenings. The patio is enclosed except for a wrought-iron gate that leads to the street, and it features trees growing up through the floor, lights strung on wires overhead, ivy on the brick walls, and giant Coca-Cola memorabilia from the 1940s nailed to old barn boards. The bar doesn't pay for bands but allows each group to pass a hat during the shows.

The Blue Wisp
318 East Eighth Street
(513) 241-9477
The Blue Wisp relocated from its Garfield Place address where it had been well known as a classic dark, smoky basement bar since 1989. On East Eighth Street the jazz club has more space—about 600 square feet of additional legroom. The Eighth Street location also has a state-of-the-art ventilation system and nonsmoking section. It has the same atmosphere and the same unbelievably great jazz, including top regional and national draws such as Cal Collins. It has jazz seven nights a week (featuring the house jazz band and its own Big Band on Wednesday), and different acts each weekend.

The Cricket Lounge
601 Vine Street
(513) 381-3000
The Cricket Lounge is in the Cincinnatian Hotel and is one of the most elegant settings in the city. It most frequently offers piano music or jazz on Friday and Saturday nights. Guests of the hotel—Billy Joel, for example—have been known to come down to the Cricket and start playing the piano.

Havana Martini Club
441 Vine Street
(513) 651-2800
The Havana Martini Club has reopened in downtown as part of the Carew Tower shops near Fountain Square. It not only has martinis and cigars, it also has live Cuban music and a buffet dinner.

The Palm Court
35 West Fifth Street
(513) 564-6465
The Palm Court is the lounge in the Hilton Netherland Plaza Hotel and is one of the most elegant spots in Cincinnati with its marble and rich wood decor. A jazz trio

plays in the lounge on weekends in this relaxing environment.

Rock Bottom Brewery
10 Fountain Square
(513) 621-1588
The 10,000-square-foot microbrewery pub and restaurant is right in the heart of downtown and offers a great setting to enjoy one of its six home-brewed beers or any of the items on its menu. During the warm months, a patio facing Fountain Square opens, offering fresh air and the sounds of water cascading off the fountain as a backdrop. It's located half a block away from the Aronoff Center.

Main Street

The Main Street entertainment area evolved in the early 1990s when two or three bars opened just north of the downtown central business district in the Over-the-Rhine neighborhood. Although most people used to shy away from that area, which was run down and crime ridden, the opening of the bars began to change that. Soon the crowds started rushing into Over-the-Rhine. Club owners, attracted by the availability of empty space and the relatively low rent, quickly followed. Before anyone knew it, the Main Street area became its own entertainment district.

The area is now the main hangout for Greater Cincinnati's singles crowd. More than one million visitors a year make it a popular entertainment destination in the city. That translates into thousands of people packing the area each weekend, streaming north from downtown after work or driving in from other parts of the city.

Although the streets and bars are jammed, this poor residential neighborhood didn't change when the bars moved in. Police patrol the area quite heavily at night, but the occasional safety problem does occur. The hit-up for money from beggars happens quite frequently, and every so often it might expand to an offer to sell some merchandise at a discounted price that is so hot, asbestos gloves are needed to handle it. So it pays to lock your car and pay attention to your surroundings when visiting Main Street.

BarrelHouse Brewing Company
22 East 12th Street
(513) 421-2337
BarrelHouse is one of the area's many microbreweries and slightly off the Over-the-Rhine Main Street entertainment district's beaten path—about 2 blocks away from Main Street on 12th Street—but not far enough to keep the crowds away. Located in a renovated print shop, the pub features a large copper bar and a Day-Glo mural of Cincinnati's skyline. It serves up 12 home-brewed beers, which are cooking and cooling in giant stainless-steel containers behind the bar, as well as live music on weekends and a wide variety of outstanding gourmet pizzas and specialty sandwiches. Hand-rolled cigars are also available.

Courtyard Cafe
1211 Main Street
(513) 723-1119
The Courtyard Cafe has a cozy courtyard in the back that is paved with cobblestones and accented with plants and trees. It is a bar and grill where you can also play darts.

Japp's
1134 Main Street
(513) 684-0007
Japp's, a longtime Main Street establishment, was purchased, underwent a renovation, and shifted its focus. It is now a New York-style salon with an added cigar section and a wine and martini menu. The club's site was once the home of a wig shop and offered wigs from "virgin nun's hair." It is affiliated with the Rhythm & Blues Cafe. Open from 9:00 P.M. to 2:00 A.M. Friday and Saturday only.

Jeckyll and Hyde's
1140 Main Street
(513) 929-4400

The club is different from most of the nightclubs in Over-the-Rhine in that it does not depend so much on bands or beer to survive—although it does offer plenty of both—and generally does not attract the barhoppers. Rather, its main attraction is pool, which can be played until 2:30 A.M. Highly competitive darts is also popular at Jeckyll and Hyde's.

Jefferson Hall
1150 Main Street
(513) 723-9008
Jefferson Hall is in a warehouse that's been converted into artist studios and a bar. It brings in live music five days a week on the hall's stage, which sits in the front window. The bar's atmosphere is big on history, with black-and-white photos and old colored postcards of Cincinnati hanging on the unpainted brick walls. Word has it the bar's name came from the original building, which was an assembly hall for secret societies.

Neon's
208 East 12th Street
(513) 721-2919
Neon's was one of the original hotspots in the Over-the-Rhine Main Street entertainment district, and it still packs in the patrons with its single-malt scotches and upstairs cigar bar, complete with walk-in humidor. Neon's has live bands scheduled randomly. Neon's doubles its size in the summer thanks to a huge outdoor patio.

Rhythm & Blues Cafe
1140 Main Street
(513) 684-0080
Despite its name, the live music played at the bar is not limited to rhythm and blues but includes all types of high-energy acts. RBC is affiliated with Japp's.

Mount Adams

Mount Adams has been one of the area's main sources for nightlife for a long time. Mount Adams residents, as diverse a group as you will find in any one area in Greater Cincinnati, choose to live up on the hill as much for the nightlife as for the location and views. The nightlife crowd is a bit of a melting pot of Greater Cincinnati—a little of this crowd, a little of that crowd.

If any one group can be pinpointed as most frequently visiting Mount Adams, it would be the arts crowd. They leave their cars at the nearby Playhouse in the Park or the art museum and walk down into Mount Adams, partly because the arts buildings are so close and partly because one of the problems with Mount Adams is finding a place to park. It's virtually all on-street parking, and finding a vacant slot to slide into can be a tough chore. And don't be surprised if your journey to and from your car takes you up or down a hill or two.

Blind Lemon
936 Hatch Street
(513) 241-3885
Blind Lemon, named after blues singer Blind Lemon Jefferson, is a small but outstanding bar. It features a partially covered, fenced-in brick garden with wrought-iron chairs and tables. It's a peaceful place to sit and listen to a band during the summer. The bonfires on cold nights are also a great attraction. Jazz and folk are the most common types of music offered.

City View Tavern
403 Oregon Street
(513) 241-8439
City View Tavern is your classic dive, with a small balcony and a great view of downtown and the riverfront. Postcards and memorabilia from guests line the walls of the tiny bar, including signs such as CHILDREN LEFT UNATTENDED WILL BE SOLD. The bar is squeezed between two homes—if it wasn't a bar, it would probably be someone's house—and more signs out on the balcony remind guests not to get too loud for this reason. The club's jukebox has hits from the 1940s to today. Food is available, although it's served on paper plates and the menu is limited.

The Incline Lounge
1071 Celestial Street
(513) 241-4455
The Incline Lounge is in the Celestial Restaurant in Highland Towers on the edge of the Mount Adams hillside. It offers patrons live jazz on Friday and Saturday and a great view of the city below. It's a bit more expensive and dressier than some of the Mount Adams bars, but it's a great place to end the evening. Its name comes from its location, which is where the old streetcar that chugged up the incline made its stop.

Longworth's
1108 St. Gregory Street
(513) 651-2253
Bar patrons get two bars for the price of one at Longworth's. A DJ plays hip-hop upstairs while live bands play downstairs. During the warmer months, reggae, folk, and acoustic music are added to the list of players on the patio. Dinner from Longworth's can also be ordered until 10:00 P.M. daily—a reason to go there in itself.

Mount Adams Bar & Grill
938 Hatch Street
(513) 621-3666
The Mount Adams Bar & Grill is popular with a lot of radio and television personalities, but it attracts all types, from yuppies to granolas, the salt-of-the-earth to guys in ties. It's a bit more upscale than what you might find on Main Street, but the atmosphere remains very down to earth. It is also one of the few bars in Mount Adams that stays open until 2:00 A.M. on the weekend. It also serves food until 11:45 P.M. on Saturday and Sunday.

Staying downtown, but want to hit the bars in Newport or Covington? Take the Southbank Shuttle for $1.00. It loops around downtown and the river area every 20 minutes until 10:00 P.M. Sunday through Thursday and until midnight on Friday and Saturday.

Northern Kentucky

While a great deal of Northern Kentucky's nightlife centers around the long row of bars, restaurants, and nightclubs along the river, there are many hundreds of corner bars and popular gathering places that aren't on the waterfront.

Bobby Mackey's
44 Licking Pike, Wilder, KY
(859) 431-5588
Bobby Mackey's specializes in country music, and his band, Bobby Mackey and the Big Mac Band, performs on Friday and Saturday as they have for more than 20 years. Two of the other attractions of the bar are the mechanical bull and an arm-wrestling machine. The bull gives cowboy-wannabes the ride of their life, and the arm-wrestling machine can break even the strongest of challengers. The bar also has a karaoke night on Thursday and has a designated-driver program where the driver gets complimentary soft drinks. Doors open at 7:30 P.M. You must be age 18 or over. (See our close-up in the History chapter for more on Bobby Mackey's.)

Coco's
322 Greenup Street, Covington, KY
(859) 491-1369
Coco's is a longtime Northern Kentucky nightspot, offering a mix of jazz, blues, and folk on the weekends in an intimate setting with exposed brick walls. During the day it serves up eclectic fare as a restaurant. You can eat until 10:00 P.M. on weekdays and midnight on Saturday. The music starts at 9:00 P.M.

Cosmo's
604 Main Street, Covington, KY
(859) 261-1330
This grill pub has live music Tuesday, Wednesday, Thursday, and sometimes Friday, with pop, rock, and classic rock bands.

Dee Felice Cafe
529 Main Street, Covington, KY
(859) 261-2365
www.deefelice.com
Stepping into Dee Felice is like stepping into the heart of New Orleans. The cafe, in MainStrasse Village, has live jazz every night. All bands play on an elevated stage behind the bar, making it easy to catch the acts. Because of the popularity, you're asked to order something to eat and are limited to two hours during dinner hours on Friday and Saturday. Reservations are suggested.

Jack Quinn's Irish Ale House & Pub
112 East Fourth Street, Covington, KY
(859) 491-6699
This bar opened in 1998 and has worked hard to re-create a real Irish pub. All the furniture and bars in the pub were custom-made in Ireland. The bar offers live Irish and folk music Wednesday through Saturday. It also has a full menu and a banquet facility.

Mansion Hill Tavern
502 Washington Street, Newport, KY
(859) 581-0100
Mansion Hill is a small neighborhood bar that is big on dishing out the blues. Some of the finest blues bands in the area can be found on stage here. Wednesday is acoustics night, Friday and Saturday have blues bands. Sunday in blues jam. During the warm months, Mansion Hill has a small outdoor courtyard.

Southgate House
24 East Third Street, Newport, KY
(859) 431-2201
The Southgate House is actually a historic site in Northern Kentucky—it's the birthplace of James Thompson, who invented the tommy gun—but it has since become one of the liveliest bars in Northern Kentucky. Many local and regional bands play at the club, but it occasionally hosts a smaller national act. The bands here, which range from country to rock, usually keep the beat up-tempo and the volume loud.

Tickets
100 West Sixth Street, Covington, KY
(859) 431-1839
Tickets is one of the top sports bars in Northern Kentucky. Located in a restored firehouse, the facility offers a variety of big- and small-screen TVs. It has a full menu for those who are hungry and some video and sports games for when the games on television get boring.

York Street Cafe
738 York Street, Newport, KY
(859) 261-9675
York Street Cafe is a coffeehouse and nightclub that has gained quite a reputation for bringing in well-known soloists and smaller acts from all over the country. The music selection is eclectic; acts include folk, alternative, jazz, swing, and blues. You can sit at tables or on couches and overstuffed chairs and put your drinks on the coffee tables.

On the River

Some of the area's most popular nightlife locations are on the river, in part because of the views they offer of downtown Cincinnati. Many of the restaurants located on the river also have bars or offer limited entertainment options after dinner hours.

The Waterfront
14 Pete Rose Pier, Covington, KY
(859) 581-1414
Owners Boomer Esiason, Cris Collinsworth, Pete Rose, Jeff Ruby, and others have made this a great place to catch sports and entertainment celebrities. The three-part Waterfront complex includes South Beach Grill, an upscale restaurant; Sunset Room for private parties; and Rhumba, an upscale dance club.

Other Places

Not every popular nightlife spot around Greater Cincinnati is located in a defined entertainment district. Here are a few that are spread throughout the area.

Allyn's Cafe
3538 Columbia Parkway
(513) 871-5779
Allyn's has any kind of beer you might want, tangy Cajun food, and a great sound system for the live music it offers four nights a week. Allyn's expanded with an addition on what was formerly the patio.

Annie's
4343 Kellogg Avenue, Anderson
(513) 321-0220
Annie's is highly popular with the area's younger crowd, as it is one of the few places that actively welcomes those age 19 and older. Plus it frequently teams up with local alternative radio stations to bring in medium-size national acts. Those with a college ID get in for half price every night. Friday is Dance Party night and Sunday becomes Sunday Night Fever disco night. The bar's concert hall holds up to 1,500 people.

The Blue Note Cafe
4520 West Eighth Street, Western Hills
(513) 921-8898
The Blue Note is actually three bars in one and almost always has two live bands playing at the same time. One bar is at the main entrance with a stage near the door, while a smaller, quieter bar with a grill that offers hamburgers and other traditional bar fare is in the middle and a third bar and stage are in the back. It has live music five days a week.

Brontë Bistro
2692 Madison Road, Norwood
(513) 731-7770
www.josephbeth.com
Located in the Rookwood Pavilion's Joseph-Beth Booksellers, it offers jazz, folk, or acoustical music on Friday night to entertain patrons while they browse through the vast selection of books for sale. The combination of books and music, along with something to drink from the Brontë Bistro, makes a wonderfully relaxing way to spend an evening.

East End Cafe
4003 Eastern Avenue
(513) 321-2627
The East End Cafe is popular with young East Siders. Located in a restored building near Mount Lookout, the bar has a large stage and space enough to pack in several hundred patrons to hear the different bands who perform there each weekend. The music is generally blues, modern rock, or cover tunes, and it's usually loud.

O'Bryon's Irish Pub
1998 Madison Road
(513) 321-5525
O'Bryon's attracts a lot of the sports-minded single sorts with a laid-back atmosphere. The 11 TVs are usually tuned in to a ball game of some sort. It offers a deck up on the roof with nine umbrella-covered tables during warm weather.

Shady's Pub
9443 Loveland-Madeira Road, Symmes
(513) 791-2753
Shady's offers a place to rock to live music out in Symmes. It offers more than 150 imported, domestic, and microbrewed beers.

20th Century
3021 Madison Road
(513) 731-8000
This club is in the former 20th Century Theater, a building that is listed on the historic register. It has some movie memorabilia in the lobby and plays live music on the weekends. It also hosts some small national acts in the theater, which can seat up to 300.

Willie's
5054 Glencrossing Way, Western Hills
(513) 922-3377

401 Crescent Avenue, Covington, KY
(859) 581-1500

8470 Montgomery Road, Kenwood
(513) 891-2204

8188 Princeton-Glendale Road, West Chester
(513) 860-4243

These restaurants/bars are owned by the loud and boisterous radio talk show host Bill Cunningham and are favorite hangouts for local sports celebrities, particularly the Covington, Kentucky, location. Several giant-screen TVs and dozens of smaller sets pack the facilities, offering views of several different games at one time. In addition to the decor, sports games such as Pop-a-Shot can be played. The Covington location also has a DJ playing dance music on Wednesday, Thursday, Friday, and Saturday nights. The club also has karaoke on Sunday and live music on Tuesday night.

HOTELS AND MOTELS

There's a story that Mark Twain, on one particularly lamentable visit to Cincinnati, stayed in a hotel with such pitiful room service that the author remarked he hoped to be staying in that same establishment when the world ended, "because there, everything arrives 10 years late." Yes, Twain later modified the barb to refer to the entire city rather than a single lodging house, but the damage to our town's innkeeping reputation was already done.

Whether this tale is apocryphal or not, Twain's century-old critique shouldn't reflect badly on today's terrific accommodations. Cincinnati, like many places, has seen an explosion of hotel and motel development in the past decade. Nearly three dozen new hotels have opened in the region, primarily in Northern Kentucky (thanks to the Newport Aquarium, the Northern Kentucky Convention Center, and the racetrack that opened in nearby Gallatin County). In all, the area has 20,000-plus hotel rooms. In this chapter, we present a range of options, with amenities and rates to suit most travelers' needs.

Among the all-around best places to stay in town are two historic downtown hotels—the Cincinnatian and the Hilton Netherland—plus the more modern downtown Westin and the Embassy Suites at the Covington RiverCenter. Two historic inns—the Best Western Mariemont Inn and the Golden Lamb Inn in Lebanon—are among a handful of country-style inns that offer a nice break from the routine. And for pure hedonistic enjoyment, it's hard to beat the Wildwood Inn Tropical Dome and Theme Suites in Florence. The spate of modern suite hotels that have sprung up in the past decade, mainly in the suburbs, also offers numerous cozy homes away from home.

Northern Kentucky hospitality gets short shrift from major national travel guides although it has 6,000 rooms all its own. Not only are most Northern Kentucky lodgings not included with Cincinnati listings, they don't even appear in the same book because regional lines are drawn at the Ohio River. But hotels in Covington and Newport are extremely convenient to downtown and boast the best views of the Cincinnati skyline and Ohio River. Most offer transportation across the bridges, although you can certainly make the 10-minute walk on a nice day. One of the newest Kentucky shoreline hotels is the luxurious Cincinnati Marriott at RiverCenter, which opened in 1999.

Know too that these waterside hotels book up early and fast for such major Ohio River events as the Riverfest fireworks and the Tall Stacks steamboat celebration. (See the River Fun chapter.) Reserving a room a year in advance is not unheard of; adding to the crunch are the Newport on the Levee, the Newport Aquarium, and the Northern Kentucky Convention Center—three tourist draws that didn't exist on this side of the river until recently.

The majority of attractive Greater Cincinnati hotels and motels are clustered in four areas: downtown and just across the river in Covington and Newport, the northeastern Interstate 71 corridor near Paramount's Kings Island, the North Central area intersected by Interstates 75 and 275, and the Florence area in Northern Kentucky. The east and west suburbs of Cincinnati have only a handful of hotels and motels, though that may change eventually on the West Side due to the advent of casino gambling in Lawrenceburg, Indiana.

If you want an authentic Cincinnati experience, your best bet is to stay downtown or across the river in Covington or Newport. If you eschew urban congestion and would rather stay at a quiet hotel with a lot to see within walking distance, head to the Best Western Mariemont Inn, a grand Tudor structure along Mariemont's delightful town square. You can catch an art film and munch on Graeter's ice cream all within a few steps of the hotel.

Whatever you do, don't book a hotel near Paramount's Kings Island amusement park on the northeast side of town, unless of course, all you plan to do during your stay in Cincinnati is ride roller coasters. During the summer, you end up paying a premium for the convenience of easy access to the theme park (not to mention the Tennis Masters Series), a pointless cost if Kings Island or pro tennis tournaments aren't your primary tourist destinations.

Transplants looking for an easy answer to "Where do I live during my first month in Cincinnati?" can turn to the many "extended-stay" properties listed below. A new player in the Cincinnati market is the Equity Corporate Housing firm, which has purchased condos in some of the city's trendiest apartment buildings and complexes and offers them for one-month leases. Since you end up paying under $60 per night for a fully furnished apartment (utilities and phone included), it's a consideration. Rooms include cable TV, VCR, sofa, dining table, linens, kitchenware, answering machine, and free local phone calls. Properties include downtown's Grofton Lofts, Greenwich on the Park, and, in the surburbs, the posh Arbors of Anderson, Arbors of Montgomery, and Harper's Point. Call (513) 771-4643.

The listings below don't cover every hotel, motel, and inn. They're meant to cover a choice of the best-quality and best-value hotels in each area. You can expect that the newer suburban hotels offer great accommodations and plenty of free parking. But they generally are in areas that are hard to distinguish from most other suburban commercial districts around the country. We include descriptions of room interiors for the unique hotels; expect the chain motels to offer four walls and a bed unless otherwise noted. Most hotels do not allow pets, but we'll let you know of those that do. All hotels and motels listed here accept major credit cards unless otherwise noted.

PRICE CODE

The pricing guides below are for weekday rates, double occupancy. You can undoubtedly find better deals through group bookings, travel discounts, or other special packages.

$	**Less than $75**
$$	**$75 to $100**
$$$	**$101 to $150**
$$$$	**$151 and more**

DOWNTOWN

Downtown is—big surprise—where the most expensive hotel rooms are generally found. Those on a budget may want to refer to the Northern Kentucky Riverfront section of this chapter. Some of the Kentucky hotels are just a 10-minute walk across a bridge from downtown Cincinnati.

The Cincinnatian Hotel **$$$$**
601 Vine Street
(513) 381-3000

This historic hotel, recently named one of *Condé Nast Traveler* magazine's top-25 hotels in America, was built in 1882 and elegantly reopened in 1987. It's within easy walking distance of downtown attractions—the Aronoff Center for the Arts and shopping at Tower Place and Macy's/Tiffany's are only a block or two away. It's also home to the exquisite Palace restaurant and the popular Cricket Lounge, with a good selection of lesser-priced offerings.

This is generally Cincinnati's most expensive hotel, with weekday rates for double occupancy at $180 and up, but such is the price of elegance. It has 146

If money is no object, head first to the Cincinnatian Hotel. Cincinnati's most expensive hotel is also its most ritzy, holding high English teas and treating guests to glimpses of the Hollywood stars who often stay here. The hotel restaurant, The Palace, is simply stunning.

rooms, meeting halls, and a well-equipped exercise room. Personal computers, in-room safes, secretarial services, voice mail, Internet access, and dataports are available for business travelers. Amenities for all guests include Roman-size tubs, bathroom phones, terry-cloth robes, 24-hour room service, complimentary overnight shoe shine, turndown service, and twice-daily maid service. The rooms, as you might expect, are stunning, with intricate wood cabinets, high ceilings, impressive vase lamps, lush quilt comforters, and roomy desk space.

If you choose what might be the city's most expensive hotel room, the Emery Presidential Suite, you'll fork over $1,500 per night. For that you get two bedrooms, a living room, a dining room, and two baths. The decor is warm tones of beechwood and stately marble, accented by two fireplaces, a wet bar, whirlpools, and surround-sound stereo system. Heck, what's an expense account for?

Famous guests have included Billy Joel, who stayed here and played the hotel lobby's baby grand at 2:00 A.M., plus Ronald Reagan, Margaret Thatcher, Tom Cruise, Dustin Hoffman, Frank Sinatra, Cher, and the Rolling Stones. And Fleetwood Mac's Stevie Nicks thrilled guests by serenading Lindsey Buckingham in the Cricket Lounge.

Another of the hotel's claims to fame is its English tea at the Cricket Lounge, for which people make reservations weeks in advance. Besides a great selection of specialty teas, you get live harp music and pastries made daily by the hotel's pastry chef.

Garfield Suites Hotel **$$-$$$$**
2 Garfield Place
(513) 421-3355

This is one of the sleepers, if you'll pardon the pun, among downtown hotels. It's only a few blocks off Fountain Square adjacent to Piatt Park, across the street from the main library. For adventuresome fare, the Universal Grille is nearby.

The 151-room hotel includes 76 two-bedroom suites plus some two- and three-bedroom penthouse suites on the 16th floor. Weekly and monthly rates are available. Two-bedroom penthouse suites are available at an appropriately lofty price of $299 a night. All rooms have kitchens, microwaves, refrigerators, and safes, and a coin laundry is on the premises. Some rooms have coffeemakers and whirlpools. Small pets are allowed for a onetime $100 cleaning fee.

Hilton Netherland Plaza **$$$$**
35 West Fifth Street
(513) 421-9100

This stately old art deco–style hotel is a National Historic Landmark. Notice the intricately carved moldings and unusual art deco accents in the large ballrooms. This is a well-preserved hotel, but because it's an older building, some rooms are cramped by modern standards. Still, they are grand enough, with lots of walnut, lush carpeting, and comfortable beds. Many rooms have bars, coffeemakers, microwaves, refrigerators, and whirlpools, plus a selection of free and pay in-room movies.

Downtown's shopping mall, Tower Place, is adjacent to the hotel (through Carew Tower), and Saks Fifth Avenue is within easy walking distance. Right across the street are Macy's and Tiffany's. Tower Place itself features shops such as Banana Republic and Brentano's bookstore. A food court on the ground floor also is popular with the downtown lunch crowd.

Amenities in the 632-room, 31-story hotel include a heated indoor pool, saunas, a whirlpool, and privileges at the Carew Tower Health & Fitness Club in the same building. The on-site restaurant is Orchids at Palm Court, one of downtown's finest.

Hyatt Regency Cincinnati $$$-$$$$
151 West Fifth Street
(513) 579-1234

This 502-room hotel in the heart of downtown is adjacent to Saks Fifth Avenue, with shopping at Tower Place nearby. The popular Champs Italian Chop House restaurant is on the ground floor, and the 22-story hotel is also a short walk from many other downtown restaurants. This is one of the few downtown hotels with a heated indoor pool, and it also has saunas and a whirlpool. The Hyatt went through a $5 million rehab, including an upgraded phone system and electronic-entry system for doors.

Millennium Hotel $$$
100 West Sixth Street
(513) 357-5800

The Millennium Hotel is one of downtown's newer hotels and one of its largest. Amenities include outdoor pool with sundeck, access to a fully equipped health club with sauna and squash courts, video rentals, laundry and valet service, gift shop, limousine service, safe-deposit boxes, complimentary cribs, and an on-site barber shop. The 872 rooms in the 32-floor high-rise are decorated in soft wood paneling and a beige/purple color scheme. Dine at the hotel's restaurant or grab a drink in the High Spirits Lounge. The hotel is directly across the street (and attached by an enclosed skywalk) from the Duke Energy Convention Center, making it popular with conventioneers.

One Lytle Place $
621 Mehring Way, on the riverfront
(513) 621-7578

A 25-story luxury high-rise overlooking Sawyer Point Park and the Serpentine Wall on the Ohio River, One Lytle Place is an "extended-stay" option (one-month minimum) that offers a dramatic view no matter which way your balcony faces—the city skyline, Mount Adams, or the rolling Kentucky hillside. We base our $ rating on the fact that one-month leases for fully furnished apartments begin at $1,665 and top out at $2,235 for a two-bedroom, river-view suite—in other words, between $55 and $75 per night. There's a rooftop sundeck, indoor heated swimming pool, exercise room, Jacuzzi, and sauna, and concierge services include valet dry cleaning and reserved garage parking. Lytle runs a free shuttle to the downtown Fortune 500 companies and other firms, though, frankly, you could hoof it to Procter & Gamble world headquarters, for instance, in three minutes.

Ramada Inn $$$
800 West Eighth Street
(513) 241-8660

This 12-story, 245-room hotel is slightly northwest of downtown (in the Queensgate neighborhood, a mixture of office parks and light industry). A popular spot for business meetings and seminars, it's also the closest hotel to the Museum Center at Union Terminal. A $5 million renovation of the interior was completed in 1998. On-site amenities include meeting rooms, an outdoor pool, restaurant, rooftop cocktail lounge, and a coin laundry. Many rooms have bars, coffeemakers, refrigerators, and whirlpools. All rooms have free Showtime. The inn offers free parking, unlike many of the downtown hotels.

Staying at least a month and enjoy living in a loft? Downtown has seen a resurgence of loft studios and one bedrooms, most notably at the Lofts at Shillito Place (formerly Lazarus department store), the Gramercy, and the Greenwich on the Park. Kitchens, laundry facilities, fitness centers, and parking available; the Gramercy even accepts cats. Call (513) 651-1661 for lease information.

Terrace Plaza **$$$**
15 West Sixth Street
(513) 381-4000
The lobby of this attractive downtown hotel is actually on the eighth floor of the building—the first seven floors and also some of the higher floors are office space. The 240 rooms and 10 suites are elegantly appointed in beige and white; some have bars, coffeemakers, and refrigerators. The outstanding services and facilities for business travelers include meeting rooms, personal computers, secretarial services, and room service.

A concierge level provides a hospitality suite with continental breakfast and afternoon hors d'oeuvres. A well-equipped exercise room and sauna are among the other on-site creature comforts. The hotel is within walking distance of a number of fine downtown restaurants. It's certainly one of the closest hotels to the Aronoff Center for the Arts.

Westin Cincinnati **$$$$**
Fifth and Vine Streets
(513) 621-7700
Centrally located directly across Fifth Street from Fountain Square, the 450-room Westin is a modem, nicely decorated hotel in line with the high standards set by Westin nationwide. This hotel was opened in 1981 and renovated in 1998, improving the lobby, all rooms, and the health club. The Westin may not have the historical character of the Hilton Netherland Plaza or the Cincinnatian, but it compensates with other amenities, such as a spacious restaurant, the Albee; convenient access to parking in an underground garage; an interesting collection of boutiques and specialty shops; and a commanding view of Fountain Square. There's an indoor pool and fitness center. The Westin's rooms are among our favorites, with comfy sofa chairs, sizable desks, and immaculate carpets.

NEAR DOWNTOWN (NORTH)

The "Pill Hill" hotels serve the University of Cincinnati main campus and the conglomeration of hospitals that give this hilltop neighborhood its Pill Hill moniker. The primary reason you'd stay in uptown Cincinnati, in fact, is if your sole destination is one of the many huge hospitals (including Children's and Shriner's) here, the university campus, or the Cincinnati Zoo.

Marriott Kingsgate
Conference Center Hotel **$$-$$$**
151 Goodman Drive
(513) 487-3800
A new player on the uptown hospitality scene, this conference center opened in 1999. A full-service Marriott with 206 rooms, the Kingsgate is located within easy walking distance of campus and is the very first major hotel to cater to prospective University of Cincinnati students and parents. Guest rooms include coffeemaker, hair dryer, iron and ironing board, and two telephones with dataports and access to high-speed Internet services. An on-site fitness center features free weights, treadmill, stair machine, stationary bike, and lockers. Dine at the excellent hotel restaurant, Bistro 151 (see the Restaurants chapter), or enjoy a drink in the Tap Room. A 550-car garage is directly connected to Kingsgate, no small favor in a congested urban neighborhood with few available parking spots thanks to commuting university students and visitors at the Pill Hill hospitals. The Kingsgate is a choice for parents visiting their campus kin, of course, but is also the closest hotel to the Cincinnati Zoo and major hospitals such as University, Shriner's, Children's, Good Sam, and Deaconess.

Quality Hotel and Suites **$$-$$$**
4747 Montgomery Road, Norwood
(513) 351-6000
Approximately a 10-minute drive from downtown Cincinnati, the Quality Hotel is

a popular business-meeting location, with some nice amenities and a hotel restaurant, Highlands, which does a fairly brisk lunch trade with nonguests. This eight-story, 146-room hotel has a heated outdoor pool and free in-room movies plus a bar, coffeemaker, microwave, refrigerator, and hot tubs in some rooms. Free continental breakfasts are available to all rooms. Airport transportation is available. Parking is ample.

Vernon Manor Hotel **$$-$$$**
400 Oak Street
(513) 281-3300

Built in 1924, the dignified Vernon Manor Hotel was the site of a scene in the Academy Award-winning movie *Rain Man* and the subject of several mentions in the movie. This is one of the best hotels that's convenient to both the Pill Hill hospital district and the University of Cincinnati.

The hotel has two fine restaurants downstairs that are popular for business lunches and great Sunday brunches. The lounge, Club 400, is a friendly spot the hotel manager describes as "a lounge where you'll still be married when you leave." The hotel's authentic reproduction of an English manor includes a panoramic view of the city from its rooftop garden. And rare is the Saturday when there aren't multiple wedding receptions going on here.

Its old-world dignity aside, the Vernon Manor in many ways has the look and feel more of an apartment building than a hotel. Fifty-six of its 168 rooms have kitchens with refrigerators and microwaves, so it's well suited for extended stays. The staff prides itself on providing friendly, informal, first-name service for folks who may have loved ones at nearby hospitals or who just like to loosen their ties after a long day of work. There's an on-site massage therapist and hair salon, as well as a fitness center and business center. Monthly rates are available.

NORTHERN KENTUCKY RIVERFRONT (JUST SOUTH OF DOWNTOWN)

The explosion of new hotels in Newport and Covington, Kentucky, is terrific news for the traveler, since competition breeds more favorable room rates and package deals. The boom has also created a ferocious competition for hotel staff: Some Northern Kentucky hotels find themselves offering college tuition reimbursement and free bus passes to keep employees!

Cincinnati Marriott at RiverCenter **$$$-$$$$**
10 West RiverCenter Boulevard, Covington, KY
(859) 261-2900

A soaring 14-story atrium and granite-columned gazebo distinguish this addition to the riverfront scene. Opened in 1999, the hotel accommodates 900 guests in 322 rooms and sits adjacent to the Northern Kentucky Convention Center. All rooms feature dual-line telephone with voice mail and dataport, cable TV, hair dryer, and iron and ironing board. The hotel restaurant, Zebo's, offers trendy bistro fare. There is an indoor pool, and a three-story health-and-fitness spa with sauna, whirlpool, and massage. A unique feature at any hotel: There's a cozy library with fireplace and high-back leather chairs and, of course, lots of reading materials. A concierge service features valet and guest laundry, safe-deposit boxes, and shoeshine, plus there is a hair stylist and gift shop on-site.

Comfort Suites Riverfront **$$**
420 Riverboat Row, Newport, KY
(859) 291-6700

This riverfront hotel features six floors with 124 rooms and is certainly one of the most economical hotels in the downtown area (especially since each room comes with complimentary continental breakfast). A fully equipped business center is open 24 hours, offering copier, fax, laser printer, and computers, plus there's a fitness room with Lifecycles, stair steppers, treadmills, and Nautilus equipment. It's an all-suite hotel, with each room boasting fridge, microwave, ironing board, and more. A sample room we saw had tones of white and green, with vaulted ceilings, framed flower prints, and dark-stained walnut cabinetry. The sofa, coffee table, and dining table were nice touches.

The Buckhead Mountain Grille restaurant is immediately adjacent, as is Don Pablo's, Joe's Crab Shack, and the Riverboat Row eateries.

This is one of the closest hotels to the $200 million Newport on the Levee entertainment complex, featuring the Newport Aquarium, the Shadowbox Cabaret comedy nightclub, a multiscreen AMC movie theater, restaurants, and shopping.

Courtyard by Marriott $$
500 West Third Street, Covington, KY
(859) 491-4000

Marriott opened this 80-room hotel in 1999. Features include indoor corridors, an indoor pool, a minigym, an on-site restaurant and lounge, and a coin laundry.

Embassy Suites Cincinnati at RiverCenter $$$$
10 East RiverCenter Boulevard, Covington, KY
(859) 261-8400

OK, it's not Cincinnati. It's not even Ohio. But it does have a breathtaking view of Cincinnati across the river. And it's one of the city's nicest hotels, combining the convenience of being a bridge away from downtown with the more relaxed feel and readily available covered parking of a top suburban hotel. This hotel also combines the two-room suites and monthly rates of an extended-stay hotel with the look and amenities of a luxury-class downtown hotel. A towering atrium lobby has marble floors and a splashing fountain that lead to glass-enclosed elevators.

The eight-story, 226-room hotel includes six two-bedroom units, meeting rooms, business center, heated indoor pool, sauna, whirlpool, sundeck for the summer months, well-provisioned exercise room, and complimentary evening beverages. Guests also receive a free full breakfast. All rooms have two TVs, hair dryers, irons and ironing boards, coffeemakers, microwaves, refrigerators, and a choice of free or pay movies. A room we saw was spacious, with dining-room table (complete with four chairs), sofa, coffee table, and more.

The hotel restaurant, the Embassy Grille, is one of our favorite continental restaurants. Nearby are also several fine restaurants and shops, including the Behle Street Cafe and several restaurants and specialty shops at MainStrasse Village in Covington.

A word of advice: When a hotel brochure proclaims the hotel is just 15 minutes from downtown, or just 20 minutes from the airport, that's usually as the crow flies. Not as the crow navigates I-75's orange barrels or as the crow stews in traffic, stuck in the baseball or football traffic along Fort Washington Way along the river.

Extended Stay America $
650 West Third Street, Covington, KY
(859) 581-3000

This extended-stay hotel opened in 1998, a newcomer in the growing market for longer-stay facilities (though single-night guests are welcome). This Extended Stay is quite near the Northern Kentucky Convention Center and only a few minutes' drive from the Newport Aquarium. The 105 rooms include efficiencies with fully equipped kitchens and two twin- or queen-size beds. There are guest laundries on-site. Weekly rates are available.

Hampton Inn $$
200 Crescent Avenue, Covington, KY
(859) 581-7800

This hotel, opened in 1997, features 151 rooms in a six-story complex. Amenities include an indoor pool and a fitness center, plus free Disney and HBO. The rooms feature king-size beds, writing desks, and plush carpeting.

Holiday Inn–Riverfront **$$**
600 West Third Street, Covington, KY
(859) 291–4300

Only a half mile from the Northern Kentucky Convention Center, this hotel balances nicely the needs of the corporate and the leisure traveler. The 153 remodeled rooms are tastefully furnished and each is outfitted with color TVs and computer dataports. There's an outdoor pool, fitness facilities, multiple meeting rooms, and the Greenery restaurant and lounge. There is a free continental breakfast.

Radisson Hotel Riverview **$$–$$$**
668 West Fifth Street, Covington, KY
(859) 491–1200

The giant scalloped cylinder in Covington is the Radisson Hotel Riverview (the former Clarion Hotel). A rotating restaurant, the Riverview, on the top (18th) floor provides a panoramic view of downtown Cincinnati and Northern Kentucky. Just a brief walk from MainStrasse Village, this Covington landmark gives you ample opportunity to get out and enjoy the fine shops and restaurants there. Or you can make the quick trip across the bridge to more attractions in downtown Cincinnati. Many rooms have commanding views of the Cincinnati skyline. Most others have nice views of beautiful 19th-century homes in Covington.

Each of the 236 rooms has its own recliner, dataport, and coffeemaker. Some rooms have microwaves and refrigerators. Jacuzzi and wet-bar suites also are available. (There are an impressive four floors devoted to nonsmoking rooms.) Other amenities include a heated indoor/outdoor pool, exercise room with sauna and tanning bed, platform tennis court, whirlpool, room service, and valet laundry service, Courtesy transportation is available to downtown and the airport. Barber and beauty shops are on-site, and plenty of free parking is available above or below ground.

Riverfront Travelodge **$**
222 York Street, Newport, KY
(859) 291–4434

A budget option as well as a consideration when all the major Northern Kentucky hotels are booked (a real possibility during Tall Stacks week as well as during major events at the Northern Kentucky Convention Center), this wellworn motel has 103 rooms and an outdoor pool. The Newport Aquarium is practically next door.

NORTHERN KENTUCKY (SUBURBS AND AIRPORT)

Some of the region's most affordable hotel rooms are found alongside the bedroom communities and sprawling retail boxes that are popping up on what was once rural farmland surrounding the Cincinnati/Northern Kentucky International Airport.

AmeriSuites Cincinnati Airport **$**
300 Meijer Drive, Florence, KY
(859) 647–1170

AmeriSuites offers 128 suites with iron and ironing board, voice mail, refrigerator, microwave, wet bar, and coffeemaker. There is a fitness center and indoor heated pool. A free continental breakfast is served. Weekly rates are available.

Ashley Quarters **$$–$$$**
4880 Houston Road, Florence, KY
(859) 525–9997

This extended-stay hotel features 70 rooms with full-size, fully equipped kitchens. There's a direct phone line in each room (select rooms have two phone lines), plus voice mail and dataports. Rooms also feature irons and ironing boards, coffeemakers, and, of course, housekeeping. There is also an on-site laundry and valet dry-cleaning service, an off-property gym, and meeting-room facilities.

Baymont Inn & Suites $$
1805 Airport Exchange Boulevard, Erlanger, KY
(859) 746-0300
Just 2 miles from the airport, this former Budgetel features rooms that include a work desk, coffeemaker, cable TV, and modem-compatible phones. Suites include a sofa, microwave, and refrigerator. Business facilities include free use of the fax machine (up to five pages), and VHS tape players are available. There is an outdoor pool, and free continental breakfast is delivered to your room.

Best Western Florence $$
7821 Commerce Drive, Florence, KY
(859) 525-0090
Just minutes from the airport, Best Western features an outdoor whirlpool spa, sauna, and workout gym. Rooms include a dining table with two chairs and cable TV. A choice of restaurants is across the street. There is a free continental breakfast.

Best Western Fort Mitchell $$$
21 Dixie Highway, Fort Mitchell, KY
(859) 331-1500
This former Holiday Inn includes a heated indoor pool, sauna, whirlpool, and exercise facilities. Other amenities include room service, valet laundry service, free airport transportation, and an on-site restaurant and lounge. The restaurant is particularly elegant for a Best Western, with linens, fine china, and other nicely appointed table settings. The 214 rooms are attractive and clean. The hotel is only 3 miles from downtown and 7 miles from the airport. Turfway Park racetrack is just minutes away.

Cincinnati Airport Marriott $$
2395 Progress Drive, Hebron, KY
(859) 586-0166
This Marriott opened in 1999 and features a restaurant, lounge pool, and business center. The 306 rooms are all outfitted with computer dataports and other amenities such as spacious work desks to attract the business traveler.

Courtyard by Marriott $$
46 Cavalier Boulevard, Florence, KY
(859) 371-6464
Five miles from the airport, the Courtyard offers an indoor pool and whirlpool, exercise room, and Jacuzzi rooms. Rooms include a work desk and coffeemaker. Three large Presidential Suites include parlor, refrigerator, microwave, two TVs, and two telephones. A full breakfast can be purchased in the Courtyard Cafe, as can cocktails in the evening.

Drawbridge Hotel $$$
2477 Royal Drive, Fort Mitchell, KY
(859) 341-2800
With 505 rooms, this is one of the largest hotels in the area. Extensive facilities include one of the largest collections of meeting rooms in Greater Cincinnati and a hair salon. There are two restaurants and a lounge here, including Josh's and Chaucer's. The hotel is 5 miles from downtown and 5 miles from the airport.

Though some rooms are in the value-price range, Drawbridge also has luxury-class rooms. A VIP concierge/corporate floor is an all-adult floor with concierge service, continental breakfast, and honor bar—and all rooms have queen-size four-poster beds. Throughout the hotel, all rooms are accessible by interior corridors. Some rooms have coffeemakers, refrigerators, and whirlpools.

The complex has two swimming pools—one indoor heated pool and outdoor pool—a sauna, whirlpool, two lighted tennis courts, exercise room, basketball court, and sand volleyball court. Available services include a masseuse, valet laundry, on-site barbershop and beauty salon, and video-game arcade. Coin laundry, free airport transportation, and children's programs are additional amenities. Ask about a variety of seasonal and year-round special packages.

Fairfield Inn by Marriott $
50 Cavalier Boulevard, Florence, KY
(859) 371-4800
This three-story, 135-room hotel provides

dependable quality as well as good value. There's a free continental breakfast. Some rooms have interior corridors and all have dataports for computers. Numerous dining options are nearby. It's only a few minutes from Florence Mall and Turfway Park, 5 minutes from the airport, and 5 to 10 minutes from downtown.

Hampton Inn **$**
7393 Turfway Road, Florence, KY
(859) 283-1600
Another great suburban hotel value, the four-story, 117-room Hampton Inn is close to Florence Mall and Turfway Park, 5 minutes from the airport, and 5 to 10 minutes from downtown. The lobby has a fairly cozy breakfast area with free continental breakfast provided. Each room also gets free movies, and half the rooms are designated for nonsmoking guests. Other amenities at the hotel include meeting rooms, an outdoor pool, and free airport transportation. All rooms are accessible from interior corridors.

Hilton Greater Cincinnati Airport **$$$**
7373 Turfway Road, Florence, KY
(859) 371-4400
One of the nicer suburban hotels in Greater Cincinnati, the Hilton Greater Cincinnati Airport—which recently underwent $5 million in renovations—has larger-than-average rooms and better-than-average furnishings. A fairly wide assortment of rooms includes some suites and others with king-size beds. Convenient to shopping at Florence Mall, the Turfway Park horse track, and a variety of restaurants in Florence, it's also only 5 miles from the airport. The Grand Cafe restaurant features a wine cellar, bakery on the premises, and live entertainment.

Amenities of the five-story, 306-room hotel include a heated outdoor pool, sauna, lighted tennis court, and exercise room, plus computer hookups for business travelers. Special services include valet laundry and free airport transportation. Some rooms have honor bars, microwaves, refrigerators, and whirlpools. The executive concierge service package includes a free continental breakfast, evening drinks, and hors d'oeuvres.

All rates quoted in the city's northern suburbs are for spring/summer; expect to pay less in fall and winter. Why? Because nearby are Paramount's Kings Island amusement park, Beach Waterpark, and Galbreath Field (home of the American Jumping Classic). And the Tennis Masters Series, one of the nation's premier tennis tournaments, is held at the sports center.

Holiday Inn–Cincinnati Airport **$$$**
1717 Airport Exchange Boulevard, Erlanger, KY
(859) 371-2233
This airport hotel offers a good combination of convenience and atmosphere. Only 2 miles from the airport and 8 miles from downtown, the six-story, 306-room hotel has a plush atrium lobby with comfy chairs, lots of greenery, and a fountain. The hotel has all interior corridors, conference facilities, a heated indoor pool, saunas, fitness center, secretarial services, free airport transportation, coin laundry, and the on-site McKenna's restaurant and cocktail lounge. All rooms have coffeemakers, irons and ironing boards, voice mail, and computer dataports. Some have whirlpools, honor bars, and refrigerators. It's one of the closest full-service Kentucky hotels to the *Argosy VI* casino and Perfect North ski slopes.

Home Suites Florence **$$**
8050 Holiday Place, Florence, KY
(859) 371-2700
Amenities at this 106-room, recently renovated hotel include room service, free airport transportation, an on-site restaurant and lounge, and an outdoor swimming pool. It's about 6 miles from the airport and 13 miles from downtown and only a few minutes from Turfway Park and Florence Mall. All rooms have coffeemakers and hair dryers. Some have refrigerators.

CLOSE-UP

Wild Times at Wildwood Inn

Imagine spending the evening in an African safari village. Or plopping down for the night in a cavern complete with stalagmites and trickling waterfalls. Or taking a Polynesian holiday to the South Pacific.

All this without ever leaving Greater Cincinnati.

You can do these trips and more at the sprawling Wildwood Inn Tropical Dome and Theme Suites, certainly the region's most imaginative hotel attraction.

Consider the Shi-Awela village (meaning "a peaceful place of rest"), an exotic and gated re-creation of a safari village in Africa. Inside the village, you encounter 12 huts, all with individual front doors and parking. The round, thatched-roof huts are surrounded by actual savanna grasses and Kenyan trees and plants, as well as a lagoon, making for what one manager describes as "a virtual-reality African vacation."

Each spacious hut features African decor, including king-size bamboo beds with mosquito netting, animal pelts, even Zulu shields. Fear not, you won't be roughing it entirely. Not with the giant projection-screen TV and CD surround-sound stereo system so readily available.

Then there's the Fabulous Tropical Dome and Tropical Garden Atrium, a great option for families. In addition to the indoor heated swimming pool, there's a kiddie pool, tubular playground, waterfall, tropical fog mist, billiards, Ping-Pong tables, picnic tables, and sundeck. The continental breakfast is on the house.

You'll also get a kick out of the Happy Days Suite, where you can bunk in a 1959 Cadillac convertible turned into a bed (fins and all) and watch a "drive-in" flick on the home theater screen (we

Hotel Ivy **$$**
30 Cavalier Court, Florence, KY
(859) 371-0081

A nice value, this hotel is nothing fancy but does provide all the basics and then some. It's close to Turfway Park racetrack and Florence Mall and less than 10 minutes from downtown. The two-story, 125-room hotel has all interior corridors, meeting rooms, an outdoor pool, privileges at a nearby health club, and airport transportation. Private office space is free to guests. Some rooms have microwaves and refrigerators, and VCRs are available for a fee. Ask about weekend rates. Weekly and monthly rates also are available.

Sheraton Hotel–Cincinnati Airport **$$$–$$$$**
Cincinnati/Northern Kentucky International Airport, Hebron, KY
(859) 371-6166

You can't get much closer to the airport than this: The hotel is right on the airport grounds (about 20 minutes from downtown). The eight-story hotel offers the recommend *American Graffiti*). There's a jukebox in the corner, a telephone booth, and—if you can believe—a four-person "diner" in one corner (complimentary snacks provided). Memorabilia from the era include pictures, records, signs, even a 1950s Coke machine.

In a tribute to the nearby Kentucky Speedway, there's the Speedway Suite. Guests relax in actual race-car seats as they experience the thrill of an auto race on the 6-foot television screen. Racing memorabilia, dozens of model cars, posters, and signs accent the area. Refreshments are available in the pit, and sleeping accommodations are beds nestled into three authentic, full-size race cars. Vroooommm.

Honeymooners and couples looking for a romantic getaway will find saucy accommodations in the Southwestern Cave Room, seemingly carved out of solid rock. "It's inspired by the spectacular Carlsbad Caverns in New Mexico," notes one brochure. The subterranean room is a trip back to the Stone Age, with animal-skin covers, prehistoric amenities, and trickling underground waterfall.

The hotel complex's 124 rooms range from plush to classic. The two-story Champagne Spa room has a spiral staircase and cathedral ceilings. The Fitzgerald Suite—as in Zelda and F. Scott—is an elegant Victorian accommodation. There's also a Wild West Suite, Oriental Suite, Polynesian Suite, and more. Rooms are outfitted with an assortment of microwaves, refrigerators, coffeemakers, and the like.

What about prices? Packages abound. For instance, the Family Package gets you the Dome Room, with free pizza, for $150 weekdays. Up to five people can rent a smaller room in the Dome for $80; if you're willing to trudge to the outside connecting rooms, it's only $59 a night. (Higher rates prevail on weekends.) The Happy Days, Speedway, and Cave suites are $235 weekdays, $285 weekends. The Safari Village costs $200 weekdays, $260 weekends. For more details call (859) 371-6300.

business traveler secretarial services, valet laundry and dry cleaning, and free airport transportation, plus conference facilities. Each soundproof room offers free movies. This Sheraton (until 2006 it was a Radisson Hotel) underwent a dramatic $10 million makeover, scaling down the number of rooms from 200-plus to 177, resulting in bigger, more comfortable spaces. The renovation produced an expanded fitness center and a new, heated indoor pool.

Super 8 Motel **$**
7928 Dream Street, Florence, KY
(859) 283-1221

2350 Royal Drive, Fort Mitchell, KY
(859) 341-2090

Dependable chain quality and a value price make this 93-room, two-story motel with interior corridors a winner. On-site services at the Florence location include a coin laundry and, in some rooms, microwaves, refrigerators, and whirlpools. Rooms, predictably enough, are plain. The Fort Mitchell location is a 106-room, three-story motel just off Buttermilk Pike, near a variety of dining options. It's also just 5 miles from downtown and 5 miles from the airport. Amenities include a small, heated pool. Weekly rates are available.

Wildwood Inn Tropical Dome and Theme Suites **$-$$$$**
7809 U.S. Highway 42, Florence, KY
(859) 371-6300
The Wildwood Inn offers one of the most complete recreation packages in Greater Cincinnati, with something to suit honeymooners, weekend escapees, or transferees looking to relocate (see our close-up about this inn earlier in this chapter).

NORTHEASTERN SUBURBS

Note that rates are generally higher during the summer months because of demand for Paramount's Kings Island and other nearby water parks and attractions.

AmeriSuites
Deerfield Crossing **$-$$**
5070 Natorp Boulevard, Mason
(513) 754-0003

11435 Reed Hartman Highway, Blue Ash **$$$-$$$$**
(513) 489-3666
The Mason AmeriSuites opened in 1999 and offers some of the best rates found in any quality hotel this close to Paramount's Kings Island. There are 128 suites with iron and ironing board, voice mail, refrigerator, microwave, wet bar, and coffeemaker. There is a fitness center and indoor heated pool. A free continental breakfast is served.

The Blue Ash AmeriSuites offers a good home away from home for the long-term business traveler or newcomer putting down roots. It's in the middle of the Blue Ash business corridor, which rivals downtown for office space. The hotel is also only 10 minutes or less from shopping at the Kenwood Towne Center or Tri-County Mall and a host of restaurants in all price ranges in the Blue Ash area.

Wooded grounds and a luxurious lobby help set this 128-room hotel apart. Offerings include a mixture of king-size-bed and double-bed rooms, all of which have bars, microwaves, free movies, refrigerators, and VCRs. Some have coffeemakers. Monthly rates and senior discounts are available.

Best Western **$$-$$$**
8020 Montgomery Road, Kenwood
(513) 793-4300
Situated amid a vast array of Kenwood shopping and dining choices, this fine hotel also has a restaurant of its own. The two-story, 152-room hotel has interior corridors, meeting rooms, heated outdoor and indoor pools, two lighted tennis courts, shuffleboard, volleyball, a sauna, whirlpool, exercise room, and cocktail lounge. Secretarial services are available. Some rooms have bars, coffeemakers, refrigerators, and whirlpools. All have dataports and voice mail. Ask about package trips to area attractions.

Candlewood Suites **$$-$$$**
10665 Techwood Circle, Blue Ash
(513) 733-0100
Candlewood's three floors offer 77 suites, both studio and one-bedroom. Each suite comes equipped with kitchen, VCR, ironing board, hair dryer, work station, and computer dataports. The decor is modern. The one-bedroom suites also feature a sofa. Room access is via indoor corridors, and amenities include a fitness center and—a rarity among Cincinnati hotels—an on-site grocery. Dining options abound nearby. Rates decrease considerably for extended stays.

Cincinnati Marriott-Northeast **$$-$$$**
9664 Mason-Montgomery Road (Interstate 71 at Fields Ertel Road exit), Mason
(513) 459-9800
This 303-room hotel serves the Paramount's Kings Island area and Cincinnati's Northeast corridor. It has 13,000 square feet of flexible meeting space, concierge-

level business rooms, a workout center, a heated indoor/outdoor pool, and many rooms with microwaves, coffeemakers, hair dryers, and irons and ironing boards. There are seven Jacuzzi suites. Other amenities include an on-site restaurant and safe-deposit boxes.

Clarion Hotel Blue Ash **$**
5901 Pfeiffer Road, Blue Ash
(513) 793-4500
This is a nicely appointed business hotel with 266 rooms in six stories. Amenities include a heated indoor pool and on-site dining room and coffee shop. Also consider breakfast just a few minutes down Kenwood Road at Marx Hot Bagels, a local favorite. The hotel offers a shuttle service to the Blue Ash–area business corridor and Kenwood Towne Centre, both of which are only minutes away. Some rooms have bars, coffeemakers, microwaves, and refrigerators.

Comfort Inn–Northeast **$-$$**
9011 Fields Ertel Road, Mason
(513) 683-9700
Comfort Inn gives you all the basics and is less than 10 minutes from Paramount's Kings Island, the Beach, and the Tennis Masters Tournament. There's also a Showcase Cinemas complex with state-of-the-art movie technology nearby. The three-story, 117-room motel has an outdoor pool, interior corridors, and meeting rooms. Numerous dining choices are nearby, and there's a complimentary breakfast. Other amenities include same-day dry-cleaning service, an on-site laundry facility for guests, and three suites with microwaves and minifridges.

Comfort Suites of Blue Ash **$-$$**
11349 Reed Hartman Highway, Blue Ash
(513) 530-5999
This 50-room suite hotel has an attractive atrium lobby decorated in a French Quarter motif with cast-iron grilles, a fountain, and lush vegetation. Rooms are spacious and come with refrigerators and free movies. Some have coffeemakers and pullout sofas, and VCRs are available for a rental fee. Other amenities include meeting rooms and an outdoor pool. Its location in the Blue Ash business corridor makes it a popular business hotel.

Courtyard by Marriott **$$$**
4625 Lake Forest Drive, Blue Ash
(513) 733-4334
The Courtyard is a no-nonsense business hotel. All 149 rooms in the three-story hotel are spacious and have dataports. Some have refrigerators. Other features include indoor corridors, a heated indoor pool, a minigym, an on-site restaurant and lounge, and a coin laundry.

Days Inn Kings Island **$$-$$$**
9735 Mason-Montgomery Road, Mason
(513) 398-3297
The two-story, 124-room Days Inn provides all the basics for Paramount's Kings Island visitors and business travelers, including meeting rooms, a pool, and a playground. Some rooms have coffeemakers, and a wide array of restaurants are nearby. A free continental breakfast is provided.

Embassy Suites Hotel **$$$$**
4554 Lake Forest Drive, Blue Ash
(513) 733-8900
This Embassy Suites in the heart of the Blue Ash business corridor makes a nice first impression with a large, luxurious atrium filled with tropical plants. The five-story, 235-suite hotel has meeting rooms, a heated indoor pool, sauna, whirlpool, and coin laundry. The on-site restaurant, Cascades, features a waterfall and babbling brook. The spacious suites include TVs, bars, microwaves, refrigerators, dataports, coffeemakers, and iron and ironing board. Guests receive a free full breakfast and complimentary evening manager's reception.

Extended Stay America **$**
4260 Hunt Road, Blue Ash
(513) 793-6750
This 71-room extended-stay hotel beats the price of other extended-stay offerings

in the Blue Ash area, albeit with smaller studio apartments. All studios have fully equipped kitchens with microwaves. The hotel also has an outdoor pool, exercise room, a sauna, and coin laundry. Weekly rates are available. Several restaurant options are within a short driving distance.

Hampton Inn Kings Island **$$-$$$**
5323 Beach Boulevard, Mason
(513) 459-8900

This hotel is close to the Beach Waterpark (one-fourth of a mile away) and Paramount's Kings Island (less than a mile). Facilities at the Mason complex include an indoor pool, a dry cleaning service, and a laundry on-site. A full 80 percent of the rooms are designated nonsmoking. Rooms include free movie channels, dataports, and interior corridor doors, and there are special Jacuzzi suites. A complimentary continental breakfast is served.

Kings Island Resort and Conference Center **$$$-$$$$**
5691 Kings Island Drive, Mason
(513) 398-0115

You won't get much closer to Paramount's Kings Island, the Beach, and the Golf Center at Kings Island without pitching a tent on the grounds (not recommended or allowed). This popular conference location has 288 rooms in two stories, with a mix of interior and exterior corridors. A full package of amenities includes two pools—one heated and one indoors—sauna, whirlpool, putting green, two tennis courts, exercise room, coin laundry, playground, free shuttle to the theme park's door (not an inconsiderable perk, saving your family both effort and the $10 per day parking charge), and on-site restaurant and lounge. Some rooms have bars, coffeemakers, microwaves, and refrigerators.

Kings Luxury Inn **$$**
10561 Mason-Montgomery Road, Mason
(513) 398-8015

Another Paramount's Kings Island-area favorite, this inn's rates reflect the seasonal influx for area attractions and events. The two-story, 104-room hotel includes meeting rooms and an outdoor pool. Some rooms have coffeemakers.

La Quinta Kings Island **$-$$**
9918 Escort Drive, Mason
(513) 459-1111

An unusual feature at this hotel is the indoor greenhouse pool and spa. Rooms include a work desk, coffeemaker, cable TV, and iron and ironing board. Suites include a recliner, microwave, and refrigerator. Business facilities include free use of the fax machine (up to five pages). There's a Lonestar Steakhouse next door, and Paramount's Kings Island is just 4 miles away. A free continental breakfast is served.

Red Roof Inn **$-$$**
9847 Escort Drive, Mason
(513) 398-3633

5900 Pfeiffer Road, Blue Ash
(513) 793-8811

The Mason Red Roof Inn is a former Best Western, a two-story, 124-room motel that's five minutes from Paramount's Kings Island. Little ones will enjoy a playground on the premises. Other amenities include an outdoor pool and coffeemakers in some rooms. The Blue Ash motel provides dependable chain quality in a nice location minutes from Blue Ash businesses. There's no on-site restaurant, but plenty of options are nearby, including the popular Marx Hot Bagels, a short drive down Kenwood Road.

Residence Inn by Marriott **$$$**
11401 Reed Hartman Highway, Blue Ash
(513) 530-5060

Always a good bet for extended stays or business trips to the Blue Ash business center, Residence Inn offers 118 nicely decorated one- and two-bedroom apartment suites. Many have fireplaces, some have two baths, and each unit has dataports and a full kitchen. There's also a complimentary breakfast.

The comfortable lobby has a fireplace. But you won't have to just sit around looking at the fire; you can avail yourself of the heated pool, whirlpool, exercise room, sports court, and volleyball court. Weekly, monthly, and seasonal rates are available, and you can bring Fido or Kitty if you also bring a $95 cleaning fee.

Springhill Suites **$$**
9365 Waterstone Boulevard, Deerfield Township
(513) 683-7797
Located near the Kings Auto Mall, this Marriott property offers one of the more affordable stays within a 2-mile perimeter of Paramount's Kings Island. The 102-room facility offers an indoor pool, a spa, and a free continental breakfast. There's a microwave and refrigerator in every room.

Super 8 **$$**
5589 Kings Mills Road, Kings Mills
(513) 398-8075
This is a solid value for visitors to Paramount's Kings Island, the Beach, and the Golf Center at Kings Island. The two-story, 202-room complex offers conference facilities, an outdoor pool, a playground, coin laundry, and video-game room. There's outdoor recreation and fishing nearby. Some rooms have refrigerators, and VCRs are available for a separate rental fee.

TownePlace Suites **$$**
9369 Waterstone Boulevard, Deerfield Township
(513) 774-0610
This extended-stay complex opened in 1999. TownePlace Suites does not offer single-night stays but is an ideal consideration for families planning to hit Paramount's Kings Island for a full week (and don't kid yourself, many families do). Like its companion Springhill Suites, it's operated by Marriott and offers many of the amenities you'd expect.

Wingate Inn **$$**
4380 Glendale-Milford Road, Blue Ash
(513) 733-1142
This very affordable 82-room, four-story hotel opened in 1999 and sits directly across from the Blue Ash Airport. There's an indoor pool, and rooms are outfitted with dataports and coffeemakers.

On the road with Fido or Muffin? You have a few—precious few—hotel and motel options (short of sneaking the poor puppy inside your room in a gym bag). Garfield Suites downtown, Residence Inn-Sharonville, Residence Inn-Blue Ash, Red Roof Inn-Cherry Grove, and Holiday Inn-Eastgate do accept pets (we've noted cleaning fees where applicable).

NORTH CENTRAL

The North Central area primarily serves business travelers, since the only notable tourism attractions are the megamalls and the Sharonville Convention Center. Many of these hotels and motels are located directly off I-75 and I-275 exits, making them convenient stopovers.

AmeriSuites **$$-$$$**
12001 Chase Plaza Drive, Forest Park
(513) 825-9035
A great suite hotel, AmeriSuites looks more like a condominium complex than a hotel. It's convenient to shopping at Cincinnati Mills and Tri-County Mall and to a host of fine restaurants. The 126 rooms include a mixture of king-size-bed and double-bed rooms, all of which have bars, microwaves, refrigerators, and VCRs. Some rooms have coffeemakers. Monthly rates and senior discounts are available.

Baymont Inn **$-$$**
10900 Crowne Point Drive, Sharonville
(513) 771-6888
You get a free continental breakfast, and the inn has all-interior corridors, meeting rooms, an outdoor pool, and video players (for an additional fee). The four-story, 130-room hotel has several dining choices nearby.

Baymont Inn & Suites **$-$$**
12150 Springfield Pike, Springdale
(513) 671-2300
Rooms include a work desk, coffeemaker, cable TV, and modem-compatible phones. Suites include a sofa, recliner, microwave, and refrigerator. Business facilities include free use of the fax machine (up to five pages). The massive Tri-County Mall is just a mile down the road. A free continental breakfast is delivered to your room.

Cincinnati Marriott Union Centre **$$$**
6189 Mulhauser Road (just off the Interstate 75 Union Centre exit), West Chester
(513) 874-7335
One of the region's newest high-rise hotels, the Cincinnati Marriott Union Centre opened in 2001. The eight-story, 295-room hotel is the centerpiece of the growing Union Centre retail-and-business development corridor in West Chester. The hotel—which largely serves such corporate giants as nearby GE Aircraft Engines and various Procter & Gamble facilities—features a business center, fitness area with indoor lap pool, concierge level, laundry valet service, safe-deposit boxes, and the favorably reviewed River City Grille restaurant. More than 200 rooms are specifically designed for business travelers, including two phone lines, telephone with voice mail, and computer modem hookup. All rooms have CNN, ESPN, HBO, clock radio, and coffeemakers. Nearby is Dave & Buster's, an entertainment/gaming and restaurant attraction, as well as numerous chain eateries.

Days Inn Sharonville **$-$$**
U.S. Highway 42 at Interstate 275 (exit 46), Sharonville
(513) 554-1400
This Days Inn provides an outdoor pool, game room, and a restaurant and lounge. There are 143 rooms served by interior corridors that include TV with free HBO and ESPN. A free continental breakfast is provided.

Doubletree Guest Suites **$$$-$$$$**
6300 East Kemper Road, Sharonville
(513) 489-3636
Doubletree is an attractive suite hotel on wooded grounds with a posh lobby and corridors at I-275 and Reed Hartman Highway, right on the Sharonville/Blue Ash border (making it a toss-up whether to place this listing in the Northeastern section or here). The three-story, 151-room hotel has all one-bedroom suites, each with a separate living room and refrigerator and some with coffeemakers. Weekly and monthly rates and a breakfast plan are available, as are personal computers and secretarial services for business travelers. Other amenities include a heated outdoor pool, whirlpool, and an exercise room.

Extended Stay America **$-$$**
11547 Chester Road, Sharonville
(513) 771-7829

320 Glensprings Drive, Springdale
(513) 671-4900

11645 Chesterdale Road, Springdale
(513) 771-2457

9651 Seward Road, Fairfield
(513) 860-5733
These extended-stay hotels for the budget-conscious include studios and efficiencies with fully equipped kitchens and guest laundries on-site. Other amenities may include outdoor pools, cable television, an exercise room, and a sauna. Weekly rates are available. Several restaurant options are within a short driving distance.

Holiday Inn Express **$**
8567 Cincinnati-Dayton Road, West Chester
(513) 755-3900
This 61-room budget version of the Holiday Inn includes such amenities as an indoor pool and complimentary breakfast bar. It provides a clean and tasteful choice for business travelers and family guests in the rapidly growing West Chester community.

Holiday Inn I-275 North **$$$**
3855 Hauck Road, Sharonville
(513) 563-8330

You have no excuse for a sedentary existence in this Holidome facility, which has a heated indoor pool, wading pool and playground, exercise room, sauna, whirlpool, and tennis, basketball, and volleyball courts. All rooms in this 275-room hotel have been refurbished, and some have refrigerators, coffeemakers, and modem hookups. Dining is at the on-site Chase Grille restaurant.

Homewood Suites by Hilton **$$-$$$**
2670 East Kemper Road, Sharonville
(513) 772-8888

Yet another slice of the suite life in the north suburbs, each room at Homewood Suites has a separate bedroom, living room, and kitchen area, and you get a free continental breakfast and an evening reception. Weekly, monthly, and seasonal rates are available, as are storage facilities—a nice twist for transferees.

A $1.5 million retrofit was completed in 1999, nicely sprucing up what was already an attractive facility. Among the 111 rooms in the three-story complex are 12 two-bedroom units. Each room has dataports, an equipped kitchen, and a video player. There are interior corridors throughout the hotel. Other amenities include meeting rooms, an outdoor pool, guest laundry, an exercise room, a whirlpool and sports court, plus secretarial services and personal computer availability with Internet access. Homewood Suites is convenient to north suburban business areas and about 10 minutes from three shopping malls. Pets up to 40 pounds are allowed with a $15 per day cleaning fee.

La Quinta Inn and Suites **$$-$$$$**
11029 Dowlin Drive, Sharonville
(513) 771-0300

This facility is one of our favorites to the north of town. The 151-room, eight-story complex includes indoor pool, whirlpool, exercise room, interior corridors, and all that you'd expect in a suite hotel. Each room features coffeemaker, iron and ironing board, hair dryer, fridge, and microwave. Add to that a billiard room, complimentary continental breakfast, and complimentary cocktails from 5:00 to 7:00 P.M. Many rooms feature a comfy sofa. For a few dollars more, you can get a kitchen suite or whirlpool suite.

Liv-Inn **$**
11385 Chester Road, Sharonville
(513) 772-7877

This 100-room hotel has all interior corridors and caters to business travelers with large rooms and convenient desks. All rooms with queen-size beds have recliners. It's only a short walk from the Sharonville Convention Center and a drive of five minutes or less (rush-hour traffic notwithstanding) to Tri-County Mall. The inn has an outdoor pool.

Quality Inn **$$**
8870 Governors Hill Drive, Landen
(513) 683-3086

This hotel is just off I-75 near Sharonville and Springdale businesses, Tri-County Mall, and the Sharonville Covention Center. The three-story, 130-room hotel with all-interior corridors was created for the business traveler, with a nice atrium lobby, large desks, meeting rooms, and dataports and coffeemakers in all rooms. VCRs are available for a fee.

Ramada Inn **$-$$$**
11171 Dowlin Road, Sharonville
(513) 772-4114

Amenities include an outdoor heated pool, meeting rooms, and complimentary continental breakfast. The hotel has a mix of rooms accessed by interior and exterior corridors. Rooms are cheerfully decorated and include dataports.

Ramada Springdale **$$-$$$**
11911 Sheraton Lane, Springdale
(513) 671-6600

Renovated in 1999, this 10-story, 276-room hotel offers luxurious rooms and monthly rates for extended-stay travelers.

Some rooms have coffeemakers and refrigerators, and all rooms have dataports. Other amenities include meeting and conference rooms, a heated indoor pool, a whirlpool, and an on-site restaurant. A megaplex movie theater and several popular restaurants are nearby, and Tri-County and Cincinnati Mills Malls are only five minutes away.

Red Roof Inn **$**
2301 East Sharon Road, Sharonville
(513) 771-5552
This motel has approximately 105 rooms. It offers standard Red Roof Inn quality and cleanliness, complimentary morning coffee, and plenty of off-site dining options nearby.

Residence Inn by Marriott **$$$**
11689 Chester Road, Sharonville
(513) 771-2525
This 144-room hotel caters to the business traveler, transferee, and other extended-stay guests. It has a mix of studios without kitchens and one- and two-bedroom suites with kitchens in a setting that looks more like a condominium complex than a hotel. All units are comfortably large and tastefully decorated. Other amenities include a heated outdoor pool, sports court and whirlpool, complimentary breakfast and evening beverages, and a coin laundry. Should you tire of cooking for yourself, numerous dining options are nearby on the Chester Road strip. Pets are allowed for a one-time $100 cleaning fee.

Sheraton Sharonville **$$-$$$**
11326 Chester Road, Sharonville
(513) 771-2080
This brand-new Sheraton (which opened in 2006) features a business center, fitness center, restaurant and bar, indoor and outdoor pools, and is located directly across the street from the Sharonville Convention Center.

Super 8 **$**
330 Glensprings Drive, Springdale
(513) 671-0556
This is a good choice for dependable quality and reasonable prices. The 120-room motel is only five minutes from shopping at Tri-County Mall and a number of closer strip centers and a variety of dining options. Amenities include coffeemakers in some rooms. Weekly rates are available.

FAR NORTH

Rustic lodgings abound in this region, but "far north" is, well, far north of most tourist attractions and Cincinnati sights that you'd want to see. If the quaint towns of Lebanon or Oxford are your destination, then you're probably right to look here.

The Alexander House **$$-$$$**
22 North College Avenue, Oxford
(513) 523-1200
This charming two-story, six-room historic country inn was built in 1869. All rooms are furnished with antiques and quilts. There are no TVs, and parking is on the street, but the charm makes this a favorite for visitors to Oxford. There is a fine restaurant here as well. Smoking is prohibited on the premises. Forget getting a reservation during graduation or parents' weekend at nearby Miami University—consider, instead, a bed-and-breakfast in Oxford (see the Bed-and-Breakfasts chapter).

The Golden Lamb Inn **$$-$$$**
27 South Broadway, Lebanon
(513) 932-5065
This beautiful historic country inn is the oldest public lodging in Ohio. In fact, it was founded in 1803 only a few months after Ohio became a state. In 1815 a two-story federal-style brick building replaced the original log tavern and today serves as the lobby and part of the second floor of today's four-story restaurant and inn.

The inn became nationally famous in the 19th century when it hosted famous literary figures and politicians of the day.

Its heyday came during the days of coach travel, when many drivers and travelers who couldn't read were simply told to stop at the sign of the Golden Lamb. One of the travelers—who surely could read—was Mark Twain. He stayed here as he rehearsed for a performance at the Lebanon Opera House. Charles Dickens also stayed here during a tour of the United States in 1842. Presidents William Henry Harrison and Ulysses S. Grant stayed here, too, as did Kentucky's famous Sen. Henry Clay.

Today, presidents tend to choose more modern establishments. But there's still plenty to love in the 18 rooms that make up the Golden Lamb Inn, especially for antiques lovers. Rooms, each of which is named after a famous guest from the past, double as museum displays until rented, showcasing the Golden Lamb's collection of Shaker furniture and Currier and Ives prints. In fact, the inn is listed as a Shaker museum—one of the few museums you also can sleep in.

You can't buy the antiques in the rooms, but plenty are available for sale at the many antiques stores along Broadway in Lebanon or in Waynesville, which is less than 10 minutes away. The gift shop at the Golden Lamb is also a popular place for its collection of reproduction antique merchandise. Fine dining is always nearby too. The Golden Lamb is probably best known these days as a fine restaurant that attracts diners from throughout the Greater Cincinnati and Dayton areas.

There is, of course, no pool, no exercise room, and no refrigerator in the room. And it probably goes without saying that they don't want pets gnawing on the antiques.

The Hamiltonian Hotel **$$-$$$**
1 Riverfront Plaza, Hamilton
(513) 896-6200

This six-story, 122-room hotel overlooks the Great Miami River in the heart of the historic section of Hamilton. Amenities include an outdoor pool and on-site restaurant, with coffeemakers, refrigerators, and whirlpools in some rooms. Guests can use the nearby YMCA's indoor pool in the winter.

Hueston Woods Resort **$$-$$$**
Ohio Highway 732 at Oxford, Hueston Woods State Park
(513) 523-6381

Frantic parents trying to book a hotel room anywhere near Miami University on graduation and parents' weekends, or during major games, might consider this often overlooked option. Operated by the Ohio State Park Resorts & Conference Center system, Hueston Woods Resort is a rustic A-frame lodge nestled in the Hueston Woods State Park. There's no lack of accommodations here—94 guest rooms with private balconies and 40 fully furnished cabins, plus indoor and outdoor pools. A dining room serves breakfast, lunch, and dinner. The campus is 10 minutes away.

Marcum Conference Center & Inn **$-$$$**
100 North Patterson Avenue, Oxford
(513) 529-2104

Like many large universities (especially those located in small college towns with nary enough hotel rooms to serve parents and visitors to campus), Miami University maintains its own conference center. Built on the campus, the inn has 92 rooms, each with a private bath, direct-dial telephone, and cable TV. An on-site restaurant serves breakfast, lunch, and dinner. There's a business center. Campus tours can be arranged at the front desk. Reservations are not taken for rooms on graduation and parents' weekends. First come, first served.

WEST

You'd think the "west" would be wildly burgeoning with new hotels, thanks to the presence of the riverboat casinos just across the border in Indiana. But the casino resorts have more than dominated the market. For alternatives, consult the Bed-and-Breakfasts chapter.

Argosy Casino Resort $$-$$$$
777 East Eads Parkway, Lawrenceburg, IN
(888) ARGOSY-7

This 300-room hotel opened in 1998 with a 200,000-square-foot pavilion decorated in a Mediterranean theme complete with palm trees. The *Argosy VI* floating casino—the world's largest inland riverboat—is docked immediately adjoining the hotel and pavilion complex, and all are serviced by a six-story, 1,800-car parking garage (this is good news for gamblers who previously had to park a mile outside of Lawrenceburg and hop shuttle buses into town).

Argosy spent $200 million on this hotel complex, and it shows. The three-level pavilion is capped with a stained-glass dome designed to look like a map of the earth; inside, hotel guests have the choice of dining in restaurants that include the Outpost Lounge, featuring African themes (including a thatched roof and African baobab trees), or the Chart Room (which is decorated with an actual cropduster airplane hanging from the ceiling). The 350-seat Passport buffet area is particularly noteworthy, as it's split into separate rooms decorated in French, Egyptian, and other Mediterranean styles, as well as in the style of the Lost City of Atlantis. The Walt Disney Company helped create the stone columns and paintings to offer the illusion of under-the-sea Atlantis. (See the River Fun chapter for more details on the casino itself.)

Belterra Casino Resort Hotel $
777 Belterra Drive, Belterra, IN
(888) BELTERRA

Who needs Atlantic City? This 15-story hotel and entertainment complex serves the town's riverboat casino and includes a concert hall that has featured Alabama, the Doobie Brothers, and the Beach Boys. The $60 weeknight rate is one of the best bargains for a full-service hotel in the region, as the resort is trying to lure gamblers to stay as long as possible (and, hey, nobody is making you gamble). There are 308 rooms, a health spa, bakery, jewelry shop, and gift shop, plus free valet parking and a three-level garage with parking for 1,300 cars. Dining options at the hotel include Jeff Ruby's Steakhouse, the Ultimate Buffet, the Aquarium Grill, and Casino Cafe. The hotel's Aquarium at Belterra is the largest private aquarium in the region, a 60-foot-long, 7,000-gallon tank that features a Pacific saltwalter coral reef and a thousand species of tropical fish. An 18-hole, 7,000-yard golf course rounds out the recreational offerings.

Grand Victoria Casino and Hyatt Resort $$-$$$$
600 Grand Victoria Drive, Rising Sun, IN
(800) GRAND11

Hyatt Corporation opened this theme resort area centered around the *Grand Victoria II* riverboat casino, flashing back to 1890s Indiana with cobblestone streets and gaslights. The 300-acre resort in Rising Sun features a hotel, health club, and Wellington's steak house, all set in a Victorian motif. In addition to the 200-room hotel/resort itself, there are small motels and many bed-and-breakfasts in the area (see the Bed-and-Breakfasts chapter), but you really shouldn't miss the resort experience. Its concert hall features the likes of Tom Jones and Wayne Newton, plus there are gift shops, the Victoria Pub, Picadilly's delicatessen, and other amenities.

Imperial House West–Cincinnati $
5510 Rybolt Road
(513) 574-6000

This five-story, 198-room motel has a mix of interior- and exterior-corridor rooms, plus an outdoor pool, exercise room, and a sauna. Meeting rooms and a coin laundry also are available. The hotel includes 32 efficiency units with refrigerators.

Quality Inn $
Interstate 74 and New Haven Road, Harrison
(513) 367-5200

This hotel provides business travelers and other visitors with a reasonable value. The two-story, 108-room structure has all-interior corridors, plus meeting rooms, secretarial services, a heated outdoor pool, a coin laundry, and a coffee shop. Some rooms have bars, and 10 efficiencies have microwaves and refrigerators. Video players are available for a fee.

EAST

Primarily bedroom communities 'round here, but if your destination is the outdoor Riverbend Music Center, Coney Island amusement park, or River Downs racetrack, then one of these accommodations—especially the Cherry Grove hotels—might work for you.

Best Western Clermont **$**
4004 Williams Drive, Cherry Grove
(513) 528-7702
Best Western Clermont is a good choice for dependable quality and value prices. The 128-room motel just off I-275 at the Beechmont Avenue exit is close to a variety of dining options, including the Olive Garden and Smokey Bones. The inn is less than 10 minutes from Eastgate Mall. Amenities include a heated outdoor pool. Riverbend, Coney Island, and River Downs are just a few minutes away by interstate.

Best Western Mariemont Inn **$**
6880 Wooster Road, Mariemont
(513) 271-2100
A little out of the way from most business destinations and attractions in Greater Cincinnati, the Mariemont Inn is still well worth the trip. Right in the heart of Mariemont, one of Cincinnati's quaintest villages, the Mariemont Inn is the only Cincinnati hotel in the *National Trust Guide to Historic Bed & Breakfast Inns and Small Hotels,* which only includes inns 50 years old or older that have maintained their architectural integrity.

This is also one of the best values among area hotels. Built in 1926, this old English-style inn has 58 rooms and antique furniture, including beds with hand-carved headboards in many rooms. It would almost be more at home in the Bed-and-Breakfasts chapter—but your hotel stay doesn't include a free breakfast. Eat breakfast here anyway, though, because the morning fare at the National Exemplar restaurant is among the best you'll find anywhere in Cincinnati.

The hotel doesn't include such modern amenities as pools or exercise rooms, but it's hard to beat for a weekend getaway or change from the usual business-hotel pace.

Hampton Inn **$**
Eastgate North Drive at
Ohio Highway 32, Eastgate
(513) 752-8584
This hotel is one of the newest on Cincinnati's far east side, which encompasses Clermont County and the thriving Eastgate Mall area. The $7 million hotel opened in 1999 and includes an outdoor pool and fitness area, plus coffeemakers and ironing boards in all 120 rooms.

Hilton Garden Inn **$-$$**
Wards Corner Drive at Interstate 275, Loveland
(513) 576-6999
The area's first Hilton Garden Inn opened in 2000. The $5 million complex, with 84 guest rooms, includes an on-site restaurant, indoor pool, a convenience store, and health club. The inn is located close to the Shriners' Oasis Golf Course and Conference Center.

Holiday Inn-Eastgate **$$-$$$**
4501 Eastgate Boulevard, Summerside
(513) 752-4400
This six-story, 247-room hotel has spacious, attractive public areas, an on-site McKenna's restaurant and lounge, and extensive conference facilities. The hotel is next to Eastgate Mall, so there's plenty of shopping nearby, including Dillard's and Kohl's department stores. Other amenities include a heated indoor pool, sauna,

whirlpool, and exercise room. Secretarial services are also available. Some rooms have bars, coffeemakers, microwaves, refrigerators, and whirlpools. Pets are allowed at no charge (but the hotel no longer allows you to leave them unattended in the room). Call for details on special rates and packages.

Red Roof Inn **$**
4035 Mount Carmel–Tobasco Road, Cherry Grove
(513) 528–2741

Another good all-around value with dependable chain quality, this Red Roof is located at the Beechmont Avenue, I–275 interchange. Its 109 rooms include several "business king" rooms with king-size beds, large desks, and dataports on the telephones. Small pets are allowed at no charge. It's close to several shopping and dining possibilities. Riverbend, Coney Island, and River Downs are just a few minutes away by interstate.

BED-AND-BREAKFASTS

Bed-and-breakfast inns in Greater Cincinnati provide a relaxing change of pace for travelers. Though they often don't have such modern amenities as swimming pools, exercise rooms, or in-room dataports, they more than make up for it in homespun charm and atmosphere. And as you can gather from the name, breakfast comes with the deal. Here are some of the better bed-and-breakfast accommodations in the region, though some of the area's well-kept secrets no doubt eluded our writers' net.

This chapter lists almost two dozen bed-and-breakfast operations in Northern Kentucky and Southeastern Indiana alone. Why so many B&Bs in a throng of tiny burgs on both sides of the Ohio River? The opening of riverboat casinos in Lawrenceburg, Rising Sun, and other Indiana riverside communities certainly had a lot to do with their emergence. Not to mention the lure of skiing at Perfect North Slopes near Lawrenceburg, and the opening of the Kentucky Speedway in Gallatin County, Kentucky. Whatever the reason, once deserted shorefront villages are now bustling.

Before you visit a bed-and-breakfast, here are some words of advice: Don't plan on just dropping in. Reservations are required at all these inns. Keep in mind that phones and TVs in the rooms are the exception rather than the rule. And if you prefer the nameless/faceless treatment, bed-and-breakfasts are a bad choice. Chances are you'll spend some time socializing with the owners and guests in the cozy common areas—and maybe make some new friends.

Travelers would do well to contact the two bed-and-breakfast associations serving the region before they book a bedroom. The Ohio Bed & Breakfast Association, (614) 868-5567, can provide a list of its Cincinnati members, all of whom are inspected regularly and must meet certain standards. The Bed & Breakfast Association of Kentucky, (859) 689-5096, doesn't actively inspect its members but does require them to provide proof of a state operator's license as well as valid health permits.

Assume that the inns listed here do not allow pets or smoking unless we've noted otherwise. Some inns do not accept credit cards—we let you know which ones—although all accept checks. In some cases, children are not allowed—again, we'll indicate when this is the case. We've gone out of our way to list toll-free phone numbers whenever available, though not just for the reason you might expect. Yes, toll-free numbers save you phone charges. But beyond that, we've found that busy bed-and-breakfast proprietors are much more likely to pick up the ringing 800/888 line than their own home phone!

PRICE CODE

This pricing guide is for weekday rates, double occupancy.

$	**Less than $75**
$$	**$76 to $100**
$$$	**$101 to $150**
$$$$	**$151 and more**

OHIO

Artist's Cottage **$$**
458 East Warren Street, Lebanon
(513) 932-5938, (888) 233-2378
This restored 1864 carriage house is operated by Jeff and Denise Bitzer. It's Denise who has carefully decorated the tiles in the cottage to give travelers the feel of an island retreat. In addition to a pool and hot tub, the Artist's Cottage features a private bath, two beds, stereo, and a gas log fireplace. Don't forget to take a gander at the

Many Ohio B&Bs offer gift certificates by way of the Ohio Bed & Breakfast Association. You can buy the certificates directly through the association at (614) 868-5567 as a handy stocking stuffer or birthday gift. The OBBA gift certificates can be redeemed at any member inn; they're purchased in $50, $100, and $200 increments.

neighboring Denise Art Studio. A full breakfast is served in the cottage.

Baird House Bed & Breakfast **$$**
201 North Second Street, Ripley
(937) 392-4918

One of two terrific bed-and-breakfasts in the tiny town of Ripley (believe it or not), Baird House Bed & Breakfast is an 1840s Civil War timepiece with a spectacular view of the Ohio River, private baths, porches galore, and an inviting rustic feel. Innkeepers Patricia and Glenn Kittles put on a gourmet breakfast and even have been known to stage musical shows for lucky guests.

Ripley itself is better known as the tobacco capital of Ohio, with its Ohio Tobacco Museum, annual tobacco auctions, and famous Tobacco Festival. That said, nonsmokers are welcome to sample a bit of rural Americana in a town where little has changed over the decades. We should note that, tobacco capital or no, there is no smoking allowed in the guest rooms. No credit cards.

Brewster Place & Antique Shop **$$**
225 North Broadway, Lebanon
(513) 933-9932

Nestled among Lebanon's famous antiques stores, Brewster Place is managed by none other than Jim Brewster (a happy coincidence, that). The 1860 structure is conveniently located downtown and features quaint two-room suites decorated with antiques, each with private bath and private entrance.

Burl Manor **$$**
230 South Mechanic Street, Lebanon
(513) 934-0400, (800) 450-0401

Hosts Jay and Liz Jorling welcome you to this mid-1800s manor, built by the publisher of Ohio's oldest newspaper, the *Western Star.* The Italianate home features a spacious parlor with crystal chandeliers, a carved central staircase, and bedrooms outfitted with period decor. All rooms have private baths. There's a gathering room as well as a game room featuring bumper pool and a film library. Outdoors there's a swimming pool, lawn croquet, horseshoes, and volleyball. Children are welcome. It's a 10-minute drive to Paramount's Kings Island amusement park. Shopping opportunities abound just a few blocks away on Lebanon's Main Street.

Hardy's Haven **$$**
212 Wright Avenue, Lebanon
(513) 932-3266

Al and Phyllis Hardy transformed this 1885 structure, the original location of March Bros. Publishing Co., into a distinctive traveler's lodging house. Located in the Victorian district next door to Hardy's Interiors & Antiques, this vintage establishment offers three suites, each with private bath, custom draperies, and antiques. One suite has access to a porch. The Hardys will serve a continental breakfast in your suite, or you're welcome to join them at their breakfast table across the street for a complete hot meal.

Hatfield Inn **$-$$**
2563 Hatfield Lane, Turtlecreek Township
(513) 932-3193

Lebanon dentist Dr. Robert Haas and his wife, Penny, operate their family home as a bed-and-breakfast. The 1810 farmhouse has been in their family for a half century, and it offers five bedrooms, all with private baths, some with hot tubs. The leisurely breakfasts sometimes last for hours, what with all the socializing, and feature scrambled eggs, biscuits with sausage gravy, and pastries. Pets may be kept in a pen outside.

Hexagon House $$
419 Cincinnati Avenue, Lebanon
(513) 932-9655
Listed on the National Register of Historic Places due to its striking six-sided exterior, Hexagon House was built in the 1850s by a local horse breeder and vet. Proprietors Eve and Jim Lennon have renovated and air-conditioned the building, furnishing it with charming antiques.

Hickory Ridge Bed & Breakfast $
1418 Germany Hill Road, Manchester
(937) 549-3563
This delightful rustic cottage, surrounded by well over 100 acres of flowers and hickory trees, is home to proprietor Sue Bradley, who prepares all the meals. The two guest bedrooms are cozy, outfitted in white carpet and linens. The one shared bath is downstairs. Lunch and dinner, afternoon teas, and snacks are all options. Don't miss a wonderful hiking opportunity, and yes, picnic lunches are provided upon request. No credit cards.

Kings Manor Inn Bed & Breakfast $-$$
1826 Church Street, Kings Mills
(513) 459-9959
Here's a remnant of the past in the place from which Paramount's Kings Island drew its name. This three-story inn was built in 1903 by Col. George King, whose family owned the King Powder Factory from which the town got its name. The inn is convenient to Kings Island, the Little Miami Bike Trail, and surrounding attractions. Owner Bob Molinaro offers a spacious living room, cozy library, sunroom, and giant wraparound porch. Three guest rooms and a two-room suite are available—all with private baths. Furnishings are comfortable and in appropriate early-20th-century styles.

Murphin Ridge Inn $$$
750 Murphln Ridge Road, West Union
(937) 544-2263, (877) 687-7446
An hour's drive from downtown Cincinnati, the Murphin Ridge Inn is one of our very favorite bed-and-breakfasts in the region. Why? It's perfect in almost every respect. The 1820 Virginia-style brick farmhouse and adjoining guest house are adroitly managed by innkeepers Sherry and Darryl McKenney. Its location, on the edge of the Appalachian foothills in Adams County and surrounded by 140 acres of countryside, allows plenty of opportunities for either leisurely strolls or serious hiking. In addition to wooded trails, the bountiful recreation amenities include an outdoor swimming pool, tennis and basketball courts, and even a charming croquet court. There's a fire pit where guests delight in the stars and conversation. Location alone, however, doesn't account for Murphin Ridge's popularity. The dining experience is unparalleled, as the inn's chef prepares regional American specialties (dinners are available, though only breakfast is included in the overnight price). The kitchen will even pack a picnic lunch for hikers. The 10 guest rooms are somewhat spartan, though lovingly furnished in custom wood furniture built by the area's best-known craftsman, David T. Smith. Each room features a private bath, while some include cathedral ceilings, porches, or fireplaces. Nine forest cabins have also been added to the complex.

Nearby is the historic Serpent Mound as well as the intriguing Amish community and bountiful shopping experiences (see the Adams County listing in the Day Trips chapter). The inn's diners reap the benefits of seasonal garden produce harvested from two vegetable gardens as well as an herb garden.

The Parker House $-$$$
2323 Ohio Avenue
(513) 579-8236
The Parker House is a historic bed-and-breakfast inn in the city neighborhood of Clifton, only a short walk from the University of Cincinnati and a brief car trip or walk from "Pill Hill" hospitals. Mark and Patricia Parker serve as proprietors of this 7,000-square-foot Queen Anne Victorian mansion that was built in the

There's lots of hoopla about the National Underground Railroad Freedom Center in downtown Cincinnati. But it's the tiny town of Ripley where participants in the Underground Railroad actually crossed into Ohio from Kentucky, a slave state. Two B&Bs, the Signal House and Baird House, are loaded with history. Go back to where freedom began.

1870s. The four guest rooms all have private baths, and the first two floors (out of three) are devoted entirely to guests' enjoyment. Breakfast is served in the original music room, with its 12-foot mural ceilings. Parking is free and available, a rare amenity in Clifton. Smoking is OK on the porch.

Queen Anne **$$**
243 South Broadway, Lebanon
(513) 932-3836
This spacious 1886 home was recently renovated to include both central heat and air-conditioning. The Queen Anne is appointed in antique furnishings and offers queen-size beds covered in handmade quilts. Hosts Mildred and Paul Crane moved their Queen Anne operation from its former High Street location in order to be within a close walk of the antiques-shopping district.

Ravenwood Castle **$$-$$$$**
Bethel Road, New Plymouth
(800) 477-1541
For a bit of Britain right here in the Heartland, get thee to Ravenwood Castle. It's a bit more of a hike than the other bed-and-breakfasts listed here, about two hours east of Cincinnati, but this medieval-castle inn is certainly worth the drive. Proprietors Sue and Jim Maxwell invite you to stay in one of their 12 guest rooms. There's a tearoom, great hall with fireplace, and gift shop. The castle is nestled in the rustic Hocking Hills, a region verily overflowing with geological wonders: waterfalls, scenic foothills, and more.

Ross B&B **$**
88 Silverwood Circle, Springdale
(513) 671-2645
One of the most affordable bed-and-breakfasts in town, Ross B&B is hosted by Joan and George Ross in a split-level home on a quiet residential street in Springdale. This could be ideal for the business traveler tired of the budget motel life. Two bedrooms are available, a single and a double, with a shared bath. Tri-County Mall and Cincinnati Mills are just minutes away for the shopper in the family. In addition to serving a full breakfast, Joan offers homemade dessert upon your arrival in the evening. No credit cards.

Signal House Bed & Breakfast **$$-$$$**
234 North Front Street, Ripley
(937) 392-1640
This early 1800s Italianate home has been expertly transformed into a quaint bed-and-breakfast by proprietor Betsy Billingsley. A three-room private suite with bath has been added to the existing two guest rooms (shared bath). Its history is one of post-Revolutionary pedigree: The Signal House was used to signal the Rev. John Rankin by lantern that the waterfront was safe to lead slaves to freedom during the heady days of the Underground Railroad. (Why not call it the Rankin House? Because that honor goes to the nearby museum honoring Rankin and the 2,000 slaves he saved—all immortalized by local Harriet Beecher Stowe in *Uncle Tom's Cabin*.)

Yes, all of Ripley drips with Civil War history, but this bed-and-breakfast is hardly just for history buffs. Four-poster beds, romantic views of the Ohio River, and one of the best breakfasts you'll ever enjoy await you in Ripley. Come on down.

Six Acres Bed and Breakfast **$$-$$$**
5350 Hamilton Avenue, College Hill
(513) 541-0873

Six Acres Bed and Breakfast is located on guess-how-many acres in College Hill, just 15 minutes from downtown. This bed-and-breakfast features well-appointed bedrooms and common areas in a newly restored 6,500-square-foot mansion. Built between 1850 and 1860, the home has a unique connection to the Underground Railroad, having been owned and built by Zebulon Strong, an abolitionist. Six Acres honors the spirit of that tradition, offering food and shelter to weary travelers. Quilting and cooking classes are also offered.

Symphony Hotel **$$**
210 West 14th Street
(513) 721-3353
Occupying the former Clyde Hotel, the Symphony Hotel is a gracious Victorian stone mansion in (unlike most bed-and-breakfasts) a distinctly urban inner-city neighborhood. Although located in the gritty urban pioneer district of Over-the-Rhine near downtown Cincinnati, this is a distinctly upscale establishment. The building itself, built in the mid-1800s, is like a trip back in time. It's been restored and refurbished, with furniture from the period in each room. Each bedroom is dedicated to an individual composer such as Mozart or Bach—hey, roll over, Beethoven.

In addition to breakfast, the establishment offers three- and four-course dinners, though the hours vary greatly—dinner is offered only on performance nights at nearby Music Hall. The management also offers many ticket/dinner/accommodation packages in conjunction with the Cincinnati Symphony Orchestra and Cincinnati Pops, which play at Music Hall. (Symphony Hotel, get it?)

The White Garden Inn **$$-$$$$**
6194 Brown Road, Oxford
(513) 524-5827, (800) 324-4925
This is Oxford's newest (and newly constructed) bed-and-breakfast, built in Victorian style and offering five bedrooms, each with a private bath. See the close-up in this chapter for details. The inn is a totally nonsmoking home, and children age 12 and over are accepted.

Yesterday Again **$$-$$$**
3556 U.S. Highway 68 North, Wilmington
(937) 382-0472
Yesterday Again is an 1826 farmhouse on the grounds of Twin Springs Farm, with 16 acres of pasture. As the name connotes, this is a return to another era, a time when people pitched horseshoes, played croquet, or simply rocked on the home's large front porch. There's still a barn, smokehouse, and chicken coop, complete with a family of chickens. Lest you tire of all this homestead atmosphere, there's a swimming pool open in summer and a hot tub open year-round. Inside the farmhouse you'll find a sunroom, dining room, and living room with a piano (feel free to play). Guest rooms, furnished with century-old brass beds and oak suites, each feature a private bath, TV, and clock radio. A fully stocked small refrigerator and microwave are located in an upstairs closet and are shared by guests. The proprietors, Skip and Judy Kirchner-Davis, welcome you along with their resident farm dog, Tisha, and resident farm cat, Calicoats. For breakfast, choose from quiche, omelets, French toast, eggs, hash browns, and bacon or sausage.

NORTHERN KENTUCKY

Amos Shinkle Townhouse Bed and Breakfast **$-$$$**
215 Garrard Street, Covington, KY
(859) 431-2118, (800) 972-7012
Built in 1854 by entrepreneur Amos Shinkle, this inn lies in the heart of Covington's historical Riverside District amid courtyard gardens. The Amos Shinkle Townhouse is ornately decorated with rich cornices, an Italianate facade with a cast-iron filigree porch, grand chandeliers, elaborate crown moldings, Italianate mantels, and oak

CLOSE-UP

A Stroll in the Garden

The White Garden Inn, ensconced in the quaint town of Oxford, blends both the traditional and the contemporary.

"The inn is a fantastic romantic getaway. It's quiet and very spacious, so couples can remain as private as they want to be," observes John Alexander, who opened this bed-and-breakfast with his wife, Linda. Built in Victorian style with a hint of Cape Cod, the structure may look vintage, but it was actually constructed in 1998.

Catering to the romantic traveler as well as parents of Miami University students—the campus is only a few miles away from the B&B—the inn sets a lofty standard. "You arrive as a traveler and leave as a friend," says John.

The house encompasses some 9,000 square feet and includes five bedrooms (all with private baths) for visitors, each decked out in a garden theme: Iva's Garden Room, which overlooks the inn's namesake, an all-white garden with gazebo; Sunshine Room, with yellow decor and pink accents; Periwinkle Room, with a huge brass bed and antique oak pieces; Autumn Rose, with an antique mahogany four-poster bed; and the Queen Anne Suite, a 700-square-foot bedroom featuring a cozy fireplace and 20-foot-high cathedral ceiling (famous faces who've stayed here include actress Geena Davis).

Each room features picturesque windows, and soft terry-cloth robes are hung in each bath for every guest's comfort. Wear one as you stroll down to a breakfast of stuffed French toast, quiche, blueberry pancakes, soufflé or southwestern egg casserole, all served at the 6-foot circular glass-top table in the dining room.

Common areas include the structure's wraparound veranda, gazebo, and the property's five acres that boast multiple gardens. The Alexanders encourage visitors to roam the surrounding countryside, a rustic setting surrounded by woods. Or take a trip into the college town of Oxford, which offers small gallery shops featuring stained glass, antique neon, and paintings.

floors. This bed-and-breakfast inn—overseen by proprietors Bernard Moorman and Don Nash—is listed by the National Trust for Historic Preservation, which requires that an inn be at least 50 years old and have maintained its historical integrity.

There's a garden and patio, and a long screened porch affords a nice view of the Ohio River and the surrounding historical district. And it's only a short walk or drive to downtown Cincinnati or antiques stores and fine dining in Covington's MainStrasse Village.

Among the seven guest rooms is a master bedroom in the main house with a private bath and four rooms in the carriage house, in which horse stalls have been redesigned as imaginative sleeping quarters for kids. All rooms have four-poster Victorian beds and telephones.

Ash-Ley House B&B **$$-$$$$**
310 East Third Street, Newport, KY
(859) 291-1114

A restored Victorian situated in the Mansion Hill Historic District, the Ash-Ley House features bedroom suites with private baths, Jacuzzi tubs, and views of the Cincinnati skyline. The grand parlor is a reminder of a more elegant, gilded era gone by; the fireplace crackles in cool weather. There is valet parking, not a minor amenity when it comes to the cramped streets of the historic district. You're within walking distance of the Newport Aquarium as well as Riverboat Row. A full breakfast is served, but continental breakfast is also available.

Back Inn Time **$$**
804 West Shelby Street, Falmouth, KY
(859) 654-6100

Located in the rustic (and sometimes flooded) town of Falmouth, the Back Inn Time bed-and-breakfast (circa 1888) features seven guest rooms, each with a private bath, cable TV, and individual heating and cooling units. One room is decorated in angelic borders, another features a Jacuzzi bath. Breakfast, served by Verda Bonar and her family in the front parlor, is usually bagels, muffins, cereal, and fruit. Smoking is permitted in designated areas.

Burlington's Willis Graves **$$-$$$**
5825 North Jefferson Street, Burlington, KY
(859) 689-5096, (888) 226-5096

A finely appointed 1830s federal-style getaway, Burlington's Willis Graves is ideal as a business traveler's retreat. It's settled in the countryside, yet just 12 minutes from the Cincinnati/Northern Kentucky International Airport. Listed on the National Register of Historic Places, the brick home is owned and operated by Nancy and Bob Swartzel. There are phones and cable in every room, and all rooms have private baths. The scenic grounds and gardens are close to horse-riding and fishing opportunities. Turfway Park racetrack is also nearby. And, yes, a man named Willis Graves built the house.

Bed-and-breakfasts aren't your standard hotels. Many B&Bs don't allow smoking, and some even refuse to allow children. And some in our guide that used to take credit cards have dropped the practice since the last edition, citing increasing Visa and MasterCard fees. So it's always best to consult the proprietor ahead of time on house rules.

Christopher's B&B **$$-$$$$**
604 Poplar Street, Bellevue, KY
(859) 491-9354, (888) 585-7085

This bed-and-breakfast is in a unique building: the former Bellevue Christian Church in the town's historic district. Brenda Guidugli spent a year stripping the sanctuary to its frame; only the floor, stained-glass windows, and painted tin roof remain in the interior. She added a balcony that wraps around three sides of the second story. There are three bedrooms with private baths—one is a suite with a living room and a two-person whirlpool. Each room has a TV with a built-in VCR and cable. An interesting note: The church congregation weighed offers from other churches before deciding that a life as a B&B was a better future for the building.

First Farm Inn **$$-$$$**
2510 Stevens Road, Petersburg, KY
(859) 586-0199

Dana Kisor and Jennifer Warner operate this bed-and-breakfast in an 1870s farmhouse well away from the hustle and bustle of the city. Set among the rolling hills on the bluffs above the Ohio River, First Farm Inn offers a fish pond as well as horseback riding. Spacious rooms are

The Golden Lamb isn't listed in this chapter, but it ought to be. Strictly speaking, it's not a bed-and-breakfast, so it wound up in the Hotels and Motels chapter. Nonetheless, the Lamb has all the historical significance and charming imagery of the finest bed-and-breakfast—sans complimentary breakfast. Consider it.

decorated with century-old handcrafted oak furniture belonging to Warner's great-grandparents and have private baths. Lest you think yourself too far from civilization, fax and Internet access are provided. Breakfast itself is anything from Grand Marnier French toast to baked southwestern eggs. You're welcome to bring your horse (pasture boarding available).

Gateway Bed and Breakfast $$
326 East Sixth Street, Newport, KY
(859) 581-6447, (888) 891-7500

This 1878 Italianate town house with floor-to-ceiling windows and decorative plaster moldings is in Newport's East Row National Historic District. Rooms are spacious and beautifully decorated, with many antique musical instruments throughout the house. Owners Ken and Sandy Clift serve a full country breakfast in the dining room. A rooftop deck is a great place to pass a summer evening—especially during the Riverfest fireworks on Labor Day weekend. There are three guest rooms, all with private baths.

The Kleier Haus $$
912 U.S. Highway 62, Maysville, KY
(606) 759-7663

Gay and Ed Kleier are the proprietors at this 1885 home, nestled among the scenic farms and rolling hills of Kentucky. There are three bedrooms, all with private baths and cable TV, plus guests are welcome to make use of the dining room, living room, spacious porch, and patio. There's a hot tub to warm you, even in winter. An old-fashioned Kentucky breakfast is served, with country ham, eggs, biscuits, and homemade jams. Stroll around Maysville, home to recent Miss America Heather Renee French, as well as the famous Clooney clan (Rosemary, George, Nick, etc.), or pop over to historic Old Washington a few minutes away. Take a walking tour of the town, established in 1786, where antiques shops abound. Also nearby is Blue Licks State Park, site of the last battle of the American Revolution. No credit cards.

Mary's Belle View Inn $-$$$
444 Van Voast Avenue, Bellevue, KY
(859) 581-8337

Talk about your truth in advertising. Mary Bickers runs this two-story bed-and-breakfast, and it certainly does boast a splendid view. The century-old home, with a deck on the second floor overlooking the Ohio River, is booked solid every year for the Riverfest fireworks. You are more likely to nab a room the rest of the year. There are three bedrooms to rent, one a suite with a Jacuzzi and all with private baths. Children are welcome.

Red Brick House $
201 Chapel Street, Falmouth, KY
(859) 654-4834

This bed-and-breakfast is also a working antiques shop that features collectibles, glassware, pottery, and books. Located in the downtown historic district directly behind the courthouse, this 1885 Victorian Gothic (in redbrick, natch) features themed bedrooms such as the Country Room, done up in dolls and antique toys; the Ming Room, with Oriental antiques; the Cherub Room, with double-poster bed; and the Tulip Room. Only the Tulip Room has a private bath. Proprietors are Gene and Joellen Kearns.

Weller Haus Bed & Breakfast $$-$$$$
319 Poplar Street, Newport, KY
(859) 431-6829, (800) 431-4287

Valerie and David Brown welcome you to these two 1880s Victorian Gothic houses in the Taylor Daughter's Historic District (only a mile or so from downtown Cincinnati). Church steeples, city streets, and stained glass are just some of the attractive sights to see from the windows of the antiques-appointed guest and sitting rooms, all equipped with private baths and phones. Weller Haus's five spacious guest rooms feature original millwork. A skylit great room, gathering kitchen, and secluded garden are other nice features.

An exquisite breakfast is served among the pattern glass, linens, laces, and porcelains of yesteryear. This isn't to say there aren't modern amenities: Consider the two double Jacuzzi suites, for instance. The location is within walking distance of fine dining along Riverboat Row and five minutes from downtown. Weller Haus is just minutes away, as well, from the Newport Aquarium.

SOUTHEASTERN INDIANA

Empire House Hotel **$-$$$**
114 South Front Street, Rising Sun, IN
(812) 438-4064

This charming restored 1816 hotel, a bed-and-breakfast, is run by innkeepers Steve and Karen Berger. It's well within walking distance to the Grand Victoria Casino. There's a river view, balcony with swing, and seven suites with private baths, cable TV, and their own entrances.

Mulberry Inn & Gardens
118 South Mulberry Street, Rising Sun, IN
(812) 438-2206, (800) 235-3097

Less than an hour's drive from downtown Cincinnati, the Mulberry Inn is one of the highlights in the quaint town of Rising Sun. The home is in the heart of the town's residential area, just a few blocks from the Grand Victoria Casino. The proprietors, Kurt and Barb Jasper, maintain a charming establishment, featuring gardens where you can watch the birds flutter while enjoying a full breakfast. The back porch offers a bucolic view as well—a world away from urban tensions. Each room includes a private bath and color TV, VCR, movies, and in-room phones. Certainly the most popular room for a romantic getaway is the Jungle Room, complete with canopy bed, fireplace, and whirlpool bath.

Rosemont Inn **$-$$$**
Indiana Highway 56, Vevay, IN
(812) 427-3050

About an hour's drive from downtown Cincinnati, the Rosemont Inn is located on the banks of the Ohio River in the historic town of Vevay. The inn—built in 1881 by James K. and Charlotte Pleasant, members of a wealthy merchant and river shipping family—is a Victorian Italianate with five bedrooms.

Each room features interior woodwork with six types of inlaid hardwood and has a private bath and fireplace. Terry-cloth robes in each room are a nice touch, and lovely antiques are scattered throughout the house. A full-service breakfast is served in the sunny dining area overlooking the Ohio River, as are late-afternoon refreshments and, in winter, a high English tea. The rose garden is particularly stunning.

Schussler House **$$$**
514 Jefferson Street, Madison, IN
(812) 273-2068

An 1849 federal/Greek revival home, Schussler House includes three guest rooms decorated in antique furniture and featuring private baths. Soft music is usually playing in the front parlor, where there's an abundance of reading material. Breakfast can include house specialties such as apple flan or caramel-glazed French toast, served in the sun-filled dining room. Hosts Ann and Larry Johnson remind you that Madison operates on eastern standard time at all times; daylight saving time does not exist in this part of the world.

Story Inn **$$-$$$$**
6404 South Indiana Highway 135, Nashville, IN
(812) 988-2273

An ideal place to stay if you're in the area shopping Nashville's famous crafts community (with 250 stores and galleries), or enjoying the recreational opportunities at nearby Brown County State Park. Guests are encouraged to travel back in time at this former general store, still decorated with toys and sundries of the 1920s. The Story Inn offers 12 bedrooms with absolutely *no* TVs, clocks, radios, or phones. The management has surrendered to the modern era only in that air-conditioning and private baths are installed. There's a common room offering a library and parlor games. Breakfast is served in the Story Inn restaurant, but make sure you take time to enjoy dinner there too. Room rates include a bottle of wine. The restaurant is consistently rated as one of Indiana's top gourmet eateries by national food magazines.

SHOPPING

Shopping opportunities abound in Greater Cincinnati. Five department store chains—Dillard's, Macy's, JCPenney, Parisian, and Kohl's—permeate the region, plus there's a dizzying variety of discount retailers and everything in between. The northern Interstate 275 corridor alone is a fertile crescent for the shop-'til-you-drop crowd. Here, within about a 15-mile area, are Cincinnati's biggest suburban shopping malls, with more than 5 million square feet of retail space combined and almost 600 stores. Each mall has plenty of satellite retailers as well, making this one of the most densely shopped areas you'll find anywhere.

Lost in the hubbub of suburban mall development is the fact that downtown Cincinnati is in the midst of a retail renaissance. Witness the first opening of a department store downtown in half a century—Macy's huge complex at Fountain Square West. Witness the opening of a ritzy Tiffany & Co. Jewelers in the new complex that also features Brooks Brothers. Witness the renovated Saks Fifth Avenue and the Tower Place mall, which boasts the likes of Brentano's, the Limited, and more. Downtown now has an estimated 1.7 million square feet of retail space with more than 400 shops—an embarrassment of riches.

Outside of downtown, trendy malls and shopping complexes are popping up everywhere, most notably Rookwood Commons, Rookwood Pavilion, and Newport on the Levee (see the close-up in this chapter).

In this chapter you'll find information about area malls, outlet stores, farm markets and flea markets, along with our favorite (among Greater Cincinnati's many) specialty food stores and wineries, bookstores, and gift shops.

Try not to blame us too much if one of these stores is gone by the time you get there. We've tried to mention only establishments with staying power, but even bright stars wink out in the fast-changing retail market.

MALLS

Downtown

Tower Place
Fourth and Vine Streets
(513) 241-7700

Just look for the tallest building downtown and you'll have found the heart of downtown Cincinnati shopping—Tower Place mall, at the base of the Carew Tower, on Fourth between Vine and Race Streets. Try parking either at the Fountain Square Garage, a city garage with entrances on Vine Street north of Fifth Street, Walnut Street south of Sixth Street, and beneath the Westin off of Vine Street just north of Fourth Street. This garage usually will serve you well, in fact, no matter where you're going downtown. Downtown isn't so big yet that you can't walk fairly easily most everywhere from one parking garage.

Inside Tower Place you'll find a nicely appointed marble and gold-trimmed mall that looks very much like a suburban shopping mall. Among the stores here are Brentano's, the Limited, Godiva, Ann Taylor, Talbots, and the I Love Cincinnati Shoppe.

The food court is above average, particularly the Big Easy, purveyor of great Bourbon Chicken and other fast Cajun dishes. And not far away in the arcade of the Carew Tower is Hathaway's Restaurant, a friendly retro excursion to an old-fashioned lunch counter.

Tower Place itself doesn't have anchor stores, but Saks Fifth Avenue at Fifth and Race Streets (the only Saks in Greater Cincinnati) is across the street.

East

Anderson Towne Center
7500 Beechmont Avenue, Anderson
(513) 232-3438
This brand-new outdoor shopping mall features the largest Kroger in the world, a Macy's, Kmart, Starbucks, Fred Meyer Jewelers, gift and furniture shops, as well as a selection of restaurants including Michael G.'s, Carrabba's Italian Grill, T.G.I. Friday's, IHOP, and Moe's Southwest Grill.

The most efficient use of your shopping time may well be to browse the Beechmont Avenue strip in Anderson. Where else, within a mile, can you find a Target, Staples, two (count 'em, two) Super Krogers, Macy's, and Kmart, plus hundreds of smaller merchandisers? It's exit 69 off the I-275 loop. Shopping nirvana.

bigg's Place Mall
4450 Eastgate Boulevard, Summerside
(513) 753-7222
Anchors include the bigg's hypermarket and Super Saver discount cinemas, plus a number of shoe and clothing shops.

Borders Complex
4530 Eastgate Boulevard, Summerside
(513) 943-0068
Here you'll find a Borders books, American Red Cross retail store, Circuit City, Office Depot, Kroger, and Kids"R"Us.

Eastgate Center
4000 Eastgate Boulevard, Summerside
(513) 943-3530
Major tenants include hh gregg electronics, Rhodes Furniture, Jo-Ann Fabrics, Michael's hobby supply, and the Original Mattress Factory. Across the way, you'll find Pets Mart, Service Merchandise, and Dick's sporting goods.

Eastgate Mall
Interstate 275 and
Ohio Highway 32, 4601
Eastgate Boulevard, Summerside
(513) 752-2290
This Clermont County mall is in one of the fastest-growing shopping areas in town. The mall itself is the area's sixth-largest, with 766,000 square feet and nearly 90 stores. Anchor stores and major attractions here include a Dillard's department store, Kohl's, Sears, JCPenney, and Victoria's Secret. The Sears is one of 13 test Sears stores in the nation, which means you will see merchandise arrive here long before the other stores. Other shops include Waldenbooks, Hallmark, Spencer's Gifts, KB Toys, and dozens more. Adjacent to the mall is a Toys"R"Us.

Eastgate Square
4370 Eastgate Boulevard, Summerside
(513) 753-3200
Anchors include Wal-Mart, Chuck E. Cheese, Sam's Club, Furniture Fair, and more.

Kenwood Towne Centre
7875 Kenwood Road, Kenwood
(513) 745-9100
Though slightly smaller (at least for the time being) than Tri-County and Cincinnati Mills malls, Kenwood Towne Centre generally enjoys the reputation as the top mall in Cincinnati. With about 2,000 fewer parking spaces than those similarly sized malls, it can present a big parking challenge at holiday time. But that doesn't keep people from coming here in droves.

Anchors of this mall, at the corner on Kenwood and Montgomery Roads, include Dillard's, Macy's, and Parisian. Other stores among the 180 at the 1.1 million-square-foot mall include the only Sharper Image and Brookstone stores in town, Benetton, Waldenbooks, the Bombay Company, Build-a-Bear Workshop, Restoration Hardware, Eddie Bauer, the Limited, and Limited Too.

Finish off with a meal at the Cheesecake Factory.

Meijer's Complex
888 Eastgate North Road, Summerside
(513) 947-0900
This strip of major retail giants includes

Meijer's grocery, Golf Galaxy, restaurants, and hotels.

Rookwood Commons
2600 Edmundson Road, Norwood/Hyde Park
(513) 531-4567

Rookwood Commons features such trendy shops as Zany Brainy, Anthropologie (an eclectic housewares outlet), and a slew of cutting-edge fashion shops. The Commons boasts some of the area's most popular new restaurants: The Pub at Rookwood Mews prepares excellent fish-and-chips, a grilled-asparagus salad, and they've got Brit brews such as Old Speckled Hen on tap. The unusual dishes served up at P.F. Chang's, such as spicy chicken enclosed in lettuce wraps, make for a lively lunch. Got a big group in your shopping party? For a Papal retreat, head to the Pope Room at Buca di Beppo, where a private table sits 16, and you're surrounded by plaster statues and portraits of His Eminence. For dessert, try Maggie Moo's, where flavorings are hand-mixed into ice cream on a chilled marble slab, then wrapped into a waffle cone.

Rookwood Pavilion
Madison and Edwards Road, Norwood/Hyde Park
(513) 396-8965

Rookwood Pavilion is not in Hyde Park but it's so much like Hyde Park that even natives confuse the issue. Actually, Rookwood Pavilion is squarely within the boundaries of Norwood, whose city officials will be quick to fill you in on this fact. This shopping center, converted from an old machine-tool factory, is a sign of rejuvenation for a city abandoned by GM and LeBlond Makino plants in the 1980s.

Rookwood Pavilion is today possibly the hottest shopping center in Greater Cincinnati, thanks largely to two very popular spots. The giant Joseph-Beth Booksellers book/restaurant/music/toy/food store is probably the all-around nicest bookstore in Greater Cincinnati. Nearby, First Watch is the best and most popular place in town for breakfast. This is also a good discount center, with Stein Mart apparel and housewares, HomeGoods discount housewares, and T.J. Maxx discount clothing. The center also has a Smith & Hawken for finer house and garden supplies and Fawn Confectionery for tasty treats. Don't miss dining at Don Pablo's, which is unlike any you've ever seen, inside the converted LeBlond Makino factory.

Skytop Pavilion at Garard's Station
5280 Beechmont Avenue, Anderson
(513) 231-0606

A bigg's anchors this shopping complex, which also features retail gift shops, a Starbucks, and various fast-food restaurants.

Sycamore Plaza
Kenwood and Montgomery Roads, Kenwood
(513) 794-9440

Across Montgomery Road you'll find Kenwood Towne Centre's discount-oriented alter image, Sycamore Plaza. This used to be called Kenwood Mall before Kenwood Towne Centre turned it into a ghost town. In its second life as Sycamore Plaza, it's one of the hottest retail properties in town. Among the 15 stores in this 345,000-square-foot center are a Barnes & Noble superstore, Macy's Furniture Gallery, Men's Wearhouse, Toys"R"Us, and Staples. It also has some popular restaurants including Max and Erma's and Johnny Rockets.

North Central

Cincinnati Mills
Interstate 275 and Winton Road, exit 39, Forest Park
(513) 671-2882

The former Forest Fair Mall has bounced back with the addition of such stores as Aeropostale, American Eagle Outfitters, As Seen on TV, Bass Pro Shops, Bath

Junkie, Bon Worth, Calendar Club, Corningware/Corelle/Revere Factory Store, Flaunt, Fragrance Depot, Games Galore, Guess? Company Store, Jones New York, London Fog Factory Store, Metropolis, Mikasa, Mystic Oyster, Nine West Outlet, Off 5th Saks Fifth Avenue Outlet, Perfumania, Rocky Mountain Chocolate Factory, Steve & Barry's University Sportswear, Zales the Diamond Store Outlet, and more. Other major attractions include SuperSaver Cinemas, bigg's, and the WonderPark amusement arcade (see the Kidstuff chapter).

Deerfield Towne Centre
Mason-Montgomery Road at Irwin-Simpson Road, Deerfield Township
No phone

This new outdoor shopping mall features merchants such as Talbot's, Sharper Image, Borders Books, Jones the Florist, Aquarium Adventures, Bombay, the Maytag Store, and a number of restaurants, including Abuelo's Mexican Food Embassy, Nothing but Noodles, Polo Grille, and the Macaroni Grill.

Tri-County Mall
11700 Princeton Road, Springdale
(513) 671-0120

Built in 1960, this was southwest Ohio's first mall and once drew shoppers from a 100-mile-plus radius. By the 1990s, sandwiched by new competition from Kenwood Towne Centre and Cincinnati Mills, it was losing shoppers fast. But remodeling has turned this mall into a vibrant center with more occupied space than any other in the city. Flanked by multilevel parking structures, this place is easy to get into and out of and provides plenty of covered parking so treasured on hot or rainy days.

Anchors in this 1-million-square-foot, 180-store mall include Macy's and Dillard's. It's pretty much of a toss-up between Tri-County and Kenwood Towne Centre as to which has the biggest or best Dillard's. Tri-County's Macy's store is slightly bigger. Other specialty stores here include Eddie Bauer, the Limited, Limited Too, and Abercrombie & Fitch.

Thirsty? Head across the road to Bahama Breeze, 325 North Commerce Way, where we count 31 different labels of the world's rums, from Bacardi Anejo to Barbancourt Reserve Speciale. The sinful Mojita Cubano cocktail (crushed spearmint, rum, and sugarcane juice) certainly takes the edge off mall shopping.

West

Northgate Mall
Colerain Avenue at Springdale Road off Interstate 275
(513) 385-5600

A lot of malls might have crumbled when they saw the likes of Cincinnati Mills and Kenwood Towne Centre moving in nearby and Tri-County undergoing a major renovation and expansion. But Northgate Mall did some rehabbing of its own to create a megamall in its own right. Anchors of this 1 million-square-foot mall include Dillard's, Sears, Macy's, and JCPenney. You'll also find such other mall favorites as Old Navy, Fragrance Factory, Cellular Connection, Art or More, Hat World, Motherhood Maternity, Sunglass Hut, and Vitamin World. A $40 million renovation was scheduled to begin in late 2006.

West Town Centre
6300 Glenway Avenue
(513) 244-3489

The other West Side shopping center includes a Dillard's, Thriftway, and a Home Depot.

Western Hills Plaza
Glenway Avenue and Werk Road

This venerable West Side institution has 34 stores in its 450,000 square feet. Major stores include Kroger, Staples, Pier One Imports, and Sears.

CLOSE-UP

Newport on the Levee

Newport on the Levee is a gigantic entertainment and retail complex located on the Newport, Kentucky, riverfront directly across from downtown Cincinnati. The mall features nightclubs, restaurants, upscale retail shops, a comedy club, bookstores, a 20-screen AMC movie complex, and even a 25,000-square-foot interactive gaming facility called GameWorks.

The 10-acre complex—located next door to the Newport Aquarium—is a retail/restaurant/entertainment behemoth, with retail shops such as American Eagle, Cold Stone Creamery ice-cream parlor, Claire's Boutique, Pretzeltime, Hot Topic, d.e.m.o., Pacific Sunwear, Journey's, Limited Too, and a Barnes & Noble 25,000-square-foot superstore with a Starbucks Cafe and patio overlooking the Ohio River.

The sprawling $200 million facility also has the Shadowbox Cabaret, a combination theater, comedy club, and rock music venue, which presents a mix of the troupe's best sketch comedy and rock 'n' roll.

The GameWorks facility sports hundreds of interactive games and virtual-reality mind-benders, including racing in miniature Indy 500 and NASCAR vehicles, old-fashioned midway games such as Skee-ball, karaoke singing, a Las Vegas–style "Wheel of Fortune," a "Jurassic Park—The Lost World" interactive challenge, electronic and video sports, and more. There's also plenty of food and drink: At the glass-enclosed contemporary restaurant Jax Grille, guests can order from the restaurant menu (meals are served throughout the gaming area as well). A specialty is toasting marshmallows at your table, over a "personalized campfire," to create s'mores, which can then be dipped into various sweet condiments. The Arena Bar located in the Sports Zone is a full-service bar specializing in martinis, manhattans, and margaritas. There's also the Hopscotch Lounge in the Pool Hall.

Among the mall's restaurants are Mitchell's Fish Market, a seafood eatery, Dewey's Pizza, Brio Tuscan Grille, and Claddagh Irish Pub.

There's a 2,000-car parking garage underneath the facility. The L&N Bridge has been converted into a pedestrian walkway—the so-called Purple People Bridge—which links the Levee with parking in downtown Cincinnati and the Great American Ball Park.

Northern Kentucky

Cincinnati/Northern Kentucky International Airport
Interstate 275 and Donaldson Road, Hebron, KY
(859) 767-3144
You might not think of an airport as a mall, but the Greater Cincinnati/Northern Kentucky International Airport easily qualifies as one. The Delta terminal features dozens of stores, including a Sportsworld, Waterstones Booksellers, the Body Shop, Destination Disney, and the area's only duty-free shop.

Crestview Hills Mall
2929 Dixie Highway, Crestview Hills, KY
no phone
Crestview Hills Mall reopened in early 2006 after an $80 million overhaul. Upscale new tenants include Banana Republic, Coldwater Creek, Talbots, and unique-to-the-area restaurants such as Doc Green's Gourmet Salads, Nothing but Noodles, and Abuelo's Mexican Food Embassy.

Florence Antique Mall
Mall Road at U.S. Highway 42, Florence, KY
(859) 371-0600
At the Florence Antique Mall, a hundred or so dealers fill up a former Swallen's store with every antique (and yes, piece of junk) imaginable.

Here's a lesson in pop culture: A favorite soda 'round here is Ale-8-One, a homegrown Kentucky soft drink now sold in Ohio as well. It's best described as a cousin of ginger ale to those who have never tested this savory and unique blend. The Wainscott family still brews Ale-8-One, and they keep the 80-year-old formula a bigger secret than Coca-Cola's.

Florence Mall
Interstate 75 at exit 180A, 2028 Florence Mall Road, Florence, KY
(859) 371-1231
The big kahuna among malls in Northern Kentucky, this 828,000-square-foot center has 130 stores. They include anchors Macy's, Sears, and JCPenney, in addition to such mall favorites as Gap, Victoria's Secret, and Waldenbooks.

Newport on the Levee
1 Levee Way, Newport, KY
(859) 581-2000
See the close-up within this chapter on this gigantic entertainment-and-shopping complex.

OUTLET SHOPPING

Down Lite Factory Store
7818 Palace Drive, Blue Ash
(513) 489-DOWN
Down Lite is an honest-to-goodness factory outlet, with sometimes deep discounts on goods from some of the nation's top catalog operations (such as L. L. Bean) and retailers.

Dry Ridge Outlet Stores
1100 Fashion Ridge Road, (Interstate 75 at exit 159), Dry Ridge, KY
(859) 824-9516
A little more than 20 miles south of Florence Mall, Dry Ridge Outlet Stores is the closest outlet mall to Cincinnati. Among the stores here are the Nike Factory Store, Liz Claiborne, Van Heusen, Nine West, Samsonite Co. Store, Leather Loft, and Bass.

Entenmann's Bakery Outlet
123 West Kemper Road, Springdale
(513) 671-2722
Ever wonder what happens to those Entenmann's baked goods that don't sell in the grocery? Here's where they

go, available at cut-rate prices and still delectable.

Esther Price Fine Chocolates Outlet
7501 Montgomery Road, Silverton
(513) 791-1833
Esther Price is southern Ohio's finest chocolate, and while you can buy a box in the refrigerator section of certain local groceries, nothing beats coming to the factory outlet itself. You get the freshest choice of creams and nougats possible and you can handpick your box. All chocolate cherries? No problem.

The Original Mattress Factory
Ohio Highway 4 at Muhlhauser Road, Fairfield
(513) 860-9988
This factory and showroom was founded by a former Serta exec who wanted to manufacture quality mattresses at outlet prices. He succeeds. Choose from standard and custom brass, iron, and wood beds. And best yet, no haggling—the prices are the same every single day. If a trip to the Fairfield factory is too far, there are many satellite shops across the tristate.

Prime Outlets at Jeffersonville I & II
1100 McArthur Road, Jeffersonville (Interstate 71 at exit 69)
(740) 948-9091
It's not quite in Greater Cincinnati, but the Prime Outlets I & II are hard to ignore and well worth the hour's drive north. Formerly called the Jeffersonville Outlet Center and Ohio Factory Shops, these megamalls have a number of ever-changing name-brand outlets. Tenants include Brooks Brothers, Tommy Hilfiger, and a huge food court so you won't go hungry.

Reading Wedding Outlets
Jefferson Avenue at Benson Street, Reading
(513) 733-3100
The neighborhood of Reading is the most centralized bargain wedding outlet experience you can find. There are some 20 businesses along 3 blocks of Benson Street and Jefferson Avenue in downtown Reading that cater specifically to brides and grooms. From wedding dresses to bridal cakes, this is the ultimate nuptial-planning center. Shops include Patricia's Weddings and Custom Cakes Unlimited, Paris Veils and Bridal Accessories, Bridal and Formal off-the-rack gowns, Precious Moments Photography, Carrousel Weddings, Oasis Florists, and Under Wraps.

Dippin' Dots, the Kentucky-made ice cream that's sold in Greater Cincinnati at only a few select locations (at such parks as Kings Island and the Beach water park), is hot stuff in Japan—far outselling any regular brand of ice cream. The dessert consists of little balls in assorted flavors, cryogenically frozen using liquid nitrogen.

FARM MARKETS

Beiersdorfer Orchard
21874 Kuebel Road, Guilford, IN
(812) 487-2695
Beiersdorfer sells apples, cherries, and pears. The cider here is delicious.

Benton Farms
11946 Old Lexington Pike, Walton, KY
(859) 485-7000
Benton Farms sells corn, beans, and pumpkins in season.

Clough Valley Maple Syrup Farms
5531 Clough Pike, Anderson
No phone
Like maple syrup? Head here, where they sift an amazing amber maple syrup from 300 trees near the Motz family home. The Motzes produce only 900 pints of dark amber but nonetheless won a blue ribbon at the Ohio State Fair. The syrup is $9.00 a

You can't call yourself a Cincinnatian till you've tried Grippo's, the local potato chip still churned out by the Grippo family of Groesbeck. You can't get the distinctive chips in a plain flavor, so don't even ask. Folks 'round here do pine for the BBQ, sweet Bermuda onion, and pepper-and-sour-cream flavors. And the belief persists that an empty Grippo's bag, if kept stuck in your back pocket, brings good luck.

pint. Sap starts running in February, and visitors are welcome at the nightly boilings.

Hidden Valley Fruit Farm
5474 North Ohio Highway 48, Lebanon
(513) 932-1869
At Hidden Valley you'll find terrific cider as well as apples, beans, corn, grapes, and pumpkins.

Iron's Fruit Farm
1640 Stubbs Mill Road, Lebanon
(513) 932-2853
Iron's is known for its red and black raspberries as well as pumpkins.

Maplewood Orchards
3712 Stubbs Mill Road, Morrow
(513) 932-7981
Maplewood sells apples, pumpkins, and apple cider. Hayrides are also popular here.

Rouster's Apple House
1980 Ohio Highway 131, Milford
(513) 625-5504
Rouster's sells the popular Krispy apples by the bushel and half bushel.

FLEA MARKETS

Caesar Creek Flea Market
Interstate 71 at Ohio Highway 73, Caesar Creek
(937) 382-1660
This indoor/outdoor market features 500 vendor spaces and offers amenities such as food and drink. Admission is $1.00 per carload.

Peddlers Flea Market
4343 Kellogg Avenue
(513) 871-3700
Peddlers Flea Market in the Columbia-Tusculum neighborhood of Cincinnati (worth a visit in itself for a gander at all those wonderful Victorian houses) is your best bet for retro and fixer-upper furniture. You're not going to find a better selection of '50s, '60s, and '70s authentic furniture outside of your grandma's attic.

Rubbish
14th and Main Streets
No phone
Kathy Holwadel and Jeff Syroney run a second-hand thrift shop unlike any other. Stroll into this downtown storefront, in fact, and you'll immediately sense a literary connection. Everything from former *Cincinnati Post* art critic Jane Durrell's manual Smith-Corona (price: $40) to books of poetry, framed prints of city landmarks by sketch artist Carolyn Williams ($20), first editions, chess sets, itty bitty book lights, even a stereo system owned by Rick Pender, arts and entertainment editor for the weekly *CityBeat* newspaper. All items are donated by local literary luminaries. But the Rubbish shop is only half the story. Described as a perpetual yard sale, the retail storefront operation is designed to help fund the non-profit agency Ink Tank, which headquarters its offices in the back half of the Rubbish location. The Ink Tank mission: to promote writing at a grassroots level as well as incubate nontraditional voices in literature and nonfiction. Playwrights, poets, journalists, romance writers, would-be authors, and published authors have all tramped through the rambling, high-ceiling space. A free WiFi service is one appeal; so too a free gathering space for book discussion groups to meet amid like minds. That and the chance to buy some really literate merchandise. A portable typewriter, anyone?

Trader's World
601 Union Road, Monroe
(Interstate 75 and
Ohio Highway 63, exit 29)
(513) 424-5708
One of the granddaddies on the local flea market scene, Trader's World was profiled in the PBS documentary *Flea Markets of America.* There are 1,200 vendor spaces and parking for 6,000 cars. Some of its major specialties are hardware and supplies (including great prices on dowels, wood knobs, and assorted doohickeys coveted by woodworkers), shoes, die-cast cars, trucks and other assorted vehicles (there are three large booths devoted just to these), plus other scattered offerings. What's hot at the flea market? Clooney memorabilia, that's what. Any item relating to Cincinnati's most famous family—the late Rosemary Clooney, actor George Clooney, and American Movie Channel's former host Nick Clooney—is fetching top dollar. A high school prom photo of George and his date, for instance, sold for $370. Admission to the grounds is 75 cents per vehicle.

Turtle Creek Flea Market
320 North Garver Road, Monroe
(Interstate 75 and
Ohio Highway 63, exit 29)
(513) 539-4497
Specialties at Turtle Creek include some 300 vendors inside, plus another 300 to 400 outside during busy seasons. Admission is free.

FOOD SHOPS

The Best of Cincinnati
484 Northland Boulevard
(513) 851-2900
Whether you're new or a native, ordering a catalog from these folks is the quickest way to taste a crash course in Cincinnati cuisine. Anything from the trademark Montgomery Inn barbecue sauce and Skyline chili to Izzy's hot mustard, Graeter's candy, and LaRosa's salad dressing can be delivered to your door.

Bilker Fine Foods
9708 Kenwood Road, Blue Ash
(513) 791-5600
They've moved from the Roselawn digs to Blue Ash, but Bilker's is still the king of kosher. Where else to go for your smoked whitefish, nova lox, or knishes and blintzes? Or a full line of kosher frozen food products from the likes of Best and Tabatchnick? Don't leave without sampling the chopped chicken liver.

Bonbonerie
2030 Madison Road
(513) 321-3399
Bonbonerie and Jenny Craig—never the twain shall meet, but oh well. This is the city's premier bakery, hands down. Scones, cheesecakes, the works—and their trifles are not to be trifled with. There's an adjoining tearoom too.

Dilly Deli
6818 Wooster Pike
(513) 561-5233
This Mariemont gourmet deli offers sandwiches and wine tastings, plus daily takeout dinner specials such as chicken tetrazzini.

Fred and Gari's
629 Vine Street
(513) 784-9000
For the best chocolate cream pie in town, try a calorie-laden slice of heaven served at Fred and Gari's, a take-out bakery and lunch spot. Their banana cream pie is no slouch, either.

Gethsemani Monastery
Gethsemani Farms, Trappist, KY
(502) 549-3117
The oldest Trappist monastery in the United States is found across the river in Trappist, Kentucky, but ordering the monks' famous cheese or fruitcake is as easy as picking up your phone—and, Lord yes, the good friars accept credit cards. The monks produce their semisoft creamy cheese based on a centuries-old European formula, available in mild, aged, or smoked—or try

all three in a sampler box of wedges. Their fruitcake is the real thing, by the way, redolent with Kentucky bourbon and aged cherries, raisins, pineapple, dates, and nuts.

Jean Paul
6660 Clough Pike, Anderson
(513) 231-2780

This is a full-service grocery with perhaps the most extensive and eclectic choice of cheeses in town, as well as a butcher's shop, deli meats, and (for the busy worker) a half-dozen hot meals prepared daily for take-home. The increased mushroom selection is terrific too—our kind of morel majority.

Jungle Jim's
5440 Dixie Highway, Fairfield
(513) 829-1919

Jungle Jim's is a huge gourmet food store with a small grocery store wrapped around it. It's also, as billed by owner "Jungle" Jim Bonaminio, "The Most Unusual Store in America." You can't miss the giant, gaudily painted animals, tropical fruits, or jungle soundtrack as you walk in. Inside you'll see singing mechanical refugees from Chuck E. Cheese's.

Besides the kitsch, you'll find great stuff for the kitchen, including what the store claims is Ohio's largest wine collection. You'll also find possibly the city's best all-around cheese, bakery, and deli shops, all under one roof. Entire ministores here are devoted to Mexican, Indian, Mediterranean, and Asian fresh foods and groceries. One grocery features foodstuffs from Denmark such as lingonberry jam, another offers Irish canned custards straight from Dublin. One Dutch co-author we could mention savors the licorice and chocolate at the Netherlands store.

Even if you didn't like eating, this place would be worth a visit just as a food museum. You can easily spend hours just looking around—and some folks do.

Keegan's Seafood
6675 Salem Road
(513) 233-5959

For the freshest salmon, lobster, and crab this side of Maine, try Keegan's Seafood in Mount Washington. Also the place to find a terrific lobster quiche, seafood lasagna, freshly made cole slaw, and more.

Marx Hot Bagels Factory
9701 Kenwood Road, Blue Ash
(513) 891-5542

Cincinnati's premier kosher bagel shop is owned and run by the flamboyant, provocative—and Catholic—John "Bagelman" Marx. The bagels? They're the closest thing you'll find to New York bagels, and the atmosphere is pretty Gotham-like too. Placing an order at the store on a Saturday morning can be a little like placing an order at the New York Stock Exchange. But it's well worth the grief. You'll come away with a bag of the best bagels this side of the Alleghenies, and much of the time they'll still be too hot to eat.

Mediterranean Foods
314 Ludlow Avenue
(513) 961-6060

This is the place to go for Arabic, Greek, Italian, and Turkish foodstuffs—with Egyptian, Moroccan, and Lebanese thrown in to boot. More than 1,600 items line the walls, from 10 types of pita bread to rices, nuts, figs, and beans. Nifty cheese selection too. Where else to find that Hungarian *kaskaval* cheese?

Newtown Farm Market
3950 Roundbottom Road, Newtown
(513) 561-2004

These folks grow their own strawberries and corn in the summer, and they carry great produce and specialty foods from around the globe. The waiting list for Michigan cherries can be a long one. Owner Bobby Palmisano, from a Cleveland produce family that goes way back, is the former produce director at Jungle Jim's. Don't miss the deli and the incredible selection of exotic canned foods and salad dressings.

The Party Source
95 Riveria Drive, Bellevue, KY
(859) 291-4007
Right across the Big Mac Bridge (Interstate 471 bridge) from downtown, this huge outlet has fast become party central for folks on both sides of the river. Besides an extensive selection of wine and other beverages, the Party Source stocks an extensive array of gourmet foods, including some great frozen hors d'oeuvres for the busy host and hostess. There's also a full plate of other party gear. And we'd be remiss if we didn't remind you that Kentucky liquor prices are quite competitive when compared to Ohio's state store operation, and the selection's far more diverse.

Saigon Market
119 West Elder Street
(513) 721-8053
Saigon Market in Over-the-Rhine is the perfect place for the occidental tourist interested in Asian foodstuffs of all sorts. Take a wok on the wild side.

Spatz Natural Life Health Food
607 Main Street
(513) 621-0347
In a city crammed with health-food and vitamin stores, Spatz stands out. First, the downtown fixture is locally owned; second, it offers far more than bottled drinks and boosters.

Wild Oats Community Market & Deli
2693 Edmondson Road, Norwood
(513) 531-8015
There's a fully loaded organic salad bar at Wild Oats, which includes sun-dried tomatoes, nuts, squashes, and all manner of olives to heap atop your field greens. Plus there's an incredible selection of imported cheeses, a sushi bar, and a bakery.

Workshops of the Restoration Society
3414 DeCoursey Avenue, Latonia, KY
(859) 491-1291
Workshops of the Restoration Society is primarily a furniture-restoring outfit, but it also devotes an entire room to goodies fresh from the Amish of nearby Adams County: jams, cheeses, breads, and more. The raspberry pie is not to be missed.

Graeter's ice-cream shops concoct a "flavor of the month" for each of the 12 months of the year. The most popular flavor? Peach, no contest. A pint of its dreamy peach, available only in July, is as tough to find as a liberal in Hamilton County. Long lines, limited supplies.

WINERIES

Burnet Ridge Winery
6721 Richard Avenue, North College Hill
(513) 522-4203
Winemaker Chip Emmerich ships in grapes from California to produce the wines that include his Purple Trillium, a prizewinning blend of cabernet sauvignon and merlot. How hot is this vintage? Emmerich found himself pouring a glass for none other than President Clinton at a ritzy fund-raising gala. Other wines bottled include Melange a Trois Chardonnay and Sonoma County Pinot Noir.

Chateau Pomije
2019 Madison Road
(513) 871-8788
Chateau Pomije is actually a wine shop; the wine is produced at an Indiana vineyard.

Henke Winery
3077 Harrison Avenue, Westwood
(513) 662-9463
Joe and Joan Henke have moved from their longtime digs in Winton Place, but they still serve up five or more varieties of wine daily at this new location. The wine is made from grapes grown in Virginia, New York, and Ohio.

Meier's Wine Cellars
6955 Plainfield Road, Silverton
(513) 891-2900
www.meierswinecellars.com
Meier's is Cincinnati's own source for cream sherry, LaBrusco, or any of the other dozen varieties of wine produced here.

Moyer's Winery
3859 U.S. Highway 52, Manchester
(937) 549-2957
Moyer's is a scenic winery and (just as notably) a restaurant, all with a picturesque view of the river, gazebos, and lots of atmosphere. Loyal patrons will be sad to learn that Ken and Mary Moyer—who have been growing the grapes and serving up regional American cuisine on the Ohio River for a quarter-century—sold the place to a group of investors. Nonetheless, the Moyer label lives on.

Valley Vineyards
2276 East U.S. Highway 22, Morrow
(513) 899-2485
www.valley-vineyards.com
You can see the wine-making process from the wine to the bottle and sample some while you're at it. Winemaking can be viewed from late August to early October, but Valley Vineyards is also open the rest of the year, offering tours of storage facilities, wine, and food. The tours are free, as is a taste of the wine. You can also get here from the Little Miami Scenic River Bike Trail. But beware: Bicyclists have been arrested for DUI in Ohio. No kidding.

Vinoklet
11069 Colerain Avenue
(513) 385-9309
Vinoklet is a winery that's also a restaurant. There's a choice of steaks, chicken, or seafood (which you can grill yourself). Dinner, wine, and dessert for a couple is $60.

BOOKSELLERS AND NEWSSTANDS

B. Dalton Bookseller
Northgate Mall, 9577 Colerain Avenue, Bevis
(513) 385-5608

Tri-County Mall, 11700 Princeton Pike, Springdale
(513) 671-3420
B. Dalton is a standard-bearer of mall book outlets. That doesn't mean these shops aren't worth a visit, however. They carry some of the area's largest selections of humor, Hollywood tell-alls, how-to books, and other specialties.

Barnes & Noble
1 Levee Way, Newport on the Levee, Newport, KY
(859) 581-2000

7800 Montgomery Road, Kenwood
(513) 794-9440

7663 Mall Road, Florence, KY
(859) 647-6400
You get what you'd expect from the Barnes & Noble chain—wide inventory, competent help, and comfortable environs. If you have a choice, head to the superstore at Newport on the Levee.

Books & Co.
350 East Stroop Road, Kettering
(937) 298-6540
This one is worth a special drive, whether you're a book lover, music lover, or coffee lover. Folks from across the region flock to Books & Co., which aggressively brings in top-name authors for signings and hosts a highly regarded music series on weekends in the store. The coffee-and-dessert shop is a must visit—and oh yes, they sell books too. Lots. The mystery, children's, and local-interest sections are particularly strong.

The Bookshelf Inc.
7754 Camargo Road, Madeira
(513) 271-9140

The Bookshelf is a smaller shop that caters to the interests of area residents, and in this upscale community (which is quite near ritzy Indian Hill), the interests would be art, antiques, fine cooking, history, and the like. There's a varied selection of general-interest texts too.

Borders Books & Music
11711 Princeton Road, Springdale
(513) 671-5852

4530 Eastgate Boulevard, Eastgate
(513) 943-0068

9459 Colerain Avenue, Northgate
(513) 245-9898
Borders is another book megastore with tons of inventory. Beyond the books, however, is a wonderfully esoteric collection of magazines. Where else can you snag the latest copy of *Flatiron News*? The stores have one of the largest folk and New Age CD inventories in town, and the children's reading section is superb.

Brengelman's Bookstore
454 West McMicken Avenue
(513) 621-4865
Here's a quirky place: It's open only on Saturday and Sunday afternoons, and the building is marked only with a small sign that says BOOKSTORE. Nonetheless, it's delightful to sink into an overstuffed couch and browse the books, both old and new.

Brentano's
Tower Place Mall, Carew Tower
(513) 723-9656
Downtowners flock to Brentano's bookstore, especially for its sizable collection of audio books-on-tape and its up-to-date business section.

Christ Church Cathedral Bookshop
318 East Fourth Street
(513) 621-1817
The bookshop inside Christ Church Episcopal Cathedral is where you'll find all manner of gift ideas for the religious and nonreligious. From bookmarks with quotable sayings to stained-glass jewelry and leather-bound Bibles, the store's selection is remarkably varied.

Cincinnati Nature Center Bookstore
4949 Tealtown Road, Glen Este
(513) 831-1711
The Cincinnati Nature Center Bookstore offers the most complete hands-on nature study you'll find in the area, with numerous educational programs for youths, including spring and fall biology programs and summer classes. The store stocks every possible nature book relating to Ohio, Kentucky, and Indiana; topics include local bird-watching, trail hiking, bicycling, and botany opportunities.

Duttenhofer's Treasures
214 West McMillan Street
(513) 381-1340
Every city has one of these, or ought to—a dusty, musty, marvelous used-book store that prides itself on maintaining a diverse collection, from first editions to campy science fiction, mystery novels to local interest books. A treasure trove, literally.

Fountain News
Fifth and Walnut Streets
(513) 421-4049
More than 130 newspapers from all corners of the globe give new meaning to the word "newsstand." Be it an Arabic weekly, the *Sunday Times* of London, or such mags as *Chicago Gardener,* you'll find it here.

Friends of the Public Library Book & Gift Shop
Public Library of Cincinnati and Hamilton County, 800 Vine Street
(513) 369-6000
There's plenty of local flavor here, with a box of "Doors of Cincinnati" notecards, hologram magnets, Cincinnati coloring books, games, puzzles, ties, and—needless to say—books. We'll let you in on a little secret: The mezzanine includes the Book Nook Cafe, which is good news for literary noshers.

May 3 is a great day to do your banking 'round these parts. The fifth month/third day of the year is somehow special to the folks at Fifth Third Bank Corp., who lay out an assortment of free goodies and punch every 5/3 at just about every branch. And hey, who's to say U.S. Bank and National City Bank customers can't snitch a free cookie?

Half-Price Books
11389 Princeton Road, Springdale
(513) 772-1511

8118 Montgomery Road, Kenwood
(513) 891-7170
We're not sure how they do it, but the hard and softcovers here really are half price—and pretty new too.

The Heritage Shop of the Historical Society
1301 Western Avenue
(513) 287-7000
The Heritage Shop of the Historical Society sells all sorts of nifty literary items, including books, toys, posters, and ornaments. Of most local interest, perhaps, is the Cat's Meow line of wood miniature buildings representing Cincinnati's unique architectural treasures: Findlay Market, Fountain Square, the art museum, the Hamilton County Courthouse, Wise Temple, Lunken Airfield, and more. The Procter & Gamble headquarters in miniature, for instance, would make a terrific gift for that Proctoid you know.

Joseph-Beth Booksellers
Rookwood Pavilion, 2692 Madison Road, Norwood
(513) 396-8965
www.josephbeth.com
The incredible diversity of the selection as well as the helpful service make Joe-Beth stand out from the crowd. Whether you're in search of the latest copy of *Punch* or an obscure fanzine, you'll find it here—as well as a friendly smile. We like to snuggle in the overstuffed armchairs, listen to the weekly live music by the likes of Katie Reider or Silver Arm, and enjoy life.

King Arthur's Court
3040 Madison Road
(513) 531-4600
This is primarily a toy store with a nicely arranged selection of educational toys and a downstairs department devoted solely to model trains, model cars, and other sorts of model projects. However, King Arthur's also carries 3,000 hardback and softcover juvenile titles, making it a substantial player on the local children's bookstore scene.

Montgomery Book Co.
9917 Montgomery Road, Montgomery
(513) 891-2227
Montgomery's is the friendly, neighborhood kind of bookseller, with one-on-one service and free coffee percolating in back. Not to imply that the store is tiny—it carries thousands of titles, from cookbooks and mysteries to children's literature and, unusual for any bookstore, a full selection of books on tape that are available to rent.

Newport Aquarium Bookstore & Gift Shop
1 Levee Way, Newport, KY
(859) 261-7444
Consider the Newport Aquarium's book shop your last chance for a last-minute gift on Christmas Day—the aquarium is open 365 days a year, including all day December 25. The aisles are littered with stuffed penguins and *National Geographic* calendars. Most interesting is the wide selection of books that focus on a variety of topics such as sea life, polar bears, sharks, seals, and more. The children's book selection is as extensive as the adult shelves, with easy-to-read picture books regarding life in the wild.

Ohio Book Store
726 Main Street
(513) 621-5142
True to its name, this is the area's niftiest display of books on Ohio, Ohio history,

Ohio cuisine, Ohio . . . well, you get the point. It also has thousands of back issues of *Life* and *Look* from 1937 on, plus copies of *National Geographic, Sports Illustrated,* and more.

Pink Pyramid
907 Race Street
(513) 621-7465
Pink Pyramid is an adult bookstore, or at least the closest thing conservative Cincinnati has to an adult bookstore outside of Larry Flynt's Hustler shop (which we have chosen not to list). Unlike the Hustler shop, Pink Pyramid has much socially redeeming value, with challenging homosexual literature and art books as well as thoughtful philosophical writings. There are also video rentals, and that is what has gotten this shop into trouble with local law enforcement on many occasions. The store is becoming something of a cause célèbre among First Amendment absolutists and local literati.

Significant Books
3053 Madison Road
(513) 321-7567
Proprietors Bill and Carolyn Downing know everything about finding obscure books and rare editions. (Case study: We went looking for a novel 30 years out of print. They searched and found a copy in Dallas within a week.)

St. Francis Bookshop
1618 Vine Street
(513) 241-7304
You'll discover anything from handpainted wooden ornaments from El Salvador to glazed ceramic peace signs at the St. Francis Bookshop. But its book collection (crossing all faiths) is notable.

The Villager
6932 Madisonville Road, Mariemont
(513) 271-0523
Not strictly a bookstore, this variety shop offers children's books, general fiction, nonfiction hardcovers and paperbacks, and the odd biography among its shelves of art supplies, greeting cards, and gift ideas.

While every other costume purveyor in town doesn't put its inventory on sale until after Halloween, the folks at the Ohio Renaissance Festival start early on marking down the chain mail, suits of armor, maces, swords, Sherwood Forest outfits, queen's dresses, and other period clothing. The festival closes in mid-October, so on the last Sunday, the knight and wizard garb is marked to deep discount. Just in time for All Hallow's Eve.

Waldenbooks
Eastgate Mall, 4601 Eastgate Boulevard, Eastgate
(513) 752-9591

Kenwood Towne Centre, 7875 Montgomery Road, Kenwood
(513) 791-0011

Western Hills Plaza, 6139 Glenway Avenue, Westwood
(513) 662-5837

Florence Mall, 2028 Florence Mall Road, Florence, KY
(859) 371-0216
If you're inside a mall in Greater Cincinnati, chances are it has a Waldenbooks. This archtypical mall bookstore covers all bases, from sports and biography to fiction and mysteries.

Whatever Works Wellness Center & Bookstore
7433 Montgomery Road, Silverton
(513) 791-9428
Whatever Works carries a first-class collection of books relating to the care and maintenance of the spirit, the soul, the karma, or whatever you'd like to call it, plus health texts, aromatherapy, classes, and more.

UNIQUE GIFT SHOPS

Boardwalk Hobby Shop
1032 Delta Avenue, Mount Lookout Square
(513) 871-2110
Need a game of Twister? Come to Boardwalk Hobby Shop, which boasts, without doubt, the city's most extensive collection of model kits and vintage toys and board games. Whether you're looking for some obscure variation of Lincoln Logs, some rare pigment of military model paint, or a vintage board game that hasn't been in the mainstream stores for decades, this delightful and nostalgic place is your best bet.

Cincinnati Art Museum Gift Shop
920 Eden Park Drive
(513) 721-5204
Surprisingly, this is the best place in town for oddball computer-related gifts. Where else to find a Macintosh CD-ROM with a font suitcase of Egyptian hieroglyphics—write a unique letter to your mummy. Or how 'bout a Dalí screen saver, featuring 25 of the artist's most bizarre visions. There's also a selection of mouse pads with famous artworks, as well as the expected repertoire of any art museum gift shop: Andy Warhol wristwatches and desk clocks, Dalí desk calendars, Museum of Modern Art appointment books, pottery and silver services, artist ties, and jewelry.

Cincinnati Zoo Gift Shop
3400 Vine Street
(513) 281-4700
Searching for a gift to please the animal lover in your family? Here you'll find animal jewelry, posters, umbrellas, clocks, music, and books. But for a unique gift, consider the ADOPT program. For $35, you can adopt a snow leopard, Bengal tiger, or whatever and help defray its weekly veterinary care and food bill. You get a packet with a color photo of the adoptee, a fact sheet, a gold ADOPT ornament, and a certificate of adoption. (The Bengal tiger, we're told, makes a great gift for any Bengals fan you know.)

Contemporary Arts Center Gift Shop
44 East Sixth Street
(513) 345-8400
Here you'll find anything from a classy rosewood and silver-plated bottle stopper to less-pricey items such as artsy umbrellas, stained glass, color Claymation clay, belts, book bags, paint sets, rubber-stamp kits, notecards, and the ever popular "Fighting Nun" puppet.

Haines House of Cards
2514 Leslie Avenue, Norwood
(513) 531-6548
Haines House of Cards is a retail store and small factory whose customers are magicians worldwide. Haines ships trick card packs as far as England, France, Germany, and Japan, and customers have included conjurers David Copperfield and Harry Blackstone Jr. The top-the-line invisible deck is $30.00, but prices range from $5.00 and up for us amateurs. Why all the fuss? The shop, opened in 1945, long ago perfected a secret formula sprayed so each playing card won't slide, ruining the trick. The recipe is still a secret today.

Hebrew Union Gift Shop
3101 Clifton Avenue
(513) 221-1875
You'll find a wide selection of menorahs in silver, ceramic, wood, stone, glass, and traditional brass as well as other Jewish items at Hebrew Union College's gift shop. This Clifton shop is also a treasure trove of local Jewish history.

I Love Cincinnati Shoppe
Tower Place Mall, Carew Tower
(513) 651-5772
Are you a fan of the UC Bearcats? A complete line of Bearcats hats, sweatshirts, and infant wear bearing the Bearcats logo is available at the I Love Cincinnati Shoppe. As is, of course, anything Queen City related, from skyline T-shirts to Reds and Bengals merchandise.

Kentucky Haus
10th Street at Monroe, Newport, KY
(859) 261-4287

Kentucky Haus, which recently moved, is the place to find all things Kentuckian, from Berea College crafts and Bybee Pottery to paintings and prints of regional scenes. Workshops on soap making, hand-painted floorcloths, and historical topics (such as Old Latonia Racetrack's place in history) are just some of the offerings at this unique treasure.

Krohn Conservatory Gift Shop
Eden Park
(513) 421-5707
When in dire need of a gift idea for gardeners, turn to our favorite old Krohn. Krohn Conservatory that is, where you'll run across bird feeders, herb plants, baskets, mailbox covers, topiary kits, and a nifty ceramic birdhouse in the shape of Noah's ark. An added benefit: This is the only place in town steamy enough that you can do your holiday shopping in T-shirt and Bermuda shorts.

The Meow Mart
6958 Plainfield Road, Silverton
(513) 984-3312
Cat lovers should head first to the Meow Mart, whose sales benefit the adjoining no-kill cat shelter, the Scratching Post. You'll find a full line of Iams cat food, notecards, jewelry, toys, teaser sticks, and more.

Natural History Museum Collectors Shop
1301 Western Avenue
(513) 287-7000
Forget educational toys. Forget boring ol' books. The gift shop at the Natural History Museum has what your kids *really* want, say a giant Darth Vader action figure or a kit to help produce special effects like in the Hollywood movies. Of course, there are more-sedate gifts too: fossils, kaleidoscopes, gemstones, Vivaldi CDs, animal prints, kids' nature books, and American Indian crafts, as well as art items from Africa and Peru. Magnet kits seem to be the most popular scientific item, with no less than seven different kits devoted to the magic of magnetism.

The One-Stop Allergy Shop
8464 Winton Road, Blue Ash
(513) 936-0224
Aahchoo! The One-Stop Allergy Shop boasts a complete (and sneeze-proof) selection of featherbeds, comforters, stuffed animals, mold and mildew removers, dust-mite prevention products, even purifiers and face masks. Your nose knows if this is the place for you.

Victorian Quilt Shop
8556 Beechmont Avenue, Cherry Grove
(513) 474-9355
Ohioans are mad for their quilts, and this is the region's definitive quilting source. Perhaps the passion dates from our Midwest farming family roots, or the fact that the state boasts as many Amish as Pennsylvania, but whatever the reason, quilting remains a top pastime among the handicraft hobbies 'round here. At Victorian, you'll find Ohio-made quilts, fabric, patterns, and supplies of all sorts, along with homespun advice. Hey, who says winners never quilt?

Wine World—Baskets Gourmet
7737 Five Mile Road, Anderson
(513) 232-6611
If you've totally run out of gift ideas, this ambitious shop, located inside a suburban strip mall, is a wonderful source. The staff can whip up any delectable combination possible for a basket. Smoked salmon pâté? Oui. Tangy salsa? Si. Pick and choose from a full selection of nuts, candies, and, of course, wine and beers of the world. The store features wine tastings too.

"Rookwood" is the name of the game at two auctions held the first weekend of every June. Fans of Cincinnati pottery fly in from all parts of the world, paying up to $75,000 for a vase without blinking twice. Some $2 million worth of Rookwood can change hands, and it's an amazing thing to watch—even if you can't afford to bid. Call the Cincinnati Art Galleries, (513) 381-2128, for details.

ATTRACTIONS

A recent study says that residents of Greater Cincinnati spend 36 percent more on entertainment than the national average. The Bureau of Labor Statistics report says tristate households spend $2,485 per year on entertainment, about 7 percent of the household budget. Nationally, families spend about $1,824 per year.

So it only goes to show that there are lots of entertainment opportunities in the area. The major attractions covered in this chapter are those not covered in other chapters of the books. You'll have to look for the Cincinnati Art Museum and the Broadway Series in the Arts chapter. Information on Reds and Bengals games can be found in the Spectator Sports chapter. But if you want to know about Paramount's Kings Island or the Cincinnati Zoo, keep reading.

The chapter is divided into four sections: Pure Fun, Pure Fun Plus (fun plus special interest/education), Museums, and Historic Attractions.

As with all our information, many of these tourist attractions change each year (adding or closing rides and points of interest or changing hours or admission charges), so to get the absolute latest information, you may want to call ahead.

Several recorded messages about current attractions are also available through different services. The Talking Yellow Pages, (513) 333-4444, has numerous specialty lines for entertainment and events: a concert line, a points-of-interest line, and a special-events line. Check the front of the Yellow Pages for a complete listing.

PRICE CODE

The following price code is based on the cost for general admission for one adult. Most sites offer considerably discounted tickets for children and seniors, and some allow discounts or free entry for members of their respective organizations.

$	**$5.00 and under**
$$	**$6.00 to $10.00**
$$$	**$11.00 to $15.00**
$$$$	**More than $15.00**

PURE FUN

Argosy VI **Free**
777 Argosy Parkway, Lawrenceburg, IN
(888) ARGOSY7

Just across the Indiana state line—about a 20- to 25-minute drive from downtown Cincinnati—is Lawrenceburg and the *Argosy VI* gambling riverboat. The *Argosy VI* is one of the largest riverboat casinos in the world (the length of a football field). It has 1,977 slot machines and 104 table games, including blackjack, roulette, Caribbean stud, minibaccarat, and craps, plus a full array of video-poker units. It is open 24 hours. Reservations are recommended. See the River Fun chapter for more details.

The Beach Waterpark **$$$**
2590 Waterpark Drive
(exit 25 off Interstate 71), Mason
(513) 398-SWIM, (800) 886-SWIM
www.thebeachwaterpark.com

Hey, we're landlocked and easily a thousand miles from the nearest sandy ocean beach. That explains the popularity of Greater Cincinnati's water parks, of which the Beach is perhaps the most notable. The Beach likes to fashion itself as Jamaican cool, as if its 35 acres sit along the coast of Kingston. Yeaaah, mon. You can bodysurf in the wave pool, hydroplane down the giant slides, take a slow cruise on single or double inner tubes, or go for a ride on the thrilling Aztec Adventure water coaster in this H_2O extravaganza. Or you can kick back on the sandy beaches, play volleyball, play in the children's water areas, or take in the live entertainment.

The park is open Memorial Day through Labor Day beginning at 10:00 A.M.; closing times vary throughout the season. Admission is $74 for a season pass for adults, $160 for a family of four. Single-day admission is $26.99 Friday through Sunday and $19.99 Monday through Thursday for adults, $10.99 for seniors and for children ages 5 to 9. Children under age 2 are free. It's immediately off Interstate 71, exit 25, across from Paramount's Kings Island. Parking costs $7.00.

Coney Island **$$-$$$$**
6201 Kellogg Avenue, Anderson
(513) 232-8230
www.coneyislandpark.com

Located off Interstate 275 at the Kellogg Avenue exit, this laid-back getaway on the banks of the Ohio River offers a fun family outing without all the cost or utter exhaustion of a day at a larger, more frenetic amusement park. Unless you go to its Sunlite Pool, it's no more than a two- or three-hour excursion. Overall, this is a popular attraction for East Siders, although a more modern water park up north, the Beach, has stolen some of its thunder regionally. Coney is also adjacent to the Riverbend Music Center and River-Downs racetrack, which makes the area one of the city's entertainment meccas.

Before 1972 Coney was *the* amusement park in Cincinnati. When Coney's owner also opened Kings Island, most of Coney's original attractions were carted off to stock the new park. But Coney was reopened as a low-key amusement park in the mid-1970s under the name "Old Coney." Many longtime residents still call it this, but the PR department discourages this usage now, preferring the current name, Coney Island, and dwelling on what it offers today, which is actually quite a lot.

Sunlite Pool at Coney is billed as the world's largest recirculating pool (200 feet by 400 feet). Although the World Recirculating Pool Council could not be reached for independent verification, suffice it to say there's plenty of room for splashing and swimming. Sunlite Pool also has a 500-foot waterslide and 180-foot water coaster.

Pedal-boat trips on Lake Como are another popular attraction at Coney. (In another entry from the Cincinnati truth-is-stranger-than-fiction department, police once engaged an assault suspect in a pedal-boat chase here.) The park also offers a fairly wide variety of rides, food services, a miniature golf course, and a large, well-equipped playground. Moonlite Gardens is a popular spot for dances that range from teen sock hops to Big Band bashes for the slightly older crowd.

Coney is also an extremely popular site for company picnics, and it hosts several major annual events: the Appalachian Festival in May and Summerfair in June (see the Annual Events chapter).

Sunlite Pool is open Memorial Day through Labor Day 10:00 A.M. to 8:00 P.M. daily. Park rides are open during this period from 11:00 A.M. to 9:00 P.M. daily. There are three different tickets you can buy for your day at Coney. The first is a combined Sunlite Pool and ride ticket. It costs $18.50 for age 4 and up, $9.95 for kids ages 2 and 3. To buy just Sunlite Pool tickets, the price is $10.95 for age 4 and up and $3.95 for kids ages 2 and 3. A rides-alone ticket is $9.95 for age 4 and up and $6.00 for age 3 and under. Parking is $6.00. (If the Ohio River is at flood stage, call first. Flood waters sometimes force Coney to close temporarily.)

Paramount's Kings Island **$$$$**
6300 Kings Island Drive
(exit 24 off Interstate 71), Mason
(513) 754-5700, (800) 288-0808
www.pki.com

No summer in Cincinnati is the same without at least one visit to Paramount's Kings Island. More than three million people check out the attractions at the area's largest amusement park each year. And each year they will find more fun and new rides as well as the long lines that come with those attractions.

In 2006 the newest attraction was not a roller coaster but rather a Nickelodeon theme park. The Nickelodeon Universe has

CLOSE-UP

A Sign of Things to Come

When Tod Swormstedt sleeps, he sees signs.

When he's awake, same thing. The Cincinnati publishing executive encounters signs, hundreds of 'em: blinking neon banners, legendary fast-food icons, classic roadside kitsch ...

Perhaps it's to be expected of a man who is championing the American Sign Museum.

"We have all the classics. The HOLIDAY INN: THE WORLD'S INNKEEPER sign, for instance, one of the great ones, with the arrow and chasing lights. And one of the early McDonald's signs, featuring a guy they called Speedy."

The enthusiastic Swormstedt is rattling off his favorites in his collection now: "There's the Dog 'n Suds porcelain neon graphic arrow, a full-size 28-foot Howard Johnson's lamplighter neon, a Goodyear opal glass image, a Hamm's Beer animated neon . . . ."

Swormstedt pauses for breath.

The American Sign Museum will launch in two stages, the curator continues. A prototype opened in a 3,400-square-foot "preview space" inside the old Essex warehouse in the city neighborhood of Walnut Hills.

The Cincinnati native's audacious concept for the permanent American Sign Museum will require lofty inside exhibition space as well as adjoining, and sprawling, outdoor display areas—thousands upon thousands of square feet.

"Our plan includes the need for a 21,000-square-foot building, but our specs virtually require we have outdoor as well as indoor space, for the outdoor signs," Swormstedt says.

As he views it, the permanent American Sign Museum will also house a sign-restoration department, including a working neon plant as well as other fabrication/restoration capabilities.

What do Swormstedt and his trade magazine company—ST Media Group—bring to the table in crafting the deal for a permanent home? Signs. Thousands of 'em. Rare and collectible placards, vintage posters, historically significant banners, roadside Americana, pop art, and pop culture creations.

As Swormstedt pitches his ambitious vision, a museum devoted to nothing less than preserving and chronicling "the front line of advertising," you begin to get the religion.

When asked "Why in Cincinnati?" Swormstedt's rapid-fire response is "Why *not* Cincinnati?" The city is home to Procter & Gamble, the largest commercial advertiser in the world. Home to dozens of turn-of-the-20th century sign makers and pioneers of the craft, billboard artists, poster-printing companies, and manufacturers of sign-related objects. And, not incidentally, home to Swormstedt's own ST Media Group, publisher of the nation's largest trade pub devoted to the commercial sign industry, the century-old *Signs of the Times* magazine. (ST Media has donated a "substantial" amount of seed money to the museum project.)

The tale of how Swormstedt's private

collection evolved into a public campaign for a new museum begins simply enough: "I was having a midlife crisis," says Swormstedt of his work at *Signs of the Times* magazine, where his grandfather and dad worked and where, currently, his brother and two cousins are employed. "I'm still on the payroll, but my focus is the museum."

Hot on the success of other cities launching special-interest museums—the International Spy Museum, Holocaust Museum, and the Newseum in the nation's capital, for instance, and the Rock and Roll Hall of Fame in Cleveland—Swormstedt is adamant his dream of a large-scale museum can work.

"On the inside of the building, we want to put signs in architectural context," Swormstedt says, describing his concept of period storefronts that line nostalgic streets. "We've already created the storefronts to display the signs."

View the collection, which spans 1880 to the present, and you begin to imagine the possibilities: Pass by a hand-painted tin sign with push-through embossed opal glass text. Check out a Chicago dry cleaner's shop window sign that's a neon clock. Move on to a countertop SHOE REPAIR sign that's an illuminated plastic panel. And next onto a Pennsylvania OPTICIAN AND JEWELER advertisement (back when those jobs were one and the same).

Rounding out Swormstedt's collection: an early "neon" fluorescent menu board; a glass chemist's sign, circa 1910; a Frank Sinatra showcard from Las Vegas, let's say 1960; a neon rooftop Gulf sign, also 1960; an Elgin Watch countertop display (featuring a motorized plastic vintage car); salesmen's sign kits; tavern and inn signs; drugstore signage; and "paper" items such as catalogs, books, blueprints, and sketches.

The collection began, and prospered, simply as a by-product of Swormstedt's magazine work. "I was not originally aware of the network of collectors in antique signs," says Swormstedt, who now sits on the board of the national Society for Commercial Archaeology. "It's a big network of collectors and some big money is being spent. Just watch on eBay. There are whole sections on porcelain, neon, and vintage signs.

"Some signs are fetching up to $10,000 each on eBay, which is the good news and the bad news. It means there is definitely an interest. But it's going to be hard for me to get more of this stuff for free."

More and more, he has to be careful of the swindlers: "There's a lot of counterfeit signs. There are all these Burma Shave signs, fakes, sitting around in antiques shops."

Swormstedt is amazed there is no current public archive or public collection of signs already in existence. "There is a neon museum in Las Vegas, but they concentrate only on preserving neon signs within the city limits of Las Vegas."

The American Sign Museum is at 2515 Essex Avenue, Walnut Hills. Call (800) 925-1110, ext. 336, or (513) 258-4020; or visit www.signmuseum.org. Hours by appointment on weekends, weekday mornings, and evenings. Admission is $10; group rates are available.

18 new rides and attractions, some featuring Dora and Blue and others relating to SpongeBob. For older kids, there is Danny Phantom and Jimmy Neutron.

In the past five years, many new rides have been added, including the Italian Job, Delirium, Drop Zone, Face Off, and Flight of Fear.

The Italian Job is a fast-track coaster that opened in 2005. Patterned after the 2003 movie of the same name, it takes riders through movie sets inspired by the film's climactic chase sequence.

Delirium reaches 137 feet during its swinging motion. Riders are faced outward in suspended seats. Drop Zone also lets you face outward as you plunge 315 feet; it is the tallest gyro drop in the world. Face Off is an inverted roller coaster with a loop that will take you to 5g force at 55 mph. Flight of Fear is an indoor coaster that takes you through a maze of loops, drops, and spins.

Some older favorite roller coasters include the Beast, Son of Beast, Vortex, Tomb Raider, Top Gun, and the good old Racer, which you can take forward or backward. The Beast and its offspring are in a breed by themselves. The older is the longest wooden roller coaster in the country and has been named tops in the wooden coaster realm by enthusiasts everywhere. The Son is the tallest, fastest, and the only looping wooden coaster. It gets to speeds of more than 78 mph. The Vortex is another old favorite. This metal twisty ride was the first six-inversion roller coaster and is quite intense, with speeds of more than 55 mph. Tomb Raider was named after the movie and is a seat-moving roller coaster where you are flipped upside down four times. It's not as great as its neighbor the Beast, but it's still a favorite of many. Top Gun will leave you dangling in midair with the cars attached on top instead of below, which makes it difficult to see where you're going.

Other favorite, less intense, rides at the park include Adventure Express, Whitewater Canyon, and Congo Falls. Scooby-Doo and the Haunted Castle is a great fun ride where you get to shoot the ghosts.

Kings Island is one of the top 15 amusement parks in the country and the largest in the Midwest. It is filled with rides, major stage productions, children's shows, movies, and dozens of restaurants and shops. It also has games, arcades, a picnic area, and its own amphitheater.

Its 1,600 acres are divided into seven theme areas and centered around a one-third-scale replica of the Eiffel Tower. (After a visit to France, local humor columnist David Wecker remarked that "they've built one of those Kings Island towers in Paris too.") The observation deck at the top of the tower, by the way, offers spectacular views of the park and surrounding area, particularly in the fall when the leaves change color.

With the addition of new coasters and thrill rides each year, the lines get a little shorter on the old tried-and-true roller coasters. Still, be prepared to wait sometimes more than two hours to get on some of the popular rides. Some of the less-intense rides have shorter lines but, generally, be prepared to stand in line to get on, or in, everything, including restaurants and food booths. Sometimes, though, two tasks can be carried out at one time. The park's managers aren't dumb—they often put food and drink booths adjacent to where people are standing in line. It's common to send one member of the family on a food or drink run while the rest of the group keeps his/her place in line. (Cutting in line, though, is expressly forbidden, and violators get kicked out of the park. That rule is strictly enforced.) Be prepared to pay a premium if you buy food—or anything else—in the park. You can bring your own food and drinks, and lockers are available so you don't have to carry it around all day.

During the summer, the solution to baking in the sizzling summer heat is a cup of Homemade brand cherry cordial ice cream from one of the vendors and catching the train to the renovated water park, opened in 2005 and renamed Boomerang Bay to reflect its Australian theme. Still the same great wave pool and kiddie pools, though. There are now more than 50 water attractions, including 30 slides and a lazy river. But best of all, there's a luxurious element with cabanas, live music, and lounge-chair waiter service.

For a family trip, gather in one of the giant inner tubes with seats and roll down Whitewater Canyon, where strategically placed workers with itchy trigger fingers explode bursts of water into the air. Strapped into your seat, there is nothing you can do but watch the water go up, watch it come down, cover your head, and get soaked. It's wonderful on steamy summer days, but on chilly or breezy days you leave the ride with chattering teeth and goose bumps the size of golf balls.

If you have children, run, do not walk, straight to Nickelodeon Universe, which includes many pint-size rides and a couple of roller coasters. The Beastie is a smaller version of the park's main attraction and the Rugrats Runaway Reptar is a suspended kids' coaster. The children's area now includes the flume ride, which has been renamed the Wild Thornberry's River Adventure. If you're a fan of Nick, the show in the children's area shouldn't be missed.

Another ride that's fun for kids and adults alike is focused on the most popular cartoon on Nickelodeon. SpongeBob SquarePants 3-D is an ocean motion ride and a 3-D attraction. The ride is located in the back of the park, near the Vortex, and not only do you get 3-D glasses, your seat moves with the action on the screen. For those of you who get seasick, some nonmoving seats are available near the front of the theater.

There are many more rides for children of all ages, including Scooby's Ghoster Coaster and Yogi's Sky Tours.

Kings Island is open daily during the spring and summer. Kings Island also is open some weekends during September and October. But call ahead and check because several area companies rent out the whole place for their employees on some of those weekends. Then it's closed to the public.

The park opens at 9:00 A.M., but rides don't start until 10:00 A.M., while the water park doesn't open until 11:00 A.M. With the hour difference, it's quite common—and a darn good idea—for people to enter the park when the gates open and go sprinting like they were late for a bus to their favorite roller coaster. Although they still have an hour until the ride opens, it's one of the shorter waits of the day for the popular coasters.

Individual tickets are $34.99 for ages 7 through 59 and $29.99 for children 4 through 6 and seniors 60 and older. Children 3 and younger get in free. It's becoming more and more difficult to take in the whole park in one day, especially for first-timers. Knowing this, the park sells tickets for the next day inside the park for $19.99. Season passes are $106.99 for adults. A season pass for a family of four is $319.96 plus $75.00 for each additional child. Season passes are also good for admission to Paramount's six other amusement parks in the United States and Canada. Parking is $9.00.

PURE FUN PLUS

Carew Tower Observation Deck **$**
Fifth and Race Streets
(513) 579-9735

It isn't the Sears Tower, but the 49th-floor observation deck atop Cincinnati's tallest building has buckled the knees of a few acrophobes. With an unobstructed view in every direction, you can watch storms roll in from the west, catch

Kings Island has a great volunteer work program. Your nonprofit group can sign you up to work a six- or eight-hour shift during the times the park needs extra staff; the group gets your pay for its programs and you get two to four free tickets for the following season.

If your children are too young to enjoy the bigger water parks, visit one of the Hamilton County parks that offer mini water parks. The best part is that admission is just $1.00 with a Hamilton County park sticker at Miami Whitewater Forest, Woodland Mound, and Winton Woods. All offer sprinkler-type water fun in a wet playground and are open daily between Memorial Day and Labor Day.

spectacular sunsets, and even stand above the clouds on some days. To get there, take an elevator to the 48th floor of the Carew Tower and then walk up one flight. Hours are 9:00 A.M. to 5:00 P.M. Monday through Friday, and 10:00 A.M. to 7:00 P.M. Saturday and Sunday.

Cathedral Basilica of the Assumption **Free**
Madison Avenue and 12th Street, Covington, KY
(859) 431-2060
www.covcathedral.com

This small-scale replica of Notre Dame is a must-see. The cathedral features a French Gothic design with gargoyles, flying buttresses, mural-size oil paintings by renowned artist Frank Duveneck, and 82 stained-glass windows, including the world's largest at 24 feet by 67 feet. (See more information on the cathedral in the Worship chapter.)

Cincinnati/Northern Kentucky International Airport **Free**
Interstate 275 and Donaldson Road, Hebron, KY
(859) 767-3144
www.cvgairport.com

More than 40,000 children take a guided tour of the airport each year. The tour includes the airport's aircraft rescue firefighting facility and a demonstration of the rescue equipment, the murals that were taken from Union Terminal, the different concourses, and the airport's own airplane, where children can explore the cockpit and instrumentation and receive an explanation of emergency procedures. Weekday tours begin at 9:30 A.M., 11:00 A.M., and 1:00 P.M. and are free. Call the marketing department for reservations two weeks in advance.

Cincinnati Observatory Center **$**
3489 Observatory Place
(513) 321-5186
www.cincinnatiobservatory.org

One of the first observatories in America, the Cincinnati Observatory was founded by Ormsby Mitchell in 1842 and remains the oldest fully operational observatory in the nation. It was originally located in Mount Adams, but pollution from the industry-rich river basin upwind forced its move to the appropriately named Mount Lookout. Samuel Hannaford designed the structure, which the University of Cincinnati physics department operated and maintained. Since it was taken over by a nonprofit group in 1999, more people are discovering this hidden treasure. The new facility is open for day and evening tours, and there are plans to convert the facility into a museum of American astronomy.

Tours of the stately domed structure that sits majestically atop Mount Lookout are available by appointment. The observatory is open on Thursday, Friday, and Saturday nights and it opens at dusk. Admission is free on Thursday.

Cincinnati Railway Co. **$$$$**
198 South Broadway, Lebanon
(513) 933-8022
www.cincinnatirailway.com

Formerly known as the Turtle Creek Railway, the railway provides an enjoyable hour-long, round-trip train ride through the beautiful rolling countryside of southwestern Ohio. While you're in Lebanon, you can enjoy a meal at the historic Golden Lamb Inn and some boutiquing and antiquing at the bounty of Lebanon's shops (see the Day Trips chapter). Trains run Saturday and Sunday April (with the

Easter Bunny Express) through October (when there are fall pumpkin rides). Santa rides are available in November and December. Trains depart at 10:00 A.M., 12:30 P.M., and 3:00 P.M. on Saturday, 11:30 A.M. and 2:00 P.M. Sunday. Fare is $17 for adults and $15 for children under age 12.

Cincinnati Zoo and Botanical Garden **$$$**
3400 Vine Street
(513) 281-4700
www.cincinnatizoo.org

Even though the zoo's financial struggles continue, with the help of very generous donors it has been making giant strides. Some of its special exhibits include a Manatee Springs exhibit, with manatees, alligators, a crocodile, turtles, birds, fish, and even butterflies.

The zoo's $6 million Vanishing Giants exhibit is housed in the renovated Elephant House with expanded outside habitats for Asian elephants, giraffes, and okapi. The Elephant House, which was built in 1905 and is listed on the National Register of Historic Places, now has new colors, and its main dome and base are lit at night.

The half acre outside the exhibit has a 38,000-gallon pool, shade trees, and grass areas. The elephant performance area has shaded seating for 420 people.

The Lords of the Arctic exhibit has an underwater viewing pool and doubles the size of the former polar bear exhibit. Besides the existing 6-foot-deep pool and the new 12-foot-deep viewing pool, there also are waterfalls and shallower pools for the bears to play in. Two bears were brought over from the Denver Zoo to join the two bears already at the zoo.

Even before all of the grow, the Cincinnati Zoo was one of the most respected zoos in the country. In particular the zoo is renowned for its collection of 100 endangered species, including 6 that are extinct in the wild. Alas, the last passenger pigeon on earth died here in 1914. The memorial to her and the last Carolina parakeet, which died here in 1918, is still on the grounds today.

The zoo is also known worldwide for its captive-birth programs with such exotic animals as Malaysian tapirs, okapis, gorillas, and white tigers. More than 100 white tigers have been born here. And the zoo is a particularly fecund place for gorillas, which have had a world-record number (47 at latest count) of captive births here. The annual Zoo Babies event in June, in which newborns of all sorts go on display, is among the zoo's most popular attractions. Newborns are on display all year at the nursery in the Joseph H. Spaulding Children's Zoo, a petting zoo that also includes the zoo's penguins and walrus (orangutans in Pampers climbing the jungle gym are a hit, and check out the subterranean view of prairie dogs and underwater view of the harbor seals).

Another popular attraction is Jungle Trails, a mock African and Asian rain forest that combines indoor and outdoor displays of rain-forest flora and fauna. You won't exactly be convinced you've been whisked off to Sumatra, but it's still quite nicely done. The wait can be as long as 30 minutes during peak times.

The Cat House (an ironic name for squeaky-clean Cincinnati) is a popular indoor exhibit of big cats from around the world in well-lit and nicely decorated glass-enclosed habitats. These vanishing animals are easy to find here.

Some of the other best or most popular displays include Insect World, a well-stocked insect house teeming with contained creepy-crawlies; Gorilla World, home of the zoo's extensive collection of lowland gorillas, headed by Colossus, a male silverback and one of the biggest lowland gorillas in captivity; Komodo

---

Two of the best places for home landscapers to get inspiration and a look at how various plants do in the Cincinnati climate are the Spring Grove Cemetery and Arboretum and the Cincinnati Zoo and Botanical Garden.

Dragons, with Indonesian lizards that are the world's largest (the zoo also holds the world record for hatching the most Komodo dragons); Big Cat Canyon, home of the zoo's white lions; the Cat Grotto, which houses the white tigers; the Nocturnal House, with everything from aardvarks to vampire bats (complete with bowls of blood for convenient sipping); Monkey Island, perhaps one of the most natural-looking habitats in the zoo, where monkeys frolic and otherwise interact, apparently oblivious to the crowds around them; the Bird House, home to many exotic and not-so-exotic birds; and the Bald Eagle, which can be found majestically perched within a large meshed-in habitat.

The Festival of Lights is held during the winter holidays from the week before Thanksgiving to January 1. More than two million lightbulbs are strung from just about everything that doesn't move and a few things that do. Ice-skating, hayrides, and ice carvings also add to a festive holiday mood.

For Halloween the zoo has a Hallzooween program with haunted trails and treats. It is held the two weekends before Halloween.

Kids also enjoy the train rides, which cost an extra $1.75 for adults and $1.50 for kids age 12 and younger. They give a good, if brief, overview of the park. Tram rides, which cost the same, last longer and are a good alternative.

With all the animals, many people forget the Botanical Garden part of the zoo. It contains an extensive collection of flora scattered throughout the site.

Admission to the zoo is $12.95 for adults, $7.95 for children ages 2 through 12, and $10.95 for seniors 62 and older, plus $6.50 for parking. You can buy a family membership for $79.00 or $65.00 for single parents; add $30.00 to include parking. (Metered street parking is also available near the zoo and is a good deal for nonmembers, but it's hard to come by.) A zoo pass gives you a first crack at new attractions (which come along fairly frequently), reduced-admission guest passes, 10 percent discount at zoo shops and educational classes, a monthly newsletter, neat-looking stickers for your car, and free admission to 100 other cooperating zoos around the country. You can get a credit for your admission toward annual membership if you visit. Strollers can be rented for $6.00.

The zoo is open daily 9:00 A.M. to 5:00 P.M. (8:00 A.M. to 6:00 P.M. from Memorial Day weekend to Labor Day weekend). Once in, you don't have to leave until 7:00 P.M. (or until 8:30 P.M. on Saturday) The Children's Zoo is open 10:00 A.M. to 4:00 P.M. The Festival of Lights holiday display is open 5:00 to 9:00 P.M. daily from late November through early January.

Fountain Square **Free**
Fifth and Vine Streets
No phone

The square is the heart of Cincinnati. It is where major events take place, such as Oktoberfest and the Reds World Series victory parties, and it's the place where downtown workers and visitors gather for lunch on warm days. The historical Tyler Davidson Fountain on the square was renovated in 2002, and the square was revamped in 2006.

Krohn Conservatory **Free**
Eden Park, access from Kemper Lane, Victory Parkway or Gilbert Avenue
(513) 421-5707

The massive conservatory, which is one of the largest public greenhouses in existence, grows 3,500 of the world's most exotic plants. The conservatory is divided into five areas. Palm House, Desert House, Tropical House, Orchid House, and a seasonal area that changes displays six times a year. The conservatory is especially popular during Easter with its lilies display and at Christmas with its poinsettias display. It's open daily 10:00 A.M. to 5:00 P.M. Donations are encouraged. There is a fee for the Butterfly show in May and June.

MainStrasse Village **Free**
Covington, KY
(859) 491-0458, (859) 357-6246
(24-hour special-event line)
www.mainstrasse.org

Cincinnati's German heritage is actually best commemorated south of the river in Covington. The 6 blocks making up MainStrasse Village in Covington is an area of restored 19th-century shops and homes retrofitted in a German motif. The area is home to several antiques shops, a playground for kids, and fine restaurants (see listings for Dee Felice Cafe and Wertheim's in the Restaurants chapter).

The Germany portrayed at MainStrasse should be known as "land of many festivals." Area businesses hold Mardi Gras in February, a Maifest in May, Goetta Festival in June, and an Oktoberfest in September (usually a couple of weeks before Cincinnati's Oktoberfest, also in September. Go figure). That should help you meet your beer, brat, and German puff pastry quota for the year. A Christmas Open House in late November is another popular attraction.

Of particular interest is the Carroll Chimes Bell Tower, a 43-bell carillon. It chimes on the hour and is followed by a miniconcert and a show of the mechanical figures in the bell tower, which act out *The Pied Piper of Hamelin*. The tower is lighted after dark from April through December.

Another attraction is the Goose Girl Fountain, a life-size sculpture of a German maiden carrying two geese to market. Greek-born sculptor Eleftherios Kardoulias threw away the mold after he made this one, so you won't see any others.

Look for MainStrasse just east of the Radisson Hotel Riverview, the giant scalloped cylinder just off Interstate 75's first Covington exit south of the Ohio River.

Meier's Wine Cellars **Free**
6955 Plainfield Road, Silverton
(513) 891-2900
www.meierswinecellars.com

Meier's offers a guided tour explaining how wine is made, with a tasting room as the pièce de résistance. OK, so Ohio wine is not exactly Bordeaux. But the video tour is free. Tours are available Monday through Saturday on the hour from 9:00 A.M. to 5:00 P.M. Take I-71 exit 12 to Montgomery Road, then head 1.5 miles west to Plainfield Road.

Newport Aquarium **$$$**
1 Aquarium Way, Newport, KY
(859) 261-7444
www.newportaquarium.com

Opening in 1999, the aquarium has quickly become a favorite attraction. The privately funded $40 million facility is on the banks of the Ohio River in Newport and has sharks, penguins, and alligators among its 11,000 animals of 600 different species.

It is the cornerstone of Newport on the Levee a 10-acre entertainment district that also includes a 21-screen AMC Theater, restaurants, and shops.

The aquarium is open 365 days a year. Hours are Sunday through Friday from 10:00 A.M. to 6:00 P.M., till 9:00 P.M. on Saturday from Memorial Day to Labor Day, and from 10:00 A.M. to 6:00 P.M. from Labor Day to Memorial Day.

Admission is $17.95 for an adult, $10.95 for a child 3 to 12, and $15.95 for seniors over age 65. Memberships are $33.90 for an adult, $19.90 for a child 12 and younger, and $29.90 for seniors over age 65.

OMNIMAX Theater **$$**
1301 Western Avenue
(513) 287-7000
www.cincymuseum.org

This state-of-the-art theater is part of the Museum Center at Union Terminal. Using special technology, OMNIMAX shows movies on a five-story, 260-degree domed screen that wraps around the seats and gives viewers a feeling of being in the picture. Some of the movies shown include a trip on the space shuttle, a dive into shark-infested waters, a trip across Alaska, and a Rolling Stones concert. A debate rages about which scene is scarier: the sharks attacking or Mick Jagger's lips enlarged on a five-story screen. Tickets are $7.25 for adults, $5.25 for children

If you are a season pass holder to Kings Island, you can enter the Water Park at 10:00 A.M., an hour before it opens, to get that great seat near the wave pool or your favorite wading pool. However, you cannot swim or go on any of the waterslides before 11:00 A.M. Ride the rides in the rest of the park and come back when you're hot and sweaty.

ages 3 through 12, and $6.25 for seniors age 65 and older. Showtimes vary depending on the day and the movie.

Purple People Bridge Climb $$$$
Newport on the Levee, Newport, KY
(859) 261-OVER

The Purple People Bridge Climb is the city's newest tourist attraction. If you're 12 and over, you can scale the bridge—140 feet above the Ohio River—on a vertical stroll up on special catwalks that have been installed for safety. Walkers are tethered with cables and wear special purple and yellow jumpsuits outfitted with helmets and radio headsets. Hours are sunrise to sunset. Tickets are $59.95 for a day climb and $79.95 for sunrise, sunset, and moonlight climbs on the span. Reservations are recommended.

Spring Grove Cemetery & Arboretum Free
4521 Spring Grove Avenue
(513) 681-6680
www.springgrove.org

There aren't many cemeteries you'd go out of your way to visit if you didn't have a loved one there, but this is one of them. Spring Grove Cemetery is renowned throughout the area for its landscaping. Maps available at the front office can help you find and identify the wide variety of vegetation. This is not just a spring or summer trip, for the landscape has been designed for year-round appeal. Grounds are open 8:00 A.M. to 6:00 P.M. daily.

Valley Vineyards Free
2276 East U.S. Highway 22, Morrow
(513) 899-2485
www.valley-vineyards.com

You can see the wine-making process from the wine to the bottle and sample some while you're at it. Wine making can be viewed from late August to early October, but Valley Vineyards is also open the rest of the year, offering tours of storage facilities, wine, and food. The tours are free, as is a taste of the wine. But the food isn't. The restaurant also has steak cookouts on Friday and Saturday nights. Hours are Monday through Thursday 11:00 A.M. to 8:00 P.M., Friday and Saturday 11:00 A.M. to 11:00 P.M. and Sunday 1:00 to 6:00 P.M. Take U.S. Highway 22 northeast to 2.5 miles south of Morrow. You can also get here from the Little Miami Scenic River Bike Trail.

World Peace Bell Free
Block between Monmouth and York Streets, between Fourth and Fifth Streets, Newport, KY
(859) 581-2971

On New Year's Eve 2000, the whole country got to see part of the area's newest attraction—the World Peace Bell. It rang in the new year in 2000 for every time zone in the world and got a few minutes on national television. Organizers of the 2000 event say the Millennium Center will become the new place to ring in the new year for area residents. The peace bell was cast in France and weighs 60,000 pounds. It is the largest free-swinging bell in the world at 12 feet high and 12 feet wide. There also is a walkway to the bell, so you can actually touch it. The bell swings every day at noon.

MUSEUMS

African American Museum of the Arts Consortium of Cincinnati, Free
Union Terminal, 1301 Western Avenue
(513) 381-0645

This is the only free museum in the Museum Center. It is located on the lower level of the terminal, near the historical society offices and the entrance to the OMNIMAX theater. It is a small facility, but it's full of historical tidbits and African-American art. The museum was established in 1993 during Black History Month. The front part of the museum features local African-American artists. In the back area of the museum is the history of black Cincinnati from 1800 to 1950 in displays of pictures and artifacts.

The museum is open from 9:00 A.M. to 5:00 P.M. Monday through Friday and 10:00 A.M. to 4:00 P.M. Saturday. It is closed Monday, Tuesday, and on holidays. Groups and tours are by appointment.

Behringer-Crawford Museum $
1600 Montague Road, Covington, KY
(859) 491-4003
www.bcmuseum.org

This museum in Devou Park has a fantastic setting overlooking the Ohio River valley. The house is rich in character, dating from 1848. And the collection is truly ancient, with items spanning back 450 million years. The museum is packed with natural and cultural memorabilia and artifacts from Northern Kentucky's past: wildlife, 19th-century history, industry, transportation, archaeology, and paleontology. Hours are 10:00 A.M. to 5:00 P.M. Tuesday through Friday and 1:00 to 5:00 P.M. weekends.

Butler County Historical Society Museum $
327 North Second Street, Hamilton
(513) 896-9930

Occupying the 1861 Victorian home of the Benninghofen family, this museum offers period decorations and artifacts gathered in Butler County from the pioneer days until the turn of the 19th century. Admission is charged for everyone age 12 and older. The museum is open 11:00 A.M. to 4:00 P.M. Tuesday through Sunday.

Chateau LaRoche $
12025 Shore Drive, Loveland
(513) 683-4686
www.lovelandcastle.com

Sir Harry Andrews began building this medieval-style castle on his heavily wooded estate outside Loveland in 1929. Today it's open to the public through the work of the Knights of the Golden Trail. It's also the perfect locale for a haunted house, which runs for three weekends in October. This Loveland landmark is open 11:00 A.M. to 5:00 P.M. weekends April through early September. Hours for the haunted house are 7:00 to 11:00 P.M. on Friday and Saturday.

Cinergy Children's Museum $$
Union Terminal, 1301 Western Avenue
(513) 287-7000
www.cincymuseum.com

The Cinergy Children's Museum at the Museum Center opened in 1998 and is a wonderful addition to Union Terminal. The museum teaches children about different concepts through play. Areas include Waterworks, Woods, Children Just Like Me, Energy Zone, Kidstown, and Little Sprouts Farm, a special play area for children under age four.

Its hours are 10:00 A.M. to 5:00 P.M. Monday through Saturday, 11:00 A.M. to 6:00 P.M. Sunday. Admission is $7.25 for adults, $5.25 for kids under age 12. Combination tickets for Union Terminal's other attractions are also available. But the best bet has to be the museum membership. It's $99.00 for families. (See the Kidstuff chapter for more information.)

Cincinnati Art Museum Free
953 Eden Park Drive
(513) 721-5204
www.cincinnatiartmuseum.com

The restored art museum has more than 118 galleries filled with paintings, prints, sculptures, drawings, photos, costumes, musical instruments, and other forms of visual arts spanning 5,000 years. (See the chapter on the Arts for more details.)

Cincinnati Fire Museum $$
315 West Court Street
(513) 621-5553
www.cincyfiremuseum.com

In 1852 Cincinnati became the first city to

use a steam fire engine, making it the model for other city fire departments, and it has collected memorabilia ever since. Located in the firehouse built for horse-drawn engines back in 1907, the museum includes a look at fire trucks over the years, the first fire alarm in Cincinnati, helmets, badges, shields, and other equipment. Children like the interactive computer displays and the wonderful hands-on displays, including a fire pole they can slide down and the cab of a 1995 fire truck that allows them to operate the sirens and lights. The museum emphasizes teaching fire prevention and includes a safe house where children are taught the stop, drop, and roll technique. Hours are 10:00 A.M. to 4:00 P.M. Tuesday through Friday and noon to 4:00 P.M. weekends. Admission is $6.00 for adults, $4.00 for children ages 2 through 12, and $5.00 for seniors age 65 and older. Older folks are kept from hogging the fire pole so the kids can have fun.

Cincinnati Museum Center $$-$$$
Union Terminal, 1301 Western Avenue
(513) 287-7000, (800) 733-2077
www.cincymuseum.org

Cincinnati's once-grand railroad station, Union Terminal, has been converted into the area's home of history. Inside the massive half-dome structure are the Museum of Natural History & Science, the Cincinnati Historical Society's Library, the Cincinnati History Museum, the Cinergy Children's Museum, and the Robert D. Lindner Family OMNIMAX Theater.

Within the Museum Center are displays showing the history of Cincinnati and the region, as well as permanent and rotating displays about the history of the world. The museum makes good use of today's technology with plenty of hands-on, interactive exhibits.

Cincinnati's history can be traced through its various stages, starting at the Ice Age. The Clues Frozen in Time display takes visitors back to the days when ice was carving out our seven hills. Visitors are led through a chilly, mist-enhanced meltwater channel of a replica glacier. Musk ox, woolly mammoths, saber-toothed tigers, and other ancient creatures that once roamed the area lurk amid the displays. A mastodon that got stuck in a salt lick struggles to get free just a few feet from the pathway.

A replica of the Cincinnati riverfront during the early years shows how the city was founded and the importance of the river to its development. The display includes a 94-foot-long replica steamboat, a reproduction of the Public Landing circa 1850, and a 50-foot model of the Miami and Erie Canal.

Visitors can walk through a man-made replica of a Kentucky limestone cave, which is so realistic that the temperature stays at a constant 52 degrees. The cave includes a waterfall, dome pit, stalagmites, stalactites, and, of course, just like real caves, live bats. (OK, so they're blocked off from the inside of the cave with Plexiglas, but they're there during some parts of the year.)

The Children's Discovery Center in the Natural History and Science Museum offers hands-on exhibits that introduce children to the human body and demonstrate how humans have adapted to and changed their environment. Various traveling exhibits can also be found at the Museum Center.

The Historical Society has one of the nation's largest regional research libraries. Restaurants and shops are available in the outer terminal if you need a break. Or the OMNIMAX theater offers movies on its giant, domed screen.

The museum is open 10:00 A.M. to 5:00 P.M. Monday through Saturday and 11:00 A.M. to 6:00 P.M. Sunday. Three-way combo tickets for the Museum of Natural History, the Historical Society, and the OMNIMAX theater are $13.25 for adults, $9.25 for children ages 3 through 12, and $4.25 for children under age 3. Two-way combo tickets are $10.25 for adults and $7.25 for children. Tickets to just one of the museums are $7.25 for adults and $5.25 for children. Membership to the

Museum Center is $79.00 for an individual, $99.00 for a family.

Gray Wireless Communications Museum **Free**
1223 Central Parkway
(513) 381-4033

Cincinnati native Powel Crosley was a pioneer in the broadcast communications industry, manufacturing affordable radios and televisions and then founding WLW radio and WLWT television so buyers had something to tune in to. Crosley was always experimenting, and many of the remnants of his experiments—both the successes and the failures—are displayed in the studios of WCET television. Other artifacts from the early days of wireless communications fill glass cabinets. The museum is open 9:00 A.M. to 4:00 P.M. Monday through Friday.

Hauck House Museum **$**
812 Dayton Street
(513) 563-9484

Hauck House is a museum about how the other half lived during the late Victorian age. Built during the Civil War, it gives an interpretive tour of how a wealthy family lived in the late 1800s. The house was the home of John Hauck, a German immigrant and prominent Cincinnatian who made a fortune in brewing. (Dayton Street was once known as Millionaires' Row.) The museum is open noon to 3:00 P.M. Friday and noon to 4:00 P.M. the last two Saturdays of the month. Group tours are available by appointment.

Hillel Jewish Student Center at the University of Cincinnati **Free**
Rose Warner House, 2615 Clifton Avenue
(513) 221-6728
www.hillelcincinnati.org

A number of relics from former synagogues are housed here, including stained-glass windows and important papers. The highlight of the museum is the Lion's Den, which has several different lions from various synagogues, including one in Newport, Kentucky. The lions apparently once guarded a Torah ark and a 6-foot memorial tablet. The museum is open 9:00 A.M. to 5:00 P.M. Monday through Thursday and Friday 9:00 A.M. to 3:00 P.M.

Indian Hill Historical Museum **Free**
8100 Given Road, Indian Hill
(513) 891-1873

Better known as the Little Red Schoolhouse, this one-room schoolhouse was built in 1874 and used until 1935. It is now a museum for historical material significant to the Indian Hill area. It's open by appointment only.

Legends Museum at Cincinnati Gardens **Free**
2250 Seymour Avenue, Norwood
(513) 351-3999

This is a memorabilia museum celebrating 50 years at the Cincinnati Gardens. During the early years, there was basketball, boxing, and hockey. The facility also served as a concert venue and has hosted such stars as the Beatles, Elvis, and Madonna. It had NBA basketball, minor league hockey, and has been home of both local Division I basketball teams. And don't forget the circus—the facility still hosts a circus each year. The museum is on the second floor of the facility and is open during Gardens' events or by appointment.

Loveland Historical Museum **Free**
201 Riverside Drive, Loveland
(513) 683-5692

The Loveland Museum displays material relevant to the history of the town, including artwork by local artists. The museum is open Friday through Sunday 1:00 to 4:30 P.M. and by appointment.

McGuffey Museum at Miami University **Free**
410 East Spring Street, Oxford
(513) 529-8380

This museum is the former home of William Holmes McGuffey and a depository of the works of McGuffey, who taught the world through his innovative *McGuffey Readers*. He was a professor at Miami University. Hours are 1:00 to 5:00 P.M. Tuesday to Sunday.

National Underground Railroad Freedom Center **$$$**
50 East Freedom Way
(513) 333-7500, (877) 648-4838
www.freedomcenter.org

The Freedom Center opened in 2004 between the Great American Ball Park and Paul Brown Stadium on the riverfront.

The center has 158,000 square feet of space, including 38,000 square feet of exhibit space, a 325-seat auditorium, a full-service cafe, and an 8,000-square-foot Welcome Hall. It tells the story of the Underground Railroad through interactive learning experiences. (See this chapter's close-up about the museum for more details about its features.)

The center is open 11:00 A.M. to 5:00 P.M. Tuesday through Sunday. Admission is $12.00 for adults, $10.00 for students and seniors, and $8.00 for children 6 through 12.

Pyramid Hill Sculpture Park **$**
1763 Hamilton-Cleves Road
(513) 868-8336
www.pyramidhill.org

If you don't want to visit a stuffy art museum to see some art, visit the Pyramid Hill Sculpture Park in Hamilton. It is a 265-acre park with 35 sculptures. You can either drive through the park or hike on one of several trails in the park. The park also offers summer programs for children. It is open 10:00 A.M. to 6:00 P.M. Tuesday through Sunday April through October. From November to March, it is open 8:00 A.M. to 5:00 P.M. weekdays and 10:00 A.M. to 4:00 P.M. weekends.

Railway Museum of Greater Cincinnati **$**
315 West Southern Avenue, Covington, KY
(859) 491-7245
www.cincirailmuseum.org

A collection of 80 locomotive and train cars sits in a four-acre rail yard in Covington, Kentucky, showing how life on the railroad used to be. Included in the collection are a rail post-office car, an open-platform business car from 1939, a Pullman troop sleeper, and a 1939 sleeping car. The museum is open 10:00 A.M. to 4:00 P.M. Wednesday and Saturday year-round and 12:30 to 4:30 P.M. on the fourth Sunday May through October.

Shawnee Lookout Archaeological Museum **$**
Shawnee Lookout Park, Cleves
(513) 521-7275

Prehistoric Indian artifacts dating from 14,000 B.C., which were discovered during archaeological digs in the area, are on display in the Shawnee Lookout Park. Admission is free with a Hamilton County Park Sticker ($5.00 per year), and the museum is open the same hours as the park.

Skirball Museum at Hebrew Union College **Free**
3101 Clifton Avenue
(513) 221-1875

Biblical sources of contemporary Jewish celebration and holidays are shown by means of displays of ancient artifacts and modern objects. The museum also displays the history of Hebrew Union College in Cincinnati. The museum is open Monday through Thursday 11:00 A.M. to 4:00 P.M., closed Friday and Saturday, and open Sunday noon to 5:00 P.M.

Taft Museum of Art **$$**
316 Pike Street
(513) 241-0343
www.taftmuseum.org

The Tafts' massive home was built in 1820 and is now a 30-room museum for the family's art collection, one of the greatest private collections in the country. Chinese porcelains from the Qing and Ming dynasties, French enamels, and paintings by Rembrandt, Duncanson, Van Dyke, Whistler, and Grandma Moses fill the home. (See the Arts chapter for details.)

Vent Haven Museum $
33 West Maple Avenue, Fort Mitchell, KY
(859) 341-0461
www.venthavenmuseum.com
Vent Haven is a museum for dummies. It houses the largest collection of ventriloquist dolls—about 500—including some that belonged to Edgar Bergen. The museum is open Monday through Friday May through September by appointment only.

Warren County Historical Society Museum $
109 South Broadway, Lebanon
(513) 932-1817
www.wchsmuseum.org
This three-story museum shows the development of southwestern Ohio from prehistoric days through the 19th century. It includes an award-winning Shaker gallery as well as an extensive genealogy library, fossil collection, Native American artifacts, and a re-creation of an 1860s village. The museum is open 9:00 A.M. to 4:00 P.M. Tuesday through Saturday and noon to 4:00 P.M. Sunday.

HISTORIC ATTRACTIONS

Dinsmore Homestead $
5654 Burlington Pike, Burlington, KY
(859) 586-6117
www.dinsmorefarm.org
The Dinsmore Homestead is a museum of real life, offering no fancy memorabilia, just an example of early Kentucky farm life from its beginnings in 1842 through the five generations who maintained it. The homestead is visitor friendly, allowing guests to wander through the main house and outbuildings such as the wagon shed, cookhouse, and wine house. The homestead is open April through December 1:00 to 5:00 P.M. Wednesday, Saturday, and Sunday. Take I-75 to Kentucky 18 and go west about 10 miles.

Findlay Market Free
Race and Elder Streets
(513) 352-6364
www.findlaymarket.org
This open-air marketplace has been the city's connection to fresh fruits, vegetables, meats, and cheeses since 1852. It's like a trip back to the early days of the last century—hot-dog links strung over wire, whole fish on ice inside a display case, every edible part of a pig, chicken, or cow cut up and being hawked by fifth-generation mom-and-pop vendors with long white aprons and pencils stuck behind their ears. The market is open year-round Wednesday through Sunday. Get there early for the pick of the produce. Findlay Market also hosts the Reds annual opening day parade.

Fort Ancient Museum $$
Ohio Highway 350 near Middleboro Road, Lebanon
(513) 932-4421
Fort Ancient is more than just the museum. The 100-acre park features prehistoric earthworks and remains of village sites built by the ancient Hopewell Indian tribe and other Native Americans since the Ice Age. The circular mounds were used as a sort of sundial calendar. The museum illustrates the religion, culture, and customs of the prehistoric Hopewell people. Picnic facilities and hiking trails are available to help make this a well-rounded day trip.

The park is open 10:00 A.M. to 5:00 P.M. Wednesday through Saturday, noon to 5:00 P.M. on Sunday. Closed October through March. Admission is $7.00 for adults, $3.00 for children ages 6 to 12. Ohio Historical Society members get in free.

Harriet Beecher Stowe House Free
2950 Gilbert Avenue
(513) 221-7900
Harriet Beecher Stowe lived in Cincinnati for 19 years, and it is here that she became familiar with the concept of slavery and formulated the thoughts and experiences that led to the writing of *Uncle Tom's*

CLOSE-UP

The Path of Freedom

The National Underground Railroad Freedom Center has taken center stage along the riverfront in Cincinnati. Saddled between the Reds' new ballpark and the Bengals' stadium, the center is dwarfed in comparison. But it is large in its mission and exhibits.

The museum, which tells the story of the Underground Railroad of slaves crossing the Ohio River to freedom, has a slave pen on its second floor. The cabin was moved from rural Kentucky and once held slaves who were ready to be sold. The center says its purpose is to recount and connect the powerful American story of freedom from slavery to issues of freedom today. The Freedom Center uses history exhibits, educational programs, research, interactive and simulation media, and live performances to inspire visitors with a renewed commitment to citizenship and civic engagement.

The struggles for freedom for all people include the Civil Rights Movement and events of the 19th and 20th century, including struggles in Poland, South Africa, and India. One of the unique experiences at the museum is the third-floor pavilion, where attendees are asked to reflect, respond, and resolve.

"What we want to do is look at history . . . and to think about it what it means for me today. What kind of things can I do today?" asks Spencer Crew, the president of the center.

"Our mission is to create a safe place for a dialogue and discussion that will inform modern-day freedom conductors," says Ed Rigaud, who helped plan and build the facility. "To eradicate the negative legacy of slavery. We will emphasize the triumphs, not the agony. If we don't engage in dialogue, there won't be healing. Until we confront it, we're not going to make much progress in a positive, productive way."

Cabin. The home where she lived for a short time features family pictures and copies of her journal and manuscripts. Hours are Tuesday and Wednesday 10:00 A.M. to 2:00 P.M. by appointment only. Donations are accepted.

Sharon Woods Park and Heritage Village **$$**
U.S. Highway 42, Sharonville
(513) 563-9484
www.heritagevillagecincinnati.org

A 19th-century village has been re-created here, with nine buildings, including a train station, a doctor's office, a church, and a jail. All of the buildings are furnished with 19th-century Ohio-made furniture and decorations. The village is open Wednesday through Saturday noon to 4:00 P.M. and 1:00 to 5:00 P.M. Sunday May through October. The village is decorated for Christmas each December and open on weekends during November and December. Admission is $7.00 for adults, $6.00 for seniors 65 and older, and $5.00 for children ages 6 through 12. Take I-275 east off I-75, or west off I-71 to US 42; go south a mile to the park entrance.

This is the slave pen that is on the second floor of the musem. It was dismantled from a Kentucky farm and rebuilt in the museum. COURTESY OF THE NATIONAL UNDERGROUND RAILROAD FREEDOM CENTER

Cincinnati is the right place for the Freedom Center, says Rigaud, even though there are racial problems here. "History supports it. Over half the escapes occurred somewhere in the Ohio River corridor. Cincinnati was the hotbed of activity."

It still is. The $110 million facility opened in August 2004, and more than 330,000 people have visited the museum since then. Even the architecture and the landscape design have special meaning. The winding curves and pathways from the Ohio River symbolize the move from the Old South to freedom in the North.

Ulysses S. Grant Homestead **$**
East Grant and Water Streets
Georgetown
(937) 378-4222
www.usgrantboyhoodhome.org

Artist John Ruthven renovated the two-story boyhood home of our 18th president. It is now owned by the state of Ohio. Memorabilia and period furnishings are displayed throughout. The home is open Wednesday through Sunday noon to 5:00 P.M. Memorial Day to Labor Day and noon to 5:00 P.M. Saturday and Sunday in September and October.

William Howard Taft Home **Free**
2038 Auburn Avenue
(513) 684-3362

This 150-year-old home is the birthplace and boyhood home of the 27th president of the United States and the 10th chief justice of the United States. Exhibits of his life are displayed. The home is run by the National Park Service and is open 8:00 A.M. to 4:00 P.M. daily.

RIVER FUN

Without the Ohio River, there would be no Greater Cincinnati. Though it may not be steeped in quite as much lore as the Mississippi, the Ohio is what ties the tristate area together historically and recreationally.

The average depth of the Ohio in front of Cincinnati is 26 feet. Flood stage is 52 feet. And, boy, do we flood! The Great Flood of 1937 decimated the city. In the spring of 1997, the river spilled millions of gallons of water into the downtown area, wiping out the Children's Museum as well as numerous riverfront businesses—a reminder that the river is never to be taken lightly, even in this age of flood walls.

The river brings good things too. Since the dams were built in 1929 (ironically to ensure a minimum water depth), river trade has increased more than 800 percent. You'll see lots of barges slowly plying their way on the Ohio any day of the week. Two-thirds of all river freight is some type of energy-producing commodity: coal, coke, petroleum. Every kilowatt of electricity in the area is produced from coal, which arrives by river barge.

All that commerce and industry has its downside, of course. The river may be beautiful, but the adjective "pristine" does not apply. "Look but don't touch" might be the best way to approach the Ohio River. Water quality has improved over the last two decades, but let's face it: Cincinnati is downriver from many industrial areas and the city itself contributes more than its fair share of pollution.

Most of the year, swimming in the river is technically OK—at least in the select areas not afflicted by a mean undertow. But during the summer months, the Cincinnati Health Department frequently issues advisories not to swim in the river because of high concentrations of bacterial nasties. At any time of year, there are hundreds of better and safer places to swim than the Ohio River. See Coney Island and the other water parks in the Attractions chapter as well as the numerous swimming opportunities outlined in the Parks and Recreation chapter.

Fishing is OK too. Fish are more numerous and healthier now than in the '70s, but all three states warn to steer clear of eating walleye, carp, channel catfish, white bass, and paddlefish caught in the Ohio. High levels of chlordane and PCBs are sometimes found in these bottom feeders. Fishing, boating, and other river sports are covered in detail in the Parks and Recreation chapter.

The centerpiece of the river is the Tall Stacks festival (due again in 2009—see the close-up in this chapter). But there's life on the river every day of the year—even when it freezes over, as it did back in the 1970s and crazy people walked from Ohio to Kentucky without benefit of a bridge!

A few years ago, if you were talking river attractions in the region, you might be talking about boating. Or Jet Skiing. Or even marine fireworks displays. Today you're talking casino gambling. In fact, one of the world's largest riverboat casinos, the *Argosy VI*, is harbored in Lawrenceburg, Indiana, a few minutes downstream from Cincinnati. That once-sleepy little town has fast become the most popular tourist destination in the region. And a bit farther along the river is the (for now) sleepy burg of Rising Sun, with yet another riverboat casino, the *Grand Victoria II*.

And now a word about the geography of the Ohio River valley and its corresponding weather patterns: If you think "Ohio" is a synonym for "flat cornfields," you couldn't be more wrong. Courtesy of the glaciers and the sweeping cut of the Ohio River, this part of Ohio is steep and hilly, making for attractive overlooks where the river and the scenic towns combine for a

	Average temperature	Average rainfall	Average snowfall
January	28	3 inches	7 inches
February	32	3 inches	5 inches
March	43	4 inches	4 inches
April	53	4 inches	
May	63	4 inches	
June	71	4 inches	
July	75	4 inches	
August	74	3 inches	
September	67	3 inches	
October	55	3 inches	
November	44	3 inches	1 inch
December	33	3 inches	4 inches

picturesque panorama—framed by paddle wheelers and other sorts of river traffic and pleasure boating.

But there's a downside: As one local television weathercaster used to quip, "Don't like the weather? Don't worry. It will change in just one minute." Indeed, the Ohio River valley weather fronts are notoriously fickle and capricious: one moment, sunny; the next, drizzling rain.

Despite all the attention the gambling riverboats are getting, they are by no means the only attractions on the Ohio River (or the Little Miami, the Great Miami, or the Licking Rivers, for that matter). Read on.

RIVERBOAT GAMBLING

Riverboat gambling is illegal in Ohio and Kentucky, but not in Indiana. A 20- to 25-minute drive from downtown Cincinnati lands you in Lawrenceburg, Indiana, home of the *Argosy VI*. The *Grand Victoria II* docks in Rising Sun, a bit farther downriver. And the Belterra Casino Resort opened near Vevay in 2000.

The *Argosy VI* floating casino quickly became the region's top tourist attraction when it opened in 1998, outpacing even Paramount's Kings Island and the venerable Cincinnati Reds—*Argosy* still ranks as the No. 1 floating operation among the 75 riverboat casinos in America in terms of monthly wagering (averaging half a billion—yes, billion—dollars a month).

The *Argosy* greeted more than eight million visitors last year. By comparison, the *Grand Victoria II* saw some three million visitors the same year, while the Belterra Casino Resort averaged 1.4 million. (Please note that all guests at the casinos must be 21 years of age or older.)

Whichever riverboat you choose from the list below, enjoy your day (or night) of gaming. Just don't go overboard.

In addition to these existing riverboat gambling operations, there are more far-flung gaming vessels such as the *Casino Aztar* in Evansville, Indiana. Consult the Indiana Tourism Board for details on these boats that seem to line the Ohio River all the way through Indiana.

Argosy VI
777 East Eads Parkway,
Lawrenceburg, IN
(888) ARGOSY7

Lawrenceburg is currently the destination of choice for most gamblers. It's closer to Cincinnati than Rising Sun and the other vessels, and the riverboat operation there is one of the biggest. From downtown Cincinnati, the quickest route

Flooding at Riverbend Music Center is practically a rite of spring; the Ohio River overflows its banks, canceling scores of concerts. With any springtime Riverbend concert, it's wise to call for a flood-stage status report before you leave.

to Indiana is (trust us) via Kentucky. Take Interstate 471 or Interstate 75 south and pick up Interstate 275 west. Immediately upon crossing the Ohio River into Indiana, take the first exit (16). From there, numerous signs point you to Lawrenceburg and the casino. (From the Cincinnati/Northern Kentucky International Airport, you're even closer—about a 15-minute drive.)

The *Argosy VI* is the length of a football field, with three decks. Not only is it one of the largest riverboat casinos in the world, it's one of the two largest passenger vessels of any kind on America's inland waterways. Passenger capacity is 4,000, with a crew of 400. The gaming areas are certainly roomier and better ventilated than those in most casinos we've seen, riverboat or otherwise. There are 104 table games and 1,870 slot machines. The tables include blackjack, roulette, Caribbean stud, minibaccarat, and craps, and there's a full array of video poker units. Plenty of ATMs are onboard. High rollers have their own stake on the third deck, the high-denomination area.

Nonsmoking areas are available. A snack shop on the third deck purveys hot dogs and sub sandwiches, and free munchies such as cheese cubes and carrot sticks are available. The adjoining resort hotel has full-service restaurants.

Indiana law no longer requires the riverboat to cruise to the middle of the river for gambling, so it remains docked. See the Hotels and Motels chapter (West section) for information on the adjoining Argosy Casino Resort.

Belterra Casino Resort
777 Belterra Drive, Belterra, IN
(888) BELTERRA

Belterra Casino Resort is located 1 mile north of the Markland Locks and Dam in Switzerland County, Indiana, near Florence and Vevay, about 45 minutes southwest of Cincinnati. Take Interstate 71 south to the Warsaw/Sparta ramp (exit 57), then follow Kentucky Highway 35 to where it intersects with U.S. Highway 42, turn left on US 42 and follow it to cross the Markland Bridge, then turn left to the casino.

The *Miss Belterra* riverboat casino, operated by the Pinnacle Corporation, measures 100 feet wide by 370 feet long, employs 1,500 people, and boasts 57 game tables and 1,350 slot machines amid the 38,000 square feet of gaming space on two levels. Table games include blackjack, craps, roulette, Caribbean stud poker, and baccarat. Other games include American Beauty, Cast for Cash, Triple Cash, Triple Play, Game King, Money to Burn, and Monopoly.

Belterra charges no admission, and it offers free live music as well. State law no longer requires the *Miss Belterra* to leave the dock.

The Center Stage Concert Hall in the nearby 15-story hotel features the likes of Alabama, Dan Fogelberg, the Doobie Brothers, Stephen Stills, Smokey Robinson, the Beach Boys, and America (ticket prices vary, usually from $20 to $50). See the Hotels and Motels chapter (West section) for information on the adjoining Belterra Casino Resort Hotel.

Caesars
Caesars Indiana Casino/Hotel,
Indiana Highway 111 on the riverfront,
Bridgeport, IN
(888) 766-2648

This Caesars casino is a bit farther downriver (about two to two-and-a-half hours), but the trip might be worth it to those in the market for pure opulence. Located a few miles from Louisville, *Caesars* is the world's largest gaming vessel. The $50 million casino offers 2,800 slot machines, as well as 140 blackjack, roulette, baccarat, and craps tables.

Opened in 1998, the boat contains an impressive 93,000 square feet of gaming space. The vessel is divided into seven themed casinos on its four decks, each representing an era in world history. State law no longer requires *Caesars* to cruise, so you can enter and leave the docked vessel at will.

Grand Victoria II
600 Grand Victoria Drive, Rising Sun, IN
(800) GRAND-11
Rising Sun is about 45 minutes from downtown Cincinnati (just follow the above directions to Lawrenceburg, then drive west on U.S. Highway 50 for 8 miles, then jog onto Indiana Highway 56, which takes you into Rising Sun). The *Grand Victoria II* is a replica of a 19th-century Victorian stern-wheeler, with 1,900 gaming positions and 1,302 slot machines. Some 80 tables offer blackjack, craps, roulette, Caribbean stud, and Let It Ride. Passenger capacity is 2,700.

Due to changes in Indiana law, the vessel is no longer required to leave its dock for gambling.

There's more here than just a casino, though. The Hyatt Corporation runs an 1890s Indiana theme resort centered around the casino. The 300-acre resort features a 200-room hotel, a health club, a Wellington's steak house, gift shops, the Victoria pub, Picadilly's delicatessen, and other amenities, all set in a Victorian motif on cobblestone, gaslit streets. A concert hall features the likes of Engelbert Humperdinck, Crystal Gale, Kansas, Wayne Newton, and Loretta Lynn. The Links at Grand Victoria is the new 18-hole golf course. Rising Sun does have some small motels and a few bed-and-breakfasts, but you really shouldn't miss the resort experience. See the Hotels and Motels chapter (West) for more information on the adjoining Hyatt casino resort hotel.

RIVERBOAT CRUISES

Dozens of riverboat cruise lines and charter services offer trips on the waters of the Ohio, from sightseeing tours to romantic moonlight voyages. Some of these charter lines' brochures claim that they require a minimum party of 20 or even 50 people. You should know that there is considerable leeway in these numbers, especially if a charter has empty seats to fill on any given departure date. Call first and negotiate. In all cases, reservations are a must. Here are some of the more popular charters.

BB Riverboats
1 Riverboat Row, Newport, KY
(859) 261-8500
BB offers dozens of package cruises—sightseeing cruises, meal cruises, holiday cruises—aboard the open-air barge *RiverRaft*, the large-capacity *FunLiner*, the steamboat-era *River Queen*, or an authentic replica of a Mark Twain stern-wheeler. Especially popular are the one-day trips to nearby scenic river towns. Packages and prices vary greatly, depending on the ship, day of the week, season, and age of the ticket buyer. A popular day trip is the cruise to Rabbit Hash, Kentucky.

Delta Queen Steamboat Co.
30 Robin Street Wharf, New Orleans, LA
(800) 543-1949, (513) 762-3390
Although based in New Orleans, the *Delta Queen* and her sisters make stops in the Port of Cincinnati. The company offers trips on the nation's only overnight paddle wheelers, including the *Delta Queen*, the *Mississippi Queen*, and the *American Queen* (the world's largest steamboat). Prices vary greatly depending on the length of the cruise, the boat, and the type of stateroom or suite. A three-night cruise can cost anywhere from $1,205 to $1,997 (all prices per person).

Queen City Riverboat Cruises
303 O'Fallon Drive, Dayton, KY
(859) 292-8687

This company offers charter and regular public cruises aboard the *Spirit of Cincinnati* and the *Queen City Clipper* paddleboats. Meals can range from a continental breakfast to a formal dinner. Theme cruises include Monte Carlo night and Italian American night. Prices vary. A two-hour lunch on the *Spirit of Cincinnati,* for instance, starts at $27.95 with a buffet.

RiverBarge Excursion Lines Inc.
Port of Cincinnati, downtown
on the riverfront
(888) 456-2206
Sure, you can do a quick hop aboard a BB Riverboat or other such boat for an excursion downriver. But if you want a *real* family adventure, try the RiverBarge Excursion Lines Inc., which operates the 750-foot-long *R/B River Explorer,* a flat-bottomed vessel that plies the Ohio River. A round-trip "River to Rails" voyage that begins in Cincinnati continues to Ripley, Marietta, Portsmouth, and other points. Finally, voyagers hop aboard vintage 1920s rail cars and take a side trip to the Hocking River Valley.

***Satisfaction II* and *Satisfaction III* Yacht Charter Services Inc.**
4609 Kellogg Avenue, California
(513) 231-9042
These two luxurious yachts are available exclusively for corporate and private functions and accommodate 10 to 150 guests. Unlike many seasonal charters, the ships are fully enclosed and are in service year-round. Prices range from $50 to $125 per person.

RIVERSIDE THEATERS

Shadowbox Cabaret
1 Levee Way, Newport on the Levee, Newport, KY
(859) 581-7625
Shadowbox Cabaret is a combination theater, sketch comedy, and rock music club, presenting a rotating schedule of shows, nightly Wednesday through Saturday. Tickets are $20, $10 for students and seniors.

Showboat Majestic
Foot of Broadway at the Public Landing, downtown on the riverfront
(513) 241-6550
Walk the gangplank to the *Showboat Majestic* for such theatrical chestnuts as *A Funny Thing Happened on the Way to the Forum* and *The Odd Couple.* The floating theater hall is housed inside an 80-year-old riverboat, a National Historic Landmark.

PEDESTRIAN BRIDGES

Purple People Bridge
Spanning the Ohio River between Newport on the Levee in Newport, KY, and Cincinnati's Bicentennial Commons
(859) 581-7529
This pedestrian-only bridge opened in 2003 and presents the opportunity to stroll across the Ohio River. It's easiest to park in the Newport on the Levee, which has a 2,000-car parking garage. Then walk across the river to Bicentennial Commons—a park encompassing Sawyer Point, Yeatman's Cove, and the Serpentine Wall (a stepped and winding concrete walkway along the river). This is also a great way to get to Great American Ball Park without paying outrageous ballpark garage fees. (See the description of the Purple People Bridge Climb in the Attractions chapter.)

John Roebling Suspension Bridge
Between downtown Cincinnati and Covington, KY
The Covington-Cincinnati Suspension Bridge opened on December 2, 1866, when 120,000 people—half the population of Cincinnati—crossed the span on foot. The bridge, engineered by John Augustus Roebling, almost didn't get built, thanks to squabbling between the two states. No one had ever constructed an overpass across so wide a river as the Ohio; the impressive stone towers, linking the arched tension cables, rise 230 feet above water. (Roebling used this bridge

design as the prototype for his Brooklyn Bridge.) During the 1937 flood, the bridge was the only span above water—barely—along the entire length of the state. The steel structure—painted blue in 1976 and officially renamed the John A. Roebling Bridge in 1983—was made famous in a scene from the Tom Cruise film *Rain Man.*

RIVER MONUMENT

National Steamboat Monument
Public Landing, downtown on the riverfront, Cincinnati
The huge red paddle-wheel replica of the riverboat *American Queen* is billed as America's only monument to the steamboat age. The 60-ton paddle wheel is positioned atop two three-story towers. Working tall stacks release steam toots every minute.

FERRIES

Two water taxis regularly cross the Ohio River in the Cincinnati area. The Anderson ferry is primarily for commuters, but it has some recreational uses. The Augusta ferry is used mostly by tourists and sightseers.

Anderson Ferry
4030 River Road, Hebron, KY
(859) 485-9210
The Anderson ferry crosses the river about every 15 minutes between Hebron, Kentucky, and Delhi just below the Trolley Tavern. Hours are 6:00 A.M. to 7:00 P.M. November through April, and 6:00 A.M. to 8:00 P.M. May through October. On Sunday and holidays, the ferry doesn't open until 11:00 A.M. The cost is $3.00 per car each way. Smart commuters know this is the shortcut from the west side of Cincinnati to the Cincinnati/Northern Kentucky International Airport. You avoid the car-strangled spanner known as the I-75 bridge.

During major events such as Labor Day's Riverfest fireworks extravaganza, the Coast Guard closes the Ohio River to all traffic (perturbing vessels on their way to Pittsburgh, no end). Pleasure boaters need to know that no-wake zones are also in effect for 3 miles each way, upriver and downriver. And alcohol on boats is absolutely prohibited.

Augusta Ferry
U.S. Highway 52, about 5 miles from the Clermont County line
(606) 756-3291
From just west of Higginsport, about 5 miles from the Clermont County line on US 52, you can catch the Augusta ferry to Augusta, Kentucky. This ferry provides the only river crossing for 63 miles between Cincinnati and Maysville. Keep a keen eye on the road for a sign that points toward the river and says AUGUSTA, KY, 1 MILE. The ferry runs 8:00 A.M. to 8:00 P.M. daily, with between three and five departures an hour, depending on the number of cars waiting. Crossing time is 10 minutes and the cost is $5.00 per car.

RIVERFEST AND TALL STACKS

The city's two biggest public celebrations—one annual, the other occurring every three years—are Riverfest and Tall Stacks. Appropriately, both are centered around the Ohio River, the lifeline of the region.

Riverfest
On the Ohio River
(513) 352-4000
A half-million people jam the riverbanks every Labor Day weekend for Riverfest, better known to locals as the 'EBN Fireworks. There's music and food, to be sure, but the highlight of the festivities is a half hour of fireworks, synchronized to rock music broadcast on WEBN (102.7 FM). The fireworks are such a big deal around

CLOSE-UP

Cincinnati's Signature Event: Tall Stacks

Mark Twain loved 'em. Charles Dickens abhorred 'em. Whatever camp you happen to fall in, there's no escaping steamboats in Greater Cincinnati during "Tall Stacks" week.

The world's largest convocation of paddle wheelers, the Tall Stacks festival hit the Port of Cincinnati in October 2006 and will appear again in 2009. The triennial occasion has become Greater Cincinnati's signature event, a nautical and musical wonder that packs the city's riverfront with a million-plus gawkers as well as 17 vintage riverboats.

The five-day extravaganza on the Ohio River shoreline—formally titled the Tall Stacks Music, Arts & Heritage Festival—also boasts national-caliber concerts. On any given day at the festival, you can expect to hear the likes of Mary Chapin Carpenter, Shawn Colvin, Dar Williams, Ricky Scaggs, Nickel Creek, B. B. King, the Del McCoury Band, Lucinda Williams, Creedence Clearwater Revisited, Emmylou Harris, Bo Diddley, Patty Griffin, Steve Earle & the Dukes, Los Lobos, Blind Boys of Alabama, and more.

In 2006 general admission passes cost $22 for the five-day event ($20 if purchased in advance with Kroger Plus card at area Kroger stores) and allowed daily in-and-out privileges to the riverfront and concerts (but not access to the boats). Children 12 and under were admitted free.

Tickets to harbor jaunts and buffet banquets—which in 2006 ranged from $20 to $78—go fast on the boats. One of the more popular vessels is the *General Jackson,* which presents Opryland-style shows multiple times each day.

Cincinnati's Public Landing is ground zero for the festival. It's there you'll find all official ceremonies and boarding access to the steamboats, as well as the stages for musicians, barbershop quartets, storytellers, and more.

Many of the regular boats returned in 2006, plus four new vessels: the *Magnolia Belle, Natchez, Belle of Cincinnati,* and *Spirit of Peoria.* For information call (513) 562-4949 or visit www.tallstacks.com.

PARTICIPATING RIVERBOATS

Belle of Cincinnati
Home port: Newport, Kentucky
The flagship of BB Riverboats, the *Belle* was built in 1988 as a casino. The excursion boat features four decks, four dining rooms, and room for 1,000 guests. She made her first Tall Stacks appearance in 2006.

Belle of Louisville
Home port: Louisville, Kentucky
Built in 1914, the 200-foot *Belle of Louisville* is one of the last original Mississippi River-style steamboat stern-wheelers in existence and is now a National Historic Landmark. She has three decks (two enclosed and one open air) and accommodates 650. The year 2006 marked her sixth consecutive appearance, having also participated in Tall Stacks in 1988, 1992, 1995, 1999, and 2003.

Celebration Belle
Home port: Moline, Illinois
The 190-foot *Celebration Belle* is the

largest luxury stern-wheeler on the upper Mississippi River, with three enclosed decks and outside deck space on the third deck. She participated in the 1999, 2003, and 2006 Tall Stacks.

Chattanooga Star
Home port: Chattanooga, Tennessee
The *Chattanooga Star* made her second appearance at Tall Stacks in 2006. This side-wheeler was built by the Hoseman family. For 10 months of the year, the *Chattanooga Star* travels the country's rivers hosting school groups on her decks and educating children about the nation's waterways.

Colonel
Home port: Galveston, Texas
The *Colonel* stern-wheeler cruises year-round out of Galveston. This Victorian paddle wheeler features imported carpeting and draperies, brass appointments, and hardwood dance floors. The *Colonel* traveled the farthest from home—1,700 miles—for her third appearance at Tall Stacks.

Delta Queen
Home port: New Orleans, Louisiana
Built in 1926, the *Delta Queen* first cruised California's Sacramento River. During World War II she was used as a ferry boat to transport military personnel between ocean vessels and naval hospitals. Cincinnati's Greene family purchased the *Delta Queen* in 1946 to operate as a passenger boat, and since 1948 the *Delta Queen* has sailed the Mississippi and Ohio Rivers as the only authentic, fully restored, overnight steamboat in the world. The four-deck vessel is a designated National Historic Landmark, and Tall Stacks 2006 marked her sixth consecutive appearance.

General Jackson
Home port: Nashville, Tennessee
Making her second Tall Stacks appearance in 2006, the *General Jackson* stern-wheeler seats 1,100 passengers on four levels. Each cruise experience lasts three hours and offers two seating options for a buffet meal and two performances of a 40-minute Opryland-style show. Based at the Grand Old Opry in Nashville, the *General Jackson* is known as "the grandest showboat of them all" because of her large, ornate Victorian Theater on the main deck.

Harriet Bishop
Home port: St. Paul, Minnesota
The *Harriet Bishop* (named for Minnesota's first schoolteacher) was purchased and christened just prior to coming to Tall Stacks 1995. She made her fourth appearance in 2006.

Magnolia Belle
Home port: New Orleans, Louisiana
A true stern-wheeler, the *Magnolia Belle* is driven solely by the power of her sternwheel. Her first Tall Stacks appearance was in 2006.

Majestic
Home port: Pittsburgh, Pennsylvania
The *Majestic* spans the length of a football field, accommodating 400 on three decks, and is actually a tug and barge combination integrated to give the appearance of a grand side-wheeler. She has made five appearances at Tall Stacks.

Continued

Mississippi Queen
Home port: Minneapolis, Minnesota
The majestic *Mississippi Queen* steamboat was inspired by Mark Twain's famous quote: "Someday, they'll build the biggest steamboat the world has ever known; and she'll be long, white, and gleaming in the sunshine. And that one shall be the Queen of the Mississippi." With seven sparkling white decks, a golden-piped calliope, and a giant red paddle wheel, she has made five consecutive Tall Stacks appearances.

Music City Queen
Home port: Nashville, Tennessee
The sister vessel to the *General Jackson,* the three-deck *Music City Queen* cruises the Cumberland River. The year 2006 was her second Tall Stacks appearance.

Natchez
Home port: New Orleans, Louisiana
The three-deck *Natchez* is one of only a half-dozen steam-powered paddle wheelers still operating. Her first Tall Stacks appearance was in 2006.

P.A. Denny
Home port: Newport, Kentucky
This three-deck authentic stern-wheeler was christened the *Scott* in 1930 and served the U.S. Corps of Engineers in Louisville for 24 years. When Charleston, West Virginia, river man Pete Denny bought the boat, he led it to a surprise victory in the 1974 Sternwheel Regatta Race in Charleston. She previously appeared at Tall Stacks in 1988, 1992, 1995, and 2003.

Spirit of Cincinnati
Home port: Cincinnati
The *Spirit of Cincinnati* stern-wheeler is owned and operated by Queen City Riverboats. Originally named the *Belle of the Lakes,* she was designed as a one-deck, open-air sightseeing boat. In 1983 a complete cabin superstructure, including the addition of a second deck, was built. She has made six consecutive appearances in Tall Stacks.

Spirit of Jefferson
Home port: Louisville, Kentucky
The *Spirit of Jefferson* features two enclosed climate-controlled dining decks and one full open deck. Her fourth Tall Stacks appearance was in 2006.

Spirit of Peoria
Home port: Peoria, Illinois
A replica of wedding cake–style boat, the *Spirit of Peoria* employs a paddle wheel as her only source of propulsion. This was her first Tall Stacks appearance.

here that the local TV stations interrupt programming to broadcast the display live. And a fantastic show it is . . . some say unequaled in America.

Tall Stacks
Downtown, on the Ohio River shoreline
(513) 562-4949
The world's largest gathering of riverboats, Tall Stacks first hit the scene in 1988 as Cincinnati's own version of the East Coast's "Tall Ships" celebrations. The assembly of riverboats is indeed a nautical wonder; the city's signature event now returns every three years and hails back to the days when river traffic made Greater Cincinnati one of the largest cities in the country. See the close-up in this chapter for details.

MORE RIVER ATTRACTIONS

Rivers are repositories of unique places. Here are some interesting sites and backwaters located along our waterways, listed from west to east.

Markland Locks and Dam
U.S. Highway 42, 5 miles west of Warsaw, KY
(859) 567-7661
This dam offers sightseers the largest drop in pool levels of any dam on the river. Visitors are welcome to an observation room and deck that overlooks the locks. If you wait a while, you should be able to see a barge come through. Displays in the observation room show how the locks work.

Rabbit Hash, Kentucky
Kentucky Highway 338 at Lower River Road
No one knows exactly how this village got its name, but it's a popular summer stop for riverboats. When boats dock, the village blacksmith demonstrates his trade. The main attraction here is the General Store, (859) 586-7744, which opened in 1831. It's a great place to stop for some sarsaparilla. It's open 10:00 A.M. to 7:00 P.M. Monday through Sunday year-round. This quirky town, by the way, got national press when a hound dog was elected as its mayor.

Harrison Tomb
Cliff Road west of U.S. Highway 50, North Bend
(614) 297-2630
The tomb of U.S. President William Henry Harrison is located, along with a monument, on Mount Nebo. From this hill the obelisk of Bedford limestone with marble entranceway rises 60 feet above the tomb, affording visitors an amazing panorama of the river and Ohio River valley. Open all year during daylight hours. Admission is free.

Bicentennial Commons at Sawyer Point and the Serpentine Wall
The snakelike steps of the Serpentine Wall, which stretch from the Public Landing to near Yeatman's Cove park, are a favorite place for kids and adults to while away summer moments along the river. At nearby Bicentennial Commons, surrounding the famous Flying Pigs sculpture at Sawyer Point, is a miniature sidewalk version of the entire Ohio River, providing interesting and not-so-interesting details. Parking is available either at the Public Landing or just off Pete Rose Way, if you're not walking from elsewhere downtown.

New Richmond
U.S. Highway 52 at Ohio Highway 132
(513) 553-4146 (City Hall tourist information)
Another pleasant stop on the river, this is the site of an annual Fourth of July festival and River Days, a three-day August event that culminates in a hydroplane race. There are also helicopter rides, Clermont County's largest fireworks display, and the Cardboard Regatta, which features canoes made from cardboard (guess which lucky contestant wins the Titanic Award). An amphitheater on Front Street on the east side of town is the site of frequent concerts on summer weekends. Two good places to eat in town are Joe's Place (home of the famous Tex White Chili) and the Landing, both located on the river along Front Street. You'll also find some nice antiques stores scattered along Front Street.

Grant's Birthplace
1551 Ohio Highway 232, Point Pleasant
(513) 553-4911
The birthplace of Ulysses S. Grant, the 18th president of the United States, was constructed in 1817 of white Allegheny pine. Less than 20 feet by 20 feet in size, this basic frame structure consists of a kitchen with a large fireplace, a living room, and a bedroom. The house is furnished with historic memorabilia and

If you enjoy the nautical ambience of marinas and waterside restaurants, take a drive along Kellogg Avenue around the (aptly named) California neighborhood of the city. Marinas, sea shanties, bait shops, and more dot this Ohio River community. It's not Catalina Island, but it'll do.

period furniture. The house's grounds form a park, which provides an excellent scenic view of the Ohio River along U.S. Highway 52. It's open April through October, 9:30 A.M. to noon and 1:00 to 5:00 P.M. Wednesday through Saturday, noon to 5:00 P.M. on Sunday. Admission is $2.00 for adults, students $1.00, children age five and under free.

Captain Anthony Meldahl Locks and Dam
2443 U.S. Highway 52, Chilo
No phone

The observation deck here, free and open during daylight hours, lets visitors watch the barges making their way through the locks. The dam is named after the captain who once owned Maple Lane Farm just across the road. He took members of a congressional committee down the 981 miles of the river in 1905 to prove the need for a system of dams to aid navigation. They agreed, and the project was completed in 1929. Actually, 12 more modern high-level structures were built after World War II to further improve navigation.

Maysville, Kentucky
U.S. Highway 52 at Aberdeen

Cross the bridge into this Kentucky town and you begin to suspect something's up. First, there's Rosemary Clooney Street. Then you see multiple references to actor George Clooney and his dad, former American Movie Channel host Nick Clooney. Yes, this and nearby Augusta are Clooneyville, and the Hollywood star as well as the rest of the famous Clooney clan still hang out here, much to the autograph seeker's delight. Another famous resident is former Miss America Heather Renee French. They're not the only reason to visit this quaint town, though—it abounds with history (Daniel Boone lived here for a while).

KIDSTUFF

It's a familiar story. Cincinnati kids grow to adulthood, move away to one coast or the other to pursue careers, and then—inevitably—return here to raise their own families.

This astounding return rate is no accident. Cincinnati is a terrific place for rearing children, as nurturing and relatively safe an environment as you'd expect to find in any midsize midwestern town. There's an added emphasis here on play and enrichment, however, and that's largely due to the voters, who diligently keep passing levies for museums and parks. Furthermore, corporate giants such as Procter & Gamble and Kroger, both headquartered here, wisely invest in any attraction that helps them lure new talent (and their families) to Cincinnati. Recent examples of corporate and public partnership include the Newport Aquarium, the Cinergy Children's Museum, and the Cincinnati Zoo's Lords of the Arctic.

City and suburban governments put an unusual emphasis on public parks—in fact, the City of Cincinnati devotes more acreage to urban parkland and green space per capita than any other metropolis in America. A complete listing of parks and recreation centers can be found in the Parks and Recreation chapter, but we've noted the public parks and playgrounds with the best attractions for kids in this chapter, along with a kid's-eye view of some popular activities that are also written up in the Attractions chapter. Unless otherwise noted, all the attractions listed here accept major credit cards. Whenever available, toll-free 800 and 888 numbers are noted.

We've distinguished those parks and museums you wouldn't want to miss as "major attractions." These are the places to head to first if time or money is an issue (although many of these attractions are free, or nearly so).

PRICE CODE

The following price code is based on the cost for general admission for one adult. Most sites offer considerably discounted tickets for children and seniors, and some allow discounts or free entry for members of their respective organizations.

$	**$5.00 and under**
$$	**$6.00 to $10.00**
$$$	**$11.00 to $15.00**
$$$$	**More than $15.00**

MAJOR ATTRACTIONS

Aronoff Center for the Arts $$-$$$$
650 Walnut Street
(513) 721-3344, (800) 294-1816
www.cincinnatiarts.org

Cincinnati's newest arts complex presents a special family series (bringing in the likes of *Sesame Street Live* and *Magic School Bus*) as well as Saturday workshops where, for instance, children are taught how to juggle or create their own costumes. Local companies such as Children's Theatre and Madcap Productions put on zany musicals and puppet performances. Enjoy the traveling road shows and the juggling acrobats who also make frequent appearances. Shows cost $6.00 to $14.00, workshops $14.00. Traveling shows cost more

The Beach Waterpark $$$$
2590 Waterpark Drive
(exit 25 off Interstate 71), Mason
(513) 398-7946, (800) 886-SWIM
www.thebeachwaterpark.com

This 35-acre water park features Aztec Adventure, the Midwest's only "water-coaster"; the Cliff waterslide (voted among the nation's top-10 water attractions by the readers of *Inside Track* magazine); Banzai racing slides; Typhoon

If you think the largest spectator sport in Greater Cincinnati is major league baseball or the NFL, you're wrong. The top draw in the region isn't an arena or stadium—it's the Kentucky Speedway in Sparta, Kentucky, which routinely gets record crowds of 60,000 or more for events. The Busch 300 set an all-time record as the largest single sporting event ever in the region, attracting 71,000 kids and parents. Vrrroommm!

body flumes; a new Volcanic Panic thrill slide; Riptide inner-tube ride; the Hidden Rapids gnarled tube ride; Watusi, an enclosed, double helix tube; the Snake River Rapids tube adventure; Twilight Zoom (a black, enclosed—and dark—tube ride); the Pearl waterfall and spa area; the Thunderbeach wave pool; and the Lazy Miami River tube ride for those who like slow rides. Jolly Mon Shores is a 10,000-square-foot water-and-sand area just for the little squirts. Splash Mountain is 30,000 gallons of heated water just for children 4 feet tall and under. For older children, there's Emerald Bay, which includes a lily-pad walk, cable-pulley ride, rope bridge, and monkey bars suspended over water. Add to this the ambience of 100 live palm trees and 2,600 tons of sand. For a festive twist, Holiday Fest at the Beach features a large outdoor skating rink. Hours are 6:00 to 10:00 P.M. Saturday and Sunday during December. Cost is $10.00; $7.50 for children. Outside of the Christmas holidays, the park is open Memorial Day through Labor Day beginning at 10:00 A.M.; closing times vary through the season, though it's generally 9:00 P.M. Single-day admission is $26.99 for adults, $10.99 for seniors and children under 48 inches tall and seniors. If you go late, the rate is $14.50 for adults after 4:00 P.M., $6.00 for children and seniors. Season passes are $74 per person.

Behringer-Crawford Museum **$**
1600 Montague Road, Covington, KY
(859) 491-4003
www.bcmuseum.org

The only museum devoted to Northern Kentucky's natural and cultural heritage, Behringer-Crawford boasts a fascinating collection of fossils and artifacts spanning 450 million years of history. There are also the Garden Railway train cars collected by a local model-train enthusiast. The museum sits atop Devou Park, which has a terrific playground and a sweeping vista of the Ohio River and Cincinnati skyline that's worth a trip in itself. Hours are 10:00 A.M. to 5:00 P.M. Tuesday through Friday, 1:00 to 5:00 P.M. weekends. The museum is closed Monday and holidays. Call ahead for schedules of special hands-on programs for kids.

Boonshoft Museum of Discovery **$$**
2600 DeWeese Parkway, Dayton
(937) 275-7431

Though a bit of a hike to the north, don't overlook Dayton's new Boonshoft Museum of Discovery, which features interactive science exhibits and labs, an EcoTrek through five environments (Ice Age, Woodlands, Sonoran Desert, Amazon Rain Forest, and Northwest Pacific Tide Pool), an indoor Wild Ohio Zoo, and the Phillips Space Theater. See the Day Trips chapter for details.

Children's Learning Center **Free**
Public Library of Cincinnati and Hamilton County, 800 Vine Street
(513) 369-6900

Housed inside the three-story annex to the downtown branch of the public library, the Children's Learning Center has quickly become a treasure for children and their parents. Opened in 1997, the center features dozens of computers loaded with educational games and—get this, parents—free Internet access to select (i.e., safe) Web sites for kids. No irritating waits in line, either; you can reserve a half-hour block of computer usage. The center is about more than computers, of course. A 420-gallon saltwater aquarium features a live coral reef. And because the center is run by librarians, books are a priority. The weekly reading programs are ambitious, from Library Babies to Pre-School Storytimes to Family Read-Aloud Time. Everything's free. A library card is required only if you want to check books out. Hours are 9:00 A.M. to 9:00 P.M. Monday through Friday, 9:00 A.M. to 6:00 P.M. Saturday, and 1:00 to 5:00 P.M. Sunday. See the Libraries chapter for more details.

Cincinnati Fire Museum $$
315 West Court Street
(513) 621-5553
www.cincyfiremuseum.com

No family with a budding firefighter should miss this restored, century-old firehouse. The museum features firefighting memorabilia and antique engines. Ring the fire bell, see a movie, and visit the safe house for fire prevention tips. And where else can junior get a chance to slide down a real fire pole or climb inside the cab of a modern fire truck that allows him (or her) to operate the sirens and lights? Hours are 10:00 A.M. to 4:00 P.M. Tuesday through Friday and noon to 4:00 P.M. weekends. Admission is $6.00 for adults, $4.00 for children ages 2 through 12, and $5.00 for seniors ages 65 and older.

Cincinnati History Museum $$
Union Terminal, 1301 Western Avenue
(513) 287-7000
www.cincymuseum.com

History? Blah, says your youngster. But wait. This history museum, operated inside the town's art deco train station, actually makes the past fascinating. There's a recreated paddle wheeler, a working radio studio, and revolving exhibits. Cincinnati in Motion is a particularly noteworthy permanent exhibit that will thrill youngsters. This massive model of Cincinnati (circa 1900 to 1940) is a miniature city unto itself, complete with working trains, inclines, and trolleys—hence the "in Motion" moniker. The Carew Tower, the city's tallest skyscraper, is 7 feet tall in this diminutive display, to give you some sense of the scale. Hundreds of downtown buildings, past and present, are represented in what's being touted as the largest urban model layout in the United States. If you want a gander at the late, lamented Albee Theater, St. Peter in Chains Cathedral, or the West End railyards, they're all here.

And it's a boo-tiful day in the neighborhood as a bunch of amiable ghouls and ghosts haunt the museum at the annual Shocktober each October. Shocktober combines a landmark location, the latest high-tech visual effects, and a fascinating, true chapter of Cincinnati history. Visitors meet the spooky "curator" Joseph Dorfeuille, who operated a "Chamber of Horrors" beneath Cincinnati's old Western Museum (the predecessor to the museum) in the 1820s. Hours of Shocktober are 6:00 to 10:00 P.M. Thursday and Friday, 4:00 to 10:00 P.M. Saturday, and 5:00 to 9:00 P.M. Sunday during the month of October. Family-friendly hours (recommended for children seven and under) are 1:00 to 4:00 P.M. Thursday and Friday, 10:00 A.M. to 2:00 P.M. Saturday, and 11:00 A.M. to 3:00 P.M. Sunday. Admission is $10.50, seniors $9.50, $7.50 for children ages 3 through 12.

Every winter the museum fills with the sounds of train whistles as Holiday Junction chugs back into town. A massive light show greets visitors as a train motif is projected on the front of the building. Inside, see more than 10,000 square feet of model train sets, plus there's a holiday train ride just for kids. Hours of the holiday fest are 10:00 A.M. to 5:00 P.M. Monday through Saturday, 11:00 A.M. to 6:00 P.M. Sunday. Admission is $7.25 adults, $6.25 seniors, $5.25 children 3 through 12.

Combination tickets for Union Terminal's other attractions are also available. See the Museum Center at Union Terminal listing for combo details.

Cincinnati Museum of Natural History & Science **$$**
Union Terminal, 1301 Western Avenue
(513) 287-7000
www.cincymuseum.com

The Cincinnati Museum of Natural History & Science contains much for the junior paleontologist to love. Of special interest to kids is the Children's Discovery Center, an interactive exhibit, and dinosaur exhibits. In 2001 the old bat cave was gutted to make way for an all-new cavern experience—and it's not one for the phobic. The exhibit pays tribute to one of the planet's last unexplored frontiers and covers 8,000 square feet on two levels, re-creating a limestone cavern with a 22-foot waterfall, bats (behind glass), and cave walls that are kept appropriately chilly and clammy. Walk through this eerily lit glacier cavern, and you'll hear the creaks and groans that real-life cavers experience. The museum also has special year-round programs for preschoolers through teens. Although we're not big gift shop fans, this one is a must. Hard-to-find chemistry and science sets, telescopes, microscopes, and other educational stuff abound. Hours are 10:00 A.M. to 5:00 P.M. Monday through Saturday, 11:00 A.M. to 6:00 P.M. Sunday. Admission is $7.25 for adults, $6.25 for seniors, $5.25 for children ages 3 through 12, and free for kids age 2 and under. Combination tickets for Union Terminal's other attractions are also available. See the Museum Center at Union Terminal listing for combo details.

Cincinnati Observatory Center **$**
3489 Observatory Avenue
(513) 321-5186
www.cincinnatiobservatory.org

The oldest fully operational observatory in the nation (since circa 1845), the Cincinnati Observatory Center is nonetheless a hidden treasure. The stately domed structure—where the National Weather Service boasts its origins—sits majestically atop Mount Lookout. Since an enthusiastic non-profit group took over the facility from the University of Cincinnati in 1999, even more people are discovering the wonders of the observatory. Director John Ventre is opening up the facility during the day and evenings for tours, and he and the board are planning to convert the facility into a Museum of American Astronomy. Tours and children's programs are available, but you need to call first. The observatory opens at dusk on Thursday and Friday nights. Admission is free on Thursday and the second and fourth Sundays of the month, and admission on Friday is $2.00 for kids under age 18 and $4.00 for adults.

Cincinnati Railway Co. **$$$**
198 South Broadway, Lebanon
(513) 933-8022
www.cincinnatirailway.com

Formerly known as the Turtle Creek Railway, the railway continues to offer an hour-long train ride through the beautiful rolling countryside of southwest Ohio. Theme trips, including Santa rides, mystery dinners, and ice-cream socials, are also available. Trains run Wednesday, Friday, Saturday, and Sunday April through October. Only weekend Santa rides are available in November and December. Trains depart at 10:00 A.M., 12:30 P.M., and 3:00 P.M. Saturday and 11:30 A.M. and 2:00 P.M. Sunday. Fare is $17 for adults and $15 for children ages 12 and under.

Cincinnati Reds Hall of Fame Museum **$-$$**
100 Main Street
(513) 765-7207

The 15,000-square-foot Cincinnati Reds Hall of Fame Museum is now open, paying tribute to the greats who pioneered the game here as well as those who contributed to the success of the Big Red Machine in the 20th century. Off-season hours are 10:00 A.M. to 6:00 P.M., closed Monday between January 1 and opening day (which is in early April). After April 1, game day hours are 10:00 A.M. to 8:30 P.M. daily; admission is $5.00 with game ticket. Non-game day hours are 10:00 A.M. to 7:00 P.M. daily; admission is $8.00, $6.00 seniors, $5.00 children.

Cincinnati Zoo and Botanical Garden **$$$**
3400 Vine Street
(513) 281-4700
www.cincinnatizoo.org

The second-oldest zoo in the country (opened in 1875), the Cincinnati Zoo is a must-see for any family. The Manatee Springs complex introduces you to Florida manatees, crocodiles, an albino alligator, snakes, and fish. The magnificent Jungle Trails exhibit transports you into the rain forests of Africa and Asia, where you'll discover families of orangutans and chimpanzees lolling about among waterfalls and banks of rolling fog. There's also the popular Komodo dragons, Colossus the gorilla, a new Wolf Words exhibit, and an Insect World exhibit that can't be beat. Even very young kids will get a kick out of the Children's Zoo and the tram that runs throughout the complex. The zookeepers even have a wicked sense of humor. For instance, when the American Movie Channel was running a marathon of *Planet of the Apes* movies, the gorilla keepers set up color TVs in the cages so the primates could watch.

For the bear essentials, check out the Lords of the Arctic habitat. This $2.7 million pavilion and miniature ocean features the underwater antics of four—count 'em, four—giant polar bears, the largest land predators on the planet, as well as miscellaneous other Arctic life-forms. As the largest of the land carnivores, a polar bear makes even the dreaded grizzly bear resemble an overfed gerbil. (Polar bears mature to the neighborhood of 1,200 pounds and 10 feet in height.) What's truly nifty about Lords of the Arctic—a 21,000-square-foot facility that includes a 12-foot-deep tank—is that, unlike polar bear environs at other zoos, you actually stroll beneath the water with the big guys beside this frosty 70,000-gallon tank. We're talking about the chance to stand just inches away, nose-to-nose; a mere couple of inches of clear glass is all that separates you from some 2,000 pounds worth of shredding and clawing machines. Update your will and bring your videocam. Destiny awaits.

Also worth your time: the Vanishing Giants elephant and giraffe exhibit, a state-of-the-art facility. The 3.5-acre complex includes a 38,000-gallon pool, lots of roaming space, and a 9,000-square-foot giraffe habitat. It's a breath of fresh air—literally—for both wildlife and zoo visitors who remember the cramped and stinky Elephant House.

The zoo's Center for the Reproduction of Endangered Wildlife (CREW) is often overlooked and also well worth a visit. It's here that biologists and scientists work to save entire species from extinction in the wild. Zoo scientists made history when they bred two Sumatran rhinoceros, giving birth to Emi. The program has bred the first caracal (a wildcat) and banded insang born in the Western Hemisphere, plus the first crowned guenon monkey, Panay cloudrat, sand cat, and pampas cat born in captivity. CREW also claims the world's first test-tube gorilla, the world's first ocelet kitten produced by embryo transfer, and the first elephant conceived and born in Ohio since the days of the woolly mammoth. Tours are arranged by appointment.

Admission to the zoo is $12.95 for adults, $7.95 for children ages 2 through 12, and $10.95 for seniors age 62 and older, plus $6.50 for parking. You can buy a family membership for $79 or $65 for single parents; add $30 to include parking. (Metered street parking is also available near the zoo and is a good deal for non-members, but it goes very fast.) A zoo pass also gives you a first peek at new attractions (which come along fairly frequently), reduced-admission guest passes, 10 percent discount at zoo shops and educational classes, a monthly newsletter, stickers for your car, and free admission to 100 other cooperating zoos around the country. You can get a credit for your admission toward annual membership if you visit. Strollers can be rented for $6.00. The zoo is open daily 9:00 A.M. to 5:00 P.M. (8:00 A.M. to 6:00 P.M. from

Memorial Day weekend to Labor Day weekend). Once in, you don't have to leave until 7:00 P.M.

Annual events include the Zoo Babies celebration in June, which stars the latest newborns; the autumn Harvest Festival, which includes a daffodil bulb sale as well as traditional harvest fair activities; and Hallzooween, which includes a pumpkin patch, hayrides, and trick-or-treating, all designed to teach the very young about animal life.

Each November and December the zoo crew flips the switch on the Festival of Lights, the largest holiday light show held at any zoo in the nation. The six-week event showcases a dazzling array of light sculptures built with two million twinkling bulbs. Hours are 5:00 to 8:00 P.M. Sunday through Thursday, 5:00 to 9:00 P.M. Friday and Saturday. Admission is $12.95 for adults, $10.95 for seniors, and $7.95 for children.

Cinergy Children's Museum $$
Union Terminal, 1301 Western Avenue
(513) 287-7000
www.cincymuseum.com

Once located in Longworth Hall 3 blocks from the Ohio River, the Children's Museum of Cincinnati found itself *under* the Ohio River during the great flood of '97. The museum found new life inside the Museum Center at Union Terminal. Now renamed the Cinergy Children's Museum, the complex features a slew of exhibits targeted for infants through age 10. The interactive, 30,000-square-foot museum includes a two-story treehouse, a waterfall, and a winding river. Built at a cost of $7.5 million, it's billed as one of the 10 largest children's museums in the world.

Your little ones will particularly like the hands-on exhibits in the water areas (though bring a set of dry clothes for them to change into). Also popular are the themed areas such as the vet's office, kitchen, diner, grocery, and more. Then move on to the building-block room, the bouncing-ball room, etc. Our kids find a four-hour visit doesn't even begin to cover the territory.

Hours are 10:00 A.M. to 5:00 P.M. Monday through Saturday, 11:00 A.M. to 6:00 P.M. Sunday. Admission is $7.25 for adults, $5.25 for kids under age 12. Combination tickets for Union Terminal's other attractions are also available. But the best bet has to be the Children's Museum membership. It's $50 for families (consider springing for the one-year parking pass, another $10, since the pass pays for itself in three visits).

Coney Island $$-$$$$
6201 Kellogg Avenue, Anderson
(513) 232-8230
www.coneyislandpark.com

Located on the banks of the Ohio River, Coney Island (also see the Attractions chapter) offers a fun family outing without all the cost or utter exhaustion of a day at a larger, more frenetic amusement park. Sunlite Pool at Coney is billed as the world's largest recirculating pool, and parents of small children will like the fact that the shallow section is huge and lifeguards are in abundance. Coney also has a new 50-foot freefall Scream Machine, a family roller coaster called the Pepsi Python, a 500-foot waterslide, and a 180-foot water coaster. Pedal-boat trips on Lake Como are a popular attraction for older kids. And the park has a miniature golf course, a Ferris wheel, and a large, well-equipped playground.

Sunlite Pool is open Memorial Day through Labor Day 10:00 A.M. to 8:00 P.M. daily. Park rides are open during this period from 11:00 A.M. to 9:00 P.M. Saturday and Sunday and noon to 9:00 P.M. on weekdays. It's $18.45 for a combo pass to both Sunlite Pool and all the mechanical rides, $16.45 for children ages 4 through 11, and $12.95 for seniors. Admission to Sunlite Pool is $11.95 for age 12 and over, $9.95 for children ages 4 through 11 and for senior citizens. Children 3 and under are free. A single season pass is $95.00, a family season pass is $320.00. Parking is $3.00. (If the Ohio River is at flood stage, call first. Flood waters sometimes force Coney to close temporarily.)

East Fork State Park **Free**
Intersection of Ohio Highways 125 and 222, between Amelia and Bethel
(513) 734-4323

Just a dozen or so miles from Cincinnati is a natural playground that's often overlooked even by longtime residents of the area. The centerpiece is East Fork Lake, which offers bountiful bass fishing and boating opportunities as well as a 200-yard-long beach (a lifeguard is on duty most weekends). There's also a campground, bridle and hiking trails, picnic shelters, and seasonal nature programs for kids (see the Parks and Recreation chapter for more details on this and other area parks). The park is open daily May through September.

Eden Park **Free**
Mount Adams
No phone

Centered in the heart of Mount Adams, Eden Park has plenty to offer adults too, like ice-skating in the winter on Mirror Lake. Of particular note is the park's Krohn Conservatory, one of the nation's largest public greenhouses. Wander through a tropical rain forest or dash under the rushing 20-foot waterfall. And although your little ones may not have much interest in orchids or floral displays, they're sure to think the cactus exhibit is pretty darned sharp (see the Attractions and Parks and Recreation chapters). Our kids also love the annual exotic mushroom show, the perfect place to entertain your little, um, fun-guys. The conservatory is open daily.

GameWorks **$-$$**
1 Levee Way, Newport on the Levee, Newport, KY
(859) 581-7529

GameWorks, a 25,000-square-foot entertainment complex, opened in 2002 and features hundreds of interactive games and virtual-reality mind-benders. The state-of-the-art facility, created by hometown hero Steven Spielberg, includes Jurassic Park—The Lost World, an interactive challenge; realistic racing in miniature Indy 500 and NASCAR vehicles; a Las Vegas-style Wheel of Fortune; and lots of electronic amusements and video sports. There's also plenty of food: The Jax Grille will serve you anywhere in the complex, or you can head to the glass-enclosed restaurant. There, the specialty is toasting marshmallows at your table over a "personalized campfire" to create s'mores, which can then be dipped into various sweet condiments. GameWorks' hours are 11:00 A.M. to 2:00 A.M. Thursday through Saturday, and 11:00 A.M. to midnight Sunday through Wednesday. It's open to all ages until 10:00 P.M. (18 and older after that). No admission charge; you pay as you play (most games cost $1.00 to $2.00).

The best night for bargain-hunters to visit Coney Island amusement park is any night of a Riverbend concert. Insiders know that the adjoining Coney and Riverbend share parking lots, and that Coney—in a deal with Riverbend—doesn't charge a parking fee to any incoming car on concert nights. That's a savings of $3.00. Plus Coney ride prices are reduced after 4:00 P.M., which makes for a real deal.

Legends Museum at Cincinnati Gardens **Free**
2250 Seymour Avenue, Norwood
(513) 351-3999

This memorabilia museum opened in 1999 to celebrate 50 years of the Cincinnati Gardens—once the town's major concert and basketball venue. Exhibits honor five decades of the country's greatest sports and entertainment stars (all of whom played the Gardens at one time or another, natch). There are exhibits, photographs, jerseys, trophies, and more. Who's included? Anybody from Barney to Richard Nixon, Madonna to Larry Bird, the Beatles to Billy Graham, even Frank Zappa and Hulk Hogan. Your family will love it, and best yet, the Legends Museum is open free of charge during all Gardens events.

Miami Whitewater Forest $
9001 Mount Hope Road, Harrison
(513) 367-4774

The park's Pirate Cove is a nifty "sprayground" with a cascading waterfall and water cannons. It's open daily May to October; hours are 11:00 A.M. to 9:00 P.M. Admission is $1.00, and there's a $1.00 parking charge unless you have an annual Hamilton County Parks parking sticker ($5.00) (see the Parks and Recreation chapter).

Museum Center $$-$$$
Union Terminal, 1301 Western Avenue
(513) 287-7000
www.cincymuseum.com

The Museum Center at Union Terminal is actually three separate museums as well as an OMNIMAX theater, all housed under one roof under a joint agreement. And what a roof it is! One of the world's largest half-domes covers Union Terminal, the classic art deco structure that served as the town's train station for half a century before finding new life as a home for homeless museums.

For clarity's sake, we've listed the three museums—Cincinnati History Museum, Cincinnati Museum of Natural History & Science, and the Cinergy Children's Museum—and the OMNIMAX under separate headings. But the terminal building itself is worth a visit, if for no other reason than the striking architecture, the giant tile murals, and—hey, kids, listen up—the antique Rookwood ice-cream parlor. Order the cookies 'n' cream, a Cincinnati favorite for generations. Also worth noting is the Cincinnati Railroad Club's exhibit in Tower A, with a view of the original tracks, diagram board, and dispatcher's desk. (A terrific insiders' tour of the terminal is included in the course "Cincinnati 101" offered by the authors of this book. See the Communiversity listing in the Higher Education chapter.)

The Museum Center is open 10:00 A.M. to 5:00 P.M. Monday through Saturday and 11:00 A.M. to 6:00 P.M. Sunday. Three-way combo tickets for the Museum of Natural History, the Historical Society, and the OMNIMAX theater are $12.50 for adults, $8.50 for children ages 3 through 12, and free for children under age 3. Tickets to just one of the museums are $7.25 for adults and $5.25 for children. Membership to the Museum Center is $99 per family and includes free admission to all museums (but not the OMNIMAX).

National Museum of the United States Air Force Free
Gate 28B, Wright-Patterson Air Force Base, Dayton, OH
(937) 255-3284

This impressive facility, the oldest military aviation museum in the world, touts itself as Ohio's most popular free attraction. We find it hard to argue. A whopping 10 acres of exhibits relate the history of flight. Among the many air/spacecraft are a real British Sopwith Camel, a B-1 bomber, and even an Apollo command module. A recent addition is the actual Air Force One that took President Kennedy on his fateful trip to Dallas. And don't overlook Discovery Hangar Five, the interactive section that teaches youngsters about the varying models of airplanes and jets as well as essential principles of flight. Kids will love crawling through planes and jets. Parents will love the price: free. Hours are 9:00 A.M. to 5:00 P.M. daily. An IMAX theater screens films about flight, but there is a $6.00 charge for admission for the IMAX (children $4.50).

National Underground Railroad Freedom Center $$$
50 East Freedom Way and Rosa Parks Street, at the foot of the Roebling Suspension Bridge
(513) 333-7500
www.freedomcenter.org

The new National Underground Railroad Freedom Center examines the issues challenging the societies of the world through a variety of high-definition videos, environmental theaters, animated exhibits, and other high-tech participatory experiences. Special programming is offered for children. Hours are 11:00 A.M. to 5:00 P.M. Tuesday through Sunday. Admission is $12.00 adults, $10.00 seniors, $8.00 children ages 6 to 12.

Neil Armstrong Air and Space Museum **$$**
Interstate 75 at Wapakoneta
(800) 860-0142

In the world of aviation and aerospace, the big guns all seem to hail from Ohio. Pioneers like John Glenn, the Wright brothers, and, of course, the first man on the moon. While Neil Armstrong still lives reclusively on his farm in Lebanon and isn't likely to make a personal appearance here anytime soon, the Neil Armstrong Air and Space Museum in Wapakoneta (the astronaut's hometown) is nonetheless a surefire winner for the family and well worth the drive. Reopened after a long closure, the expanded facility includes numerous Apollo and Gemini mission artifacts: space suits, launch pad memorabilia, even actual capsules. A planetarium shows slides and films about outer space. You can't miss the museum from the interstate; it's the only huge concrete dome in town. Hours are 9:30 A.M. to 5:00 P.M. Tuesday through Saturday, noon to 5:00 P.M. Sunday. Admission is $7.00 for adults, $3.00 for students, free to age five and under. And don't even think about visiting on July 20, the anniversary of the moon walk.

Newport Aquarium **$$$**
1 Aquarium Way, Newport, KY
(859) 261-7444
www.newportaquarium.com

The newest fish attraction in Cincinnati is the Newport Aquarium. Sharks, piranhas, Antarctic penguins, and Asian fish abound—11,000 examples of sea life in all. Five acrylic tunnels let you walk under and into the ocean, and get up close and personal with toothy denizens of the deep.

The $40 million aquarium features some 60 exhibits involving nearly one million gallons of salt and fresh water. The kids will especially love Pirate Theater, a Spanish galleon turned movie theater. Special educational programs for children are arranged in conjunction with schools and groups (call for details). The focal point is the permanent exhibit Surrounded by Sharks, an unnerving introduction to the most menacing predators on the planet. Yes, we're talking sharks, some 75 of them—swimming, circling, never sleeping, waiting to snap up dinner. Visitors can actually stroll beneath the water with these big guys—inside the long plastic tunnels or along see-through acrylic floors—standing just inches away.

The new Hidden Treasures of the Rainforest Islands environment is a two-story immersion exhibit that re-creates a rain forest in Indonesia. Other permanent exhibits include Dangerous and Deadly, which features piranhas, poison dart frogs, toxic stonefish, electric eels, lionfish, and cottonmouth snakes. Bizarre and Beautiful includes Mandarinfish, wolf eels, and a giant Pacific octopus. Coral Reef highlights emperor angelfish, porcupine fish, and honeycomb morey eels. And the Kingdom of Penguins tank features dozens of king and gentoo penguins.

The aquarium is open 365 days a year, 10:00 A.M. to 6:00 P.M. daily. Admission is $17.95 for adults, $15.95 seniors, and $10.95 for children 3 to 12. Annual passes are $33.90 per person, $29.90 seniors, and $19.90 children 12 and under.

Ohio Renaissance Festival **$$$$**
Ohio Highway 73 at Harveysburg
(513) 897-7000
www.renfestival.com

This replica of a 16th-century town offers both youngsters and the young-at-heart a charming trip back to a time that was nowhere near as cheery as it's portrayed today. The 30-acre complex comes complete with roving jesters, kings, queens, magicians, singers, and the like. The elephant rides are a particular hit with kids (we wonder how many medieval English towns actually had elephants, but no matter), as are the daring displays of swordplay and the knights jousting atop horses and adorned in full armor.

Added in 2001 was a 65-foot galleon that's an authentic replica of a ship that would have sailed in the 16th century. Indeed, pirates swing from the rigging during the daily stunt shows. Nearly 100 performers appear daily on 11 stages: They include daredevil acrobat Daniel—Duke of Danger, a pair of singing nuns, Solitaire the Sword Swallower, Wyndsong the Snowdragon puppet, and the Daring Devilinis. A favorite highlight is the Muditorium, where three not-so-bright fellows sling mud at each other while cracking jokes. Rides include the Seahorse, Wild Boar, Crow's Nest, and the dragon Quintain. Some 130 craft merchants offer up their wares and talents (leather goods, glassblowing, weaving, coin minting, and such), and food booths are always good for a leg of mutton or the odd mug of mead. There's also a torture chamber, complete with racks, chains, and the odd executioner. And you thought education had to be boring.

A few cautions: Some of the live stage shows can be a bit, well, bawdy for the very young. And never, ever attempt a day at the festival if it has rained within the past 24 hours. Instead of being submerged in the medieval, you'll sink into the mudieval. The festival is open weekends, August through October (and also on Labor Day), 10:30 A.M. to 6:00 P.M. Admission is $16.99 for adults, $9.99 for children 5 through 12, and kids younger than 5 get in free.

Old Crosley Field **Free**
Interstate 71 at Interstate 275 interchange, Blue Ash
(513) 530-0047

Take a trip back to a time before there were free agents and prima donna baseball players. This re-creation of Cincinnati's original Reds ballfield features the playing green and scoreboard reconstructed in precise detail. They've even got some of the original Crosley Field seats here. At Old-Timers Day each July, thousands of fans come here to watch the greats from the past play a reunion game.

OMNIMAX Theater **$$**
Union Terminal, 1301 Western Avenue
(513) 287-7000
www.cincymuseum.org

If you've never taken your kids to an OMNIMAX movie, do it here. Think "movie screen combined with planetarium" and you've got a sense of this intriguing film format, shown above moviegoers' heads on a domed ceiling. The wraparound theater encases the viewer with whatever is showing, from sharks to volcanoes to the Rolling Stones. Warning: The loud sound system may be too intense for the very young, and young children may also be intimidated by the steep tiers of seats. Show schedules vary (and even scheduled shows may be already booked by a large group), so call first. Tickets are $7.25 for adults, $5.25 for children.

Paramount's Kings Island **$$$$**
6300 Kings Island Drive
(exit 24 off Interstate 71), Mason
(513) 754-5700, (800) 288-0808

This is the Big Draw. After the casinos, and just before the Cincinnati Reds, Paramount's Kings Island theme park is the reason tourists drive and fly into Greater Cincinnati. Why? Some roller-coaster enthusiasts claim it's the finest park in the country for thrills and hills—most notably the record-setting Beast and the Son of Beast wooden coasters. Families say the fantasyland caters to young children, which is certainly true enough. And everyone enjoys the clean, safe atmosphere. Yes, you will have to endure security check-ins and purse inspections, but this is the price of safety.

The newest coaster at Paramount's Kings Island is the Italian Job, an interactive stunt coaster that opened in 2005. The theme park's first interactive family ride is Scooby-Doo and the Haunted Castle. Riders travel through the castle equipped with Fright Light ghost blasters to zap ghosts and collect points. Also new at the park: SpongeBob SquarePants 3-D, an ocean motion ride and 3-D attraction in which riders strap on viewing goggles and plop into moving seats for a motion-simulator movie experience; Delirium, a spin-and-swing ride that rockets riders 137 feet in the air and also sways them in a 240-degree arc; and Tomb Raider: The Ride, a multisensory adventure in which park guests explore a tomb before strapping into the only possible vehicle of escape. Ice caves and boiling red lava follow. In 2004 the theme park opened Boomerang Bay, a water resort and park. The water park is free with Kings Island admission.

In addition to the new rides, Kings Island mainstays remain:

Coasters: Adventure Express, a runaway mine-train ride; The Beast, the world's longest roller coaster; Face/Off, a suspended, floorless coaster (a face-to-face inverted thrill ride racing at 55 mph through three 70-foot loops, forward and backward); Flight of Fear, an indoor linear induction coaster with a 54 mph takeoff; the Racer, forward and backward coasters (running on matching dual tracks); Son of Beast, the world's tallest and fastest roller coaster; Top Gun, a steel suspended ride; and Vortex, a steel looping coaster with six inversions.

Wet rides: White Water Canyon, an inner-tube raft ride through rushing water; Congo Falls, a churning boat ride down a five-story waterfall; and the Wild Thornberrys River Adventure log flume.

Other rides: the 315-foot-tall Drop Zone, the world's tallest free fall; Eiffel Tower, a one-third scale replica of the original; the classic Carousel, built in 1926 with 20,000 sheets of 23-karat gold; spinning Monster; the Scrambler on the midway; Dodgem bumper cars; Flying Eagle scooters; the Viking Fury swinging pirate ship; and the Zephyr carnival swing ride.

Kid stuff: In the 2006 season Kings Island opened a completely revamped children's area to replace Hanna-Barbera Land and Nickelodeon Central. The new area is called Nickelodeon Universe and include 18 rides for kids, including Avatar, a first-of-its-kind spinning family roller coaster, a Plankton free-fall ride; a Danny Phantom ride that places riders on their stomachs to fly like superheroes; a Blue's Clues attraction that lets children ride in "Blue" shaped cars; a Bikini Bottom and SpongeBob's Pineapple attraction; a Dora the Explorer train ride; Jimmy Neutron bumper cars; a Little Bill gentle coaster for tots; and a Nick-Go-Round Carousel. Be sure to hop aboard the Rugrats Runaway Reptar, the world's first junior inverted roller coaster (a 25 mph ride with ski-lift style seats suspended below the track).

Pay-per-experience rides: A few rides cost extra beyond the admission price. Aerial Helicopters Flight Team is a helicopter tour of the park, in flights lasting from 2 to 45 minutes (prices range from $25 to $155 per rider). Days of Thunder is a go-kart raceway experience ($2.00 to $5.00). Xtreme Skyflyer is a ripcord free fall that lets you feel what it's like to hang glide or skydive ($45).

Where are you most likely to encounter long lines? The 10 most frequently ridden rides in a past survey were: the Racer (No. 1), Adventure Express, Vortex, Beast, Top Gun, Phantom Theater (recently replaced by Scooby-Doo and the Haunted Castle), Beastie (due to be rethemed in 2006), Flight of Fear, Congo Falls, and Viking Fury.

In addition to the park's regular summer season, Kings Island reopens in October for FearFest, a serious monthlong haunt (for age 12 and up) as the park is populated with crazed clowns, vampires, and mummies.

Ghouls just want to have fun at the region's most haunting Halloween experience. With supernatural special effects and spooky illusions galore, the experience can be petrifying: Lightning strikes the Eiffel Tower, fog rolls in across the fountains, and malevolent vampires, mummies, apparitions, and skeletons roam the theme park. Menacing attractions include a terrifying Victorian mansion, a three-ring carnival of souls, an asylum run by its inmates, and a crypt where you'll find yourself shouting for your Mummy. There's more. The antique car ride becomes Route 666. Coney Mall becomes Coney Maul, a creepy experience featuring a walk-through maze. And the Beast becomes "Sleepy Hollow," a foggy parade of shadows.

Due to the intense nature of this horror show, FearFest is not recommended for children under age 12; no costumes permitted. Fearfest runs from 7:00 P.M. to midnight Saturday, 7:00 to 10:00 P.M. Sunday through October. Admission is $25.99.

For kids under 12, consider Kings Island's Trick or Treat Spooktacular—held every Halloween weekend—which is an easygoing family outing and trick-or-treat extravaganza on International Street. It's included with regular park admission.

In the 2005 season a Cincinnati favorite returned after more than a decade's absence. Winterfest—a holiday mainstay for generations at the theme park—was reintroduced as a multimillion-dollar winter wonderland. Park patrons could ice-skate atop the Royal Fountain and gawk at the Eiffel Tower, all decked out as a gigantic Christmas tree. Also featured: millions of twinkling lightbulbs, a White Christmas Express train ride, parades, holiday foods and crafts, and more. Hours of Winterfest are 4:00 to 9:00 P.M. weekends from Thanksgiving weekend through mid-December, then nightly through the rest of December. Tickets are $17.99 for specific day tickets, $24.99 general admission.

Kings Island offers a Baby Care Center for changing and feeding, stroller rentals, and first-aid stations. A dining tip: Our favorite of the park's 30 restaurants and snack shacks is Bubba Gump's because (1) it's a comfortable, roomy cafeteria where the family can spread out, and (2) the menu features cocktail shrimp, fish-and-chips, and salads. Who needs a burnt burger and pesky gnats at an outdoor shack?

The park is open Memorial Day through Labor Day weekend from 9:00 A.M., but rides don't start until 10:00 A.M. Closing times vary throughout the season (it really is worth staying for the fireworks), as do operating times in the spring, fall, and winter. Keep in mind that weekdays may be best for smaller children, as the lines on weekends can try the patience even of older folks.

Individual tickets are $34.99 for "adults" 7 through 59 and reduced admission ($29.99) for children 4 through 6 and seniors 60 and older. It's becoming more and more difficult to take in the whole park in one day, especially for first timers. Season passes are $106.99 for adults. A season pass for a family of four is $319.96, plus $75.00 for each additional child. Season passes are also good for admission to Paramount's other amusement parks in the United States and Canada. Parking is $9.00.

Parky's Farm **$**
Winton Road and Lake Forest Drive, Springfield Township
(513) 521-7275

Parky's Farm at Winton Woods, a combination play farm and petting zoo, is one of the nicest mostly free attractions around, with goats, sheep, chickens, horses, and other farm animals in abundance. Pony rides ($2.00) and a playground inside a barn (admission $2.00) are also available. Parky's Farm Fair Days in mid-July is a nifty festival featuring kiddie tractor pulls, outdoor movies, lumberjack exhibitions, and more. In October "Halloween Nights" tell the story of Halloween to your offspring in a nonfrightening way, with its glowing ghosts and whimsical witches, a walk-through light show boasting 250,000 bulbs, fanciful family-friendly characters, hayrides, storytelling, campfires, and magic shows. Hours are 6:00 to 10:00 P.M. Sunday through Thursday, 6:00 to 11:00 P.M. Friday and Saturday. Admission is $4.00, children age 2 and under free.

The playbarn is open noon to 7:00 P.M. daily from Memorial Day through Labor Day, with limited weekend hours at other times. The park is open dawn to dusk all year and admission is free except for a $1.00 parking pass or your $5.00 annual Hamilton County Parks parking sticker.

Playhouse in the Park **$**
962 Mount Adams Circle
(513) 421-3888
www.cincyplay.com

The Playhouse is a terrific resource, with family shows such as the magical "Abracadabra," juggling presentations, and an annual production of *A Christmas Carol*. The best of these shows is the Saturday morning series just for kids, the Rosenthal Next Generation Theatre Series; anyone—puppets, storytellers, singers, even Winnie the Pooh—might show up. Shows run on Saturday at 10:30 A.M., 12:30 P.M., and 2:00 P.M. from October through May. Also ask about the creative dramatics classes for kids ages 5 through 10.

Seasongood Nature Center **$**
Woodland Mound Park, Nordyke Road, Anderson
(513) 474-0580

This is a small natural-history and nature center with several interesting exhibits. Located on the grounds of Woodland Mound Park, the center is open Wednesday through Sunday 11:00 A.M. to 6:00 P.M. in March, April, October, and November and daily 11:00 A.M. to 7:00 P.M. from May through September. Admission is free, though parking costs $1.00 unless you've bought a $5.00 parking pass good for a year at all Hamilton County parks. (See the Parks and Recreation chapter.)

Sharon Woods Park and Heritage Village **$-$$**
11450 U.S. Highway 42, Sharonville
(513) 563-9484
www.heritagevillagecincinnati.org

Three attractions make this giant park a mile south of Interstate 275, exit 46, a particularly great place for kids: The Sharon Centre, Heritage Village, and a small water park. Sharon Centre is a state-of-the-art, multipurpose facility featuring interactive education exhibits focusing on the geology and natural history of Sharon Woods Gorge and the surrounding area. Displays include wildlife; fossils; the Buckeye Pool, where visitors come eye to eye with wildlife; and even a life-size walk-through sycamore tree. Heritage Village has restored 19th-century buildings brought from other parts of southwestern Ohio, including a doctor's office exhibiting Civil War medical equipment and a barn with period equipment. On weekends, kids are invited to participate in crafts such as weaving, tin punching, quilt patchworking, and candle dipping. The village is open Wednesday through Friday noon to 4:00 P.M. and 1:00 to 5:00 P.M. Saturday and Sunday April through October.

In October the historical Heritage Village transforms into the hysterical "Haunted Village," as all the different village buildings take on an eerie atmosphere after dark. Look for a headless horseman, ghost train, haunted graveyard, spooky séance, trick-or-treat bags loaded with favors, hayrides, straw maze, and more. The event is suitable for family members of all ages. Hours are 6:00 to 10:00 P.M. Friday and Saturday, 5:00 to 9:00 P.M. Sunday. Admission is $8.00 adults and children, free for children 3 and under.

Each December Sharon Woods opens its outdoor Christmas light display, Holiday in Lights. You don't even have to bundle up your little elves—you can view the more than 200,000 lights strung along 500 trees from the comfort of your car. Illuminated, moving characters range from Santa to Godzilla to 10-foot toy soldiers. Holiday hours are 6:00 to 10:00 P.M. Sunday through Thursday, 6:00 to 11:00 P.M. Friday and Saturday. Admission is $10.00 per car.

Admission to the water park, which includes an elephant fountain and different kinds of boats, is $1.00; it's open the same dawn-to-dusk hours as the park. Admission to the park is free, provided you have a $1.00 daily parking pass or a $5.00 annual Hamilton County Park District pass. Go ahead and get the pass: It's

CLOSE-UP

Zak Morgan: The City's Only Grammy-Nominated Kids' Performer

Zak Morgan is pausing beside a bustling Mount Washington community park, just two streets over from the house where he grew up. As kids of all ages scurry up and down the wooden play sets, howling with laughter, Morgan is speaking to his chosen profession, which would be . . . well, exactly that:

Playing like a kid and howling with laughter.

For the benefit of the IRS 1040, Morgan is likely forced to list his occupation as "children's singer and songwriter." But the job description doesn't approach the Mount Washington resident's varied career paths—or his ambitious goals.

Morgan obtained one of his loftiest goals in 2004, receiving the coveted Grammy nomination for his newest album, *When Bullfrogs Croak.*

Cross Dr. Seuss with Shel Silverstein, toss in a smidgen of a grade school educator, a G-rated stand-up comic, and a folk musician, and you'll arrive at Zak Morgan, children's artist. The sought-after performer plays gigs across the country each year, at hundreds of auditoriums, arts festivals, and libraries.

Accompanied by infectious guitar riffs, Morgan's onstage storytelling is loaded with wordplay and puns that leave even the adults in the audience chortling against their will. The musician's lyrics are innocent and yet sophisticated, all in the same universe. Take a tune such as "When Bullfrogs Croak"—an ode to the passing of a bullfrog and the eternal cycle of life:

> *When bullfrogs croak,*
> *The smell will travel.*
> *When bullfrogs croak,*
> *It finishes the circle, you see.*
> *When bullfrogs croak,*
> *With guts in the gravel,*
> *It's Mother Nature's way,*
> *I'm sure you'll agree.*
>
> —Lyrics by Zak Morgan

Morgan, born in Cincinnati in 1970, lived here all the way until 1989, when he shipped off to Kenyon College. After graduation came a stint on a Wyoming dude ranch, a defining moment when he first began to entertain kids with impromptu escapades, followed by a job at a Manhattan publisher, where he reintroduced himself to children's literature. Then, a return to Cincinnati, where all these exposures cohesively unified.

Where does Morgan believe his songwriting ability originates? Looking to the family tree, Morgan—who began writing and playing music at the age of 13—identifies some likely candidates: "Probably it's most rooted in my grandpa. He would tell stories, just make them up, and the kids would gather round," recalls Morgan, adding that he also inherited his grandfather George's irreverent—nay, audacious—sense of humor. Grandpa George would invent yarns, limericks, even whole new words. "Those influences are just all brewing around in me."

As the songwriter/performer crisscrosses Cincinnati—and much of the rest of America—in his Honda Odyssey minivan, he brings an unrestrained stage presence to school auditoriums and concert halls alike. At a Cincinnati Zoo appearance, he launched into the show with passionate fervor, partnering with a giant chicken. And at a 20th Century Theater party to kick off his new CD, he even invited his Grandma Lucille onstage to sing a duet.

"The theme of my show is reading and exercising the imagination. It's such a gift, imagination, and reading is a great way to tap into it," says the star of stage and snotdom. Vocabulary expansion is stressed as well, and that's little surprise with lyrics such as "the leopard's pernicious, and you look delicious . . . ." (The *Bullfrog* cover booklet even includes a "Zakland's Unabridged Dictionary.")

All this said, there's a whole lot more to the typical Zak Morgan show (if a word like "typical" can be used in conjunction with such craziness) than the basic ABCs: costumes, props, surprise guests, whooping horns, witticisms, and more. "I try to bring the kid out in everyone, even the parents. I don't want to patronize the kids, or dumb down. You can't reach kids by patronizing them," notes Morgan. "That's especially true with fourth and fifth graders, who are trying so hard *not* to be a kid."

The album is certainly not patronizing: its lush lyrics and humorous references offer listeners a unicornacopia of material.

"No frogs, insects, chickens, or children were zapped, scratched, or roasted during the making of *When Bullfrogs Croak,*" Morgan laughs.

Topics such as nose picking, growing pains, and schoolhouse bullies weren't off-limits on *Bloom,* his first album, as Morgan quantified the essence of a child's life. "The nose picking," he's quick to point out, "well, that's only *semi*-autobiographical."

As the interview winds to a close at the Mount Washington park, two girls have recognized Morgan and begin pestering him for autographs, a cacophony of motion and excitement. "You're Zak Morgan! Zak Morgan! Zak Morgan!" they chime in electrified unison. "I can't believe it's really *you,*" exclaims the younger of the pair, a bobbing six-year-old.

In no time, the singer whips out his signature blue felt-tip and his promotional flyer, gladly obliging the duo with autographs. It must become a hardship, we suggest, to endure such kinetic accosting from the preschool set. Zak Morgan merely grins, as is his way.

the best entertainment investment in Cincinnati. (See the Parks and Recreation chapter.)

Stricker's Grove **$$**
11490 Hamilton-Cleves Road, Ross
(513) 738-3366

Even many longtimers don't know about the region's "other" amusement park, Stricker's Grove. That's because this private park is largely closed to the public, placing its emphasis on company picnics and corporate functions. But two days each summer, Ralph Stricker opens his doors wide: the Fourth of July and the second Sunday in August. There are 17 rides, including two roller coasters, the Tornado and the Teddy Bear. Admission is $7.00 (all rides included as well as free soft drinks and parking).

Sunrock Farm **$$**
103 Gibson Lane, Wilder, KY
(859) 781-5502

One of the most ambitious petting zoos around, Sunrock Farm allows kids to milk a goat, gather eggs from the chicken coop, and hand-feed the farm animals. Family tours are conducted from 2:00 to 3:00 P.M. weekdays and 2:00 to 4:00 P.M. weekends. "Family Tours" (minimum of eight people) are $8.00 for each person. Reservations are required. Ask about the hayrides.

Tristate Warbird Museum **$$**
Clermont County Airport, 4021 Borman Drive, Batavia
(513) 735-4500

What budding pilot doesn't love fighter planes? The Tristate Warbird Museum features a P-51 Mustang, an AT-6D Texas trainer, a TBM-3 Avenger torpedo bomber, a twin-engine B-25 Mitchell bomber, a Corsair fighter, and more. Also on display: an English barracks like something out of *12 O'Clock High*. Hours are 10:00 A.M. to 3:00 P.M. Saturday, 4:00 to 7:00 P.M. Wednesday. Admission is $8.00, $5.00 students and veterans, free for veterans in uniform.

UnMuseum **$$**
44 East Sixth Street
(513) 345-8400
www.contemporaryartscenter.org

The top floor of downtown's contemporary arts center is now the UnMuseum, designed for children age five and up. The UnMuseum showcases interactive art and emphasizes participatory experiences. It's also got a terrific arts-and-crafts center, with free clay, posterboard, art supplies, neon-colored foam, beads, and more. Hours are 10:00 A.M. to 6:00 P.M. Wednesday, Thursday, and Friday; until 9:00 P.M. on Monday; 11:00 A.M. to 6:00 P.M. Saturday and Sunday; closed Tuesday. Free from 5:00 to 9:00 P.M. Monday; other times it's $7.50 adults, $6.50 seniors, $5.50 students, and $4.50 children 3 to 13.

OTHER FUN PLACES FOR KIDS

American Classical Music Museum & Hall of Fame **Free**
4 West Fourth Street
(513) 621-3263

Oh, all right, perhaps "fun" isn't the operative word here. But kids ought to be exposed to something more in the world of music than Braindead Maniacs or whatever the latest punk rage is, and this is the place to do it. There's a Hall of Fame, a gift shop, and displays for the Cincinnati Symphony Orchestra and the Cincinnati Opera. Hours are 10:00 A.M. to 4:00 P.M. Monday through Friday.

Big Pig Gig **Free**
Various locations, downtown and in the suburbs

If junior tugs at your shirt sleeve and asks, "What the heck is that giant pig over there?" he's probably referring to one of the remnants from a giant porcine public art project titled the Big Pig Gig. Call it our very own Days of Swine and Roses, wherein hundreds of 5-foot-high fiberglass porkers—decorated by local artists—were bolted to sidewalks downtown and in front of just about every museum and park. Why would Cincinnati go hog wild and install the 500-pound sculptures? Once the nation's largest pork-packing center, the city earned the moniker "Porkopolis" and hogged it for the first half of the 19th century: Cincinnati slaughterhouses supplied the tables of the British Navy and even Queen Victoria's royal table. There was no garbage collection in the 1800s because of the swine that freely roamed the downtown city blocks, eating as they waddled (prompting Frances Trollope to bash Cincinnati in her famous *Domestic Manners of the Americans* as a barbaric urban center where residents lived with livestock). The Big Pig Gig officially ended in 2001, but many of the tongue-in-cheek creations—which include such characters as Hamlet, Pigaletto, Pigasso, Porkemon, Dr. Frankenswine, Pig-mailion, and Road Hog—remain in place today. Look for them in front of Museum Center alone, as well as scattered through downtown and in front of the various corporations that first sponsored the artworks.

The Children's Room **Free**
Anderson Regional Branch Library, 7450 State Road, Anderson
(513) 369-6030

The Children's Room opened in 1998 as part of a major expansion at the Anderson Regional Branch Library. The expansive space features computers with Internet access (kid-safe Web sites only), color terminals loaded with educational software, stuffed toys, a sunroom with benches for leisurely reading, and—of course—rows upon rows of children's books (check out the special Fairy Tale department). Of particular interest are the substantial audiovisual offerings, including children's books on tape, stacks of Disney videos, and music storybooks. There's also plentiful programming for tots, toddlers, and preschoolers: Library Babies is for 6- to 18-month-olds, Toddler Time is for ages 18 to 36 months, and Preschool Storytime is for children ages three to five. Hours are 10:00 A.M. to 9:00 P.M. Monday through Thursday, 10:00 A.M. to 6:00 P.M. Friday and Saturday.

Cincinnati/Northern Kentucky International Airport **Free**
Interstate 275 and Donaldson Road, Hebron, KY
(859) 767-3144
www.cvgairport.com

An airport, you're thinking, are these guys nutballs or what? But some 40,000 children take a guided tour of the city's international airport each year. The tour includes the airport's aircraft rescue firefighting facility and a demonstration of the rescue equipment, the murals that were saved from Union Terminal, the different concourses, and the airport's own airplane, where children can explore the cockpit and instrumentation and receive an explanation of emergency procedures. Tours begin at 9:30 A.M., 11:00 A.M., and 1:00 P.M. Call the Communications Department for reservations two weeks in advance.

Creation Museum and Family Discovery Center
Intersection of Kentucky Highways 20 and 338, Petersburg, KY
(859) 727-2222
www.answersingenesis.org

Let's be up front about this: The Creation Museum, slated to open soon, has a religious agenda. But this $14 million, 95,000-square-foot facility wants to entertain as well as evangelize. A series of exhibits will present what organizers believe is the simple, factual account of the history of the world, as described in Genesis, the first book of the Bible. Life-size replicas of dinosaurs, a DNA exhibit, and fossil displays are included. Wings of the museum will examine scientific fields such as astronomy, biology, and archaeology from a fundamental biblical perspective. The complex will emphasize children's programs and educational workshops. The museum is funded by the national organization Answers in Genesis, which plans to move its headquarters to the site (an analysis in the *Cincinnati Enquirer* indicates this will be the largest totally private museum ever opened in the region). Hours of operation and admission prices were not available at press time.

Dave & Buster's **$-$$**
11775 Commons Drive, Springdale
(513) 671-5501

More than 200 interactive and carnival games, a ski simulator, and more make this complex a popular destination. The size of a football field, Dave & Buster's also features bowling, simulation golf, and an on-site restaurant. In case you're contemplating the old dump-and-run, forget it—the management strictly enforces the rule that all children and teens must be accompanied by an adult over 25. Only two kids per guardian are allowed. Hours are 11:30 A.M. to midnight weekdays, 11:30 A.M. to 2:00 A.M. Friday and Saturday (but no one younger than 21 is allowed in after 10:00 P.M.). There is no admission charge; you pay per game.

Eastgate Adventure Golf **$$**
3232 Omni Drive, Eastgate
(513) 753-8000

This place combines a souped-up version of miniature golf with ever-popular go-kart racing. Adventure Golf includes waterfalls and other man-made hazards that make it a little more interesting than putt-putt. Eastgate is open March through October 10:00 A.M. to 11:00 P.M. daily. The cost is $6.50 for adults and $4.50 for children 12 and younger for Adventure Golf ($1.00 less before 6:00 P.M. on weekdays), $4.00 for adults and children for the go-kart rides. Kids must be at least 56 inches tall to ride the go-karts. Birthday packages and other group rates are also available.

Eastgate is easy to see from the road but can be hard to find once you get off. Take the Eastgate Boulevard exit off Ohio Highway 32, then head south on Eastgate Boulevard to a right onto Aicholtz Road, followed by another right onto Omni Drive.

Highfield Discovery Garden **$**
10405 Springfield Pike, Woodlawn
(513) 771-8733

Highfield Discovery Garden is a brand-new facility designed especially for small kids. The two-acre playground is themed to children's literature—Frog and Toad pond, Harry Potter garden, and more. A fabricated 25-foot tree is full of crawling and climbing tubes. It's open Tuesday through Sunday 10:00 A.M. to 7:00 P.M. (call first if the mercury dips below freezing; the gardens may close for safety reasons).

La Comedia **$$$$**
765 West Central Avenue, Springboro
(800) 677-9505

We admit at the outset, this place is a "dinner theater." But despite the dreaded label, La Comedia has been presenting quality family shows for almost a quarter of a century. As the downtown theater troupes indulge more and more in the explicit and avant-garde, La Comedia happily produces *The Wizard of Oz* and *The King and I*. The theater is by no means amateur, auditioning for casts in New York City and elsewhere. In fact, a recent survey ranked La Comedia as the nation's fourth-largest dinner theater. All perfomances include lunch, brunch, or dinner, and prices range from $44 to $59 ($25 for children 11 and under).

Midway Theater **$**
210 West Plane Street, Bethel
(513) 734-2278

This classic piece of Americana, located in the heart of the tiny village of Bethel, features premier flicks at bargain prices. The Midway is the last of a breed, the small-town independent movie house. The building itself is historic as well, about 70 years old. You can catch first-run films such as the latest *Harry Potter* for just $4.00.

Pyramid Hill Sculpture Park **$-$$$**
1763 Hamilton-Cleves Road, Hamilton
(513) 868-8336
www.pyramidhill.org

Take your kids to see sculpture at the art

museum and you have to leap back while they issue that huge, collective yawn. Take 'em to the Pyramid Hill Sculpture Park and you'll earn an entirely different reaction. They'll think the Stonehenge-style slabs and other massive carved rocks are awesome. One of the few outdoor sculpture museums in the United States, Pyramid Hill is located on the estate of a philanthropist who's building his collection one massive stone at a time. Each December Holiday Lights on the Hill features more than one million lights illuminating this sculpture park. Hours of the light display are 6:00 to 10:00 P.M. nightly. Cost is $12 per carload, $14 on weekends. The park is open April through November, 10:00 A.M. to 4:00 P.M. Saturday and Sunday. Admission is $4.00, $1.50 for children.

Rosemary Clooney House Museum **$**
106 East Riverside Drive, Augusta, KY
(606) 756-2603

The Rosemary Clooney House Museum, the home of the late singer and entertainer, is a fun family diversion. The home features the largest display of costumes and memorabilia from the film *White Christmas.* Rosemary isn't the most famous Clooney to once live in this tiny river town, by the way: Her relatives include American Movie Channel host Nick Clooney and Hollywood actor George Clooney. Hours of the museum are 10:00 A.M. to 5:00 P.M. Saturday, 1:00 to 5:00 P.M. Sunday, with weekday tours by arrangement.

Spring Grove Cemetery and Arboretum **Free**
4521 Spring Grove Avenue
(513) 681-6880
www.springgrove.org

Visit a cemetery with the kids? Most definitely, at least in the case of this particular graveyard. Spring Grove's name includes the word "Arboretum" and it's actually a place that's full of life. People regularly get married here (renting the chapel costs

Cincinnati has more than its share of festivals, but the Greater Anderson Days fest each July in Anderson is one of the kid friendliest. There are old-time carnival rides, easygoing live music, and a Rozzi family fireworks show. Best yet, for the family budget, it's just about all free. See the Annual Events chapter for details.

$450), and Spring Grove offers a busy social calendar year-round featuring ice-cream socials, big band concerts, nature walks, and more. At 733 acres, Spring Grove is the nation's second-largest cemetery, and it's where Cincinnati's rich 'n' famous go to rest—the cemetery's rolling hills are chock-full of historic landmarks and lush gardens, fantastic crypts, and awesome headstones. Among those buried here are a speaker of the House of Representatives, a secretary of the treasury under Lincoln, a chief justice of the United States, nine Ohio governors, 25 Cincinnati mayors, the parents of two U.S. presidents, 36 Union generals, a grocer (Bernard Kroger, who founded Kroger's), and two guys named William Procter and Joseph Gamble (they ran a soap company you may have heard of). Grounds are open 7:00 A.M. to 6:00 P.M. daily.

WonderPark **$-$$**
Cincinnati Mills, Forest Park
(513) 671-0100

Cincinnati's newest theme park, WonderPark stars a two-story indoor roller coaster. The family entertainment center features a rain-forest theme and 100 video arcade games, amusement rides, and more, geared to children ages 2 to 12. It's open noon to 6:00 P.M. Sunday through Tuesday, 10:00 A.M. to 8:00 P.M. Wednesday and Thursday, and 10:00 A.M. to 9:00 P.M. Friday and Saturday. Tickets are $1.00 to $2.00 per ride.

OUTDOOR PLAYGROUNDS

The best playground generally is the one closest to you, but here's a listing of some other playgrounds in the area. See the Parks and Recreation chapter too.

Airport Playfield **$**
Corner of Beechmont and Wilmer Avenues
(513) 321-6500
This playground near Lunken Airport includes brand-new and extensive play equipment, tunnels, and jungle gyms for kids. Admission is $1.00 and well worth it. The adjacent walking/biking trail and airport also help make for an all-around fun and educational outing.

Fleischmann Gardens **Free**
Comer of Washington and Forest Avenues
No phone
Dozens of tiny parks—Annwood, the Wulsin Triangle, Buttercup Valley, Geier Esplanade—pepper the Cincinnati metro area. But Fleischmann Gardens, located on the former estate of the founder of the Fleischmann Yeast Co., is our favorite tiny park for families. The slab-stone trail is an easy hike for even the youngest ones—call it, um, the path of yeast resistance.

Juilfs Park **Free**
8249 Clough Pike, Anderson
(513) 474-0003
The playground here is fully loaded, with numerous climbing, sliding, digging, and swinging options. The Anderson Park District puts on free movies under the stars on some summer evenings here, which make for a great family outing. Call for details.

Sawyer Point **Free**
Corner of Pete Rose Way,
Wyoming Street, and Eastern Avenue
No phone
Look at this park as Cincinnati's bicentennial gift to its kids. The beautiful and fully equipped playground with separate areas for big- and little-kid play, the Serpentine Wall, and historical attractions at the Bicentennial Commons nearby make for a fine outing for the kids.

Spirit of Mount Washington Park **Free**
Mears Avenue at Beechmont Avenue
No phone
This incredibly elaborate park rivals any Discovery Zone for its tubes and slides, and best yet, it's free. The huge wooden castle was built by a Thousand Hands committee of community volunteers, and their loving touch shows in the craftsmanship. Your tykes won't ever want to leave.

Woodland Mound Park **Free**
Nordyke Road, Anderson
(513) 474-0580
A "sprayground" opened at Woodland Mound in 2001 that features a 16-foot tree with two slides, whimsical and spraying blue herons, frogs, and turtles. The sprayground incorporates no standing water, making parents of toddlers happy, and includes adjacent picnic tables and concession sales. In addition to several small swing and slide areas, Woodland Mound has a large, fully equipped play area with tunnel slides, jungle gyms, and plenty of sand. It also has a nice kid-size nature trail adjacent to Seasongood Nature Center.

SPECIAL EVENTS AND ENRICHMENT OPPORTUNITIES

Watch weekend sections in the local newspapers for calendars of upcoming events for children. Here are a few regular events and educational programs worth attending.

Artrageous Saturdays
Raymond Walters College,
9555 Plainfield Road, Blue Ash
(513) 745-5705
Five shows each season cover a broad spectrum of performing arts, including classical, contemporary, and ethnic dance; folk, orchestral, and chamber music; and

children's theater. Artists not only entertain but take the time to inform kids about the art form. All shows are presented at 11:00 A.M. and 2:00 P.M. on Saturday. Call for dates, ticket prices, and a season brochure.

Calico Theatre $
Clermont College, 4200 Clermont College Drive, Batavia
(513) 732-5281

Friday evening and Saturday morning performances are designed for kids and are offered six times a year starting in the fall. The series covers a range of performing arts, including music, dance, juggling, puppets, and illustrated theater. Ticket prices are $3.00, but series tickets and group rates of $1.00 per kid for groups of 25 to 100 are available.

Carnegie Visual and Performing Arts Center
1028 Scott Boulevard, Covington, KY
(859) 491-2030

The Carnegie provides a place for emerging artists to show their art and perform plays, but it also runs some ambitious childhood learning programs. That includes bringing in volunteer artists to teach classes, and a hands-on arts program in the Biggs Early Learning Center.

Chateau LaRoche $-$$
12025 Shore Drive, Loveland
(513) 683-4686
www.lovelandcastle.com

This is a one-fifth-scale replica of a medieval castle. Really, no kidding. Chateau LaRoche, also known as the Loveland Castle Museum, offers tours to the public 11:00 A.M. to 5:00 P.M. weekends April through early September. Admission is $2.00 (kids age 12 and younger $1.00). During October, take an eerie Halloween stroll through the candlelit castle during the nightly Scary Knights Tour. Admission is $6.00, $5.00 age 12 and under. Most notable for youngsters, however, are the way-cool overnight sleepers. Scouts, school, and other groups populate this place at night, along with the odd ghost and rattling chain. The overnight sleepers are arranged through area schools and Scout groups ($150 for school groups and Scout troops up to 25 people).

Children's Choir of Greater Cincinnati
7865 Tyler's Way, West Chester
(513) 759-0644

The Children's Choir of Greater Cincinnati is actually six choirs (divided by age group and ability) that include children in grades 2 through 12. The choir has gone on tours across America, Canada, and England, and it's truly an underestimated and unrecognized resource. Call for information on how to join.

Children's International Summer Village
11 Glendale Square, Glendale
(513) 771-7200

Some 70 children from 15 nations arrive at the Children's International Summer Village each year. The kids (ages 11 to 18), from Canada, Guatemala, Sweden, Indonesia, and a host of other countries, spend a month each summer getting to know each other's cultures. Villagers communicate nonverbally through games and hand motions. Founded on the belief that world peace begins with the children, the nonprofit program also sends dozens of Cincinnati children to all points on the globe. Families traditionally contribute $1,800; the Summer Village program, which finds sponsorships among local business, picks up the rest of the tab. Notable grads include former congressman and U.S. Trade Representative Rob Portman (who, as a seventh grader, traveled to a Swedish summer village for a month).

Cincinnati Art Museum $$
953 Eden Park Drive
(513) 721-5204
www.cincinnatiartmuseum.org

The museum offers a variety of programs aimed at kids and families, including Saturday performances by Madcap Puppet Theatre and other local children's performers. Tickets are $9.00 adults, $7.00 children.

Cincinnati Children's Theatre
Taft Theatre, Fifth and Sycamore Streets
(513) 569-8080
www.thechildrenstheatre.com
Besides school-day field-trip performances, the Children's Theatre also puts on popular weekend family performances in March, April, and December.

Cincinnati Nature Center **$**
4949 Tealtown Road, Glen Este
(513) 831-1711
www.cincynature.org
The nature center offers the best hands-on nature study you'll find in the area, with numerous educational programs for youths, including spring and fall biology programs and summer classes. Besides the 1,425 acres of trails, there's a well-stocked library and an educational building with lots of great stuffed specimens. Open daylight to dusk.

Cincinnati Park Board
950 Eden Park Drive
(513) 352-4080
Several great events, such as Halloween hikes and enrichment classes, are offered at Cincinnati parks through the park board. A schedule of events is available.

Cincinnati Symphony Orchestra **$$**
Music Hall, 1229 Elm Street
(513) 381-3300
www.cincinnatisymphony.org
The orchestra presents Young People's Concerts for school field trips and Lollipop Concerts for children ages four through nine on two Saturdays a year. Watch newspaper calendars for details; better still, call ahead for times because tickets go fast. Admission is $4.50 for children and $7.00 for adults. The Cincinnati Youth Symphony Orchestra, a group of young performers under the leadership of CSO veterans, tours area high schools on a rotating basis to expose students to works of the masters. The Youth Symphony performs one joint concert with the CSO each year. And the popular Peanut Butter & Jam sessions take musicians into churches and schools across the area for Saturday morning concerts that appeal to both preschoolers and toddlers.

College-Conservatory of Music
Preparatory Program
University of Cincinnati
(513) 556-2595
Among noteworthy graduates of this preparatory program are ballerina Suzanne Farrell, actress Sarah Jessica Parker, and Tchaikovsky medalist violinist Alyssa Park. Options in this prestigious program, offered by one of the nation's leading conservatories, include private and group instruction in dance, musical theater, drama, and orchestral and chamber music. Among the most popular programs are the Suzuki violin program, Kindermusik, and the Children's Choir. A brochure is available.

Drake Planetarium **$**
Norwood High School, 2020 Sherman Avenue, Norwood
(513) 396-5560
One of the region's last remaining planetariums in an age of high-tech gimmickry and OMNIMAX spectacles is open to students across Greater Cincinnati. Funded by the National Science Foundation and NASA, this regional gem offers astronomy programs for 40,000 students annually.

Duke Energy Train Display **Free**
139 East Fourth Street
(513) 287-1500
The Duke Energy Train Display is a mammoth toy train layout and light display found in the lobby of the Cincinnati Gas & Electric Building. Kids will love the scale replicas of circus trains and festive, snow-covered towns. Best yet, youngsters get free cookies. Hours are 8:00 A.M. to 6:00 P.M. Monday through Saturday, noon to 5:00 P.M. Sunday, through December.

Flying Cloud Academy of Vintage Dance
3738 Eastern Avenue
(513) 733-3077

These folks became famous in such TV miniseries as *North and South* and the movie *Glory,* providing backdrops of vintage ballroom dancing. If you want to expose your teenager to various dance styles, from the Civil War through the Victorian era and the Roaring Twenties, this is the place. No Twist lessons, sorry. The academy also conducts an annual one-week dance seminar on the campus of Miami University.

Hamilton County Park District
10245 Winton Road, Greenhills
(513) 521-7275
www.greatparks.org

The county park district hosts special events and classes for kids year-round at parks throughout the area. Animal lore, storytelling, crafts, and kite-flying lessons are just a few examples. Most activities are free. Look for the park district's semi-monthly "Evergreen" inserts in the Sunday *Enquirer,* or call for times and details.

Heritage Programs **$$$$**
1301 Western Avenue
(513) 287-7031

The monthly motorcoach odyssey arranged by the Heritage Programs project of the Cincinnati Historical Society offers some of the most fascinating, and offbeat, views of the city. Volunteer historians who know their stuff lead you on ventures into the city's Historic Houses of Worship, Over-the-Rhine's German Heritage, and—always a favorite with teenagers—a spooky Haunted Cincinnati. Tickets for the Thursday and Saturday tours range from $25 to $75 and often include lunch at a historic restaurant.

Madcap Productions Puppet Theatre
1 Eden Park Drive
(513) 721-2787

Madcap is one of four giant puppet theater troupes in the country; this one was founded two decades ago by Jerry Handorf, a protege of Jim Henson. These are slightly off-center plays, tongue firmly placed in cheek (they recently staged a version of *Hansel & Gretel* titled *Two Crummy Kids,* told from the witch's point of view). The 14-foot giant puppets—ogres, sharks, lizards, and even a genie or two—will certainly wow your kids. Madcap performs in the public schools but also offers regular performances at the Cincinnati Art Museum.

Noah's Ark Farm **$**
401 Kentucky Highway 10, California, KY
(859) 635-0803

If your child ever wanted to meet an emu, stroke a llama, or encounter exotic pigs, macaws, horses, and ferrets, this is the place to go. Tours include teaching children the proper care and feeding of the animals, including the opportunity to bottle-feed small creatures. Hours are 10:00 A.M. to 6:00 P.M. Wednesday through Sunday, April through November. There's also a live nativity scene in December. Admission is $3.00 per person (all ages), with an additional charge of $2.00 for pony rides.

Prop Shop Tour **Free**
Playhouse Scenery Shop
2827 Gilbert Avenue, Walnut Hills
(513) 421-3888

It's little surprise that the Playhouse in the Park doesn't have the space inside the cramped theater in Mount Adams to store the varied scenery, props, and costumes from all its years of performances. Rather,

The title of "largest holiday light show organized by a private homeowner" goes to Robert Niederman. In 2001 the dairy farmer bought the locally famous Rudd family display, which included one million bulbs, and combined it with his own. The free display is open nightly each December at 4972 LeSourdsville–West Chester Road in Liberty Township. Call (513) 887-0725 for details.

all these wonderfully intriguing (and sometimes massive) theatrical trinkets are housed inside a former roller-skating rink. One weekend a year, in mid-February, the Playhouse offers rare (and free) tours of its huge scenery and props shop. Kids of all ages will get a kick out of it.

St. Rita Haunted House **$$**
Exit 14 off Interstate 75 at Glendale-Milford Road, Evendale
(513) 771-1060
www.srsdeaf.org
The St. Rita Haunted House is the area's largest haunted house, occupying an authentic Civil War-era farmhouse that includes 16 rooms of fright—including a bedroom of despair, funeral parlor, chamber of motion, foyer of doom, and Jack the Ripper room—all loaded with costumed characters. At a special children's matinee, the lights stay on and the monster masks come off. Costumes are encouraged. The monthlong haunting, a quarter-century tradition, benefits St. Rita School for the Deaf. Hours are 7:00 to 10:00 P.M. Sunday, Wednesday, and Thursday, and 7:00 to 11:00 P.M. Friday and Saturday, through the month of October. Admission is $8.00.

Wolff Planetarium **$**
Trailside Nature Center, Burnet Woods
(513) 751-3679
This tiny planetarium (seating 20 or so) is generally unknown even to longtime residents of the Clifton neighborhood where it's located. Programs on the season's stars are offered on Friday night and selected afternoon shows on weekends. Reservations are a must. The planetarium is not recommended for children under the age of five or those scared of the dark.

YMCAs of Greater Cincinnati
Each Y in the area offers a range of swimming, gymnastics, karate, and other education programs for kids. See the Parks and Recreation Chapter for a rundown on all the Ys in the area, as well as assorted youth sports.

TOY STORES AND BOOKSTORES FOR KIDS

The area has many good conventional toy stores, such as Toys"R"Us, locally based Johnny's Toys chain, and Kay-Bee Toy and Hobby shops in many malls. Bigg's Hypermarkets and Meijer also carry a wide selection of toys at good prices. What follows is a list of stores whose offerings go well beyond the usual to include particularly useful selections of educational or other high-quality toys and books for children.

Barnes & Noble
Newport on the Levee, Levee Way, Newport, KY
(859) 581-2000

7800 Montgomery Road, Kenwood
(513) 794-9440

9891 Waterstone Boulevard, Deerfield Township
(513) 683-5599
These stores have great collections of children's books and software, plus ample opportunity to try out software or CDs before you buy. Readings of children's books are offered throughout the year. Call for schedules.

Borders Books & Music
11711 Princeton Road, Springdale
(513) 671-5852

4530 Eastgate Boulevard, Eastgate
(513) 943-0068
Borders is another book megastore with a great selection of kids' books. Wee Read every Monday at 10:00 A.M. is for ages two through four, and for older kids there's Kids Storytime every Saturday at 11:00 A.M.

The Disney Store
Kenwood Towne Centre, 7875 Montgomery Road, Kenwood
(513) 984-4775

Northgate Mall, 9501 Colerain Avenue, Bevis
(513) 385-7520

Florence Mall, 2028 Florence Mall Road, Florence, KY
(859) 647-7791
No longer must parents travel all the way to Florida or California to blow a wad on Mickey and friends. These stores have got the goods. Be prepared . . . your kids will find these stores and they will make you take them there.

Joseph-Beth Kids
Rookwood Pavilion, 2692 Madison Road, Norwood
(513) 396-8965
www.josephbeth.com
For a bookstore, this is also one great toy store. It wins hands down in the contest for most comfortable and inviting children's book department, even in a city with three book superstore chains and numerous other kids' bookstores competing head-to-head. A stair-step amphitheater area gives kids and parents a cozy place to sit and read. The store also has regular readings for kids at 11:00 A.M. Saturday.

King Arthur's Court
3040 Madison Road, Oakley Square
(513) 531-4600
If you want to take it easy on yourself and your kids, do your Christmas shopping at King Arthur's Court, which has the best selection of high-quality toys in Greater Cincinnati. It also carries some of the usual Sega and Nintendo ware and other conventional toy store merchandise. You will pay more for many comparable items than at Toys"R"Us, but you'll also find a nicely arranged selection of educational toys and a downstairs department devoted solely to model trains, model cars, and other sorts of model projects.

Once Upon a Child
2733 Madison Road
(513) 871-8700

5138 Glencrossing Way
(513) 451-7600

9898 Colerain Avenue
(513) 385-3034

9727 Montgomery Road, Montgomery
(513) 791-1199

8087 Connector Drive, Florence, KY
(859) 282-8922
These stores get our vote for best toy bargains in town. They carry slightly used but hardly dented toys, previously worn but immaculate outfits. Why pay retail for Oshkosh and other premium name brands?

THE ARTS

Cincinnati has some of the oldest and most respected cultural institutions in the country, of which we boast with a great deal of pride. The symphony and pops are world renowned. The theater community is prominent enough to draw Edward Albee to town to direct. Broadway shows regularly stop here. The ballet, May Festival Chorus, and Cincinnati Boychoir are recognized nationally. And dozens of community theaters and art galleries offer local artists a chance to demonstrate their talents.

For newcomers, trying to take it all in can be a bit overwhelming. We have a suggestion, though. The best way to get a taste of Greater Cincinnati's arts offerings is during the Fine Arts Sampler Weekend in mid-February. It is the biggest and perhaps the most fun arts showcase of the year. More than 70 visual and performing arts events are held for free as part of the kickoff for the annual Fine Arts Fund fund-raising campaign that benefits the city's major cultural institutions. The events are held at 35 locations throughout the area, so it's impossible to take them all in, but going through the full listings of the events that run in the daily and arts papers and carefully planning out your weekend is all part of the fun.

The rest of the year, you can become familiar with the arts scene through functions such as Final Friday, a tour and social event that takes place in the abundance of art studios in Over-the-Rhine. It is held the last Friday of the month.

If you have artistic talent, you can further your education through the University of Cincinnati College-Conservatory of Music (CCM) or the School for the Creative and Performing Arts (SCPA). CCM offers more than just music, despite its name. And the SCPA, which stages legendary theatrical productions, offers educational and practical experience for schoolchildren in grades 4 through 12 who are interested in vocal and choral music, graphic and visual arts, dance, and creative writing. Students from SCPA perform regularly with the ballet and pops. SCPA was created in 1973 as an alternative school for the artistically inclined and is called Cincinnati's most important institution by pops conductor Erich Kunzel. It has grown in both size and stature in those two decades, with student performances making national tours and graduates heading off to Broadway. Some of the school's most famous graduates include members of the pop group 98 Degrees: Drew Lachey, Nick Lachey, and Justin Jeffre.

The most important name to know in Cincinnati arts is that of the Corbett family. Ralph and Patricia Corbett's establishment of the Corbett Foundation has resulted in contributions of more than $50 million toward maintaining and improving the arts in Greater Cincinnati.

ARTS ORGANIZATIONS

Perhaps because of its lengthy history and continual evolution, Cincinnati is one of just five of the top-50 U.S. population markets that doesn't have a central arts agency. Rather, we have several organizations that help pull together all of the arts efforts in town. For the most part, they get along well, and together they keep the area's arts strong.

Arts Consortium
1301 Western Avenue
(513) 381-0645

The Arts Consortium is the city's premier African-American arts organization. It has a dual focus of education and presentation, which it accomplishes through not only theater performances but also photography, art, theater, and dance classes. The center, which also has a gallery, recently reinstated its theater programming and expanded its performance space for more stage and seating room.

Cincinnati Arts Association
650 Walnut Street
(513) 241-SHOW
www.cincinnatiarts.org
The Cincinnati Arts Association is the central organizing and operating organization for the area's largest venues: Music Hall, Memorial Hall, and the Aronoff Center for the Arts. It keeps the abundance of performing arts shows that fill the city's calendar from becoming a tangled mess and competing against each other.

Fine Arts Fund
2649 Erie Avenue
(513) 871-2787
www.fineartsfund.org
The Fine Arts Fund is the organization behind the annual drive of the same name. The drive helps keep the quality of Cincinnati's arts at its high level by collecting more than $8.4 million annually in contributions that go to the art museum, ballet, opera, Playhouse in the Park, symphony, Contemporary Arts Center, May Festival, and Taft Museum. A Projects Pool also offers grants to smaller organizations in the area. The Fine Arts Fund puts on the Fine Arts Sampler Weekend each February (see the Annual Events chapter).

Northern Kentucky Arts Council
Robbins and Scott Streets, Covington, KY
(859) 491-2030
This arts organization in Northern Kentucky is based out of the Carnegie Visual and Performing Arts Center. The center offers educational opportunities for young people ages 4 to 17. It also hosts multiarts performances and events including music, drama, and plays in its 750-seat theater.

VENUES

Aronoff Center for the Arts
650 Walnut Street
(513) 721-3344
www.cincinnatiarts.org
Cincinnati got a new cultural core in October 1995 when the $82 million Aronoff Center for the Arts opened to rave reviews and packed houses. Since then, performances of some sort have taken place almost nightly in one of the center's three performance halls: the 2,700-seat Procter & Gamble Hall, the 150-seat Fifth Third Bank Theater, and the 450-seat Jarson-Kaplan Theater.

The center is now the performance home for the ballet, the School for the Creative and Performing Arts, and the Contemporary Dance Theater. It's also the theater for some of Cincinnati's stagings of Broadway Series productions.

Many arts lovers wondered if the opening of the Aronoff Center would eventually doom Music Hall and the Taft Theater, which previously hosted the ballet and Broadway Series shows. But the love of performing arts in Cincinnati has proven great enough that none of the venues are suffering. In fact, Cincinnatians now get to see even more high-quality performances.

And if bringing more arts options to the area wasn't enough, the center is also close to numerous restaurants and entertainment-oriented businesses that have cropped up all around the building in an area known as Backstage. The businesses offer enough pre- and post-theater entertainment opportunities that it's now possible to stay downtown after work and not be bored in the few hours until the show starts—or after it ends.

Patricia Corbett Theater
University of Cincinnati, Clifton Heights
(513) 556-4183
The Corbett Theater underwent a major renovation and expansion to modernize the facility, which is the frequent site of

CLOSE-UP

Fins to the Left . . . Meet Cincy's Most Popular Rock Singer

Every summer Cincinnatians break out the Bermuda shorts and Styrofoam shark fins when Jimmy Buffett comes back to town in what has become a rite of summer.

Buffett and his Coral Reefer Band have performed about 40 times in Greater Cincinnati, in fact. Some 700,000 area Parrotheads have flocked to Buffett's concerts over the past decade, making the scruffy singer the most popular Riverbend act ever.

What makes Buffett such a hit year after year? Perhaps it originates in the fact that the "Parrothead" phenomenon launched here. The term was coined by Coral Reefer Band member Timothy Schmit at a TimberWolf concert in 1983, back in the days when a Buffett appearance would cause barely a blip on anybody's radar screen. (He played his first outdoor show here to fewer than 6,000.) Then fate intervened: Schmit jumped onstage and likened the TimberWolf crowd, all dressed in parrot paraphernalia, to Deadheads—adapting the term "Parrotheads." A legend was born.

Year after year Buffett returned and the Parrotheads flocked. At the singer's height in the mid-1990s, he sold out four- and five-night series at Riverbend Music Center, earning a million dollars for each week's run. Buffett even recorded his live album, *Feeding Frenzy,* at Riverbend, and—of course—the hit "Fins" goes to the length of mentioning Cincinnati by name.

As the Pirate greets age 60, he's still able to refashion Riverbend into Margaritaville, if only for a few nights. Expect the crowd to continue sporting foam lobster hats, tacky Hawaiian shirts, and inflatable plastic sharks. The menu? Coronas and cheeseburgers in paradise, of course.

musical and theatrical performances by the University of Cincinnati's College-Conservatory of Music as well as regional and national acts.

Abigail Cutter Theater
1310 Sycamore Street
(513) 632-5910
The Cutter Theater is located in the School of the Creative and Performing Arts and is the main center for theatrical and musical performances by the school's students.

Memorial Hall
1225 Elm Street
(513) 241-7469
Memorial Hall is the smaller sister to Music Hall (see below), sitting next door to the historical facility. Memorial Hall offers a more intimate setting, and it is the home of the Cincinnati Chamber Orchestra.

Music Hall
1241 Elm Street
(513) 721-8222

Music Hall is the grande dame of Cincinnati's arts venues. This architectural masterpiece dates from 1878 and has seen some of the world's greatest musicians and artists grace its stage. Despite the opening of the Aronoff Center, it remains one of the key arts locations, serving as the home of the Cincinnati Symphony Orchestra, Cincinnati Pops Orchestra, and May Festival. It's also arguably better than ever as a musical venue now that it doesn't have to share its stage with the ballet and other theatrical organizations. An acoustic backdrop was added, improving the sound in the three-tiered hall. However, the Cincinnati Ballet continues to perform the *Nutcracker* at Music Hall each holiday season.

Playhouse in the Park
962 Mount Adams Circle
(513) 421-3888
www.cincyplay.com

While many of the nation's regional theaters struggle to survive, Playhouse in the Park is thriving and has achieved national recognition, winning a Tony Award in 2004. Started in 1960, the theater recently underwent a massive renovation and expansion, and it has more than 18,000 subscribers for its performances.

The Playhouse, which likes to refer to its productions as "great theatre in a great theater," is actually two theaters, the 629-seat Marx Theater and the 220-seat Thompson Shelterhouse Theater. Every seat is a good seat in both theaters. Marx Theater holds six major productions that run three or four weeks each. Thompson Shelterhouse has four or five productions that run about two and a half weeks each.

The Playhouse, sometimes referred to as PIP, tries to offer something each season to please the area's wide theatrical tastes, so the productions range from Shakespeare to modern musicals. The selections are usually well balanced, though, and theatergoers generally find something they like.

It is also home of the annual debut of the nationally renowned Rosenthal Award winners for new playwrights, as well as the immensely popular annual production of *A Christmas Carol*. Plays run nightly except Monday from September through May. Matinees are on Saturday, Sunday, and Wednesday.

Murray Seasongood Pavilion
Eden Park, access from Kemper Lane, Victory Parkway, or Gilbert Avenue
(513) 352-4080

This outdoor venue named for a former Cincinnati mayor is regularly the site of both theatrical and musical performances. The pops often performs free concerts in the natural amphitheater, located in the beautiful setting of Eden Park. Some bench seating is available near the stage, which sits down the hill from both the art museum and Playhouse in the Park.

Showboat Majestic
Public Landing
(513) 241-6550
www.cincinnatilandmarkproductions.com

The *Showboat* is owned by the city and managed by Cincinnati Landmark Production. The majestic venue has plays and musicals on the historic riverboat/floating theater Wednesday through Sunday between April and October. Productions feature some of the best semiprofessional and community theater talent in the area. A performance on the *Showboat* also offers a historical look at theater, as the boat is an authentic riverboat performance hall that was pushed up and down the river by a paddle wheeler 80-plus years ago to stage performances at different cities along the way.

Looking for a cheap but sophisticated date? Tickets are marked down to half price at noon the day of the performance for Playhouse in the Park and the symphony. Or try the ballet's half-price matinees on Saturday afternoon.

Taft Theater
Fifth and Sycamore Streets
(513) 721-8883
http://taftevents.com
The Taft is one of the venues for concerts, comedy shows, and other productions. It also is the home of the Children's Theater of Cincinnati.

MUSIC

Cincinnati Boychoir
1926 Mills Avenue, Norwood
(513) 396-7664
www.cincinnatiboychoir.org
The 120-member choir is one of the world's largest boys choirs. Members not only perform locally but also sing everywhere from California to Austria and in such hallowed venues as Carnegie Hall and the Crystal Cathedral. When they aren't traveling the world, the Boychoir can be seen performing in concerts at Music Hall each May or brightening the holiday season at various venues each December.

The Boychoir has auditions three times a year for boys in grades three through nine. Two of its members have studies with the Vienna Boy Choir School. In 2003 the choir toured Ohio instead of the world to celebrate the state's bicentennial.

Cincinnati Opera
1241 Elm Street
(513) 241-2742
www.cincinnatiopera.org
The Cincinnati Opera is the second-oldest opera company in the country. It presented its first performance on June 27, 1920, in a converted band shell at, of all places, the Cincinnati Zoo. The company's fame and fortune grew during World War II when highly talented European performers from New York's Metropolitan Opera and other large companies couldn't get home and were looking for summer work. The Cincinnati Opera was the only summer opera company at the time, so area residents were treated to the best. Fostering new and young talent became a Cincinnati Opera tradition that continues to this day.

The opera, which performed at the zoo until moving to Music Hall in 1972, stages four productions a year (all with English "surcaps"—the Cincinnatian term for surtitles projected above the stage) with leading national and international performers. It fills Music Hall to 99 percent of capacity for the concerts, so tickets are sometimes difficult to obtain. It also offers an introduction performance for children.

Since 2005 the opera has been under the artistic direction of Evans Mirageas.

Cincinnati Pops Orchestra
1229 Elm Street
(513) 381-3300
www.cincinnatipops.org
Conductor Erich Kunzel and the pops perform 20 times a year from September to May in the glorious Music Hall and then mix their spirited music with the sounds of the outdoors 10 times each summer at the Riverbend amphitheater. There is nothing quite like listening to the pops under a starry summer sky.

No matter what the venue, though, the pops offers highly entertaining concerts. Entertainers such as Doc Severinsen, Roy Clark, Andrew Lloyd Webber, Peter Frampton, the Chieftains, and Ray Charles have teamed up with the pops to create a fascinating and most enjoyable mixture of classical and modern sounds. The pops also entertains audiences by combining its outstanding symphonic music with lasers, projections, fireworks, fire and water, and hot-air balloons.

So far, 63 concerts with well-known entertainers have been recorded and released on CDs or tapes. The CDs of the pops performing with the late Henry Mancini are best-sellers. Kunzel, who was *Billboard* magazine's top crossover artist for four straight years, also was named top classical album maker by *Billboard* in 1995 for *Magical Music of Disney.* Kunzel also leads the National Orchestra each

Memorial Day and Fourth of July during its concert in Washington, D.C.

Cincinnati Symphony Orchestra
1229 Elm Street
(513) 381-3300
www.cincinnatisymphony.org
Led by conductor Paavo Jarvi, the CSO dazzles audiences from September to May with 50 concerts at the elegant Music Hall and then 6 concerts in the relaxed, outdoor amphitheater at Riverbend during the summer. As a special treat during the summer, a scaled-down version of the symphony sets up in various city and county parks and gives free concerts.

Since its founding in 1894 (making it the fifth-oldest orchestra in the country), the symphony has awed music lovers all over the world. It was the first U.S. symphony orchestra to be selected to tour Europe, and it has been invited back numerous times. It was also the first guest symphony orchestra ever invited to the Festival Casals during the 25th anniversary celebration in Puerto Rico. The CSO also regularly sells out American venues outside of Cincinnati, such as Carnegie Hall during its annual visit to New York.

When the symphony isn't going to the best places, the best people come to Cincinnati to perform. Guest conductors and performers over the years have included Vladimir Horowitz, Beverly Sills, Benny Goodman, Marian Anderson, Sir Thomas Beecham, Enrico Caruso, Pablo Casals, Arthur Rubenstein, Itzhak Perlman, Yo Yo Ma, Isaac Stern, and Ezio Pinza.

Paavo Jarvi is an Estonian native who is the 12th music director. Jarvi has been a guest conductor for a number of other orchestras. He is the son of Detroit Symphony Orchestra's director Neeme Jarvi, and Jarvi's appointment in Cincinnati was the first time in history that a father and son headed two major American orchestras.

The CSO is also in the forefront of new ideas, experimenting with video screens during performances to enhance the visual aspects of the concerts.

The Cincinnati Symphony Orchestra first performed on January 17, 1895. Conductor Frank A. Van Der Sticken opened with Mozart's Symphony in G Minor. The next evening he became the first conductor to stage an all-American concert by devoting the evening strictly to American composers.

The Kentucky Symphony Orchestra
P.O. Box 72810,Newport, KY 41072
(859) 431-6216
www.kyso.org
Formerly named the Northern Kentucky Symphony, this orchestra has grown by leaps and bounds in the last few years. It performs at the Greaves Concert Hall at Northern Kentucky University but also branches out and plays at Devou Park and the Covington Cathedral. Besides the full 90-piece orchestra, it has several smaller groups, including the Flood Wall Jazz Quartet, Men in Black Brass Quartet, Newport Ragtime Band, and KSO Boogie Band. Tickets to performances are $20 to $25.

May Festival Chorus
1241 Elm Street
(513) 621-1919
Billed as "The Oldest Continuing Choral Festival in the Western Hemisphere," the May Festival was formed in 1873 and is now world renowned. More than 200 average Joes and Josephines with good voices rehearse year-round for two weekend performances in May at Music Hall and the Cathedral Basilica of the Assumption. The chorus also travels and performs in venues such as Carnegie Hall and often hosts world-class guest artists and conductors.

Director James Conlon is also the principal conductor of the Paris Opera and has conducted national telecasts for the Metropolitan Opera and the National Symphony's Fourth of July concert. Conlon, who speaks four languages and "gets along" in several others, won France's Bellan Film Prize for his musical direction of the film version of *Madame Butterfly* in 1995.

If you miss the May performances, the chorus offers Carolfest, singing traditional holiday carols and Christmas favorites each December. The annual family holiday concert is presented as a gift to the city from the chorus.

Auditions are held in September and January.

Northern Kentucky University Choirs
NKU, Louis B. Nunn Drive, Highland Heights, KY
(859) 572-6399
Under the guidance of Randy Pennington, Northern Kentucky University has established three choirs, each of which is gaining a reputation as one of the area's most up-and-coming groups in its category. The NKU Chamber Choir, for instance, received an invitation to perform at the prestigious gala for arts patron Patricia Corbett in 1997 and to perform at Sing Cincinnati and the Kentucky Education Association convention. The Chamber Choir is the university's elite choral ensemble and is auditioned at the beginning of each fall semester, along with the nine-member Vocal Jazz Ensemble. The Northern Chorale is the third of NKU's choirs. The groups are made up of NKU students, although not all of them are music majors. Some are just students who like to sing.

Frustrated over a hot show that's sold out? You should know that no concert or event is ever really "sold out" in Cincinnati, since ticket scalping is perfectly legal and scalpers can be found in the Yellow Pages under "Ticket Agencies." You'll pay a price for a hot performer, though: Jimmy Buffett tickets at the ticket agencies, for instance, cost anything from $85 for a lawn seat all the way up to $750 for a pavilion seat (when the original face value of a ticket was just $37 to $59).

University of Cincinnati College-Conservatory of Music
Patricia Corbett Theater, University of Cincinnati
(513) 556-6638
Dating from 1867, CCM is one of the three oldest schools of music in the United States. It enjoys a strong reputation among the top tier of American conservatories, particularly for its innovative operas and its top-ranked philharmonic orchestra. Some of its graduates include Al Hirt, Tennessee Ernie Ford, James Levine, Eddie Albert, and Lee Roy Reams. Many concerts are free.

Smaller Orchestras

With one of the best music schools in the country at our doorstep and limited opportunities to perform with the symphony or the pops, area musicians have formed numerous small to midsize orchestras. Despite not having the budget of the major orchestras, they offer excellent music at a fraction of the admission price in addition to a more casual approach. Their concerts are well attended, some with several thousand people.

Among the smaller orchestras are the **Hamilton-Fairfield Symphony,** (513) 895-5151, which performs at Miami University's Hamilton branch or the Fairfield Performing Arts Center; and the **Middletown Symphony,** (513) 424-2426 (www.middletownsymphony.com), which performs at MU-Middletown. The Middletown Symphony is conducted by Carmon DeLeone, who also is the longtime conductor of the Cincinnati Ballet's orchestra.

DANCE

Cincinnati Ballet
1555 Central Parkway
(513) 621-5219
www.cincinnatiballet.com
One of the nation's top-10 professional companies, the Cincinnati Ballet is known

nationally for its diverse repertoire of contemporary and classic dance works. Thirty-five dancers and a full orchestra perform five subscription-series ballets between September and May and 10 highly popular *Nutcracker* performances each Christmas.

The Cincinnati Ballet mixes its performances with such ballet classics as *Swan Lake* and *Romeo and Juliet* and modern dance numbers such as *L*, the tribute to Liza Minelli. The orchestra is led by longtime musical director Carmon DeLeone, who not only conducts but also composes scores for some of the ballet's original works.

In 1997 Victoria Morgan became artistic director of the company, the first female to hold this position. The ballet has had only seven artistic directors since its founding in 1958, but four of those have come and gone since 1990. The hiring of Morgan created stability within the company without sacrificing the quality of performances. She was formerly a dancer for Ballet West in Salt Lake City and the San Francisco Ballet and served as resident choreographer and ballet mistress for the San Francisco Opera, the second-largest opera company in the country.

Contemporary Dance Theater
1805 Larch Avenue, College Hill
(513) 591-1222

The Contemporary Dance Theater offers modern dance concerts, including numerous touring dance events. Operating for more than 30 seasons, the CDT brings in such nationally known companies as the Liz Lerman Dance Exchange and Urban Bush Women. Performances take place at the Jarson-Kaplan Theater in the Aronoff Center for the Arts and at the College Hill Town Hall.

THEATER

Broadway Series
Aronoff Center for the Arts,
650 Walnut Street
(513) 621-2787

***Billboard** magazine was born in Cincinnati more than 100 years ago at a Vine Street saloon. William Donaldson and James Hennegan, whose family still operates a local printing company, began the publication that is now the music industry's charting guide.*

Cincinnati is a regular stop on the traveling productions of popular Broadway shows. Shows that have been performed at the Aronoff Center since its opening in late 1995 include *Miss Saigon, Cats, Grease, Damn Yankees, Stomp, Rent, Phantom of the Opera,* and *Hello, Dolly!* to name a few. The Broadway Series productions are so popular that tickets are sold in packages, and nearly 15,000 people have become season subscribers.

Cincinnati Shakespeare Company
717–719 Race Street
(513) 381-2273
www.cincyshakes.com

Established in 1995, the Cincinnati Shakespeare Company offers area residents a taste of Shakespeare with eight shows a year. The CSC performs at the site of the old Movies Theater downtown and has been well received in the years it has been staging the events, with more than 900 annual ticket subscribers now packing the theater. Although the performances are classical Shakespeare, they are sometimes done with a bold twist. In a performance of *Hamlet,* for instance, the title role was played by a woman. Tickets are $22.

Ensemble Theater of Cincinnati
1127 Vine Street
(513) 421-3555
www.cincyetc.com

Cincinnati's off-Broadway professional theater on Vine Street offers world and regional premiere works ranging from drama to comedy by national and regional playwrights. The ETC season runs from September to June. Ticket prices range from $26 to $32.

Community Theaters

Dozens of community theaters operate year-round throughout Greater Cincinnati, including 20 that form the Association of Community Theaters. ACT began in 1955 and has been the center for the area's community theaters. All the community theaters use local, unpaid talent and perform an average of four times a year. Despite the lack of high-priced talent, most of the performances are of high quality. Many groups perform in local school or college auditoriums, although the larger groups, including Footlighters, the Mariemont Players, Stagecrafters, and the Wyoming Players, have their own theaters. Shows average between $5.00 and $15.00 for admission.

College Theaters

Miami University Theater
Center for Performing Arts, Miami University, Oxford
(513) 529-3200
Students from the school perform musical and theatrical shows during the school year as well as during the summer. During the summer, the cast of the shows include semiprofessional, community, and student members.

Northern Kentucky University Theater
Northern Kentucky University, Highland Heights, KY
(859) 572-5464
The NKU Theater stages numerous theatrical shows during the academic year at the NKU Corbett Theater on the school's campus.

University of Cincinnati College-Conservatory of Music
Patricia Corbett Theater, University of Cincinnati, Clifton Heights
(513) 556-4183
Although CCM is better known for its musical productions, it also offers theater, opera, and dance performances. Its Hot Summer Nights repertory theater programs are very popular.

Xavier University Theater
3800 Victory Parkway
(513) 745-3939
Xavier's student theater offers performances in the Xavier University Center Theater on the Xavier campus.

ART MUSEUMS

Cincinnati Art Museum
953 Eden Park Drive
(513) 721-5204
www.cincinnatiartmuseum.org
The Cincinnati Art Museum is well known for its exhibits from civilizations spanning the globe. You will find a mummy from 300 B.C. Egypt, a Vincent van Gogh masterpiece, and modern art as part of the museum's permanent collection. It's one of the oldest museums west of the Allegheny Mountains—its building dates from 1866 and the museum was started in 1876.

The museum has more than 118 galleries filled with all sorts of visual arts, including paintings, prints, sculptures, drawings, photos, costumes, and musical instruments from the last 5,000 years.

A recent addition to the art museum is the $10 million Cincinnati Wing. The new exhibit space includes 15 galleries representing some 18,000 square feet; the premier exhibit is The Story of Art in the Queen City, with supplemental displays such as Making Their Mark: Drawings and Watercolors by Cincinnati Artists, and Extraordinary Gifts: Selected Paintings from the Procter & Gamble Company. An installation by Mark Fox titled *Dust* is also on display, addressing the very notion of the impulse to collect and the forces that destroy permanence.

The Cincinnati Wing showcases 400 objects and paintings by such artists as Hiram Powers, John Twachtman, Thomas Worthington Wittredge, Lilly Martin Spencer, Robert S. Duncanson, Frank

Duveneck, Henry Farny, Elizabeth Nourse, Edward Potthast, Joseph Henry Sharp, and others. It also has Rookwood Pottery ceramics (such as Maria Longworth Nichols Storer's "Crushed Vase"), furniture, clocks, and sculpture.

On view at the museum include works by Claude Monet and Pablo Picasso. Other displays of note include Andy Warhol's *Pete Rose,* Persian architecture dating from 480 B.C, marble carvings dating from 2500 B.C. to 2400 B.C., an unparalleled collection of Nabataean art, and Jin dynasty wood carvings.

One World Wednesdays are held the first Wednesday of each month and highlight a different world culture each month with art, music, food, and wine. Cost is $8.00 for nonmembers; free to members.

Museum hours are 10:00 A.M. to 5:00 P.M. Tuesday through Saturday and noon to 6:00 P.M. Sunday (closed Monday). Admission is free. Membership, which includes plenty of perks and discounts, starts at $35.

Rosenthal Center for Contemporary Art
44 East Sixth Street
(513) 345-8400
www.contemporaryartscenter.org

In 2003 the Contemporary Arts Center moved to a brand-new building in downtown Cincinnati. The old center gained infamy for its Robert Mapplethorpe exhibit, which caused the curator to be charged with, and subsequently acquitted of, pandering obscenity.

But with the new building, hopefully Cincinnatians can put that episode behind them. For more about the museum, see the close-up later in this chapter.

Miami University Art Museum
Patterson Avenue, Oxford
(513) 529-2232

Georges Rouault's "Miserere" folio is the highlight of the university's museum, which also displays an extensive camera collection, sculptures, paintings, 1840s textile and wallpaper designs, and 20th-century American art. The museum houses an international collection of folk, pre-Columbian, and African art. Admission is free and hours are 10:00 A.M. to 5:00 P.M. Tuesday through Friday, noon to 5:00 P.M. on Saturday.

Not only do the art museums have beautiful art, they also have some of the neatest gift shops with items from all over the world, especially the Taft Museum and the Cincinnati Art Museum. It's a great way to get a quick gift for someone—and you don't even have to pay an entry fee into the museum to get into the store!

Taft Museum of Art
316 Pike Street
(513) 241-0343
www.taftmuseum.org

Although it is not as well known as the Cincinnati Art Museum, the Taft Museum definitely has as nice a collection of art—and it's more accessible to those staying downtown. The Taft Museum offers beautiful art in a beautiful setting.

The Taft Museum recently completed a $22.8 million renovation. The renovation added lighting and a much-needed parking garage to the facility.

The elegant house was the former home of Charles and Anna Taft, whose love for art included European masters. The Tafts invested in art during their well-traveled lives, making their home one of the greatest private art collections in the world.

It includes works from Holland's golden age (including Rembrandt), portraits from 18th-century England, landscapes from France, and paintings by Frank Duveneck, a native Cincinnatian.

There is an ivory carving of the Virgin and Child dating from the 13th century and once lost from the Abbey Church of Saint-Denis; Chinese porcelains from the Qing and Ming dynasties; and French enamels.

The Tafts bequeathed the collection and the house to the city. The 175-year-old home, once owned by Nicholas Longworth, was where Charles's half brother, William Howard Taft, accepted the Republican nomination for president. The house now has 30 exhibit rooms for the Tafts' art collection.

Hours are 11:00 A.M. to 5:00 P.M. Tuesday through Friday; 10:00 A.M. to 5:00 P.M. Saturday, and noon to 5:00 P.M. Sunday. Open till 8:00 P.M. on Thursday. Admission is $7.00 for adults and $5.00 for seniors age 65 and older and students. Children 17 and younger and museum members get in free. Admission is free for everyone on Wednesday and Sunday.

GALLERIES

Greater Cincinnati has dozens of galleries featuring local, regional, and national artists. Although the west end of Fourth Street was once the gallery area, artists now flock to the historical-but-somewhat-rundown Main Street area in Over-the-Rhine.

Not all local art is hanging in a gallery or museum, though. Downtown is filled with more than two dozen sculptures, statues, and fountains, all displayed in the name of public art. Many sit in front of office buildings or in the downtown parks. A self-guided Public Art Walk tour brochure of the works is available at the downtown library.

A&J Art Gallery
8113 Connector Drive, Florence, KY
(859) 371-2578
A&J is an authorized Bradford Exchange Dealer and features originals, limited-edition prints and plates, dolls, and collectibles. It is open 10:00 A.M. to 5:30 P.M. Tuesday through Thursday, 10:00 A.M. to 7:00 P.M. on Friday, and 10:00 A.M. to 4:00 P.M. on Saturday.

Arts Consortium
1301 Western Avenue
(513) 381-0645
The Arts Consortium has a dual focus of education and presentation. The center, which renovated and expanded its facility several years ago, offers photography and art exhibits at its gallery. Exhibits have included works by Annie Ruth and Michael Thompson in conjunction with the consortium's 25th anniversary. The consortium also has a satellite facility at the Museum Center called the William Mallory Afro-American Museum. Hours are 9:00 A.M. to 5:00 P.M. Monday through Friday, 10:00 A.M. to 4:00 P.M. Saturday.

Carl Solway Gallery
424 Findlay Street, West End
(513) 621-0069
Sculpture, paintings, and prints from nationally and internationally recognized artists form the core of this avant-garde collection. The gallery, open for more than 30 years, is well known outside of the area and draws considerable interest. It is a member of the Art Dealers Association of America. Hours are 9:00 A.M. to 5:00 P.M. Monday through Friday, Saturday noon to 5:00 P.M.

Carnegie Visual and Performing Arts Center
1028 Scott Boulevard, Covington, KY
(859) 491-2030
The Carnegie Arts Center offers five galleries that change exhibits on a regular basis. It is one of the largest galleries in the area and one of Northern Kentucky's premier art centers. The building is itself a work of art, built in 1902 with funds from Andrew Carnegie and now on the National Register of Historic Places.

Cincinnati Art Galleries
225 East Sixth Street
(513) 381-2128
The gallery, located a block from the Aronoff Center, offers the country's largest Rookwood pottery auctions and displays Rookwood along with 19th- and 20th-century paintings and art glass. Hours are 9:00 A.M. to 5:00 P.M. Monday through Friday and 10:00 A.M. to 4:00 P.M. Saturday.

Closson's
10100 Montgomery Road, Montgomery
(513) 891-5531
This gallery is among the area's most esteemed. The gallery has been in business for about 140 years, making it one of the oldest continuously operating art galleries in the country. The gallery features regional and local works, 19th- and 20th-century American paintings, and Far Eastern and West African art and prints by Cincinnati native John Ruthven and internationally known John Stobart. Most of the works are collector's quality. Hours are 10:00 A.M. to 6:00 P.M. Monday through Saturday, 10:00 A.M. to 8:00 P.M. Thursday, and noon to 5:00 P.M. Sunday.

DAAP Galleries
University of Cincinnati
(513) 556-2839
DAAP (College of Design, Architecture, Art, and Planning) has three galleries on campus. Each location has a distinct mission. The Dorothy W. and C. Lawson Reed Jr. Gallery is on the fifth floor of the Aronoff Center for Design and Art and focuses on the disciplines represented in the academic programs of DAAP, showcasing current work in those fields of study brought in from outside the College of DAAP. The Meyers Gallery focuses on topics of interest to the university as a whole, while DAAP Galleries Downtown focuses on the work of local and regional artists. In addition, faculty and student work from the College of DAAP is showcased periodically at all three galleries. The on-campus galleries are open from 10:00 A.M. to 5:00 P.M. Monday through Friday. DAAP's downtown gallery is at 628 Sycamore Street and is open 11:00 A.M. to 6:00 P.M. Monday through Friday.

Golden Ram Gallery
6808 Miami Avenue, Madeira
(513) 271-8000
This gallery rotates the works of various artists throughout the year. Most of the featured art works are local artists' originals. Its hours are 10:00 A.M. to 5:00 P.M. Monday through Friday, 10:00 A.M. to 2:00 P.M. Saturday.

Laura Paul Gallery
4460 Lake Forest Drive, Blue Ash
(513) 651-5885
You can find numerous one-of-a-kind works at this gallery. Exhibits have included works by Enrico Embroli, Roger Muhl, Sandra Kaplan, and Jim and Clay Wainscott. It's open from 10:00 A.M. to 5:00 P.M. Monday through Friday, or by appointment.

Malton Gallery
2643 Erie Avenue, Hyde Park
(513) 321-8614
www.maltongallery.com
Abstract and realist images by local and nationally known artists are the heart of Malton's collection. More than 100 painters, printmakers, and sculptors are represented, some emerging, others well established. It has six major exhibitions each year. Hours are 11:00 A.M. to 5:00 P.M. Tuesday through Saturday, and by appointment.

Maritain Gallery
127 West Loveland Avenue, Loveland
(513) 683-1152
Exhibits by various artists rotate through this gallery, which is open from 1:00 to 4:00 P.M. Sunday through Friday. It has four exhibitions each year.

Mary Baskett Gallery
1002 St. Gregory Street, Mount Adams
(513) 421-0460
This gallery features contemporary Japanese ceramics and contemporary Asian art as well as fine prints. It's the second decade for the gallery at the St. Gregory Street location. Hours are by appointment only.

Miller Gallery
2715 Erie Avenue, Hyde Park
(513) 871-4420
The Miller has one of the largest collections of 20th-century American and Euro-

CLOSE-UP

An Artsy Building Full of Art

The Contemporary Arts Center is not only known for the art inside: The building itself is art through its architecture.

The six-floor high-rise building that houses the Lois & Richard Rosenthal Center for Contemporary Art was touted by the *New York Times* as a "breakthrough design in the use of space to punch up contemporary art" and by *Newsweek* as "perfect . . . for a museum devoted to the 'art of the last 10 minutes.' "

The $34 million project resembles nothing so much as boxes of different colors and dizzying diagonal shapes, almost haphazardly stacked as in some kind of 3-D jigsaw puzzle.

London architect Zaha Hadid, known for her modernist designs described as "controlled explosions," employs tinted glass, black aluminum, and concrete in the innovative structure. Her self-described "urban carpet," at the junction of the sidewalks at Sixth and Walnut Streets, is a layer of cement that flows into the lobby and then escalates upward to form the curved back wall of the facility.

"The three scariest words in America, to a lot of people, are 'contemporary,' 'art,' and 'museum,' " observes the Rosenthal Center's director, Charles Desmarais. "We want to surprise people who visit with pleasurable sensations. We want them to know this is a place where they can think differently, where they are *expected* to think in different ways."

The museum's street corner accessibility and location inside the urban core are in keeping with a mission to connect everyone, not just the privileged few, to the arts. That's one of the reasons the 87,000-square-foot facility is extremely transparent—the bank of 20-foot-high windows literally invites passersby on the street to glimpse inside. Entrance to the street-level lobby is free; this public space (Desmarais calls it an "urban park") includes the center's store, a coffee cafe, tables and chairs, and information kiosks. The lower basement level features a 150-seat black-box theater and performance space for dance, music, movies, and drama.

The second, fourth, and fifth floors represent gallery space—a matrix of hovering cubes and intersecting trapezoid modules—while the third floor is devoted to office space for the staff. The sixth floor incorporates the UnMuseum for children age five and up, showcasing interactive art and emphasizing participatory experiences.

The first new art museum building to

pean artworks in the city. It has painting, sculpture, and decorative art by local, national, and international artists. Hours are 10:00 A.M. to 5:30 P.M. Monday through Saturday.

Northern Kentucky University Gallery
NKU, Fine Arts Building,
Highland Heights, KY
(859) 572-5148

Two galleries of works by NKU

open in Cincinnati in 117 years, the undulating structure is energetic, almost inducing a sense of motion. The welded steel stairways—ramps with no columns or cables to hold them up—seem to float in midair, a sea of elevated cross-sections weaving in patterns as they ascend to the upper floors and finally toward the atrium skylight above.

Some gallery areas are of a typical size, but patrons can suddenly encounter loft spaces where the ceilings soar 25 feet high.

The Rosenthal Center is international in its origins, designed by an architect born and raised in Iraq, named for its Jewish patrons, and—for the premiere exhibit—boasting an array of artists from all parts of the world.

Lois and Richard Rosenthal, the center's primary benefactors, are the publishing brains behind such national magazines as *Writer's Digest, Family Tree Magazine,* and other craft and specialty pubs. The Rosenthals sold their Cincinnati media company, F&W Publications, in order to focus on community and arts endeavors (it was a gift from the Rosenthals that recently allowed the Cincinnati Art Museum to cease charging admission).

The Rosenthal Center is the latest incarnation of the Contemporary Arts Center (CAC), which left its cramped gallery space on the second floor of a Fifth Street office building. The CAC has its roots in the Modern Art Society, founded in 1939 as one of the first American institutions devoted to displaying art of the moment. Over the years the center introduced Ohioans to such artists and creators as Laurie Anderson, Pablo Picasso, Jasper Johns, Dale Chihuly, Nam June Paik, I. M. Pei, and Andy Warhol. The CAC may be best remembered, for good or ill, for the controversy over a display of Robert Mapplethorpe photos a decade ago, which included photographs of nude children and homoerotic imagery and resulted in the arrest of the center's director, Dennis Barrie, for pandering obscenity (he was later acquitted of those charges).

The Rosenthal Center for Contemporary Art is at 44 East Sixth Street, downtown Cincinnati. The center and museum store hours are 10:00 A.M. to 6:00 P.M. Wednesday, Thursday, and Friday, until 9:00 P.M. on Monday; 11:00 A.M. to 6:00 P.M. Saturday and Sunday; closed Tuesday.

Admission is $7.50 adults, $6.50 seniors, $5.50 students, $4.50 children 3 through 13. Monday nights are free after 5:00 P.M.

For more information, call (513) 345-8400 or visit www.contemporaryartscenter.org.

students, faculty, and local and regional artists are open from 9:00 A.M. to 6:00 P.M. Monday through Friday or by appointment.

Patricia Weiner Gallery
9393 Montgomery Road, Montgomery
(513) 791-7717

This gallery focuses on 19th- and early 20th-century American and European paintings as well as contemporary art. There is an emphasis on Cincinnati golden age artists. You may view the exhibits from 11:00 A.M. to 5:00 P.M. Tuesday through Saturday or by appointment.

Pendleton Art Center
1310 Pendleton Street
(513) 852-2766
www.pendletonartcenter.com
More than 250 artists working in a variety of mediums house their studios in this beautifully renovated building. It claims to be the world's largest collection of artists. Studios are open for Final Fridays from 6:00 to 10:00 P.M. or by appointment. Second Look Saturdays are held from noon to 4:00 P.M. the Saturday following Final Fridays. You can catch a free shuttle from Pendleton and Reading Roads parking lots.

Ran Gallery
3668 Erie Avenue, Hyde Park
(513) 871-5604
Progressive exhibits by varying artists are featured here. The gallery specializes in 19th- and 20th-century American and Cincinnati art. You can view the displays from 10:00 A.M. to 6:00 P.M. Tuesday through Friday and 11:00 A.M. to 4:00 P.M. Saturday.

Raymond Gallery
3508 Edwards Road, Hyde Park
(513) 871-9393
This gallery features original cartoons by Cincinnati's Pulitzer Prize-winning editorial cartoonist Jim Borgman, as well as original drawings from his comic strip, *Zits*. It also has cartoons by Jeff Stahler, cartoonist at the *Cincinnati Post*, and Emerson, whose strip also is in the *Post*. The gallery is open from 10:00 A.M. to 5:00 P.M. Tuesday through Saturday.

Row House Gallery
211 Main Street, Milford
(513) 831-7230
The excellence of John Ruthven, Mill Pond Press, and Greenwich Workshop art is the focus here. The gallery occupies two old row houses. Hours are 10:00 A.M. to 5:00 P.M. Monday through Friday (open till 7:00 P.M. Thursday) and 10:00 A.M. to 4:00 P.M. Saturday.

Ruthe G. Pearlman Gallery
1212 Jackson Street
(513) 562-6262
Students of the Art Academy of Cincinnati exhibit their work here every spring. The Ruth G. Pearlman Gallery has rotating shows by regional and nationally known artists—often those who have either studied or taught at the art academy. Hours are 9:00 A.M. to 9:00 P.M. weekdays and 9:00 A.M. to 5:00 P.M. Saturday and Sunday.

Square Framer and Gallery
8179 Princeton-Glendale Road, Hamilton
(513) 868-7926
It has limited-edition prints by Bev Doolittle and others. The gallery is open from 10:00 A.M. to 5:00 P.M. weekdays (till 6:00 P.M. Wednesday), and 10:00 A.M. to 4:00 P.M. on Saturday.

Studio San Giuseppe
College of Mount St. Joseph,
Ziv Art Building, 5701 Delhi Road, Delhi
(513) 244-4314
Works by Mount St. Joseph students are featured here along with outside work that the college brings in to parallel its curriculum. Hours are 10:00 A.M. to 5:00 P.M. Monday through Friday and 1:30 to 4:30 P.M. weekends.

Thomas More College Art Gallery
Thomas More College,
333 Thomas More Parkway,
Crestview Hills, KY
(859) 341-5800
This is the gallery for the college's students as well as outside artists. It's open 9:00 A.M. to 9:00 P.M. Monday through Thursday, 9:00 A.M. to 4:30 P.M. on Friday, 10:00 A.M. to 4:00 P.M. Saturday, and 2:00 to 8:00 P.M. Sunday.

Weston Art Gallery
Seventh and Walnut Streets
(513) 977-4165

Inside the Aronoff Center for the Arts, the Weston exhibits a variety of art styles by local, regional, and national artists. Open 10:00 A.M. to 5:30 P.M. Tuesday through Saturday (except on performance evenings, when it is open till 8:00 P.M.) and noon to 5:00 P.M. on Sunday (when it is open until 7:00 P.M. on performance evenings).

York Street Cafe Gallery
Eighth and York Streets, Newport, KY
(859) 261-9675

This art gallery is on the third floor of the highly popular York Street Cafe, so you can sip exotic coffees before you tour the art. The gallery rotates exhibits in a variety of media and is open six days a week when the restaurant is open. Closed on Monday.

ANNUAL EVENTS

Each weekend in the warm weather, the people of Greater Cincinnati trek out to one festival or another. Many residents love festivals, and there are plenty to satisfy them—whether it be church-related or a cultural event or just a reason to come downtown to eat and listen to music.

Then during the months when it is too cold to go to outside festivals, we love to make our way to the convention center for shows about homes, gardening, and boating. Although many people claim there is never anything to do in this town, we offer this chapter as an argument against those claims.

There is no way we can include all the annual events in this chapter. Besides the many church festivals, many communities have "Taste of" or "Day of" celebrations as well as holiday celebrations. And although we list the once-a-year sporting events, remember that there are numerous sports teams in the city that can provide hours of fun as well. (See the Spectator Sports chapter.)

For a listing of the smaller annual and onetime events, check *CityBeat*'s "Calendar" section or the *Post*'s or *Enquirer*'s weekend sections. Downtown Cincinnati Inc. publishes a downtown directory that includes events such as special holiday festivities. To get a copy, call DCI at (513) 421-4440.

A note: Be sure to read about Tall Stacks, the world's largest gathering of steam riverboats, in the River Fun chapter. Staged every three years, this nationally renowned event and its accompanying festivities are a Cincinnati tradition and should not be missed.

JANUARY

African Culture Fest
Museum Center at Union Terminal
(513) 287-7000
This festival includes unique African arts and crafts and African cuisine and also features activities for children and adults. It takes place during Martin Luther King Jr. weekend. Admission is free.

Bridal Show
Northern Kentucky Convention Center, 1 RiverCenter Boulevard, Covington, KY
Preparing for a June wedding? Browse the hundreds of booths and exhibits at the Bridal Show for ideas and services to help your wedding run smoothly and make it that much more special. Fashion shows feature the latest and most glamorous wedding gowns. You can interview photographers, DJs, bands, and bakers and find the best bridal registry, all in one place. And nearly every booth offers some sort of giveaway, including honeymoon trips to exotic locations. Admission is $9.00. Grooms are welcome.

Cincinnati World of Wheels
Duke Energy Convention Center, Fifth and Elm Streets
(513) 352-3750
The finest to the funkiest in automotive creations will show up for this weeklong event: dragsters, classic cars, model cars, street rods, monster trucks—just about anything with four wheels. Television and music personalities make appearances, signing autographs and posing for pictures. Admission is $11.50, $4.00 for children age 12 and younger.

The Golf, Hunting, and Fishing Show
Duke Energy Convention Center, Fifth and Elm Streets
(513) 281-0022

For two weekends in January, enthusiasts can have their fill of their summertime hobbies. Admission is $10 a day for adults. Kids are free.

Travel Sports & Boat Show
Duke Energy Convention Center, Fifth and Elm Streets
(513) 281-0022

This is one of the most popular events held at the convention center each year. While the snow falls outside, the mid-month show gives you a chance to get away—or at least spend a week dreaming about burying your toes in some sandy beach, photographing exotic animals in the wilds of Africa, or zooming across the water in a new boat. Travel agencies give away trips, and you can watch hunting and fishing demonstrations or buy a boat or almost any kind of sports equipment. Admission is $10.00 for adults, $3.00 for children age 13 and younger.

FEBRUARY

BockFest
Various venues along the Main Street entertainment district
(513) 421-2337

Almost 50 restaurants, bars, and shops in Over-the-Rhine take on a Renaissance flair for the annual BockFest, the traditional Queen City celebration of bock beer, bockwurst, and the coming of spring. Admission is free (but, of course, the brewskies aren't). A parade includes pigs and media celebrities—sometimes one and the same.

CFA Championship Allbreed Cat Show
Duke Energy Convention Center Ballroom, Fifth and Elm Streets
(513) 241-1152

For nearly five decades the nation's coolest cats have gathered in this ballroom to compete for top honors as the best of their breed in this prestigious national event. More than 20 breeds compete. Vendors and exhibitors from all over the country create a supermarket of cat-related products designed to make you laugh or make your tabby purr just a little louder. Tickets are $5.00 for adults, $4.00 for seniors, and $3.00 for children age 15 and younger.

Cincinnati Auto Expo
Duke Energy Convention Center, Fifth and Elm Streets
(513) 281-0022

This show includes new cars and prototypes as well as motorcycles. Admission is $9.00 for adults and $2.00 for children age 13 and younger.

Fine Arts Funds Sampler
Various venues
(513) 230-5000
www.fineartsfund.org

Enjoy a smorgasbord of cultural samplings at this event, where all the area's cultural and arts organizations team to show off their wares and kick off their annual fund-raising campaigns. More than 75 events take place in more than 35 locations throughout the area during the two-day, midmonth celebration. The symphony, ballet, May Festival Chorus, opera, and School for the Creative and Performing Arts all perform. The Cincinnati Art Museum, Playhouse in the Park, and Contemporary Arts Center open their doors. Guitar-a-thons, short films, plays, hands-on art lessons, and other smaller events fill out the weekend. All activities are free, with most lasting less than an hour. It's a great way to get an idea of what's available in terms of culture.

MARCH

Antiques Show and Sale
Sycamore High School, 7400 Cornell Road, Sycamore
(513) 852-1901

More than 75 dealers gather at the high school to show and sell antiques. We're talking high-quality, top-of-the-line antiques here, not flea market goods. The weekend event is sponsored by the Montgomery Women's Club. Admission is $5.00.

Celtic Lands Culture Fest
Museum Center at Union Terminal, 1301 Western Avenue
(513) 287-7000

Isn't this the luck of the Irish? The annual Celtic Lands Culture Fest at Museum Center features folklore, crafts, and the music and dance of the Emerald Isle. Highlights include the local dance troupe, the McGing Irish Dancers, as well as area musicians participating in the Battle of the Celtic Bands. Food and craft vendors fill out the rest of the terminal rotunda. Admission is free.

Cincinnati Heart Mini-Marathon
Downtown
(513) 281-4048
www.heartmini.org

It's not the Boston Marathon, but the 5K and 15K races draw big crowds. The races begin and end at Fountain Square. The event, which benefits the Heart Foundation, also offers a fitness expo, speakers, and a kid fun run. A 10K walk and a 20K skate are also held. It's free; pulled muscles cost extra.

Folk Art & Craft Show
11355 Chester Road, Sharonville
(513) 771-7744

More than 100 of the nation's most talented traditional artisans display their fine crafts, folk art, furniture, wood carvings, baskets, quilts, jewelry, and more. Admission is $6.00 for both days of the show, and an opening collectors' preview is $7.00.

Good Friday Stair Climb
30 Guido Street, Mount Adams
(513) 721-6544

For over 135 years, more than 10,000 Catholics have climbed the 200-plus steps from the foot of Mount Adams to Immaculata Church, praying the rosary on each step and accepting communion at the top.

Home & Garden Show
Duke Energy Convention Center, Fifth and Elm Streets
(513) 281-0022

This popular weeklong show runs in early March, just about the time you're beginning to realize spring isn't too far away and it's time to once again begin planting and working in the yard. Collect bulbs, perennials, annuals, seeds, or just ideas. Water gardens, landscaping, decks, shrubs, trees, and anything that has to do with homes and gardens can be found at the show. Admission is $11.00 for adults and $3.00 for children age 13 and younger.

International Wine Festival
Duke Energy Convention Center, Fifth and Elm Streets
(513) 241-3434
www.winefestival.com

Seminars, luncheons, and, of course, tastings are featured in this three-day event, which is held at the beginning of the month. Hundreds of wines from around the world compete for a gold medal. If you want to learn more about wine, choose from seminars such as "The ABCs of Wine—and More" and "Blending Food and Wine." The festival benefits the classical music station WGUC and other charities. Admission packages range from $50 to $65 for Grand Tasting events, seminars, and parties. Individual prices for seminars and tastings also are available.

Lane's End Stakes
Turfway Park, Florence, KY
(859) 371-0200, (800) 733-0200

For years this Kentucky Derby prep race was known as the Jim Beam Stakes. The name has changed several times, but it remains the richest Kentucky Derby prep race in the country. The $500,000 race is run five weeks before the derby and regularly features at least one Triple Crown race winner, such as Lil E. Tee and Prairie Bayou. As at the derby, fancy hats are the order of the day for women. Admission is free, although there is reserved seating with varying prices depending on how good the seats are. What you spend at the betting window is up to you.

Maple Syrup Festival
Farbach-Werner Nature Preserve, Poole Road and Colerain Avenue, Colerain
(513) 521-7275
One weekend each March, park naturalists tap trees, cook up some flapjacks, lead hikes, set up a model Indian camp, and show films. It's a fun, educational treat for kids, who can also satisfy a sweet tooth or two. Admission is free, but a $5.00 Hamilton County Park pass or a $1.00 daily park pass is needed.

St. Patrick's Day Parade
Downtown
(513) 922-2230
Although Greater O'Cincinnati has a decidedly German heritage, the area's St. Patrick's Day parade is reportedly the second largest in the country—no blarney. Arrive early in order to claim a prime street-side viewing location, as sidewalk space can be hard to find. Lawn chairs, coolers, and leprechauns welcome.

APRIL

Cincinnati Flower Show
Coney Island, Anderson
(513) 872-5194
www.cincyflowershow.com
This is the largest, most prestigious open-air flower-and-garden festival in the country, and the only North American flower show endorsed by the Royal Horticultural Society of Great Britain. *Good Morning America* says it is "one of the most beautiful events in the world."
Growers, florists, and designers from around the world display exhibits and give clinics and seminars plus an afternoon tea. About 35,000 people flock to the show, which runs the last weekend in April. General admission is $20.00, $5.00 for children ages 3 through 12. There may be an additional admission charge for some seminars and clinics. Parking is $3.00.

Krohn Conservatory Easter Display
Krohn Conservatory, 1501 Eden Park Drive
(513) 421-5707
If Easter is a time of hope, the special display in the Krohn's giant greenhouse creates hope for those eager for spring. One whole wing of the cross-shaped greenhouse is reserved for the display, in which hundreds of blooming lilies are placed before a backdrop of lush greenery. Fountains, with water trickling down carefully placed rocks, add audible pleasure to the wonderful sights and smells. The display lasts the entire month. Admission is free.

Opening Day
Great American Ball Park
(513) 765-7000
Nowhere in the world is there anything like the Reds' opening day in Cincinnati. More work is missed than on any other unofficial holiday. A festive atmosphere permeates downtown as everyone wears red, dons baseball caps—even with business suits—and catches the Findlay Market Parade, which is an event unto itself. The parade rolls through the streets of downtown before the Reds game and includes two teams of giant Clydesdales pulling wagons, bands, marchers, and former Reds players.

Party in the Park
Bicentennial Commons
(513) 579-3191
These huge outdoor parties are held every other week, on Wednesday night. The festivities begin at 5:30 P.M., just as the work crowd is loosening the ties and packing up the briefcases. The Party in the Park takes place near the Serpentine Wall and features musical entertainment and refreshments.

Q102 Parties at the Point
Bicentennial Commons
(513) 763-5686
The Q102 parties alternate Wednesday nights with the Party in the Park (see above). Bands play in the P&G Pavilion and refreshments are served beginning at 5:30 P.M.

WCET Action Auction
Televised on Channel 48
(513) 381-4033
This event, which raises more than $1 million for WCET, is a combination of a Sotheby's auction and the Home Shopping Network. A variety of merchandise—some of it quite valuable—is contributed by local residents interested in benefiting the public television station. All kinds of great bargains can be had.

MAY

Appalachian Festival
Coney Island, Anderson
(513) 232-6701
www.appalachianfestival.org
They don't make things like they used to, except for the Appalachian Festival, the largest Appalachian craft show in the nation. For 30 years now, festivalgoers have found themselves taken back to another era by 150 exhibitors who show how things were done in the hills. There's handmade furniture, stained glass, copper water fountains, quilts, braided rugs, leather goods, dolls, broom-making and woodworking demonstrations, music, storytelling, and lots of down-home food, all during one weekend in the middle of each May. Three stages provide endless entertainment to go with the shopping. Admission is $7.00 for adults, $3.00 for seniors age 65 and older, and $2.00 for children age 12 and younger. Tickets for some of the concerts are separate. Parking is $4.00.

Butterfly Show
Krohn Conservatory, 1501 Eden Park Drive
(513) 352-4086
www.butterflyshow.com
The conservatory is festooned with flowers that attract butterflies and is filled with species of this beautiful animal that fly around freely. Admission is $6.00 for adults and $4.00 for children; $5.00 for seniors.

The *Delta Queen*'s Annual Spring Return
Public Landing
(800) 543-1949
During the first week in May since 1946, the giant *Delta Queen* steamboat has returned to her home port of Cincinnati to be greeted with festivities, people in period costume, and Dixieland bands. The ship docks at Public Landing and fills the air around downtown with calliope music. Check with your travel agent if you'd like to go for a spin.

Flying Pig Marathon
Downtown
(513) 721-PIGS
www.flyingpigmarathon.com
This "fun" marathon made its debut in the area in 1999. More than 6,000 people participated in this 26.2-mile race in its first year. Besides runners from all over the world, the event also has a wheelchair division and allows walkers. On the day before the race, there's a fun run for children.

Indianapolis 500
Indianapolis Motor Speedway, Indianapolis, IN
(317) 484-6700
www.indy500.com
"The Greatest Spectacle in Racing" is just two hours away, and many race fans—and non-race fans who are just looking for a great big party—make the drive along Interstate 74 to the western side of Indy for the Memorial Day weekend event. It is much more than just the race, trust us. Tickets for reserved seats range from $70 to $150 and must be ordered at least one year in advance unless you want to purchase them from a scalper—then the price is up to you. General admission tickets never sell out. They cost $20 and can be purchased up to and including the day of the race.

Kentucky Derby
Churchill Downs, Louisville, KY
(502) 636-4400
www.kentuckyderby.com
For those who just can't resist wild hats and mint juleps on the first Saturday in May, Greater Cincinnati is only two hours from Louisville and the first leg of the Triple Crown. A parade of cars can be found each derby weekend heading down Interstate 71 toward Louisville. Admission to the infield, which is a party that you have to experience once in your lifetime, costs $40.

Maifest
MainStrasse Village, Sixth and Main Streets, Covington, KY
(859) 491-0458
The village's celebration is a nod to the German tradition of welcoming the first spring wines. It's held every third weekend in May, with plenty of food and entertainment at hand. There also are arts and crafts. Admission to the village is free but food is not.

May Festival
Music Hall, 1241 Main Street
(513) 381-3300
You'll hear great sounds at the oldest continuing choral and orchestral music festival in the country, dating from 1873. The all-volunteer May Festival Chorus is made up of 250 average Joes and Josephines (that is, nonprofessional singers) with great voices who perform to the accompaniment of the Cincinnati Symphony Orchestra. Top-name opera singers are brought in as soloists, along with the University of Cincinnati College-Conservatory of Music Choir, and Chorale, the Conservatory's Children's Choir, and the Cincinnati Boychoir. The festival is spread over two weekends. Preconcert buffet dinners ($20) and preconcert recitals (free) are also part of the fun. Various subscriptions are available. Single tickets are $11 to $60.

The flowers and plants displayed at Krohn Conservatory during its special shows are for sale once the shows have ended.

Taste of Cincinnati
Garfield Park, Fourth and Pike Streets
(513) 421-4272
www.tasteofcincinnati.com
Taste of Cincinnati, held every Memorial Day weekend, is the oldest continuously running food-tasting event in the nation, starting back in 1979. More than 50 of the best restaurants in Cincinnati set up booths along Central Parkway downtown and offer a smorgasbord of their finest fares, with items costing between $1.00 and $7.00. More than 400,000 people try everything from prime rib to lobster to a dozen different types of cheesecake and listen to continuous live music on three different stages.

JUNE

Child Wellness Fair
Coney Island, Anderson
(513) 934-1900
Kids and health are the focus of the three-day convention, which turns Coney Island into a giant playground featuring interactive sports, arts, computers, gymnastics, museums, and more in 17 themed play pavilions. Admission is free.

Concours D'Elegance Car Show
Ault Park, at the end of Observatory Avenue
(513) 271-4545
www.ohioconcours.com
This isn't your average car show. Since 1978, 200 of the rarest, most exotic, and most valuable cars from around the country have gathered for this highly regarded event. An art show and brunch round out the day. Cost is $20 for adults, free for children age 12 and younger. Proceeds go to the Arthritis Foundation.

CLOSE-UP

The Top Annual Festivals in Ohio

Goodness, try picking the state's top annual festivals. A tough choice when you consider the Whistle Pull Festival in Cleveland (hundreds gather to pull antique nautical whistles), the Wood Stove Festival in Urbana, the Grindstone Festival in Berea, the Lilly Pad Festival in Thornport, or even the Llama Country Rally in Galion.

All fascinating fests, we're sure. But here's our choice—so hit the National Road, the old Lincoln Highway, or any of the other roadways that transverse Ohio for these favorites (most have been around a minimum of two decades).

Festivals come in all shapes and sizes. But rarely do they come in a .45-caliber. For more than 40 years, they've been celebrating **Annie Oakley Days** in Greenville with shooting contests and appearances by the First Ohio Cowboy Mounted Shooting Association, as well as the expected parades and other fest mainstays. (Oakley, as it happens, is Greenville's most notable native daughter.) We wouldn't advise bachelors to try any corny pickup lines on the local beauty who's been crowned Miss Annie Oakley, however; she wins the title each year for her deadly aim. Gate 5 off Ohio Highway 121, County Fairgrounds, Greenville. Late July. Admission is $2.00 (your little pistols get in free if they're under age 16); (937) 547-0400; www.annieoakleyfestival.org.

For more than a decade, a total of 21 ball clubs from seven states have played at the annual **Ohio Cup Vintage Baseball Festival.** The game is played according to the rules from the year 1860, with players dressed in authentic uniforms. Ohio Village, 1982 Velma Avenue, Columbus. Early summer. Admission is $7.00 for adults and $3.00 for children ages 6 to 12; (614) 297-2679.

One of the largest Independence Day celebrations in Ohio comes courtesy of the **Centerville Americana Festival.** For more than three decades, the region's biggest July 4th parade has unveiled 125 floats and units and a wallop of a fireworks show. East Franklin Street at Virginia Avenue, Centerville. July 4. Free; (937) 433-5898; www.americanafestival.org

A couple of thousand people get really steamed every summer. What's more, they love every minute of it. The annual **Darke County Steam Threshers Reunion** gathers antique steam engines,

Frontier Days
111 Race Street, Milford
(513) 831-2411

The festival offers four days of food, rides, and live music as it has since 1962. More than 150,000 spectators take themselves back to the days when Milford was the wild frontier. A parade, one of the largest in the state, kicks off the festival on Thursday. Admission is free.

Greek Panegyri Festival
7000 Winton Road, Finneytown
(513) 591-0030

Each mid-June the area gets a taste of Greek music, food, and religion at the Greek gas engines, and tractors. Look for a flea market, antiques, log sawing, and, needless to say, tractor races. And that's not a bunch of hot air. York Woods, U.S. Highway 127 at Ansonia. Early July. Admission is $5.00 per day, with age 12 and under free; (937) 538-3676.

It ain't got that swing if it ain't got that twang. That's the message behind the annual **Vince Combs' Bluegrass Festival,** a testament—now well in its second decade—to one musician's vision of the perfect folk musical confab. Headliners include bluegrass legends and Grand Ole Opry stars. There are also jam sessions, dancing, and clogging to boot. Greene County Fairgrounds, downtown Xenia. Late July. Admission is $20 a day; (937) 372-7962.

The Dublin Irish Festival is Ohio's largest annual Celtic fest, and where else would it be but in Dublin? Hundreds of performers celebrate the Emerald Isle's culture, music, and dance, with continuous activities on eight stages. Coffman Park, 5600 Post Road, Dublin. Mid-August. Admissions is $10 for a single admission and $22 for a weekend pass; (614) 410-4545; www.dublinirishfestival.com.

The tiny village of Bowersville, population 260, specializes in living in the past at the annual **Grasshopper Train Festival.** You see, they don't have a train. Haven't had. Not for at least three-quarters of a century. No grasshoppers, either, for that matter. Organizers tick off what they do have: A parade gets the melee going, and square dancing on the street carries the festivities into the wee hours. Lock up the women and children, and call out the public safety officers—that would be the good firefighters at the Jefferson Township Volunteer Fire Department, the sponsor of the event. They note the Grasshopper Fest also features a garden tractor pull, a miniature version of the monster truck pull that's the best thing since the cow-chip contest. Bowersville Train Depot on Main Street, Bowersville. Early June. Free; (937) 453-2518.

What better place to find an Oktoberfest than in a German Village? The **German Village Oktoberfest** showcases polka to pop, oompah-pah to rock, on three stages. Teutonic fare and goods, arts and crafts, and a "glockenspiel" imported from Milwaukee are also featured at this event, which attracts 35,000 annually. German Village, Front and Sycamore Streets, Columbus. Mid-September. Admission is $8.00 for adults, $5.00 for seniors, and free for age 12 and under; (614) 221-8888; www.germanvillage.com.

Panegyri Festival at Holy Trinity-St. Nicholas Greek Orthodox Church. Art shows and other festival activities fill in the time between gyro eating and Greek dancing. Look for the "I've fallen and can't reach my ouzo!" T-shirts. Admission is $2.00.

Homearama
Various subdivisions
(513) 851-6300

Each year the Homebuilders Association of Greater Cincinnati stages a Street of Dreams, with builders from around the area purchasing a lot in an upscale subdivision and designing a home in the $400,000 to

$1 million range. Landscapers and interior designers compete for honors as well. The homes, many of which are sold by the time of the show, are then open to the public for two weeks of tours. Cost is $8.00 if you're age 13 or older or $650,000 to $950,000 if you buy a house while you are there.

Italian Festival
Riverboat Row, Newport, KY
(859) 292-3666
www.cityofnewportky.org

The free festival in celebration of the Italian heritage in Newport's community has lots of Italian food, music, games, and a study of the history of Italians in Newport.

Juneteenth Festival
Mirror Lake and Seasongood Pavilion, Eden Park
(513) 631-7289

Juneteenth Festival celebrates the end of slavery. The free event includes music, crafts, and a children's area with games and face painting.

Kids' Fest
Sawyer Point
(513) 621-9326

This festival has existed for three decades just for kids. It has hundreds of hands-on activities, from water-balloon battles to computer games to milking cows to making slime. Ooooh, how fun! Admission is free.

Oldiesfest
Butler County Fairgrounds, Ohio Highway 4 and Fairgrove Avenues, Hamilton
(513) 699-5945

Every spring, radio station WGRR (103.5 FM) brings back good old rock 'n' roll by importing greats from the past. Stars such as Chuck Berry, Jan and Dean, Frankie Valli and the Four Seasons, KC and the Sunshine Band, America, the Mamas and Papas, Brenda Lee, the Rascals, and Little Richard have appeared in previous years. The concert is free, although a ticket is needed to get through the gate; contact WGRR at (513) 321-1035 for tickets.

P&G Concert Series
P&G Pavilion, Bicentennial Commons
(513) 852-5876

In conjunction with WKFS 107.1 FM, Procter & Gamble and the Cincinnati Recreation Commission organize a series of free concerts at the P&G Pavilion in Bicentennial Commons beginning in June. The groups are local bands.

Summerfair
Coney Island, Anderson
(513) 531-0050
www.summerfair.org

More than 250 artists from around the nation gather here to display and sell their paintings, sculptures, and crafts, while country, jazz, and pop bands fill the air with music. Great bargains can be had. Special shows and art lessons are available for children during the weekend affair. The whole fair takes place around the already-entertaining venues at Coney Island, so if the mid-June heat bogs you down, take a dip in the pool or a ride on the pedal boats. Restaurants and arcade games are also available. Admission is $7.00. Children under age 12 are admitted free. Parking is free.

Used Book Sale
800 Vine Street
(513) 369-6035
www.cincinnatilibrary.org

It's hard to imagine used books drawing such attention, but since 1972 they've become one of the city's main summer attractions. The main public library sets up outside tables filled with hardbacks, paperbacks, and records. Thousands of people jam elbow to elbow around the assortment of textbooks, fiction, nonfiction, classics, romance, and more, searching for—and in some cases fighting over—books at giveaway prices. On the final day of the five-day event, the library sells large shopping bags for $5.00 and allows shoppers to fill the bags with whatever is left. Great for bookworms or casual readers, the sale offers wonderful bargains and raises money for the library.

JULY

Blues Fest
Sawyer Point
www.cincyblues.org
(513) 684-4227
Two days of music on three stages: the main stage, acoustic stage, and gospel stage. Cost is $5:00 for adults; free for children and Blues Society members.

Clermont County Fair
Off U.S. Highway 50, Owensville,
(513) 732-1657, (513) 732-0522
www.clermontcountyfair.org
All the fun and activities you associate with a county fair converge on the fairgrounds the last week in July. The fair, held a month earlier than other county fairs in the area, costs $8.00 a day or $25.00 for a weekly pass. Children ages 6 to 11 get in for $3.00 per day or for $10.00 with a weekly pass.

Greater Anderson Days
Beech Acres Park,
6910 Salem Road, Anderson
(513) 474-0003
Anderson's annual community festival is organized on a bit larger scale than your average neighborhood block party. The famous Rozzi family (think Riverfest) explodes $35,000 worth of fireworks across the skies above the mall, and that's only part of the fun. The annual Anderson Fireman's Festival is held concurrently with carnival rides, games, and live bands such as Ooh La La and the Greasers, Brothers First, and Clyde Brown of the Drifters. It's free, though there are charges for individual rides.

HomeFest
Location varies, Northern Kentucky
(859) 331-9500
This is the Northern Kentucky equivalent of Cincinnati's Homearama (see entry in June). Each year, about 35,000 people visit a subdivision in Northern Kentucky in which area home builders create a street of dream homes (which sell for as much as $500,000 to $1 million) and compete for a series of honors. Interior designers and landscapers also get to show off their best work. The tour costs $7.00; children age 12 and younger attend for free with an adult.

Newport Arts and Music Festival
Newport riverfront
(859) 441-3139
Local and regional art and music are the highlights of this festival, along with food and walking tours.

Pioneer Days Rendezvous
Caesar Creek Pioneer Village,
3999 Pioneer Village Road, Waynesville
(513) 897-1120
The lifestyle of the early settlers is re-created and celebrated at the Caesar Creek Pioneer Village during Pioneer Days. Costumed pioneers roam throughout the 1800s village. The event is free. Food or gifts purchased at the many booths will cost you, though.

St. Rita School for the Deaf
Summer Festival
1720 Glendale-Milford Road, Evendale
(513) 772-7005
www.srsdeaf.org
This event during the first weekend of the month is the crown prince of the over 70 Catholic church festivals held throughout the year in the area. More than 100 booths are set up on the school campus, with local celebrities leading emceeing events and working the booths. Prizes totaling more than $50,000 are given away.

U.S. Air and Trade Show
Dayton International Airport, Dayton, OH
(937) 898-5901
www.usats.org
The home of the Wright brothers and birthplace of aviation (no apologies to North Carolinians) goes supersonic each year with its air show. The Blue Angels, the army's Golden Knights precision para-

chute team, wing walkers, stunt pilots, endless flybys—that's just what's going on in the air. On the ground are hundreds of military planes spanning several generations. Parking at the U.S. Air Force Museum at Wright-Patterson Air Force Base and stopping in for a tour before catching a shuttle bus makes for an even greater aviation experience. Admission is $19 for adults, $16 for seniors age 65 and older and kids ages 6 through 11. Shuttle rides are $2.00. The show is only an hour north of Cincinnati off Interstate 70.

Vent Haven ConVENTion
Drawbridge Estates Premier Villager Hotel, Buttermilk Pike exit off Interstate 75, Fort Mitchell, KY, and the Vent Haven Museum, 33 West Maple Avenue, Fort Mitchell, KY
(859) 341-0461
www.venthaven.com
Normally, we wouldn't urge you to spend the weekend with a bunch of dummies. But make an exception for the annual Vent Haven ConVENTion, the world's oldest and largest gathering of ventriloquists. Talent shows, workshops, and collectibles dealers are featured as well as public performances. Tours of Fort Mitchell's Vent Haven Ventriloquism Museum are included. It's $50 per day to attend selected workshops, the museum tour, and evening shows; $115 for the entire convention, $95 for each additional family member.

AUGUST

County and state fairs
Various sites
You'll find just about everything you ever wanted in a fair—tractor pulls, grandstand entertainment, demolition derbies, rides, carnival events, animal exhibits, arcades, and plenty of food—at any of the area's abundant events. They include the Ohio State Fair in Columbus; Kentucky State Fair in Louisville; Hamilton County Fair in Carthage; Boone County Fair in Burlington, Kentucky; Kenton County Fair in Independence, Kentucky; and Campbell County Fair in Alexandria, Kentucky.

Delhi Skirt Softball Game
5125 Foley Road, Delhi
(513) 956-7000
For two decades, cigar-chomping, beer-chugging members of the Delhi fire and police departments, Price Hill Lions Club, and Delhi Athletic Association have dressed in skirts and played a softball game against celebrity teams. There is a pregame activity with the Bengals cheerleaders and fireworks after the game. The hilarious event raises over $20,000 annually for Delhi families in need.

Great Inland Seafood Festival
Riverboat Row, Newport, KY
and Yeatman's Cove, Cincinnati
(513) 761-9911
www.greatinlandseafoodfestival.com
Greater Cincinnati is 14 hours away from the ocean. Still, 15 top local restaurants show how good area seafood dishes can be at this festival. Live entertainment joins the culinary extravaganza, which attracts about 150,000 people. Admission is free; nibbling will cost you. Food runs from $1.00 for a sampling to $9.95 for a full lobster dinner. A $4.00 round-trip river shuttle is available between the two locations.

Midwest Regional Black Family Reunion
Bicentennial Commons
(513) 742-9378
www.midwestbfr.com
This massive celebration of African-American heritage, culture, and pride draws people from all over the region. The two-day event, which is organized by the National Council of Negro Women, features a parade, food, festivities, and national and local entertainment celebrating the legacy of the African-American family. The midmonth event, which draws 250,000 people along the riverfront, is free.

Renaissance Festival
Ohio Highway 73, Harveysburg
(513) 897-7000
www.renfestival.com
Belly-up to the Round Table for a leg of mutton or steak on a stake every weekend between late August and mid-October. Jousting, 16th-century costumes, strolling minstrels, shows on five stages, more than 130 craft booths, food and drink fit for a king, and everything from the Renaissance period except the crown of Henry VIII go into the festival. Tickets are $16.99 adults, $8.99 for children ages 5 through 12, and free for children younger than age 5.

River Days
New Richmond Riverfront, New Richmond
(513) 684-1253
Rides, arts, crafts, entertainment, and plenty of food are part of the river celebration in this old river town. A 5K run, the largest fireworks display in Clermont County, and hydroplane races on the river top off the two-day event, usually held at the end of the month.

Western & Southern Financial Group Masters and Women's Open
Lindner Family Tennis Center at Kings Island, Mason
(513) 651-0303
www.cincytennis.com
During the first two weeks in August, the men's tennis world turns to Cincinnati for the $2.45 million Western & Southern Financial Group Masters. The 64-player field regularly draws the sport's top 10 male players, as well as massive crowds of about 160,000 during its weeklong stay in Cincinnati.

The Tennis Masters added a women's event in 2004. Playing the week after the men's tournament, 30 women compete to win $170,000. This was not the first time women played in the tournament. They played from 1899 to 1973 and returned for one year in 1988. Tickets are between $10 and $42 per session.

Union Centre Boulevard Bash
Union Centre Boulevard, West Chester
(513) 579-3187
www.unioncentreblvdbash.com
It was only matter of time before the northern suburbs of Cincinnati got a festival of their very own. The three-day music and food festival is coordinated by the Downtown Council. It was started in 2003.

SEPTEMBER

Celtic World Festival
Coney Island, Anderson
(513) 533-4822
www.cincinnaticelticfestival.com
For two days the arts and culture of the Celtic lands—Ireland, Scotland, Wales, Brittany, and Galicia—are celebrated with bagpipe bands, Irish and Scottish dancers, and traditional foods at Coney Island. More than 200 dance and instrumental competitions draw as many as 500 performers. The *feis* (pronounced "fesh"), the Irish word for festival, is organized by the Cincinnati Irish Cultural Society. Admission is $9.00. for adults, $8.00 for seniors, and $2.00 kids ages 5 to 12. Parking is $4.00.

Comair Mini-Grand Prix
Fifth Street
(513) 271-4545
Local companies race five-horsepower go-karts around downtown streets to help raise money for the Arthritis Foundation. To enter, call the Arthritis Foundation at the number above—if it doesn't call you first, looking for your support.

Country Applefest
Downtown Lebanon
(513) 932-6585
www.countryapplefest.com
Pick your own Granny Smith, Jonathan, or Delicious apples. Sample apple pies, apple juices, and other apple treats as you stroll through the farmers' market or craft and antiques stores.

Felicity Gourd Festival
Ohio Highway 33, Felicity
(513) 876-2859
This 20-plus-year-old festival features a quilt-and-flower show, gourds of all sorts, and a parade. The day is capped off with fireworks. Admission is $1.00 for adults and 50 cents for children age 12 and younger.

Harvest Festivals
Various venues
The Greater Cincinnati area has a rich farming heritage, and the harvest is still celebrated with several festivals, including those at Sharon Woods Village, Caesar Creek Pioneer Village in Waynesville, and the Cincinnati Zoo. The events feature folks in period costumes, hayrides, Appalachian music, clogging, lumberjacks, crafts, and, of course, food. The most famous festival event of all may be the Harvest Home Fair Parade held in Cheviot. More than 200 displays take more than three hours to make their way through the streets of the small town. People put their chairs out along the parade route days in advance to save their viewing place. And nary a politician has ever missed a chance to be seen in the parade.

Midpoint Music Festival
Main Street, Over-the-Rhine
(513) 831-4219
www.midpointmusic.com
The Midpoint Music Festival showcases a weekend of alternative rock played by 200 bands from both coasts and Canada. The event takes place on 13 stages and tents in the Main Street entertainment district in Over-the-Rhine. Participating clubs include the Blue Wisp, Courtyard Cafe, Jefferson Hall, Harry's, Jekyll and Hyde's, Kaldi's, Mr. Pitiful's, Neon's, RBC, and Red Cheetah. Cost is $10 per night, $25 for three-day pass.

Oktoberfest-Zinzinnati
Downtown
(513) 579-3194
www.oktoberfest-zinzinnati.com
Everybody's German during Oktoberfest-Zinzinnati. More than 500,000 people jam 6 blocks downtown during mid-September to sing, dance, stuff themselves with sauerkraut, bratwurst, schnitzel, and strudel, and wash it all down with thousands of gallons of beer. Revelers have consumed as many as 168,000 mettwurst and bratwurst at the celebration.

Six entertainment stages, 50 food vendors, and a children's area keep the whole family busy for two days. It is the nation's largest authentic Oktoberfest, dating from 1976. Although the event is free, food prices range from $1.50 to $8.00. A 10K Volksmarch helps walk off some of the strudel.

And if that isn't enough, an Oktoberfest in MainStrasse Village in Covington, Kentucky, takes place during the first weekend after Labor Day. Still want more? Check out the Lawrenceburg Strassefest in Lawrenceburg, Indiana, or the Germania Society's Oktoberfest in Colerain Township.

Riverfest
On the Ohio River, downtown
(513) 749-3764
For more than 20 years, 500,000 people have jammed the riverbanks on both sides of the Ohio each Labor Day weekend to bid farewell to summer with an outdoor celebration that is capped by the Toyota/WEBN fireworks. Food, activities, and nationally known entertainment on numerous stages set up on both sides of the river make this one of the best annual events in the area. An air show was added to get partygoers used to looking up in the sky before the big bang. Admission is free, except in Newport, where there's a $1.00 charge along its riverfront.

20 Days & 20 Nights Festival
1200 Main Street, Over-the-Rhine
(513) 621-4700
www.cincinnatiarts.com
The 20 Days & 20 Nights Festival—which likens itself as something akin to a "Spoleto on steroids"—is a three-week arts fest

that takes place at dozens of different Greater Cincinnati stages, museums, galleries, clubs, and parks. Before the doors close on this nonstop arts festival, you'll be able to indulge in as many as 60 irreverent and fringe events ranging from wild performance art and hip poetry parties to sexy Latin jazz and raucous rock opera. The events are often free or almost always at a discount if you've purchased the festival's 20/20 Passport for $40.

Valley Vineyards Wine Festival
2276 East U.S. Highway 22, Morrow
(513) 899-2485
www.valley-vineyards.com
Try your hand at making your own vintage in the amateur wine-making contest, or let your feet's creative juices flow in the grape-stomping contest. The three-day event extends over a Thursday, Friday, and Saturday. Plenty of food is available to go with the wine. Admission is free, but wine tastings and food are extra. Camping also is free if you don't want to drive after all that wine tasting.

OCTOBER

Cincinnati Antiques Festival
Sharonville Convention Center, 11355 Chester Road, Sharonville
(513) 871-9543
www.cincinnatiantiquesfestival.org
Nearly 50 nationally recognized antiques dealers bring out the best of the past at this show, which has existed for more than 40 years. Only the best-quality antiques are found at the show. Admission is $10 for the weekend-long event.

Haunted houses
Various venues
Dozens of haunted houses can be found around the Halloween season, ranging from nonscary for small children to those good enough to qualify for an Oscar. The most popular ones are held at St. Rita School for the Deaf, 1720 Glendale-Milford Road, Evendale; Immaculate Heart of Mary, 7820 Beechmont Avenue, Anderson; Phillips Chapel CME Church, 282 Main Street, Addyston; Fountain Square, where the city puts on the Scare on the Square; and Cincinnati Mills, Interstate 275 and Winton Road, Forest Park.

Kitchen Bath & Design Show
Northern Kentucky Covington Center, Covington, KY
(513) 281-0022
Pick up some great home-decorating and renovation ideas for the two most popular areas of the house. The fanciest toilets and tubs imaginable are on display. Admission is $8.00 for adults, $3.00 for children age 13 and under.

Light Up Cincinnati
Downtown
(513) 579-3191
Downtown buildings turn their lights on, making the skyline sparkle. A photo contest is held by radio stations and camera stores with divisions for amateurs and professionals. Prizes are cash and cameras, and outstanding photos of the city have resulted.

Ohio Sauerkraut Festival
Main Street, Waynesville
(513) 897-8855
www.waynesvilleohio.com
Since 1969 Waynesville, a 19th-century English village with more than 35 antiques shops, has paid homage to one of the tastiest of festival foods: sauerkraut. During the second weekend in October, 250,000 people flock to the small city to enjoy the more than 400 arts and crafts exhibitors, entertainment, and sauerkraut served every imaginable way. It's better than it sounds.

Run Like Hell
F&W Publications, 1507 Dana Avenue
(513) 533-9300
For a different twist to Halloween, the Run Like Hell is a 5K race that starts at 7:00 P.M. and travels through the Walnut Hills Cemetery. The run is followed by a party

with food, beer, live music, and a costume contest. The $18 prerace or $30 day-of-the-race entry fee benefits the Cystic Fibrosis Foundation.

Simply the Best
Union Terminal
(513) 398-6660
All of the restaurants voted best in *Cincinnati Magazine*'s annual "Best and Worst" edition gather in the rotunda of Union Terminal and cook up samples of their award-winning fare. The $40 admission fee covers parking, drinks, and samples, and the proceeds go to charity. A true social scenario in casual clothes, the late-month event also offers other "bests" from the magazine, such as massages and golf lessons.

NOVEMBER

Beaujolais Nouveau
Mount Adams
(513) 381-2378
Beaujolais Nouveau is the celebration of the first wine of the year. Mount Adams celebrates with a parade and specials at all the businesses in town.

Cincinnati Entertainment Awards
Taft Theatre, Fifth and Sycamore Streets
(513) 562-4949
The annual Cincinnati Entertainment Awards, organized by the alternative weekly *CityBeat,* is the local version of the Grammys and the Tonys all wrapped into one; the charity bash honors local theatrical and musical achievements. Headline acts have included the Afghan Whigs, the most famous entertainment export from these parts since Jerry Springer. The evening is generally crammed with performances by local favorites as well, including Rob Fetters, Big in Iowa, Throneberry, and Watusi Tribe. WLW's Jim Scott shares the emcee honors with WEBN's Mojo Nixon. (That's sort of like pairing the Rev. Billy Graham with Howard Stern, but so be it.) It's all for charity—proceeds benefit LINKS, Lonely Instruments for Needy Kids. Admission is $10.00, $12.50 at the door.

Festival of Lights
Cincinnati Zoo, 3400 Vine Street
(513) 281-4700
Live reindeer, a nativity scene with live animals, Santa, holiday shopping, Hanukkah activities, and *two* million Christmas lights turn the zoo into a winter wonderland. The show runs mid-November through the first week in January. Don't forget your skates to get that first taste of ice-skating on the zoo's rink. Zoo admission is $11.50 for adults and $6.00 for kids ages 2 through 12, and $9.00 seniors age 62 and older.

Holiday In Lights
Sharon Woods, Sharonville
(513) 769-0393
www.holidayinlights.com
Animated storybook characters, Santa and his reindeer, snowball-throwing snowmen, and more take shape from 150,000 lights. This drive-through display features a special holiday soundtrack that can be tuned in on the car radio. The cost is $10 per carload. The show runs mid-November through January 1.

Krohn Conservatory Holiday Show
Eden Park, access from Kemper Lane, Victory Parkway, or Gilbert Avenue
(513) 421-5707
The Crib of the Nativity manger scene with live animals outside of the conservatory is one of the big attractions of the holiday season. Inside, chrysanthemums and poinsettias bloom and you can enjoy them for free.

'Tis the Season in the City
Fountain Square
(513) 684-4945
Beginning in late November, Fountain Square is transformed into a holiday wonderland, with an ice-skating rink, hot-chocolate stands, a Santa's Workshop, live reindeer, a romantic gazebo, old-

fashioned streetlamps, and the fountain itself, which glows with thousands of miniature lights. Oh, and, of course, Santa has a special chair where good little boys and girls can tell him what's on their wish list. Various onetime events are scheduled. Skating admission is $2.00. Skate rental is $1.00.

DECEMBER

Boar's Head and Yule Log Festival
Christ Church, 318 East Fourth Street
(513) 621-BOAR
www.boarsheadfestival.com
The Boar's Head Festival is one of the oldest continuing festivals of the Christmas season, held since 1940. It tells the story of the birth of Christ symbolically through a medieval feast. More than 250 actors, jesters, singers, and musicians perform the story representing the victory of the Christ child over evil. Admission is free, but tickets must be obtained at the church in early December. The event is held the weekend after Christmas, which sometimes is in January.

Carolfest
Music Hall, 1241 Elm Street
(513) 621-1919
www.mayfestival.com
Get in the spirit of the season by listening to the booming, high-quality harmonies of the May Festival Chorus, the Youth Chorus, and other guests as they belt out holiday favorites during the first week of the month. Tickets are $10.00 for adults and $5.00 for children age 12 and younger. Fa-la-la-la-la, la-la . . .

A Christmas Carol
Playhouse in the Park, Eden Park, 962 Mount Adams Drive
(513) 421-3888
www.cinciplay.com
Another artistic favorite of the Christmas season is the performance of Charles Dickens's *A Christmas Carol* at the Playhouse in the Park. Tickets, which range from $31 to $51 for adults, are very hard to come by but well worth the effort, even for Scrooges. The show runs all month.

Duke Energy Train Display
139 East Fourth Street
(513) 287-1500
One of the world's largest portable O gauge miniature railroads is displayed every December, taking up a majority of the lobby in the Duke Energy Building. More than 200,000 people view the display, which has been an annual event for more than 50 years. If the viewing line is long, some of the display can be seen at the window on Fourth Street. The trains roll from the day after Thanksgiving until New Year's Eve. Hours are 8:00 A.M. to 6:00 P.M. Monday through Saturday and noon to 5:00 P.M. on Sunday.

***The Nutcracker* Ballet**
Music Hall, 1241 Elm Street
(513) 621-1919
Every year the Cincinnati Ballet performs *The Nutcracker.* This holiday favorite has instantly sold out since 1974, so be prepared to stand in line as soon as tickets go on sale. Tickets cost $12 to $58. The performance, which runs for two weeks, is well worth the effort to get tickets, though.

RedsFest
Duke Energy Convention Center, Fifth and Elm Streets
(513) 352-3750
Meet some of the players and get psyched up for the Cincinnati Reds' upcoming season. The event allows season ticket holders and other fans a chance to hang around with coaches and players as well as get autographs and pictures. Admission is $7.00 for adults, $5.00 for children.

Reindog Parade
Mount Adams
(513) 381-2878
Mount Adams goes to the dogs in early December. Dogs are dressed as reindeer, complete with antlers and a red nose, if

the dog doesn't mind. A costume contest and parade top off the event.

St. Nicholas arrives at MainStrasse Village
Sixth and Main Streets, Covington, KY
(859) 491-0458
St. Nicholas, or "Sinterklaas" as he's known in the Old World, comes on his white horse to visit children at 5:30 P.M. on his feastday. He hands out treats to the children awaiting him at the fountain on MainStrasse.

World's Largest Office Party
Hyatt Regency, 151 West Fifth Street
(513) 961-1702
One of the social events of the season, with dozens of celebrity bartenders and live bands, is held in the middle of the month at the Hyatt Regency Hotel. The after-work affair benefits a local charity. Admission is $10.

New Year's Events
Greater Cincinnati offers hundreds of options for New Year's Eve, depending on how you like to celebrate—wild and crazy or dressed up and dignified. All the downtown hotels offer New Year's parties, as do the nightclubs on the riverfront. Prices of the events vary greatly depending upon how gala the event is. Those parties thrown by radio stations are very popular. The black-tie event held by the symphony is one of the most luxurious and includes a concert and dinner; call (513) 621-1919.

DAY TRIPS

We've spent all this time convincing you that Cincinnati is such a great place that you'd never want to leave. Now, we're going to tell you how to get away. Go figure.

Actually, you'll find plenty of good reasons to leave Cincinnati, at least for a day. Because the city is centrally located in one of the nation's most densely populated regions, it's just a short drive to many attractions.

This chapter organizes day trips by the four cardinal directions. We've limited ourselves to trips you can make in roughly two hours or less by car. And even at that, we couldn't include everything. For shorter excursions within the Greater Cincinnati area, see listings in our other chapters, including Attractions, Parks and Recreation, and River Fun.

Here's one simple rule for this chapter: If an attraction in a nearby town is duplicated just as well in Cincinnati, you won't read about it here. And one word of warning: If you're taking day trips north or west, take along a hot cup of joe or someone to keep you alert. The scenery along Interstates 71, 74, and 75 north and west of Cincinnati is not exactly invigorating, though the destinations are worthwhile. Heading south or east, you're more likely to enjoy the rolling hills.

Happy trails.

NORTH

Dayton

It's getting harder all the time to tell where Cincinnati ends and Dayton begins along I-75, as West Chester to the south and Warren County to the north make their inevitable trek toward urban convergence. But once you hit the Interstate 675 interchange, you're in Dayton for sure. That's also the road you'll want to take to some of Dayton's chief attractions.

Dayton's greatest claim to fame, of course, is being the home of the Wright brothers. Orville and Wilbur had the sense to take a nice trip to the far more picturesque Outer Banks of North Carolina to make their historic flight, and somehow their airplane has made it onto North Carolina license plates. Nonetheless, that first airplane was designed in Dayton at the Wright Brothers Bicycle Shop. Aviation is today the source of Dayton's principal attraction—the National Museum of the United States Air Force—and much of its economy, as the home of Wright-Patterson Air Force Base, still the largest air base in the world and the primary aerospace research-and-development center for the U.S. Air Force.

Daytonians also invented the cash register (John Patterson), the automatic ignition for cars (Charles Kettering), and the daytime talk show (Phil Donahue). Please, stop them before they invent again! But the area's chief attractions harken back mainly to the Wright brothers. For more information, contact the Dayton Area Chamber of Commerce, 1 Chamber Plaza, Dayton, OH 45402, (937) 226-1444; or the Dayton Visitors' Bureau, (800) 221-8234.

Boonshoft Museum of Discovery
2600 DeWeese Parkway
(937) 275-7431

The former Dayton Museum of Discovery, the Boonshoft Museum is a totally redone complex featuring interactive science exhibits and labs for children of all ages. The all-new EcoTrek takes visitors on a journey through five environments (Ice Age, Woodlands, Sonoran Desert, Amazon Rain Forest, and Northwest Pacific Tide Pool). The indoor Wild Ohio Zoo boasts 75 furry, feathery, and finny creatures that call the state home. The Phillips Space Theater offers planetarium and laser shows. And the Egyptian Room is a dandy pyramid scheme that includes a real sarcophagus. The Boonshoft's Pacific Tidal Pool features creatures typically found off the coasts of Oregon, Washington, and California. Residents of the exhibit include frilled sea anemone, ochre sea stars, leather starfish, a giant gumboot chitin (a mollusk described as a snail without a shell), and a California sea cucumber. Another popular exhibit features Shiloh, a young male North American river otter who was originally found swimming in a suburban backyard pool. (The Northern American river otter is a marine mammal native to Ohio.) Hours are 9:00 A.M. to 5:00 P.M. Monday through Friday, 11:00 A.M. to 5:00 P.M. Saturday, noon to 5:00 P.M. Sunday. Adult admission is $8.50, $7.00 for seniors, $7.00 for children ages 2 to 12.

Carillon Historical Park
2001 South Patterson Boulevard
(937) 293-2841

You can't miss the giant Deeds Carillon (that's a bell tower), which is Ohio's largest. But the park is also home to an interesting collection of historical exhibits, including an old lock that was part of the original Miami & Erie Canal, the Newcom Tavern (Dayton's oldest building), a one-room schoolhouse, a gristmill, and a covered bridge. A replica of the Wright Brothers' Bicycle Shop and a plane the brothers built in 1905—two years after the Kitty Hawk flight—also are on display. The park is open 9:30 A.M. to 5:00 P.M. Monday through Saturday and noon to 5:00 P.M. Sunday. A carillon concert takes place on Sunday afternoon. Admission is $8.00 for adults, $7.00 seniors. $5.00 for children ages 3 through 17.

Cox Arboretum
6733 Springboro Pike
(937) 434-9005

A stunning green sanctuary with dozens of herb and water gardens, Cox Arboretum is full of meandering streams and picturesque walking bridges. A popular spot for weddings (which explains those hikers in tuxedos), Cox Arboretum is open daily; admission is free.

Dayton Dragons
Fifth Third Field, on the riverfront
(937) 228-2287

A grass playing field. An intimate arena boasting just 7,230 seats. A two-tiered baseball stadium small enough to hear chatter from the dugouts. It's the Fifth Third Field, home to the Dayton Dragons, a single-A Midwest League baseball team. An attractive alternative to the massive Cincinnati Reds stadium, the ballpark is part of a sizable reconstruction project along Dayton's riverfront, dubbed RiverScape. There are walking paths and parks along the shorefront of the Great Miami River, and a giant fountain shoots streams of water 200 feet in the air during games. Game times are generally 2:00 P.M. Sunday or 7:00 P.M. weeknights and Saturday. Tickets are $6.00 to $10.00.

National Museum of the United States Air Force
Wright-Patterson Air Force Base, Area B
(937) 255-3284

Pigs are about the only thing you won't find flying around here. This is the largest aviation museum in the world, holding more than 200 aircraft, missiles, and other sorts of identified flying objects. Unidentified flying objects and their inhabitants are kept in the deep freeze elsewhere on the base, according to legend.

But, seriously, you'll find plenty of real-life aircraft to keep you busy all day. Displays include early models built by the Wright brothers and such famous World War I craft as the Sopwith Camel along with B-29 Superfortresses from World War II, including the plane that dropped an A-bomb on Nagasaki in 1945. Other aircraft of special interest include a German V-2 rocket that fell short of Britain and into the North Sea, a German Junker, and presidential airplanes including the Air Force One that took JFK on his fateful trip to Dallas. Video loops help illustrate several of the displays. An auditorium shows three films about flying. The museum has a good mix of hands-on and hands-off exhibits. Best of all, it's free.

The IMAX theater gives you the experience of an actual space flight through its six-story screen. Admission is $6.00, $5.50 for seniors age 60 and older, $4.50 for students, and $4.50 for kids age 3 and up.

This place is big. Be prepared to do some walking, and bring a stroller for the little ones. Hours are 9:00 A.M. to 5:00 P.M. daily except Thanksgiving, Christmas, and New Year's Day.

Paul Lawrence Dunbar House
219 North Paul Lawrence Dunbar Street
(937) 224-7061
This Victorian residence was home to one of America's most famous black poets and authors. Dunbar was born of former slaves in Dayton in 1872 and rose to prominence in American literature before he died in 1906 at age 33. The house holds Dunbar's library, manuscripts, and personal effects. Hours are 9:30 A.M. to 4:30 P.M. Wednesday through Saturday and noon to 4:30 P.M. Sunday from Memorial Day through Labor Day. Fall and winter hours vary, so call ahead. Admission is $5.00, $3.00 for students.

Schuster Performing Arts Center
Second and Main Streets
(937) 228-3630
This brand-new performing arts high-rise is the pride of Dayton and the new home of the city's Philharmonic Orchestra, Dayton Opera, Dayton Ballet, the Human Race Theatre Company, and the Dayton Contemporary Dance Company. Broadway touring shows also arrive here frequently.

SunWatch
2301 West River Road
(937) 268-8199
SunWatch is a reconstructed prehistoric American Indian village of the 13th century. It includes an audiovisual presentation in the visitor center that explains the history of the excavation at this site and how most archaeologists work, which is somewhat different from how Indiana Jones did it. Here you'll find displays that include a thatched-roof council house, a typical dwelling, numerous artifacts, replicas of Indian clothing, and a scale model of the village that shows how SunWatch worked as a sun calendar for its inhabitants. Hours are 9:00 A.M. to 4:30 P.M. Tuesday through Saturday, noon to 4:30 P.M. Sunday. Admission is $5.00, $3.00 for ages 6 through 17 and 60 and older.

Trapshooting Hall of Fame and Museum
601 West National Road, Vandalia
(937) 898-1945
Vandalia is one tough place to live if you're a clay pigeon. Here is where you'll find exhibits that trace trapshooting history and honor such famous markspersons as Annie Oakley. It's the only known museum in the world devoted to the sport. Admission is free. Hours are 9:00 A.M. to 4:00 P.M. Monday through Friday. The museum is closed weekends and holidays. The Amateur Trapshooting Association, at the same address, holds its annual Grand American World Trapshooting Tournament here each August.

United States Air and Trade Show
Dayton International Airport,
Interstate 75 at exit 63
(937) 898-5901
This show is held each July and is the most international thing about the Dayton International Airport. Started in 1975, the show has fast become one of the most important aviation events in the world, attracting more than 250,000 visitors a year. Daring stunts and displays of state-of-the-art aircraft make this a must-see for anyone even remotely interested in flight. Call ahead to find out the time and day of precision stunt performances by the Air Force Thunderbirds.

Lebanon

Every region has its classic small town. Here, it's Lebanon, Ohio, chock-full of

Americana and nostalgic quaintness. Lebanon is also a great shopping and dining experience—you could easily make a day of it. Here you'll find the Golden Lamb, Ohio's oldest eatery and inn (see the Restaurants and Hotels and Motels chapters for details).

The town itself is handsome, full of tree-lined streets and imposing regal homes. The shopping district features one of the region's largest collection of antiques and art shops; you'll discover streets just packed with other eclectic and exciting stores, as well as the publishing offices of the *Western Star,* the oldest newspaper west of the Alleghenies. Contact the Lebanon Chamber of Commerce for a shopping brochure: (513) 932-1100. Of particular note along the brick sidewalks and pavements are the following attractions and shop.

Cincinnati Railway Co.
Lebanon Station, 198 South Broadway
(513) 933-8022
www.cincinnatirailway.com.
The scenic Cincinnati Railway Co. offers round-trip excursions from Lebanon Station on weekends June through December. Each October the Pumpkin Patch Express is a two-hour train ride that includes a trip to a farm where families can pet animals, go inside a corn maze, pick a pumpkin, and take a hayride. Train rides with Santa during the holidays are also a big hit. The restored 1950s diesel engine and passenger coaches generally depart 10:00 A.M., 11:30 A.M., 1:00 P.M. and 2:30 P.M. Saturday; 11:30 A.M., 1:00 P.M., and 2:30 P.M. Sunday. Tickets are $15 for adults, $13 for children age 12 and under. Advance registration is required.

Liberty Western
23 West Main Street
(513) 933-0900
OK, Ohio isn't exactly the open prairie. But, hey partner, if you want to round up the cattle for a drive, head here first to outfit yourself in a complete line of western hats, boots, and clothing. Giddyup.

Pines Pet Cemetery
764 Riley Wills Road, just off U.S. Highway 48
(513) 932-2270
On the drive out of town, consider a stop at Pines Pet Cemetery, where more than 10,000 of our only-slightly-other-than-human friends rest in peace. We're talking goldfish, skunks, and horses too, as well as at least three people who chose to rest for eternity beside their beloved Fido and Tuffy. The fascinating grave markers and monuments alone are worth the stop.

Oxford

If Andy Hardy had gone to college in Ohio, he would have picked the charming university town of Oxford. Its traditional redbrick buildings blend with a quirky modern downtown to form what is truly one of the area's most pleasant day trips. The scenery on the way is certainly bucolic enough, with lots of rolling hills peppered with soybean and corn fields, but the true payoff is the impressive architecture that awaits in town. Poet Robert Frost once called the Miami University campus the prettiest academic institution he ever saw, and it is. (Transplants from New England will want to head here pronto to get a Yankee fix.)

Nearby is the tiny hamlet of **Millville,** the birthplace of Kenesaw Mountain Landis, the first commissioner of Major League Baseball, best known for banning eight White Sox players (including Shoeless Joe Jackson) for conspiring to fix the 1919 World Series with the Cincinnati Reds. We hasten to point out that White Sox players, not Reds players, were involved in the scandal and that Pete Rose was nowhere in sight. The frame house where Landis was born in a living room is still there, at 2705 Ross-Hanover Road.

Greene County

Just east of Dayton, Greene County offers interesting attractions that are worth a trip or two of their own.

Blue Jacket
Stringtown Road, Xenia
(937) 376-4358
www.bluejacketdrama.com
This summertime outdoor drama at Caesar's Ford Park Amphitheater may not be exactly accurate historically. But it's an interesting show, featuring the story of Marmaduke van Swearingen, a white boy allegedly captured by the Shawnee at age 17 who became war leader for the Indian nation. Regardless of his ancestry, Blue Jacket was a crackerjack strategist who beat Gen. Arthur St. Clair in Indiana. Show times are 8:00 P.M. nightly June through Labor Day. Tickets are $14.00 for adults and $10.00 children 12 and under on Tuesday through Saturday, and $9.00, $6.00 children, on Sunday. The amphitheater is 5 miles east of Xenia. Take U.S. Highway 42 northeast from Cincinnati or I-71 north to U.S. Highway 68 and follow the signs to Blue Jacket.

Clifton Mill
75 Water Street, Clifton
(937) 767-5501
Journey to the tiny village of Clifton anytime during the month of December and you're sure to encounter the state's largest private Christmas illumination. Indeed, how could you miss it?

Clifton Mill, the largest operating gristmill in America, transforms its surrounding grounds and river gorge into a winter wonderland adorned in festive lights. Millions of lights. Legendary lights.

The mill's owner, Anthony Satariano, is certainly no dim bulb. After all, he's managed to turn a mere flour mill, miles off any beaten track, into an immense tourist destination that attracts 75,000 visitors each holiday season to the rural hamlet of Clifton (population 165). It takes six industrious individuals more than three months to string the 3.2 million bulbs.

You should plan to be there precisely at 6:00 P.M., when the lights are switched on in a single moment. To witness the mill, its 18-foot waterwheel, and the surrounding snow-covered acreage convert instantly from utter darkness into a magnificent array of light is a heart-pounding experience. The crowd of children actually utters a collective "whoosh."

Satariano also runs a virtual Santa Claus museum next to the mill, with more than 3,000 figures of St. Nick on display—all collected over a 30-year period. Many are mechanical and clockwork figures from long-shuttered Ohio department stores, which make for a nearly living, breathing North Pole experience. "Just like Clifton, Santa Claus is timeless," observes the ebullient Satariano.

Outside amid the lights, model trains chug around handcrafted buildings, which are scale miniature replicas of landmark structures in the village, as well as a Ferris wheel, a 1950s used-car lot, and a drive-in movie theater that actually screens vintage film clips.

In addition to the annual Yuletide extravaganza, there's a year-round restaurant, the Millrace, and the inevitable gift shop where the biscuit and pancake mixes are available for procurement.

Clifton Mill itself was built in 1802 and served as a critical supplier of flour and cornmeal for the Union army during the Civil War. One of the early owners of the mill, which sits on the Little Miami River, was John Patterson, a founder of Dayton's giant National Cash Register (NCR) corporation.

If you visit the mill in the spring or summer, you can take the $1.00 tour, which includes samples of the pancake mix produced there. The holiday display switches on every night from the day after Thanksgiving until December's end (with the exception of Christmas Day). Hours are 6:00 to 9:30 P.M. Admission is $7.00 for anyone over the age of six, free to those six and under.

National Afro-American Museum and Cultural Center
1350 Brush Row Road, Wilberforce
(937) 376-4944

The National Afro-American Museum, a gleaming glass-and-stone structure, houses some 10,000 square feet of exhibits. A permanent exhibit is the centerpiece of the museum: From Victory to Freedom: African-American Life in the Fifties tracks the changes for the post–World War II generation. A 25-foot-high photo mural surrounds the exhibition hall, while multiple displays relate how African Americans slowly made inroads across all aspects of society, from religion and baseball to jobs and voting. There are re-creations of a small-town front porch, a kitchen complete with Crosley and Philco appliances, a chapel, even a barbershop called Whaley's transplanted from Columbus ("haircuts $1.50").

A '57 Chevy reminds viewers that there was a black middle class and a baby boom in the 1950s. The Chevy, which still runs, was chosen after museum researchers discovered the year and make was the most popular new auto purchase in America's black community during the 1950s.

Hours are Tuesday through Saturday 9:00 A.M. to 5:00 P.M. Admission is $4.00 for adults, $1.50 for students.

Yellow Springs

This is the closest thing you'll find to a 1960s theme park. This tiny village is home to Antioch College, a small liberal arts college with the emphasis on liberal. It has a reputation for excellent education and as a place where the revolutionary '60s meet the politically correct new millennium. Not so many years ago, the college instituted a code of conduct requiring express verbal permission prior to each phase of the courtship process. Ohio's very conservative Republican senator Mike DeWine actually grew up on the outskirts of town but lists his hometown as Cedarville. Such is Yellow Springs's reputation.

Politics aside, this place is fun, with some good restaurants and specialty shops, as well as a terrific nature preserve.

Bookplate Inc.
253½ Xenia Avenue
(937) 767-2042

This unique bookery (actually, a division of the weekly *Yellow Springs News* published at the same address) personalizes classic editions and offers Antioch Publishing bookplates.

Glen Helen Ecology Preserve
405 Corry Street
(937) 767-7375

Glen Helen is adjacent to the Antioch campus and across the road from downtown. Along the 26 miles of trails in this 1,000-acre preserve, you can find the Yellow Spring itself, plus Yellow Spring Gorge and the Little Miami River, a National Scenic River that's a little more scenic here than along stretches near Cincinnati. A trailside museum, gift shop, raptor center, and riding center are among other attractions.

Rita Caz Jewelry Studio
202 Xenia Avenue
(937) 767-7713

Creative handmade jewelry and artisan work is sold here.

Winds Cafe
215 Xenia Avenue
(937) 767-1144

This popular eatery serves meat, pasta, and vegetarian dishes from around the world.

Yellow Springs Pottery
220 Xenia Avenue
(937) 767-1666

Yellow Springs Pottery presents decorative and functional stoneware and porcelain, focusing on the work of several area artists.

Young's Jersey Dairy
6880 Springfield-Xenia Road
(937) 325-0629

At Young's Jersey Dairy, the Young family has been scooping the competition since 1958. That's the year the retail operation opened, although the farm has been in the family since the late 1800s.

Young's remains a working dairy farm today and features ice cream concocted by implementing a 14 percent butterfat mix of pasteurized milk, cream, and sugar. The ice cream is created in batches of 5 to 10 gallons, then it's wheeled into a giant freezer hooked up with a high-velocity wind machine that instantly chills the delectable mixture to 30 degrees below zero. (This immediate deep freeze prevents ice crystals from forming inside the mix, an unfortunate event that purportedly dampens the creaminess in some other brands.)

You'll find dozens of flavors, from bubble gum to fudge brownie, chocolate chip cookie dough to strawberry cheesecake, and cotton candy to something called a cow paddy. (It's double-dark chocolate cookie pieces and toffee.) Other popular items include the calfshake (regular), cowshake (thick), and bullshake (large). We'll testify, however, to the lure of the turtle sundae, two scoops of pralines and cream dripping with hot fudge and caramel sauces.

Two restaurants and a bakery add to the fray, as do minigolf, batting cages, and a driving range. You can mo-ove over and meet Elsa and her friends. The social factor is huge: Men have proposed to their future wives here. Booths and tables seat hundreds yet lend themselves to comfortable chats with strangers. Don't miss the original store's soda counter, where you can strike up a conversation with your neighbor, or the sociable front porch with picnic tables.

Columbus

If you haven't been to Columbus in about 10 years, you're in for a surprise. The "Cowtown" label put on this place in the 1970s by a local alternative newspaper no longer fits so well. For example, the trendy Short North district on High Street was several years ahead of Cincinnati's Main Street.

Keep in mind that this boom has been financed in no small part by the taxpayers of the rest of Ohio, thanks to the evergrowing state government. As long as we're paying for it, we may as well stop in and enjoy it once in a while. Some highlights are listed below. The Experience Columbus Hotline, (614) 221-CITY, can provide more information on these attractions.

Cartoon Research Library
Ohio State University,
17 West 17th Avenue
(614) 292-0538

You'll never look at the Sunday comics the same after a visit to this, the nation's largest library devoted to *Peanuts, Blondie,* and more. The facility's annual Cartoon Festival of Art features workshops by nationally known cartoonists. The center is open 9:00 A.M. to 5:00 P.M. weekdays. Admission is free.

Center of Science and Industry
333 West Broad Street
(614) 228-COSI

The Center of Science and Industry (COSI to locals) isn't where you may have last visited it. In 1999 the entire museum relocated onto a 17-acre site on the riverfront. The new facility boasts three times the area of the museum's floor space in its former downtown digs, spanning the length of nearly four football fields. Exhibits in this $125 million structure include six "learning worlds" (Adventure, Ocean, Life, Gadgets, Progress, Space), which feature anything from a street scene circa 1962 with live actors to an Indiana Jones-style adventure in the Valley of the Unknown. Themed restaurants include the Atomicafe and the Gadget Cafe, where you're encouraged to disassemble a radio or toaster while you wait for your meal. Theaters include the Extreme Screen Theater, Dome Theater, Motion Simulator, and Simulation Zone.

The center is open 10:00 A.M. to 5:00 P.M. Wednesday through Saturday, noon to 6:00 P.M. Sunday, with theaters, restaurants, and gift shop remaining open until 9:00 P.M. on Friday and Saturday. Admission is $12.50, $10.50 for individuals 55 and older, and $7.50 for kids ages 2 through 12.

Columbus Zoo and Aquarium
9990 Riverside Drive, Powell
(614) 645-3400

The Columbus Zoo and Aquarium offers creature features that its Cincinnati counterpart doesn't. Highlights include the Wings 'n Play Things Park, an insect-themed playground; the Florida Coast display; an African Forest: Congo Expedition rain-forest park; a restored 1914 carousel complete with 52 exotically carved horses; and the Pachyderm Building, the world's largest indoor elephant exhibit.

The zoo's aquarium is one of only three facilities outside of Florida to care for and display West Indian manatees (seen inside the Manatee Coast exhibit, a 190,000-gallon indoor habitat). The facility also houses one of the largest breeding populations of Lake Victoria cichlids in the world. Discovery Reef, a 100,000-gallon saltwater aquarium, incorporates sharks, stingrays, and brightly colored fish. Thousands of pieces of man-made coral and wave-producing equipment combine to offer visitors a scuba diver's view of the ocean life that surrounds a coral reef. And a touch pool invites guests to touch coastal animals such as horseshoe crabs, sea stars, and sponges. The Live Coral Reef exhibit features a simulated submersible research station, the R.V. *Battelle*. Other residents at the aquarium include penguins, alligators, Australian lungfish, and turtles.

Hours are 9:00 A.M. to 5:00 P.M. daily. Admission is $9.00 for adults, $7.00 for seniors, $5.00 for children ages 2 through 11.

Franklin Park Conservatory and Botanical Garden
1777 East Broad Street
(614) 645-TREE

Housed in a 12,500-square-foot glass structure built in 1895 in the style of London's Crystal Palace are a simulated tropical rain forest, Himalayan Mountains habitat, desert, Pacific island water garden, and tree fern forest. Other displays include a bonsai garden and an orchid collection. It's open Tuesday through Sunday 10:00 A.M. to 5:00 P.M. (Wednesday till 8:00 P.M.). Admission is $6.50 for most folks, $5.00 for individuals age 61 and older and students, and $3.00 for kids ages 2 through 12.

Jack Nicklaus Museum
2355 Olentangy River Road
(614) 247-5959

The "Greatest Game" and its greatest player are honored at the Jack Nicklaus Museum. Legendary players, famous personalities, and recreational golfers are featured in displays, which include memorabilia collected by the United States Golf Association. Hours are 9:00 A.M. to 5:00 P.M. Monday through Saturday, 1:00 to 5:00 P.M. Sunday. Admission fee is $10.00, seniors $7.00, students $6.00.

King Arts Complex
867 Mount Vernon Avenue
(614) 645-5464

The King Arts Complex, the largest and most heavily programmed facility in America dedicated to Dr. Martin Luther King Jr., presents music, art, and human rights programs throughout the year. Hours are 9:00 A.M. to 5:00 P.M. daily. Admission is $6.00.

Motorcycle Hall of Fame Museum
13515 Yarmouth Drive, Pickerington
(614) 856-1900

Vrroomm! Motorcycle enthusiasts such as Jay Leno hang out among the hundreds of classic motorcycles housed at the Motorcycle Hall of Fame. Hours are 8:30 A.M. to 5:00 P.M. daily. Admission is $3.00 for adults, $2.00 for seniors, and free to children age 16 and under.

Ohio Historical Center and Ohio Village
Interstate 71 and 17th Avenue
(614) 297-2310

This is the core museum of the Ohio Historical Society, open year-round 9:00 A.M. to 5:00 P.M. Monday through Saturday and 10:00 A.M. to 5:00 P.M. on Sunday and holidays except Christmas, New Year's Day, and Thanksgiving, when it's closed. The best attraction here is the Ohio Village, a re-created Civil War–era town that represents a typical county seat during the 1860s. The village is open January through November 9:00 A.M. to 5:00 P.M. Tuesday through Sunday. Admission is $5.00, $3.20 for those age 62 and older, $2.50 for kids ages 6 through 12.

Ohio State Fair
Celeste Center and Ohio State Fairgrounds, 17th Avenue exit off Interstate 71
(877) 646-3247, (614) 644-3247

Spectacular midway rides, goofy rodeo clowns, a crazy carnival atmosphere, and king-size country and pop draws such entertainment as Alabama, 98 Degrees, and Alan Jackson. What other event could we be talking about but the venerable Ohio State Fair? The 150-year-old happening, held each year throughout the month of August, is the state's biggest tourist draw.

Rides and attractions on the midway include Figure-Eight Racing, the Model Train Show, Pig Races, and Skyscraper (carts spinning in a 360-degree circle, creating the same 4g force you'd feel in a fighter jet). There are also multibreed horse shows, a youth horticulture fair, livestock competitions, rodeos, daily parades, nightly concerts, and stunt shows. The least-busy days are Tuesday, Wednesday, and Thursday, if you want to avoid the crowds. (Almost a million visitors come to the fair annually.)

Hours are 9:00 A.M. to 10:00 P.M. all through August. The midway is open 10:00 A.M. to midnight Friday and Saturday, 10:00 A.M. to 11:00 P.M. Sunday through Thursday. Admission is $8.00 for adults, $7.00 for children ages 5 to 12 and seniors 60-plus. Children under age 5 admitted free. All kiddie rides take one $1.00 coupon, spectacular rides take two $1.00 coupons, and superspectacular rides take three $1.00 coupons.

Ohio Statehouse
Broad and High Streets
(614) 752-6350

Check out the architecture in the Ohio Statehouse, which is considered one of the best examples of the Doric style in the United States. A painting of the Great Seal of Ohio is in the center of the rotunda dome. There's also a collection of historical documents and portraits of Ohio's noted governors and U.S. presidents.

The rotunda is open for tours from 9:30 A.M. to 3:00 P.M. Monday through Friday and noon to 3:00 P.M. Saturday and Sunday. The Senate chamber is open Monday through Friday 9:00 A.M. to 4:30 P.M. when the Senate is not in session. Admission as a visitor is free—if you want to come here as an elected representative, it will cost you plenty.

***Santa Maria* Replica**
Batelle Riverfront Park, Marconi Boulevard and Broad Street
(614) 645-8760

This is a museum-quality, full-scale replica of the flagship of the city's namesake. Visitors get a feel for the life of a 15th-century shipmate. It's open April through December, Wednesday through Friday 10:00 A.M. to 3:00 P.M., Saturday and Sunday noon to 5:00 P.M. Admission is $3.00 for adults and $1.50 for kids ages 5 through 17.

The Thurber House
77 Jefferson Avenue
(614) 464-1032

It's his world, and welcome to it: Take a tour of author James Thurber's Victorian home, restored as a literary center and bookstore featuring the works of the famed Columbus humorist. Hours are 1:00 to 4:00 P.M. daily. Tours are $2.00.

If you're going to Columbus, save some time for shopping on the way there or back. A popular stop is the outlet malls at the Jeffersonville exits off Interstate 71.

Wexner Center for the Arts
1871 North High Street
(614) 292-3535
This may well be Ohio's most cutting-edge performance venue, featuring offbeat art and photo exhibitions, the annual Avante Garage Music and Film Festival, a hilarious "B Movie A Go-Go" film festival screening such gems as *Creature with the Atom Brain,* and specially commissioned plays by New York and European writers. Hours vary by season. Admission is $5.00.

The Wilds
14000 International Road, Cumberland
(740) 638-2286
North America's largest conservation preserve, the Wilds is an ecological habitat that spans 14 square miles with no cages and features roaming giraffes and other wildlife. Hours are 9:00 A.M. to 5:00 P.M. daily, May through October. Admission is $10.00 for adults, $9.00 for seniors, $7.00 for children.

Central Ohio

Amish Country
Amish Country Visitors Bureau
(330) 893-3000
Holmes County features one of the largest settlements of Amish in America, and indeed, a trip to this hilly farm community is like a journey back in time. Horse and buggies, barn raisings, community quilts, they're all here. Towns such as Berlin and Charm feature quaint craft, quilt, and furniture shops. While in Charm, stay at the Charm Countryview Inn, owned by a Mennonite family, or the Amish Country Inn. Don't miss the town of Sugarcreek, known as the Switzerland of Ohio for its 13 cheese factories and homes styled after Swiss chalets.

Amphicar Owners Club Swim In
Grand Lake St. Mary's, Celina
No phone
There's only one Ohio festival where you can expect to hear much tech talk about the physics of aquaplaning and such odd expressions as "dipping the headlights." And that would be the annual Amphicar Owners Club Swim In, which takes place each summer in Celina. Some 40 to 50 of these peculiar amphibious vehicles drive in—or dive in—for the event. There's both a street parade on wheels and a floating parade, where the Amphicars coast single file under a one-lane bridge that leads to the lake.

The Amphicar was manufactured in Berlin (Germany, not Ohio) from 1962 to 1967; only 3,000 were ever produced, with about 500 remaining worldwide. It's the only nonmilitary amphibious vehicle ever made on an automobile production line, with glorious rear fins rising higher than any American classic car produced. The watertight steel craft can sail along the highway at 70 mph (or at eight knots on the water); enthusiasts have succeeded in some serious ocean crossings (San Diego to Catalina Island, for instance).

How did the Swim In land in Celina after many years in New York State? There's chatter in official club literature that claims Celina was determined the "actual exact and true navigational center" of its membership. (That would be latitude 40.5555 degrees north by longitude 84.6061 degrees west, for those of you voyaging to Celina.)

Annual WACO Aircraft Reunion
Wynkoop Airport, Mount Vernon
No phone
If you overhear somebody chatting about Wacos or "flying the Koop," you've undoubtedly run across some barnstorming enthusiast or a daring biplane pilot. These folks flock each summer to Wynkoop Airport in Mount Vernon, home to the Annual WACO Aircraft Reunion and Fly-In.

It's all thanks to the WACO Aircraft Company, which first opened for business in the early 1920s, capitalizing on the daredevil pilot exhibitions then sweeping the country. The manufacturer was founded in Lorain by Elwood "Sam" Junkin and Clayton Bruckner along with a well-known barnstormer of the era, Buck Weaver (thus the moniker WACO, short for Weaver Airplane Company).

The biplanes were specially designed and reinforced to endure the aerial histrionics and loopy loops favored by the crazed pilots of the day. By 1929 the firm had evolved into the most prolific producer of light aircraft in the nation.

Today a few bold enthusiasts keep the legacy of the original Waco biplanes alive. A trip to Mount Vernon and Wynkoop Airport for the Reunion and Fly-In gives new meaning to the expression "on a wing and a prayer."

Bicentennial Barn
7848 Columbus Road, Mount Vernon
No phone

You can't drive far in Ohio without encountering a "bicentennial barn," part of a project sponsored by the Ohio Bicentennial Commission to celebrate the state's 200th birthday in 2003. This century-old barn is owned by Raymond and Dixie Luzader and is used to house quarterhorses. Harley Warrick, best known for the Mail Pouch logos he painted on barns across America decades ago, consulted on the ambitious enterprise. Since that initial endeavor, barn painter Scott Hagan has crisscrossed the state, painting a representative edifice in each of Ohio's 88 counties. Each of the distinctive red-white-and-blue bicentennial logos measures 20 by 20 feet and took 18 hours—and seven gallons of paint—to complete.

(In Hamilton County, the bicentennial barn is located in Colerain Township. The century-old black barn is owned by Township Trustee Bernie Fiedeldey, who bought it in 1995—leaky roof, sagging floor, and all. The barn, constructed of ash trees sawed in half, is the original, with a stone foundation. Now that it has a new, solid floor, it's the site of barn dances in addition to its bicentennial barn status. It's located at 7941 East Miami River Road.)

"Y" Bridge
Downtown Zanesville
No phone

If you've ever received a postcard displaying an aerial photograph of a rather odd-looking Y bridge and the trademarked phrase "Turn Right in the Middle of the Bridge," then you've received your mailing from a visitor to Zanesville, Ohio.

The only Y bridge in the world, this forked treasure boasts three ends where U.S. Highway 40 (the old "National Road") crosses the confluence of the Licking and Muskingum Rivers. The structure, first built in 1814, is unique because—as *Ripley's Believe It or Not* accurately noted—it's the only place in the world where it is possible to cross the bridge and yet stay on the same side of the river.

The best viewing (short of a helicopter or airplane) is from Putnam Overlook, located off Pine Street. The steamboat *Lorena* cruises on the river during the summer months, offering a different perspective of the bridge.

The bridge, located in the center of town, is actually the fifth incarnation of the structure to be built in the same location. The noted midwestern bridge-builder Carl Schumacher came to town to live during one of the bridge construction periods, contracted pneumonia, and died—the only known fatality of the Y Bridge.

Zanesville, once the state capital of Ohio in the early 1800s, is also known as the home of the Zane Grey Museum and as home to Roseville and Weller art pottery (the town's nickname is "Clay City"). Zane Grey, the famed author of paperback western tales, grew up here.

Newark

Longaberger Basket Company
Ohio Highway 16, on the north edge of Newark
(740) 322-5588

Own a Longaberger basket? Or just covet one? Either way, head to Longaberger Land, also known as the basket company's world headquarters in Newark. We won't give you directions. Suffice to say, when you pull up to the 12-story office building in the shape of a Longaberger basket (160 times life-size), you're there. Americans, especially yuppies, have fallen in love with the handwoven baskets—with their plastic protectors, lids, and pewter tie-ons—making Longaberger one of Forbes's top-500 private companies in America. In addition to the headquarters (which features displays in the lobby) and nearby factory, there's the Longaberger Golf Club and the Longaberger Homestead, with restaurant and interpretive center. Hours of the retail shops and for tours are 9:00 A.M. to 5:00 P.M. Monday through Saturday and noon to 5:00 P.M. Sunday.

SOUTH

Lexington, Kentucky

Hold your horses. Or ride them if you wish. But if it's horses you like, run, don't trot, to Lexington. You won't be alone. Queen Elizabeth II, sheiks from Dubai, and other assorted royalty like to visit to check out the equestrian action. We've included several excellent horse-farm tours as well as other outstanding attractions.

The Greater Lexington Convention and Visitors Bureau can provide you with more information. Contact it at 301 East Vine Street, Lexington, (859) 233-1221.

American Saddlebred Museum
4093 Iron Works Parkway
(859) 259-2746
Gen. Robert E. Lee rode a saddlebred horse, and Mr. Ed was one. Those are two good reasons why horse lovers will want to check out this museum, dedicated to Kentucky's only native breed and the oldest registered American breed of horse. The museum offers a multi-image theater show, hands-on exhibits, and gift shop. The museum is open 9:00 A.M. to 5:00 P.M. Wednesday through Sunday. Admission is $9.00 for adults, and $6.00 for children ages 7 through 12.

Claiborne Farm
Winchester Road, Paris
(859) 233-4252
One of America's most famous horse farms, this is where mile record-holder Secretariat retired to stud and is buried. His memory lives on in more than 300 offspring. Tours are available by appointment only.

Historic & Horse Farm Tours
3429 Montavesta Drive
(859) 268-2906
This tour company has a monopoly on Calumet, the farm with the red-trimmed white barns that produced eight Kentucky Derby winners. The normal three-hour tour hits Calumet, the Keeneland racetrack, and a broodmare farm. A tour van picks up visitors at most hotels in the area. Daily tours start at 9:00 A.M. and the cost is $30. Do call in advance because there's sometimes a wait of two weeks or more.

Keeneland Race Course
4201 Versailles Road
(859) 254-3412
Yes, they also race horses in Lexington. In fact, you'll find many travel agencies in Cincinnati that are keenly aware of this fact and offer group tours during Keeneland's scant six weeks of racing each year—three in April and three in October.

Keeneland has been called the most beautiful horse track in the world, with its manicured grounds and dogwood-shaded paddock. A dozen derby winners have been acquired through Keeneland's July and September yearling sales, another big draw for serious horse traders and wannabes.

The spring season generally opens the first Friday in April and runs five days a week (all but Monday and Tuesday). The fall season opens the second Saturday in October and runs five days a week (Monday and Tuesday off). General admission is $3.00 (no charge for simulcast races). Reserved seats vary by day and season. The rails and paddock are preferred areas for people watching, so consider the general admission ticket. If you want to eat at the Keeneland restaurant, make your reservations far in advance.

Kentucky Thoroughbred Center
3380 Paris Pike
(859) 293-1853

Not to be confused with the Kentucky Thoroughbred Park, this is a working Thoroughbred training complex with a 1-mile training track and 900-seat sales pavilion. A one-hour tour gives visitors a behind-the-scenes look at the industry. Tours are offered at 9:00 A.M., 10:30 A.M. and 1:00 P.M. Monday through Friday, 9:00 A.M. and 10:30 A.M. Saturday, from April 1 through October 31. Cost is $10.00, $5.00 for kids age 12 and younger.

Lexington Center
430 West Vine Street
(859) 233-4567

They also like their basketball in Lexington, and this is where it's played. In fact, some people think that the basketball world revolves around this 23,000-seat arena. But you'll also find Cincinnatians taking the trip down I-75 for major concerts.

Mary Todd Lincoln House
578 West Main Street
(859) 233-9999

This restored home is the first site in America to honor a first lady. The house offers a unique look into the early years of the wife of Abraham Lincoln. The house was originally a brick tavern constructed in 1803 and was renovated into a family dwelling by Mary's father in the 1830s. The house contains many period furnishings and personal effects of Mary's. Public tours are offered March 15 through December 1, Monday through Saturday, 10:00 A.M. to 3:30 P.M. Admission is $7.00 for adults, $4.00 for children 6 through 12.

Shaker Village of Pleasant Hill
U.S. Highway 68, 25 miles southwest of Lexington
(859) 734-5411

Pleasant Hill is the largest restored Shaker village in the United States, with 33 19th-century buildings on 2,700 acres of farmland. It was established in 1805 by a group of the United Society of Believers in Christ's Second Coming, otherwise known as the "Shakers" because of the dances that were part of their religious ceremonies. A re-creation of a Shaker service here provides a demonstration.

With the exception of a handful of people in New Hampshire, there are no more living Shakers. That's largely because the sect believed in segregation of the genders. Their rather stringent rule of no offspring put a crimp in growth of the church. The only time Shaker men and women congregated was during church services, and one of the minister's duties was to make sure nothing untoward took place during those energetic dances.

The Shakers also believed in a simple, economical lifestyle, demonstrated by the unadorned simplicity of their furniture and housewares. Little did they know these items would become hip and trendy a century later. Alas, the Shakers themselves died out and the village was closed in 1910, well before they could profit from their flair for design. The village was restored in the 1960s and today is open for tours year-round.

A self-guided tour of the whole village takes about two hours. Included are working furniture, weaving, candle-making, and broom-making studios. Lodging is also available in 15 restored buildings.

The village is open daily, except Christmas Eve and Christmas Day, 10:00 A.M. to 5:00 P.M. Some exhibition buildings are closed November through March. Admission is $12.50 for adults, $7.00 for kids ages 12 through 17, $5.00 for kids ages 6 through 11.

Three Chimneys Farm
Old Frankfort Pike
(859) 873-7053
The late Seattle Slew, the 1977 Triple Crown winner, stood at stud at this picturesque farm. Call for times when the farm is open to the public. Tours are by appointment only Tuesday through Saturday.

Bourbon County, Kentucky

No trip to the Bluegrass State is complete without touching on the Bourbon Trail, a string of distilleries stretching across central Kentucky.

More than 90 percent of the country's bourbon is produced here amid the rolling bluegrass landscape—call it wine country without the wine. That's right, the amber liquid calls Old Kentucky its home, and a half dozen or so distilleries in the state proudly open their doors to visitors year-round for intoxicating tours and programs.

Though technically bourbon can be produced anywhere, Kentucky is the only state allowed to place its name on the bottle. Originally shipped through Bourbon County, barrels were stamped with the county's name and soon this Kentucky whiskey became known as bourbon. The alcohol is barreled as a clear liquid, like vodka, and changes color during the aging process inside the charred oak barrels.

Many distilleries are located in or around Bardstown, called the Bourbon Capital of the World, in part because the area's water supply boasts very high limestone content and low iron, somehow making it a perfect ingredient to distill bourbon. Each September the annual Kentucky Bourbon Festival in Bardstown is a five-day event that attracts tens of thousands (call 502-348-3623 for details). Bardstown is also home to the Oscar Getz Museum of Whiskey History (502-348-2999).

Thanks to bourbon's aroma, any distillery tour is a treat for the senses, full of aromatic copper and steel tanks, vanilla scents, and caramel bouquets. Be forewarned: Most tours involve walking and climbing stairs, so wear comfortable shoes.

Heaven Hill Distilleries
1311 Gilkey Run Road, Bardstown
(502) 337-1000
Founder Evan Williams was known for his hospitality, toting a jug of whiskey to town meetings where he was an early government trustee. Later, members of the Jim Beam family, including Jim's brother Park, would practice their craft here.

The Bourbon Heritage Center denotes the history of the distillery's flagship bourbon, Evan Williams. You can watch the film *Portrait of Heaven Hill,* experience interactive exhibits, visit a working rickhouse (the facility where the barreled bourbon is aged), and enjoy a free "Taste of Heaven" in the barrel-shaped tasting room. There's a gift shop on-site as well, with copper and oak crafts. You can purchase a frontier jug of Evans Williams Master Select Bourbon personalized with your name. The Heaven Hill Trolley can shuttle you through a tour of Old Bardstown. Free hourly tours are offered Tuesday through Saturday 10:00 A.M. to 4:00 P.M., Sunday noon to 3:00 P.M. (no bourbon tastings or sales on Sunday).

Jim Beam's American Outpost
Kentucky Highway 245, Clermont
(502) 543-9877
Farmer Jacob Beam and his son David Beam began to hit their stride selling in the early 1800s. During Prohibition, the Beam family was forced to take up growing citrus fruit in Florida, but they returned to the bourbon business here when Congress declared the booze could flow again.

The visitor center offers an abbreviated look at the bourbon-making process through exhibits that trace the 200-year history of the distilling family. All tours are self-guided. Free tastings are offered in a stately mansion once occupied by Jim Beam's son. Displays include the world's smallest working still and an antique version dating from the Revolutionary War era. Open and free to the public Monday through Saturday 9:00 A.M. to 4:30 P.M., Sunday 12:30 to 4:00 P.M. (no tastings on Sunday).

Maker's Mark
3350 Burks Spring Road, Loretto
(270) 865-2099

Any bourbon tour would likely begin first with Maker's Mark, which has been producing its bourbon whiskey (they spell it "whisky" in honor of the company's Scottish roots) since 1840, complete with its signature red wax on the bottle cap. The distillery is listed in the *Guinness Book of World Records* as the oldest operating bourbon distillery on the planet. Robert Samuels brewed his first batch in 1780 for personal use. Samuels's grandson, T. W., erected the family's first commercial distillery on the family farm in 1840. The name Maker's Mark comes from the tradition of fine English pewter; makers only put their mark on their finest pieces.

The distillery is located on scenic 850-acre grounds framed by magnolias and sugar maples. On display are an antique fire engine in the fire department, the original owner's Victorian house, a road tollhouse, a quart house (believed to be the nation's oldest remaining retail whiskey store), barrel warehouse, still house, and visitor center. In the gift gallery you can buy a small bottle (if you're 21 or older) and plunk it in the "dipping booth," creating a customized red-wax sealed bottle that you can sign and date. Free tours are conducted Monday through Saturday mornings at 10:30 and 11:30, and afternoons at 12:30, 1:30, 2:30, and 3:30. Sunday tours are conducted afernoons only from March to December at 1:30, 2:30, and 3:30. (No liquor sales on Sunday.)

Wild Turkey Distillery
1525 Tyrone Road, Lawrenceburg
(502) 839-2182

The brand is named for the wild turkey hunts favored by the first owner of the distillery. Begin at the visitor center, located in a former worker's house, then take one of the four one-hour distillery tours offered on weekdays only. In the summer months the tour might not include the fermentation room (Wild Turkey shuts down production in the hottest months of the year). On display are various artifacts related to the company's history as well as segments on the distilling process. Free tours are offered Monday through Friday at 9:00 and 10:30 A.M., and at 12:30 and 2:00 P.M.

Woodford Reserve
7855 McCracken Pike, Versailles
(859) 879-1812

Elijah Pepper birthed his golden brown elixir here in 1812. Later, French wine merchant Leopold Labrot and Frankfort banker James Graham formed Labrot & Graham on the site. The current owner, Brown-Forman Corp. (owners of Jack Daniel's in Tennessee), reopened this 19th-century distillery a decade ago; the $14 million complex is a National Historic Landmark. The visitor center offers an introductory film plus exhibits, photos, and artifacts about the history of Kentucky bourbon.

A restaurant and gift shop feature wine racks made from whiskey barrels, among other bourbon-inspired fare. The 78-acre site includes all aspects of bourbon production. Begin your tour with a stroll through the facility where the sour mash bubbles in unique cypress fermenting tanks. The distilling room, dating from 1840, features copper pot stills just like ones used a century ago. Other exhibits reflect on the art of coopering the barrels and offer a walk through the only surviving stone aging warehouse in America. The tour ends with samples of bourbon balls.

Open Tuesday through Saturday 9:00 A.M. to 5:00 P.M., Sunday 12:30 to 4:30 P.M. Tours are conducted Tuesday through Saturday at 10:00 A.M., 11:00 A.M., 2:00 P.M., and 3:00 P.M.; Sunday tours are conducted April to October only at 1:00, 2:00, and 3:00 P.M. Admission is $5.00 (includes a tasting and souvenir shot glass) for 18 years old and up. Children are free (but no tasting).

Louisville, Kentucky

The Kentucky Derby at Churchill Downs is clearly the big draw, but there's more to Louisville than mint juleps and fast horses. Note, the "s" in Louisville is silent. So are all the vowels when natives pronounce it. The correct pronunciation is "Louie-ville" for out of towners and "Lou-a-vull" for natives.

While in town, check out the West Main Street Historic Cultural and Arts District between the 500 and 900 blocks downtown. This is the largest collection of 19th-century cast-iron storefronts this side of SoHo in New York City.

You can contact the Louisville Convention and Visitors Bureau at (800) 626-5646.

Churchill Downs
700 Central Avenue
(502) 636-4400
Lexington may have all the horses, but Louisville's got the big race. The Kentucky Derby, the first and foremost leg of the Triple Crown, is run the first Saturday of each May. The derby has been run on this course since 1875. The track hosts other Thoroughbred races from the last week in April to the first week in July and from the end of October to the end of November.

The waiting list for Kentucky Derby tickets is long, but you can always join the throngs in the infield. Your best bet for a grandstand seat is any day but derby day. Admission is $2.00, $1.00 for seniors, children 12 and under free, for both clubhouse and for grandstand.

The Kentucky Derby Museum, (502) 637-1111, is adjacent to Gate One at the racetrack and houses numerous racing artifacts and a 360-degree audiovisual recreation of the derby. The museum is open Monday through Saturday 9:00 A.M. to 5:00 P.M., noon to 5:00 P.M. Sunday. Admission is $9.00, $8.00 for those age 55 and older, and $3.00 for kids ages 5 through 12.

Louisville Slugger Museum
Hillerich & Bradsby Co.,
800 West Main Street
(502) 585-5226
This stop will surely clear the bases for any baseball fan in your household. If you played baseball as a kid, you probably went through your share of Louisville Sluggers. That is, unless you were a post-1970 aluminum bat kid and you didn't, like Robert Redford in *The Natural,* hand-turn your own bat out of a tree felled by lightning. So there's nostalgia galore here, including a bat used by Babe Ruth.

The museum is open to the public for tours Monday through Saturday 9:00 A.M. to 4:00 P.M. Admission is $8.00 for adults, $7.00 for seniors, $4.00 for children ages 6 to 12. No bat production on Saturday.

The Dean Martin Festival, held each June in Steubenville, pays a reverential tribute to all things possibly connected to Steubenville's native son. There's a film festival, Dino impersonations, Catholic masses, and, oh yes, lots and lots of martinis. That's **amore!**

EAST

Adams County

Adams County may be one of Ohio's poorest in money terms, but it's among the state's richest in attractions and natural beauty—including one of the nation's largest and most elaborate prehistoric Indian mounds, southwest Ohio's most beautiful nature preserve, and one of the region's favorite getaways.

Blake Pharmacy
206 North Market Street, West Union
(937) 544-2451

This unpretentious drugstore houses one of the state's few remaining authentic soda fountains. Ask and they'll gladly prepare you a raspberry or vanilla Coke, made the way our parents remember it. Some 30 weddings have been performed in the aisles of this drugstore, if for no other reason than it's the most notable tourist attraction in sleepy West Union. Hours vary by season, so call ahead.

Keim Family Market
2621 Burnt Cabin Road, Seaman
(937) 386-9995

Our favorite of the many Amish farm markets in the area. You'll find the predictable home-baked goods and cheeses, but also some offbeat spices, jams, and jellies (take home the pecan apricot). Take time to swing in the numerous gazebos and gliders that are for sale on the property. Hours are Monday through Friday 8:00 A.M. to 6:00 P.M., 8:00 A.M. to 5:00 P.M. Saturday.

Lewis Mountain Herbs
2345 Ohio Highway 247, West Union
(937) 549-2484

Judy Lewis has been tending her herb farm for well over a decade now. The greenhouse complex and gift shop feature hundreds of well-known and exotic fresh herbs for cooking, medicinal purposes, and just plain nibbling. The farm is located atop a hillside (you'll know you're near it when you pass the volunteer firehouse) and is a perfect spot for a picnic or Kodak moment. Hours are generally Monday through Saturday 9:00 A.M. to 4:00 P.M., but we've arrived at 3:00 P.M. and found the place shuttered. Call ahead.

Miller's Farm
906 Wheat Ridge Road, West Union
(937) 544-8524

Harry and Leah Miller are the proprietors of this wonderful, and ever expanding, operation. The "bulk foods" aren't all that bulky, but you're welcome to cart home as much as you like (bring a big, empty ice cooler). One building houses the bakery, full of molasses cookies and Amish pies. Another building is devoted to jams, jellies, noodles, chips, cereals, candies, and cheese (sample the horseradish or vegetable herb yogurt cheeses). Quilts and Amish dresses are also on sale. The third building houses all the lovingly crafted woodworkings: chairs, lazy Susans, toys, and the like. Watch out for the horse you-know-what in the parking lot, which can have as many buggies as cars some days. Hours are 9:00 A.M. to 5:00 P.M. Monday through Saturday. Each Labor Day weekend, there's a blowout benefit cookout for the local Amish school.

Murphin Ridge Inn
750 Murphin Ridge Road, West Union
(937) 544-2263, (877) MURPHIN

This country inn in a restored 1810 house is one of the best quick getaways from the Cincinnati area or a good place to stop in for a meal while visiting the area's other attractions.

The inn has 10 rooms, two with fireplaces and all furnished with antique reproductions by the Workshops of David T. Smith, the Cincinnati area's foremost maker of reproduction furniture. One room is used as an art gallery to show the work of Adams County artists. Nearby on Wheat Ridge Road is Miller's Farm (see previous listing), with Amish baked goods and crafts. Innkeepers Sherry and Darryl McKenney can direct you to other craft and food stores.

The setting is quiet and pastoral, with plenty of privacy and three hiking trails on-site. More modern amenities include a pool and tennis court. Meeting rooms are available, and the entire inn can be reserved with sufficient notice. Meals are good Amish country cooking and moderately priced. But keep in mind that the county is dry.

Make reservations before you go and make them several months in advance of fall foliage season in mid- to late October.

Serpent Mound
Ohio Highway 73, 4 miles northwest of Locust Grove
(937) 587-2796
Atop a ridge along Brush Creek, this mound, in the shape of a snake with an egg in its mouth, is nearly a quarter-mile long and as high as 5 feet in spots. The best view is from the observation tower, but keep in mind that the prehistoric Indians didn't have this luxury when building the mound. A museum and picnic facilities also are on-site. The park is open daily 9:30 A.M. to 5:00 P.M. Memorial Day through Labor Day, and 10:00 A.M. to 5:00 P.M. daily the rest of the year. Admission is $5.00 per private vehicle, $4.00 if the passenger is age 65 or older.

Augusta, Ripley, Maysville, and Old Washington

Augusta, Old Washington, and Maysville in Kentucky, with Ripley tucked in between on the Ohio side of the river, make up a foursome of picturesque river towns along a 20-mile span of the Ohio River, and they're well worth a trip.

You can visit each of these cities separately over time, or, if you're ambitious, you can hit them all in a day. Follow U.S. Highway 52 and its parallel highway on the south shore of the river, Kentucky Highway 8. You can cross the river via the bridge between Aberdeen, Ohio, and Maysville or via ferry ($5.00 each way) between US 52 just west of Higginsport and Augusta. The ferry is the only river crossing in the 63 miles between Cincinnati and Maysville. Keep a keen eye on the road for a sign that says AUGUSTA, KY, 1 MILE and points toward the river. The ferry runs 8:00 A.M. to 8:00 P.M. daily.

The William Harsha Bridge, the newest cable span on the Ohio River, is found near the town of Aberdeen. Linking US 52 on the Ohio side with KY 8 on the south side, the bridge provides quick access to Kentucky.

AUGUSTA, KENTUCKY

This pretty river town in Kentucky, which dates from 1780, was inadvertently built on the burial ground of an ancient vanished race of unusually large Indians. Residents regularly unearth shards of pottery and arrowheads when they plant their begonias.

While in town, eat at the **Beehive Tavern,** 101 West Riverside Drive, a restored 1796 building with a fantastic restaurant operated by Cuban native Luciano Moral. Call (606) 756-2202. And don't miss the **Rosemary Clooney House Museum** (read about it in the Kidstuff chapter).

RIPLEY, OHIO

Ripley, believe it or not, is Ohio's only burley tobacco market. As you drive in on US 52, you'll pass row after row of the deadly weed planted all the way to the river. Annual auctions are held here from morning to early afternoon from mid-November to January, except for Christmas week.

This is also home to the **John Rankin House** (follow the signs off US 52 on the west side of town), where the Rev. John Rankin, in cahoots with a farmer on the Kentucky shore, helped more than 2,000 slaves to freedom during the 1850s and 1860s. Documentary evidence confirms an account in *Uncle Tom's Cabin* of a runaway slave girl, Eliza, who escaped pursuers to the Rankin House by leaping from ice floe to ice floe along the Ohio River with a baby in her arms. The Rankin House is open noon to 5:00 P.M. Wednesday through Sunday from Memorial Day through Labor Day and the same hours on weekends only during September and October.

Make time for a stop at **Moyer's Winery,** a scenic winery and (just as notably) a restaurant about 15 miles past Ripley in Manchester, 3859 US 52, (937) 549-2957. There are lots of gazebos and porches on which to sip wine, or lemonade if you're the designated driver. Open Monday through Thursday 11:30 A.M. to 8:30 P.M. and Friday and Saturday 11:30 A.M. to 10:00 P.M.

MAYSVILLE, KENTUCKY

One of the oldest settlements on the Ohio River, Maysville was settled in 1784 by the Virginia legislature as a supply point for settlers coming down the Ohio River. Daniel Boone's family operated a tavern here for a while, and some of his relatives are buried behind the **Maysville Public Library,** 221 Sutton Street.

While in Maysville, you'll want to try transparent pie, a puddinglike dessert peculiar to this area. Transparent-pie central is **Magee's Bakery,** 212 Market Street, (606) 564-5720, open Tuesday through Saturday 9:30 A.M. to 5:00 P.M.

Burley tobacco is big here too. In fact, it's the world's second-largest burley market after Lexington. Auctions are conducted from mid-November through mid-January, except Thanksgiving and Christmas weeks.

Antiques shops, galleries, and boutiques dot the center of this charming little river town. The place to eat is **Caproni's,** (606) 564-4321, at the foot of Rosemary Clooney Street next to the railroad depot.

For more information, call or write the Maysville-Mason County Chamber of Commerce, 15½ West Second Street, Maysville, KY 45106, (606) 564-5534.

OLD WASHINGTON, KENTUCKY

This charming village, located just a few minutes south of Maysville, is brimming with quaint gift, antiques, and furniture shops—not to mention history. Established in 1786, Old Washington is home to a couple dozen structures stretching along 5 blocks of Main Street, including inns, row houses, and brick mansions featuring lush gardens. Shops of particular note include the **Carousel Shop, Phyllis' Antiques** (including lamps and dollhouses), the **Strawberry Patch** (crafts and teddy bears), and the **Washington Hall Shops** (all gathered inside an 18th-century hotel). Call the Washington Visitors Center at (606) 759-7411 for details on guided tours.

Marietta

If you're looking for a true sense of history, legacy, and lore along the Ohio River, head to Marietta, a picturesque waterfront town established in 1788 as the first permanent settlement in the Northwest Territory. Marietta lies in the heart of the Ohio River Scenic Byway, which encompasses 452 miles and passes through 14 counties.

Parts of the original Ohio Company fortification remain, as does the Castle, a stellar example of Gothic revival architecture and a museum that offers guided tours and exhibits of regional artifacts. And Harmar Village is linked to downtown Marietta by a historic railroad bridge that is open to foot traffic. It's in Marietta that you'll encounter the Ohio River Museum, which immerses visitors in the legacy of the river and the paddle wheelers that plied their trade on its waters. Consider an overnight stay at the Lafayette Hotel, located at the confluence of the Ohio and Muskingum Rivers. It's on the National Register of Historic Places.

Campus Martius Museum
601 Second Street
(740) 373-3750

This facility highlights population migration in Ohio's history. It's built on the site of the original fort that established Marietta. Gen. Rufus Putnam's house and the Ohio River Land Company Office remain from that fortification and are enclosed within the museum. Open 9:30 A.M. to 5:00 P.M. Wednesday through Saturday, noon to 5:00 P.M. Sunday (closed winter months). Admission is $7.00 for adults, $3.00 for children ages 6 to 12, free to children age 5 and under.

The Castle
418 Fourth Street
(740) 373-4180
Once the home of Ohio senator Theodore Davis, the Castle boasts an octagonal tower, trefoil attic window, and stone-capped spires. Inside, the building is furnished with items of historical signifigance to the area. One-hour tours of this Gothic revival mansion, which is listed on the National Historic Register, are offered on the half hour. Open 10:00 A.M. to 4:00 P.M. Monday, Thursday, and Friday, 1:00 to 4:00 P.M. Saturday and Sunday. (Open daily in summer months.) Admission is $5.00 for adults, $4.50 for seniors, $2.50 for children ages 6 to 17, free to children age 5 and under.

Ohio River Museum
601 Front Street
(740) 373-3717
Three buildings are devoted to the history of the river named the Ohio by the Iroquois and called *La Belle Rivière* ("the Beautiful River") by the French. One building focuses on the natural history of the Ohio, while another is devoted to steamboats and the third explores the enduring relationship between residents and river. Outside, on the Muskingum River, visitors can tour the *W. P. Snyder Jr.,* the last intact steam-powered stern-wheeler towboat in America. Open 9:30 A.M. to 5:00 P.M. Saturday, noon to 5:00 P.M. Sunday and holidays. Admission is $7.00 for adults, $3.00 for children ages 6 to 12, free to children age 5 and under.

Does anybody really know what time it is? Not in Indiana, apparently, where some of the state's counties don't observe daylight saving time. It causes some confusion, especially if you're taking a day trip where you can easily arrive in a given county an hour earlier than the county you departed from. For the record, Dearborn County (which is part of Greater Cincinnati) switches to eastern daylight time with the rest of us.

WEST

Nashville, Indiana

Nashville, the county seat of Brown County, is one of the tristate area's major arts-and-crafts centers, with more than 90 specialty shops, 7 antiques stores, 10 art galleries, 16 restaurants, and a dozen ice-cream and candy stores. It's a pretty sweet life for the town's 700 inhabitants, who cater to the thousands of visitors who flock here mainly from Cincinnati and Indianapolis. Of particular culinary interest is the Ordinary, a restaurant that is anything but (try the pheasant and other colonial dishes).

Fall foliage season in mid- to late October is peak season. And the town is packed. Late spring and summer are the best times to visit if you just want to check out the art and entertainment. Holiday shopping season is also popular without being quite as hectic as October.

Horse-drawn carriage rides are available from Alexander Carriage Rides on the North Van Buren Street main drag. Two country music halls also beckon fans from miles around. The Country Time Music Hall, a mile east of town on Indiana Highway 46, is in a hand-pegged barn. The Little Nashville Opry, three-quarters of a mile southwest of town on IN 46, brings in big name acts from March to November.

For more information, contact the Brown County Chamber of Commerce at 37 West Main Street, Nashville, IN 47448, (812) 988-6647.

Brown County Art Gallery Association
1 Artist Drive
(812) 988-4609
The association presents excellent art exhibits featuring artists from Nashville's earliest art colony days of the '20s and '30s. It's open 10:00 A.M. to 5:00 P.M.

Monday through Saturday and noon to 5:00 P.M. on Sunday.

Brown County State Park and Abe Martin Lodge
Indiana Highway 46
(812) 988-7316
Located 2 miles east of Nashville, this park and lodge are popular stops for visitors. Cabins are basic, but family cabins have cooking facilities. Rates are very reasonable. Book way in advance for the fall foliage season.

The Story Inn
6404 South Indiana Highway 135, Story
(812) 988-2273
The tiny hamlet of Story (pop. 7), about 10 miles from Nashville, features a wonderful restaurant housed in an old tin-sided general store. Antique tools and toys line the shelves, but the real star of the place is its regional American menu; the fare is delicious and modestly priced. The restaurant is consistently rated as one of Indiana's top gourmet eateries by the national food magazines. The Story Inn is also a B&B that offers 12 bedrooms with absolutely *no* TVs, clocks, radios, or phones.

Indianapolis, Indiana

How many reasons are there to visit Indy? At least 500 or so. Indianapolis is a city of plains, trains, and automobiles. Besides the famed Indy 500, there's the world-class Children's Museum—the city's No. 1 tourist attraction not counting that little motor jaunt around an oval track—a major-league museum of Native American and western plains art, and the thriving Broad Ripple district with its music clubs and trendy pubs.

Children's Museum
3000 North Meridian Street
(317) 921-4000
Sure, Cincinnati's got one too. But this is perhaps the biggest and best children's museum in the world. Next to the Indy 500, it's the city's biggest draw. Major attractions include the SpaceQuest Planetarium and the Lilly Center for Exploration, designed by teens for kids to explore a variety of topics. Dinosaur replicas; full-scale and model trains; a carousel with goats, giraffes, and lions in addition to horses; and a performing arts theater are other big attractions.

The museum is open 10:00 A.M. to 5:00 P.M. daily. Admission is $11.50, $10.50 for those age 60 and older, and $6.50 for ages 2 through 17. The planetarium costs an extra $2.00, and the carousel is 50 cents a go-round.

Circle Centre
49 West Maryland Street
(317) 681-8000
This huge retail-and-entertainment complex covers 2 downtown blocks and features plenty of shopping opportunities as well as restaurants, nightclubs, and theaters.

Conseco Fieldhouse
125 South Pennsylvania
(317) 917-2727
The Pacers play here. Call the number above for tickets, which aren't particularly hard to come by unless the Pacers are playing the Chicago Bulls.

Eitetjorg Museum of American Indian & Western Art
500 West Washington Street
(317) 636-9378
The western collection includes works of Georgia O'Keeffe, Frederic Remington, and members of the original Taos, New Mexico, art colony. The Indian collection includes crafts and artifacts from throughout North America. The museum is open Tuesday through Saturday 10:00 A.M. to 5:00 P.M. and Sunday noon to 5:00 P.M. (The museum opens on Monday in the summer, as well.) Admission is $7.00, $6.00 for those age 65 and older, $4.00 for students with ID, and $4.00 for kids ages 5 through 17. The family rate is $10. Admission costs more during special events.

Indianapolis Motor Speedway
4790 West 16th Street
(317) 481-8500

You may have heard of the Indianapolis 500. Every year on the Sunday before Memorial Day, around a half-million people jam this 2.5-mile oval to watch cars going around in circles very fast. Time trials in early May are another big draw—you can see the cars without so many other people around. There's also an 18-hole golf course inside and around the track, but forget tee times on Memorial Day weekend.

Call after April 1 for a ticket order form for the Indy 500. Return the form ASAP, as ticket availability is based in part on how early you apply. Prices range from $30 to $100 (for the paddock penthouse).

The Auto Racing Hall of Fame and Museum, appropriately enough, is here too, displaying many of the winning cars and related memorabilia. A film about the track's history and highlights is shown every half hour. The museum is open daily 9:00 A.M. to 5:00 P.M. Museum admission is $3.00, $1.00 for children ages 6 to 15. A bus tour of the track is another $3.00.

Indianapolis Zoo and White River Park
1200 West Washington Street
(317) 630-2030

From Siberian tigers and polar bears to whales and dolphins, just about every species can be found here. White River Park, where the zoo is located, also encompasses the Indiana State Museum and IMAX Theater, Victory Field (home to the Indians AAA ball team), and the National Collegiate Athletic Association (NCAA) Hall of Champions Museum. The zoo is open 9:00 A.M. to 4:00 P.M. Monday through Thursday, and 9:00 A.M. to 5:00 P.M. Friday, Saturday, and Sunday. Admission is $10.95, $6.95 for students and seniors.

If you're an architecture buff, drive over to Columbus, Indiana, where city planners showed considerable foresight in hiring some of the 20th century's most notable architects—I. M. Pei, Eliel and Eero Saarinen, and Cesar Pelli among them—to design the library, city hall, and other civic structures.

Madame Walker Center
617 Indiana Avenue
(317) 236-2099

This restored four-story theater is embellished with the African and Egyptian motifs loved by Madame C. J. Walker, America's first female self-made millionaire, who also was black. This was once the place where Louis Armstrong and Dinah Washington performed and today is the center of a district of small jazz clubs. "Jazz on the Avenue" takes place here every Friday evening. Tours are available by appointment. Admission is free, but special-event admissions vary.

RCA Dome
100 South Capitol Avenue
(317) 262-3410

One of the few air-supported domed stadiums in the United States, this one is home to the Colts and site of numerous concerts and conventions that draw Cincinnatians. It also houses the National Track and Field Hall of Fame. Check local papers for a list of events.

Union Station
123 West Louisiana Street
(317) 631-2221

Other cities have turned their railroad terminals into museums and malls or allowed them to be shuttered altogether. Here, Union Station is now a fully functioning hotel, where you can sleep in one of 26 authentic Pullman train cars.

PARKS AND RECREATION

Even most longtime residents of Greater Cincinnati haven't taken advantage of the numerous recreational opportunities in this area. Besides beautiful parks with lots of activities, there are rivers and lakes that provide hours of relaxation and recreation. And, of course, there are the standard sport and health clubs that can be found in most towns. Information about all of these pursuits can be found in this chapter.

PARKS AND NATURE PRESERVES

Though it's one of the nation's oldest and most developed industrial areas, Greater Cincinnati is blessed with an abundance of well-preserved natural beauty, thanks to some forward-thinking local governments and private philanthropists. In addition to numerous locally run parks with extensive recreation facilities, you'll find thousands of acres of nature preserves that offer limited access to humans so as to offer unlimited access to the flora and fauna. The Cincinnati area is also home to at least five state parks. Combined, these green spaces provide the opportunity to enjoy just about every outdoor pursuit imaginable, including backpacking, biking, canoeing, Frisbee golf, hunting, fishing, downhill and cross-country skiing, and more.

Foresight obviously was once a hallmark of the city of Cincinnati and Hamilton County governments, since this most densely populated portion of the tristate area has some of the best and most extensive parks and parkland. Taxpayers in the surrounding counties are a little tighter with a buck, and their governments got into the parkland acquisition game later, when land was more expensive. The outlying counties do have parks, certainly. But most of the parkland outside Hamilton County is owned by the state of Ohio or Kentucky. The Cincinnati Nature Center, one of Clermont County's largest parks and one of the most beautiful nature preserves in the area, is privately owned.

With the opening of the Ronald Reagan Highway in 1997, many of the Hamilton County parks became more accessible to people from all over Cincinnati. Never has a concrete roadway done more for people who enjoy green spaces. The highway passes directly by the entrances of many of the region's best parks (Sharon Woods, Winton Woods, Lake Isabella, Kroger Hills Prairie, and Richardson Forest Preserve, for example) and provides links to many more.

Greater Cincinnati has more parks than we could possibly cover here. So what follows is a listing of the best parks in Ohio and Northern Kentucky—ones you might drive out of your own neighborhood or out of your way to visit. Unless otherwise noted, parks are open to the public year-round, dawn to dusk.

Ohio

CINCINNATI

The city of Cincinnati alone has more than 100 parks with thousands of acres of green space ranging from 1-square-block playgrounds to 1,466-acre Mount Airy Forest, the first municipal forest in the United States.

> *How small is the smallest park in the city of Cincinnati park's system? Thornton Triangle boasts an incredible 0.01 acreage. Located on the West Side at Gracely and Thornton Avenues in Sayler Park, the triangle was acquired by transfer in 1912 when the equally diminutive burg of Fernbank was annexed. The park's only notable feature is that it contains a zinc and cast-iron fountain of a Native American facing the sun.*

Airport Playfield
Beechmont and Wilmer Avenues
(513) 321-6500

Part of the Cincinnati Recreation Commission facilities, this park lets you watch the planes take off from Lunken Airport as you walk or bike along the park's 6.5-mile trail or play the par 3 golf course and driving range. Bike rental is available if you don't want to bring your own. Children will love the Land of Make Believe, one of the more extensive playgrounds in the area.

Ault Park
End of Observatory Avenue
(513) 352-4080

The pavilion at this 143-acre Cincinnati park is a Hyde Park landmark. The attractively landscaped park is a great place for walks, Frisbee tossing, and picnics. Each April it also becomes the site of the Greater Cincinnati Flower and Garden Show, the nation's largest outdoor garden show.

Bicentennial Commons, Sawyer Point, and Yeatman's Cove
Between the Ohio River and Pete Rose Way
No phone

These adjacent parks offer the best all-around recreation facilities of any city park. Among the attractions at the 22-acre Bicentennial Commons, opened during the city's 200th anniversary in 1988, are a superior playground, a dozen tennis courts, sand volleyball courts, the famous/infamous Flying Pigs sculpture, fishing piers, a rink for roller-skating and ice-skating, a boathouse and rowing center, and the Procter & Gamble Performance Pavilion, site of free summer concerts (check the entertainment section in local newspapers for shows).

The Serpentine Wall along the edge of Yeatman's Cove is a great place for warm-weather lolling, frolicking, and river watching. Parking costs $2.00, but it's well worth the investment. Or you can park for free at the Public Landing at the western edge of the parks.

Burnet Woods
Clifton Avenue and Dr. Martin Luther King Drive
(513) 352-4080

Across the street from the University of Cincinnati and Hebrew Union College, this park is a natural favorite with college students. But the 89-acre park is also popular with locals for its hiking trails, picnic shelters, small lake, and nature center.

Eden Park
Access from Kemper Lane, Victory Parkway, or Gilbert Avenue
(513) 352-4080

The park's name came from the land's original owner, Nicholas Longworth, who called it the Garden of Eden. One trip here and you'll see why. Though it's not loaded with recreation areas, this 186-acre Mount Adams park is one of the most beautiful urban parks in the United States. Eden Park gets four stars as a place to take a date for a picnic.

The park also is the center of the city's cultural life, as home to the Playhouse in the Park, Seasongood Pavilion, Krohn Conservatory, and Cincinnati Art Museum. (See the Arts and Attractions chapters.) The pavilion band shell is the site of frequently packed summer concerts in the Seasongood Concert Series. (Check the entertainment listings in local newspapers for times and details.) Krohn Conservatory, one of the nation's largest public greenhouses, offers a tropical rain forest, a rushing 20-foot waterfall, plus orchids, floral displays, a cacti exhibit, and more.

Mirror Lake here is the most picturesque place in Cincinnati for winter ice-skating.

Mount Airy Forest
5083 Colerain Avenue
(513) 352-4080

This 1,466-acre park was the first municipal forest when established by the city of Cincinnati in 1911. Today it's a natural haven and playground for West Siders, with miles of hiking trails, a Frisbee-golf course, numerous picnic shelters, and play areas. Mount Airy Arboretum features displays of azaleas, flowering crab apples, lilacs, and rhododendrons. The forest itself boasts a million hardwoods and conifers. The giant "medieval castle" that you can see from Mount Airy Forest is actually a masonry wall that hides 14 water towers sitting atop the highest point in Hamilton County.

Mount Echo Park
Off Elberon Avenue, Price Hill
(513) 352-4080

This park offers one of the best views of the Ohio River valley, including downtown. With several shelters, it's a great place for family outings and picnics. There's a small playground and basketball and tennis courts.

HAMILTON COUNTY

Hamilton County Park District draws people from all over the tristate because of its beauty and convenience to residents in and outside of the county. And it keeps people coming back because you get a lot of bang for your buck.

Not only does Hamilton County operate 19 parks totaling nearly 15,000 acres, but it charges the same annual $5.00 parking fee to residents and nonresidents alike ($1.00 for a onetime pass). What's more, the county's biggest and best parks—Miami Whitewater Forest, Winton Woods, Sharon Woods, and Woodland Mound—are quite convenient for residents of Dearborn, Butler, Warren, and Clermont Counties, respectively. All parks are open dawn to dusk, 365 days a year (some visitor centers and gift and nature shops are closed holidays). Pets on leashes are permitted in all parks.

The county offers an extensive program of special events and enrichment activities at the parks. Watch for the park district's "Evergreen" insert, which comes out in the *Cincinnati Enquirer* every two months. For other scheduling or event information, call the Hamilton County Park District at (513) 521-PARK, ext. 67, or check out its Web site, www.greatparks.org.

Juilfs Park
8249 Clough Pike, Anderson
(513) 474-0003

This Anderson Township park, which attracts its fair share of folks from the west side of Clermont County, has one of the East Side's best playgrounds, plus soccer and baseball/softball fields and a walking trail. It also has tennis, basketball, and volleyball courts.

Miami Whitewater Forest
Access from New Haven, Dry Fork, and Oxford Roads, Harrison
(513) 367-4774

This 4,279-acre park is the largest in the Hamilton County Park District. In addition to more than 3 miles of nature paths, it has a 7.8-mile multipurpose jogging/bicycling/skating/walking trail, a 1.2-mile inner loop for the less adventurous, horseback riding

---

i

Your kids will love the three Hamilton County Parks that have "spraygrounds": Miami Whitewater's Parky's Pirate Cove, Winton Woods' Parky's Ark, and Woodland Mound's Parky's Wetland Adventure. These water parks for kids ages 2 to 12 are open from 11:00 A.M. to 8:00 P.M. every day from Memorial Day through Labor Day. Admission is $1.00 with a $5.00 annual park sticker.

Some of the Hamilton County Parks also have winter sports facilities. You can go ice fishing or ice-skating at Miami Whitewater Forest, Sharon Woods, Triple Creek, Winton Woods, and Woodland Mound. Sledding hills are located at Miami Whitewater, Sharon Woods, and Winton Woods. Of course, you have to bring your own equipment.

trails, a boathouse and lake, boat fishing, campground, Frisbee-golf course, playgrounds, a visitor center, gift shop, and snack bar. Pirate Cove is a fun "sprayground," with a cascading waterfall and water cannons. Located in northwest Hamilton County, the park is also easily accessible to residents of Dearborn County, Indiana, just off exit 3 of Interstate 74.

Sharon Woods Park and Heritage Village
11450 U.S. Highway 42, Sharonville
(513) 563-9484
www.heritagevillagecincinnati.org

One of the larger and better-equipped Hamilton County parks, Sharon Woods is also popular with visitors from Butler and Warren Counties. The 730-acre park is a great site for fossil hunting . . . but don't take them home with you. Other attractions include a hiking and biking trail around the lake, a fitness trail, a boathouse, and many picnic areas. The Gorge Trail provides a good 1.25-mile nature hike past small waterfalls. The water park includes an elephant fountain and pedal boats.

Within the park is Heritage Village, which has restored 19th-century buildings brought from other parts of southwest Ohio, including a medical office exhibiting Civil War medical equipment and a barn with period equipment. The village varies its schedule depending on the season. Call (513) 563-9484 for more information and hours of operation. Admission to the village is $7.00 for adults, $6.00 for seniors, $5.00 for children ages 5 to 12, and free for kids age 4 and younger.

Winton Woods
Winton Road and Lake Forest Drive
Greenhills
(513) 521-7275

This 2,465-acre park, which completely surrounds the city of Greenhills, is the biggest and most popular park in the Hamilton County Park District. Because it's only a few minutes from the county line, it's also popular with Butler County residents.

The park has a 3-mile paved hike/bike trail (bike rental is available), a bridle trail, and a riding center on the south side of Winton Lake. It also has a dozen picnic areas, a 1-mile fitness trail, a boathouse, nine shelters, an 18-hole Frisbee-golf course, and a regular golf course.

Parky's Farm, a demonstration farm, is a great attraction for kids, with goats, pigs, chickens, ponies, and other farm animals in abundance. Pony rides ($2.00), wagon rides ($2.00) and an indoor playground inside a barn (admission $2.00) are also available. (See the Kidstuff chapter.)

Woodland Mound Park
Access from Kellogg Avenue or Nordyke Road, Anderson
(513) 474-0580

Stephen Ostrander, author of *Natural Acts Ohio,* rates the view from Woodland Mound among the best scenic overlooks in Ohio. But there's more to do here than look around. The park has a great playground, two low-key hiking trails of 1 mile and 0.5 mile, a well-regarded golf course, an outdoor concert area where the Cincinnati Symphony Orchestra and the Cincinnati Pops have occasional free concerts, ballfields, and a snack bar. Because it is on a steep hillside over the river, Woodland Mound almost always has a good enough breeze to fly a kite.

Woodland Mound also has a "sprayground," a small water park for children ages 2 to 12 with waterslides, animals, and shooting water.

The Seasongood Nature Center includes nature exhibits, wildlife-viewing windows, and a gift/bookshop.

BUTLER COUNTY

Hueston Woods State Park and Nature Preserve
Ohio Highway 732, College Corner
(513) 523-6347

This 3,596-acre forest straddles the Butler and Preble county line just off OH 732, north of Oxford. It has a popular lodge and restaurant, golf course, picnic areas, camping, fishing, swimming pools, a nature center, and a pioneer farm museum. A 200-acre nature preserve within the park is a great place for hiking and bird-watching (150 species have been spotted here). The park also has a lake for boating. Boat rentals are available.

CLERMONT COUNTY

Cincinnati Nature Center
4949 Tealtown Road, Glen Este
(513) 831-1711
www.cincynature.org

The beauty of this private, nonprofit nature preserve inspired the 1969 book *The Inland Island* by Josephine Winslow Johnson. Today that name is more apt than ever. The 1,425-acre preserve is an oasis of nature encircled by rapid development in western Clermont County.

Hiking is the main activity here, since the center is dedicated purely to conservation and outdoor education. You can choose from 15 miles of trails that range from the wheelchair-accessible Stanley Rowe All Persons Trail to some fairly long and steeply sloped trails. Scenery runs the gamut from open meadows to fairly deep woods, though most of the center is a relatively young second-growth forest. Do pick up a trail map at the Rowe Building, because it's not hard to get lost in the winding trails. Take it from one who knows.

The nature center is of special interest to birders, who have sighted 153 species of birds here. Rare (to this area) badgers and coyotes also have been spotted. And the park is home to the endangered Indiana bat and the blue-spotted salamander. Novice gardeners will enjoy the Herb Wall, a collection of well-labeled cultivated herbs. You'll find 237 kinds of wildflowers blooming here at various times of the year.

The nature center and gift shop in the Rowe Building have perhaps the area's best collection of nature books. The nature center is open daily. Admission is $3.00 weekdays and $5.00 on weekends for adults, $1.00 for children. Members get in free; membership is $35 per year for an individual and $60 annually for a family and includes a 10 percent discount at the gift shop.

A scenic walkway leading from the Rowe Building along Powel Crosley Lake is a favorite gathering spot for families with kids, who feed bread crumbs to always-hungry fish and turtles.

East Fork State Park
Intersection of Ohio Highways 125 and 222, between Amelia and Bethel
(513) 734-4323

East Fork is a large (8,420-acre) but relatively underdeveloped state park in eastern Clermont County. The public beach is covered with a mix of fine pebbles and sand. There are picnic shelters, a campground, hiking trails, a 5-mile mountain bike trail, and 55 miles of bridle paths. The lake, with its five launch ramps, offers bountiful bass fishing and boating opportunities.

Stonelick State Park
2895 Lake Drive, just east of Milford in Wayne
(513) 734-4323

This is the smaller and lesser used of the state parks in Clermont County. The 1,058-acre park offers picnicking, hiking trails, and swimming. It also has camping. Restrooms and hot water are available so you don't have to rough it entirely. Reservations can be made to (866) 644-6727. Stonelick Lake offers boating and fishing (bass, bluegill, and crappie).

Union Park
Glen Este-Withamsville Road and Clough Pike, Eastgate
No phone

This is by far the best equipped of the

locally run parks in Clermont County. It includes a walking trail (no bikes, puuhh-lease), a playground, and basketball courts. Look for the Vietnam-era helicopter at the corner of the park, which is part of a Vietnam veterans memorial.

WARREN COUNTY

Caesar Creek State Park
4020 North Clarksville Road, Waynesville
(513) 897-3055
One of the largest and best-developed parks in Ohio, Caesar Creek's 10,771 acres feature a large man-made lake with several boat ramps, a swimming beach, a campground, hunting and fishing opportunities, numerous picnic areas, hiking and bridle trails, and scenic overlooks. The visitor center displays fossils and Indian artifacts from the site and provides information about the area's history. An original log cabin from 1807 located on this site became the anchoring attraction for Pioneer Village, a collection of other (mostly Quaker) homesteads from the late 1700s and early 1800s that have been rebuilt or relocated from other parts of the park.

Northern Kentucky

Big Bone Lick State Park
3380 Beaver Road, Union, KY
(859) 384-3522
We knew you must be wondering, so here's how this park got its name: Archaeologists found a bunch of big bones of prehistoric animals who were drawn to the salt lick here. Today, this 525-acre state park off US 42 and Kentucky Highway 338 is the site of mock archaeological excavation sites that help recount the real archaeological work that was done here. Trails lead to dioramas of prehistoric beasts and a view of a herd of bison on the park grounds. A discovery trail was built to overlook the bison. It's worth the trip just to see the baby bisons born there each year.

The park has a new museum to display the history of Big Bone Lick Park, which includes bones and other items uncovered at the site. The first phase of the facility was finished in 2004. Two other phases will be built as the state makes money available. The museum is open 9:00 A.M. to 5:00 P.M. on the weekends year-round and weekdays from 9:00 A.M. to 5:00 P.M. from April to October. The museum is free.

This nicely developed park also has miniature golf, tennis, hiking trails, a campground, and fishing. Crafts, music, and children's activities are offered throughout the summer. Call for details.

Devou Park
Access from Western Avenue or Kentucky Highway 1072, Covington, KY
(859) 431-2577
Another great urban park, Devou has possibly the best view of any park in the area, taking in the downtown Cincinnati skyline and the houses of old Covington. Devou's playground has the most beautiful view you can get while pushing a kid on a swing. The 550-acre park also has a golf course, tennis courts, a lake, and picnic areas. The Behringer-Crawford Museum features exhibits about Northern Kentucky's natural and cultural heritage, including a fascinating collection of dinosaur-era fossils and Ice Age artifacts.

RETREATS

Although parks are great for communing with nature, retreats are becoming a more and more popular option for recharging the batteries in a pristine environment. Below are some of the area's more popular nature retreats.

Grailville
932 O'Bannonville Road, Loveland
(513) 683-2340
www.grailville.org
Owned and operated by the Grail, a private nonprofit organization with its origins in the Grail women's movement,

which started in the Netherlands in 1921, Grailville is open to anyone, but its literature specifically notes that "nature lovers" will appreciate the 300 acres of organic gardens and fields, the pond and pine grove, creeks, and the nature trail for hiking. Grailville recently built a labyrinth, a spiritual path that leads you to the center of a spiraling or regularly swirling pattern.

Overnight accommodations and meals can also be arranged for groups of up to 71 people. Reservations are required.

Milford Spiritual Center
5361 South Milford Road, Milford
(513) 248-3500
www.milfordspiritualcenter.org
The center offers individual and group retreats at its 37-acre complex on the banks of the Little Miami River. Opened by the Society of Jesus in 1927, it promotes quiet solitude via nature walks and other programs. Call for information on the different types of retreats.

BIKING

In addition to the public bike trails listed below, some of the region's more considerate communities cater to bicycle riders. Blue Ash and Madeira have a berm-side bike trail along Kenwood Road, and Indian Hill has an extensive network of on- and off-street trails intended for horseback riding. Maps are available at the Indian Hill Rangers Station, 6525 Drake Road, (513) 561-7000.

Early (very early!) one Sunday morning every August, the streets of Cincinnati and Covington—which include some extremely challenging hills—become a bike route as part of the 20-mile Morning Glory Ride (for detailed information, check out newspaper calendars or your local bike shop). Bike shops also can provide information and application forms for the Cincinnati Cycle Club and maps of local trails.

California Junction Trail
5400 Kellogg Avenue, California
(513) 231-8678
This pleasant bike trail runs through California Woods Nature Preserve for about 1 mile. Mountain bikers and in-line skaters use the trail as well. The nature preserve has naturalists on hand to tell you what flora and fauna are in season at the time you're choosing to bike the trail.

Little Miami Scenic Trail
22 miles through numerous counties
No phone
By far the longest and best bike trail in the region is the Little Miami Scenic Trail, a paved bikeway that runs 50 miles along a former railroad track from Milford in Clermont County through Loveland in Hamilton County and into Green County.

Along the trail you will find the Fort Ancient State Memorial, a museum honoring the Fort Ancient prehistoric mounds, which are a National Historic Landmark.

Construction at Fort Ancient ended, oh, say 2,000 years ago. But it began again in 1997 to expand the Fort Ancient Museum to four times its original size. The $3.5 million project was completed in 1998, with the museum encompassing the entire prehistory of the Ohio Valley. The complex features dioramas, computer interactives, and even a 15,000-square-foot garden featuring the crops grown by the early cultures.

The gently rolling trail here has some beautiful deeply wooded sections and some extremely ugly industrial and post-industrial sections. The prettier sections are between Miamitown and Kings Mill, where you're almost assured of spotting at least one bluebird (once rare to this area)

If you're looking for outdoor recreation, head straight for the Little Miami River in the Loveland area. Not only does it have the best bike trail in the area, you also can rent canoes and get on the river.

during a summer trip. Sections where you'll want to keep your head down and just concentrate on pedaling include parts of the trail between Milford and Miamitown and between Kings Mill and Morrow.

The best staging areas are in downtown Loveland and at the Schoolhouse Restaurant, 8031 Glendale-Milford Road, Camp Dennison, which graciously lets bikers use its parking lot, located adjacent to the trail (and it's not fussy about serving meals to sweaty bikers). The Schoolhouse is about a mile from the Milford end of the trail, and it's easier to start here than to fight the traffic from wherever you can find parking on Milford Road. Bikes for the bikeless are available for rent at stores along the trail in Loveland and Miamitown. Note that although biking is the primary use of this trail, it's also for hiking, in-line skating, and horseback riding. Bikers need to be alert for all these slower-moving users and prepared to dodge the occasional horse pie.

Shaker Trace Trail
Miami Whitewater Forest, Dry Fork and Oxford Roads, New Haven
(513) 367-4774

You can rent bicycles as well as tandems and in-line skates at the visitor center. One particularly nifty feature for cyclists on the 7.8-mile trail is the "courtesy cart" that patrols the trail and is outfitted with emergency patch kits for flat tires and offers first aid and cool drinking water. There is a shorter 1.2-mile loop near the visitor center.

BOATING

If it floats, Cincinnatians love it. You'll find plenty of outlets for sailing, canoeing, rafting, tubing, kayaking, and other boating sports on the region's abundant lakes and rivers. The season is generally May through September, but many boat-rental outlets will open early or stay open through October if the weather's nice. (Be advised: Although boat-rental outfits are plentiful, few if any rent powerboats or Jet Skis because of liability and insurance considerations.)

Between sunrise and sunset, powerboaters and Jet Ski riders on the Ohio River are subject to a no-wake zone between Interstates 75 and 471. There's no specific speed limit, but law enforcement agencies from both sides of the river will use common-sense judgment to determine if watercraft are making too many waves. No-wake zones are in effect 24 hours a day near floating marinas, riverfront restaurants, and other riverfront businesses. Offenders can be fined $65 in Ohio and $15 to $100 in Kentucky.

Operating a boat while under the influence is illegal and punishable by fines and jail time similar to those for DUIs.

Ohio requires boat licenses and registration, with fees ranging from $12 to $93. Your boat dealer can arrange for the license. Boat trailers must be licensed through state license agencies. Kentucky requires boat licenses, which range from $15 to $28 and are sold by the county clerk's office in the county where the boat is docked. You only need a license from one state—the one where the boat is docked.

Need access to a boat-launching site? Free ramps include the Riverside Public Ramp, the California Ramp, and Yeatman's Cove Public Landing in Cincinnati, the New Richmond Public Ramp in New Richmond, and the Foster Public Ramp in Foster.

The following listings include outfitters (offering everything from rentals to guided tours) as well as boating locations.

Caesar Creek State Park
4020 North Clarksville Road, Waynesville
(513) 897-1050

A large man-made lake offers a scenic day of boating or fishing. Waterskiers and powerboat enthusiasts, in particular, flock to this 2,800-acre lake designed for unlimited-horsepower watercraft (there are no no-wake zones). There are five launch ramps around the shoreline, the two largest just near the park office near the entrance. The park has limited boat rentals.

Cincinnati Kayaks Downtown
255 McCormick Place, Mount Auburn
(513) 582-4031
This outfitter offers Ohio River kayak cruises and adventures on the serene Licking River ($20 and up). Boat rental includes an experienced guide and safety instructions. Special rates are available for Riverfest and Tall Stacks.

East Fork State Park
Intersection of OH Highways 125 and 222, between Amelia and Bethel
(513) 734-4323
East Fork's lake offers bountiful bass fishing and boating opportunities. The 2,100-acre man-made reservoir has five launch ramps, with the largest near the park office. There are no boat rentals.

Kincaid Lake
Rural Route 1, Falmouth, KY
(859) 654-3531
The Kentucky State Park system manages this 183-acre lake, which features a dock with 38 slips, launching ramps, and rental fishing boats and pontoons ($7.00 a day and up).

Lake Isabella
Off Loveland-Madeira Road, Loveland
(513) 791-1663
This 28-acre lake features a full-service boathouse with rowboat rentals ($8.45 and up), a fishing pier, and canoe access to the Little Miami River.

Miami Whitewater Forest Lake
Access from New Haven, Dry Fork, and Oxford Roads, Harrison
(513) 367-4774
Miami Whitewater Forest Lake is an 85-acre man-made body of water, built in 1971 by damming a woodland creek. A boathouse rents rowboats, pedal boats, and canoes for fishing and other recreational activities. The cost is $8.45 for an hour.

Morgan's Ft. Ancient Canoe Livery
5701 Ohio Highway 350, Oregonia
(513) 932-7658
www.morganscanoe.com
You'll find canoes, kayaks, and rafts for rent here. Prices vary seasonally and are quoted on request.

Rivers Edge
3928 U.S. Highway 42, Waynesville
(937) 862-4540, (800) 628-2319
Rivers Edge rents both canoes and kayaks for journeys on the Little Miami River. The kayaks are of the touring variety (as opposed to the more familiar white-water version), and are perfectly suited to the easier-going Little Miami (easier going, that is, compared to the Colorado rapids). Experts provide instruction at the shore before departure, and there's also a video to watch about safe kayaking. Rivers Edge does not, however, provide guides for your river trip. Rental fee is $21 per kayak for up to six hours. Canoe rental varies on how long you have it out, but for a four-hour trip, for instance, the cost would be $36.

Sharon Woods Lake
11450 U.S. Highway 42, Sharonville
(513) 521-7275
Sharon Woods Lake was constructed in 1936 by damming Sharon Creek. A boathouse rents rowboats, canoes, pedal boats, and hydrobikes for recreational activities. The cost is $8.45 for an hour.

Stonelick State Park
2895 Lake Drive, just east of Milford in Wayne
(513) 625-7544
Stonelick Lake—a long and smooth 181-acre body of water—offers boating and fishing, with extensive stocks of bass, bluegill, and crappie. It's one of the area's quietest lakes, thanks to a policy of no gas motorboats (small sailboats and electric motors are allowed, as are canoes or rowboats). It has one small launch ramp. The camp office rents pedal boats and canoes for $5.00 an hour.

Strictly Sail Inc.
10766 Kenwood Road, Kenwood
(513) 984-1907
www.strictlysailinc.com
Besides selling boats, Strictly Sail offers sailing lessons. Call for more information and rates.

Winton Woods Lake
Winton Road and Lake Forest Drive
Greenhills
(513) 521-7275
This 188-acre lake underwent an extensive restoration project in the last few years, restoring 37 more acres of lake surface area. The boathouse rents rowboats, canoes, pedal boats, and hydrobikes for recreational activities. The cost is $8.45 an hour.

BOWLING

Cincinnatians will constantly argue about the better place to live: East Side or West Side. If you're a bowler, however, there's no contest. The West Side, with its traditional family values and working-class origins, has spawned the city's finest bowling lanes. Below are our favorites (from both sides of town). A complete list of area bowling centers (they no longer refer to themselves as alleys) is available from the Greater Cincinnati Bowling Association, (513) 761-3338 or www.gcbabowl.org.

AMF King Pin Lanes
7735 Beechmont Avenue, Anderson
(513) 231-8010
Little kids and their parents flock to King Pin, with its terrific "Bumper Ball" leagues on 48 lanes. Your three-year-old (and his/her older siblings) can join the junior league. And yes, it also has adult leagues and a lounge too.

Brentwood Bowl
9176 Winton Road
(513) 522-2320
www.brentwoodbowl.com
Around since the '60s, Brentwood Bowl offers 48 lanes as well as multiple leagues for men, women, seniors, and children. Some 200 kids, ages three to seven, bowl every Saturday morning. On Saturday afternoons the Bowl hosts what may be the area's largest league for the mentally and physically disabled. Billiards, video games, and a restaurant round out the experience. There's a nursery for any toddlers too young to pick up a ball.

Cherry Grove Lanes
4005 Hopper Hill Road, Cherry Grove
(513) 528-7888
www.cherrygrovesportscenter.com
What doesn't Cherry Grove have? There's a pro shop, sand-lot volleyball, billiards, arcade, darts, a sports bar, and an outdoor bar and grill. And, oh yes, 34 lanes with automatic scoring.

Colerain Bowl
9189 Colerain Avenue, Groesbeck
(513) 385-8500
Colerain Bowl, on the busy Colerain Avenue shopping strip, has 36 lanes. It offers Thunder Alley glow bowling and karaoke on the weekends.

Glenmore Bowl
3716 Glenmore Avenue
(513) 661-5394
One of the area's oldest lanes, Glenmore opened its doors in 1927. A sense of history, yes, but the Bowl's 10 lanes are state-of-the-art, refitted synthetic lanes. A neat bar too.

Madison Bowl
4761 Madison Road
(513) 271-2700
All 32 lanes at Madison are open 24 hours a day. A lounge, snack bar, and restaurant means you never have to leave.

Strikes & Spares
8032 Blue Ash Road, Deer Park
(513) 891-9355
This center offers 12 lanes, with leagues playing every night. There's a restaurant, bar, and video games.

Super Bowl
510 Commonwealth Avenue, Erlanger, KY
(859) 727-2000
There are billiards, games, and a pro shop in addition to 64 lanes. This is where Kentuckians go to bowl.

Western Bowl
6383 Glenway Avenue
(523) 574-2222
The promised land. Or rather, promised lane. The Western Bowl, with 68 lanes, stands above all the rest. It bills itself as Cincinnati's largest bowling center and is host to the Hoinke Classic, a nationally known tournament that lasts 10 months a year, attracts 50,000 entrants, and gives away $2 million in prize money. It's open 24 hours a day, with free nursery care. Western Bowl also has a restaurant, four bars, and a game emporium. Next door there is a miniature golf course with an ice-cream parlor that is open from April through October.

FISHING

Local anglers fish the lakes and rivers of the region throughout the year, even if it means cutting a hole in the ice. To fish from a boat on the Ohio, you need a special Ohio River fishing license, which is only issued by the state of Kentucky (Kentucky claims all but a few feet of the river on the Ohio side as its property). A three-day fishing license is $12.50, a 15-day license is $20.00. They can be obtained at sporting-goods and fishing-tackle retailers. If you want to fish from the Ohio shore, all you need is a regular Ohio driver's license. Or if you want to fish from the Kentucky side, all you need is a regular Kentucky driver's license.

Fish are more numerous and healthier in the Ohio now than in the 1970s. But all three states warn to steer clear of eating walleye, carp, channel catfish, white bass, or paddlefish caught in the river. High levels of chlordane and PCBs are sometimes found in these bottom feeders.

Other assorted rules and regs: Snagging is generally illegal for all fish except carp and select forage fish. Poisons, firearms, electricity, and chemicals as fishing devices are prohibited by all three states. It is illegal to release exotic species of fish into the Ohio or its tributaries. Frogs may not be shot except with a bow and arrow. Turtle traps must be marked with the name and address of the owner. It is unlawful to possess more than 100 crayfish unless you are a licensed bait dealer. And lastly, anglers may use no more than two fishing lines.

All that said, here are a few places where you can spend a great day throwing out a line. We've indicated where boat rentals are available.

Caesar Creek State Park
4020 North Clarksville Road, Waynesville
(513) 897-1050
Caesar Creek's sizable 2,800-acre lake features lots of coves, inlets, and bays that promote bountiful bass fishing. Saugeye and walleye are also stocked annually. Caesar Creek is open 6:00 A.M. to 11:00 P.M. year-round, but the lake is open 24 hours a day for those who like to get in the boat well before dawn. On a state park lake, no fishing license is required for anglers age 16 and younger. Adults can obtain a fishing license at Wal-Mart, Kmart, or a local fish-and-tackle store. There is no fee for fishing at the lake. Parking is free.

East Fork State Park
Intersection of Ohio Highways 125 and 222,
between Amelia and Bethel
(513) 734-4323
East Fork's 2,100-acre reservoir is a favorite of local bass anglers, especially from shore in the spring. East Fork is open 6:00 A.M. to 11:00 P.M. year-round. No fishing license is required for anglers age 16 and younger. Fishing licenses can be obtained at Wal-Mart, Kmart, or a local fish-and-tackle store. There is no fee for fishing at the lake, and parking is free.

CLOSE-UP

Cornhole: The Classic Cincy "Sport"

Cornhole. Any out-of-towner is left scratching his head over what this word might refer to. Is it a foodstuff? An agricultural reference? A vaguely naughty phrase?

Cincinnatians, of course, know the true meaning of cornhole. The homegrown bag-toss game, which some suggest was even invented here, requires few tools: some beanbags, a box with a hole in it, and . . . well, that's it, really.

On the West Side, where the game first emerged, they actually play full-fledged cornhole tournaments. In Bridgetown, Cheviot, and Covedale, to name a few, the game is played with fervor year-round (some residents have 2-by-4 cornhole boxes permanently set up in their basements).

Few West Side summer festivals don't sport some version of the game. And there's even a Web site, www.cornholegame.org, run by Mount Healthy's Cornhole Game Association. There, you can purchase game sets (though exotic and intricately designed cornhole game boxes have begun popping up on the East Side in gift shops and mom-and-pop woodcraft stores).

The game's origin (and name) comes from early players on the city's farms who filled work gloves with spare corn kernels to create the beanbags. Soon added was a slanted board with a grapefruit-size hole—hence, the "corn" and the "hole."

Today the game can still be played one-on-one, but more often teams of two or more compete. A successful toss through the hole, creatively termed a "cornhole," is worth 3 points; the first side to reach 21 points wins. An "ace" (merely getting the bag on the board) is worth 1 point. A "Mary Ellen" is a toss that falls short of the board.

Kincaid Lake
Rural Route 1, Falmouth, KY
(859) 654-3531
Kincaid Lake covers 183 acres and is stocked with crappie, bluegill, and more.

Lake Isabella
Off Loveland-Madeira Road, Loveland
(513) 791-1663
This 28-acre lake is stocked with adult channel, blue and shovelhead catfish, and rainbow trout. It's ideal for the first-time fisherman or fisherwoman, because an Ohio state fishing license is not required and friendly staff members are on hand to help you learn the ropes. The lake is a pay-fishing lake ($7.50 and up, depending on how many trout you bag) and is stocked every Friday. You can rent a rowboat for $8.45 and up.

Miami Whitewater Forest Lake
Access from New Haven, Dry Fork, and Oxford Roads, Harrison
(513) 367-4774
Fishing is by rental boat only and electric trolling motors are permitted. You can rent a rowboat, pedal boat, or canoe. The cost is $8.45 an hour. There's also a bait-and-tackle shop. Bank fishing is allowed only in the cove adjacent to the visitor center. In the winter, ice fishing is allowed.

Sharon Woods Lake
11450 U.S. Highway 42, Sharonville
(513) 521-7275
Those in the know say this 35-acre lake has the best bass fishing of any county-owned lake in the region. Fishing is by rental boat only, and electric trolling motors are permitted. A boathouse rents rowboats, canoes, pedal boats, and hydro-bikes. The cost is $8.45 an hour. There's also bank fishing along the pier.

Stonelick State Park
2895 Lake Drive, just east of Milford in Wayne
(513) 625-7544
Stonelick Lake offers bountiful bass, bluegill, and crappie. The lake is relatively small for a state park, just 200 acres, and quiet (gas motorboats are forbidden). Stonelick is open 6:00 A.M. to 11:00 P.M. year-round.

Winton Woods Lake
Winton Road and Lake Forest Drive, Greenhills
(513) 521-7275
This 188-acre lake underwent an extensive restoration project in the last few years, restoring 37 more acres of lake surface area. The boathouse rents rowboats, canoes, pedal boats, and hydrobikes for recreational activities. The cost is $5.66 for a half hour up to $11.32 for the entire day. Bluegill, crap-pie, bass, and channel catfish are stocked.

FRISBEE GOLF

The tristate is home to some great Frisbee-golf courses. The 18-hole Frisbee course at Woodland Mound is the area's most attractive; although the holes aren't long, they can be unforgiving. City and county parks with notable Frisbee-golf facilities are:

Embshoff Woods & Nature Preserve (nine holes)
4050 Paul Road, Delhi
No phone

Miami Whitewater Forest (nine holes)
Access from New Haven, Dry Fork, and Oxford Roads, Harrison
(513) 367-4774

Mount Airy Forest (18 holes)
5083 Colerain Avenue, Mount Airy
(513) 352-4094

Winton Woods (18 holes)
Winton Road and Lake Forest Drive, Springfield
(513) 521-7275

Woodland Mound (18 holes)
Access from Kellogg Avenue or Nordyke Road, Anderson
(513) 474-0580

HIKING/BACKPACKING

There are literally dozens of options for both the amateur and the seasoned hiker in the region. Wherever you choose to hike, do pick up a trail map at the visitor centers or park offices, because it's easy to get lost on some of the more winding trails. Other warnings: There are two poi-sonous snake species in the tristate area: the copperhead and the timber rattler. Neither is aggressive, and in fact there are no reports a backpacker has ever been bitten. Still, it's wise to hit the encyclope-dia if you don't know what these two snakes look like, and pack a snakebite kit. Those with an abnormal fear of snakes, venomous or otherwise, should wait until after the first frost in fall—you won't see a single slithering creature.

Caesar Creek State Park
4020 North Clarksville Road, Waynesville
(513) 897-1050
Caesar Creek has 43 miles of easy to rugged trails, all excellently maintained. The terrain is incredibly varied, ranging from meadows to gorges. A wheelchair-accessible trail begins near the dam over-look. The Little Miami Trail can also be accessed near Corwin, north of the park.

The most notable landscape features are waterfalls, as well as Caesar Creek Lake and Caesar Creek Gorge, formed by glacial meltwater and over 180 feet deep. The Gorge Trail is tough; for easier hikes, consider the Flat Fork Ridge/Wellman Meadows Trail. Day-issue permits are available for fossil collecting from the visitor center.

Cincinnati Nature Center
4949 Tealtown Road, Glen Este
(513) 831-1711
Hiking is the main activity at this 1,425-acre nature preserve. You can choose from 15 miles of trails that range from the wheelchair-accessible Stanley Rowe All Persons Trail to some fairly long and steeply sloped trails. Terrain ranges from open meadows to fairly deep woods. Note to bird-watchers: Some 150 species of birds have been spotted here. You also can find 237 kinds of wildflowers blooming here at various times of year.

Cowan Lake State Park
729 Beechwood Road, Wilmington
(513) 289-2105
A perfect park for the beginner. There are 5 miles of trails; the Emerald Trail is considered easiest, the Lotus Cove Trail moderate. The terrain, shaped by a glacier 10,000 years ago, varies from shale to lily ponds. Fossils abound. There are 200 campsites on four loops located on the north side of Cowan Lake. Conveniences include restrooms and shower stations, as well as a park.

East Fork State Park
Intersection of Ohio Highways 125 and 222,
between Amelia and Bethel
(513) 734-4323
East Fork has 40 miles of trail showcasing the park's fascinating rock formations, stone terraces, and meandering streams. Several sites of both the Adena and Hopewell Indian cultures remain, dating from 3,000 years ago. All vestiges of the gold mines that once operated here in the 1860s, however, are gone. As is, we presume, the gold. There are no lodges or cabins, but select campgrounds do feature electricity and hot showers. Park rangers on horseback patrol the trails, a security feature unavailable at some of Ohio's other state parks. Carrying your own drinking water supply, or a purifying system, is a must. Wear bright clothes to discourage any confusion a hunter might have between you and a buck.

To decide which of the trails to hike (many favor the Back Country Trail, a three-day adventure) and where to access them, call first. Oh, if you're wondering who the Steve Newman Worldwalker Perimeter Trail is named after, Cincinnati's Newman recently walked around the globe and wrote a book about it called *Worldwalker.*

Fort Thomas Landmark Tree Trail
South Fort Thomas Avenue at Carmel Manor Drive, Fort Thomas, KY
No phone
The Fort Thomas Tree Commission can be thanked for preserving the city's most beautiful old-growth forest. Its 1.1-mile trail winds across lush green slopes, offering views of wood bridges and at least 15 different species of trees (including buckeyes), plus wildflowers and numerous birds. Bikes are not permitted on this trail.

Hueston Woods State Park and Nature Preserve
Ohio Highway 732, College Corner, Oxford
(513) 523-6347
A National Natural Landmark, the preserve offers all the amenities: lodge, campsites, cabins, and more. Hit the restrooms and drinking fountain at the start of Big Woods Trail. Terrain is tall timber, primarily beech and sugar maple—don't miss autumn here if you like to gawk at colorful leaves. And if you visit at the end of winter, you're sure to be offered some freshly tapped maple syrup. The 200-acre nature preserve within the park is a great place for hiking and bird-watching. One

hundred and fifty species of birds have been spotted here, including hawks and woodpeckers. Wildflowers put on amazing displays in almost every season.

Little Miami Scenic Trail
22 miles through numerous counties in Ohio
No phone
The best bike trail in the region is also a walking-and-hiking trail. The Little Miami Scenic Trail is a paved bikeway that runs nearly 22 miles along a former railroad track from Milford in Clermont County through Loveland in Hamilton County and into Morrow in Warren County. Watch out for fast-moving bikes.

Miami Whitewater Forest
Access from New Haven, Dry Fork, and Oxford Roads, Harrison
(513) 367-4774
At 3,906 acres, this is the largest park in the Hamilton County Park District. There are 3 miles of nature paths, a 7.8-mile walking trail, and a 1.2-mile inner loop for the less adventurous.

Mount Airy Forest
5083 Colerain Avenue, Mount Airy
(513) 352-4094
Though city parks aren't often known for their hiking trails, the ones at Mount Airy are superb. At 1,466 acres, Mount Airy is the largest municipal park and forest in the nation. There are miles of hiking trails through a forest that boasts a million hardwoods and conifers.

Shawnee Lookout Park
Miamiview Road just outside of Cleves
(513) 521-PARK
The park's self-guided trails are marked with numbered stakes that are keyed to brochures, which are available by calling ahead. Terrain is hills, woods, ravines, and creeks, with some terrific overlooks offering a panoramic view of three states as well as the Ohio and Great Miami Rivers. Both the Little Turtle and Blue Jacket Trails offer restrooms and drinking water and are good for the beginning hiker. Archaeology buffs will appreciate the 12-acre fort built by an ancient people, with walls built atop steep slopes.

Stonelick State Park
2895 Lake Drive, just east of Milford in Wayne
(513) 625-7544
Stonelick includes shelters, a modern campground with tent sites, and 7 miles of foot trails. Warning: Much of the hiking trails are on level, poorly draining soil. During the late winter and spring, it's soggy, but it's one of the best places to spot butterflies or wildflowers, if you're so inclined. Terrain is primarily flat forest.

HORSEBACK RIDING

Cincinnati may not quite be in Bluegrass horse country, but equestrian pursuits are still quite popular. The village of Indian Hill is known for its extensive network of horse trails, maps of which are available at the village offices, 6525 Drake Road, (513) 561-6500. See the Parks section above for public parks offering horse trails.

The following stables offer lessons and, where we've so noted, trails open to the public for a fee. Specific age cutoffs for lessons for children are also noted, but most teach riding to any child able to mount a pony and stay seated without the aid of a parent. The hours of these stables vary incredibly, depending on what month of the year it is, whether they are running pony camps, and other seasonal factors. So it's best to call first. All do stay open year-round, but in some months, only for boarding purposes.

East Fork Stable & Lodge
2215 Snyder Road, Batavia
(513) 797-7433
East Fork Stables teaches English saddle, western, and endurance saddle riding lessons for kids and adults, beginners to advanced. Lessons are available for $20 to $45 per hour. The four-day summer pony

camps for kids teach all aspects of riding, grooming, and horse care for $225. You can also hop a horse and ride East Fork's 50 miles of trails for $45 for 1.5 hours. There's an overnight camping lodge and cabins available for $100.

Little Miami Scenic Trail
22 miles through numerous counties in Ohio
No phone
The Little Miami Scenic Trail runs nearly 22 miles along a former railroad track from Milford in Clermont County through Loveland in Hamilton County and into Morrow in Warren County. Although primarily a trail for bikers and hikers, horseback riding is also encouraged.

Winton Woods Riding Center
10073 Daly Road, Greenhills
(513) 931-3057, (513) 728-3551, ext. 366
The center is in Winton Woods, which is part of the Hamilton County Park system. It offers riding lessons in English, western, jumping, and dressage. The center also offers a day camp in the summer for $250 and horse shows throughout the horse show season. Trail rides cost $29 for 75 minutes.

YMCA Western Ranch Camp
Camp Ernst, Boone County
(859) 586-6181
www.ymcacampernst.org
The YMCA Western Ranch Camp is a summer riding camp for youngsters ages nine and older. Camp is $425, with a $25 discount for Y members, and is offered at various times during the summer.

MALL WALKING

Just about every mall in the area has a walking program. Call the mall office nearest you for details (see the Shopping chapter). By far the most challenging and popular mall walk is at the 1.8-million-square-foot Cincinnati Mills (at the Forest Park exit off Interstate 275). In this vast expanse, mall walkers can be found all day, not just in the early morning hours.

ROCK CLIMBING

One of the newer recreational pursuits to hit our area is rock climbing. Several businesses offer instruction and will rent the equipment needed for the climb.

Climbing Wall
Miami University Outdoor Pursuit Center, Oxford
(513) 529-6888
Students and nonstudents alike can do a "Try Climb" at the facility for just $4.00. Then if you like it, you can take a class at $25 each to learn more about rock climbing. After that, the climbing is $2.50 once you pay the $8.00 to get in the recreation center.

RockQuest
3475 East Kemper Road, Sharonville
(513) 733-0123
RockQuest has more than 18,000 square feet of climbing surface with something for both beginners and advanced rock climbers. It has textured and sculpted walls. Cost is $14.00 daily with a $4.00 shoe rental and $4.00 harness rental. There is an instruction course for $5.00, for which reservations are required.

ROWING

Cincinnati Rowing Center
Bicentennial Commons at Sawyer
(513) 352-3660
The Cincinnati Rowing Center at Sawyer Point offers classes and facilities for rowing indoors. It has a rowing tank inside the building, which is in the basement of the Montgomery Inn Boathouse.

SKIING

In addition to the tristate's two downhill skiing resorts with man-made snow, you can try cross-country skiing at three Cincinnati parks. Trails at **Mount Airy Forest,** 5081 Colerain Avenue, are available free to cross-country skiers on the weekends. The **Neumann Golf Course** at 7215 Bridgetown Road and **California Golf Course** at 5920 Kellogg Avenue offer cross-country skiing and equipment rental when the snow is 4 inches or deeper.

Perfect North Slopes
19640 Indiana Highway 1
Lawrenceburg, IN
(812) 537-3754, (513) 381-7517 in Cincinnati
www.perfectnorth.com
With 70 acres of tree-lined trails and wide open slopes, Perfect North is the region's top skiing facility. There are five chairlifts and seven rope tows, a ski school, a "slow skiing" zone for nervous novices, and much more. The pro shop can outfit you with any equipment you need, available for rental or purchase, and also specializes in boot repair, waxing, and binding. The resort, which uses man-made snow when Mother Nature doesn't cooperate, offers skiing all day every day and late nights on the weekends, racing clinics, and racing camps. Season passes are available for $312 in the off-season to $480 in peak season. A single lift ticket on weekends is $40.

SOCCER

Cincinnati has more soccer players per capita than anyplace else in the United States. Youth soccer is extremely popular, but it's not the whole story. Here are some active centers in Greater Cincinnati.

Cincinnati Sports Club
3950 Red Bank Road, Fairfax
(513) 527-4000
www.cincinnatisportsmall.com

Kolping Society
10235 Mill Road, New Burlington
(513) 851-7951
www.kolpingcincinnati.com

Soccer City
5770 Springdale Road, Colerain
(513) 741-8480
www.indoorsoccercity.com

Wall2Wall Soccer
846 Reading Road, Mason
(513) 573-9898
www.wall2wallsoccer.com

Western Sports Mall
2323 Ferguson Road, Westwood
(513) 451-4900
www.westernsportsmall.net

SOFTBALL

Softball is so big in Cincinnati that an estimated 1,200 softball teams are fielded each year—and that's probably a conservative estimate. The Cincinnati Recreation Commission, 805 Central Avenue, (513) 352-4000, organizes some mighty good amateur baseball leagues that may include former minor and major leaguers. Local recreation commissions (see subsequent section), employers, churches, and bars organize softball teams or can help set you up. The following softball complexes also organize leagues:

Amateur Slow-Pitch Softball
10400 Hamilton-Cleves Highway
(513) 738-3636

Cincinnati Softball Center
10701 Campbell Road, Harrison
(513) 367-0266

Queen City Softball Complex
9267 Cincinnati-Dayton Road,
West Chester
(513) 777-8638

Softball City Sports Complex
620 Mason Road, Taylor Mill, KY
(859) 581-0510

SWIMMING

Check the Yellow Pages under "Swimming Pools" for public and private swim clubs, and see the listings for recreation centers and YMCAs below.

RECREATION CENTERS AND COMMISSIONS

Greater Cincinnati is a hotbed of softball, soccer, and volleyball. Call or visit one of the local recreation centers listed below for information on their specific programs.

Ohio

CINCINNATI

Bush
2640 Kemper Lane, Walnut Hills
(513) 281-1286

Camp Washington
1201 Stock Street
(513) 681-6046

Clifton
320 McAlpin Avenue
(513) 961-5681

Ebersole
5701 Kellogg Avenue, California
(513) 231-6617

English Woods
1976 Sutter Avenue, Fairmont
(513) 481-7264

Evanston
3204 Woodburn Avenue
(513) 861-9417

Hartwell
8275 Vine Street
(513) 821-5194

Hirsch
3630 Reading Road, North Avondale
(513) 751-3393

Kennedy-Woodford
6065 Red Bank Road, Kennedy Heights
(513) 631-5625

Krueck
270 West McMillan Avenue, Clifton
(513) 861-6572

LeBlond
2335 Eastern Avenue, East End
(513) 281-3209

Lincoln
1027 Linn Street, West End
(513) 721-6514

McKie
1655 Chase Avenue, Northside
(513) 681-8247

Millvale
3303 Beekman, Cumminsville
(513) 352-4351

Mount Auburn
270 Southern Avenue
(513) 381-1760

Mount Washington
1715 Beacon Street
(513) 232-4762

North Avondale
617 Clifton Springs Avenue
(513) 961-1584

North Fairmount
1660 Carll Street
(513) 471-3727

Oakley
3882 Paxton Avenue
(513) 321-9320

Over-the-Rhine
1715 Republic Avenue
(513) 381-1893

Pleasant Ridge
5915 Ridge Avenue
(513) 731-7894

Price Hill
959 Hawthorn Avenue
(513) 251-4123

Sayler Park
6720 Home City Avenue
(513) 941-0102

Winton Hills
5170 Winneste Avenue
(513) 641-0422

SUBURBAN AREAS

Anderson Park District
(513) 474-0003

Blue Ash Recreation Center
4433 Cooper Road
(513) 745-8550

Blue Ash Sports Center
11540 Grooms Road
(513) 745-8586
A replica of the old Crosley Field was rebuilt on this site using the original seats.

Cheviot Recreation Commission
3837 Carrie Avenue
(513) 481-2835

Crescentville Recreation Center
12153 Crescentville Road
(513) 671-2191

Evendale Recreation Center
10500 Reading Road
(513) 563-2247

Forest Park Recreation Department
(513) 595-5252

Glendale Lyceum
865 Congress Street
(513) 771-8383

Green Township Parks and Recreation
6303 Harrison Avenue
(513) 574-8832

Greenhills Golf & Tennis Club
14 Enfield Road
(513) 589-3585

Greenhills Recreation Department
11000 Winton Road
(513) 589-3581

Hamilton (City) Parks and Recreation
(513) 868-5874

Hamilton County Park District
10245 Winton Road
(513) 521-PARK, ext. 67

Mariemont Swimming Pool
6000 Mariemont Avenue
(513) 272-0593

Mariemont Tennis Courts
3928 Plainville Road
(513) 561-8711

Montgomery Park
information and reservations
(513) 891-2424

Montgomery Swimming Pool
7777 Sycamore Avenue
(513) 791-0148

North College Hill Pool
End of Grace
(513) 522-5488

Watch for Hamilton County Park district's "Evergreen" insert in the Cincinnati Enquirer *every two months. The insert lists special events and enrichment activities.*

Norwood Recreation Commission
2605 Harris Avenue
(513) 531-9798

Sharonville Recreation Department
Adult & Youth Sports
(513) 563-9072
Sports Hotline
(513) 563-4257

Springdale Parks & Recreation Department
11999 Lawnview Avenue
(513) 671-6260

Northern Kentucky

Boone County (KY) Recreation Department
(859) 334-2117

Covington (KY) Community Center
1008 Lee Street
(859) 491-2220

Covington (KY) Recreation Department
859) 292-2151

Florence (KY) World of Sports (Sports Complex)
7400 Woodsport Drive
(859) 371-8255

Fort Mitchell (KY) Parks & Recreation
267 Grandview Drive
(859) 331-9118

Fort Thomas (KY) Recreation Department
Armory Recreation Center
950 South Fort Thomas Avenue
(859) 781-1700

Newport (KY) Recreation Department
(859) 292-3686

Petersburg (KY) Community Center
6517 Market Street
(859) 586-8318

YMCAs

In addition to city recreation centers and commissions, community YMCAs are the other major source of year-round activities for kids and adults. Two dozen YMCAs serve the tristate. Virtually all of them offer whirlpools, saunas, and child care for adults using the facilities. Amenities and special fitness equipment for each Y are listed below. See also www.cincinnatiymca.org.

Ohio

HAMILTON COUNTY

Blue Ash YMCA
5000 YMCA Drive
(513) 791-5000
The Blue Ash Y has two indoor pools and one outdoor pool in addition to Nautilus equipment, free weights, a group cycling room, an indoor running track, and a basketball court. The ambitious tots exercise program features Pee Wee Play, Gym Tots, and Pre-Tumbling. For kids ages three to five, there are Little Leagues for indoor soccer and other sports, plus arts and crafts and, if you can believe it, basic cooking classes for five-year-olds. For older children, there are the usual hockey, football, and gymnastics, but lessons in ballet and tap dancing are offered too.

Central Parkway YMCA
1105 Elm Street
(513) 241-5348
This well-equipped downtown Y has one indoor pool, Nautilus and Hammer Strength equipment, free weights, two gyms, an indoor track, four racquetball courts, handball courts, an indoor golf driving room, and free parking for members. It also has massage therapists and personal weights instruction available by appointment. Suburban Y members can work out for free here. Classes are offered in step aerobics, powerfit, and

such esoteric activities as cardio boxing, ninjutsu, and scuba diving.

Clippard YMCA
8920 Cheviot Road, Colerain Township
(513) 923-4466
The Clippard Y has a nice mix of indoor and outdoor amenities. Inside are a pool, full gym, group cycling room, health and wellness room with cardiovascular workout equipment, Nautilus equipment, and free weights. Outside are pools for adults and kids with a water play area. An indoor water park was added in 2003, complete with a waterslide, walking channel, and spray features.

Powel Crosley Jr. YMCA
9601 Winton Road, Springfield
(513) 521-7112
An indoor and an outdoor pool, three outdoor tennis courts, two outdoor sand volleyball courts, four racquetball courts, a group cycling room, a one-fifth-mile walking/running trail, gymnasium, and Universal and Nautilus equipment are available at this large and popular Y. It also has an indoor water park.

Gamble-Nippert YMCA
3159 Montana Avenue, Westwood
(513) 661-1105
Both indoor and outdoor swimming pools are available at this West Side Y, along with racquetball courts, Nautilus equipment, and free weights.

Lincoln Heights Center YMCA
1100 Lindy Avenue
(513) 563-6822
You'll find a gymnasium, weight room, and outdoor pool here.

M.E. Lyons YMCA
8108 Clough Pike, Anderson
(513) 474-1400
This very active Anderson Y has both indoor and outdoor pools, a family fitness center with cardiovascular workout equipment, an indoor track, Nautilus equipment and free weights, six tennis courts, five racquetball courts, and a gym. There's a full range of swim, gymnastics, and wrestling classes, plus the more unusual tae kwon do, scuba diving, and the hot new sport in town, in-line hockey.

Melrose YMCA
2840 Melrose Avenue
(513) 961-3510
Facilities here include a gymnasium, an indoor pool, Universal and Nautilus equipment, free weights, a youth recreation center, a multipurpose room, a computer lab, and two club rooms.

Richard E. Lindner YMCA
Sherman and Walter Avenues, Norwood
(513) 731-0115
The Norwood Y has an indoor pool, outdoor pool, gymnasium, racquetball courts, Nautilus equipment, and free weights.

West End YMCA
821 Ezzard Charles Drive
(513) 241-9622
The West End Y has a weight room, gymnasium, game room, and Nautilus equipment. There's no pool, but there is a host of youth programs in this youth-oriented facility.

Williams YMCA
1228 East McMillan
(513) 961-7552
The Williams Y serves the university area with Nautilus equipment, a basketball court, indoor swimming pool, indoor track, racquetball court, studio cycling, stretching area, and boxing program.

BUTLER COUNTY

Fairfield YMCA
785 Nilles Road
(513) 829-3091
Facilities here include an indoor pool, full gymnasium, free weights, and Nautilus equipment. It also has aerobic classes and racquetball courts.

Hamilton Central YMCA
Second and Market Streets, Hamilton
(513) 887-0001
This Y has an indoor pool, Cybex machines, and two indoor tracks. It also has a cardiovascular theater, cycling room, free weights, steam room, and whirlpool, as well as handball and racquetball courts.

Hamilton West YMCA
1307 Northwest Washington Boulevard, Hamilton
(513) 869-8550
The Hamilton West Y has an indoor pool, Cybex machines, and an indoor track.

CLERMONT COUNTY

Camp Felicity YMCA
1349 Lenroot Road, Amelia
(513) 876-4473
An outdoor pool and running track are among the features at this camp for underprivileged children between the ages of 11 and 14. Ys from around Greater Cincinnati send people to this camp each summer.

Clermont YMCA
2075 Frontwheel Drive, Batavia
(513) 724-9622
Indoor and outdoor pools are available here, along with an outdoor playground, indoor track, full gymnasium, Universal and Nautilus equipment, free weights, nursery, and multipurpose room. It also has sports programs for adults and children.

WARREN COUNTY

Countryside YMCA
1699 Deerfield Road, Lebanon
(513) 932-1424
www.countrysideymca.org
This is by far the biggest and best-equipped Y in the region. The building, which of itself occupies five acres, sits on 126 acres of land. Outdoor amenities include two heated pools, tennis courts, a sand volleyball court, a 1.5-mile nature trail, baseball and soccer fields, a half-mile track, a picnic pavilion, three playgrounds, and garden plots available to members at no extra cost.

Inside are Nautilus equipment, free weights in a light-weight room and a heavy-weight room (for serious grunting and groaning), a circuit training room, three pools, a track, racquetball courts, tennis courts, a game room with a pool table and table tennis, a regulation dance floor, three gymnasiums, and a snack bar.

Northern Kentucky

Camp Ernst YMCA
7615 Camp Ernst Road, Burlington, KY
(859) 586-6181
www.ymcacampernst.org
An operating western ranch, Camp Ernst has a well-regarded summer camp for boys and girls ages 9 through 16. Among the gigantic playthings are a harness Zip Line and a giant bouncing balloon on the lake.

Campbell County YMCA
1437 South Fort Thomas Avenue, Fort Thomas, KY
(859) 781-1814
This Y has an indoor and three outdoor pools, Nautilus equipment, free weights, and racquetball courts.

Kenton County YMCA
5262 Madison Pike, Independence, KY
(859) 356-3178
An outdoor-only facility, the Kenton County Y has a pool and volleyball, tennis, and basketball courts.

R.C. Durr YMCA
5874 Veterans Way, Burlington, KY
(859) 534-5200
This Boone County Y has indoor and outdoor pools, a gymnasium, a Nautilus and free-weight room, and a full set of cardiovascular fitness equipment.

Southeastern Indiana

Dearborn County YMCA
404 Green Boulevard
(U.S. Highway 50), Aurora, IN
(812) 926-6262
The Y offers classes in aerobics, youth sports, and tumbling, as well as day-camp programs and sports leagues. Call for sites and details.

YWCA

While YMCAs have always been open to women, the area YWCA is nonetheless a potent force in terms of its aggressive stand on women's health issues (breast cancer awareness, domestic abuse counseling and shelters, and so on). It also offers a number of services and recreational opportunities for both men and women.

Downtown Center YWCA
898 Walnut Street
(513) 241-7090
www.ywca.org
The downtown YWCA offers a pool, health club facilities, gym, sauna, and indoor walking track. The Fitness Center offers classes in health and wellness as well as self-defense. Classes include aerobics, water aerobics, cardio kick boxing, spinning, yoga, and warm water flexibility. It also has girls' basketball and volleyball leagues.

HEALTH CLUBS AND SPORTS CENTERS

Area residents tend to pick their health club based on geographic convenience. Local Yellow Pages list hundreds of such clubs. For tourists and travelers who are in town for only a few days, we've culled a short list of clubs that don't require monthly or annual membership, although you may need to belong to an affiliated club or association. We've included hotels that have major health and fitness facilities for their guests. (See the Health Care chapter for fitness facilities run by and at local hospitals.)

Bally Total Fitness
4780 Cornell Road, Blue Ash
(513) 469-0090

9675 Montgomery Road, Montgomery
(513) 984-4811

3694 Werk Road, Western Hills
(513) 922-1731
All but the Blue Ash location have an indoor swimming pool and racquetball courts. All three have a track, weight-training equipment, and stair machines. Child care is available. You must have a Bally membership, but it can be to any club in the United States.

Cincinnati Sports Club
3950 Red Bank Road, Fairfax
(513) 527-4550
www.cincinnatisportsmall.com
The Cincinnati Sports Club is a full-feature health club: cardiovascular fitness center, Cybex machines and free weights, indoor and outdoor pools, one-fifth-mile indoor running track, and basketball, squash, racquetball, and tennis courts. The club is part of the Sports Mall, a multipurpose sports facility with two indoor soccer fields, five indoor batting cages, a snack bar, a rehabilitation/sports-medicine clinic, gymnastics training, and aerobics classes. It recently opened a "children-only" fitness center inside the building. All the equipment in the center is adjusted for children from kindergarten to eighth grade.

Nonmembers must belong to the International Racquetball and Squash Association in order to use the facilities.

Drawbridge Hotel
2477 Royal Drive, Fort Mitchell, KY
(859) 341-2800
Certainly the place for exercise buffs to stay if they want to be near the Cincinnati/Northern Kentucky International Air-

port. It offers no less than three swimming pools (one indoors), tennis courts, sandlot volleyball, a fitness room, a whirlpool, a sauna, and more. See the Hotels and Motels chapter for more information about lodging at Drawbridge.

Embassy Suites Cincinnati at RiverCenter
10 East RiverCenter Boulevard, Covington, KY
(859) 261-8400
This facility provides an indoor pool, a sauna, and a fully outfitted fitness center. Even better, for joggers, it's next to the riverfront and beautiful Riverside Drive.

Gold's Gym
4030 Smith Road, Hyde Park
(513) 533-GOLD
There are multiple locations of this gym near major shopping areas in Cincinnati. Besides Hyde Park, there is one in Eastgate, Beechmont, Western Hills, and on Colerain Avenue. The facilities have all the workout machines one could want as well as classes in spinning, yoga, and pilates. Gold's also offers tanning and saunas.

The Gym at Carew Tower
441 Vine Street
(513) 651-1442
www.thegymatcarewtower.com
This is certainly the most conveniently located health club to major downtown hotels such as the Westin, Hilton Netherland Plaza, and Hyatt. The club offers a 40-foot lap pool, Cybex machines, free weights, an aerobics room, and a full set of cardiovascular workout equipment such as stationary bikes, stair machines, NordicTrack, and rowing machines. There's also a steam room, whirlpool, and sauna. Nonmembers can spend the day for $10.

Hilton Netherland Plaza
35 West Fifth Street
(513) 421-9100
You'll find an indoor pool and a health club offering free weights, an aerobics room, and a full set of cardiovascular workout equipment, including stationary bikes, stair machines, and rowing machines.

Hyatt Regency Cincinnati
151 West Fifth Street
(513) 579-1234
Use the indoor pool and in-house health club at the Hyatt or take a quick stroll to any number of downtown health clubs, such as the Gym at Carew Tower (listed above).

Living Longer Performance Center
5400 Kennedy Avenue
(513) 351-3000
A bargain $8.00 per day allows nonmembers the full use of these facilities, which include a wide range of virtual-reality bikes, cardiovascular workout equipment, Nautilus equipment, free weights, and tanning beds. It is a quick 10-minute drive from downtown, right up Interstate 71.

Millennium Hotel
150 West Fifth Street
(513) 357-5800
The Millennium offers a full-service health club for its guests, plus the use of the outdoor rooftop pool (in season).

Victory Lady Fitness Center
9351 Colerain Avenue
(513) 923-3334

433 Ohio Pike, Anderson
(513) 528-2434
A women-only health-and-fitness center, Victory Lady caters to women who want to work out without getting checked out.

Facilities include an indoor swimming pool, free weights, Hammer Strength equipment, Lifecycles, stair machines, electronic treadmills, personalized programs, and private showers. Nonmembers can get one free visit if they mention they've seen the club's ad in the Yellow Pages. Members of the International Racquetball and Squash Association or any of the 400 Allied Health Association clubs nationwide get unlimited access.

Westin Cincinnati
Fifth and Vine Streets
(513) 621-7700
The Westin hotel's fitness center has an indoor pool, whirlpool, and workout room for the convenience of its guests.

GOLF

Golf in Cincinnati has become a sport for all people. Around town, players at the tees range from the professionals at Kings Island to the par 3 beginners at Reeves golf course. People in Cincinnati play golf all through the year. If there is a nice day in December or February, you will find people on the links all across the area.

Greater Cincinnati has more than 100 golf courses of various levels. Shaker Run Golf Course in Lebanon is considered to be the most difficult course in Greater Cincinnati. More than 30,000 rounds were played at the course in 2002. Many other courses also have 30,000 to 60,000 rounds each year.

We're not sure why there are so many golf courses in Greater Cincinnati—it's not exactly a place people come for a golf vacation. Maybe it's the weather, which allows for long golf seasons, or maybe people here just enjoy the game.

Everybody seems to play, though. Don't be surprised if you can't get in touch with certain business executives in their offices during the first few warm spring days. Plenty of local business takes place on the links. And if you need a building inspected, check the back nine. That's where a local television station found then-county building inspectors a few years ago, teeing it up on taxpayer time.

Some of the courses are private; most are public. And a surprising number are part of a residential golfing community. It seems you can't build a housing development around here these days without including a golf course. (See the Neighborhoods chapter.)

We've put together a comprehensive list of public courses in Greater Cincinnati by area, with basic information about each one. The distances and par are from the back tees. Prices are all for 18 holes unless otherwise specified. Reservations at courses in the Hamilton County Park District (City of Cincinnati) can be made up to 14 days in advance by calling (513) 651-GOLF.

CENTRAL

Avon Fields Golf Course
4081 Reading Road
(513) 981-0322

Owned by the city of Cincinnati, this 80-year-old course is the oldest municipal golf course west of the Allegheny Mountains. Located in the heart of the city, it is accessible from all parts of town. The 5,081-yard, par 66 course offers straight and simple fairways played over a rolling terrain. There are no par 5 holes on the course, with the longest hole being a 432-yard par 4, one of 12 par 4s the course has to offer. Although the course can be played by beginners, the small target greens make the course more of a challenge for experienced players. The greens and fairways are bentgrass.

The greens fee is $20 for riding, $16 for walking. For reservations, call (513) 651-GOLF up to 14 days in advance. A driving range and pro shop are available.

Beach Creek Golf Club
1831 Hudepohl Lane
(513) 522-8700

Beech Creek is one of many 9-hole courses in Greater Cincinnati that can be adapted to an 18-hole course through the use of different tees. The course measures 3,000 yards through 9 holes, so it's good if you're looking for a quick game or don't want to walk long distances. The course has its challenges, though, and a grove of beech trees in the middle of the fairway on the fifth hole. Both are scenic but demand good shooting. The greens fee is $25 on weekdays, $27 on weekends with a cart. Reservations are suggested.

Blue Ash Golf Course
4040 Cooper Road, Blue Ash
(513) 745-8577

This scenic course is owned by the city of Blue Ash and is playable at all levels of ability. The course is tree lined and well bunkered by both sand and water. Water hazards, in fact, come into play on 9 holes (including no. 1 and no. 18), which can make for a terrible (or a wonderfully ego-boosting) way to begin and end a round. Hole no. 1 requires a drive over two creeks that cut through the fairway, while hole 18 is a 525-yard par 5 that ends at a creek that cuts right in front of the green. Hole 6 may be the toughest because of the lake that sits next to the green. The par 72 course runs 6,643 yards, with four par 5s.

The greens fee is $27 every day, and the cart fee is $13 per person. Reservations can be made seven days in advance by Blue Ash residents and seven days in advance by nonresidents after 9:00 A.M. Practice greens and practice bunkers are available.

Glenview Golf Course
10965 Springfield Pike
(513) 771-1747

Glenview has been recognized as one of the country's 50 outstanding public golf courses according to *Golf Digest*. The course is owned by the city of Cincinnati and located in a rural setting with beautiful bluegrass fairways and bentgrass greens. It has five tees on each hole. From the back tees, the course plays 7,024 yards with a par of 72. An additional 9 holes were recently added, giving the course 27 holes, each a par 36, each with two par 5s, but each with its own characteristics. The East Course ends with a 563-yard par 5. The West Course and South Course each have two almost identical holes that play over water hazards, one just 181 yards and the other 205 yards in length.

Greens fees are $29 riding and $21 walking. For reservations, call up to seven days in advance. A pro shop and driving range are available.

Greenhills Village
14 Enfield Street, Greenhills
(513) 589-3585

This tiny par 3 9-hole course runs just 1,100 yards, but it's a mature course with lots of large trees and hilly terrain. All the greens are elevated, adding to the challenge by making approach shots critical. Greenhills Village is a great course for beginners who are developing their skills, or for those in search of a very quick round of golf. The greens fee is $14 for 18 holes. There are no carts.

Sharon Woods Golf Course
11355 Swing Road, Sharonville
(513) 769-4325

Sharon Woods is the oldest of the seven courses owned by the Hamilton County Park District, dating from 1938. The par 70 course runs 6,633 yards, with the 468-yard third hole running uphill all the way. As one might gather from the name, the course is carved out of a heavily wooded section of a local park, making mature trees a regular hazard. The round ends with a beautiful but demanding 431-yard par 4. The greens fee is $23 every day. The cart fee is $12. Reservations can be made five days in advance.

Winton Woods/Meadow Links
10999 Mill Road, Greenhills
(513) 825-3701

This course in Winton Woods is owned by the Hamilton County Park District. The 9-hole, midlength course, which features bentgrass fairways and greens, stretches over 2,110 yards, with a par of 31. The course is spread out wide, which is good for players who by choice or by chance spread the ball all around the fairways. It is more of a challenge than most 9-hole courses, though. Water is in play on 4 of the 9 holes, including the 303-yard no. 9 hole, where water sits just off the tee.

Because the course sits in the middle of a local park, mature trees abound.

The greens fee is $12.00 every day, and the cart fee is $6.25 per person. Reservations can be made five days ahead of time. Juniors pay just $6.00.

Also offered at Meadow Links is the Golf Academy, with a 49-station covered and heated driving range, a natural turf practice area of different course scenarios, an indoor auditorium and learning center, special programs that are free to the public, and a complete lesson program for all skill levels. A pro shop that specializes in custom club fitting is available, as well as a snack bar.

Winton Woods/Mill Course
1515 West Sharon Road, Greenhills
(513) 825-3770

This long, rolling course sits in Winton Woods Park and has bentgrass fairways and greens and five water hazards. The Mill was renovated in 1993 and includes a clubhouse for the challenging 6,376-yard, par 71 course. Its no. 2 hole is a 513-yard par 5 that makes a sharp 90-degree turn to the left.

The greens fee is $22.00 every day, and the cart fee is $12.50. Reservations are accepted five days ahead of tee times.

Wyoming Golf Club
81 Mount Pleasant Avenue, Wyoming
(513) 821-8226

Although it has only 9 holes, the course at this 101-year-old private club fools newcomers with its difficulty. It is not a pitch-and-putt course—a creek runs through five holes, and there are three par 5 holes, including one 465 yards long and another 555 yards long. The course is somewhat exclusive, although not to the point where nonmembers can't find a member to host them for a round. The course is 3,160 yards long with par 36. The greens fee is $30 and the cart fee is $14. A driving range, practice areas, swimming pool, and platform tennis courts are also available.

If you're just learning how to play golf, the Meadow Links Golf Academy can help you. Located in Winton Woods, the academy has both natural and artificial practice areas. It also offers special rates for juniors and offers free clinics in the summer. Call (513) 825-3701 for information.

EAST

California Golf Course
5920 Kellogg Avenue
(513) 231-6513

This 60-year-old course, which is owned by the city of Cincinnati, is edged with heavy woods, and the trees spill over into the narrow fairways, creating the need for precise aim. The course is played over a rolling terrain and is built around two massive holding basins for the city's waterworks, which offer water hazards along with a beautiful setting. It sits high above the Ohio River too, creating scenic overlooks of the Kentucky hills. The par 70 course is 6,227 yards long but straightforward with only one par 5—the 480-yard no. 2 hole—and one hole with a dogleg. The back nine has only one par 3.

The greens fee is $27.50 riding and $17.50 walking. For reservations, call up to seven days in advance. A restaurant and pro shop are available.

Deer Track Golf Course
6160 Ohio Highway 727, Goshen
(513) 625-2500

This 6,352-yard, par 71 course features one of the area's few island greens. One of the course's 16 lakes surrounds the green on the par 3 157-yard 15th hole. The course also has 47 sand traps. Permanent weekend tee times are available. The weekend greens fee is $25. The cart fee is $10.

Eagles Nest Golf Course
1540 Ohio Highway 28, Goshen
(513) 722-1241

Eagles Nest is flat, easy to walk, and offers open fairways, elevated greens, and a sampling of all hazards, including so much water that scuba gear may be necessary. The 156-yard par 3 no. 7 hole isn't much more than a tee, a lake, and a green. The 299-yard par 4 no. 3 hole also goes over a lake. The toughest hole may be no. 9, which has water off the tee and water around the green, forcing a good drive and a good approach shot. The course features rye and bluegrass and runs 6,100 yards with a par of 71.

Greens fees are $20.50, and the cart fee is $11.00 per person. Reservations are accepted seven days in advance. A pro shop and driving range are available.

Hickory Woods Golf Club
1240 Hickory Woods Drive, Lowland
(513) 575-3900

The course is short, just 6,200 yards long, but deceiving. The front 9 holes are fairly open, but the back 9 combine hills, woods, and streams on just about every hole. Par is 70. Bluegrass and rye grass are combined on the fairways, while greens are bentgrass. Hole no. 8 seems to stretch on forever, doglegging left and right, with 580 yards between the tee and the green. Possibly ruining the day, the 18th hole is a 472-yard par 5 that requires a drive over water. The greens fee is $38 and includes a cart. Reservations can be made seven days in advance.

Indian Valley Golf Course
3950 Newtown Road, Newtown
(513) 561-9491

Sitting along the banks of the Little Miami River, this 6,284-yard, par 72 course is flat and ideal for older golfers or beginners. The holes range from the 130-yard, par 3 no. 5 to the 523-yard, par 5 no. 14. Water comes into play on two holes, 3 and 15. The greens fee is $19. The cart fee is $11. Reservations are required.

Little Miami Golf Center
3811 Newtown Road, Newtown
(513) 561-5650

Owned by the Hamilton County Park District, Little Miami offers two 9-hole courses, both of which are flat, simple, short, and great for beginners. The regulation-length course is a par 35 that stretches 3,204 yards and features a 592-yard, par 5, two par 3s, and six par 4s that range from 274 to 400 yards. The par 3 course is 882 yards with a par of 27.

The greens fees are $11.00. The cart fee is $6.25 per person. Discounted junior rates are $6.00. Reservations are needed for weekend mornings only and can be made five days in advance. A pro shop and driving range are available.

O'Bannon Creek Golf Club
6842 Ohio Highway 48, Loveland
(513) 683-9100

This private course features rolling terrain and plenty of trees along 6,513 yards, offering a par of 70. Greens fees are $35 weekdays, $40 weekends. The cart fee is $14. A driving range and practice green are available.

Reeves Golf Course
Beechmont and Wilmer Avenues
(513) 321-2740

The Reeves course is owned by the city of Cincinnati and is adjacent to the Lunken Airport playfield, so it's not uncommon for corporate jets, private planes, helicopters, or even the Goodyear blimp to fly overhead. The course is level, easy to walk, and offers no water hazards. The par 70 course, with rye fairways and bentgrass greens, is 6,371 yards long and features elevated greens that make approach shots critical. Almost all of the holes are straight and not exceptionally long, with the 471-yard no. 10 and the 477-yard no. 4 the longest.

The greens fee is $16 for riding, $13 walking. For reservations, call (513) 651-GOLF up to 14 days in advance. A lighted practice area and heated driving-range stalls are available. Tennis courts and softball fields are nearby.

Reeves also has a 9-hole par 3 executive course. Greens fee for that is $7.25.

Vineyard Golf Course
600 Nordyke Road, Anderson
(513) 474-3007

The Vineyard is the "resort course" of the seven owned by the Hamilton County Park District. It features bentgrass tees, fairways, and greens in a rolling, scenic, and heavily wooded setting near Woodland Mound Park. The par 71 course has three lakes that come into play on six holes and 45 white-sand bunkers running throughout its lengthy 6,789 yards. Some holes, such as the no. 2, which stretches for 553 yards, is protected by all three hazards: lake, trees, and bunkers.

The greens fee is $29.50 every day, and the cart fee is $12.50. Reservations can be made 10 days ahead. The golf course is rated four out of five stars by *Golf Digest*.

WEST

Aston Oaks
1 Aston Oaks Drive, North Bend
(513) 467-0070

This scenic course was designed by the Nicklaus Group and is part of a housing development along the Ohio River. The no. 12 hole overlooks the river. The course's signature hole is the no. 16, which crosses a creek three times before hitting the green, which is along a 10-foot-high rock wall. Three of the course's holes run along the creek.

Greens fees for the course are $35 weekdays and $45 on weekends and include the cart, which is mandatory.

Circling Hills Golf Club
10240 Carolina Trace Road, Harrison
(513) 367-5858

This course on the far-western edge of Cincinnati is a flat, links-style course with two lakes and numerous bunkers spread over 6,350 yards. It is easily walkable, although a couple of holes seem to go on forever. The 434-yard no. 3 hole doglegs to the left and is later followed by the 565-yard par 5 no. 5 hole, which requires a chip shot over a creek to make the green. The course has four par 5s including the no. 16, which is 570 yards, and the no. 7, which is 495 yards.

The greens fee is $23 daily, and the cart fee is $13. A driving range, pro shop, and practice greens are available. Reservations can be made seven days in advance.

Delhi Hills Golf Course
1068 Ebenezer Road, Delhi
(513) 941-9827

This small 9-hole par 3 course covers just 2,600 yards and has no sand traps but plenty of hills. It has been family owned and operated since 1958 and is excellent for practicing iron shots. The greens fee is $7.50 for 9 holes and carts are $5.00.

Dunham Golf Course
1951 Dunham Way, Price Hill
(513) 251-1157

The city of Cincinnati owns this course, which is ideal for juniors or beginners. It stretches just 1,310 yards, with a par of 29, so it's convenient for those looking for a fast game or looking to work on their short game. Hills and valleys make each hole unique, with holes ranging from the 83-yard no. 3 to the 259-yard no. 9.

The greens fee is $14.75 for riding, $10.00 for walking; carts are reserved for seniors only. For reservations, call (513) 651-GOLF up to 14 days in advance.

Fernbank Golf & Tennis Club
7036 Fernbank Avenue, Saylor Park
(513) 941-9960

This 9-hole, executive-style course runs 2,198 yards with flat, wide-open fairways and a par of 31. The course is easy to walk and good for beginners, with two holes less than 92 yards. The 391-yard no. 8 and 419-yard no. 9 holes are exceptions to the short course. Greens fees are $7.50

for 9 holes weekdays, and $9.50 for 9 holes weekends. There are no riding carts, although pull carts can be rented for $2.00. Play is on a first-come basis.

Hartwell Golf Club
Caldwell Drive and May Street, Hartwell
(513) 821-9855
The 9-hole course offers tight, tree-lined fairways covering 2,439 yards. The hilly terrain helps push par to 34. Rye fairways and bentgrass greens are featured. The no. 3 hole is the course's longest, stretching 408 yards. Greens fees are $8.00 for 9 holes weekdays, and $15.00 for 18 holes weekends. Cart fees are $7.00 per person on weekends, $6.00 weekdays.

Hillview Golf Course
6954 Wesselman Road, Mack
(513) 574-6670
This scenic, family-owned course sits atop a hill on the city's west side and features several lakes. The par 71 course is 5,435 yards long. Greens fees are $14.75 before 3:00 P.M. weekdays and $16.50 before 3.00 P.M. on weekends. The cart fee is included in the above rate, which is for 9 holes.

Miami View Golf Club
8411 Harrison Avenue, Whitewater
(513) 353-2384
The first two holes of this private course are a 477-yard par 4 and a 435-yard par 4, possibly making for a long day for short hitters. The rest of the par 71 course features rolling hills and three lakes through its 6,506 yards. Fees are $30 weekdays and $35 weekends. Cart fee is $12.50 per person. The club also has a driving range, putting green, practice fairway, and chipping green.

Miami Whitewater Forest Golf Course
8801 Mount Hope Road, Harrison
(513) 367-4627
A lot of wildlife roams this scenic, Hamilton County-owned par 72 course. It sits adjacent to a lake, but that simply adds to the beauty of the course because water comes into play on only one hole, no. 9. The course is straightforward and good for beginners, but it is long, stretching 792 yards. None of the par 4 holes is less than 335 yards, and four are more than 400 yards long. The greens fee is $22.00 every day, and the cart fee is $12.50. A pro shop and driving range are available.

Neumann Golf Course
7215 Bridgetown Road, Bridgetown
(513) 574-1320
Neumann is the most popular course in Greater Cincinnati, with an estimated 95,000 rounds played here each year. The 40-year-old course, which is owned by the city of Cincinnati, features three 9-hole courses: Red, 2,913 yards long, par 35; White, 2,944 yards long, par 36; and Blue, 3,156 yards long, par 35. The 27 holes are all over rolling, wooded terrain. The Red Course features a 465-yard par 5 that bends to the right around a grove of trees, forcing golfers to either go over or around it. The White Course includes one of the few holes with water, the 307-yard no. 2, which has water just off the tee. The Blue Course has two of the toughest back-to-back holes, with a 390-yard no. 7 that goes over water, followed by a very long 612-yard par 5.

Greens fee is $26.00 for riding, $16.50 for walking. A driving range and pro shop are available. For reservations, call up to seven days in advance.

Pebble Creek Golf Course
9799 Prechtel Road, Bevis
(513) 385-4442
Trees and bentgrass tees, greens, and fairways make this rugged, hilly course lush. The course runs just 5,848 yards, although it includes four par 5s, with the longest hole the 520-yard no. 11. Greens fees are $31 weekdays and $41 weekends for the par 71 course. The cart fee is included. Reservations can be made seven days ahead of tee time.

Robin's Nest Golf
8300 Dry Fork Road, Harrison
(513) 367-6280
www.robinsnestgolf.com
This is a perfect course for a quick 9 holes. The par 3 course is nice and straight with not many hazards and trees. The holes range from 105 to 200 yards. Cost is $8.00 for walking and $12.50 for riding. The course also provides night golf for $12.00 per person with a minimum of 12 people.

Shawnee Lookout Golf Course
2030 Lawrenceburg Road, North Bend
(513) 941-0120
You can see three states from the 12th tee of this scenic, hilly Hamilton County-owned course that overlooks the Ohio River. Deer and other wildlife roam the heavily wooded course. No holes on the front 9 of this par 70, 6,001-yard course extend beyond 365 yards. The holes, though, are crooked as can be, with dogleg and Z-shaped fairways throughout. A small creek runs through the course, coming into play on half the holes, and a small lake complicates the 159-yard par 3 no. 5 hole.

The greens fee is $20.00 every day, and the cart fee is $12.50. Reservations can be made 10 days in advance.

Woodland Golf Course
5820 Muddy Creek Road
(513) 451-4408
Woodland is a short, 9-hole course, but it's hilly and it features a little bit of all types of hazards that require accurate tee shots. The 2,206-yard, par 34 course is owned by the city of Cincinnati and has only two par 3 holes. The greens fee is $14.25 for riding, $9.00 for walking. For reservations, call up to seven days in advance. The old farmhouse clubhouse adds to the rustic atmosphere.

NORTH

Fairfield Green
2200 John Gray Road, Fairfield
(513) 858-7750
This 6,290-yard, par 70 course is flat and easily walkable, but almost half its holes have water hazards. Hole no. 16, a 393-yard par 4, features a green surrounded on three sides by water, while water and trees pack the 543-yard par 5 no. 3. The greens fee is $23 every day, and the cart fee is $13. Reservations can be made seven days in advance. Putting greens and tennis courts are nearby.

Hueston Woods Golf Course
6961 Brown Road, Oxford
(513) 523-8081
Situated in Hueston Woods State Park, this course is filled with mature trees. Featuring bluegrass fairways and bentgrass greens, it is a very long 7,005 yards, with a par 72. Water comes into play on three holes, but two of them—the 208-yard no. 16 and the 201-yard no. 18—require drives over the drink. The 11th hole is the longest, stretching a whopping 567 yards.

Greens fees are $19 weekdays and $27 weekends. The cart fee is $12 per person. Reservations can be made any time before the tee time. A pro shop and driving range are available.

Pleasant Hill Golf Club
6847 Hankins, Middletown
(513) 539-7220
This flat course is used a lot by leagues and senior golfers. It features shorter par 5s and longer par 4s on its 6,586 yards. Par is 71. Greens fees are $23. The cart fee is $12. A driving range, pro shop, and practice areas are available.

Potters Park Golf Course
417 Hamilton-New London Road, Hamilton
(513) 868-5983
A tight, undulating course, Potters Park

features small greens, few bunkers, and long par 3s over its 5,449 yards. Par is 69. The greens fee is $16 weekdays and $20 weekends and the cart fee is $10 weekdays and $12 weekends.

Vista Verde Golf Club
4780 Millikin Road, Hamilton
(513) 868-6948
Eight miniature ponds sit within this 5,900-yard, par 70 course that features elevated tees and no bunkers. All greens are surrounded on three sides by trees or placed on hills and are sand based for quick drainage. The greens fee is $29 and includes a cart. You can see fox, deer, and pheasant in abundance on the course.

Walden Pond
6090 Golf Club Lane, Indian Springs
(513) 785-2999
Walden Pond opened in 1997 and was designed by Michael Hurdzan. It now hosts the women's Mid-American Conference championship each spring. The course has bentgrass greens and fairways. Its clubhouse is a mansion built in 1831. Greens fees range from $46 to $64 and include a cart. The course does have twilight specials.

Weatherwax Golf Course
5401 Mosiman Road, Middletown
(513) 425-7886
Weatherwax, which was designed by Arthur Hills and was rated in 1992 by *Golf Digest* as one of the top-75 public courses in the country, has four 9-hole courses—Woodside, Meadows, Valley View, and Highlands—that can be arranged six different ways. Each course has five sets of tees, creating 30 different ways to play the course. The two main courses, Woodside and Meadows, combine for a very long 7,174-yard par 72 from the back tees. Valley View and Highlands combine for a lengthy 6,756-yard par 72.

The course completed a $2.2 million renovation in 1998 that included a switch from bluegrass to bentgrass fairways, elevated tees, and new sand traps. The greens fee is $24 weekdays, $26 weekends, and the cart fee is $12 per person. A driving range and practice area are available, along with a limited pro shop.

Wildwood Golf Club
5877 Ross Road, Fairfield
(513) 874-3754
Wildwood is a semiprivate club built inside a residential community. It offers restricted hours for public play. The course is a regulation length 9-hole, 3,160-yard, par 35 course. It has two sets of tees on each hole, though, creating the option to play 18 holes. The 396-yard no. 4 becomes a 459-yard no. 13 with the second tee. The 489-yard no. 9 becomes a 399-yard no. 18. The course, which has bluegrass fairways and bentgrass greens, is tight and hilly. The greens fee is $19.50 during the week and $25.00 on the weekend, and the cart fee is $13.00. Check for availability of public play.

NORTHEAST

Crooked Tree Golf Course
5171 Centennial Oak Drive, Mason
(513) 398-3933
Plenty of mature trees, lakes, and rolling terrain make Crooked Tree especially picturesque. The 6,415-yard course, which features bentgrass throughout, starts off with a 535-yard par 5 that doglegs to the right and then back to the left. The turn is made after a 540-yard par 5 in which a creek runs down the middle of the fairway and wraps around the green. There are six par 3s and four par 5s in the par 70 course, and drives must be made over a lot of rough on several holes before reaching the fairway.

The greens fee is $40 on weekdays, $43 on Friday, and $47 on Saturday and

Sunday. It includes a cart. Crooked Tree, which is part of a residential development, also has one of the largest pro shops in the area. Reservations can be made seven days ahead. A driving range and clubhouse restaurant and bar are also available.

Golf Center at Kings Island
6042 Fairway Drive, Mason
(513) 398-7700
The Golf Center at Kings Island is everything you could imagine in a day of golf, giving amateur golfers a chance to see how they might fare against the pros. Until 2002 it was home to the annual PGA Seniors tournament and has hosted 25 professional championships since it was built. It has two courses: the 27-hole larger Grizzly and the smaller 18-hole Bruin, both designed by Jack Nicklaus.

The championship Grizzly course runs up to 6,800 yards (for 18 holes) and cuts no slack throughout. Mature trees and dozens of sand bunkers are spread throughout the course, and there's water on at least six holes. And, as a final exam, hole no. 9 on the west 9 is a 546-yard par 5 that doglegs left over a large lake that has eaten up more than its share of pro players. Greens fees, which include a mandatory cart, are $40 Monday through Thursday, $50 on Friday, and $60 on weekends and holidays.

The Bruin is a 3,428-yard, par 60 midlength course, with 6 par 4s and 12 par 3s. Water comes into play on just one hole of the Bruin, which is flatter, straighter, and much more direct than the Grizzly. Greens fees for the Bruin are $13 weekdays, $14 weekends. Carts are $11.50.

If you're downtown and looking for a quick round of golf with a view, head over to Devou Park Golf Course in Covington. It is hilly, so use a cart, but enjoy a view of Cincinnati's skyline from some of the holes.

Reservations for both the Grizzly and the Bruin can be made 10 days in advance for weekends. Reservations can be made 21 days in advance for weekdays. Eight tennis courts, a driving range with grass tees, and practice bunkers are available. The upscale restaurant and bar is a good place to wrap up the day.

Kingswood Golf Course
4188 Irwin Simpson Road, Mason
(513) 398-5252
A large lake and rolling fairways are featured on the squeezed 5,834 yards at Kingswood. The course has a par of 71, and water comes into play on three holes. The 454-yard par 4 no. 2 hole is wedged between nos. 3 and 8, requiring precision placement or a trip onto a neighboring fairway. Greens fee is $22. The cart fee is $11 per person. Reservations can be made seven days in advance.

Shaker Run Golf Club
4961 Greentree Road, Lebanon
(513) 727-0007, (800) 721-0007
http://shakerrungolfclub.com
Just about every shot in the bag is needed to work through this 6,965-yard Arthur Hills-designed course, which was ranked by *Golf Digest* as No. 82 out of 100 greatest public golf courses in 2003. In 2005 the course hosted the U.S. Amateur Public Links Championship. The course is heavily wooded throughout and dotted with water hazards on 11 of the 18 holes. Bring your trunks, because you'll go for a swim at least once. It opens with a 567-yard par 5, and if that doesn't get you off to a bad start, the par 3 no. 5 requires a drive that carries 240 yards over water onto a green that hugs the water. The turn is made after a 435-yard par 4 no. 9 that follows the water's edge before turning right, carrying over more water and onto a green that is just about an island. The round ends with a 420-yard par 4 that drives over water in order to reach the fairway. Par is 72.

Greens fees are $65 weekdays and $76 weekends, with the cart. Reservations can be made 14 days in advance, and a 48-hour cancellation notice is required.

TPC at River's Bend
316 Winding River Boulevard, Maineville
(513) 677-0550
www.tpcatriversbend.com
The jewel in the crown of Cincinnati golf. The course, designed by Arnold Palmer, is the new host of the Kroger Classic Champion's Tour Event. It was named *Golf Digest*'s Best New Private Course in 2002. The private course, opened in 2001, is in a natural setting with rolling hills and many changes in elevation. The length of the course is 7,180 yards.

Twin Run Golf Course
2505 Eaton Road, Hamilton
(513) 868-5833
This par 72 course stretches a lengthy 6,551 yards over rolling farmland but is playable by golfers at all levels. A clubhouse offers a snack bar and pro shop. The greens fee is $16 weekdays, $20 weekends, and the cart fee is $12. Reservations for weekend tee times are taken on the Monday before the weekend. No reservations are needed during the week.

Western Row Golf Course
Mason-Montgomery Road, Mason
(513) 398-8886
Western Row is one of the most highly played clubs in the area because of its flat, hazardless course. With the par 72 course running a lengthy 6,746 yards, it has its challenges, particularly the four par 5s, all of which are more than 500 yards. Those seeking tee times sometimes have to compete with leagues and outings. Greens fee is $22. The cart fee is $12 per person. Reservations are required for weekends only.

NORTHERN KENTUCKY

A.J. Jolly Golf Club
U.S. Highway 27, Alexandria, KY
(859) 635-2106
Campbell County owns this scenic par 71 course, which features an abundance of water hazards, including a 250-acre lake. The par 71 course, which stretches out over 6,200 yards, includes a lengthy 558-yard par 5 on the no. 9 hole. The greens fee is $22 and a cart is $12. Reservations for all seven days of the week can be made up to eight days in advance.

Boone Links Golf Course
19 Clubhouse Drive, Florence, KY
(859) 371-7553
www.boonelinksgolfcourse.com
This 27-hole course is owned by Boone County and is open year-round for diehard golfers who don't mind cold weather. The course is straightforward, with no tricky holes, although five par 5s can be found through the 27 holes, including a 490-yard par 5 on the first hole. The course runs 6,724 yards and can be played with three different configurations.

The greens fee is $23 and a cart is $12. Reservations can be made seven days in advance. A pro shop and restaurant are available.

Devou Park
1344 Audubon Road, Covington, KY
(859) 431-8030
Devou Park's course is part of a larger city park that offers great views of the downtown Cincinnati skyline. It is played over 6,000 yards with a par of 70. The fairways are a combination of rye and bluegrass, while the greens offer bentgrass. The course is straightforward and playable by all levels. It has just one par 5, the 523-yard no. 4, although the hole is straight.

The greens fee is $22.00 every day, and the cart fee is $12.50 per person. A pro shop, restaurant, and bar are available. Reservations can be made seven days in advance.

Kenton County
3908 Richardson Road, Independence, KY
(859) 371-3200
Kenton County has three courses that share a common clubhouse: Fox Run, Pioneer, and Willows.

Fox Run is the largest and nicest, heavily wooded with bentgrass tees and greens and 9 holes with water hazards. The rolling terrain stretches 7,055 yards, including a 558-yard 18th hole that doglegs right and left and then requires a good approach to the green, which sits behind a lake. Par is 72. That can make for a tough ending to a day on the links. The greens fee is $43 Monday through Thursday, $46 Friday through Sunday, and includes a cart. Fox Run offers a driving range, a warm-up range, and a putting green.

The Pioneer is the original of the three courses owned by Kenton County and is the most playable by the average golfer. Fairways are wide, and only three holes have water hazards. Water on the 202-yard, par 3 no. 13, though, leaves no room for error, and the water on the 369-yard, par 4 no. 4 forces drivers to either do their best Tiger Woods impersonation or pull up short and hit an iron over the water. Bentgrass tees and bluegrass fairways mark the course, which has only one par 5, and that isn't until the 17th hole. The greens fee is $24 for the 6,059-yard par 70 course. The cart fee is $13.

The Willows has a very demanding back 9. Six holes on the front 9 feature water. The par 72 course runs 6,791 yards, and the 398-yard no. 4 hole is played over water twice. The greens fee is $27 every day, and the cart fee is $13.

On all three courses, Kenton County residents may schedule weekend tee times 10 days in advance and nonresidents must wait until 9 days out. During the week, reservations are scheduled 7 days in advance for everyone.

Lassing Pointe Golf Course
2260 Double Eagle Drive,
Boone County, KY
(859) 384-2266

Bentgrass tees and fairways highlight the long 6,724 yards of the par 72 Lassing Pointe, near Union. The course was rated as the best public course in Kentucky by *Golf Digest* in 1999 and by *Golf Week* in 2003. The course has some of the largest greens in the area, with four to six sets of tee boxes for each hole. The day starts with the course's longest hole, a 555-yard par 5.

The greens fee is $37 and a cart is $12 per person. Reservations can be made 7 days in advance for weekdays, 9 days for Saturdays, and 10 for Sundays. A fully stocked pro shop, practice range, and short-game center are available.

Meadowood Golf Course
1911 Golf Club Drive, Burlington, KY
(859) 586-0422
www.meadowoodgolf.com

This 9-hole course is 2,600 yards and has a par of 35. The greens fee is $11.00, and the cart fee is $7.00. Reservations are available, as is a pro shop.

Twin Oaks Golf Course
East 43rd and Michigan, Covington, KY
(859) 581-2410

Its flat course with wide Bermuda grass fairways stretching over 6,396 yards attracts 100-plus corporate outings every year. Large trees, four lakes, and numerous bunkers make the par 70 course challenging, though. There are only two par 5s in the 18 holes: a 560-yard hole at no. 16 and a 516-yard hole at no. 5. The back 9 runs along the Licking River.

The greens fee is $24 every day, and the cart fee is $16. Reservations for two tee times can be made two weeks in advance.

World of Sports
7400 Woodspoint Drive, Florence, KY
(859) 371-8255

This course, owned by the city of Florence, is a par 58 executive course. It has 14 par 3s and 4 par 4s for quick rounds. Several holes are tricky, especially for beginners, requiring golfers to go over a lake. The greens fee is $17.50. The cart fee is $12.50 per person. No reservations are required. Also offers a driving range and a pro shop.

SOUTHEASTERN INDIANA

Elk Run Golf Club
Soap Hill Road, Aurora, IN
(812) 926-3595
This small, 9-hole course runs just 2,480 yards but has only two par 3 holes. It is a good course for beginners. The greens fee is $20 for 18 holes, including a cart. Tee times are on a first-come basis.

Grand Oak Golf Club
370 Grand Oak Drive, West Harrison, IN
(812) 637-3943
A premium is placed on accuracy on this tight, target course. Elevated tees and bentgrass fairways run throughout the scenic, par 72 course, which stretches 6,528 yards through mature trees. Five holes include water hazards. The course begins with a 390-yard par 4 that requires play over water, which can start the day with a splash. The 555-yard par 5 no. 16 is actually U-shaped, requiring some tricky shooting.

Greens fees with carts are $38 weekdays and $43 weekends. Reservations are accepted 14 days in advance. A driving range and short game center are available, and club repair is handled in the pro shop.

Indian Lakes
7234 East Indiana Highway 46, Batesville, IN
(812) 623-GOLF
The emphasis in the name is on Lakes. Six of the course's 9 holes are over water—and not just a stream or trickle, but a lake. Rolling hills and tree-lined fairways help make the course difficult as well as scenic. The large greens help ease the strain. Greens fees at the course, which is part of a residential resort, are $13 weekdays and $15 weekends. Carts are free for resort members and $12 per person for non-members. Call ahead for tee times.

Links at Grand Victoria
600 Grand Victoria Drive, Rising Sun, IN
(800) 472-6311
Billed as the only Scottish links-style course in the area, this 6,400-yard course is at the Grand Victoria Casino. It has bentgrass tees, fairways, and greens as well as sweeping bunkers and winding lakes. It also has views of the Ohio River. The course was designed by Tim Liddy. Greens fees, which include a cart, are $50 Monday through Thursday and $57 Friday through Sunday.

Sugar Ridge Golf Club
2010 State Line Road, Lawrenceburg, IN
(812) 537-9300
The course at Sugar Ridge is very hilly and long (at 7,000 yards it is one of the longest courses in the area) with a par of 72 and secluded fairways. Heavily wooded, it is named after the abundance of sugar maples around the course. A lot of wild animals wander around the course, which offers four sets of tees on each hole. The 17th hole is a 600-yard par 5 with a green surrounded by bunkers, one of four par 5s. Greens fees, which include a cart, are $32.00 weekdays and $39.50 weekends. Reservations can be made up to one week in advance.

Vineyard Golf Club
Indiana Highway 250, Rising Sun, IN
(812) 594-2627
This 18-hole course runs 6,172 yards with a par of 72, but it may be difficult for beginners. The par 4, 250-yard 17th, for instance, leads to a peninsula green. Greens fees are $27 during the week and $30 on weekends. The cart fee is included.

SPECTATOR SPORTS

Even if many people don't know much about the city of Cincinnati, most have heard of our sports teams. While the professional teams seem to be "letting" other cities' franchises enjoy some success right now, the future is full of promise. Both the Cincinnati Reds and Bengals have new facilities downtown (see the close-up in this chapter on the Great American Ball Park), and hope springs eternal.

Of course, many people know that the Cincinnati Reds were the first Major League Baseball team and have won several World Series Championships. The Cincinnati Bengals have played in the Super Bowl twice. Besides those two main sports, we have minor league baseball and horse racing. And each year the area hosts one of the top nine tennis tournaments in the world.

Basketball fans in Greater Cincinnati get to see some great hoops with some of the top college teams in the country right here. Each year several of the area colleges find their way into the top 25 and even into the top 5. All the colleges win more than 20 games and make it to the NCAA tournament most years.

Besides the major sports, there are various sports events in the Queen City each year, including ice-skating and gymnastics. We've hosted world and national skating and gymnastic championships and just about every post-Olympic event that skates or tumbles. Our sports scene includes the NCAA basketball tournament, the NCAA hockey tournament, Olympic hockey team exhibitions, NBA basketball, and NHL hockey games, and even the rodeo, indoor motorcycle racing, monster-truck tractor pulls, and professional WWE big-time wrestling with Texas cage, to-the-death, last-man-in-the-ring, world championship, no-holds-barred, heavyweight title matches—assuming you consider these activities sports.

The Flying Pig Marathon has become a surprise big event on the Cincinnati's sports scene. Started in 2000, the marathon has quickly become a favorite event for spectators and runners. Held in May, the race route takes the 7,500 runners all over Cincinnati and into Northern Kentucky and ends at Yeatman's Cove downtown. The race's Web site, www.flyingpigmarathon.com, gives you information on how to register and the route the race takes; it even offers hints on how to be a good spectator.

The Kentucky Speedway is another big addition to the sports menu. Opening in 2000, the speedway quickly became one of the hottest tickets in town. The speedway is in Sparta, Kentucky, about a half hour south of the Cincinnati area. It is a 1.5-mile tri-oval with room for about 70,000 spectators.

Not only are sporting events vital to the immediate area's economy and psyche, they are probably our major regional attraction. Fans regularly travel hundreds of miles from Indiana, Kentucky, Ohio, West Virginia, and even Tennessee to watch the Reds and Bengals play.

Regionalism also can be found in the followers of college sports. Although most people in Greater Cincinnati are University of Cincinnati (UC) and Xavier University fans, there also are contingencies of Ohio State, Kentucky, and Indiana fans in the community. Of course, more fans for Kentucky are found in the south, more for Ohio State north of town, and more Indiana fans are obvious once you cross the border to Indiana. But as a whole, many alumni of all major area colleges show their colors in town.

One last reminder before you get into the listing of sport clubs—this chapter is called *Spectator* Sports. If you're more into participating in sports, check out the Parks and Recreation chapter.

BASEBALL

Cincinnati Reds
Great American Ball Park
(513) 421-4510, (800) 829-5353
www.reds.com

Baseball and Cincinnati are synonymous. This is the place where the professional game originated, where the first night game was played after President Franklin Roosevelt threw a switch at the White House to turn on the ballpark lights, where hometown hero Pete Rose became the all-time hits leader, and where opening day each April is an unofficial holiday celebrated with a parade.

It is the place where the Big Red Machine once dominated the game, winning six Western Division titles, four National League titles, and two World Series. It is the place where five World Series trophies rest, where the first National League team to go wire-to-wire, staying in first place every day of the season, resided, and where some of baseball's greatest players and managers call home.

In fact, as summarized by Lonnie Wheeler and John Baskin in their book *The Cincinnati Game,* "If there is one city whose removal from the face of baseball history would [disfigure] it beyond recognition, it is Cincinnati."

When the Reds (née the Red Stockings) began playing professionally in 1869, the team put together a 130-game winning streak before suffering its first loss, setting high standards for the game and particularly for Cincinnati. We didn't like to lose then, and that's still true today. The team continued to roll until 1871, when it was discontinued by the owners for six years because of (does this sound familiar?) increased salary demands.

By 1919, though, the Reds were back on top of the baseball world, winning their first World Series over the Chicago White Sox, a team that became better known as the Black Sox because some team members accepted bribes from gamblers to throw games. Although a cloud and a question mark hung over that World Series title, the Reds didn't let it stop them in their search for glory, playing in eight more World Series (1939, 1940, 1961, 1970, 1972, 1975, 1976, and 1990) and winning four of them. During those years, some of the game's all-time greatest players wore Reds uniforms: Rose, Johnny Bench, Frank Robinson, Joe Morgan, Tom Seaver, Ernie Lombardi, Ted Kluszewski, and Buck Ewing.

If you stand in the "Gap" at Great American Ball Park, you can watch the river and the game at the same time. Be careful, though, because when a home run is hit, fireworks come out of the riverboat smokestacks nearby.

The area's contribution to Major League Baseball is not limited to just Reds players: Almost 250 Greater Cincinnati natives have made it to the major leagues, either as players or managers. Today, more than a dozen local players are in the majors, including Ken Griffey Jr.

Former greats Buddy Bell, Dave Parker, Leon "Bull" Durham, Joe Nuxhall, Jim Bunning, Kent Tekulve, Walter Alston, Jim Frey, Don Zimmer, and others helped the area collect 32 national amateur baseball titles and more than 50 state high school baseball championships.

The hopes of Reds' fans were high when the new ballpark opened in 2003, but it was a disappointing season. Another manager was fired and eventually also the general manager. But people in Cincinnati never give up on the Reds and are supportive of the new general manager Wayne Krivsky. Louisville Riverbat coach Dave Miley was hired to be manager in 2004. The team will be focusing mostly on developing young talent because even with the new managers, the budget hasn't substantially increased.

Barry Larkin retired after the 2004 season. Ken Griffey Jr. is the headliner on the team, but he has been plagued by health issues. Younger players on the

CLOSE-UP

It's a Home Run

"Rounding third and heading for home"—the neon letters outside Great American Ball Park beckon you. The famous words were spoken by longtime Reds broadcaster Joe Nuxhall, who said them at the end of each ballgame.

Nostalgia such as that phrase and many other memories of the tradition of baseball in Cincinnati are what fans will find in the Cincinnati Reds' new ballpark. Great American Ball Park opened along the Ohio River in 2003.

The retro vintage stadium, built at a price tag of some $300 million, is full of unique touches, such as the 50-by-20-foot art deco limestone relief, *The Spirit of Baseball,* which depicts the romance of baseball through a young boy's eyes.

There also are bronze statues in Crosley Terrace, the main entrance, which include a pitching Joe Nuxhall, catching Ernie Lombardi, hitting Frank Robinson, and on-deck Ted Kluszewski. Giant tile mosaics include Tony Perez and other Big Red Machine greats.

"The Gap," a 35-foot break in the stadium's superstructure along the third-base line, opens up views of downtown from inside the ballpark and allows pedestrians downtown a view of the proceedings. The huge scoreboard is the third largest in Major League Baseball. All seats face home plate and have cup holders. And natural grass replaces artificial turf.

The Hall of Fame and Museum is on the west side of the ballpark in the former center field of Riverfront Stadium. It includes plaques depicting former Reds players and relics of the team. It also features interactive displays.

Great American has 42,263 seats—20

team include Adam Dunn and Bronson Arroyo.

The majority owner of the team and its chief executive officer is Robert Castellini. Marge Schott was the tough-as-nails, dogloving, sometimes admirable, sometimes embarrassing owner of the team until 1998. She was punished for repeatedly making racial, ethnic, and sexist comments. The fellow Major League Baseball owners forced Marge to sell majority ownership of the team.

Although Marge is gone, some of her legacy will stay with the team. For instance, it was important to her to keep baseball affordable for families.

The Fan Cost Index done by the *Team Marketing Report* rated the Cincinnati Reds the lowest in 1998. The price for four tickets, two beers, four soft drinks, four hot dogs, two programs, and two souvenirs was $89.97. The highest was the New York Yankees, where a family of four would spend $148.56.

The new ballpark still has seats for as little as $5.00. Ticket prices currently range from $5.00 to $215.00.

Tickets can be ordered by calling the numbers listed above or purchased with a service charge from any Ticketmaster outlet in the country. Locally, Ticketmaster's number is (513) 562-4949. Tickets and other memorabilia are also available at the Reds Dugout gift shop in the lobby of the percent fewer than its predecessor, Cinergy Field—and they're all red. Some seats are only 50 feet away from home plate, which is closer than the batter is to the pitcher. The price for these prime seats is $175 to $215 per ticket. But that includes VIP parking, access to the private lounge, in-seat food and beverage service, and extra-wide padded seats.

Other premium seats cost $42.00 to $60.00. Average ticket prices run $5.00 to $30.00. During the season, you can also rent private suites from $2,040 to $11,900 for 35 to 170 people (includes the catered buffet).

Not only does the new ballpark have great seats, the food has been upgraded. The chow includes Montgomery Inn pulled pork and BBQ-chicken sandwiches and Skyline Cheese Coneys. There also are several restaurants in the ballpark. The Machine Room lounge serves fried baloney and bone-in-pork sandwiches, a half-pound steak burger, and chimichangas; heck, even deep-fried Twinkies on a stick are on tap. The locally brewed Red Legg Ale is available in the restaurant as well. This restaurant is open for lunch 11:00 A.M. to 2:00 P.M. weekdays and on game days with a ticket to the game.

Soft drinks may be brought into the ballpark, as long as the soda is packaged in clear plastic bottles and the seal isn't broken. Soft-sided coolers (no hard-shell coolers) are permitted, subject to inspection, but dimensions can't exceed 16 by 16 inches. Radios are OK, smoking isn't, and don't even think about turning your camera or video recorder onto the game action.

And no, it isn't called Great American because of the great American tradition of baseball in Cincinnati. The Great American Insurance Company, owned by former Reds majority owner Carl Lindner, paid $75 million for the privilege of putting its name on the building.

Westin Hotel at Fifth and Vine Streets downtown.

The Reds games are televised locally on Time Warner's Fox Sports Ohio. The commentators for those games are George Grande and Chris Welch. WLW radio (700 AM) provides outstanding Reds coverage, with Hall of Famer Marty Brennaman and Steve Stewart telling it like it is—good or bad, whether anyone likes it or not.

Marty and Steve also provide a fix for diehard baseball fans during the long winter months between the World Series and spring training with a weekly *Hot Stove League* talk show on WLW that concentrates on baseball only. And if you think there is nothing more disappointing than a rain delay, you're in for a pleasant surprise if you're within earshot of a radio. Marty and Steve fill in the time with entertaining and hilarious stories about the game and take questions on what they refer to (for reasons known only to themselves) as the Banana Phone.

Florence Freedom
8100 Ewing Boulevard, Florence, KY
(859) 594-HITS
www.florencefreedom.com

The Florence Freedom is a Frontier League (minor league) team that started in 2003. The first year, the team played at Miami University Hamilton, but a new stadium was built along Interstate 75 near U.S. Highway 42 in Florence and opened in 2004. Tom Browning, former Cincinnati Reds pitcher, was manager of the team in its inaugural year. Many local college baseball players were included on the team's roster. The team has open tryouts in the spring and starts playing in May. Ticket prices range from $5.00 to $9.00 per game.

FOOTBALL

Cincinnati Bengals
1 Bengals Drive
(513) 621-3550
www.bengals.com

A new coach and a new stadium have brought some optimism back to the Cincinnati Bengals. Marvin Lewis was hired before the 2003 season, and he led the team to an 8-8 season. The fans were back in the stadium, and the cheers of "Who Dey" were heard throughout the city. In 2005 the Bengals' record was 11-5, and they won the AFC North Division.

Before the Cleveland Browns moved to Baltimore, Baltimore first approached Bengal owner Mike Brown. It could have been the Bengals who moved to Baltimore. But Brown turned down the deal, saying his first priority wasn't to make as much money as he could and that he was committed to Cincinnati. Before he moved the team, he said he would first give the people of the city a chance. That meant asking them to pay for the construction of a football-only stadium. So in November 1996 the fans matched Brown's commitment by overwhelmingly passing a sales tax increase to pay for the stadium. Construction of the ultramodern Paul Brown Stadium was completed in 2000, just 3 blocks west of Cinergy Field.

But although fans gave Brown his support in the future of the franchise, many fans still question his management skills. The team has never had a winning season while he has been general manager. Each year, however, hope springs eternal. At the NFL draft, Brown has made some picks that should have helped the team. None of the draft picks ever seem to work out the way the team had hoped. And in the meantime, Brown has developed a reputation of being a tightfisted monarch, king of the family-owned business, who is unwilling to dip into the free-agent market and sign high-price players.

Although it's still a long way away, our thoughts are starting to drift toward the playoffs and—could it be?—a return to the Super Bowl. The Bengals have twice made it to the Super Bowl, losing each time to the San Francisco 49ers, darn it, in two of the closest Super Bowl games ever. Some of the greatest players ever to wear Bengals stripes played in those Super Bowls, including Boomer Esiason, Tim Krumrie, Isaac Curtis, Ken Anderson, and Anthony Munoz, the first Bengal to make it into the Hall of Fame. Future greats may lead the team back to the big game, and the city will be thankful they are ours.

Ticket prices for Bengals games don't come cheap. If you prefer to see the team play for a lot less, summer camp is at Georgetown College in Georgetown, Kentucky, about 70 miles south of Cincinnati, near Lexington, Kentucky.

COLLEGE SPORTS

University of Cincinnati
2624 Clifton Avenue, Clifton Heights
(513) 556-2287

Basketball tends to dominate the sports scene at UC, with the Bearcats regularly ranked in the top-20 teams in the nation. The University of Cincinnati once dominated college basketball around the time Oscar Robertson walked the campus, winning the NCAA tournament twice in the early 1960s. The Bearcats then fell into a long drought, but under the leadership of fiery head coach Bob Huggins, it became a formidable power once again. With his "play harder longer" motto, Huggins led his teams to the top of college basketball polls and made them regulars in the

NCAA tournament. He even took his team to the NCAA Final Four in his third year at the helm.

Huggins was never without controversy, though. There were a few disappointing seasons, and then "Hugs" got a DUI. He was let go from his contract by the new UC president. The team was taken over by assistant coach Andy Kennedy for the 2005–06 season. Former assistant coach Mike Cronin was hired in 2006

This is an important time for UC, who just left the Conference USA for the Big East Conference. Two other conference schools, Louisville and South Florida, moved with them. There they will have to compete against Villanova, Syracuse, and the University of Connecticut.

UC plays at the 13,000-seat Fifth Third Arena at the Shoemaker Center, and tickets for the games are difficult to come by. There has been talk of trying to expand seating at the facility to squeeze in more fans, but it hasn't happened yet. The university has a somewhat unusual arrangement with its season ticket policy, whereby those who want season basketball tickets must also buy season football tickets. The ticket trick was a way to boost attendance and support for the football program.

UC's football program saw a transformation in 2004. Rick Minter was fired after the disappointing 2003 season, and the university hired Ohio State assistant coach Mark Dantonio. He was the defensive coordinator with Ohio State for three years, including the national championship season in 2002. Games are played at Nippert Stadium on the UC campus.

Xavier University
3800 Victory Parkway
(513) 745-3411

The Musketeers of Xavier University, a private Jesuit college of just 6,500 students, has become one of college basketball's elite powerhouses. And it has done so with class, remaining free of NCAA sanctions and graduating every player who played as a senior since 1986.

Starting with coaches Bob Staak, Pete Gillen, and Skip Prosser, Xavier has taken its program up a notch on the success ladder each year and now finds itself regularly named one of the top-20 teams in the country (and no longer overshadowed by its state-supported neighbor, UC). In 2004 assistant coach Sean Miller took over when Thad Matta left for Ohio State.

The Muskies, who play in the powerful Atlantic 10 Conference, offer an exciting, fast-paced game with plenty of fast breaks and a lot of in-your-face pressure defense. This strategy has served the team well, taking it as far as the Elite Eight in the NCAA tournament and sending players such as Brian Grant, David West, and Tyrone Hill into the NBA.

Xavier used to play its home games off-campus at the 10,000-seat Cincinnati Gardens, but in 2000 a 10,000-seat $40 million convocation center called the Cintas Center became its home court. Tickets are harder to get, with as many as 6,500 people buying season tickets, leaving only a handful after students, faculty, and alumni scoop up most of those remaining.

Miami University
Oxford
(513) 529-3924

Miami is known in the football world as the Cradle of Coaches, with coaching legends Bo Schembechler, Woody Hayes, and Ara Parseghian, among others, getting their start in Oxford. The RedHawks—known as the Redskins until political correctness prevailed—came back to the winning side in the 2003 season when quarterback Ben Roethlisberger put Miami back in the top 10 and into a bowl appearance. The team finished with a 13–1 record and won over Louisville in the GMAC Bowl in Mobile, Alabama. Roethlisberger decided to enter the NFL draft after his junior year and was chosen as a first-round draft pick..

The university's basketball program gets overshadowed by UC's and Xavier's but is a strong program. Under coach

Every year for the Crosstown Shootout, the game between the University of Cincinnati and Xavier University's men's basketball teams, sponsored by Skyline Chili, the restaurant sells special Crosstown Shootout basketballs in the weeks before the game.

Charlie Coles, the RedHawks went to the Elite Eight in the NCAA tournament in 1999. Wally Szerbiak, who led the team to national prominence, was the No. 1 pick in the NBA draft in 1999.

The team has had five straight 20-win seasons and four trips to the NCAA tournament in six years, and they continue their winning ways. The RedHawks often make a run for the Mid-American Conference title. They play at Millett Hall on the Oxford campus.

Other Colleges

Northern Kentucky University
Highland Heights, KY
(859) 572-5193

The success of the area's basketball teams doesn't stop at the Division I level. NKU was the runner-up in the NCAA Division II Tournament in 1997 and 1998.

The Lady Norse, however, won the Division II National Championship in 2000 and have been a dominant team on the Division II level. At times, the women have attracted more attention than the men's program, but now both programs find themselves in the spotlight each year.

NKU has taken a hard look at starting a football program but has not made the commitment yet.

Thomas More College
Crestview Hills, KY
(859) 341-5800

Both the Saints' football and basketball programs tend to get overshadowed by all of the high-powered teams in the area, but they're contenders in their own right with a Division III program. The basketball program has done so well, in fact, it has drawn players talented enough to go on to the professional ranks in Europe or to the Continental Basketball Association. One of its most famous recruits was a local player from Covington Latin High School named David Justice, who decided to stop playing basketball and concentrate on playing baseball and is now a retired major league player.

Thomas More just started its football program in 1990 and found immediate success. The team has only had one season with a losing record—in 1998.

College of Mount St. Joseph
5701 Delhi Road
(513) 244-4311

Mount St. Joseph, which also plays on the Division III level, also started its football program in 1990 and competes regularly with Thomas More. Both schools are small (and academically challenging), and the games don't draw much of a crowd, but they have started a good little annual rivalry.

Ohio State University
Columbus
(800) GO-BUCKS

Fans in the area really pay more attention to what happens with Ohio State University football. When OSU plays at home, I-71 is jammed with Greater Cincinnati residents, who beat a path to Columbus to watch the Buckeyes (the fanaticism stops at the river, though). Trying to get a ticket to the Horseshoe, aka Ohio Stadium, is a tough task, but a call to (800) GO-BUCKS is worth the try.

The Ohio State Buckeyes have become a national powerhouse in the last several years. They won the title of national champions in 2002. In the 2003 season the team competed in the Fiesta Bowl and beat number eight Kansas State.

They ended up number four in the last national polls of the season.

But it's the Ohio State basketball team who made the headlines in 1999, making it to the Final Four for the first time since 1968. It has been in the NCAA tournament every year since, and the team was the Big 10 regular season champion in 2002.

University of Kentucky
Lexington, KY
(859) 257-1818

The neighboring state school to the south, the University of Kentucky, barely missed making it to the Final Four in 1999, after winning the national championship in 1996 and 1998. People from all over Kentucky drive to watch the Wildcats play basketball at Rupp Arena. The loyal fan base trickles over a little bit into Ohio, although there seems to be a rivalry between fans of Ohio sports teams and those who support Kentucky. Local sports talk show callers often badmouth Kentucky fans and anything said about Kentucky can quickly flood the phone lines with defensive Big Blue supporters. It takes good connections or a friendly scalper to get a ticket to Rupp Arena for a Wildcats game. To try, though, call the number above.

The UK football team also is finding its own again. It revived some national attention when the Wildcats went to the Outback Bowl in Tampa, Florida, in 1998. Tim Couch, the quarterback on the team, was the top draft pick in the NFL draft in 1999.

SOCCER

After several failed attempts at professional soccer in town, a team came to Greater Cincinnati in 1997—the Cincinnati Riverhawks. The team didn't bring the expected attendance and fizzled out. In 2005 a new team was started by a former Northern Kentucky University soccer player. The Cincinnati Kings (www.cincinnatikings.com) are a second division United States Soccer League team that plays home games at Xavier University. The team consists mostly of former Cincinnati-area college soccer players and a few foreign players from England and the Netherlands.

HORSE RACING

Racing fans can find live racing in the Greater Cincinnati area most of the year. With a thoroughbred track on both sides of the river and a harness track in Lebanon, there is no shortage of betting opportunities. And both Turfway Park and River Downs also show races from around the country and beyond through simulcasting on TV screens. Race fans can bet on those from their warm seats in the clubhouses of the tracks.

But for those people who are racing purists, Greater Cincinnati is only two hours away from Louisville, and a parade of cars heads down I-71 each Kentucky Derby weekend. In the spring and fall, area fans also enjoy taking weekend trips to Keeneland race course in Lexington, Kentucky.

Turfway Park
7500 Turfway Road
(just off Interstate 75),
Florence, KY
(859) 647-4711, (800) 815-2808
www.turfway.com

Turfway Park in Northern Kentucky holds meets in September and October and December through the first of April. Turfway likes to think it offers "Major League Horse Racing" and for good reason: It's the 11th most lucrative racetrack in the country, according to *Thoroughbred Times Statistical Review,* with an average daily purse of $175,000. Those statistics by themselves are major league, but the track also hosts special events such as the Lane's End Stakes, one of the richest Triple Crown prep races in the country.

This $500,000 race is run six weeks before the Kentucky Derby and four recent winners—Lil E. Tee, Prairie Bayou, Hansel, and Summer Squall—have gone on to win a Triple Crown race.

Turfway also has another big race day in September with the Kentucky Cup Day of Champions.

The track also houses the area's largest restaurant (reservations are suggested), with a very good menu, tables that overlook the track, and personal TV monitors at each table for close-ups of the race or for watching simulcast races.

A section known as the Race Book is for serious bettors and includes more than 600 TV monitors to keep up with what's going on at other tracks around the country. The track also has a betting guide to help beginners at the track.

Admission is free, although a charge is required for the dining room, with a $7.00 minimum. Parking also is free.

River Downs
6301 Kellogg Avenue, Anderson
(513) 232-8000
www.riverdowns.com

River Downs has been offering Thoroughbred racing for more than 70 years, running every day except Wednesday from mid-April through Labor Day. The best local horses can be seen regularly, but twice a year River Downs draws horses from around the country with the $100,000 Bassinet Stakes and the $200,000 Miller Genuine Draft Cradle Stakes.

The track, which sits along the riverfront and next to Coney Island and Riverbend Music Center, underwent a $14 million renovation a few years ago and now offers an enclosed, air-conditioned grandstand in which lunch and cocktails can be ordered. Since the track runs during the warmer months, most of the track's seating is in an outdoor grandstand, where bettors can see, feel, and smell the action.

The track also offers simulcasts of seven races from Thistledowns in Cleveland and offers a betting card that is a combination of the River Downs and Thistledowns races.

The River Downs Race Book betting area similcasts races from around the country as well as Australia and Hong Kong.

Admission for live racing is $3.00 for the clubhouse and $2.00 for the grandstand. Upper grandstand seating is free. Parking is free in designated areas.

Lebanon Raceway
Ohio Highway 63, Lebanon
(513) 932-4936
www.lebanonraceway.com

Lebanon Raceway is open for harness racing from January through May and October through December. You can watch the trotters from a glass-enclosed, climate-controlled grandstand. Check with the track for post times. To get to the track, take the Lebanon-Franklin (Ohio Highway 123) exit off I-75 and go east about 8 miles. Admission and parking are free.

AUTO RACING

Auto race fans can find plenty of speed at the area's two small oval tracks or its long drag strip. Or the greatest spectacle in racing, the Indianapolis 500, is just two hours away, and hard-core race fans and speed novices alike often spend Memorial Day weekend each year in Indianapolis watching the race.

Florence Speedway
12234 U.S. Highway 42, Florence, KY
(859) 485-7591
www.florencespeedway.com

Florence Speedway in Northern Kentucky offers short-track racing for sprint cars, modifieds, and late-model stock cars. The track is 9 miles west of I-75 on US 42 in Florence and runs early spring to late fall, weather permitting. Ticket prices vary depending on the event.

Kentucky Speedway
Kentucky Highway 35, Sparta, KY
(606) 578-2300, (888) 652-RACE
www.kentuckyspeedway.com

The 1.5-mile track, with seating for more than 66,000 people, cost $152 million and opened in 2000. The track wants to eventually become a NASCAR Winston Cup track. Besides its 65,989 grandstand seats, there are 50 luxury suites, 210 seats in the private club, and more than 2,000 seats in the exterior club. The track itself is a tri-oval, 70 feet wide with a 12-foot shoulder. The back stretch is 1,600 feet long.

Each event has a different ticket cost. For more information, call the above toll-free number. There also is a ticket office in the Drawbridge Villager Premier Hotel in Fort Mitchell.

Edgewater Sports Park
4819 East Miami River Road
(513) 353-4666
www.edgewaterrace.com

Edgewater Sports Park offers local drag racing when the weather permits between February and November. Admission is $5.00 on Friday night and $10.00 Saturday night. Take Interstate 74 to Rybolt Road and go west 2 miles on Harrison Avenue to East Miami River Road.

TENNIS

Tennis Masters Series Cincinnati
250 East Fifth Street, Suite 1610
(513) 651-0303
www.cincytennis.com

During the first two weeks in August, the tennis world turns to Cincinnati for the $3 million Tennis Masters Series tournament. The event is one of nine Tennis Masters tournaments held around the globe.

Being part of such an elite group makes Cincinnati part of a regular stop for many of the world's top players, including Andre Agassi, Roger Federer, Andy Roddick, and Lleyton Hewitt.

The tournament, played at the ATP Center in Mason, is the only non-Grand Slam tournament with three permanent stadiums. These large seating areas make it a great place to watch tennis and are highly popular with the players because more fans can watch them play. More than 170,000 people pack the courts during the weeklong event. Many others also can watch the tournament on national television on a daily basis.

In summer 2004 women began competing again in Cincinnati. The Women's Tennis Association tournament precedes the men's event in July. It is a tier III event, which means it will have a 30-person singles draw and feature 1 of the top 10 players in the world and 3 of the top 20 players.

Much more than tennis goes on during the tournaments. Dozens of corporate hospitality tents and vendors with every type of specialty tennis product available pack the groups around the ATP Tennis Center.

For the men's tournament, individual single-day tickets range from $14 to $36. All seats in the lower section are sold as part of series packages. A weekend package of five sessions, including the finals on Sunday, is $164. A package for the main tournament is $250. The women's series costs from $99 to $149 for the full series.

You also can become one of the 1,000 volunteers who work the tournament each year. Call (513) 651-2872 about volunteering opportunities. The tournament is run by a nonprofit organization, Tennis Cincinnati, and proceeds from the tournament—about $300,000—are donated each year to the Children's Hospital in Cincinnati and the Tennis for City Youth. By the end of 2004, the tournament had donated more than $5.9 million to charity.

The Met Tournament
Lunken Playfield, Beechmont and Wilmer Avenues
(513) 321-1772
For tennis on a smaller scale, the city's annual Met Tennis Tournament is held each summer at Lunken Playfield on the East Side. The tournament determines the city's amateur champions.

OTHER SPORTS EVENTS

Madison Regatta
Ohio River, Madison, IN
(812) 273-0549
www.madisonregatta.com
High-powered hydroplanes gather each summer for the Madison Regatta on the Ohio River. It's like the Indy 500 on water. The race is run in June or early July, weather permitting. An occasional late-spring flood sometimes pushes the date back to later in the summer. General admission tickets are $20 in advance and $25 the weekend of the race, VIP passes are $145 with parking and $125 without, and pit passes are $20.

RELOCATION

Greater Cincinnati makes up eight counties in three states, but the suburbs keep expanding farther away from the center of the city.

New neighborhoods are being created yearly and the housing boom just never seems to stop. The four counties in Ohio (Hamilton, Warren, Butler, and Clermont), three counties in Kentucky (Boone, Campbell, and Kenton), and Dearborn County in Indiana have all seen a lot of new home construction. All green spaces in communities are being filled with new subdivisions and the farmland in outlying counties is quickly being converted into suburbs as well.

Hamilton County Regional Planning Commission said that the metropolitan area had 2 million people in 2004; that's an 8 percent increase from 2000, when the population was 1.85 million.

Most of that growth is in the suburbs. Hamilton County is only expected to have a 1 percent increase between the year 2000 and 2010. But Butler, Clermont, and Warren Counties are expected to have more than a 10 percent increase in population during that same time. And the growth is even higher in Northern Kentucky's Boone County, which is estimated to grow by 16.5 percent between 2000 and 2010. Campbell and Kenton Counties will have a more modest growth with 1.3 percent and 4.6 percent, respectively.

There are some areas of Greater Cincinnati that are expected to experience a decrease in population growth—mostly the urban areas in the central part of the city and Covington and Newport.

One reason for the expected overall population increase is that people are discovering Greater Cincinnati is a good place to raise a family, especially compared to other large cities. That's one reason *Places Rated Almanac* ranked Greater Cincinnati as America's Most Livable City in 1993 and why the suburb of Blue Ash was listed in *50 Fabulous Places to Raise a Family* in 1993 and 1996. It's why so many sports figures who come to play for the Reds or Bengals end up staying here, even though their careers take them to other cities during playing season.

And it's cheaper. The median price of existing homes in Greater Cincinnati is $142,500 compared to $156,900 in Atlanta and $182,900 in Raleigh/Durham, North Carolina. Cincinnati also is below the national median price of homes, which is $184,100.

Greater Cincinnati offers house styles from ultracontemporary to historic and a wide range of neighborhood types. Some river communities have hardly changed since the days of paddle wheelers. Some neighborhoods are like their own small towns. There are golf course communities and enclaves of Victorian and antebellum homes on streets with gas lamps. But best of all, even the most distant suburbs are only 25 minutes from downtown, allowing residents to be near the city but still live in a very rural setting. And none of the neighborhoods are far from community or county parks, churches, or shopping.

Greater Cincinnati also has a wide variety of schools from which to choose, with 50 public school districts and more than 250 private schools. There are schools that place a heavy emphasis on religion and those that place a heavy emphasis on the arts. There are preparatory schools that require students to take Latin, while others have strong vocational programs. There are schools for the deaf and schools for the learning disabled. Wherever you live in Greater Cincinnati, you won't be far from a school that meets your child's needs. See the School and Child Care chapter for more information.

The most important thing to know if

you're looking for a home in Greater Cincinnati is that the East Side and the West Side (Vine Street is the dividing point) are as polar-opposite communities as any one city could have. The West Side is the working-class side, with lunch buckets, bowling balls, old homes handed down for generations, and people who drink beer and grill burgers on the back porch while listening to the Reds on the radio, where everyone went to school with each other and where there's a church and/or bar on just about every street corner. The East Side is the suit-and-tie side, with art galleries and upscale shopping centers, where people drink imported beers on the back deck of their new and expensive homes and where they can afford Bengals tickets and BMWs. People joke about the differences between the two sides of town, but we're all really just one big happy family. Sort of.

A real estate agent should be able to help you find what you are looking for. Many agencies in Greater Cincinnati have computerized listings of all the homes for sale in the area.

If you want to get a head start finding a home, check the homes section in the *Cincinnati Enquirer* or one of the local real estate magazines or TV shows. Many families like to first find an area they would feel comfortable in and then search for a home within that area. The **Greater Cincinnati Relocation Services,** (513) 271-4900, www.gcrs.com, provides fully furnished apartments for a day, week, or month in both Cincinnati and Northern Kentucky if you want to take your time looking. (Also see the Hotels and Motels chapter for furnished apartments and extended-stay options.) See the Senior Services chapter for retirement communities.

Although we couldn't possibly mention all the multitudes of communities that make up Greater Cincinnati—some communities, such as O'Bryonville, in fact, aren't even recognized by city officials—we've tried to give a brief description of most of the larger communities in the area. The Greater Cincinnati and Northern Kentucky maps in the front of this book will help you locate some of these communities.

NEIGHBORHOODS

In the City

There are more than 2,000 residential units downtown, ranging from apartment flats and town houses to luxury condominiums. And more units are being built annually as the city tries to lure life back from the suburbs.

Because of the higher price of real estate, however, living downtown is typically more expensive than in the suburbs. Small, one-bedroom apartments will begin renting for around $600 a month. The new townhomes are expected to sell beginning at around $100,000. Luxury condos start at $350,000 and can go up to $1 million. With Interstates 75, 71, and 471 all intersecting downtown, residents have easy access to other parts of town. There's been talk for several years of building a large grocery store downtown, but for now residents must go outside the area for all but minor grocery shopping. Still, if living in the center of the city is your dream, with arts and entertainment within a short walk, downtown is where you should be.

BETTS-LONGWORTH

One of the up-and-coming areas in the heart of the city is this historic neighborhood in West End on the western edge of downtown. Although most of West End remains lower income, efforts by city officials to create moderate-income housing in the area have created a miniboom of renovations and new construction. Old, historically significant single-family houses with detailed woodwork are being restored, and clusters of single-family row houses were built. The city, which offers financial incentives to both builders and buyers, likes to feature these homes in an annual parade of inner-city homes known as Cityrama. Some of the first homes built in the area—along Central Avenue north of Ninth Street—now sell in the $110,000 range, more than double their original value.

MOUNT ADAMS

As one of Cincinnati's entertainment districts, Mount Adams offers one of the city's unique urban settings. Located just east of downtown, the neighborhood features tall, thin houses and apartment buildings wrapped tightly around an L-shaped hillside that offers views of either downtown or the river. Other homes, all loaded with charm and character, line the neighborhood's narrow, winding streets and steep hills and mix seamlessly with the numerous trendy restaurants, bars, boutiques, and arts and crafts shops. Residents of this lively community have the luxury of being connected to large and beautiful Eden Park, which offers not only lush greenery but also many of the area's arts centers.

Like the rest of the communities in the central part of the city, Mount Adams is in the Cincinnati Public Schools District. Few families live in Mount Adams, though; many of the residents are empty nesters, young business executives who like to walk to work, or people who want to be in the center of the entertainment action. Vidal Sassoon has a home here. His wife is from Greater Cincinnati and his hairstyling products are manufactured by Procter & Gamble. The average home price here is $542,000 but can be more, depending on the quality of the view and the size and condition of the house.

OVER-THE-RHINE

With the largest collection of Italianate buildings in the country, Over-the-Rhine adjoins downtown to the north and is fast becoming one of the city's trendiest places to live. With its incredible 19th-century architecture, the entire Over-the-Rhine area has earned a listing in the

Mount Adams got its name from former president John Quincy Adams, who in November 1843 traveled 1,000 miles for the dedication of the Cincinnati Observatory. The 76-year-old Adams delivered a two-hour history of astronomy. Locals were so impressed they changed the site's name from Mount Ida to Mount Adams.

National Register of Historic Places; in fact, it's the largest National Historic District in the nation. Once the home of thousands of German immigrants, the community is reminiscent of a century-old neighborhood. It earned its name because residents had to cross over the canal that ran through downtown, which reminded them of the Rhine River in their homeland.

Over-the-Rhine is also a local historic district, which means that architectural controls and guidelines can make the restoration of buildings more difficult and slow. Advocates of low-income housing, who fear that a rush of new development would force the poor from their homes, are also slowing the process, but the city is working on creating a zoning plan that would make the community a mixture of lower-income to upper-middle-income homes. Much of the area is currently low-income housing, although artistically renovated apartments and flats in the $70,000 to $250,000 range are slowly becoming available on the eastern side of the neighborhood, especially around Main Street, where coffeehouses, art galleries, and trendy nightclubs abound.

LIBERTY HILL

This area includes small two- and three-bedroom homes built on a tree-lined hillside that offers a unique overlook of downtown and is still within walking distance of the central business district. The homes have become popular with do-it-yourself types, who buy them for as little

CLOSE-UP

All the Wright Moves

Lots of Ohio houses were built in the 1950s. But only a few have the Wright stuff.

The Boulter House is one of five southwest Ohio structures designed by architect Frank Lloyd Wright.

There are a total of three homes in Cincinnati designed by the famed American architect; this one is located at 1 Rawson Woods Drive, in the historic Clifton "Gaslight" District just north of downtown. (The Historic Preservation Association occasionally conducts tours.) Known as the Boulter House, this 2,700-square-foot "Usonian" house, constructed of concrete block and plate glass, includes Philippine mahogany that's stained Taliesin red, one of Wright's signature colors. All the built-in furniture and some freestanding pieces—fitted desks, beds, dressing tables, bookshelves, benches, and cupboards—were also designed by the architect, another trademark effect. Even the drapes are Wright originals.

The home was built for Cedric and Patricia Boulter in 1954, just a few years before the architect's death in 1959. The Boulter family resided there until 1989, when the house was purchased by a University of Cincinnati urban-design professor.

as $50,000 and modernize them, adding large windows and decks to take advantage of the view.

Central Suburbs

MOUNT AUBURN

Immediately north of downtown, Mount Auburn offers an abundance of frame and brick homes built sturdily upon a hillside. Many homes in this older neighborhood, which was one of the area's original hilltop suburbs, have views of downtown and the river. Although some homes have not been properly maintained over the years, their affordability and character are making them popular with do-it-yourselfers and are leading to a rebirth of the community. Homes here average about $91,000 but can quickly increase in value. Mount Auburn is served by the Cincinnati Public Schools system.

WALNUT HILLS

Sitting east of Mount Auburn is one of the area's oldest and most fashionable communities. It is also in the Cincinnati Public Schools system. In the early days this splendid neighborhood was home of the city's "upper crust," and some majestic mansions still remain in the eastern portions of Walnut Hills. Many of the old, elegant buildings, especially those near Eden Park and in east Walnut Hills, have been renovated and are in superb condition.

Overall, the community offers diverse home styles and attracts a wide variety of residents with its ancient trees, wide streets, and large lawns. The average price of a home is $232,000, although some sections of the community, which are targeted

The Boulter House is listed on the National Register of Historic Places. The split-level residence includes a two-story living room, a study with a cantilevered balcony, a suspended staircase, and a guest suite.

Unlike most of Wright's Usonian homes—single-story structures with various wings sitting on flat lots—the Boulter House is two stories high and sits on a sloping half-acre lot. Wright, who championed an organic design that rooted homes in their natural settings, envisioned his Usonian homes (a term derived from the "United States of North America") as affordable housing for a democratic America.

The Boulter House joins two others, in Amberley Village and Indian Hill, as Cincinnati's three Wright homes. A fourth Wright structure, the Meyers Medical Clinic, is located in Dayton, and a fifth, the Westcott apartment building, is found in Springfield.

There are a total of 12 Wright structures in Ohio: three are located in Canton, and the others are spread out in small towns across the northern part of the state.

Wright designed and built almost 500 buildings during his prolific career, though 1 in 5 has been destroyed over the decades through neglect or new development.

by those with lower incomes, offer more modest homes on small lots. In fact, prices can range from as low as $40,000 to millions for a mansion.

CLIFTON

Another of Cincinnati's landmark historic neighborhoods is home to some of the area's oldest upper-class families, University of Cincinnati professors, and many physicians who practice in "Pill Hill," the area's nearby medical community. Clifton, which sits about 10 minutes north of downtown, is dominated by the elegant stone mansions built by 19th-century business barons looking to move away from the masses. But more moderate frame and brick homes also fill the neighborhood's wide streets, most of which are lined with large, stately trees and lit by old-fashioned gas lamps. Modern condominiums and single-family residences can also be found, particularly around the Windings, which is a converted massive, castlelike home that belonged to William Neff, who amassed a great fortune in pork packing. The Windings became a girls' school after Neff left and is now divided into six luxurious condominiums, with newer multilevel homes surrounding it.

Homes here, which are serviced by the Cincinnati Public Schools, average $202,000, although prices can range up to around $650,000. Residents can relax in majestic Mount Storm Park, which was also once a private residence, or Burnet Woods. Or they can visit the community's business district, which includes several trendy restaurants and nightclubs as well as the Esquire Theater, an old-time movie house that brings in art and cultural films that can't be found at the megaplexes.

CORRYVILLE

This neighborhood is dominated by the University of Cincinnati, and many of the large but less stately homes built near the campus in eras past have since been turned into affordable multiunit rentals or fraternity or sorority houses. Many entertainment businesses geared toward the college crowd line sections of Corryville. Still, those who prefer to live with the young, hip crowd can find home bargains that average $62,000 in this neighborhood.

AVONDALE

Avondale is also one of the area's early 1900s "gaslight" communities and is highly popular because of its central location and easy access to the interstates. The community sits between I-71 and I-75 and just south of the Norwood Lateral and offers single- and two-family homes in a wide range of prices and architectural styles. Like some of the other older and larger communities in the area, Avondale has split into two distinct sections: north and south. The northern section has older, well-kept homes and has maintained its European characteristics, quaint charm, and century-old feel. Beautiful landscaping and a strong and active neighborhood association keep the area attractive to families and young professionals. Homes average $125,000, but can range from $45,000 to $600,000, and children attend Cincinnati Public Schools. The southern half of the community, which is anchored by the Cincinnati Zoo and its proximity to the area's medical community, has fallen on harder times, although efforts to rebuild this section of Avondale are ongoing.

NORWOOD

Perhaps the greatest community rebirth story in the area belongs to Norwood, one of the largest independent cities in Greater Cincinnati. Once a center for Greater Cincinnati's industrial and manufacturing businesses, the community suffered when many of its older plants closed their doors in the 1970s and 1980s. Some thought was given to incorporating Norwood into the city of Cincinnati, which surrounds it on all sides. Norwood, though, worked to rebuild itself, and went as one headline put it, "from fizzle to sizzle in eight years." It is now home to an upscale retail center, numerous professional business parks, and hundreds of houses fashionable enough to attract young families looking for nice, modest two- and three-bedroom homes. Although older, most homes have been well maintained by the blue-collar owners who worked at the factories, and they now sell for around $107,000. The 22,000 residents in the 3-square-mile city also benefit from nine city parks, easy access to both I-75 and I-71, and their own school system.

PLEASANT RIDGE

Like Norwood, Pleasant Ridge is a comfortable, old community dating from 1795 and offers many affordable homes. Pleasant Ridge includes several mansions and stately homes that once belonged to Cincinnati's aristocratic families, but the community remains unpretentious and the homes moderately priced, averaging $154,500. First-time buyers find the central location, convenient highway access, neighborhood shopping, and community swimming pool to be major assets.

DEER PARK AND SILVERTON

Just north of Pleasant Ridge along I-71 are these middle-class communities. Both offer modest ranch and Cape Cod-style single-family homes, averaging around $119,000. Many first-time buyers stay on once they discover the conveniences of the business district, the central location, and the down-to-earth benefits and lifestyles each community affords. Deer Park maintains its own school district, while Silverton children attend Cincinnati Public Schools.

BLUE ASH

Farther north along I-71 is Blue Ash, the area's second-largest business district, with nearly 2,000 businesses and a daytime population of more than 70,000. But when the workers leave, fewer than 13,000 people and a great little community remain. As we noted above, Blue Ash was once listed as one of the *50 Fabulous Places to Raise a Family*. And for good reason. The city collects an abundance of taxes from the businesses and then turns around and spends the money on improving the community. The city's community center has an Olympic-size swimming pool, a whale-shaped children's wading pool, and twisting tube slides. A scale replica of Crosley Field, the former home of the Reds, is in the Blue Ash Sport Complex, along with 10 baseball fields and 6 soccer fields. The community common areas are always lush with greenery. The city also offers residents a nature park, amphitheater park, their own golf course—one of the best public courses in the country—and even an airport. There are free special events in the town square and memorial park.

Once people move into Blue Ash they don't want to leave, so finding a home in the 7.7-square-mile city can be difficult. Almost all of the homes are new and contemporary and sell for an average of $225,000. Children attend the highly regarded Sycamore schools. The Raymond Walters College branch of the University of Cincinnati is also located in Blue Ash.

SHARONVILLE

Located along I-75 just south of the Interstate 275 interchange, Sharonville is best known for its business and entertainment district. This community of 13,200 just added a 56,000-square-foot convention center to go with its hotels, retail areas, and nightclubs, making it a frequent destination for travelers. Residents, though, like the area for its quiet subdivisions, which feature many newer multilevel homes that are valued around $150,000. Home prices can range from $50,000 all the way to $200,000, though. Residents take great pride in keeping their homes nicely landscaped.

SPRINGDALE

The focal point of nearby Springdale is its shopping district. Residents with shopping on their minds are thrilled by the abundant retail options in the area, which is anchored by the massive Tri-County Mall and includes hundreds of small and large stores in the smaller plazas and strip malls that branch out along its heavily traveled retail corridor. And, if that's not enough, Cincinnati Mills sits just 5 miles away and Northgate Mall just 10 miles away. A wide mixture of residential properties also can be found within Springdale's 6 square miles. Homes here sell for around $132,000 and are popular with families, who are attracted by the town's proximity to the I-75 and I-275 interchange, its location within the Princeton School District, and its community center, which offers a pool and tennis courts to the community's 10,700 residents.

GLENDALE

Southeast of Springdale is the tiny village of Glendale, one of the area's most distinctive neighborhoods. Glendale was the first planned community in the area and one of the first in America. Laid out in 1851, it is today the only national landmark community in Ohio.

Glendale looks like it still belongs in the 19th century. This splendid community has worked hard at maintaining its parklike setting, with gas streetlamps on winding lanes and distinctly elegant homes with stone walls or white rail fences surrounding the large, beautifully landscaped lawns. Even new homes are built on larger lots and are required to keep within the architectural parameters set by the community's original plan. Many of the homes are older—in fact, some of the original homes are still standing and sell for around $283,000, which tends to be higher than comparable homes in other neighborhoods. Prices generally start around $100,000 and extend to $800,000. But residents benefit from Princeton schools and the community's beauty.

ARLINGTON HEIGHTS AND LINCOLN HEIGHTS

Found farther south on I-75, both of these are lower-income communities. Both neighborhoods have a wide range of single- and two-family homes, most of which are offered as rental properties. Currently only 30 percent of the homes in Lincoln Heights are owned by their occupants, although there are concerted efforts to increase home ownership through grants, discounts, guidance from a business specializing in home rehabbing, and the coordination of the Lincoln Heights Housing Committee. Homes can be purchased for around $50,000 in Lincoln Heights and about $78,000 in Arlington Heights.

EVENDALE, READING, AND LOCKLAND

These middle-class communities all sit just off I-75, offering residents easy access to the rest of the area. These towns were once part of a burgeoning industrial valley and feature many well-built brick and frame houses that were home to generations of hard-working families who earned livings in the local industries. Those houses are now attracting young families who are looking for affordable first homes.

Evendale, which is best known as the location of GE Aircraft Engines, placed very strict limitations on new development from the early 1950s until the 1980s, creating a demand for land from which it is now benefiting. Sixty percent of the homes in Evendale are less than 8 years old, while the remaining 40 percent are 25 to 35 years old. Prices range from $100,000 to $1 million. The average selling price is about $289,000.

The Reading area was once farmland but is now being developed with spacious new homes that average around $116,000. Prices are bolstered by the town's numerous historic homes, located particularly in the northern section known as Reading Heights. Reading has its own school system.

Lockland, which has suffered the most from the loss of industry, has sturdy homes in the $75,000 price range. Lockland residents are very proud of their schools, which they fought hard to maintain through the down times.

AMBERLEY VILLAGE

Amberley Village takes its name from a village in England and is one of the area's most distinctive and prestigious communities. Carefully planned by its citizens and government, Amberley works to preserve its rural, wooded characteristics and spacious atmosphere. Just 3,200 residents live within its 5 square miles. Professionals and executives are attracted to this quiet and peaceful neighborhood located 12 miles north of downtown. Many of the homes in this elegant community were built on at least one acre of land and are secluded behind tall hardwoods and well-established foliage, but you can also find contemporary, custom-built estates. Rollman Estates subdivision was a recent Homearama site (see the Annual Events chapter). Home sales here average $408,000, but can reach the $1 million mark.

BOND HILL, PADDOCK HILLS, AND ROSELAWN

Some of the most centrally located communities in the area, these three are anchored by their proximity to Cincinnati Gardens. Much of Bond Hill and Paddock Hills is middle- to lower-income and offers a wide range of single- and two-family homes and apartments. Bond Hill's homes cost an average of $79,000; Paddock Hills homes cost an average of $164,000. The Old Bond Hill section of Bond Hill, though, still features Victorian and Queen Anne-style homes set in wooded areas. Roselawn is a well-kept community, featuring many English and early American styles of homes on beautifully landscaped lawns that sell for an average of $103,000.

ST. BERNARD AND ELMWOOD PLACE

St. Bernard and Elmwood Place, which are located along the western edge of I-75, were originally developed for families working at nearby businesses such as P&G's Ivorydale and Nu-Maid margarine, in the heart of industrial Mill Creek Valley. Homes in St. Bernard average $105,000 and in Elmwood Place average $57,000 and are still popular among those working in the area.

WINTON PLACE AND WINTON HILLS

Of all the communities in Greater Cincinnati, neighboring Winton Place and Winton Hills comprise the largest land area, but only a small portion of it is for homes. Just 2,600 residents live in Winton Place, while just 6,000 reside in Winton Hills. The average house in Winton Place is about $77,000. The communities offer a little of everything—residences, industry, commercial businesses—although much of the area is taken up by the ELDA landfill, which was closed and capped in 1998. The massive and elegant Spring Grove Cemetery also rests within the two communities, lending beauty to the neighborhood.

CARTHAGE AND HARTWELL

These are the northernmost communities within the city limits of Cincinnati and offer homes in a wide variety of sizes and architectural styles. Much of the development of these two communities came in the years following World War II, when families built homes to be near the local industries. The area still maintains a somewhat commercial and industrial nature, although it has some rural aspects. For instance, squeezed between the homes and businesses in Carthage, where houses average $70,000, is the Hamilton County Fairgrounds. Homes in Hartwell, which offers some hilly areas with spectacular views of the residential valley below, average $92,500.

Many, but not all, suburban communities give you credit for local income taxes you pay where you work. Check with your city hall to make sure you don't have to pay taxes in both places.

WYOMING

This historic village traces its roots back to 1861, and more than 300 homes in this splendid community are listed on the National Register of Historic Places. Comprising just 2.5 square miles, Wyoming is one of the most distinctive neighborhoods in the area, with old Victorian homes—some with carriage houses—sitting back off the wide streets edged with ancient trees. The area's 8,300 residents take great pride in the community's school system, which is one of the best in the state, and neighbors frequently get together for civic club activities and community-wide social events. Home prices average $298,000; Wyoming is easily accessible from I-75 and the Ronald Reagan Highway.

FINNEYTOWN

Finneytown is an attractive, family-oriented neighborhood of 13,000 residents who maintain an independent school system and are active in the affairs of the community. A mixture of homes can be found here, most dating back 30 to 35 years and ranging from a modest $55,000 to $260,000. The average is $140,000. A central location and proximity to I-75 and the Ronald Reagan Highway make it easy for residents to get to all other parts of town.

MOUNT AIRY

Mount Airy is a quiet neighborhood with smaller homes, many of which were built in the late 1940s. The homes are still in good condition and are moderately priced, although newer, higher-priced homes in the area have bumped the average price of a house to $136,000. Mount Airy, which sits on one of the highest hills in the area, includes massive Mount Airy Forest, where residents and people from all over the city come to hike through its hills and towering hardwoods.

COLLEGE HILL AND NORTH COLLEGE HILL

College Hill and neighboring North College Hill trace their roots back to the days when two colleges were located on their hilltop, which was then far enough away from the city to allow for proper studying. These now-densely populated areas have many older homes in a variety of sizes as well as many pleasant apartments. Young families are drawn here by the abundance of attractive and sturdy starter homes. Homes in North College Hill tend to be a bit smaller and sit on smaller lots; the average price is $92,000. College Hill homes average $108,000. Residents also find the proximity to Interstates 75 and 74 attractive, as well as the busy business district and the community school district.

GREENHILLS AND FOREST PARK

Energetic residents of these communities love their proximity to Winton Woods, the 2,400-acre county park that offers numerous recreational opportunities, including golf, fishing, and baseball fields. For those residents who prefer shopping to sports, Cincinnati Mills is nearby. Both communities also offer their residents historical places to live.

Greenhills was created in the 1930s as one of 25 experimental residential developments around the country established by the federal government as a means of easing problems brought on by the Great Depression and to study the relatively new concept of community planning and design. The government based its plans for the 1.5-square-mile community on the garden cities of England. Although most of the homes are of a size more typical of the 1930s, they are still in good shape, averaging $128,000, and are highly attractive to young couples searching for ideal starter homes.

Forest Park also began as a planned community and has since developed into the third-largest city in Hamilton County. Houses on the classic older tree-lined streets average $127,500, but homes can be found to match every taste and budget. In addition to having Winton Woods in its midst, Forest Park also offers its 18,600 residents several public parks and recreational facilities within its 5.5 square miles.

Residents of both communities are served by the Winton Hills School District, the culmination of a merger in the early 1980s of the Forest Park and Greenhills School Districts.

Eastern Suburbs

HYDE PARK

One of the city's oldest and most prestigious neighborhoods is Hyde Park. Most of the homes in this lovely community are older and full of character and personality, with leaded and stained-glass windows and doors, intricate woodwork, and lush landscaping. Massive, castlelike stone mansions from eras past sit back on secluded hillsides. But houses of every size and style can be found here, and even the simplest of frame houses seem to exude a bit more character in Hyde Park. Homes tend to be higher priced than in other areas, averaging $368,000 but with some selling in the millions of dollars.

Along with churches, day-care centers, and shopping areas, Hyde Park offers some of the area's most interesting specialty shops and trendy restaurants. Residents frequently browse the town square's stores on warm days, stop by Graeter's for ice cream, and sit on tree-shaded park benches near the gently flowing fountain. They are also surrounded by two of the area's largest parks, Alms Park and Ault Park, which are packed on summer days by young families and health enthusiasts.

MOUNT LOOKOUT

Neighboring Mount Lookout is similar to Hyde Park with a fashionable town square and many large, old homes. Singles, young professionals, and even families find the many remarkable older homes and row-house condominiums in this area attractive. The average home price is $309,500. Mount Lookout's town square offers a glimpse of the diversity, style, and tastes of the community, with everything from an old-fashioned deli and grocery shop that has been in the same location for decades, to trendy coffeehouses, used-book stores, and even a movie theater/ restaurant where moviegoers are shown current films while being served dinner at tables. This is where you'll find one of the area's favorite "dives," Zip's, which serves arguably the best hamburger and fries in the city.

Mount Lookout also has the distinction of being the home to the area's only observatory. The Cincinnati Observatory Center was relocated from Mount Adams in order to give astronomers a clearer view of the heavens. (For information on the observatory, see the Attractions and Kidstuff chapters.)

COLUMBIA-TUSCULUM

Down fashionable Delta Avenue toward the river, Columbia-Tusculum was once a steamboat-manufacturing town. This riverside community is one of the oldest in Greater Cincinnati and is well known for its renewal and restoration of the old, sturdy frame houses from the steamboat era. Some of the homes are even decorated with steamboat themes to match the area's history. Young couples love the Victorian homes—"painted ladies," as they are known because of their colorful exteriors. Not all of the homes in the community have been renovated, though, so houses average around $161,500, although beautifully built bargains in need of some work can be found for less than that. A few contemporary homes and modern row-house condominiums, some of which offer river views, can also be found.

MOUNT WASHINGTON

The focal point of Mount Washington, located on the easternmost fringe of the city of Cincinnati, is its massive water tower. Sitting on the highest point on the East Side, the tower, with its revolving beacon, can be seen from all parts of Greater Cincinnati. During the Christmas season, rows of lights are strung down its smooth sides, creating a beautiful sight. Beechmont Avenue, one of three main thoroughfares into downtown Cincinnati from the East Side, slices its way through Mount Washington and its business district, which is lined with old-fashioned stores and modern new retail establishments. Many small apartment buildings and large complexes can be found along Beechmont, which is served by all of the major East Side bus routes.

On the narrow streets off of Beechmont sits an assortment of homes, many built in the 1940s after World War II and occupied by the same families for several decades. Homes here can be found for around $145,000, a price that is increasing regularly as young couples seeking to be near desirable but more expensive Anderson are moving in. Children here are served by Cincinnati Public Schools and can play Frisbee or swing in nearby Stanbery Park.

ANDERSON

This is one of the fastest-growing communities in the area, thanks to good schools, access to interstates and major thoroughfares, proximity to major retail areas, availability of large tracts of land, the presence of Mercy Hospital Anderson, and a commitment by township leaders not to sacrifice the town's natural beauty for the sake of more development. In an effort to preserve its rural, wooded character and prevent the desire for development from spinning out of control, township officials set aside more than 200 acres of land as a natural setting. This unique foresight has made Anderson one of the most beautiful communities in which to live. Homes and even entire subdivisions seem to be carved into scenic hills and virgin woodlands rather than being built on them.

Anderson's 38 square miles were mostly modest farmland as little as 15 years ago. Most of the homes here are new, but they come in a wide variety of architectural styles, prices, and sizes. The average sale price is $256,500 but custom homes are being built regularly and sell for $500,000 and more.

Many of the 42,000 residents in this family-oriented community regularly get together to enjoy the activities offered throughout the year, such as free family movies shown on a large screen at two local parks during the summer and an annual festival put on by the Anderson Park District. The Forest Hills School system, one of the best in the state, serves the Anderson area. Residents also enjoy the township's eight local parks and three upscale golf courses.

NEWTOWN

Nearby Newtown offers the benefits of small-town living with the benefits of a larger community. Founded in the early 1700s, Newtown remains in many ways a quaint little village, with a gas station and a popular ice-cream stand on the village's main corner. Within its 3 square miles are many small, older homes, but there's also an abundance of large estate homes, most of which are in the sprawling Ivy Hills subdivision. Houses average about $91,500. The village's schoolhouse is still standing, but children now attend the highly regarded Forest Hills Schools.

BATAVIA AND AMELIA

Greater Cincinnati's growth has overtaken these two rural communities in Clermont County; they are becoming increasingly popular because of their remoteness but easy accessibility from I-275. Batavia's history can be traced back to the 1830s when it was a gold-mining town, albeit a short-lived one. Still, the historic old village survived and now offers residents the beauty of a small town in the country that is not too far removed from civilization. The town's 2,000 residents live in a mixture of historic homes—some nearly 200 years old—in the heart of town and in newer homes with acreage built in subdivisions on the town's fringes. Homes cost an average of $169,000. Residents are served by the growing West Clermont School District and enjoy the availability of the University of Cincinnati's Clermont County branch.

Amelia too is a small town that has become a popular destination for those looking to get away from city life. Many young families have moved into the town's 3 square miles, buying older historic homes or newer multilevel houses in recently built subdivisions. The average house costs about $151,000.

UNION TOWNSHIP

Residents of Union Township are attracted by its proximity to local interstates, its mix of historic homes and new home subdivisions, and abundant shopping options. The township includes the ever-growing Eastgate community, Glen Este, Mount Carmel, and Withamsville. Homes average $173,000. Much of the growth in these areas has occurred over the last 10 years in conjunction with the development of the Eastgate shopping area, a booming retail mecca anchored by Eastgate Mall and including hundreds of large discount stores, specialty shops, restaurants, and hotels. Residents of Union Township are also blessed with the presence of the Cincinnati Nature Center, one of the most serene sites in all of Greater Cincinnati.

MILFORD

Milford traces its roots back to 1788 when early settlers fell in love with the area, which sits snuggled between the Little

Miami River and East Fork River. It still remains a somewhat rural community, but with easy access to I-275 and U.S. Highway 50, it has become popular with those who like the seclusion of country living. New homes and condominiums have created a variety of housing options for the 6,100 residents, with properties available for around $169,000. Milford is an exempted village, outside the governing influences of the county, and as a result has its own school system and its own governing council made up of community leaders who have protected the small-town feel by maintaining three municipal parks and a preserve along the Little Miami River for hiking and picnicking.

INDIAN HILL

Indian Hill is unquestionably the most upscale community in Greater Cincinnati. This onetime farming community still has working dairy farms, but they share the village's 20 square miles with $3 million estates. Homes here are second to none in Greater Cincinnati, and many sit back from the roads on rolling, heavily wooded hillsides. Houses with their own tennis courts and pools and even their own horse stables are not uncommon. Horse-crossing signs are posted throughout the community, and it is not unusual to see residents horseback riding along its narrow, winding roads.

Indian Hill's 5,000 residents take great pride in living here and work hard at preserving their community's rural and secluded character. Most actively participate in the village's activities and operations. Although a full-time village manager handles day-to-day operations, most decisions are made by an elected council of community residents. Seven garden clubs help keep the common areas beautifully landscaped year-round, and Indian Hill Exempted Village Schools, one of the best school systems in the state, always has an abundance of parent volunteers.

Indian Hill is home to many of Greater Cincinnati's wealthiest families, and it shows in the average sale price of residences, which is around $1.2 million. Homes in the village, though, can range from $350,000 to $4 million and more. *Worth* magazine, a national financial publication, ranked Indian Hill as No. 102 on its list of America's 300 Richest Towns in 1996—no surprise to most Cincinnatians.

TERRACE PARK

The scenic Little Miami River splits Indian Hill and neighboring Terrace Park, which is reminiscent of a New England village, with its stately trees, colonial homes, and neatly divided streets that are named after famous colleges. The village covers just 1.5 square miles and is one of the most sought-after communities in which to live. Offering a strong historical flavor, old-world charm, and highly regarded Mariemont schools, many of the 2,100 residents don't want to leave Terrace Park once they locate here. Homes range from $90,000 to $500,000-plus. The average sale price is about $464,000.

MARIEMONT

Mariemont is another quiet, peaceful community whose homes are in high demand. This tiny, 1-square-mile community, which is one of the area's earliest planned communities, is listed on the National Register of Historic Places. It is an English-style village, complete with an all-English Tudor town square, and filled with colonial and Georgian-style homes. Most homes here are priced around $324,000, but this community of 3,100 has become so popular that housing is very difficult to find. Although small, the village is served by its own school system, which is one of the best in the state.

OAKLEY AND MADISONVILLE

The communities are becoming highly popular areas with young couples and singles because of their affordable housing options and their proximity to restaurants, shopping, and some of the trendiest parts of town. These suburban communities

Looking for a home loan? Consider one of the smaller banking operations in town such as Mt. Washington Savings & Loan. Such cottage industries rarely, if ever, sell their mortgages to a bigger bank. Plus, many of these S&Ls don't charge private mortgage insurance (PMI).

remain mostly middle to lower income, but many attractive homes with charming features such as hardwood floors and front porches can be found for moderate prices. Housing in Madisonville is priced around $70,000, while in Oakley, which has experienced a great jump in housing values, home sales average $171,500.

MADEIRA

Another small but popular community is Madeira. The community, which covers just 3.7 square miles, tries hard to maintain its small, country-town atmosphere. Its focal points are a tiny railroad depot, from the days when trains regularly stopped here, and a busy business district, which houses cozy restaurants and interesting specialty shops. Madeira is very much a family-oriented community that takes great pride in its school system. The area's 9,000 residents enjoy a mixture of home styles and sizes (most of which sell for around $230,000) and take an active part in protecting the quality of the community by strictly controlling development, virtually prohibiting commercial projects, and restricting exterior signs—including real estate SOLD signs.

KENWOOD

The pulse of this affluent community just north of Madeira is its chic retail area, which features Sycamore Plaza and the Kenwood Towne Centre, the area's most upscale and most popular mall. Kenwood features much more than shopping though, with mature trees, well-landscaped lawns, and homes of all styles and sizes, all of which seem to spill over with charm and personality. It is easily accessible via I-71 and is a favorite with families in the middle- and upper-middle-income brackets. Homes here typically sell for around $241,000. Schoolchildren are served by one of four school districts—Madeira, Indian Hill, Deer Park, or Cincinnati Public Schools—depending on which section of the community they live in.

MONTGOMERY

Neighboring Montgomery, which stretches north to I-275, offers homes in a spacious environment that the community's residents have worked hard to preserve through high standards and strict zoning requirements. The 9,800 residents who live within its 5 square miles enjoy a wide variety of home sizes and architectural styles and feel good about sending their children to Sycamore schools. Homes in this upscale family community can be found for around $403,000. Montgomery's city square, known as Olde Montgomery, sets the standards with its English Tudor buildings and 19th-century-village feel, and the flavor and quality carry over to the rest of the community. Olde Montgomery offers residents some of the most interesting upscale shops and restaurants, including the original Montgomery Inn restaurant (see the Restaurants chapter).

LOVELAND

Loveland is a mecca for active residents, with the luxury of having within its borders one of the area's busiest and most beautiful exercise areas. The Loveland Bike Path stretches for 22 miles along the shoreline of the Little Miami River, offering runners, walkers, bikers, and in-line skaters a beautifully scenic setting in which to exercise. This community of 6,000, which sits just northeast of the I-275 and I-71 interchange, is one of Greater Cincinnati's fastest growing, and it takes great pride in its green spaces and its location next to the scenic Little Miami River. Housing here comes in all price ranges and sizes—

there's even a castle (see the Chateau LaRoche listing in the Attractions chapter)—but homes generally can be purchased for around $198,000. Primary and secondary schoolchildren are served by the town's own school system.

NEW RICHMOND AND MOSCOW

Along the riverfront on the East Side are these two original river towns. New Richmond is in many ways still reminiscent of an old river town, with historic buildings and old woolen mills that still operate. Park benches underneath large shady trees line the riverbanks along the village's downtown business district. And the 2,500 residents have carefully planned the community's growth, accepting new developments while making sure not to upset its image as a "uniquely historic river town." Home prices range from $45,000 all the way to $500,000; they average $147,000. New Richmond residents are quite proud of their independence. The village is an exempted village, meaning it is exempt from county influences, both political and educational. Its school system, New Richmond Exempted Village Schools, is one of the richest in the state. Residents here are never far from recreational opportunities, with eight municipal parks in the town.

Moscow is perhaps best known as the location of the Zimmer Power Plant, which was originally designed to be nuclear powered but was converted at great expense to coal power before the first atom was split.

Western Suburbs

PRICE HILL

Immediately west of downtown is this historic community, one of the first hillside communities settled as the city's affluent citizens fled from the smoky downtown basin to the scenic hills. Like its eastern counterpart, Mount Adams, J-shaped Price Hill offers great views of the river and downtown, and many of its distinctive 19th-century houses are now being renovated after years of wear. Today Price Hill is home to 40,000 residents, mostly middle class and many of whom have had homes in the community through several generations and can trace their roots back to the time when 60 percent of the neighborhood was made up of German-Catholic or Irish-Catholic families. Many brick, frame, and Victorian homes with large front yards and large front porches are available for around $63,000. Price Hill, which is served by Cincinnati Public Schools, is fully developed, so there are no new homes in the area.

Mount Echo Park sits on Price Hill's southeastern hilltop and offers splendid views of the river, Northern Kentucky, and downtown Cincinnati.

COVEDALE

A few newer condominium developments can be found here, in one of the smallest communities in town, but one that also offers Victorian homes. Homes within Covedale's 73 acres average about $112,000.

DELHI

The community of Delhi is well known for its gardens. For some unknown reason, more commercial greenhouses are located in Delhi (pronounced by locals as Dell-high) than any other section of Cincinnati, and many of the homes in this bedroom community have lovely, well-kept flower gardens. The houses here tend to be older, with mature trees and foliage. In addition, there are several higher-income subdivisions on the western side, some offering wonderful vistas of the river and Northern Kentucky. Homes here sell for an average of around $150,000 and are served by the Oak Hills School District. The 30,000 residents within Delhi's 10 square miles also work hard at protecting their community, and have stuck together strongly in their battles with the airport

Getting a new puppy to go along with your new home? Ohio law requires that dogs three months and older be licensed. Cincinnati law also requires dogs to be on a leash if they are outside of your yard. And a pooper-scooper law is enforced locally, meaning you have to immediately clean up any calling cards your pooch leaves in your neighbor's yard or the local park.

about overhead flight patterns. Delhi also has the distinction of being the home of the College of Mount St. Joseph, one of the oldest colleges in the area.

CAMP WASHINGTON AND FAIRMOUNT

North of downtown and to the west of I-75, Camp Washington is home of some of the city's oldest industrial businesses, The average home price is $47,000. Fairmount has many less expensive homes and two of the city's low-income housing developments. The average home price is $30,000.

CHEVIOT AND WESTWOOD

Nearby Cheviot and Westwood are older neighborhoods dominated by Cincinnati's German-Catholic heritage. Residents of Cheviot take great care of their splendid little community through an independent municipal government that is filled by elected officials from within the community. Founded in 1818, this simple, conservative neighborhood of just 1 square mile sits high on the western hillside and offers its 9,600 residents a small-town atmosphere with mature trees and well-preserved colonial-style homes that are available for around $100,000. Neighboring Westwood has a wide variety of distinctive older homes dating from the late 1800s that average around $109,000, as well as some more expensive multilevel homes built in newer subdivisions. The streets in Westwood are clean and secluded, and shopping, churches, and day care are close by, as is Mount Airy Forest, Cincinnati's largest and most beautiful wooded area. Both communities are served by Cincinnati Public Schools.

WESTERN HILLS

Western Hills is well known as the area's baseball breeding ground, with 10 Western Hills High School graduates who played in the major leagues, including Pete Rose, Don Zimmer, and Russ Nixon. But residents like the 12.5-square-mile community for the charm of its older homes, its community offerings such as two parks and a swimming pool, and its strong German heritage, which is still evident today. The area's 30,000 residents live in affordable homes that cover a variety of architectural styles and sizes, with many of the homes sitting on larger lots. The average sale price is $172,000. The Western Hills section of Glenway Avenue serves as the main retail district for the entire West Side. The community is served by Cincinnati Public Schools, but parts of Western Hills extend outside Cincinnati city limits and into Miami, Delhi, and Green Townships, which can have an impact on taxes.

WHITE OAK AND MONFORT HEIGHTS

These two are growing rural communities, where the rolling hills that just a few years ago were farmland have been converted to upscale subdivisions with multilevel homes priced at around $150,000 to $350,000. However, the average price of a home is about $195,000 in Monfort Heights and $175,000 in White Oak. Both of these peaceful communities are served by Northwest Schools and Oak Hills Schools. The west side of the communities adjoins parts of Mount Airy Forest. Monfort Heights has just 8,100 residents within its 6 square miles, while White Oak is a shade smaller, with 7,400 residents on 6 square miles.

COLERAIN

Colerain Avenue, one of the largest and busiest retail districts in Greater Cincinnati, is the heart of Colerain. The district is anchored by massive Northgate Mall and contains hundreds of specialty stores spread throughout dozens of strip malls, plazas, and freestanding buildings for several miles in both directions. Colerain, which is located to the west of I-275 at U.S. Highway 27, is the largest geographic township in Ohio at 45 square miles, although most of the residential development is south of I-275.

On the east side of the township, homes average around $133,000. On the west side, homes average $184,000. Although a few larger estates and many farms are located on the gently rolling hills north of I-275, that area has yet to be mass-developed by home builders, but it's just a matter of time. Northwest Schools serves Colerain's 57,000 residents. It must be noted that Colerain is the repository for much of Greater Cincinnati's trash. The Rumpke landfill, or "Mount Rumpke" as it is known, is the highest man-made peak in Ohio, and it hasn't even reached capacity yet, although it is expected to in the not-too-distant future.

HARRISON

Harrison sits as close to Indiana as possible while still remaining in Ohio. Many people find this area highly attractive because of the affordability of homes, some of which are brand-new and others that date from the 1800s, and the great care the community takes in preserving its rural, wooded character. Some parts of the community, which is served by Southwest Schools, have minimum acreage requirements for homes. The city maintains four recreational playfields and two pools. Just 12,000 people live within Harrison's 12.5 square miles. The average house sells for $178,500.

OTHER WEST SIDE COMMUNITIES

Like Cincinnati itself, many smaller river towns were founded in the area's early developmental period and are now West Side communities of Greater Cincinnati. These include Sedamsville, Riverside, Sayler Park, Fernbank, Addyston, and, perhaps most notably, North Bend. North Bend is the final resting place of President William Henry Harrison and the birthplace of President Benjamin Harrison. Although some new estate homes with wonderful vistas of the Ohio River are being built in these communities, most remain small towns with older homes, many dating from the 1800s. All of the communities are served by Three Rivers Schools, and are near Shawnee Lookout Park. Home prices range from $40,000 to $160,000.

Northern Suburbs

FAIRFIELD

Fairfield is a medium-size town of 44,000 residents that Greater Cincinnati expanded out to and is now connected to, but like other local independent communities, it's very much its own entity. Many residents of Greater Cincinnati are attracted to this city, which is 18 miles north of downtown, and its population has more than doubled in the past 10 years. New apartments and single-family homes that average around $166,000 have been built within its 20.5 square miles to meet the demand. Billed as the "City of Opportunity," Fairfield gives its residents an opportunity to get involved, and they usually do, with 20 community organizations keeping the city clean, well run, and well cared for. The city has four parks and is close to Mercy Hospital Fairfield. Residents can find most everything they want at the hundreds of restaurants, businesses, retail stores, and hotels that line both sides of Ohio Highway 4, which slices through the core of the city. Fairfield has its own city schools, which are highly

Greater Cincinnati is made up of many municipalities and counties in three states. The most important thing to know is that it is not long-distance to call most of Greater Cincinnati, but you must use the area codes to call across state lines. Area codes are 513 for Ohio, 859 for Kentucky, and 812 for Indiana.

respected and have recently expanded to meet the growth.

WEST CHESTER

About 15 miles north of downtown, north of the I-75 and I-275 interchange, is West Chester, one of the fastest-growing and most prestigious areas in Greater Cincinnati. The soft, rolling hills that were farms just 15 years ago now feature some of the most luxurious estate home developments in the area. Home prices in this distinctive community average $233,500, although homes can be found near the $1 million range. This 35-square-mile area has become so popular and grown so fast, its highly regarded Lakota School District had to build two new high schools and turn the old high school into a junior high in order to meet the demand.

MASON

Mason grew by thousands of homes in the 1990s and now is one of the biggest northern suburbs. Residents and town officials, though, have kept the secluded, 14-square-mile community from becoming overdeveloped by maintaining more than 190 acres for parkland, four parks, two lakes, baseball and soccer fields, and hiking trails. The area's 15,000 residents send their children to Mason Schools, and thrill-seeking residents love having Kings Island in their backyard. The average house in the community costs $305,000.

Northeastern Suburbs

SYMMES

Symmes lies northeast of the I-71 and I-275 interchange. The area's 13,000 residents have seen an explosion of growth in recent years, and the township's 9.7 square miles are now 70 percent developed. Still, large, upscale single-family homes continue to be built here, and it has been the site of several recent Homearama shows. Estate homes, town homes, and condos are all under construction, as are retail and commercial developments. School options can be puzzling, as three school districts—Sycamore, Indian Hill, and Loveland—service different parts of the township. All three school systems, though, are outstanding, so residents can't lose. Older homes can be found for as little as $35,500, while newer ones can cost as much as $600,000. Most, though, sell for $406,000.

LANDEN

Within Symmes is Landen, a planned community designed in 1975 that is a mecca for nature lovers, as it is centered around a heavily wooded 100-acre park that includes an 8-acre lake and a network of hiking and biking trails. The homes in this remarkable community are mostly custom built and located in the Kings School District. Home prices here average $184,000 but can top $500,000.

LEBANON

Lebanon is an old city, founded in 1796, that is being rediscovered as the suburbs push outward. Residents love the rustic, small-town charm, and its century-old main street, which is packed with dozens of antiques stores and the highly popular Golden Lamb restaurant and hotel (see the Restaurants and Hotels and Motels chapters). The city even has its own train, adding to its 19th-century atmosphere. Distinctly elegant homes from the 1800s can be found here, as well as some newer homes, most priced around $194,000. Although located 29 miles north of downtown, residents find the area very accessible off I-71. About 11,000 people make their home here, including astronaut Neil Armstrong.

Northern Kentucky

It used to be that homes in Northern Kentucky were more affordable, and in recent years many new people have flocked to the area. But the housing prices have increased steadily over the last few years. Now the biggest thing Northern Kentucky has to offer is space. There are still some large tracts of land undeveloped in the outer parts of the suburbs.

COVINGTON, KY

Covington is by far the largest city in Northern Kentucky and, with a population of 41,000, is the third-largest city in the state behind Louisville and Lexington. This river city is located directly across the Ohio from downtown Cincinnati and is connected by the historic Roebling Suspension Bridge. Towering office buildings and luxurious hotels that carry the Cincinnati business environment across the river distinguish Covington's downtown area from all others in Northern Kentucky and give it the look and feel of a true city.

Covington has all of the markings of a city its size too, with businesses, retail districts, and nightlife spots. Its residential communities are one of its key attractions, though. Historic Victorian homes can be found throughout the older sections of the city, where rehabbing of the stylish homes, with their century-old charm, is common. Many of the homes are on the National Register of Historic Places, including most of those in the Historic Riverside Drive District, which is filled with antebellum southern mansions, 130-year-old row houses, and Civil War–era homes. New upscale condominium complexes are also being built in Covington, particularly on its hillsides, which have fantastic views of Covington's river basin and downtown Cincinnati. The MainStrasse area in Covington is also very popular because of its quaint setting, its German village feel, and a retail district that offers numerous specialty shops and cozy restaurants (see the Attractions and Shopping chapters).

Being such a large city, Covington has its share of middle-income and poorer areas as well, so homes average around $84,000 but can range in price from $30,000 all the way up to $400,000. Families here are served by Covington schools. The city's west side includes Devou Park, a 704-acre playground with an 18-hole golf course, picnic area, and one of the area's best overlooks of downtown Cincinnati and downtown Covington. Several other golf courses are located in the southern parts of Covington. St. Elizabeth Medical Center North is also located in the city.

NEWPORT, KY

Large mansions can be found in neighboring Newport, another landmark historic neighborhood that is directly across the river from downtown Cincinnati. Three bridges connect Newport to Cincinnati, so residents on the north side of the river flow into Newport to enjoy all its entertainment spots. Newport's reputation as the area's "Sin City," garnered in the 1930s when it was more popular than Las Vegas for gambling and prostitution, is waning as a result of the community's efforts over the last 20 years to clean itself up and turn itself around. Besides the aquarium and Newport on the Levee, the entertainment hotspots center around "Riverboat Row," a lineup of floating and land-based restaurants and bars. Diners flock to Riverboat Row year-round to grab a bite to eat, watch the boaters on the river, and catch the spectacular vistas of the Cincinnati skyline.

Some of the city's many residential neighborhoods feature remarkable Victorian, Queen Anne, Italianate, and colonial revival homes that are more than 100 years old. The Mansion Hill and Gateway districts of the city are both listed in the National Register of Historic Places. Most residents, though, live in smaller homes that can range in price from $50,000 all the way to $200,000. The average house sells for $118,000. Newport has its own school system.

BELLEVUE, KY

Adjacent to Newport is Bellevue, a small town whose roots date from 1870. This charming river town of 6,300 is centered around its old-fashioned business district, which runs right along the river and includes a generations-old pizza parlor and a candy store where they still make all of the sweets by hand. A number of homes in this 1-square-mile town date from the early 19th century, particularly in the fashionable Bonnie Leslie area, which offers well-maintained brick houses with large trees and river and city views. Homes here, most of which are 50 and 60 years old, average $84,500. Residents of Bellevue are particularly proud of their schools, displaying banners that read TIGER TOWN (in honor of their sports teams) on streetlights around town.

DAYTON, KY

Dayton, next in the string of small river towns, also offers old-time charm, with numerous patio-style homes, some of them located on a hilltop that offers wonderful river views. Dayton is one of the area's older communities, and its 6,000 residents are a combination of lifelong residents and new families. The average house sells for $64,500. Some families live in apartments that were built in the town's old high school.

FORT THOMAS, KY

One of the most exclusive communities in Northern Kentucky is Fort Thomas, which sits on the hill above the Ohio River and was a longtime military outpost. Known as the "City of Beautiful Homes," Fort Thomas offers houses in a wide variety of sizes and architectural styles, all well maintained with mature trees and plush landscaping. Many have panoramic vistas of the river and the eastern side of Cincinnati. Homes here, some of which are more than 120 years old, are priced around $168,000, and it's not unusual to find a $60,000 two-bedroom home sharing a narrow, winding street with a large $200,000 home. Nor is it unusual for a home to sell before it's even listed; word of mouth is often enough to attract a buyer. The 15,000 residents of this quiet, peaceful community are quite proud of their schools, which are some of the most competitive in sports in the state, and are comforted by the presence of St. Luke Hospital East located in the city.

HIGHLAND HEIGHTS, KY

Northern Kentucky University is the focal point of Highland Heights, which is located at the southern end of I–471. The community is the third-fastest-growing community in the tristate and has grown by 50 percent in the last six years, and the smaller, 1960s Cape Cods and ranch-style homes that sell for around $60,000 are now being mixed with newer multilevel homes that range up to $180,000. The average home sells for $106,000. Many condominiums are being built in the area, as well as a large number of retail establishments along US 27, which cuts through the heart of the city. The city's civic center provides residents with a wide variety of activities.

WILDER AND SOUTHGATE, KY

Nearby Wilder was found to be the fastest-growing community in Northern Kentucky in the most recent census. More than 2,500 residents now live in the tiny community along the Licking River because of the boom in condominium and apartment communities. Most homes sell for around $115,000. Southgate is also becoming an attractive area, particularly with first-time buyers because older, more traditional homes are available for moderate prices. The average is $95,000.

ALEXANDRIA, KY

Twelve miles south of downtown on US 27 in Campbell County is Alexandria, a growing city of 7,100 residents. Established in 1856, Alexandria is becoming one of the area's fastest-growing communities, thanks to the recently completed AA Highway connecting Alexandria (the only town in the Greater Cincinnati area the highway touches) to the East Coast. East of Alexandria, large tracts of land can still be bought, and a small-town atmosphere is still pervasive. Homes here are available from $60,000 to $400,000, but with all the new home construction, the average home costs $163,000. Alexandria is also home of the Campbell County Schools District, which serves most of the county's residents, as well as A.J. Jolly Park, where residents can enjoy golf, baseball, swimming, camping, and fishing.

COLD SPRING, KY

Area residents are also discovering Cold Spring, a tiny community of 3,400 along US 27 that is sprouting new subdivisions and condominiums. Homes can range from $70,000 to $250,000. The average home costs about $151,500.

FLORENCE, KY

Florence, located just off I-75, has quickly become the second-largest community in Northern Kentucky, with nearly 20,000 young individuals and large families attracted to its proximity to the Cincinnati/Northern Kentucky International Airport, businesses, and the largest retail district south of the river. The Florence Mall is the heart of the retail district, and it is surrounded by hundreds of smaller and medium-size stores and large, big-box users such as Sam's, Wal-Mart, and Target. Almost all of the homes in this area have been built within the past 15 years and are available for around $156,000. Homes range from $70,000 to $400,000, and numerous condominiums and apartments are also available. Florence is in the Boone County School District.

To advertise the new mall in Florence, Kentucky, the red and white water tower was painted with the words FLORENCE MALL. But because it was on government property and couldn't advertise a private enterprise, the M was repainted to a Y-apostrophe. Now the city wears the Southern saying FLORENCE Y'ALL as a badge of honor.

UNION, KY

Union, just southwest of Florence, has also grown by leaps and bounds. It is the sixth-fastest-growing city in Greater Cincinnati. Subdivisions of homes are going up all over the former farm country, and retail stores are following suit. The average house now costs $260,000. Union is served by the Boone County School District and has its own high school—Ryle High School.

ERLANGER, KY

Erlanger is also one of Northern Kentucky's largest cities, as well as one of its oldest. Sitting along I-75, this community of 17,000 has its own independent school system and one of the largest movie theaters south of the river, the Showcase. Many older homes are spread around town and sell for an average of $132,500.

CRESTVIEW HILLS, KY

Crestview Hills, on the south side of I-275, is a smaller, more rural, but certainly not sleepy community. Crestview Hills Mall is located within the community's 3 square miles, as is Thomas More College, one of the most exclusive private colleges in the area. The neighborhood's 2,500 residents live in a mixture of older homes with mature trees and newer single-family homes in subdivisions, with an average price of about $198,000.

EDGEWOOD, KY

Many young families are attracted to Edgewood, a relatively new community at the bottom of the I-275 circle freeway. The community's 8,500 residents enjoy newer homes built on spacious lots. The average home sells for about $219,000, but homes that sell for as much as $1 million can be found here. St. Elizabeth South Hospital is located within the community's 4 square miles.

FORT MITCHELL, KY

Fort Mitchell is a highly desirable neighborhood in Northern Kentucky. Located off I-75, it has many well-cared-for older homes priced around $202,000 as well as estate communities with custom-built houses. Children attend Beechwood Independent Schools, which are some of the best in the state. Fort Mitchell also offers a wide variety of dining and entertainment options and is the home of the Drawbridge Villager Premier Hotel, a highly popular hotel, convention, and entertainment complex that features several restaurants, nightclubs, and more.

LAKESIDE PARK, KY

Next to Fort Mitchell is small—just 2 square miles—but quite tranquil Lakeside Park, with its six lakes spread out among 14 residential developments. This lovely neighborhood offers its 3,000 residents classic older homes as well as some newer homes that have been built to match the classic tradition of the rest of the community. Most homes are priced around $173,000. Residents are quite active in keeping the community beautiful through a civic association and even hand out awards to residents who do the most to beautify their property.

VILLA HILLS, KY

Villa Hills was rated the area's most livable neighborhood in a study by *Cincinnati Magazine* in 1994 and has adopted the slogan "A special place to live." This is easy to understand, as the small community, which overlooks the river on the western side of Kenton County, provides its 7,400 residents with distinctive new homes, wonderful views of the Ohio River, and one of the lowest crime rates in the area. It is also a favorite neighborhood for sports stars and other personalities. Home prices here have shot up to around $232,000.

FORT WRIGHT, PARK HILLS, AND CRESCENT SPRINGS, KY

Fort Wright and Park Hills are small communities, but they feature beautiful, large traditional homes (valued at around $140,000 to $190,000) on wooded hillsides, and they adjoin Devou Park. Crescent Springs, to the south, has smaller traditional homes that are attracting many younger families and some new construction. More than 3,600 residents now live in this small town along I-75, whose history dates from the 1850s. The average house in Crescent Springs costs about $162,500.

OTHER KENTUCKY COMMUNITIES

Many other smaller, older towns can be found along the river in Northern Kentucky: Bromley, Ludlow, Silver Grove, and Melbourne. Homes in these communities tend to be older, and the towns are truly small towns, with families who have lived there for several generations.

Southeastern Indiana

LAWRENCEBURG AND AURORA, IN

Southeastern Indiana boasts a number of small river towns, including Lawrenceburg and Aurora. Lawrenceburg's 4.5 square miles are being converted into a major tourist attraction because of the opening of a gambling casino on its riverfront (see the River Fun chapter). The 4,000 residents get 3 million visitors to the casino each year. Homes in Dearborn County, which includes Lawrenceburg and nearby Aurora, average $183,000.

HIDDEN VALLEY LAKE, IN

Just outside of Lawrenceburg is Hidden Valley Lake, a planned residential development built around a 150-acre lake and an 18-hole golf course. It's becoming an upscale bedroom community for business executives who seek to get away from the city.

OTHER INDIANA COMMUNITIES

Brookville Lake, Greendale, and Bright, are attractive communities for those who don't mind the commute because they all offer a lot of land for development, outstanding property values, and a very rural setting. Homes here generally start around $80,000 and range upward to $250,000.

GOLF COURSE COMMUNITIES

Golf and Greater Cincinnati seem to be intertwined, although we aren't sure why. (If you doubt it, see the Golf chapter and count the number of courses for yourself.) Realizing this—and it didn't take long—developers began building whole communities around golf courses. The risk of a broken window from an errant tee shot is easily outweighed by being able to walk out the back door and onto the back nine or, as is the case with some die-hard duffers, the justification for owning your own golf cart.

Wynnburne Park, now Western Hills Country Club, was the area's first country club community, chartered in 1912 and platted in the 1920s. The developer boasted it was "only a mashie shot away" from the golf course. Many courses followed, and many more will. The area still has enough large tracts of inexpensive farmland available that developers can afford to build both homes and a golf course.

If living on the links is what you're looking for, ask your real estate agent to give you a tour of one of the following subdivisions: Ivy Hills in Newtown; Coldstream in Anderson; the Oasis in Loveland; Wildwood in Fairfield; the Golf Center at Kings Island; the Heritage Club, Fairway at Pine Run, Eagle View, and Crooked Tree in Mason; Beckett Ridge and Wetherington in West Chester; Walden Pond in Indian Springs; Shaker Run in Lebanon; Deer Run in Miami; Pebble Creek in Colerain; the Traditions in Burlington, Kentucky; Triple Crown in Union, Kentucky; and Hidden Valley Lake in Dearborn County, Indiana.

All these communities offer upper-income single-family residential properties, and a few have multifamily residential, condominium, and landominium properties.

LIVING ON THE WATER

The Ohio River may not be the Carolina coast, but it is water. And for those who don't like to be landlocked or who like to sleep on a real waterbed, the river is the only place to reside. Twelve harbors along the river have slips that allow for full-time residence on houseboats. The slips, with individual electrical and water hookups, can be rented by the season or by the month. Prices vary depending on the harbor. Of course, if you live on a houseboat and don't like where you are, it's a heck of a lot easier to pack up and move.

Four Seasons Marina, 4609 Kellogg Avenue, (513) 321-3300, and Watertown Yacht Club, 1301 Fourth Avenue, Dayton, Kentucky, (859) 261-8800, are two marinas that offer shelter from the noise and traffic of the river as well as electrical hookups, fuel, and a parking lot for those excursions inland.

BUILDERS AND DEVELOPERS

Greater Cincinnati has an abundance of home builders and developers who can provide everything from small, modular homes to custom homes that begin at $1 million.

If you're into that rustic atmosphere, you can choose among several log-home builders who offer different styles: hand-cut, hand-hewn logs, machine cut and smoothed logs, and on. . . . If you're looking for a custom-built home, a good place to see the work of several builders at the same time is the annual Homearama show in Cincinnati or the HomeFest show in Northern Kentucky. Builders and developers purchase lots in a newly developed, very upscale subdivision and try to one-up each other with amenities, luxury, landscaping, and decorating. See the June section of the Annual Events chapter for more details.

If you have questions about a certain builder or developer, try checking with the Home Builders Association of Greater Cincinnati, (513) 851-6300, or the Northern Kentucky Home Builders' Association at (859) 331-9500.

Many new subdivisions will have a model home or two and an on-site agent who can tell you all about the community and help you purchase a home there. Be aware, though, that on-site agents work for the builder or the real estate company that is marketing the community, although by law they must treat you fairly and honestly. However, if you want someone to represent your best interests, get your own real estate agent.

REAL ESTATE AGENCIES

In addition to the major franchises, Greater Cincinnati has dozens of small or independently owned real estate agencies—far too many to list here. The following list is an overview of the area's real estate offices.

Bischoff Realty Inc.
3620 Glenmore Avenue, Cheviot
(513) 662-1990
This small but rapidly growing real estate company has carved out a niche for itself by becoming an expert on homes on the west side of Greater Cincinnati.

Century 21 Garner Properties
5285 Madison, Independence, KY
(859) 525-6777
www.northernkentuckyhomes.com
This independently owned real estate broker has offices in Florence, Independence, and Falmouth. It has a relocation department and has been in business since 1980.

Century 21 Thacker & Associates
4851 Wunnenburg Way, West Chester
(513) 874-1264
The company has a relocation department in its office. Its UIP Referral Network links it to the thousands of offices in the Century 21 chain nationwide, making relocation easier.

Coldwell Banker West Shell
8040 Hosbrook Road, Kenwood
(513) 794-9494

3260 West Bourne Drive, Western Hills
(513) 922-9400
www.cbws.com
Coldwell Banker became the dominant real estate company in Greater Cincinnati in 1997 when it bought West Shell Realtors, which had been the area's largest firm. With the consolidation of offices and shifting of agents now complete, CBWS has 19 offices spread throughout Greater Cincinnati. The national presence allows for easy communication with people relocating from another city with a Coldwell Banker office. It also offers mortgage services.

Coletta & Associates
3917 Edwards Road, Hyde Park
(513) 871-1600, (800) 718-1611
www.colettarealtors.com
This small, boutique agency focuses on the area's East Side. It has become a popular alternative to the large agencies.

Comey & Shepherd Inc.
6901 Wooster Pike, Mariemont
(513) 561-5800
www.comey.com

Comey & Shepherd has a network of about 200 sales associates who offer citywide service. Its *Home Tour* television program is a visual tour of local homes that airs on the local cable network. Comey also offers PropertySource, (513) 271-HOME, a telephone listing service that gives detailed descriptions of each of its listings. Relocation services, an in-house mortgage assistance group, and a home warranty program are available. In addition to its Mariemont headquarters, Comey & Shepherd has offices in Anderson, Hyde Park, Montgomery, Clifton, Wyoming, and West Chester.

First Agency Group
1419 Alexandria Pike, Fort Thomas, KY
(859) 441-0877

24 Whitney Drive, Milford
(513) 831-3744
www.realtymarketplaceonline.com

First Agency Group has been serving area home buyers and sellers since 1979 with auctions and consulting.

Jim Huff Realty Inc.
334 Beechwood Road, Fort Mitchell, KY
(859) 344-4616, (800) 313-4833
www.huff.com

Jim Huff Realty, the third-largest real estate company in Greater Cincinnati, has been a dominant force in the real estate industry for more than 25 years. Locally owned and operated, Huff Realty has rapidly grown to include more than 400 sales associates and 13 offices serving the entire tristate area.

Jordan Realtors
7658 Montgomery Road, Kenwood
(513) 791-0281

3960 Montgomery Road, Norwood
(513) 531-4740
www.jordanrealtors.com

This small agency was founded in 1966 and concentrates on the East Side. Still family owned, the offices' 30 agents offer "professional services with a personal touch." Although its two offices are on the same road, they are far enough apart to allow agents to cover a wide portion of the East Side. The agency also offers marketing analysis, relocation services, and home appraisals.

RE/MAX
Multiple locations
www.remax.com

RE/MAX is a well-known national real estate agency with 24 independently owned and operated businesses throughout Greater Cincinnati. Being part of a nationwide organization allows for communication with thousands of offices around the country, making relocating to or from Greater Cincinnati easier.

Sibcy Cline Realtors
8040 Montgomery Road, Kenwood
(513) 984-4010
www.sibcycline.com

Sibcy Cline is the largest independently owned real estate company in Greater Cincinnati with more than 1,200 Realtors and 23 sales offices in the area. The agency offers other services to help in the buying and selling process, including a guaranteed sales program, relocation and auction departments, and a financial services and mortgage department. The agency publishes its own *Listings* magazine monthly and offers a ListNet site on the World Wide Web that shows interior as well as exterior pictures of listed homes. It also has the Listing Line, a telephone listing service that provides a complete description of all listings.

Star One Realtors
6875 Fountains Boulevard, West Chester
(513) 779-5900
www.starone.com

Star One is one of the area's fastest-growing real estate companies. It has expanded to nine offices throughout the area and gained quite a reputation for service, quickly becoming the third-largest agency in terms of sales and transactions. In 2001 the agency completed more than 5,000 transactions. The offices cover all of Greater Cincinnati; Star One has a relocation division and a commercial division.

REAL ESTATE PUBLICATIONS

Numerous real estate magazines list area properties for sale. Most of them contain listings of a variety of real estate agencies (those who pay for space), although some larger agencies print their own magazines with just their own listings. Almost all these publications are free and can be picked up at area grocery and convenience stores. In addition, several TV shows feature available properties (check local TV listings), and real estate agents Mike Rose and Michael Bastian host a radio program on various real estate topics, including listings, on WKRC (550 AM) each Saturday between 7:00 and 8:00 P.M.

Coldwell Banker Real Estate Guide

Coldwell Banker publishes this magazine of its own local listings monthly. It's available as an insert in the *Cincinnati Enquirer* as well as at local grocery and convenience stores.

For Sale by Owner

This free publication, which comes out every other month, previews homes throughout the area that owners choose to put up for sale without the help of a real estate agent.

Greater Cincinnati Relocation Guide

Real estate agencies publish this glossy magazine in cooperation with the Greater Cincinnati Chamber of Commerce. It includes some community profiles, relocation information, feature articles, and general information about the city. The guide is available through most real estate agencies or can be purchased at some bookstores for $8.00.

Harmon Homes

Harmon publishes one magazine for Ohio and Indiana and another for Northern Kentucky. Both include listings for condominiums and land and come out twice a month.

Listings

Sibcy Cline Realtors' magazine provides information on homes listed by the agency.

Real Estate Week

The *Cincinnati Enquirer* offers a special advertising biweekly publication with listings and articles on home maintenance and care, moving, and other related topics. It's available at all Kroger grocery stores.

The Real Estate Book

This glossy publication gives clear, all-color looks at hundreds of homes for sale around the area.

APARTMENT COMMUNITIES

Greater Cincinnati has an abundance of apartment and rental communities for those who are looking for a place to live without buying. While there are far too many to list here, we've offered a sampling of what's available in different areas. Many apartment communities are clustered with other apartment communities, so if one isn't exactly to your liking, there may be more options nearby. The average apartment rental in the city is $572 per month.

You can pick up a copy of *Greater Cincinnati & Northern Kentucky Apartment Rental Guide* for more information on the numerous apartment communities around Greater Cincinnati. Temporary and corporate housing are included in this colorful, pocket-size guide, which comes out every two months. *Apartments for Rent* also features apartment-complex ads and is published every two weeks. Both publications are free and available at racks in grocery and convenience stores. You can also check www.cincirents.com for homes and apartments.

Aspen Village
2703 Erlene Drive, Western Hills
(888) 307-0665
Aspen Village is two communities, both offering spacious one- and two-bedroom apartments at an affordable price, starting at $350 a month. The communities share three outdoor pools, three tennis courts, a Nautilus fitness center, and playground. Leases as short as three months are available for apartments that include fireplaces, and heat is paid for in some units. Pets less than 20 pounds are welcome. The communities are located off Queen City Avenue near I-75, on major bus routes.

Charleston of Blue Ash
4870 Hunt Road, Blue Ash
(513) 793-4090
The Charleston is located in the heart of "fabulous" Blue Ash, just a short walk from Memorial Park and the city's quaint shopping district. One-, two-, and three-bedroom units are available from $815 to $1,085 a month. Some two-bedroom units have two full bathrooms. Other units have wraparound balconies, built-in bookshelves, washer/dryer hookups, gas heat, and oversize soaking bathtubs. Pets are welcome. Furnished corporate housing is also available in the complex.

Eastgate Woods
4412 Eastwood Drive, Batavia
(513) 752-2727
These English Tudor buildings are in a beautifully landscaped and heavily wooded area adjacent to the popular Eastgate shopping area. Each building has a private entry and apartments have private balconies and extra storage space. Clubhouse facilities, a swimming pool, 24-hour emergency service, and short-term leases are available. Seven different floor plans are available, with one-bedroom units starting at $320 and two-bedroom units at $405.

Fourth & Plum Apartments
231 West Fourth Street
(513) 241-7272
www.4thandplum.com
These loft-style and warehouse apartments are unique and in the middle of downtown. The 193 units include studios, one-bedroom, and two-bedroom apartments. The prices range from $540 to $895 a month. Amenities include a rooftop pool that is heated, a fitness facility, and parking.

Harper's Point
8713 Harperpoint Drive, Symmes
(513) 489-1160
Located in one of the most desirable areas of town, Harper's Point offers one-, two-, and three-bedroom town homes and apartments with a rough-hewn look with cedar shakes, loft spaces, woodburning fireplaces, plush landscaping, and duck-filled ponds. Units, which range from $640 to $1,240 a month, include vaulted ceilings, washer/dryer hookups, and extra storage space. The clubhouse has a pub for parties. Short-term leases are available on furnished units, and pets up to 40 pounds are welcome. Residents are near the popular Shops at Harper's Point and get a discount at the Club at Harper's Point.

Highland Ridge
1400 Highland Ridge Boulevard
Highland Heights, KY
(859) 781-2900
This community near Northern Kentucky University has one- and two-bedroom units with three distinctive floor plans, wood-burning fireplaces, washer/dryer included, and extra storage. A fitness center and clubhouse are available to residents, as well as a pool, sundeck, and tanning beds. Pets are welcome and short-term leases are available.

One Lytle Place
621 East Mehring Way
(513) 621-7578
One Lytle Place puts residents right along the riverfront in the heart of downtown and offers spectacular views. The 26-story

building has 11 different spacious floor plans for one- and two-bedroom units, starting at $860 a month. The highly secured building also has a rooftop observation deck, concierge, covered parking, hot tub and sauna, heated pool, and exercise and fitness center. Pets are welcome. Bicentennial Commons park is at the building's back door. A free access shuttle is available to drive residents around downtown or to nearby shopping areas.

Paddock Club
8000 Preakness Drive, Florence, KY
(859) 282-7444
Paddock Club is right in the middle of one of the busiest areas in Greater Cincinnati—just west of the Florence Mall and its surrounding retail district and just south of Turfway Park racetrack. The one-, two-, and three-bedroom apartments start at $599 a month and offer decorator wall coverings, washer/dryer hookups, gas log fireplaces, and garages with automatic door openers. Community areas include a clubhouse, hot tubs, sauna, tanning beds, indoor racquetball courts, weight room, and swimming pool. Pets are welcome.

Panorama
2375 Montana Avenue, Western Hills
(513) 481-1234
Located in the middle of a large apartment area on Montana Avenue in Westwood, Panorama stands out with its luxurious amenities. All apartments have large balconies, central air, and ceiling fans, and heat and hot water are paid for. Two-bedroom units have fireplaces and three-bedroom apartments have washer/dryer hookups. Panorama is on a major bus route convenient to I-74, I-75, and I-275. You can bring your cat.

Village of Coldstream
996 Meadowland Drive, Anderson
(513) 474-4907
www.coldstreamapts.com
Coldstream is located in a parklike setting in the highly desirable area of Anderson. It offers one-, two-, and three-bedroom apartments and town homes. The brick or stone colonial buildings, built by upscale specialists Towne Properties, have spacious floor plans, large walk-in closets, extra storage space, and washer/dryer hookups. Heat is paid for. Plenty of social activities take place at the clubhouse, tennis courts, volleyball courts, fitness center, and swimming pool. Pets up to 20 pounds are welcome. Units start at $580 a month and go to $1,025 a month.

Williamsburg of Cincinnati
200 West Galbraith Road, Hartwell
(513) 948-2300
Williamsburg of Cincinnati is one of the largest and nicest apartment communities in Greater Cincinnati, offering studio, one-, two-, and three-bedroom units. Within the heavily wooded 110-acre community just 1 mile west of I-75, renters find three designer swimming pools for socializing or cooling off, a fitness center, sand volleyball court, tennis courts, guest rooms for visitors, and washer/dryer hookups in some units. Some units offer fireplaces, built-in bookcases, and carports or garages. One-bedroom lofts include spiral staircases. Short-term leases are available. Dry cleaning is available through the concierge service, and there is a restaurant on site. Most large dogs are welcome. Studio units rent for $515 a month, with one-bedroom units at $590, two-bedroom units at $690, and three-bedroom units at $970 a month.

Woodridge
3977 Woodridge Boulevard, Fairfield
(513) 874-1988
Woodridge is a combined community of four smaller communities—Woodridge Crossing, Woodridge Knoll, Woodridge Point, and Woodridge Glen—that sit in a wooded setting in Fairfield, off OH 4 near the I-275 exit. Large two-bedroom apartments begin at $709 a month and include cathedral ceilings, private balconies, controlled building access, mini and vertical

blinds on the windows, and vanities in the master bathroom. Each building has laundry facilities, or washer/dryer hookups are available. Woodridge is near Tri-County Mall and Cincinnati Mills restaurants, and bus routes. The communities are operated by Associated Land Management Group.

UTILITY SERVICES

Gas and Electric

Duke Energy
139 East Fourth Street
(513) 421-9500, (513) 287-2400 TDD-TTY
www.cinergy.com
Duke Energy operates the gas and electric utilities for Greater Cincinnati north of the river and Southeastern Indiana. To report gas leak emergencies, call (513) 651-4466. To report a power outage, call (513) 651-4182.

Union Light Heat & Power Co.
107 Brent Spence Square, Covington, KY
(859) 421-9500
In Northern Kentucky, Duke Energy does business as ULH&P. For electrical problems, call (513) 651-4182 or (800) 543-5599. For gas leaks or other problems, call (513) 651-4466 or (800) 634-4300.

Water

Boone County (KY), (859) 586-6155
Butler County, (513) 887-3061
Cincinnati, (513) 591-7700
Clermont County, (513) 732-7970
Northern Kentucky Water Service District, (859) 578-9898
Warren County, (513) 925-1377

Sanitation and Garbage Removal

Municipalities in the Greater Cincinnati area contract with individual companies to collect trash. Residents are billed through user fees or taxes. If you live in an unincorporated part of a county, though, you may well be on your own. Generally, the sanitation and garbage removal in Greater Cincinnati is handled by Rumpke, (513) 742-2900; CSI (513) 771-4200; or Waste Management of Greater Cincinnati, (800) 343-6047.

Sewers

Butler County Sewer Department, (513) 887-3061
Clermont County, (513) 732-7970
Cincinnati/Hamilton County Metropolitan Sewer District, (513) 352-4900 days, (513) 244-5500 nights/weekends
Warren County Water Department, (513) 925-1377

Telephone

Cincinnati Bell
201 East Fourth Street
(513) 565-2210, (513) 397-9611 TDD-TTY
Cincinnati Bell is the primary telephone service in Greater Cincinnati. It offers a multitude of additional services beyond basic phone service. For phone repair, call 611, or (513) 566-1511 from a cellular phone or (513) 397-9611 for TDD-TTY hearing impaired service.

Cable TV

See the Media chapter for complete information about cable TV.

SENIOR SERVICES

The older adult population of the tristate area has its share of community activities and programs. Nearly one-quarter of the area's population is older than 50, making older adults Greater Cincinnati's largest population group. In recent years assisted-living facilities have been added in all areas of the tristate and more are being planned. To keep up with issues facing older adults, there are free publications you can pick up for at libraries, senior centers, and at some stores.

Those age 60 and older qualify for a Golden Buckeye Card, a special discount card honored by thousands of restaurants, retailers, and attraction sites across Ohio that entitles holders to reduced prices and special offers. Call (800) 422-1976 for a card. Those age 62 and older qualify for a Golden Age/Golden Eagle passport that offers free entry to national parks and 50 percent discounts on user fees. Call (513) 684-3262 for a $10 card.

Many golf courses offer senior rates during nonpeak hours. Some restaurants have special senior menus. Those 65 and older can ride the Metro for reduced fares. Banks have special accounts for people who are age 50 and older.

SERVICES

The Alzheimer's Association
644 Linn Street, Suite 1026
(513) 721-4284

The Alzheimer's Association provides relatives and friends of those afflicted with Alzheimer's disease with information, support-group meetings, and telephone counseling.

Arthritis Foundation,
Ohio River Valley Chapter
7124 Miami Avenue
(513) 271-4545

This chapter of the Arthritis Foundation is a local branch of the national organization and provides information and support for those with arthritis. The chapter offers self-help classes and support groups and also teaches aquatic classes at various locations in the community.

Cincinnati Area Senior Services
644 Linn Street, Suite 1020
(513) 721-4330
www.senserv.com

The staff here has compiled a comprehensive list of services for those age 60 and older. Many of the services, including a senior transportation service, make it possible for less-active adults to continue living at home. The program also operates five senior centers and meal sites throughout the city. Some of the other services include the Guardianship Assistance Program (an adult protective service), medical transportation, Meals on Wheels, an adult daytime care center, a health-testing program, and Alzheimer's disease information.

Clermont Senior Services
2085 Front Wheel Drive, Batavia
(513) 724-1255
www.clermontseniors.com

Clermont Senior Services offers a complete listing of information, resources, and services such as social and recreational activities, nutrition information, residential facilities, and medical programs for Clermont County residents age 60 and older.

Council on Aging, Southwestern Ohio
175 Tri County Parkway, Sharonville
(513) 721-1025
www.help4seniors.org

The statewide program helps those age 60 and older with the special problems and concerns associated with the senior years.

Eldercare Locator
644 Linn Street
(800) 677-1116
This central referral service of the Area Agencies on Aging helps families access nationwide information about health, homemaking, nutrition, transportation, legal matters, and other community-based services especially for older adults.

Elderlife at Deaconess Hospital
311 Straight Street at Clifton Avenue
(513) 559-2340
A free health and wellness program from Deaconess Hospital, Elderlife offers discounts on prescription drugs and vision, hearing, and dental care, in addition to transportation, physician referrals, and seminars for seniors. It also has Lifeline, a 24-hour emergency response system.

Medicare Hotline
(800) 282-0530
Nationwide Insurance Company provides this phone line to answer questions about Medicare.

Ohio Department of Aging
50 West Broad Street, ninth floor
Columbus
(614) 466-5500
www.goldenbuckeye.com
This agency has information and distributes Golden Buckeye discount cards.

Pro Seniors Inc.
7162 Reading Road, Suite 1150
(513) 345-4160, (800) 488-6070
www.proseniors.org
Older persons with legal and long-term-care problems can get assistance at this United Way agency. Pro Seniors also offers legal advice, referrals, and representation and helps find nursing homes and home care for those in need. It publishes a free guide on selecting a home-care provider and investigates nursing-home complaints.

Senior Care Preferred
3200 Burnett Avenue, Clifton
(513) 585-6462
A membership program that provides discounts and education for seniors. It is affiliated with the Health Alliance, a group of hospitals in Cincinnati.

Senior Services of Northern Kentucky Inc.
1032 Madison Avenue, Covington, KY
(859) 491-0522
www.seniorservicesnky.com
Senior Services is a clearinghouse of information, resources, and services for seniors living in Northern Kentucky. Topics it can provide information on include social and recreational activities, nutrition, residential facilities, and meeting medical needs. It also operates 12 senior centers throughout the area and a volunteer program.

Social Security Administration
550 Main Street, Room 2000

1050 Hospital Drive, Batavia

6553 Winford Avenue, Hamilton

15 East Sunnybrook Drive, Cincinnati

8275 Youell Street, Florence, KY
(800) 772-1213
www.socialsecurity.gov
These offices handle all inquiries regarding Social Security. All five offices share the same telephone number.

Visiting Nurse Association
2400 Reading Road
(513) 345-8080

2220 Grandview Drive, Fort Mitchell, KY
(859) 344-1661
www.thevna.org
Hospice, respite, and private-duty nurses

WMKV radio station is for senior citizens. Found at 89.3 FM on your dial, the station plays music from the '40s and '50s and nothing from after 1956. The station also has live call-in shows about caregiving and medical issues pertaining to seniors. The station is located at Maple Knoll Village and uses a lot of senior volunteers.

are available through the Visiting Nurse Association, which offers short-term care to relieve family caregivers. This United Way agency offers sliding fees and hourly rates.

RESIDENCES

Choosing a place to live is never easy. The Council on Aging Housing Coordinator, 644 Linn Street, Suite 1100, Queensgate, (513) 721-7670, provides information on housing options for older adults, including congregate living, subsidized apartments, shared housing, and home-matching opportunities. A separate Passport Program may pay for in-home nursing care and supportive services for low-income persons.

The Cincinnati Metropolitan Housing Authority, (513) 721-4580, is the city's low-income housing unit. It offers low-income senior housing at Marquette Manor, 1999 Sutter Avenue, Fairmont, and 11 other communities within the city.

The following area facilities offer a variety of independent and assisted-living options.

Asbury Woods Retirement Villa
1149 Asbury Road, Anderson
(513) 231-1446
The villa is an independent-living facility with 50 one- and two-bedroom apartments. A villa van shuttles residents to preplanned social activities. A caterer serves meals once a week.

Aspen Amber Park Retirement Community
3801 East Galbraith Road, Deer Park
(513) 745-7600
www.aspenretirement.com
Independent, assisted-living, and temporary stays are available here. Each apartment has a balcony or terrace and full kitchen (or three meals a day and snacks are available). Housekeeping services, laundry and linen services, transportation, and a full activity program are available. All utilities except telephone are included. Respite stays are available.

Atria Highland Crossing
400 Farrell Drive, Fort Wright, KY
(859) 341-0777
Residents have the choice of assisted or independent living in studios and one- and two-bedroom units, with weekly housekeeping, two hot meals daily, and 24-hour emergency assistance.

Baptist Village of Northern Kentucky
3000 Riggs Avenue, Erlanger, KY
(859) 727-4448
Baptist Village residents have an option of independent or assisted living in cottages or apartments on 21 scenic acres. The village has 108 units and 100 nursing-home beds. Security is available 24 hours a day, as well as emergency services, planned activities, and housekeeping. Subsidized assisted living also is available. The community is developing condominium units.

Batavia Nursing and Convalescent Inn
4000 Golden Age Drive, Batavia
(513) 732-6500
This facility welcomes Medicare and Medicaid residents. Short-term care is available, along with physical and occupational therapy, skilled nursing, and independent living. The center has 216 beds.

Bayley Place
990 Bayley Place Drive, Delhi
(513) 347-5500
Residents here receive independent assistance in daily living tailored to their needs. Bayley Place's motto is "for those who don't need nursing care, but who would appreciate an occasional helping hand." In/outpatient physical, occupational, and speech therapy are available. Tiered pricing and short-term respite care are available, and no admission fee is required. It is sponsored by the Sisters of Charity. It also offers the Terrace apartments for seniors with memory impairment.

Beechknoll Community
6550 Hamilton Avenue, North College Hill
(513) 522-5516

Beechknoll offers both assisted and independent living in studio or one-bedroom apartments. Three meals are served daily. An Alzheimer's disease and dementia unit is available. The facility is Medicare and Medicaid approved. Respite stays are welcome.

Berkeley Square
100 Berkeley Drive, Hamilton
(513) 856-8600
Berkeley is a 64-acre community with more than 110 cottage homes, ranging from one bedroom to three bedrooms. Thirty-seven apartments are also available for rent, and there are 50-bed nursing and 25-unit assisted-living wings. The community includes a town hall, swimming pool, whirlpool, exercise room, library, craft room, gift shop, and dining room. Up to three meals served a day. The acreage also has five stocked fishing lakes.

Brookwood Retirement Community
12100 Reed Hartman Highway, Blue Ash
(513) 605-2000
Residents here receive independent- and assisted-living, skilled, or intermediate nursing care. Brookwood is approved for Medicare and has 101 Medicaid beds. Respite stays are available. The community has 254 units with apartments and single rooms.

Chesterwood Village
8073 Tylersville Road, West Chester
(513) 777-1400
This community offers cottages for independent living. Each two-bedroom, two-bath cottage has an attached garage and an enclosed porch. A central clubhouse for parties and community-sponsored social events is located on the grounds. Other services include transportation and activities. Emergency response systems are monitored. A 74-bed nursing home opened in 1999 and assisted-living units opened in 2001. It is Medicaid and Medicare certified.

Colonial Heights and Gardens
6900 Hopeful Road, Florence, KY
(859) 525-6900
www.colonialheightsandgardens.com
Independent and assisted living is available to residents here in five apartment sizes. Meals, housekeeping, and on-site nurses are available. Utilities, except phone, are paid. The 173-unit facility is on 17 acres near the Florence retail area.

Cottingham Retirement Community
3995 Cottingham Drive Sharonville
(513) 563-3600
Cottingham has independent- and assisted-living apartments, a skilled-nursing area, an early-stage dementia center, and a temporary/respite program. A beauty salon, branch bank, general store, indoor pool, cafe, and chapel are all on-site. Physical, occupational, and speech therapy are offered. Cottingham has Medicare beds in its nursing area.

Deupree Community
3983 Rosslyn Drive
(513) 272-0600
Deupree offers independent living in one-, two-, or three-bedroom apartments. Health care services and security are available in addition to an active social program. It is owned by the Episcopal Retirement Homes. Deupree Community also has independent-living, assisted-living, and nursing beds at 4001 Rosslyn Avenue. Altogether, there are seven levels of care, including one for those with memory loss.

Eastgate Village
776 Old Ohio Highway 74, Eastgate
(513) 753-4400
Eastgate has 150 independent studio and one- and two-bedroom apartments and two-bedroom deluxe units. A nurse's aide is on call 24 hours a day. Three meals are prepared daily; other amenities include housekeeping and laundry, a beauty salon, a health club, Jacuzzi, greenhouse, library, chapel, and Sunday Mass. Pets are welcome.

Evergreen Retirement Community
230 West Galbraith Road
(513) 948-2308
Another independent- and assisted-living facility, with skilled-nursing care available, Evergreen has one- and two-bedroom apartments in country cottages lining a golf course. Immediate occupancy is available with 12-month leases, and no endowment is necessary. Extra storage and transportation are available.

Garden Manor Extended Care Center
6898 Hamilton–Middletown Road, Middletown
(513) 424-5321
This facility is set up for independent and assisted living, and extended care also is available. Residents live in one- or two-bedroom apartments. There are gardens to walk in, planned trips, a central dining hall, movies, bingo, and a swimming pool.

The Hillrise
1500 Groesbeck Road, College Hill
(513) 541-4268
Hillrise offers 137 independent-living apartments. Emergency assistance is available 24 hours a day. This affordable community is centrally located and adjacent to the community business district and major bus routes.

Judson Village Retirement Community
2373 Harrison Avenue, Westwood
(513) 662-5880
This facility on 30 wooded acres offers independent and catered living. Nursing care is available 24 hours a day. Full therapy services, a chapel, greenhouse, arts-and-crafts workshop, wood shop, beauty shop, barbershop, and bank are also available. It is Medicare/Medicaid certified.

Llanfair Retirement Community
1701 Llanfair Avenue, College Hill
(513) 681-4230
Llanfair offers Cape Cod–style cottages and apartments on 14 wooded acres. Independent- and assisted-living options are available. Skilled nursing is also available, along with a supportive unit for Alzheimer's patients. Transportation, 24-hour emergency services, and activities are provided. The center is Medicare and Medicaid certified and accredited by the Continuing Care Association Commission. It offers guest stays and respite care. Although Llanfair is part of the Presbyterian retirement communities, it has an interdenominational chapel.

Mallard Cove
1410 Mallard Cove Drive, Sharonville
(513) 772-6655
Residency requires no endowment or entrance fee. Mallard has studio and one- and two-bedroom apartments, a 24-hour-a-day staff, transportation, and one to three meals a day and snacks. Housekeeping services, laundry and linen services, transportation, and a full activity program are available. All utilities except telephone are included. A 24-hour emergency call service is in place. Assisted-living services are also available.

Manorcare at Woodridge Retirement Communities
3801 Woodridge Boulevard, Fairfield
(866) 295-4786
Woodridge's services include assisted and independent living with three daily meals, nursing assistance on call 24 hours a day, housekeeping, transportation, a barber/beauty shop, and chapel. It is Medicare certified. Rent is monthly, and no endowment fee is required.

Maple Knoll Village
11100 Springfield Pike, Springdale
(513) 782-2400
Maple Knoll Village has operated for 160 years and was recently voted one of the top-20 continuing-care retirement communities in the country. Independent and assisted living are available, as are intermediate and skilled nursing care. It offers manor homes, cottages, and apartments. A health-and-wellness center, heated

swimming pool, fitness room, and whirlpool are included. Radio station WMKV operates from the village.

Marjorie P. Lee Retirement Community
3550 Shaw Avenue
(513) 871-2090
Features here are independent and assisted living, skilled nursing care, and dining and housekeeping services. It is accredited by the Continuing Care Association Commissions and is part of Episcopal Retirement Homes Inc.

Mason Christian Village
411 Western Row Road, Mason
(513) 398-1486
Mason Christian Village has 283 cottages, 73 apartments, 60 assisted-living beds, and 62 skilled-nursing beds. It is Medicare and Medicaid approved and is sponsored by the Christian Benevolent Association.

Mercy Franciscan at Schroder
1302 Millville Avenue, Hamilton
(513) 867-4100
This center offers independent and assisted living with skilled nursing and a special Alzheimer's disease unit.

Mercy Franciscan Terrace
100 Compton Road, Wyoming
(513) 761-9036
This facility, which is part of the Franciscan Health Systems of Cincinnati Inc., offers skilled nursing, assisted living, and independent living. Temporary stays are available. An indoor swimming pool, chapel, exercise programs, physical therapy, and rehabilitation services are available.

Mercy Franciscan at West Park Retirement Community
2950 West Park Drive, Westwood
(513) 451-8900
West Park offers assisted and independent living, a skilled-nursing unit, meals, a bank, chapel, barber/beauty shop, and free transportation to nearby shopping areas. Temporary stays are available. West Park is part of the Mercy Health Partners.

Mercy St. Theresa Center
7010 Rowan Hill Drive, Mariemont
(513) 271-7010
The center offers assisted living, nursing care, and Alzheimer care in a congregate-living environment. Services here include personal and nursing care, subacute rehabilitation care, and special care for the memory impaired. It is Medicare certified and a member of the Mercy Health Partners.

Mount Healthy Christian Home Inc.
8097 Hamilton Avenue
(513) 931-5000
Sponsored by the Christian Benevolent Association, this home offers independent and assisted living and nursing care. It is Medicaid approved.

New England Club
8135 Beechmont Avenue, Anderson
(513) 474-2582
Amenities and services in this upscale independent-living community include three meals a day, housekeeping and linen service, free transportation, paid utilities, and a resident manager. No buy-in fees are required. Month-to-month rent is available.

North Hill Court Shared Family Living Home
6920 La Boiteaux Avenue, North College Hill
(513) 931-2567
This large home has 16 rooms for independent living, with residents sharing the rest of the home. Three meals are served each day. Laundry and housekeeping are available.

Northgate Park Retirement Center
9191 Round Top Road, Bevis
(513) 923-3711
Residence at Northgate Park requires no entrance fee. The center has no steps or elevators. Each apartment has a kitchenette, patio, and wood-burning fireplace, and residents are offered a flexible meal plan, 24-hour security, transportation service, satellite TV, and a barber/beauty shop.

Philada Apartments
7732 Greenland Place, Roselawn
(513) 761-5544
The facility has 37 studio and one-bedroom apartments for independent living. Each apartment has its own kitchen. Laundry facilities are available. Rent is based on income.

St. Paul Lutheran Village Inc.
5515 Madison Road
(513) 272-1118
www.stpaulvillage.com
Residence at St. Paul's requires no entrance fee. The facility offers independent living in a studio or one-bedroom apartment, and transportation, meals, a laundry, and a beauty parlor are available.

Scarlet Oaks Retirement Community
440 Lafayette Avenue, Clifton
(513) 861-0400
www.scarletoaksretirementcommunity.com
This facility, located in an upscale residential gaslight district, has operated since 1909. It offers one- and two-bedroom independent-living apartments and personal support for those needing assistance. It has a 70-bed nursing unit, welcomes respite/short-term stays, and has no entrance fees. It is Medicare certified and is part of the Deaconess Longterm Care.

SEM Terrace
5371 South Milford Road, Milford
(513) 248-1140
SEM Terrace offers independent living in a congregate environment on 55 wooded acres. Three meals a day are available. Home health care is another option. The center is on one level, and pets are permitted.

One of the largest senior bowling leagues in the country is at Western Bowl. Older adults from all over bowl on Thursday morning. The league has door prizes and fills all of the 68 lanes at the bowling center.

SEM Villa
201 Mound Avenue, Milford
(513) 831-3262
SEM Villa is a congregate-living facility. Three meals a day, home health care, transportation, activities, monthly rates, and rental assistance are available. Small pets are welcome.

Seasons Retirement Community
7300 Dearwester Drive, Kenwood
(513) 984-9400
Seasons offers independent and assisted-living options in large apartments. Skilled nursing is also available, should the need arise. The community is located near the upscale Kenwood Towne Centre, Sycamore Plaza, and dozens of restaurants.

Sunrise Assisted Living
9090 Montgomery Road, Kenwood
(513) 745-9292
Sunrise is a 67-unit assisted-living facility that opened in 1997. Services include meals, housekeeping, transportation, and barber/beauty shop.

Sutton Grove Retirement Community
1131 Delliuia Drive
(513) 231-0008
Residents at Sutton Grove have access to a garden, transportation, an exercise room, a chapel, an emergency call system, a barber/beauty shop, and laundry facilities. Pets are welcome.

Town Square Apartments
4719 Alma Avenue, Blue Ash
(513) 984-1131
Town Square is an independent-living facility with 50 one- and two-bedroom apartments within 2 blocks of a major shopping area.

Twin Towers
5343 Hamilton Avenue
(513) 853-2001
Twin Towers, which is located on 125 wooded acres, was started by the United Methodist Church in 1899. Residents in this large community can choose from

one-floor patio homes, all with garages, or studio and one- and two-bedroom apartments. Assisted-living and nursing-home care also are available. An indoor pool, whirlpool, and craft rooms are among the amenities. Monthly rates are available. Twin Towers is Medicare and Medicaid certified and approved by the Continuing Care Association Commission.

Valley Creek Retirement Community
10620 Montgomery Road, Montgomery
(513) 984-4045
Valley Creek, which sits in the heart of upscale Olde Montgomery, offers independent living in one- and two-bedroom apartments. Management is on-site. Transportation is available, and an intercom entry is required for security. Storage also is available.

Victoria Park Retirement Community
1500 Sherman Avenue, Norwood
(513) 631-6800
Services here include skilled nursing care and assistance with bathing, dressing, and medication supervision. A nurse's aide is on call 24 hours a day. Three daily meals are served, and short-term stays can be arranged. The center offers weekly housekeeping and laundry service, daily planned activities, transportation, a barber/beauty shop, and 24-hour security.

Western Hills Retirement Village
6210 Cleves-Warsaw Road
Western Hills
(513) 941-0099
These independent-living apartments have 24-hour security and emergency services. Residents may take advantage of daily activities and religious services, along with free cable TV, housekeeping, laundry, and transportation. Covered parking is available. Skilled and intermediate nursing, and occupational, speech, and physical therapy are available. The center does not require an entrance fee.

ACTIVITY CENTERS

Greater Cincinnati and Northern Kentucky have dozens of activity centers for older adults that offer cultural, recreational, and social activities geared specifically to their age group. Seniors can try their hand at ceramics, painting, crafts, and other hobby interests or get involved in aerobics or exercise programs, bowling, dancing, and bingo. Programs are open to anyone age 60 and older.

The city of Cincinnati Recreation Commission and the Senior Services of Northern Kentucky together have 40 senior activity centers, meaning there is probably one pretty close to where you live. To find the senior center nearest you, contact the Cincinnati Recreation Commission at (513) 352-4000 or Senior Services of Northern Kentucky at (859) 491-0522.

Other centers, most of which are community based, include:

Anderson Senior Center
7970 Beechmont Avenue, Andersonn
(513) 474-3100

Cincinnati Area Senior Services Centers and Meal Sites
1720 Race Street, (513) 381-3007

644 Linn Street, (513) 721-4330

2010 Auburn Avenue, (513) 621-8733

601 Maple Avenue, (513) 751-3530

Colerain Senior Citizens Center
4300 Springdale Road, Bevis
(513) 741-8802

Green Township Senior Citizens Center
3620 Epley Road, Monfort Heights
(513) 385-3780

Hillrise Senior Center
1500 Groesbeck Road, College Hill
(513) 542-9344

Loveland Friendship Center
227 East Loveland Avenue, Loveland
(513) 783-7049

The College of Mount St. Joseph's program Life-Learn is a noncredit educational program for mature learners. It provides a number of courses including computers, religion, art, genealogy, and history. For a registration fee of $35, seniors can take any course they want during each session. For more information call (513) 244-4525.

Maple Knoll Village Center
for Older Adults
11199 Springfield Pike, Springdale
(513) 782-2400

Marielders Senior Center
6923 Madisonville Road, Mariemont
(513) 271-5588

North College Hill
Community Senior Center
1586 Goodman Avenue,
North College Hill
(513) 521-3462 (TDD accessible)

North Fairmount Seniors Center
1769 Carll, North Fairmount
(513) 921-3920

South Fairmount Seniors Center
1860 Queen City Avenue
South Fairmount
(513) 921-5809

Springfield Township Community
Senior Citizen Center
9158 Winton Road, Finneytown
(513) 522-1154

Sycamore Senior Center
4455 Carver Woods Drive, Sycamore
(513) 984-1234

VOLUNTEER, EMPLOYMENT, AND EDUCATION OPPORTUNITIES

You'll find ample opportunities to get involved in volunteer activities in Greater Cincinnati. Volunteering offers the double benefit of helping the community and keeping you vital and involved. We have suggested a few centers and services to get you started. Most of the agencies and organizations previously mentioned in this chapter would be other good sources to contact for specific interests. And don't overlook cultural, educational, and youth-oriented groups, which are described in other chapters in this book and are always looking for extra hands.

AARP Senior Employment Services
700 Walnut Street
(513) 721-0717

Retired Senior Volunteer Programs
(RSVP) Cincinnati Area Senior Services
644 Linn Street
(513) 721-4330

Senior Services of Northern Kentucky
1032 Madison Avenue, Covington, KY
(859) 491-0522

Service Corps of Retired Executives
(SCORE)
550 Vine Street
(513) 684-2812

HEALTH CARE Ⓗ

If you have to get sick somewhere, the Cincinnati neighborhoods of Clifton, Mount Auburn, and Avondale would be good places to do it. The area's biggest hospitals and a cluster of smaller or specialty hospitals are located in these neighborhoods north of downtown, an area collectively known as "Pill Hill" in the health-care community. There are plenty of other suburban and rural hospitals, including affiliates of the Pill Hill hospitals, that serve the rest of the Greater Cincinnati area.

Cincinnati hospitals are well known regionally and nationally for quality care. University Hospital's two Air Care helicopters, for example, provide emergency service as far as 150 miles away. Cincinnati's Children's Hospital Medical Center is among the largest and busiest children's hospitals in the United States. And Cincinnati's Shriners Hospital for Children is one of only a few in the country and provides treatment for severely burned children, mostly free of charge.

Cincinnati also has a reputation as a cradle of medical research. Albert Sabin developed the first oral polio vaccine at the University of Cincinnati and Children's Hospital. Henry Heimlich was chief of surgery at Jewish Hospital when he developed his famous maneuver and started an institute in Cincinnati to help fund other research. The first medical laser laboratory was established by Leon Goldman at Children's Hospital, and the first argon laser surgery in the United States was done here. The University of Cincinnati opened the Genome Research Institute in 2003 after obtaining hundreds of millions of dollars in federal grants. Some 450 researchers at the 360,000-square-foot biotech facility in Reading will hunt for better treatments for heart disease, obesity, cancer, and other ills.

All this combined means Cincinnati is a major destination for "medical tourists"—that is, out-of-town patients visiting here for medical treatment. Cincinnati's hospitals injected $363 million into the local economy during 2003, according to Cincinnati Chamber of Commerce estimates.

The consolidations that are happening here and elsewhere as a part of the managed-care philosophy are helping fuel the "centers of excellence" concept, in which each hospital concentrates on an area or areas of expertise. Of course, which hospitals are "centers of excellence" in which specialties remains a point of debate. Several Pill Hill hospitals lay claim to that title in such areas as cardiac and cancer care and even rehabilitation. The descriptions below note areas where hospitals have identified their strengths.

Generally, you should know that the major "health alliances" (translated: consolidations) in Greater Cincinnati are the Health Alliance of Cincinnati—which includes University Hospital, St. Luke hospitals, and Jewish Hospital—and the Tri-Health Alliance, which includes Good Sam and Bethesda North. The Mercy Health Partner systems is also a major player, involving the half-dozen Mercy hospitals from Fairfield to Anderson. Most other hospitals are on their own, for the moment.

You should also know that the state of Ohio has canned the CON (Certificate of Need) laws, which deterred new hospital openings by requiring that any proposed hospital prove there was a need in the market for its services. The demise of the CON regulations means the state is ripe for the opening of specialty, "boutique" hospitals that cater to exclusive needs—say, a niche hospital just for expectant mothers, or one just for hip-replacement surgery.

HOSPITALS

Bethesda Hospital
10500 Montgomery Road, Montgomery
(513) 745-1111

The Bethesda system was begun in 1896 by seven German Methodist deaconesses to minister to the needs of the sick and poor. Today it is part of a system of health-care centers and offices throughout Greater Cincinnati. It's also affiliated with Good Samaritan Hospital through Tri-Health Alliance, thereby consolidating some management and health services. Bethesda shocked many when it announced in 2000 that it was closing its primary hospital in the city proper, Bethesda Oak. That leaves the suburban Bethesda, first opened in 1971, as the system's sole remaining full-service acute-care hospital.

Bethesda has the second-largest cardiac program in Hamilton County, and it recently was ranked the best heart hospital in Ohio, Kentucky, and Indiana in a study that reviewed clinical quality outcomes.

Bethesda has announced a $150 million expansion. Construction of a new seven-story patient tower is now under way and will be completed in 2007. The entire project, including outpatient expansion and renovation, will let the hospital increase inpatient capacity by 400.

Currently, Bethesda is a 270-bed hospital that serves the northeastern suburbs and beyond. It's the largest and busiest suburban hospital in the tristate area. It provides a full range of inpatient and outpatient surgery, including general medical care, maternity care, a Level II Special Care Nursery, intensive care and coronary care units, physical rehabilitation, cancer treatment, cardiac rehabilitation, and a breast-care center. It has the second-busiest adult emergency room in Greater Cincinnati after University Hospital in Clifton. On or near the Bethesda campus are five physician office buildings and an outpatient surgery center.

Community services at Bethesda include a paramedic-training program. The hospital also comprises Bethesda Warren County, the only 24-hour emergency and diagnostic services facility in Warren County. For its part, the Bethesda system has the most extensive network of suburban offices and treatment centers of any Cincinnati hospital system, including centers in Eastgate, Fairfield, and Warren County that provide diagnostic and physical therapy services.

Children's Hospital Medical Center
3333 Burnet Avenue
(513) 636-4200

When kids get very sick in Cincinnati, Children's Hospital Medical Center is usually the one to treat them. This hospital has the busiest pediatric emergency room and the most outpatient visits and performs the most surgical procedures of any children's hospital in the United States. Founded in 1883, this 423-bed hospital currently ranks fifth in overall pediatric admissions nationwide, behind only children's hospitals in big metros such as Boston and Philadelphia. It also has by far the busiest emergency room of any kind in Greater Cincinnati. Children's 100 pediatric residents make its residency program one of the largest of any kind in the United States. Children's ranked among the top-10 best hospitals in the country for pediatric care, according to the most recent *U.S. News & World Report* guide to America's best bospitals.

Children's recently completed a $128 million expansion, building new clinical research areas, an education and conference center, and new parking lots. And another $115 million research tower will add 1,000 more jobs by its completion in 2007.

Children's Hospital is a regional hospital, with 15 percent of its patients coming from outside Greater Cincinnati. It's the only Level I pediatric trauma center serving southwestern Ohio, Northern Kentucky, and Southeastern Indiana. And Children's provides specialized medical and surgical services in such areas as diagnosis of rare and complex diseases, and laser neurosurgery. Services also include a child-abuse treatment team, craniofacial and other plastic and reconstructive surgery, a lead-poison clinic, and bone marrow, heart, and kidney transplants.

Achievements by Children's Hospital's researchers include development of the Sabin oral polio vaccine and a bubble oxygenator to make open-heart surgery possible. Current research by the hospital's 26 research divisions focuses on cystic fibrosis, prevention of premature births, kidney disorders, sickle cell disease, juvenile rheumatoid arthritis, and many other conditions.

Children's also has many satellite locations for urgent care, including facilities in Anderson Township, Fairfield, Mason, and West Chester.

The Christ Hospital
2139 Auburn Avenue
(513) 585-2000

The Christ Hospital was founded in 1889 through the philanthropy of Procter & Gamble cofounder James Gamble and the work of Methodist missionary Isabella Thoburn. It is still a regional health center, treating more adult patients from outside Hamilton County than any other Pill Hill hospital. But it treats plenty of Cincinnatians too.

Christ Hospital ranked in the top-50 best hospitals in the country for cardiac care in *U.S. News & World Report*'s guide to America's best hospitals.

Christ Hospital, until recently a member of the Health Alliance of Cincinnati and now on its own, is known as "Greater Cincinnati's heart hospital," and it leads the region in open-heart surgeries. The hospital's other specialties include cardiovascular services, women's services, orthopedics, cancer care, and spine care. Christ also offers teaching programs in the hospital. The programs include school of nursing and internal medicine residency.

Facilities include cardiac catheterization and endoscopy labs and Greater Cincinnati's first positron emission tomography (PET) scanner. The hospital also has outpatient-testing facilities in Delhi, Mason, and Blue Ash.

Christ Hospital is completing a $77 million construction project that will double the size of the emergency department and add a multistory "heart tower" for cardiac care. Two floors of the hospital are dedicated to women's health. Obstetrics and gynecology make up about 30 percent of the hospital's patient care.

Christ Hospital's psychiatric program is the largest in a private hospital in Ohio and includes an eight-bed psychiatric intensive-care unit and a 16-bed senior adult mental health unit specializing in care for patients age 60 and older.

i

The largest Ronald McDonald House in America is located next to Children's Hospital. The home lets parents of extremely sick children stay overnight for just $5.50. The $9 million facility, which opened in 2001, employs five full-time staffers and includes a cafeteria, children's theater, and 48 guest rooms.

Deaconess Hospital
311 Straight Street
(513) 559-2100

Deaconess was founded in 1888 when the ministers of several German American Protestant denominations founded the Deaconess Society. Today this 255-bed hospital provides a wide range of medical, surgical, and health services.

Deaconess is the orthopedic leader in Cincinnati thanks to invasive surgery suites and contributions from the community. Deaconess has also opened the Regency Hospital on the fourth floor as an acute-care hospital to care for long-term, medically complex patients.

Primary focus areas include cardiac services, orthopedic services, geriatric psychiatry, surgical weight loss, and surgical services. On-site specialty centers include Deaconess's Arthritis Center,

Back Treatment Center, Breast Care Center, Cincinnati Joint Replacement Center, and Cincinnati Laser Center. Other specialized programs include sports medicine and allergy treatment.

Dearborn County Hospital
600 Wilson Creek Road, Lawrenceburg, IN
(812) 537-1010

Dearborn County is a 144-bed hospital founded in 1959 that serves residents of Southeastern Indiana through its central Lawrenceburg facility and medical office buildings in Rising Sun and Harrison. Its medical and surgical services include diabetes education and support classes, hospice, laparoscopic and laser surgery, lithotripsy for kidney stones and gallstones, and a full range of diagnostic and imaging services. Other services include an infant/child safety program.

Dearborn's long-term expansion plan will end in 2009 with a new state-of-the-art three-floor patient tower. Just recently Dearborn opened the doors to its new subacute unit. Built above the hospital's O'Brien Wing, the new unit occupies more than 10,000 square feet and has 12 resident rooms, its own rehabilitative therapy gym, a lounge, and a dining room as well as other clinical and public areas. Currently Dearborn is converting its original subacute unit into a medical/surgical floor. The converted unit will include 15 private patient rooms, some of which will be designed for the care of ventilator patients.

Drake Center
151 West Galbraith Road
(513) 948-2500

Drake Center fills the gap for patients who are too sick for nursing homes but don't require the services of an acute-care hospital. Drake Center is one of only a handful of hospitals in the nation dedicated solely to providing rehabilitation and long-term skilled nursing care.

Funded largely by a special Hamilton County tax levy, Drake offers a sort of long-term care safety net to Hamilton Countians that few people in the United States have. If you have a severe accident or injury and you live in Hamilton County, Drake will be there to provide rehabilitation, whether you can pay or not.

Drake has special multidisciplinary teams to treat spinal cord and brain injuries and the area's largest ventilator unit to treat persons with severe respiratory conditions. Services include occupational therapy, physical therapy, therapeutic recreation and speech-language pathology, psychological counseling, and community reentry assistance.

Facilities include an aquatic therapy pool and on-site living areas to help patients adapt to disabilities in a home setting before leaving the hospital. Rehabilitation engineers are available to help patients adapt their homes to their disabilities before discharge. A behavioral medicine program at Drake combines several disciplines to help persons learn to cope with or overcome chronic pain and return to work.

Drake also offers support groups to help families cope with arthritis, Guillain-Barre syndrome, Huntington's disease, head injuries, respiratory conditions that require ventilators, and other conditions.

Fort Hamilton Hospital
630 Eaton Avenue, Hamilton
(513) 867-2000

Fort Hamilton is a 307-bed hospital that provides a full range of medical and surgical services to residents of southern Butler County, including cardiac catheterization and rehabilitation, full diagnostic and imaging services, laser surgery, a cancer treatment center, and occupational and physical therapy. Its maternity services are equipped to handle not only routine deliveries, but high-risk pregnancies and emergency situations as well.

The hospital also has a freestanding SurgiCenter for outpatient surgery and an employee assistance program and employer-sponsored sick-child care program.

Good Samaritan Hospital
375 Dixmyth Avenue
(513) 872-1400

Good Samaritan is the largest private hospital in Greater Cincinnati and has more licensed beds (nearly 700) and births per year than any other single hospital facility in the area. It's affiliated with Bethesda hospital through the TriHealth Alliance in which it has consolidated administrative and some medical services. Founded in 1852, it's also among the oldest hospitals in the area.

Good Sam has one of only three local Level III neonatal intensive care units. A $5 million face-lift served to improve the city's busiest maternity service. The hospital is devoting an entire floor to its expanding neonatal intensive care unit, while filling another floor with private recovery rooms for mothers and babies.

The hospital lists its Comprehensive Heart Center as another center of excellence. The 43-bed center includes a coronary care unit, three cardiac catheterization labs, two open-heart surgical suites, a pacemaker clinic, a vascular lab, diagnostic testing facilities, and full cardiac rehabilitation services.

Good Sam also has a Level I Trauma Center—one of two (along with Children's Hospital) in Greater Cincinnati verified by the American College of Surgeons. The Trauma Center has specialists in all areas of bodily injury. The hospital also has developed a fast-track service to treat patients who come to the emergency room for nonemergency care, primarily indigent patients who use the ER for routine care.

The 40-bed inpatient Rehabilitation Center, one of the largest in Cincinnati, is certified by the Commission on Accreditation of Rehabilitation Facilities in comprehensive inpatient rehab, spinal cord injury, brain injury, outpatient medical rehab, work hardening program, infant and early childhood development program, and residential/supervised living.

Other programs and services include a Molecular Diagnostics Center that develops new tests based on the latest developments in recombinant DNA technology, an occupational health program, a comprehensive cancer program, inpatient psychiatric units, neurosurgery, and outpatient assessment and membership programs for seniors.

Jewish Hospital
4777 East Galbraith Road, Kenwood
(513) 686-3000

With the closing of the original Jewish Hospital on Pill Hill, this has become Jewish's primary patient facility. The origins of Jewish Hospital date from the cholera epidemic of 1849, which convinced Cincinnati Jews of the need to raise money for a hospital to treat indigent Jews. The founders also wanted to make sure no Jew would be buried without another Jew there to say Kaddish, the prayer for the dead, and prevent deathbed conversions to Christianity by Jews anxious to receive some kind of religious rite.

Today Jewish Hospital remains one of Greater Cincinnati's most respected hospitals, treating persons of all religious faiths. Among its medical and surgical services and facilities are a coronary care unit, a diabetes management program, and outpatient surgery. There is also an oncology unit and stem cell transplant program, as well as an open-heart surgery unit. Senior citizen care services include an osteoporosis diagnostic and a senior wellness program. Jewish also provides adolescent-outpatient chemical dependency services.

Mercy Hospital (Anderson)
7500 State Road, Anderson
(513) 624-4500

Residents of Anderson, Newtown, Mount Washington, and southeastern Clermont County are served by this 186-bed hospital located just off Five Mile Road. Mercy Hospital Anderson was recently chosen as one of the country's top 100 in a study conducted by HCIA-Sachs, a health-care information research company.

Among medical and surgical services

and facilities are the Cancer Center, which offers an extensive range of outpatient cancer therapies and counseling; the Family Birthing Center with birthing suites; and the Cardiovascular Training Center, offering comprehensive cardiac rehabilitation and a full range of diagnostic and emergency cardiac care services.

Mercy Anderson also features the Center for Women's Health, which is equipped with advanced technology and staffed by a team of physicians, nurses, and technologists. The hospital opened a new heart surgery wing in 2006, offering open-heart surgery options on the east side of town for the first time. In 2001 Mercy Anderson opened a sizable outpatient-care facility to increase its ability to handle outpatient, same-day surgeries.

Mercy Hospital (Clermont)
3000 Hospital Drive, Batavia
(513) 732-8300

A 151-bed general, medical/surgical acute-care hospital founded in 1973, Mercy offers diagnostic and imaging services, intensive care treatment, cardiac rehabilitation, laser surgery, one-day surgery, psychiatric inpatient and outpatient units for adult and adolescent treatment, and physical, respiratory, and occupational therapy.

Clermont Mercy was among the first in Greater Cincinnati to perform laparoscopic (laser) gall bladder surgery. The hospital is also known for its inpatient psychiatric care programs, psychiatric day treatment programs for adolescents, comprehensive cancer treatment/linear accelerator, and physical/occupational health therapy services. It is one of a half-dozen Mercy Health Partners hospitals in the Greater Cincinnati area.

Mercy Hospital (Fairfield)
3000 Mack Road, Fairfield
(513) 870-7000

Built in 1978, Mercy Hospital Fairfield provides the same medical services as many Mercy hospitals in addition to an executive fitness program, CancerCare center, and a pulmonary rehabilitation program. The 194-bed hospital recently added a Family Birth Center, featuring 15 birthing suites, each with a Jacuzzi, TV and VCR, two operating rooms for C-sections, a Level I nursery for stabilizing high-risk infants, and 24-hour anesthesia and neonatal coverage.

Mercy Fairfield has been expanding over the years to keep up with patient demands. Since 2002 Mercy has doubled the size of the hospital to include a renovated emergency department, an expanded intensive-care unit, an updated main laboratory, a new admitting area, and other improvements.

The Mercy Ambulatory Surgery Center next to Mercy Hospital Fairfield is one of the most highly used, freestanding surgery centers in the country. Utilizing the latest in techniques and equipment for outpatient surgery (endoscopy, pain management, laser procedures), it enjoys a 98 percent satisfaction rate from patients.

Mercy Hospital (Mount Airy)
2446 Kipling Avenue
(513) 853-5000

This 269-bed hospital was founded in 1971 to serve residents of northeastern Cincinnati and nearby suburbs. The hospital's "Comeback Team" rehabilitation unit and Cardiac Care Unit offer extensive diagnostic, surgical, and rehabilitation services. Inpatient and outpatient cancer care is provided in a hospital-based cancer program and a freestanding radiation therapy facility that have received joint accreditation by the American College of Surgeons.

The Pain and Work Rehabilitation Center uses a behavioral approach to ease chronic pain without reliance on medications. Surgical services include use of laser equipment in orthopedic, gynecological, and other surgical procedures.

Mercy Hospital (Western Hills)
3131 Queen City Avenue, Western Hills
(513) 389-5000

This 267-bed hospital offers an array of services, including 24-hour emergency care, orthopedic care, the Eye Center,

Women's Health Center, hospice, and intensive-care unit. The Women's Center provides mammography services, with an enhanced follow-up process with results in 24 to 48 hours. Mercy Western Hills uses a new computer-aided detection (CAD) or "second look" system that enhances exam interpretations.

Middletown Regional Hospital
105 McKnight Drive, Middletown
(800) 338-4057
Serving central Butler County, this 310-bed hospital was founded in 1917 and has one of the busiest adult emergency rooms in Greater Cincinnati as well as a fast-track urgent care center for noncritical patients. Services include a Level II maternity center with birthing suites, cardiac catheterization and rehabilitation, industrial medicine, sports medicine services, and a specialized endoscopy center.

Middletown Hospital has begun construction on its new $195 million health and technology campus. The 70-acre area will include a hospital, a medical office building, and facilities for outpatient services such as surgery and cardiology. Construction of this new hospital is set to be completed in 2008.

Northkey Community Care Center
502 Farrell Drive, Covington, KY
(859) 578-3200
This nonprofit inpatient facility serves severely disturbed youth ages 5 to 17. The hospital coordinates treatment with outpatient mental-health providers, local school special education programs, pediatricians, and state social service agencies. The 51-bed main hospital is a refurbished facility originally built in the 1950s. A therapeutic living area on a wooded hillside overlooks the Ohio River valley and Cincinnati skyline.

Services include psychiatric and psychological evaluation and treatment; individual and group psychotherapy; family therapy; art, music, and recreational therapy; a behavior management program; aftercare coordination; and specialized treatment groups dealing with sexual abuse, loss and grief, substance abuse, social-skills training, values clarification, and anger/stress management.

St. Elizabeth Medical Center North
401 East 20th Street, Covington, KY
(859) 292-4000
Founded in 1861 and managed jointly with St. Elizabeth Medical Center South in Edgewood, Kentucky (see listing below), this facility is part of Northern Kentucky's largest hospital system in terms of licensed beds, budget, and emergency-room visits. Employee job satisfaction here is greater than at any hospital, according to an independent survey that included several Pill Hill hospitals. St. Elizabeth notes that employee turnover in the combined hospital system has been consistently lower than the average for Greater Cincinnati hopitals.

Services provided at St. Elizabeth North include inpatient and outpatient chemical dependency treatment, Northern Kentucky's only inpatient hemodialysis unit, and a long-term skilled nursing-care unit.

St. Elizabeth Medical Center South
1 Medical Village Drive, Edgewood, KY
(859) 344-2000
St. Elizabeth South, founded in 1978, has Northern Kentucky's only open-heart surgery program and manages a busy cardiac catheterization program for the St. Elizabeth hospitals and St. Luke East and West hospitals. The Cancer Care Center at St. Elizabeth South is the largest outpatient cancer treatment program in

i

Which hospitals boast the best cafeterias? The urban weekly* Cincinnati City-Beat *answered this critical question in a recent taste test. The paper's prognosis: The Rooftop Cafe at Shriners Hospital for Children tops the chart, while the Helen Gill Lindner Dining Room at Good Sam is a close second. We'll have a ham and rye, stat!

CLOSE-UP

Alternative Health Care: The Road to Wellville

What began in the monasteries of China and the streetfront shops of Clifton Heights is now going mainstream. Alternative medicine is being practiced to an ever-greater extent by Greater Cincinnati's hospitals and doctors; in fact, it's become a big moneymaker for the medical establishment: Call it I-Ching meets "cha-ching."

Almost all local hospitals now offer some form of alternative health-care treatment (massage therapy and biofeedback, for example). But some hospitals are taking it one step further. In Anderson, Mercy Hospital Anderson recently opened one of the nation's largest "wellness centers," the massive Mercy Center for Health and Wellness (aka "the Healthplex"), directly across the street from the hospital. There's more. Mercy Hospital Fairfield runs another large wellness center. In Blue Ash, there's the TriHealth Fitness & Health Pavilion, run jointly by Good Samaritan and Bethesda Hospitals.

The wellness complexes offer the usual fitness basics: weight rooms, exercise machines, treadmills, spas, pools, and other traditional gym fare. It's the holistic aspect—treating the mind and spirit as well as the body—that makes these centers different from Joe's Gym down the road. The wellness program at Mercy Hospital Anderson, for instance, offers anything from biofeedback to reflexology and therapeutic touch.

There's a whole lot of wellness shaking down. Behind it all, say local doctors and nurses, is this simple philosophy: The cure to certain ailments lies within yourself, not inside a pill bottle—that perception and attitude can indeed triumph where pharmaceuticals fail—and a three-pound organ, the brain, is at the crux of many a cure. Of course, keeping it in perspective, much of this "alternative" medicine isn't all that new or New Age; it's Far Eastern medicine that predates "traditional" Western medicine by as much as 50 centuries.

As the line between orthodox and unorthodox medicine continues to blur, some hospitals prefer to call "alternative" medicine "complementary" medicine. They don't like the implication of an either/or situation, that patients must somehow choose between going with a traditional or an alternative treatment. Certainly when it comes to a major medical crisis—emergency-room treatment, surgery, trauma—the services of a trained MD are a must. Hospitals are merely acknowledging with these wellness centers that when it comes to the everyday aches and pains of life (as well as certain chronic diseases such as arthritis), you might do better to seek solutions outside the hospital corridors.

By one estimate, at least one Cincinnatian in three is trying some form of alternative medicine. Some local employers' medical plans will even cover acupuncture, chiropractic, reflexology, yoga, and other unusual forms of care. Greater Cincinnati also has dozens of shops and outlets where you can learn more about your options, most notably

Whatever Works Wellness Center & Bookstore in Silverton (a wonderful store full of resources and supplies and especially notable for its aromatheraphy collection) and Spatz's Natural Life Health Food downtown. (See the write-ups on both in the Shopping chapter.)

The most popular forms of alternative medicine in Greater Cincinnati? We compiled this list with the help of hospitals, the Academy of Medicine, and other sources.

Acupuncture. A linchpin of Chinese medicine for centuries, it's based on the premise that inserting needles at various points in the body will, through energy meridians, influence the course of certain diseases. Studies have indeed shown that acupuncture provides short-term relief of pain by releasing endorphins (naturally produced substances that resemble morphine). It's also been shown to alleviate asthma. There are many acupuncturists listed in the local Yellow Pages.

Aromatherapy. This is a relatively new term for the ancient practice of using aromatic herbs and fragrances to treat illness. The Egyptians whipped up a perfume of cinnamon and clove to ease stress. Muslims in the 12th century inhaled sandalwood to relieve migraines. The Greeks favored cypress odor to overcome depression. The theory: The part of the brain that receives and processes smells, the limbic system, also controls vital body functions, including hormone secretion. Certain odors can stimulate the release of certain hormones. Whatever Works in Silverton is an excellent outlet if you're considering aromatherapy.

Biofeedback. "Biofeedback teaches you how your body works. It helps deal with panic attacks, stimulates relaxation response, and we see just phenomenal results with high blood pressure," says Anita Schambach, a registered nurse who specializes in the technique. Essentially, biofeedback allows you to gain voluntary control over normally involuntary body functions by observing electronic sensors that let you measure and, ideally, control heart rate, skin temperature, and blood pressure.

Biomagnetics. According to Jeff Bathiany, whose Fort Thomas practice is "attracting" all sorts of attention, biomagnetics is simply the theory that magnets, placed on the body for lengthy periods of time, ease the aches of carpal tunnel syndrome and other ills. (His catalog offers magnetic necklaces, bracelets, watchbands, belts, even foam insoles for foot pain.)

Chelation. Championed by Cincinnati's own Jane Heimlich (wife of Dr. Henry Heimlich), this therapy involves dripping a synthetic amino acid into a vein to remove toxins. The method, as well as ozone therapy (a combination of ozone and oxygen to combat disease), are outlined in Jane Heimlich's book, *What Your Doctor Won't Tell You,* a guide to alternative medicine.

Chiropractic. This is a medical practice based on the belief that misaligned vertebrae can impair the nervous system and lower the body's resistance to disease. Thus, spinal manipulation can cure various ailments and aches. Consult the Yellow Pages for a list of chiropractors.

Continued

Chunging (pronounced chun-ging). This Korean regimen of simple exercises and breathing techniques will help what ails you, even serious diseases such as diabetes, according to Dr. Yungjo Chung, the Cincinnati-based author of *Chunging: The Cleansing Side of Medicine*. Chung should know; he struggled with diabetes until he came across this method, which stresses getting bad things (like pills) out of the body (in contrast with traditional Western medicine, which is largely drug based).

Hypnotherapy. As a therapy, the belief is that hypnosis enables a patient to gain direct control of normally involuntary bodily responses and functions (such as the immune system). The Yellow Pages list hypnotherapists.

Qigong (pronounced ki-gong). Once the quiet regimen of monks in China, the practice of this 5,000-year-old healing method is spreading. Proponents say the daily routine of movements can battle arthritis, depression, heart disease, and other chronic illnesses. In practice qigong simply means a long period of daily effort of holding postures that employs exercise, visualization (or imagery), and affirmation/prayer, according to Luke Chan, the Cincinnati-based author of *101 Miracles of Natural Healing* and the area's leading authority on qigong.

Rubenfeld Synergy. It's all about talking and touching, says Candee Lawson, a certified Rubenfeld Synergist who runs a Mount Healthy practice. Ilana Rubenfeld developed this body-mind method, which blends compassionate touch and psychotherapy, to deal with her own debilitating back spasms. The Rubenfeld Synergy Method combines elements of Gestalt therapy, hypnotherapy, Alexander Technique, and Feldenkrais Method. "RSM accesses stored emotions and memories in the body which may result in energy blocks, tensions, and imbalances," says Lawson.

Northern Kentucky. The Family Birth Place here is also the busiest maternity unit south of the river, with 2,700 births annually. All the rooms at the Family Birth Place allow mom and baby to stay in the same room from delivery until they go home. Other services include a Work Rehabilitation Center, hospice program, a women's wellness center, and candela laser surgery for removal of skin lesions.

Watch your step. The leading cause of injury deaths around here is falls, according to a Hamilton County Health Department report. A full 30 percent of all accidental deaths are caused by falls, twice the national average. Following falls are poisonings and drug overdoses, accidental gunshots, traffic accidents, suffocations, fires, and drownings.

St. Luke Hospital East
85 North Grand Avenue, Fort Thomas, KY
(859) 572-3100

St. Luke East is a 310-bed general medical and surgical acute-care hospital. It is part of an alliance that includes its St. Luke West affiliate in Florence, Kentucky, and the Christ Hospital and University Hospital in Pill Hill.

Services and facilities at St. Luke East include inpatient and outpatient alcohol and chemical dependency treatment, birthing suites, a comprehensive cancer treatment center (the first in the region to be recognized by the American College of

Surgeons), cardiac diagnosis and rehabilitation, infertility services, and centers for sleep disorders, diabetes, skilled nursing, and women's health care.

St. Luke Hospital West
7380 Turfway Road, Florence, KY
(859) 962-5200

St. Luke West, affiliated with St. Luke East and allied with the Christ Hospital and University Hospital, is a 177-bed hospital whose services include cardiac diagnosis and rehabilitation, cancer care, an employee-assistance program, psychiatric inpatient care, day treatment and partial hospitalization programs, a sleep disorders center, and a work-conditioning program for rehabilitation.

Shriners Hospital for Children
3229 Burnet Avenue
(513) 872-6000

This is a regional referral hospital providing acute and rehabilitation care free of charge for severely burned children primarily from a 1,000-mile radius around Cincinnati. It was founded in 1964 and opened its current facility adjacent to Children's Hospital Medical Center in 1992.

The 30-room hospital is funded primarily by a Shriners Hospitals endowment fund, which also pays for transport of children to the hospitals. Patients, who must be referred by a physician, have come to the hospital from 40 states and many nations.

Research programs at the hospital have helped improve survival rates of severely burned children nationwide. When the program began, a child with 40 to 50 percent total body surface burn had only a 50 percent chance of survival. Today a child with burns on 85 percent of his or her body has the same chance of living. A patented high-calorie diet for burn victims was developed here and is now available everywhere.

The hospital also provides occupational therapy, reconstructive surgery, a school reentry program, and summer camp program for former burn patients.

Achooo! From the day you arrive, you'll hear tell of the dreaded "Cincinnati Sinus." Indeed, a recent survey showed we have more ear, eye, nose, and throat specialists per capita than any other city in America, just to satisfy all the suffering sneezers. What causes our sinus ills? Some say it's the Ohio Valley weather system, trapping inversion layers. Others cite the region's peculiar molds and pollens.

Summit Behavioral Health
1101 Summit Road
(513) 948-3600

This state psychiatric hospital provides acute, intermediate, and long-term residential care. Services include a full range of psychiatric and psychological therapy, plus medical, occupational therapy, and religious and social services.

The University Hospital
234 Goodman Street
(513) 584-1000

The oldest of all Greater Cincinnati hospitals, University Hospital is by most measures the biggest too. Founded in 1823, it is one of the area leaders in number of licensed beds (more than 700), number of adult emergency-room visits annually, and number of inpatient admissions. Within the past few years, University has severed its ties, ironically, with the University (as in the University of Cincinnati). It is now a private, nonprofit hospital.

University's cardiovascular care program includes research, education and clinical care, the Heart Emergency Room, a cardiac transplantation/heart failure program, and an adult congenital heart disease program. The neurosciences center at University treats patients referred from all over the world for brain tumors, stroke, epilepsy, and aneurysms. And the University Hospital Trauma Center was the region's first Level I trauma center.

When it comes to accidents, the three most accident-prone neighborhoods in the area are Lockland, Elmwood Place, and Cleves, according to a Hamilton County Injury Surveillance Report. Among the safest neighborhoods: Forest Park and Blue Ash.

The hospital provides round-the-clock physician coverage in every surgical specialty, anesthesia, and intensive care. Since 1984 the University Air Care two-helicopter medical team has transported more than 12,000 patients within a 150-mile radius. And the Barrett Cancer Center at University, a national research site, allows local cancer patients access to many cutting-edge treatments not available at other hospitals in the city or even the state.

University provides probably the most comprehensive range of services of any Greater Cincinnati hospital, including the aforementioned cancer prevention, treatment, and research services; liver and pancreas transplantation; a birthing center that provides obstetrics and gynecology for high-risk moms and babies; an AIDS-related disorders center; an inpatient burn care unit; a sensory disorders center; ear and eye banks; a stroke ER; and a sickle cell center.

Veterans Affairs Medical Center
3200 Vine Street
(513) 861-3100
Founded in 1954, this hospital serves United States military veterans. Special services include an AIDS clinic, an amputee prosthetic clinic team, a chronic-pain program, and a women's clinic.

URGENT-CARE CENTERS

A step down from hospital emergency rooms, these urgent-care centers generally offer minor emergency treatment and off-hour medical care for nonemergency illness.

Bethesda Warren County
1618 Deerfield Road, Lebanon
(513) 745-1436
A full-scale, freestanding, around-the-clock emergency room.

Children's Urgent Care at Outpatient North
9560 Children's Drive, Mason
(513) 636-6800
Open 7:00 A.M. to 11:00 P.M. Monday through Friday, noon to 7:00 P.M. Saturday, and 11:00 A.M. to 7:00 P.M. on Sunday.

Mercy Harrison
10450 New Haven Road
(513) 367-2222
Open 24 hours a day.

Mercy Health Solutions
4404A Glen Este-Withamsville Road
Summerside
(513) 752-9610
Open 8:00 A.M. to 5:30 P.M. Monday through Friday, 9:00 A.M. to 12:30 P.M. Saturday, and closed Sunday.

Mercy Health Center-Mason
(Urgent Care and Occupational Health)
7450 Mason-Montgomery Road, Mason
(513) 701-2100
Open 8:00 A.M. to 7:30 P.M. Monday through Friday, 8:30 A.M. to 4:30 P.M. on Saturday and Sunday.

HOSPICE CARE

Hospice of Cincinnati
4310 Cooper Road, Blue Ash
(513) 891-7700

Hospice of Northern Kentucky
1403 Alexandria Pike, Fort Thomas, KY
(859) 441-6332

PHYSICIAN REFERRAL SERVICES

These services are popular with newcomers seeking physicians in a particular specialty in their area of town. Physician referral lines in some cases will also refer you to physicians based on the type of insurance they accept. A listing of Greater Cincinnati physician referral services and their sponsoring hospitals (when not already in the name) follows.

Nurse On Line (Fort Hamilton)
(513) 867-2222

TriHealth Ask-A-Nurse
(Bethesda and Good Samaritan)
(513) 569-5400

MEDICAID AND OTHER INSURANCE

How do you pay for all this health care? If you're lucky, you're covered by an employer health plan. But, as is true just about everywhere, finding insurance coverage for individuals is tricky business in Greater Cincinnati.

Many insurers in the area offer health insurance for individuals, but there are some caveats. If you or a family member has a history of medical problems, you will either be turned down or pay a very steep rate. In Ohio, HMOs are required to allow individuals to enroll once a year regardless of their medical history or employment status. But rates are high.

The Greater Cincinnati Chamber of Commerce offers one of the best and most affordable "group" plans around, provided you're self-employed or own a business, are healthy, and join the chamber. (The same goes for many smaller chambers such as the Anderson Area and Clermont Chambers.)

Medicaid is available to qualified unemployed persons and administered through county human-services departments throughout Greater Cincinnati.

SCHOOLS AND CHILD CARE

Greater Cincinnati has some 50 public school districts and nearly 300 private schools. Perhaps nowhere in the country are schools changing as profoundly as they are here.

In Ohio, legal skirmishes over public schools and how they should be funded boiled over. Traditionally the public school system has been funded by local property taxes. Critics and school officials have long challenged the fairness and equity of funding that relies on variable local property values as well as the goodwill of the electorate to pass school levies. The Ohio Supreme Court finally agreed, ordering the legislature and governor to—within one year—replace reliance on property tax with some other funding system (almost certainly more state monies and a corresponding tax increase). By 2004 the court had thrice scrapped the statehouse's proposals and ordered legislators back, as it were, to the chalkboard. The long-term effect of all this legal wrangling? In theory, poorer urban school districts will one day gain equal footing with posh suburban districts.

For newcomers to Ohio the issue has some very real and unsettling implications. If you move to an area that has an impressive and well-funded school district today, things could change dramatically in the future. Funding may be cut or you may have to come up with supplemental local monies to maintain current school spending. At the same time, many districts that are cash-poor today will be in for a windfall when reform is implemented in the next year or so. Stay tuned.

On the Kentucky side of the river, changes already are in motion. The Kentucky Education Reform Act, now in its second decade of implementation, has helped equalize funding among school districts and launched a host of controversial educational reforms. The verdict by the national media on KERA is overwhelmingly positive, but polls show a majority of Kentuckians view it negatively. Largely, opposition centers around multigrade grouping and nontraditional teaching methods instituted as part of the reform.

Private schools are numerous and strong in the region. One in four students in Hamilton County attends a private school, a higher proportion than in any metropolitan area in the state and two-and-a-half times the national average. The affluent city neighborhoods of Hyde Park and Mount Lookout top the list of communities where more residents send their children to private rather than public schools, according to a recent study. Enrollment in nondiocesan private schools is growing four times faster than in public schools in the tristate. And enrollment in diocesan Catholic schools is growing twice as fast as in public schools. With 58,000 students, the Archdiocese of Cincinnati already runs the ninth-largest Catholic school system in the nation. It's also the biggest school system of any kind in Greater Cincinnati, with 8,000 more students than Cincinnati public schools. Another roughly 12,000 students attend schools run by the Diocese of Covington.

i

Wonder why your public school never seems to schedule practices, games, or extracurricular activities on a Wednesday night? It's part of an unwritten "Dark Wednesday" agreement with the local Catholic church. The decades-old gentlemen's agreement assures that high school students are free to attend services and church youth groups.

The choices are obviously many. What follows are highlights of some of the best, biggest, and most popular public, private, and charter schools in Greater Cincinnati.

PUBLIC SCHOOLS

When choosing a school district, parents will want to consider many factors, such as per-pupil spending, student/teacher ratio, average daily attendance rate, dropout rate, and student body size. Parents will encounter the Ohio Ninth Grade Proficiency Test because a student must pass all five sections of this test (writing, reading, math, science, and citizenship) to receive a high school diploma; this is a closely watched barometer of a district's academic standing. Students have 11 chances to pass the test and may even continue taking the test after finishing their senior year of high school.

The Ohio Department of Education also mails school district "report cards" to two million parents of Ohio schoolchildren. The report cards (fair's fair, the kids have to endure them too) measure attendance rates, graduation rates, school funding, test scores, and other data. In Greater Cincinnati the Madeira, Loveland, Indian Hill, Forest Hills, Mariemont, Sycamore, Mason, Milford, and Wyoming districts met all 18 performance standards—scoring in the top of the state's 600 districts.

Ohio

Funding for Ohio's school system is, for the moment at least, based mostly on property taxes, though a few school districts have passed income taxes to partially fund their budgets. The current system favors districts with strong industrial tax bases or pricey residential real estate. Poorer school districts, particularly rural districts, fare much worse. Though it's technically supposed to help equalize per-pupil spending, the state funding formula actually adds to the inequities in some cases because it grandfathers in funding levels from decades ago. Challenges to similar funding systems have prevailed elsewhere in the country, including Indiana and Kentucky.

The solution usually involves a system in which one mill (1/1000th of a dollar) of property tax generates the same revenue for a school district regardless of the value of real estate there. State funding makes up the difference for poorer school districts. In Ohio such a system would mean that to keep state funding at current levels, state support for many of the richest school districts would have to be eliminated.

Adding to the current financial woes of many Ohio schools is the state's property tax rollback system. Under this system, a school tax levy always raises roughly the same amount of money as when first passed, even as property values increase later. Only new development can actually increase school funding without a new levy. As a result, all but a handful of lucky school districts must constantly come back to voters for new levies as inflation increases their costs but not their tax revenues.

Despite the complexity and inequity of its funding system, Ohio still manages to have some pretty good schools. And Greater Cincinnati has some of the best schools and school districts in the state.

HAMILTON COUNTY

Results of the latest Ohio Ninth Grade Proficiency Test reflect that Cincinnati Public Schools, the area's largest public school system, performed better than any other urban school system in Ohio.

Cincinnati Public Schools students, however, continue to lag behind those in the more affluent suburban districts. Top scorers among the area's suburban districts included Indian Hill, Madeira, Sycamore, Loveland, Mariemont, Wyoming, and Forest Hills.

Cincinnati Public Schools
230 East Ninth Street
(513) 363-0000

With 40,000 (down from 50,000 a decade ago) students, Cincinnati Public Schools make up by far the largest public school system in the area. Give the Cincinnati Public Schools an A, or at least a high B, for effort. Unfortunately, this is still an urban district, with all the problems associated with big urban school districts.

The district has tried to alleviate these problems by inviting the business community to take the lead in telling the district how to solve its problems. Specifically, the Cincinnati Business Committee, a group of 27 heads of some of the city's major public and private companies, has taken an active role in advising the district, if not in actually sending any of their children there. The CBC appointed the Buenger Commission, which recommended some fairly fundamental reforms in the management of the school district. Most of the major recommendations have been carried out, including:

- Reducing central school administration by 70 percent.
- Hiring a private sector executive to run nonacademic, i.e., business, operations.
- Establishing greater accountability for teachers, principals, and administrators—this has been done through more frequent job appraisals and a pay-for-performance system, in which employees of schools that improve graduation rates and test scores can get up to 4 percent merit raises.
- Upgrading vocational education programs.
- Establishing a training academy for educators.

Academically, the district has big challenges. Overall performance numbers paint a mixed picture. Districtwide, about half of Cincinnati students go on to college—not bad for an urban district.

Also noteworthy is that in Cincinnati the middle school concept is being phased out. Instead, students will be grouped in grades K through three, four through six, and seven through eight in order to link students with the same teachers over a longer period of time. The student/teacher ratio is 18.5 to 1, daily attendance is 83 percent, and the dropout rate is 9 percent. Despite its funding woes, it should be noted that the Cincinnati district's per-pupil spending is a very respectable $6,692. Of course, much of that goes for such things as crosstown transportation, which suburban districts don't have. And the expenses of magnet programs (more on these below), which might seem like frills, are part of a court-mandated desegregation program.

Despite a relatively attractive pay scale (starting salary is $27,600), Cincinnati Public Schools—the fifth-largest employer in town—still often get the last pick of teachers. This isn't just because it's an urban district with urban troubles but also because Cincinnati is often the last district in the area to hire new teachers each year. Enrollment levels are either so unpredictable—or so poorly predicted—that many teachers are hired in September or October, weeks after the school year has begun.

Now, a word about the Cincinnati Public Schools' magnet program. And that word is "terrific." These specialty schools attract children from across the city and include the Academy of World Languages, Hughes Center (a communications school that also offers math, science, Paideia, and a Zoo Academy), Jacobs Center (math and science), Fairview (teaching German), Clark (Montessori), Schiel (arts), Quebec Heights (math and science), Withrow (international studies), and the School for the Creative and Performing Arts (one graduate is actress Sarah Jessica Parker).

In addition to these citywide schools, there are magnet programs in select neighborhood public schools (primarily Montessori, Paideia, language, and college prep programs); entry to the neighborhood programs is limited to those living in certain parts of the city.

Because these magnet schools (so named for their "attraction") are so highly regarded, there is understandably a scramble to win a place. Beginning with the 2006 school year, prospective students must go to the school they want and sign up.

Deer Park Community Schools
8688 Donna Lane, Deer Park
(513) 891-0222
This blue-collar school district northeast of Cincinnati is one of the smallest in Hamilton County, with 1,600 students in three elementary schools and one junior-senior high.

Finneytown Local Schools
8916 Fountainbleu Terrace
(513) 728-3700
Finneytown has traditionally been one of the best school districts on the west side of town and, by the numbers, one of the most productive districts in the state.

Forest Hills Local Schools
7550 Forest Road, Anderson
(513) 231-3600
This 8,000-student school district is one of the larger and better-known suburban districts in Greater Cincinnati and one of the more efficient.

Indian Hill Exempted Village Schools
6855 Drake Road, Indian Hill
(513) 272-4500
Indian Hill is Cincinnati's wealthiest, and one of the nation's poshest, community—home to Carl Lindner and other top executives of Cincinnati's major companies. Not surprisingly, the schools aren't too shabby. Per-pupil spending is among the highest in Greater Cincinnati. A countrywide survey by a *Washington Post* education reporter named Indian Hill High School as the fifth most-challenging school in the nation, encouraging students to excel academically.

Lockland City Schools
210 North Cooper Avenue, Lockland
(513) 563-5000
A small, 800-student, working-class school district in north central Hamilton County, Lockland has just one elementary school and one junior-senior high.

Loveland City Schools
757 Lebanon Road, Loveland
(513) 683-5600
This school district in northeastern Hamilton County also crosses into parts of Clermont and Warren Counties.

Madeira City Schools
7465 Loannes Drive, Madeira
(513) 985-6070
The Madeira school district has a mix of longtime residents, newer families with kids, and middle- and upper-income residents.

Mariemont City Schools
6743 Chestnut Street, Mariemont
(513) 272-7500
The villages of Mariemont, Fairfax, and Terrace Park make up this district, which includes a mix of upscale and blue-collar residents.

Mount Healthy City Schools
7615 Harrison Avenue, Mount Healthy
(513) 729-0077
This is a 4,000-student district in a working-class area on the west side of town.

North College Hill City Schools
1498 West Galbraith Road,
North College Hill
(513) 931-8181
This is a blue-collar school district on the west side of town.

Northwest Local Schools
3240 Banning Road, Groesbeck
(513) 923-1000
With more than 10,000 students, this is the second-largest school district in Hamilton County and one of the largest in the area.

Norwood City Schools
2132 Williams Avenue, Norwood
(513) 396-5520

The largely urban Norwood district has a reasonably good tax base.

Oak Hills Local Schools
6479 Bridgetown Road, Green Township
(513) 574-3200
Oak Hills is a hardworking school district in the best of the West Side tradition.

Princeton City Schools
25 West Sharon Road, Glendale/Sharonville
(513) 771-8560
Princeton's district is among the most economically diverse suburban districts in the city.

Reading Community City Schools
1301 Bonnell Avenue, Reading
(513) 554-1800
This small, middle-class, 1,400-student district with two elementary schools and one junior-senior high enjoys strong community support.

St. Bernard-Elmwood Place
105 Washington Avenue, St. Bernard
(513) 641-2020
With 1,300 students, this is one of the smaller school districts in Hamilton County.

Southwest Local Schools
230 South Elm Street, Harrison
(513) 367-4139
Southwest's 4,000 students attend six elementary schools, one junior high, and one senior high school.

Sycamore Community Schools
4881 Cooper Road, Blue Ash
(513) 791-4848
Sycamore's 6,000-student district covers the upscale suburbs of Blue Ash, Montgomery, and Sycamore and is generally recognized as among the best in Greater Cincinnati.

Three Rivers Local Schools
92 Cleves Avenue, Cleves
(513) 941-6400
This 2,300-student district on the far western side of Hamilton County is experiencing an influx of upscale residential development that is filling three elementary schools to capacity.

Winton Woods City Schools
1215 West Kemper Road, Forest Park
(513) 619-2400
Winton Woods is a large, 4,500-student district with six elementary schools, one middle school, a ninth-grade school, and a senior high.

Wyoming Public Schools
1603 Springfield Pike, Wyoming
(513) 772-2343
Wyoming is generally regarded as among the best—if not the best—school districts in Greater Cincinnati.

BUTLER COUNTY

Nearly every school district in this fast-growing area of Greater Cincinnati has spending levels well below the state average. Still, it turns in decent results and keeps attracting new students.

Fairfield City Schools
211 Donald Drive, Fairfield
(513) 829-6300
This middle-class community has a fairly wide range of income levels and expectations for its schools.

Lakota Local Schools
5030 Tylersville Road, West Chester
(513) 874-5505
Serving the rapidly growing West Chester community, this is one of the largest and fastest-growing suburban school districts in Ohio.

CLERMONT COUNTY

Clermont County schools serve an ever-growing student population, thanks to intensive land development.

Batavia Local Schools
800 Bauer Avenue, Batavia
(513) 732-2343
Batavia's school district is growing, with

one elementary school, one junior, and two senior highs that serve a fairly diverse community of blue- and white-collar residents in an area that's next in line for big-time suburban sprawl.

Bethel-Tate Local Schools
200 West Plain Street, Bethel
(513) 734-2238
This 2,100-student rural/blue-collar district in eastern Clermont has three schools—elementary, middle, and high.

Clermont Northeastern Local Schools
2773 Ohio Highway 131, Batavia
(513) 625-5478
There are 2,000 students in two elementary schools, one middle, and one high school.

Goshen Local Schools
6785 Goshen Road, Goshen
(513) 722-2222
Goshen is a blue-collar suburban/rural district in northern Clermont that serves students in three elementary, one junior high, and one high school.

Milford Exempted Village Schools
3 Eagles Way, Milford
(513) 831-1314
Milford's district has four elementary schools, a middle school, a junior high, and a high school and is one of the biggest and wealthiest districts in Clermont County in terms of community demographics.

New Richmond Exempted Village Schools
1139 Bethel-New Richmond Road, New Richmond
(513) 553-2616
This wide-ranging district covers most of southern Clermont County.

West Clermont Local Schools
4578 East Tech Drive, Amelia
(513) 943-5000
Strong community support helps account for an $11 million expansion covering four of the district's eight elementary schools, its two junior highs, and two high schools.

Williamsburg Local Schools
145 West Main Street, Williamsburg
(513) 724-3077
Williamsburg's school district has room to grow thanks to passage of a bond levy and renewal of an operating levy.

WARREN COUNTY

Warren is a pretty solid county for schools. Funding levels are similar to those in Clermont County, and Warren has the same combination of rapid population growth and largely tax-abated industrial development as Clermont.

Kings Local Schools
5620 Columbia Road, Kings Mills
(513) 398-8050
The Kings Local district has had an excellent record of community support, with five of six money issues passing in recent years.

Lebanon City Schools
25 Oakwood Avenue, Lebanon
(513) 934-5100
Lebanon's fast-growing district comprises three elementary schools, one intermediate (grades four and five), one middle, and one high school.

Little Miami Local Schools
5819 Morrow-Rossburg Road, Morrow
(513) 899-3408
Enrollment in Little Miami schools has increased appreciably. In 2006 voters approved a $62.5 million bond issue to build and expand schools.

Mason City Schools
211 North East Street, Mason
(513) 398-0474
Mason's district has four elementary schools, a middle school, and a high school.

Kentucky

The Kentucky Education Reform Act has dramatically improved the image of Kentucky schools nationally. Kentucky has always exerted considerable control over

Everybody is rushing to the burbs, it seems. The fastest-growing school districts (as charted by student-body growth in the past decade): Boone, Campbell, Lakota, Mason, and Forest Hills.

its local school districts and, under KERA, state micromanagement of local school affairs has grown.

Beechwood Independent Schools
50 Beechwood Road, Fort Mitchell, KY
(859) 331-1220
This small district has both its schools—a K-through-6 elementary and a 7-through-12 secondary school—in the same location.

Bellevue Independent Schools
215 Center Street, Bellevue, KY
(859) 261-2108
Bellevue's district includes an elementary school and a high school.

Boone County Schools
8330 Kentucky Highway 42, Florence, KY
(859) 334-4400
Boone County Schools is a rapidly growing district that serves students in 10 elementary schools, 4 middle schools, 3 senior highs—Boone, Conner, and Ryle—and one vocational school, an alternative high school, and an adult-ed school.

Campbell County Schools
101 Orchard Lane, Alexandria, KY
(859) 635-4161
This district includes six elementary schools, one middle school, and a new high school.

Covington Independent Schools
25 East Seventh Street, Covington, KY
(859) 292-5800
Covington is an urban district facing urban challenges with innovative programs.

Dayton Independent Schools
200 Clay Street, Dayton, KY
(859) 491-6565
The Dayton school district serves 1,400 students with an elementary and a high school.

Erlanger-Elsmere Independent Schools
500 Graves Avenue, Erlanger, KY
(859) 727-2009
This small district puts the emphasis on community schools.

Fort Thomas Independent Schools
2356 Memorial Parkway, Fort Thomas, KY
(859) 781-3333
Fort Thomas's district has the parental involvement and high expectations that go along with one of Northern Kentucky's most upscale communities.

Kenton County Schools
20 Kenton Lands Road, Erlanger, KY
(859) 344-8888
With more than 12,000 students, this is one of Northern Kentucky's largest school districts.

Ludlow Independent Schools
525 Elm Street, Ludlow, KY
(859) 261-8210
This urban river-town district has one elementary, one junior high, and one high school.

Newport Independent Schools
Eighth and Washington Streets
Newport, KY
(859) 292-3023
Newport's district serves an urban community with three elementary, one junior high, one high school, and special schools that include a vocational school and an adult learning center.

CHARTER SCHOOLS

Charter schools in Ohio are quasi-independent public schools. Charter schools are a relatively new experiment in the school-choice movement, a third option to traditional public and private institutions. They operate under fewer state regulations and without preexisting union contracts and state tenure laws. Their mere existence has sent a shudder through urban school systems such as Cincinnati Public Schools, which fear even more competition and brain drain. (Kentucky and Indiana, for their part, do not authorize charter schools.)

Some distinctions that differentiate charters from the traditional public model: The school boards aren't elected but appointed by the school's founder or founders. The state can revoke a school's funding if the charter school fails to fulfill its contract or fails student achievement goals and state testing. The tuition-free schools—which serve 4,000 students in Cincinnati—tend to have smaller classes and longer school days and to stress innovative teaching.

Hope Academy
1805 Miles Road, Springfield Township
(513) 825-2441
Four schools modeled after the regionally famous Hope Academies in Cleveland (which were begun as part of the state's controversial voucher program there), the Hope Academy in Cincinnati is championed by Cincinnati city councilman Phil Heimlich. Serving K through 12, the four academies—Riverside, Academy of Cincinnati, Southern Academy, and the Life Skills Center—opened in the 2000 school year.

International College Prep Academy
244 Southern Avenue, Mount Auburn
(513) 241-1141
This school serves 500 students in grades K through six, stressing strong academics and discipline.

Oak Tree Montessori
20 East Central Parkway
(513) 241-0448
Oak Tree Montessori is a charter community school. Oak Tree accepts children from age six weeks through the sixth grade and offers before- and after-school care for children. For students age six weeks up to age five, tuition is charged. It is a public school (no tuition) for grades K through six.

W.E.B. DuBois
1812 Central Parkway, Over-the-Rhine
(513) 651-9624
DuBois requires 180 students to attend 10 hours a day for 250 days a year and take martial-arts classes as part of physical education. Lunch and uniforms are free.

PRIVATE SCHOOLS

Many of the schools listed here have waiting lists and competitive entrance requirements.

Nearly one out of four Hamilton County schoolchildren attends a private elementary or high school—making the county one of the top five in the nation in terms of private-school mania, according to the most recent U.S. Census.

Some 14 percent of kids attend private school in Clermont County. In Warren it's 13 percent, and in Butler it's 12 percent. Across the river in Northern Kentucky, 26 percent of Kenton County kids attend private, while 25 percent of Campbell and 18 percent of Boone kids go private. In Dearborn it's 11 percent.

East Side neighborhoods heavily influence the demographic. In Hyde Park and Mount Lookout, for instance, 7 out of 10 children go to private schools. In the village of Indian Hill, it's 4 out of 10.

Some private schools are all male or all female. We indicate in the listing when this is the case.

Ohio

Adath Israel School
3201 East Galbraith Road,
Amberley Village
(513) 792-5082
Adath Israel is a Conservative Jewish religious school associated with Adath Israel Synagogue. It serves 180 students from preschool to seventh grade. Although a majority of the students are of the Conservative

Jewish faith, there is some mixture of Reform and Orthodox in the student body, according to school officials.

Archdiocese of Cincinnati
100 East Eighth Street
(513) 421-3131

The archdiocese runs the largest school system of any kind in Greater Cincinnati, the ninth-largest system of Catholic schools in the United States, and one of the few parochial systems nationwide that is still growing (the addition of a 14th high school is a distinct possibility). Interestingly, at least 12 percent of its students are not Catholic.

The district operates 72 elementary schools and 12 other high schools. We've listed the high schools here.

- Badin High School, 517 New London Road, Hamilton
- Elder High School, 3900 Vincent Avenue (male)
- Fenwick High School, 3800 Center Road, Middletown
- LaSalle High School, 3091 North Bend Road, Monfort Heights (male)
- McAuley High School, 6000 Oakwood Avenue, College Hill (female)
- McNicholas High School, 6536 Beechmont Avenue, Mount Washington
- Moeller High School, 9001 Montgomery Road, Kenwood (male)
- Mother of Mercy High School, 3036 Werk Road, Westwood (female)
- Mount Notre Dame High School, 711 East Columbia Avenue (female)
- Purcell Marian High School, 2935 Hackberry Street, East Walnut Hills
- Roger Bacon High School, 4320 Vine Street, St. Bernard
- Seton High School, Glenway and Beech, Price Hill (female)

(Please note that in addition to schools run by the archdiocese, you will find some Catholic schools listed elsewhere in "Private Schools." These schools are independently operated by the Jesuits, Franciscans, or other religious orders.)

Cincinnati Country Day School
6905 Given Road, Indian Hill
(513) 561-7298

The most expensive and one of the most prestigious private schools in Greater Cincinnati, this school has classes for early childhood through high school. Admission is competitive except for the developmental preschool program. Tuition assistance and scholarships are available.

Cincinnati Hills Christian Academy
11300 Snider Road, Symmes
(513) 247-0900

The academy is an increasingly popular nondenominational Christian school with 1,300 students in K through 12. Scripture is integrated into the curriculum through classwork and weekly religion classes. Advanced-placement courses are available in English, chemistry, and biology. New facilities include a fine-arts center and tennis complex.

Cincinnati College Preparatory Academy
1141 Central Parkway, West End
(513) 684-0777

This charter stresses a college-driven focus, serving 400 students in K through 12. Students begin physics lessons, for instance, in kindergarten. Later grades continue to stress the math and science focus. Uniforms are required.

Cincinnati Waldorf School
745 Derby Avenue
(513) 541-0220

Emphasizing multisensory learning and movement activities in all subject areas, this is one of 500 Waldorf schools in the United States and the only one in Greater Cincinnati. Fine-arts programs are integrated throughout the curriculum. The school has 100 students in preschool through the fourth grade.

St. Rita School for the Deaf
1720 Glendale-Milford Road, Evendale
(513) 771-7600

St. Rita serves 145 students from age two months through 12th grade, providing comprehensive education from birth on for deaf students. It's the nation's only privately funded school for the deaf that encompasses birth to 12th grade in a residential program.

St. Ursula Academy
1339 East McMillan Street
(513) 961-3410
St. Ursula's is an independent female Catholic school, with 650 students in grades 9 through 12. It places strong emphasis on community service and preparation for college.

Saint Ursula Villa
3660 Vineyard Place
(513) 871-7218
The Villa serves 500 students from preschool through the eighth grade, centering on a Catholic-oriented, college prep education. The school is independent from the archdiocese and stresses a strong extracurricular program and team sports. The campus is located on a 21-acre former estate in Mount Lookout.

St. Xavier High School
600 West North Bend Road
(513) 761-7600
This all-male Jesuit school, known as "St. X" by most Cincinnatians, is the city's oldest and largest private school in addition to being one of its most prestigious. Classroom instruction for its 1,400 students remains traditional, but the school uses interdisciplinary offerings and team teaching. A $12.6 million addition includes a science wing, chapel, and gym.

The Seven Hills School
5400 Red Bank Road
(513) 271-9027
Insiders may jokingly call this the "Seven Bills School," but it's actually only the second-most expensive private school in Greater Cincinnati. The 1,000-student school consists of preschool through 12th grade. About 15 percent of its student body receives financial aid. The school boasts having students from 60 Cincinnati zip codes. The emphasis is naturally on college prep, with special concentration on fine and performing arts and global education.

Only a few private schools in Cincinnati top $6,000 in annual tuition. They include Cincinnati Hills Christian Academy, Summit Country Day, Ursuline Academy, St. Ursula Academy, St. Ursula Villa, St. Xavier High School, the Seven Hills School, and the Cincinnati Country Day School.

The Springer School
2121 Madison Road
(513) 871-6080
Springer has 200 students ages 6 to 14 and provides a comprehensive program for children with learning disabilities that focuses on teaching the skills and strategies they need to return to the traditional classroom. Customized programs include work with a variety of professionals. This is one of the most expensive private schools in Greater Cincinnati, but financial aid and grants are available, and most children return to traditional classrooms in community schools after three years.

Summit Country Day School
2161 Grandin Road
(513) 871-4700
This 1,000-student school is another of the area's most prestigious private schools (as well as the third most expensive), and has the only independent Catholic K-through-12 program in the city. The high school has a comprehensive array of advanced-placement programs. Foreign language instruction begins in the Montessori kindergarten and continues through grade 12.

Trinity Episcopal School
7190 Euclid Road, Madeira
(513) 984-2215
This small (20 students) Episcopal school specializes in education for students with

diagnosed neurological disorders, particularly ADD/hyperactivity disorder, in preschool through eighth grade. Individually guided education is tailored to each student's needs.

Ursuline Academy of Cincinnati
5535 Pfeiffer Road, Blue Ash
(513) 791-5791
Ursuline is a century-old Catholic college-preparatory school. This 635-student high school places emphasis on leadership and decision making. The school's modular schedule and open environment promote responsible decisions and time management. The school has been honored for excellence by the U.S. Department of Education.

Yavneh Day School
8401 Montgomery Road, Kenwood
(513) 984-3770
With a student body of 400, preschool to eighth grade, Yavneh serves Conservative, Reform, Orthodox, and nonaffiliated Jewish students. The school stresses an academic program of general education and Judaic studies.

MONTESSORI SCHOOLS

Montessori schools, which stress individually guided instruction through discovery, are very popular for preschool and primary education in Greater Cincinnati. Below are some of the more popular programs. In addition, some magnet elementary schools in the Cincinnati public school system offer Montessori programs.

Mercy Montessori Center
2335 Grandview Avenue
(513) 475-6700

The New School
3 Burton Woods Lane
(513) 281-7999

Sands Montessori
6421 Corbly Avenue
(513) 357-4330

Xavier University Montessori Lab
3800 Victory Parkway
(513) 745-3424
Xavier is one of the few colleges in the country to offer a master's degree in Montessori education, and this is the lab school that helps train Montessori educators. The lab school has a long waiting list.

Kentucky

Calvary Christian School
5955 Taylor Mill Road, Covington, KY
(859) 356-9201
This college preparatory school, affiliated with Calvary Baptist Church, serves grades K through 12. The 650-student school places an emphasis on the phonetic reading program in the primary grades, individual character development, and the fine arts. There are computer and science labs as well as a theater stage.

Covington Latin School
21 East 11th Street, Covington, KY
(859) 292-5864
This is a unique college prep program for academically talented students, who usually enter in the eighth grade and graduate by age 16. The program compresses junior and senior high into four years. Begun as a boys school in 1923, it now has a coed enrollment of about 180 students.

Diocese of Covington
947 Donaldson Highway, Covington, KY
(859) 283-6200
The Covington diocese operates a system with 11,500 students in 31 elementary and 9 secondary schools. Value-based education with an emphasis on traditional instruction along with technology and cooperative learning are hallmarks.

Villa Madonna Academy
2500 Amsterdam Road, Villa Hills, KY
(859) 331-6333
A relatively small school with 130 students, this nearly century-old college prep program for grades 1 through 12 is nonetheless notable for being run by Benedictine sisters, known for the quality of their teaching, and for its academic consistency. Tradition doesn't necessarily mean old-fashioned. The nuns' computer curriculum, with Internet access for all, is nationally recognized.

CHILD CARE

Finding reliable, competent child care in any city is a challenge. In Greater Cincinnati, that challenge is made all the more formidable by a confluence of factors beyond the control of the average parent. The U.S. Census reports that 45,552 Greater Cincinnati children under the age of six live in homes where both parents (or the only parent) works. Yet in the entire tristate, there are only about 45,000 available slots for children in day-care settings. In other words, this is a tight market for finding available child-care openings. And it's going to get tighter.

In a national survey published by *Working Mother* magazine, day cares in Ohio, Kentucky, and Indiana all won lackluster ratings—Ohio the lowest of all. Furthermore, a recent day-care study shows area child-care workers can only expect to earn $7.18 an hour before taxes—about what a McDonald's fry chef earns here on average.

Child-care centers must be licensed by the state in Ohio, Kentucky, and Indiana. That said, in Ohio especially, the loopholes are infamous. And since the far majority of the area's day-care centers are found on the Ohio side (Hamilton County alone has about 1,300 child-care centers and home providers, with slots for 18,000 children and 2,000 infants), this is a problem worth addressing in some depth. Understand that Ohio is still in the midst of the Republican revolution that swept the nation a few years back. Conservative legislators and the governor are cutting, or at least certainly not increasing, funds for children's services. And services such as inspections of day-care facilities are a "luxury" the administration can't afford. Yes, the Ohio Department of Human Services is required by state law to inspect all day-care centers in Greater Cincinnati and elsewhere twice a year. At least one of those two inspections must be unannounced. However, a study published in the *Cincinnati Enquirer* showed that numerous centers do not receive the two inspections and that, indeed, the state keeps no record of how often this requirement is met.

The Department of Human Services, for its part, counters that it is struggling to keep up with inspecting a burgeoning number of day-care centers (4,000 in Ohio, as opposed to 3,000 just a decade ago) with no increase in its staff of 38 inspectors statewide. Department officials claim the lack of inspections doesn't affect safety although, mystifyingly, no Ohio state office is actually required to keep statistics on accidents and deaths in child-care centers.

Ohio is currently one of six remaining states that does not regulate home-based day care (as long as it involves six or fewer children). The six-pack rule effectively means the vast majority of the state's home day-care providers don't have to meet any requirement, regulation, or inspection—not even a Health Department checkup on kitchen and sanitary facilities.

The only time home care is regulated is if the home is "certified"—which it must be if the care is subsidized by a state or federal program—or licensed, a requirement only if seven or more children are watched at one time. Action for Children, a nonprofit watchdog organization, estimates that three-fourths of children in home-based day care here are under unregulated care.

The demand for child care in the region is expected to increase as more single parents move into the workplace. More than 47,000 tristate children currently live in homes where one or both parents are on welfare. What happens next, and the impacts on the quality and availability of child care in the area, is an open question. Certainly, as the laws of supply and demand take hold, costs will rise. (Right now, child care in Greater Cincinnati runs about $129 on average per week for infants, $100 for toddlers, $95 for preschoolers, and $86 for school-age children.)

In Kentucky, as a result of the welfare reform legislation and its looming consequences, the state is actively contracting with churches and other religious organizations to operate child-care facilities. Kentucky city, county, and state governments can funnel tax money to nonprofit corporations set up by churches as long as the funds are used for child care and other nonreligious purposes. The upshot: If you're looking for child care in Kentucky, consider calling local churches. You do not have to become a member of the church or denomination in order to have equal access to these state-funded care centers.

Babysitting services are few and far between, with the Yellow Pages listings being largely devoted to pet sitters.

Cincinnati has a full complement of youth organizations to help keep your kids busy after school, in the evenings, or on weekends. They include the Boy Scouts, (513) 961-2336; Girl Scouts, (513) 489-1025; and the Boy's/Girl's Club, (513) 421-8909. It's also worth contacting Big Brother/Big Sister, (513) 421-4120, for details on its mentoring program.

That's the overview of child care in Greater Cincinnati. Here are some nuts and bolts about resources to locate quality child-care providers. The very first phone call you make should be to Comprehensive Community Child Care, better known in the area as the 4Cs, (513) 221-0033. Funded by local businesses and the United Way, the 4Cs assists families on both sides of the Ohio River in finding child-care options. The agency will help you sift through the possibilities of au pairs, home providers, and day-care centers. The agency refers to 398 area centers, 665 home providers, 622 preschools, and 582 after-school programs. The 4Cs has also launched a Quantum Leap Campaign, with a goal of helping create and accredit new day-care centers as well as adding 200 home providers to its accredited registry.

Some of the larger chain care and education centers in the area include Compass Schools Children's World Learning Centers, Kinder Kare Learning Centers, Biederman Education Centers, Bright Horizons, the Goddard Schools, and Little Red School Houses. You can find a complete listing of commercial ventures under "Child Care Centers" in the Yellow Pages. The *Cincinnati Business Courier* publishes an annual listing of the largest child-care centers in the area in their annual list directories.

In Ohio as well as Kentucky, church-run day nurseries and preschools are another option. The long lines of parents who traditionally wait to sign up for such programs are a solid indication that the child-care programs run by the region's churches are equal or sometimes superior to commercial ventures. Check under "Churches" in the Yellow Pages.

The YMCA of Greater Cincinnati is the largest day-care provider in the region, operating 85 care centers on both sides of the Ohio River for kids two months through 12 years of age, and is well worth a phone call. (See the Parks and Recreation chapter for the number of your nearest Y.)

A number of public and private schools offer extended day care as part of their curricula. Keep in mind, however, that a major shift in how Ohio's schools are funded is on the horizon (as we noted in the introduction to this chapter), and these latchkey programs may be among the first to feel the ax in the school year that changes eventually take effect. That said,

Ohio school districts currently offering extended care include: Cincinnati Public Schools, Deer Park, Fairfield, Finneytown, Forest Hills, Indian Hill, Lockland, Mariemont, Milford, Mount Healthy, Northwest, Norwood, Oak Hills, Princeton, Reading, St. Bernard, Sycamore, and Wyoming. In Kentucky, school districts offering latchkey programs include Beechwood, Bellevue, Boone, Campbell, Covington, Erlanger, Fort Thomas, Kenton, and Ludlow.

Many private schools offer after-school care programs. They include Cincinnati Country Day, Cincinnati Hills Christian Academy, Cincinnati Waldorf School, St. Ursula Villa, the Seven Hills School, Summit Country Day, and Villa Madonna Academy, as well as many Catholic archdiocese grade schools. (See the Private Schools listings earlier in the chapter for contact numbers for all these district, diocesan, and private schools.)

During the summer, of course, many of these schools are closed. Consider options such as the Cincinnati Recreation Commission, (513) 352-4000, which will care for the children of working parents all day during the summer. The children must be between the ages of 6 and 12. The care takes place in the community recreation center nearest the child's school. Other summer options include the area's many day camps, many run by the Cincinnati Park Board (including Nature Camp, Preschool Discovery Morning, and Adventure Camp), the Hamilton County Park District, Anderson Park District, the Cincinnati Nature Center, and any number run by the YMCA. (See the Parks and Recreation chapter for contact numbers for the various park boards and districts as well as Ys.)

Your best summer resource may well be *All About Kids,* a free monthly magazine available in most grocery stores. Its March issue each year is devoted largely to a comprehensive and up-to-date "Summer Camp Directory," which includes most day, overnight, sports, special needs, and academic camps as well as art, music, and dance camps.

If you're moving to town to work for a major corporation, you may be in luck. Companies such as Procter & Gamble, Chiquita, and Kroger have taken the lead in making sure their employees' children are properly looked after. And six area employers—AT&T, Deloitte & Touche, GE Capital Services, IBM, Citicorp, and Ethicon Endo-Surgery Inc.—have pooled $640,000 to improve day-care options for their workforces, believing that worry-free employees are productive employees. If you're not working for one of the Fortune 500 companies, you still ought to inquire with your firm's human resources director about any company child-care plans (or subsidies) that might exist.

Most area hospitals, universities, and the local arms of federal agencies such as the Internal Revenue Service offer their employees some kind of on-site center or other resource. United Way funds a number of day-care centers, including Fairmount Day Care Center, Madisonville Day Care Center, Wesley Child Care/Infant Toddler Center, and New Beginnings Child Care Inc. The United Way requires all centers it funds to be accredited by the 4Cs.

Here are some practical first steps you can take as you actually begin to weigh the value of one day-care center against another. State law in both Ohio and Kentucky does require that inspection reports be posted in visible locations at day-care centers for parents to see. You can also write the agency and obtain a report of any given day-care center. In Ohio write the Ohio Department of Human Services, 65 East State Street, Columbus, OH 43215. In Kentucky contact the Cabinet for Human Resources, Office of the Inspector General/Division of Licensing and Regulations, 275 East Main Street, Frankfort, KY 40621. Neither state agency encourages telephone queries.

As you consider day-care centers, be aware that in addition to state and 4Cs accreditation, about 10 percent of local child-care centers go to the trouble of becoming accredited by the National Association for the Education of Young

Children, an important distinction.

Knowing a day care is licensed or accredited is all well and good, but it doesn't absolve you of the need to check out the child-care provider yourself. The best way to shop for child care is to call ahead to arrange for a visit the first time, then make a second visit unannounced. Any center or provider that has a problem with unannounced visits is probably one to avoid. On any visit, watch how staff members speak to the children; see if they are more concerned with a smudged wall than with comforting an unhappy child. Are emergency fire procedures in place? Find out which is the nearest hospital and the neighborhood's average 911 response time (this is public information published regularly in the local papers).

Ask the center about its ratio of child-care workers to the number of children in a class. Find out how, and how often, staff will formally communicate to you (either by oral or written report) on your child's socialization success and other benchmarks.

Check with the Cincinnati Better Business Bureau for a record of complaints. Also check the public library's newspaper database to see if favorable, or unfavorable, stories have appeared about a child-care center you are considering.

Finally, be aware that "day care" and "preschool," in this region at least, are nowhere near the same thing. A private day-care center, even one that claims to offer some kind of "preschool" program, doesn't have to conform to any state educational requirements. If you want your child to attend a licensed, legitimate preschool, make sure it's one accredited by the state Department of Education.

Good luck. And may the 4Cs be with you.

HIGHER EDUCATION

The largest private employer in Cincinnati isn't Procter & Gamble or Kroger or even Chiquita Banana. It's the University of Cincinnati, and that fact alone says volumes about how vital higher education has become in the mind-set of Greater Cincinnati. The area offers everything from a huge state institution to a midsize Jesuit university to a dozen smaller colleges, both public and private. You can choose from a full range of campuses: urban, suburban, even rural. And the quality and breadth of majors and academic study paths are as diverse as the student populations themselves.

Xavier University, Miami University of Ohio, and the College of Mount St. Joseph, in particular, are notable academic institutions. But there's something for everyone.

No discussion of higher education in Cincinnati can go very far without delving into what the University of Cincinnati—the second largest educational institution in Ohio—has to offer. And that's a lot. UC leads as a nationwide pioneer in cooperative education, giving students valuable on-the-job training and contacts while they're still in school. And the campus has gone high tech; engineering students, for instance, participate in interactive lectures with NASA researchers thousands of miles away.

Meanwhile, the research arm of the university continues to grow. Thanks to its budding Center for Obesity and Nutrition Research (funded by $1 million annually in federal grants), UC is assembling a star team of scientists who may transform "America's eighth fattest city" into a national center for obesity research.

UC opened its Genome Research Institute in 2003. Some 450 researchers at the 360,000-square-foot biotech facility hunt for better treatments for heart disease, obesity, cancer, and other ills.

The area's state schools also offer some special bargains, one being the reciprocity agreement between UC, Cincinnati State Technical and Community College, and Northern Kentucky University that allows Ohio residents in Hamilton, Butler, Warren, Clermont, and Brown Counties to attend NKU at Kentucky-resident rates and Northern Kentucky residents to attend UC or Cincinnati State at Ohio-resident rates. To qualify, Ohio students must complete associate's degree programs in their home state, then transfer. (Excluded from the reciprocity deal are electronics, engineering technology, industrial technology-construction, manufacturing engineering technology, nursing, and social work majors.) Students from Southeastern Indiana may also qualify for in-state resident rates at these Ohio and Kentucky institutions. Admissions offices can provide more details.

Branch campuses of UC and Miami offer lower tuition rates than the main campuses, and they provide classes that in most cases transfer to four-year degrees at the main campuses. Cost per quarterly credit hour at UC's Clermont College is less than 80 percent of the cost at the main campus, and the cost at UC's Raymond Walters campus in Blue Ash is less than 90 percent. At Miami's Middletown and Hamilton branch campuses, annual undergraduate tuition is about a third lower than at the main campus in Oxford. All Miami branch campus credits transfer to the main campus, but you need to check the course listings for UC's branch campuses to see which credits will transfer there.

A further advantage if you choose to study here: Cincinnati's institutes of higher learning do cooperate with each other. The Greater Cincinnati Consortium of Colleges and Universities allows students at the 13 member private and public schools

The most expensive Cincinnati colleges for in-state undergraduates? Xavier's tuition tops out at $23,000, Thomas More is $17,600, Miami University is $9,500, and UC is $8,900. Better bargains are found at Northern Kentucky University ($5,000), the smaller colleges, and the extension campuses of UC (Clermont College and Raymond Walters College).

to take courses at any of the other schools if they're not offered at their home institutions. Consortium members include the Art Academy of Cincinnati, Athenaeum of Ohio, Cincinnati Bible College & Seminary, Cincinnati State, Chatfield College, College of Mount St. Joseph, Hebrew Union College/Jewish Institute of Religion, Miami University, Northern Kentucky University, Thomas More College, University of Cincinnati, Wilmington College, and Xavier University.

Greater Cincinnati colleges are also long on convenience. Many of them offer evening and weekend programs. Chatfield College and the Cincinnati branches of Wilmington College have centered their entire programs around working adults.

Chances are you can study at a Cincinnati university without spending much on gas either. Even the campuses of UC have branches at some area high schools and off-site office centers, including a shopping center storefront campus in Summerside and the Union Township Administration Building in West Chester. And Chatfield College offers classes in North Fairmount.

Everyone, in fact, seems to be branching out. The newest and fastest-growing satellite campuses can be found on the far East Side, and that's not surprising, since the East Side—along with the northern suburbs—boasts some of the fastest-growing residential communities in the tristate. Wilmington College recently added an East Side branch in the Eastgate Mall area near Anderson, for instance. And Clermont College in Batavia, a satellite of UC, recently launched a massive expansion program. Enrollment at Clermont, already up 40 percent since the beginning of the last decade, sparked construction of a $10 million complex housing 43,000 square feet of additional classroom space.

The listings in this chapter cover the major traditional colleges in the area along with some alternatives to traditional colleges—among them, Cincinnati State, Communiversity, and the Union Institute, perhaps the nation's most innovative alternative-education institution. You'll also find a section on continuing adult education as well as trade and technical schools.

In short, whatever your educational need, whatever your time frame and financial constraints, you'll find the solution at one of Greater Cincinnati's numerous houses of higher education. Read on.

COLLEGES AND UNIVERSITIES

Art Academy of Cincinnati
12th and Jackson Streets
(513) 721-5205

The Art Academy of Cincinnati is one of five museum schools in the United States (the academy actually predates the Cincinnati Art Museum). It was founded in 1869 as the McMicken School of Art, an early department of what would become the University of Cincinnati in 1873. But the founders felt the art school should be separate from the university and affiliated with the art museum when the museum opened in 1885. The academy gained use of the old Mount Adams Public School on St. Gregory Street in 1979, and classes are now held at both locations.

The Art Academy offers associate's and bachelor's degrees in design and fine arts and is the only college offering the bachelor of fine arts degree in the area. Of its 200 students, more than 80 percent attend full-time. Coursework includes digital design, printmaking, metalworking, hot-glass design, sculpture, and photo design.

The academy is a member of the Alliance of Independent Colleges of Art and Design, which includes such prestigious schools as the museum schools in Washington, Chicago, and Boston; the Rhode Island School of Design, and the School of the Visual Arts in New York. Academy students are eligible to spend a semester in a similar program at other member schools for credit.

Athenaeum of Ohio/
Mount St. Mary's Seminary
6616 Beechmont Avenue, Anderson
(513) 231-2223

The Athenaeum of Ohio is an accredited center of education providing programs of preparation for and development in ministry within the Roman Catholic tradition. It also offers a certificate in lay ministry and prepares men for the permanent diaconate and priesthood. It was inaugurated in 1829 by the first bishop of Cincinnati (along with Xavier University, which later split to form its own Jesuit-run campus).

The Athenaeum offers master's degrees in divinity, theology, biblical studies, religion, and pastoral counseling. Public lectures and exhibits, choral presentations, and noncredit courses for the public round out the academic offerings.

Chatfield College
20918 Ohio Highway 251, St. Martin
(513) 875-3344

The mission of Chatfield College is to make a liberal arts education available to people who might not succeed in college if Chatfield did not exist. Most of the 300 students, whose average age is 31, are first-generation college students from Cincinnati and Appalachian counties east of the city. The private two-year college offers the associate of arts degree with concentrations in business, health and human services, child development, commercial art, and liberal arts. In addition to classes at its main campus, Chatfield offers courses each semester at its Cincinnati Branch, North Fairmount Community Center, 2569 St. Leo Place, North Fairmount, (513) 921-9856.

The college has an open admissions policy, accepting any student who has a high school or college transcript or a GED certificate. Classes usually meet only once a week during daytime or evening hours to accommodate work schedules. The academic year includes two 15-week semesters during fall and spring and a shorter summer session.

Cincinnati Christian University
2700 Glenway Avenue
(513) 244-8100

Cincinnati Christian University (formerly Cincinnati Bible College & Seminary) prepares students who will take full-time ministries within their local churches or who want ministry-related careers or want to be volunteer leaders in their churches. The private college, supported by Christian churches and Churches of Christ, was created in 1924 by the merger of institutions in Cincinnati and Louisville, Kentucky.

Situated on the highest hilltop overlooking downtown Cincinnati, the 40-acre campus includes a mix of modern buildings and traditional structures from the 1870s. Faculty members have studied at more than 80 universities, and more than 60 percent have or are working toward doctorates. Of the nearly 900 students, two-thirds attend full-time.

The college offers associate's, bachelor's, and master's degrees. Programs include Bible, general studies, and church music, plus emphases on youth ministry, ministry to the deaf, early childhood education, teacher education, music education, journalism, and psychology. This is another private school with budget-minded tuition, which runs about $1,000 less than the state universities in Ohio.

Cincinnati College of Mortuary Science
645 West North Bend Road
(513) 761-2020

The Cincinnati College of Mortuary Science is the oldest college of mortuary education in the United States. It was founded in 1882 by Joseph H. Clarke and has grown to have an international reputation. CCMS is accredited by the Ohio Board of Regents and is authorized to offer instruction leading to the bachelor of mortuary science and the associate of applied science degrees.

The college's approximately 130 students come from 30 states and several foreign countries. After graduation, many pursue employment as funeral directors and embalmers, but others take jobs in such areas as pathology, anatomy, forensics, grief counseling, and mortuary science education.

Cincinnati State Technical and Community College
3520 Central Parkway
(513) 569-1500

Attending Cincinnati State Technical and Community College is just about a sure way to land a job. Indeed, local employers say the school can't produce grads fast enough to meet the demand. Praised by national magazines and even former vice president Al Gore, the public two-year community college—now the fourth-largest college in Cincinnati—boasts a 98 percent job placement rate for its technical graduates in fields ranging from laser electro-optics and civil engineering to health care and aviation maintenance.

Cincinnati State, formerly known as Cincinnati Technical College, offers a wide range of associate's degrees and an extensive cooperative education program. More than 600 employers hire Cincinnati State students for co-ops alone. Among the most popular degrees are dental hygiene, chef technology, restaurant management, hotel management, culinary arts, turfgrass management, massage therapy, and environmental technology. Of the college's 7,700 students, more than 50 percent attend part-time.

Cincinnati State offers the world's first college degree in cemetery management. The degree is offered in partnership with the Cincinnati College of Mortuary Science.

College-Conservatory of Music
Calhoun Street at Clifton Avenue
(513) 556-6000

While the College-Conservatory of Music is technically a part of the University of Cincinnati, we list it individually because it is a completely separate institution with its own admissions office and own specific entrance requirements (which include auditions). Already one of the top conservatories in the country, the century-old CCM has undergone a $98 million renovation and expansion. It has an enrollment of 1,200 students, plus 1,800 in preparatory programs, and offers 100 degree programs. Studies run from ballet to classical guitar, electronic media to harpsichord, and jazz to stage design.

Among its alumni and former attendees are opera diva Kathleen Battle, Suzanne Farrell (one of the century's great ballerinas), and the late popular musicians Al Hirt, Tennessee Ernie Ford, and Frank Zappa. CCM ensembles have made acclaimed tours in recent years to New York, Europe, and the Far East. Closer to home, CCM events number nearly 900 annually.

CCM's campus includes the Corbett Center for the Performing Arts, with a 740-seat, fully equipped proscenium theater complete with organ for recitals. There are numerous smaller theaters and studios for smaller chamber recitals, opera, ballet, and drama.

College of Mount St. Joseph
5701 Delhi Road
(513) 244-4200

This coeducational Catholic liberal arts college was founded in 1920 by the Sisters of Charity of Cincinnati. "The Mount," as it's known by many Cincinnatians, offers career-oriented programs for traditional and nontraditional students in day, evening, and weekend schedules. About half of the college's 2,100 students are nontraditional, meaning they are older than 23 and more than five years out of high school. More than half attend part-time and more than two-thirds are women. The percentage of freshmen who graduate in five years is 68 percent, well above the national average of 48 percent.

Students may choose from more than a dozen associate's degrees, 40 bachelor's degrees, 3 master's degrees, 8 preprofessional programs, and several certificate programs. Ninety-nine percent of science program graduates who apply to medical schools are accepted. Physical therapy is another rapidly growing major at the college. And cooperative education programs are available to full-time students in all majors.

The college offers several outreach programs. Project EXCEL provides support services to help students with learning disabilities succeed at the college. Project SCOPE is a summer program of college orientation and enrichment for black high school students. The college also offers a summer residency program for high school women to introduce them to career opportunities in math and sciences and prepare them for college study in these fields.

The College of Mount St. Joseph is about 7 miles southwest of downtown Cincinnati on a 75-acre site overlooking the Ohio River and across the river from the Greater Cincinnati/Northern Kentucky International Airport. The new Jean Patrice Harrington Student Center includes a 2,000-seat arena where the equally new men's basketball team will play. College facilities also feature a new state-of-the-art health sciences center and a new student administrative-services center.

God's Bible College
1810 Young Street
(513) 721-7944

The college provides preparation for ordained and lay ministry and offers associate's and bachelor's degrees to its student body of 250.

Hebrew Union College–
Jewish Institute of Religion
3101 Clifton Avenue
(513) 221-1875

Hebrew Union College was established in 1875 by Rabbi Isaac Wise, the founder of American Reform Judaism, as the first institution of Jewish higher education in the United States. It has been an intellectual center of Reform Judaism ever since and houses the Reform movement's library and archives collections. HUC is also a leading center for study, training, research, and publication in the Bible, ancient Near Eastern languages, Hellenistic studies, rabbinics, Jewish religious thought and philosophy, and modern Jewish history. The campus's Skirball Museum–Cincinnati Branch exhibits art and artifacts from 4,000 years of Judaic cultural tradition. Not least among its roles is offering master's programs to more than 120 students of Jewish and other faiths.

Although it is one of the area's smaller colleges, HUC has a prominent place in the history of the city and the world. During the Holocaust, HUC literally saved the lives of many European Jewish scholars who faced death in Nazi-occupied Europe by bringing them to the Cincinnati campus. It also became a successor to many of the Jewish institutes of higher learning destroyed in Europe. In 1972 HUC participated in the ordination of the first female rabbi. Today about 50 percent of the college's rabbinic students are women. The college also trained the first Reform rabbi in Israel, ordained in 1980, and the first Israeli woman rabbi, ordained in 1992.

Recent research milestones for HUC include using computer analysis to unlock secrets of the Dead Sea Scrolls and rescuing from near extinction the ancient Aramaic language, the original language of several books of the Bible and the Talmud and of Jesus Christ and his apostles.

The college merged in 1950 with the Jewish Institute of Religion in New York,

Looking for a guaranteed job on graduation? The paper science program at Miami University is one of only eight in the nation and, during the past 15 years, has found work for 100 percent—yes, 100 percent—of its graduates each and every year. The average starting salary for a student with a graduate degree in paper science, an engineering degree specific to the forest-products industry, is $49,000.

where a second campus of the college remains. The merged school opened a Los Angeles campus in 1954 and a Jerusalem campus in 1963. In conjunction with the University of Cincinnati, HUC also operates the Center for Ethics and Contemporary Moral Problems, where international scholars research and debate ethical issues. A program analyzing ethics in the media (or the lack of them) has garnered national attention.

Ivy Tech State College
500 Industrial Drive, Lawrenceburg, IN
(812) 537-4010
Ivy Tech is part of a network of 22 two-year technical colleges in Indiana that provide college-level, job-oriented training in both certificate and associate's degree programs. Of the 800 students on the Lawrenceburg campus, more than two-thirds attend part-time, and the average age is 30.

Programs include accounting, office administration, business administration, computer information and systems technology, electronics technology, industrial technology, manufacturing technology, medical assistant training, a practical nursing certificate, and an associate's degree in nursing. In response to the area's booming riverboat casino and tourism industry, a hospitality curriculum includes hotel management, food service, and restaurant training.

Tuition is the lowest of any community or four-year college in the state. Residents of the Kentucky counties of Boone, Carroll, Gallatin, and Trimble also pay Indiana in-state rates.

Maysville Community College
1755 U.S. Highway 68, Maysville, KY
(606) 759-7141
Founded in 1967, this two-year college offers associate's degrees in a variety of technical and academic fields. The student body numbers 1,200.

Miami University
301 South Campus Avenue, Oxford
(513) 529-1809
Founded in 1809, Miami has a reputation as one of the best deals in college education. It was recently ranked 22nd among the top-50 best public universities in the nation by *U.S. News & World Report* and 35th on *Money* magazine's annual list of the top-100 best college buys. Students at the Hamilton branch, 1601 Peck Boulevard, (513) 785-3111, and the Middletown branch, 4200 East University Boulevard, (513) 727-3200, get an even better deal their first two years—about two-thirds of the main campus tuition rate. Enrollment is more than 21,000 overall, with 2,200 on each of the branch campuses. More than 100 students also attend Miami's John E. Dolibois European Center in Luxembourg.

This state school's reputation as a "Public Ivy" has helped make it one of the most popular state campuses and the toughest to get into. The middle 50 percent of enrolled freshmen ranked in the top 7 to 23 percent of their high school classes.

Renowned for its beauty, the heavily wooded main campus is dominated by the modified Georgian style popular in the 19th century. Miami's King Library, which owns more than two million volumes and is the largest building on campus, recently underwent a $2 million renovation.

Miami places an emphasis on senior faculty teaching undergraduates, including freshman and sophomore courses. Eighty-five percent of freshman classes are taught by faculty who hold the highest degrees in their fields. More than 82 percent of all students graduate in five years and 75 percent in four, both well above national averages. More than 76 percent of graduates who apply to medical or law schools are accepted.

Among the best recognized of a comprehensive array of programs and majors are accounting, English, environmental and life sciences, history, international studies, paper science (one of eight such programs in the country), and political science. The program's 240 students live and study together in a historical section of the campus. The Page Center for Entrepreneurship offers cutting-edge business courses such as "Guerrilla Marketing" and "New Venture Creation." Be it a class on making money with the Internet or a course that encourages innovation and risk, the Page Center is definitely not your father's business school.

Miami is also the only primarily noncommuter campus in the Cincinnati area, so it provides the option of "going away" to college without having to go very far. About two-thirds of Miami students come from Ohio, the rest from 42 other countries and other parts of the United States. Though less than an hour's drive from downtown Cincinnati or Dayton, Miami dominates the tiny college town of Oxford—population score: students 18,011, townies 8,500. (One word of caution. "Tiny" isn't always synonymous with "safe"; the Oxford campus, in some years, has had as many rapes and assaults as the urban UC campus. And the university was recently taken to task by no less a judicial body than the U.S. Supreme Court for obfuscating its campus crime reports.)

Northern Kentucky University
Nunn Drive, Highland Heights, KY
(859) 572-5220

NKU offers deep-discount pricing in the Greater Cincinnati college market, with state-resident undergraduate tuition less than half that of state institutions across the river. And since many Ohioans in Greater Cincinnati can pay in-state rates at NKU, at least for their last two years of college, many do.

Of course, NKU isn't just cheap. It also offers a solid education in a wide range of programs and all classes are taught by faculty, not student assistants. Programs include aviation administration (one of the few programs in the country), education, information systems, journalism, and radio/television, management, marketing, mathematics and computer science, nursing, and theater. The college also offers preprofessional programs in dentistry, engineering, law, medicine, pharmacy, physical therapy, veterinary, and wildlife management in conjunction with the University of Kentucky at Lexington.

Of particular note is the communications department, which has a state-of-the-art Macintosh computer lab, an award-winning weekly paper, and, most notably, WNKU-FM, a public radio affiliate where news-reporting students can obtain some real-life newsroom experience.

At the graduate level, NKU offers its well-respected Salmon P. Chase College of Law, an MBA program, a combination juris doctor/MBA program, and public administration and nursing degrees.

Founded in 1968, NKU is the newest of Kentucky's eight public universities. Of NKU's 14,000 students, more than 60 percent attend full-time, but the university caters to large numbers of nontraditional students from both sides of the river.

Among the wide range of intercollegiate athletic programs—baseball, softball, tennis, cross country, men's golf, men's soccer, women's volleyball, and others—are NKU's Division II men's and women's

One of the hottest tickets on campus at Northern Kentucky University is the "Two-day Film School," a crash course on movie-making that imports Hollywood producers, directors, and screenwriters as faculty.

basketball programs, which compete as the Norse in the Great Lakes Valley Conference.

Southern State Community College
100 Hobart Drive, Hillsboro
(937) 393-3431
Founded in 1975, this institution—serving 1,800 students—offers degree certificates and associate's degrees in agriculture, business, marketing, and other endeavors.

Thomas More College
333 Thomas More Parkway, Crestview Hills, KY
(859) 344-3332
Thomas More College is a Catholic liberal arts college affiliated with the Diocese of Covington, Kentucky. The campus is just minutes from downtown Cincinnati.

Thomas More was founded in 1921 as a teacher-training school for young women and became coeducational in 1945. The college offers 23 bachelor's and 23 associate's degree programs. Through the Thomas More Accelerated Degree Program (TAP), students with 60 credit hours of previous college work can obtain a bachelor's degree in business administration in 18 to 20 months by attending class one day per week and a small group meeting one day per week. More than 60 percent of the 1,500 students at Thomas More attend full-time. About 150 live on campus.

Students tend to come out of their programs well prepared, as demonstrated by one graduating class where 83 percent of the accounting graduates passed the CPA exam on their first attempt, 100 percent of the nursing graduates passed the National Council Licensure Examination, and 100 percent of education majors taking the National Teachers Examination were successful.

The Union Institute
440 East McMillan Street
(513) 861-6400
The Union Institute is a private university that offers bachelor's degrees and PhDs. Most of the 1,500 students are in their 30s and 40s, and the flexible "university without walls" offers these busy working professionals the chance to complete a degree while maintaining a career. The institute uses the word "learner" rather than student to emphasize its objective of active rather than passive learning. Tutorial-guided study options and a minimum number of residential seminar meetings throughout the year permit flexible scheduling.

Union Institute students include educators, law-enforcement officers, health-care administrators, substance abuse counselors, government officials, corporate managers, and more. The most frequently chosen majors? Psychology, business, education, and criminal justice.

Students, who are as likely to be from across the world as across town, work one-on-one with faculty, primarily by phone and computer modem. Notable grads include author Rita Mae Brown (author of *Rubyfruit Jungle*), pioneer child-care author Grace Mitchell (who's also the mother of attorney F. Lee Bailey), and Clarissa Estes, author of the best-selling *Women Who Run with Wolves.*

Located in a historic Tudor building in Walnut Hills, the Union Institute was founded by 10 college presidents in 1964 as a vehicle for educational research and experimentation and has focused its efforts on programs for the highly motivated adult learner. The curriculum and students alike are nontraditional, with an emphasis on self-directed study. In fact, when *U.S. News & World Report* compiled a list of schools with the highest proportion of classes with fewer than 20 students, the Union Institute ranked No. 1 (99 percent of its classes), beating out Yale and Harvard.

The Graduate College in Cincinnati confers only doctorate degrees. Undergraduate programs for bachelor of arts or bachelor of science degrees are also offered here and in Miami, Florida; Sacramento, California; and Los Angeles. Both graduate and undergraduate students generally enter as mature adults. Admission for graduate school, in fact, is conditional upon demonstration of extensive prior learning from work or other experience or study. A learner's committee may grant credit for that prior learning.

For undergraduates, programs in 50 areas of concentration are individually designed with the help of a full-time professor who serves as academic adviser. Courses emphasize active problem solving in a seminar rather than passive note taking in class. "Learning Agreements," which include group agreements and individual agreements, outline specific academic goals and objectives. Students have the option to choose letter grades or receive narrative evaluations of work performed under these agreements. An undergraduate's entire degree plan culminates in completion of a senior project that can take many forms but is expected to include an oral presentation to a final review committee.

The Graduate College likewise requires individually tailored plans. Each learner's program is developed in consultation with faculty and advisers. A faculty committee helps evaluate learners' past and present learning to ensure the work is of doctoral quality.

No credits are counted. Rather, learners move through a series of stages, with faculty members serving as facilitators. The unique program includes an entry colloquium during which learners, faculty, and consultants live and work together for 10 days away from their normal routines. Over the following 24 months or longer, learners choose from among 50 seminars offered annually.

During the program, learners must spend 10 days in peer meetings and 15 days at seminars. The rest of the work is faculty-guided independent study based upon each individual's Learning Agreement. The process culminates in a Project Demonstrating Excellence, which may be a formal dissertation or may take other forms.

Tuition for the private university is moderate and within 20 to 30 percent of what UC and Miami charge.

University of Cincinnati
2624 Clifton Avenue
(513) 556-6000

The University of Cincinnati made its first major mark on U.S. education in 1906, when it created the first cooperative education program in the world through its College of Engineering. UC counts among its alumni former president and later Chief Justice William Howard Taft, author Thomas Berger, and sports greats Sandy Koufax and Oscar Robertson. Faculty have included Albert Sabin, developer of the oral polio vaccine, and Neil Armstrong, the first man on the moon.

The current UC president, Nancy Zimpher, came aboard in 2003 as the school's 25th president in 184 years—and first female chief. Zimpher is dealing, like every other public college president, with a challenging economy and decreased state funding (a decrease of almost $18 million since 2001).

"We need to build in the community a better understanding of the university's prominence nationally," said Zimpher in an early interview with *Cincy Business Magazine*. "In some respects, Cincinnati doesn't know what it has here." She promised a new emphasis on obtaining federal research grant dollars rather than regularly raising tuition.

Despite budget constraints, the university boasts some standout colleges:

UC's College of Law was ranked one of the top-50 law schools in the country in a recent *U.S. News & World Report* study. The magazine, which placed the UC college among the likes of Stanford and Columbia, cited its 93 percent passage rate for bar exams as well as the rate of grads employed nine months after graduation—94 percent. The college is the fourth-oldest continually operating law school in the country, after Harvard, Yale, and the University of Virginia.

UC also has a top-notch engineering school and industrial-design program. Its undergraduate business and MBA programs, while lacking the prestige of Ivy League or other major programs around the country, have gained national attention for their own spin on cooperative education—having students act as consultants for small businesses and providing in many cases very successful solutions. And the College of Design, Architecture, Art and Planning is arguably one of the finest in the country.

In all, UC offers 87 doctoral, 120 master's, 147 bachelor's, and 90 associate's degree programs in a wide range of disciplines, most with an eye toward landing students a job in the real world. For its part, Procter & Gamble, the largest company in Cincinnati, recruits heavily from the UC campus, primarily in the chemistry and health research departments. A new journalism department opened in 2005, marking the first time UC offered such a degree.

UC grinds out more sheepskins each spring than anybody else. Yet it remains a complete mystery, even to its own students and faculty. How do you get a grip on this behemoth? We always say the way to a university's heart is through its bank account. The university's top-5 sources of revenue are Ohio taxpayers, student tuition, federal grants, income from sales, and endowment gifts, totaling about $500 million a year. The top money-makers on campus are, in order of rank, the University Bookstore, the dorms/dining halls, the parking lots/garages, intercollegiate athletics, and the Shoemaker Arena.

And if you're in a lunchroom debate over which UC sports bring in the most Bearcat bucks, the top three athletic programs in terms of revenue are football, men's basketball, and women's basketball.

UC traces its origins to 1819, when the Cincinnati College and the Medical College of Ohio were founded. In 1870 the city of Cincinnati founded the University of Cincinnati, which later absorbed the medical college and several other institutions. For years UC was the second-oldest and second-largest municipal university in the country, until it became a state university in 1977.

This largely commuter school has just under 34,000 students, slightly less than two-thirds of whom attend full-time. Only about 3,000 students live on campus and another 750 live in nearby sorority and fraternity houses. That puts parking at a premium in the tightly packed Clifton Heights neighborhood north of downtown, UC's location.

Another addition to the fray: The campus is constantly being renovated and expanded (students joke that UC actually stands for Under Construction). A decadelong expansion plan includes a $150 million Campus Life Complex (with restaurants, workout rooms, and shops), a new hotel and conference complex, the $46 million Vontz Center for Molecular Studies, a concert amphitheater, and, thankfully, more green space in the form of grass quads. Right now, wrecking cranes and yellow tape are the order of the day, and entire departments are often moved overnight. Nothing is where you think you left it yesterday. Check the daily student paper, the *News-Record,* regularly for updates.

UC's branch campuses—Clermont College, 4200 Clermont College Drive, Batavia, (513) 732-5200; and Raymond Walters College, 9555 Plainfield Road, Blue Ash, (513) 745-5600—offer both two-year associate's degrees and programs that can lead to four-year degrees either at UC's main campus or elsewhere. There are 3,600 students at Raymond Walters and 2,000 at Clermont, so neither branch is what you'd call small. Surprisingly, many branch campus students find that their credits transfer more easily to NKU than to UC's main campus. Among the popular programs at the branches are allied health and veterinary assistant training at Raymond Walters and criminal justice at Clermont College. The Clermont campus also offers the option of individualized study, in which students learn outside the classroom. Its "Weekend College" allows students to complete a course in only three weekends, studying such topics as child care administration and effective oral communication. The "Telecourse" program broadcasts to students in their homes via public television. For information on UC's College-Conservatory of Music, see the separate entry.

UC is also known for research. The Carnegie Commission ranks it as one of only 75 Research I universities among 5,000 institutions of higher learning in the United States. Among firsts developed whole or in part at UC are the first antihistamine, Benadryl, by George Reiveschl; the first electronic organ, by Winston Koch; the first YAG laser to remove brain tumors; the first baccalaureate degree program in nursing; the first emergency medicine residency program; and the first degree program offered via satellite (health planning).

The biggest federal research contracts, in descending rank, come from: National Institutes of Health, U.S. Navy, National Science Foundation, U.S. Army, Environmental Protection Agency, Department of Energy, U.S. Air Force, Defense Advanced Research Projects Agency/Pentagon, Department of Justice, and Housing and Urban Development. Other federal contractors include NASA, the National Security Agency, and the Defense Special Weapons Department. In other words, don't mess with your prof; he might be armed with a death-ray gun.

A new first-of-its-kind degree program—legal nurse consultant—attracted national headlines. The program turns trained nurses into paralegals, in response to the increasing involvement of lawyers and legal issues in health care. After September 11, 2001, UC began offering biological and chemical terrorism courses through its College of Applied Sciences.

UC has a notable intercollegiate sports program, especially Division I football and basketball. The basketball program ended its two decades in the wilderness of mediocrity between the Oscar Robertson era and current successes when Bob Huggins—now departed—was named basketball coach in 1990. Since then, UC has made several Final Four and Final Eight appearances. The best sports news of all: In 2005 UC joined the Big East Conference and entered into league competition against the likes of Syracuse, the University of Connecticut, Rutgers, Seton Hall, Villanova, Georgetown, and Notre Dame.

Wilmington College
3 Triangle Park Drive, Sharonville
(513) 772-7516

The focus of the Cincinnati branches of Wilmington College is the adult working student. The Sharonville campus is a branch of a private four-year liberal arts college established in 1870 by the Religious Society of Friends in Wilmington and is less than an hour's drive to the northeast. The college has just added an East Side campus in the Eastgate Mall area near Anderson.

Of the Sharonville campus's nearly 400 students, more than 90 percent attend part-time. All services, including admissions and registration, are handled at times designed to mesh with work schedules. Offices are open until 8:00 P.M. Monday through Thursday and 8:30 A.M. to noon Saturday. Faculty and administrators strive for flexibility in coping with absences due to work or family demands. And as many as 30 credit hours may be earned through the College-Level Examination Program (CLEP), Advanced Placement (AP), proficiency examinations, or experiential learning assessment.

The branches offer programs leading to bachelor of arts degrees in accounting and business administration with marketing or management concentrations. Students also able to take courses on the main campus may choose from additional majors. One course track that garnered national attention is the first equine studies program in the tristate. Classes include horse anatomy, reproduction, and physiology. The college provides a half-million-dollar equine center with stable accommodations for 24 animals, but students have to bring their own horse.

Xavier University
3800 Victory Parkway
(513) 745-3301
Xavier University was established in 1831 by the first bishop of Cincinnati, Edward Fenwick, and named the Athenaeum. After the first Jesuits arrived to staff the school in 1840, the name was changed to St. Xavier College. Originally in downtown Cincinnati, St. Xavier College moved to its present location in 1919. In 1930 the name was changed to Xavier University, reflecting the school's new growth and development.

Today Xavier offers associate's, bachelor's, and master's degrees in a wide range of programs, with strength in such areas as communications arts, business administration, education, psychology, and pre-med/vet studies in life sciences. Seventy-eight percent of Xavier grads who apply for medical or veterinarian school get in. Xavier prides itself on its small class sizes, averaging 23 students. It is primarily a commuter school, half of whose roughly 6,500 students attend full-time and half part-time.

As a private school, tuition is naturally steeper here than at surrounding public institutions, but 80 percent of students receive some form of financial aid. Service scholarships also provide some top students with full rides in return for regular weekly service to the community. For that matter, most Xavier academic programs contain some service component, in keeping with Xavier's Jesuit tradition. At the graduate level, Xavier students are sometimes surprised to find that they don't pay that much more than state school students when they take into account that Xavier's graduate programs tend to be less bloated with needless course requirements.

EXTENSION CAMPUSES

The following are extension campuses of the large Greater Cincinnati universities—often, tuition at these extension branches is far less than on the main campus, yet credits are easily transferred if you decide to complete your degree on the main campus.

Chatfield College's
North Fairmount Campus
2569 St. Leo Place
(513) 921-9856

Clermont College (University of Cincinnati's Clermont County Campus)
4200 Clermont College Drive, Batavia
(513) 732-5200

Miami University's Hamilton Campus
1601 Peck Boulevard, Hamilton
(513) 785-3111

Miami University's Middletown Campus
4200 East University Boulevard, Middletown
(513) 727-3200

Northern Kentucky University's Covington Campus
1401 Dixie Highway, Covington, KY
(859) 572-5220

Raymond Walters College (University of Cincinnati's Blue Ash Campus)
9555 Plainfield Road, Blue Ash
(513) 745-5600

Wilmington College's Eastgate Campus
4360 Ferguson Drive, Eastgate
(513) 943-3600

ADULT CONTINUING EDUCATION

Whether you're a senior citizen in search of an adult-ed class, or a young professional looking to bolster your resume with a noncredit career course, Cincinnati abounds in opportunities. Even far-flung Ohio institutions such as the University of Findlay and Wright State offer classes at area hotels and high schools.

Antonelli College
124 East Seventh Street
(513) 241-4338
Antonelli College offers numerous courses in photography and art, with an emphasis on trade skills.

Art Institute of Cincinnati
1171 East Kemper Road, Tri-County
(513) 751-1206
This school trains students for careers in graphic design, visual arts, interactive Web design, advertising, and commercial art, and offers associate's degrees.

Beckfield College
16 Spiral Drive, Florence, KY
(859) 371-9393
Beckfield College (the former Kentucky Career Center) offers bachelor's degrees in applied science and associate's degree programs in computer repair, paralegal studies, court reporting, and medical office technology.

Brown Mackie College
1011 Glendale Milford Road, Woodlawn
(513) 771-2424

309 Buttermilk Pike, Fort Mitchell
(859) 341-5627
Two area campuses offer courses in video production, computers, accounting, and the like.

Chefs' School at Cooks' Wares
Harper's Point, 11344 Montgomery Road, Symmes Township
(513) 489-6400
Classes here are taught by local notable chefs from five-star restaurants here and elsewhere.

Cincinnati Academy of Design
1310 Pendleton
(513) 961-2484
The Cincinnati Academy of Design offers courses in illustration, art direction, design, and computer graphics.

Communiversity
Class locations vary
(513) 556-6932
Communiversity is the region's most ambitious adult education program, coordinated by UC's Department of Continuing Education. It's where "community meets university" through noncredit classes meeting at such far-flung locations as the Cincinnati Observatory, area gardens and parks, art galleries, downtown stock brokerages, Music Hall, even Sharon Woods Golf Course. Hundreds of courses are offered each year in the broad categories of art, astronomy, business and career, communications and literature, computer skills, culinary arts, fitness, home and garden, language, law and finance, music, needle arts, sports adventures, studio arts and handicrafts, theater and dance, and travel.

Area and national experts are recruited from the community to teach the classes.

You must be 18 or older to attend Communiversity classes. Course costs range from $20 to $200, but most classes are free to senior citizens. The easiest way to get a listing of Communiversity courses is through local branch libraries, which display course brochures.

Conversa Language Center
817 Main Street
(513) 651-5679
Conversa Language Center teaches language classes, primarily for travelers and businesspeople (it's no accident that Procter & Gamble is an easy walk away).

Cooking School at Jungle Jim's
5440 Dixie Highway, Fairfield
(513) 829-1919
A demonstration cooking school operates at the city's most unusual grocery (see Jungle Jim's in the Shopping chapter for details on the grocery).

Communiversity may well offer the town's most lively and fun courses. Topics include "Celtic Art and Ornaments" (taught by Celtic artist Cyndi Matyi), "The Joy of Soy Cooking," and "Rock Climbing for Beginners." There's also a rather intriguing little course titled "Cincinnati 101," an introduction to the city that is led by the authors of this book.

DeVry University
8800 Governors Hill Drive
(513) 583-5000

Offers master's and bachelor's degrees in business administration.

Elderhostel
Campus of Northern Kentucky University
Highland Heights, KY
(859) 572-5220

Northern Kentucky University's Elderhostel program offers dozens of courses, taught by community experts and, sometimes, NKU faculty members. No grades or quizzes, but you have to be at least 55 years old to participate. Topics range from "The Cincinnati Story: Toni Morrison's *Beloved*" to "Riverboat Boom: Big Cities, Little Burgs." Costs are generally in the $300 to $400 range, but that includes meals.

Gateway Community Technical College
1025 Amsterdam Road, Covington, KY
(859) 292-3930

790 Thomas More Parkway, Edgewood, KY
(859) 341-5200

90 Campbell Drive, Highland Heights, KY
(859) 441-4500

This is one of the largest vocational schools in Northern Kentucky, with three campuses and a 98 percent graduate placement rate. The school offers associate's degrees. Courses include air-conditioning, auto body, automotive, carpentry, child development services, computer-aided drafting, cosmetology, electronics, accounting, machine tools, masonry, office technology, and welding. The Edgewood campus offers coursework in medical office technology, pharmacy technology, practical nursing, and medical assisting. The Highland Heights campus offers courses in diesel technology, electrical technology, industrial electronics technology, printing, desktop publishing/electronic prepress, art/graphic design, and art/production art.

Greater Cincinnati Film Commission Film School
602 Main Street
(513) 784-1744

Occasional courses are offered in writing, producing, directing, budgeting, and distributing movies. (Some courses are taught by Hollywood director Don Simmons, whose past students include Spike Lee, Quentin Tarantino, and Robert Rodriguez.)

Great Oaks Institute of Technology & Career Development
3254 East Kemper Road, Sharonville
(513) 771-8881

For 30 years Great Oaks has offered programs to enhance workplace skills. Four campuses (Diamond Oaks in Dent, Laurel Oaks in Wilmington, Live Oaks in Milford, and Scarlet Oaks in Sharonville) offer vocational training for 35 affiliated school districts, and serve high school juniors and seniors from 40 high schools. Approximately 70,000 adults also receive vocational training each year. Great Oaks provides training in 50 vocational programs, including aviation, carpentry, air-conditioning repair, computers, and food service. The Sharonville Scarlet Oaks campus also offers a Center for Employment Resources and a Corporate Technology Conference Center.

Indiana Wesleyan University
9286 Schulze Drive, West Chester
(765) 881-3601

This Indiana university offers nursing classes in Greater Cincinnati, usually meeting one evening per week.

ITT Technical Institute
4750 Wesley Avenue, Norwood
(513) 531-8300
ITT Technical Institute offers associate's degree programs in computer-related fields.

Lower Price Hill Community School
2104 St. Michael Street
(513) 244-2214
Offers adult education through an agreement with Cincinnati State. Classes usually meet only once a week during daytime or evening hours to accommodate work schedules.

Mount Vernon Nazarene University
11260 Chester Road, Sharonville
(513) 761-1291
Offers a master's degree in management and bachelor's degrees in business administration, accounting, and office administration.

National College of Business
6871 Steger Drive
(513) 761-1291

7627 Ewing Boulevard, Florence, KY
(859) 525-6510
The National Business College offers degrees in accounting, business management, legal and executive secretarial, computer applications, medical assisting, and travel and tourism. The Florence campus also offers a variety of diplomas, including new programs in medical transcription and medical billing and coding. The college is part of National Business College, which has 14 campuses in Kentucky and Virginia.

Ohio Center for Broadcasting
4790 Red Bank Road, Madisonville
(513) 271-6060
The Ohio Center for Broadcasting offers career training in radio, television, and other broadcasting-related fields.

Ohio Learning Network
(614) 995-3240
www.oln.org
More than a thousand Cincinnatians study abnormal psychology, environmental law, or accounting at colleges in Columbus and Cleveland, all without leaving the city. This distance-learning network, run by the Ohio Board of Regents, combines the resources of some 20 Ohio colleges and universities to offer virtual-classroom credits.

Southwestern College of Business
8095 Connector Drive, Florence, KY
(859) 282-9999

9910 Princeton-Glendale Road, West Chester
(513) 874-0432
This school, with two campuses on opposite ends of the tristate, provides degree certificates, diplomas, and associate's degrees in a variety of business fields.

University of Phoenix
9050 Centre Pointe Drive, West Chester
(513) 772-9600
Offers bachelor's, master's, and doctorate degrees in business.

***Writer's Digest* Correspondence School**
1507 Dana Avenue, Evanston
(513) 531-2690
These mail correspondence courses for fledgling writers and novelists are known worldwide.

LIBRARIES

Cincinnati-area libraries are a model of regional cooperation, thanks to the Greater Cincinnati Library Consortium, (513) 751-4422, a group of 44 college and university, public, school, and special libraries with more than 10 million books and 50,000 periodicals. A library card from any member library allows you to borrow materials directly from any of the others. Then you can return what you borrowed to the closest member library, and it will get routed back to the right place.

At least part of the local library system's success is due to the fact that Hamilton County early on consolidated all its libraries into one system, avoiding duplication of staff and expenses. (By comparison, Cleveland's Cuyahoga County has nine public library systems.)

Library systems in the surrounding suburban counties have branch systems of their own. Anyone with library cards from these systems also can obtain a free Hamilton County library card, and an estimated 10 percent of the Hamilton County system's circulation is attributable to non-county residents.

At the center of the region's public library system is the Public Library of Cincinnati and Hamilton County, the oldest public library west of the Alleghenies. It was founded in 1853, 16 years before the Reds, which gives you an idea of its lofty place in Cincinnati history. Nationwide, it ranks second in per capita circulation among major public library systems in the nation and fourth in total collection overall. While the library's per capita circulation ranks it ahead of the New York and Chicago public libraries (and many others), local librarians are nonetheless upset with their No. 2 slot—for 17 years, you see, the Cincinnati/Hamilton County library consistently placed No. 1, until Denver claimed the top spot in a recent ranking.

More impressive news came in recently, when a national survey showed the Public Library of Cincinnati and Hamilton County ranked first in the nation for circulation per card holder, and also ranked first in holdings per capita (10.9 items per person, more than double of the library in second place, Queens, New York). In one recent year the library circulated 14,861,011 items total.

If you plan to use the Public Library of Cincinnati and Hamilton County, get ready to enter the information age. The card catalog is computerized, using CINCH (Computerized Information Network for Cincinnati and Hamilton County).

The heart of the 40-library system—with its 403,531 registered users—is the main branch downtown, which holds more than 10 million books, periodicals, maps, books on tape, CDs, and CD-ROMs. You can also research your family tree in one of the nation's largest—and from all appearances most heavily used—genealogy centers.

A block-long annex to the downtown branch, opened at a cost of $44 million, offers a plethora of services. The Magazines and Newspapers section includes 18,000 newspapers and periodicals, and the Public Documents and Patents section is one of only three at U.S. libraries to offer the complete U.S. Census records. The dazzling Children's Learning Center includes dozens of computers and free Internet access (see the Kidstuff chapter for more details). The Library for the Blind and Physically Handicapped offers a full range of services for the disabled, including CINCH workstations with voice and braille capability. This annex is connected to the main library by a skywalk.

Plastic library cards allow librarians to tally your withdrawals—and instantly discover your overdue misdemeanors—with a swipe of the card. The plastic cards also allow you Internet access at all branches (you need to ask for a PIN code, however). Don't like to read? You can use your card to borrow up to six videos, four CD-ROMs, and 20 CDs at one time. DVDs are also available.

Other useful services that accompany your card include INFOFAX, wherein a page from any printed resource at the downtown branch can be faxed directly to your home or business. And if you find yourself in a hospital or—even more unhappily—in a prison, the public library will still serve you through its Books by Mail program. The program serves patients in nursing homes and retirement centers, as well as others who find their movement restricted.

What's the most popular item at the Public Library of Cincinnati and Hamilton County? DVDs, no question. In one recent year library users borrowed more than 1.5 million DVDs—up 86 percent from the previous year. The largest branch library, in terms of circulation? The Anderson branch on the East Side.

With a card from most public libraries, you can check out or even order books and materials in collections of local college libraries.

PUBLIC LIBRARIES

Aurora (IN) Public Library
414 Second Street, Aurora, IN
(812) 926-0646

Boone County (KY) Public Library
Main Branch, 7425 U.S. Highway 42, Florence, KY
(859) 371-6222

Lents Branch, 3215 Cougar Path, Hebron, KY
(859) 586-8163

Walton Branch, 24 South Main Street,
(859) 485-6777

Campbell County (KY) Public Library
Main Branch, 3920 Alexandria Pike, Cold Spring
(859) 781-6166

Fort Thomas Branch, 1000 Highland Avenue
(859) 572-5033

Newport Branch, 401 Monmouth Street
(859) 572-5035

Clermont County Public Library
Main Branch, 180 South Third Street, Batavia
(513) 732-2128

Amelia Branch, 58 Maple Street
(513) 752-5580

Bethel Branch, 111 West Plane Street
(513) 734-2619

Goshen Branch, 6678 Ohio Highway 123
(513) 722-1221

Milford Branch, 1099 Ohio Highway 131
(513) 248-0700

New Richmond Branch, 103 River Valley Boulevard
(513) 553-0570

Owensville Branch, 2548 U.S. Highway 50
(513) 732-6084

Union Township Branch, 4462 Mount Carmel-Tobasco Road
(513) 528-1744

Williamsburg Branch, 594 Main Street
(513) 724-1070

Kenton County (KY) Public Library
Main Branch, 502 Scott Street, Covington
(859) 491-7610

Erlanger Branch, 3130 Dixie Highway
(859) 962-4000

Independence Branch, 6477 Taylor Mill Road
(859) 962-4030

Lane Public Library System
Main Branch, North Third and Buckeye Streets, Hamilton
(513) 894-7156

Fairfield Branch, 701 Wessel Drive, Fairfield
(513) 858-3238

Lawrenceburg (IN) Public Library
123 West High Street
(812) 537-2775

Lebanon Public Library
101 South Broadway
(513) 932-2665

Mason Public Library
200 Reading Road
(513) 398-2711

Public Library of Cincinnati and Hamilton County
Main Library, 800 Vine Street
(513) 369-6900

Anderson Regional, 7450 State Road
(513) 369-6030

Avondale, 3566 Reading Road
(513) 369-4440

Blue Ash, 4911 Cooper Road
(513) 369-6051

Bond Hill, 1703 Dale Road
(513) 369-4445

Cheviot, 3711 Robb Avenue
(513) 369-6015

Clifton, 351 Ludlow Avenue
(513) 369-4447

College Hill, 1400 West North Bend Road
(513) 369-6036

Corryville, 2802 Vine Street
(513) 369-6034

Covedale, 4980 Glenway Avenue
(513) 369-4460

Deer Park, 3970 East Galbraith Road
(513) 369-4450

Delhi Hills, 5095 Foley Road
(513) 369-6019

Elmwood Place, 6120 Vine Street
(513) 369-4452

Forest Park, 655 Waycross Road
(513) 369-4478

Green Township, 6525 Bridgetown Road
(513) 369-6095

Greenhills, 7 Endicott Street
(513) 369-4441

Groesbeck, 2994 West Galbraith Road
(513) 369-4454

Harrison, 10398 New Haven Road
(513) 369-4442

Hyde Park, 2747 Erie Avenue
(513) 369-4456

Loveland, 649 Loveland-Madeira Road
(513) 369-4476

Madeira-Indian Hill-Kenwood,
7200 Miami Avenue
(513) 369-6028

Madisonville, 4830 Whetsel Avenue
(513) 369-6029

Mariemont, 3810 Pocahontas Avenue
(513) 369-4467

Miami Township,
8 North Miami Avenue, Cleves
(513) 369-6050

Monfort Heights, 3825 West Fork Road
(513) 369-4472

Mount Healthy, 7608 Hamilton Avenue
(512) 369-4469

Mount Washington,
2049 Beechmont Avenue
(513) 369-6033

North Central Regional,
11109 Hamilton Avenue, Pleasant Run
(513) 369-6068

Northside, 4219 Hamilton Avenue
(513) 369-4449

Norwood, 4325 Montgomery Road
(513) 369-6037

Oakley, 4033 Gilmore Avenue
(513) 369-6038

Pleasant Ridge, 6233 Montgomery Road
(513) 369-4488

Price Hill, 3215 Warsaw Avenue
(513) 369-4490

Reading, 9001 Reading Road
(513) 369-4465

Roselawn, 7617 Reading Road
(513) 369-6045

St. Bernard, 4803 Tower Avenue
(513) 369-4462

Sharonville Regional,
10980 Thornview Drive
(513) 369-6049

Symmes Township Regional,
11850 East Enyart
(513) 369-6001

Walnut Hills, 2533 Kemper Lane
(513) 369-6053

West End, 805 Ezzard Charles Drive
(513) 369-6026

Westwood, 3345 Epworth Avenue
(513) 369-4474

Wyoming, 500 Springfield Pike
(513) 369-6014

Salem Public Library
535 West Pike Street, Morrow
(513) 899-2588

PRIVATE LIBRARIES

In addition to a vast array of public libraries, Cincinnati has an interesting assortment of private libraries to which the public has at least limited access. Here are a few.

Athenaeum of Ohio Maly Library
6616 Beechmont Avenue
(513) 231-2223
This Roman Catholic seminary features the Eugene H. Maly Memorial Library, with more than 94,000 volumes in theology, Biblical studies, pastoral counseling, bioethics, and other religious studies. The rare book collection dates from the 13th century. The library is open to the public.

Cincinnati Art Museum Library
920 Eden Park Drive
(513) 721-5204
Certainly the source in the city for books by and about painters, sculptors, and other artists, the Cincinnati Art Museum Library is a much-used resource by artistic types. You may enter at no cost if you have a valid library card from the Public Library of Cincinnati and Hamilton County. No borrowing allowed, but there is a photocopier on-site.

Cincinnati Historical Society Library
1301 Western Avenue
(513) 287-7000
The Historical Society Library dates from 1831 and includes 40,000 books, 50,000 pamphlets, 2,500 maps, 2,300 periodicals, and 6 million feet of film, much of it relating to regional history. Rarities include books bound in jeweled silver, a flat wooden map of the world, and the Hauck Rare Book Collection. There are also extensive genealogical resources, including Cincinnati birth, baptism, marriage, death, cemetery interment, and property ownership records spanning two centuries, as well as many local high school and college yearbooks. Upstairs in Tower A is one of the nation's largest libraries devoted to railway history.

Cincinnati Library for the Blind & Physically Handicapped
800 Vine Street
(513) 369-6900
If you have trouble reading a traditional book or gazing at a standard computer screen, then this is the place for you. It's the Cincinnati Library for the Blind & Physically Handicapped, which celebrated 100 years of service to Cincinnati's sight impaired. The library is also for seniors who need large print or audiocassette books, or anyone who has trouble reading a traditional book. If your vision is poor, or if you have a medical condition—or even a reading disability—you may well qualify for books. Each day, the facility's nine librarians pack up and deliver more than a thousand talking books to patrons across Greater Cincinnati. The collection includes 37,500 audio cassettes along with 12,000 braille books. The Library for the Blind was founded in 1901 by two sisters—Georgia D. and Florence B. Trader—as only the fourth such library in the nation. In 1944 Helen Keller herself visited at a commemoration ceremony. Today the facility remains one of 56 regional libraries that comprise the National Library Service for the blind and handicapped.

The most fascinating library in town isn't open to the public. A shame. The Klosterman Magic Library in Goshen has been touted by no less than Smithsonian *magazine as the world's largest collection of books on prestidigitation and witchcraft. David Copperfield is a regular here, as are other pros. The library is owned by Ken Klosterman, who owns the huge Klosterman Bakery, and has a part-time curator.*

Cincinnati Stake Family History Library
5505 Bosworth Place, Norwood
(513) 531-5624

This treasure trove, operated by the Church of Jesus Christ of Latter-day Saints and open to the public, is devoted to helping in genealogical research. Major databases include the Ancestral File, a church-managed computer file that contains millions of names and their links to ancestors and descendants. The International Genealogical Index lists places and dates of birth for millions of people, as well as marriages, dating from the 1500s. And the Social Security Death Index lists millions who have died in the United States since 1962.

Civic Gardens Center of Cincinnati Library
2715 Reading Road
(513) 221-0981

You should find the answer to most any gardening question you may have in this collection of noncirculating books. A $35 annual membership entitles you to full use of the library, plus gives you access to the newsletters, lectures, classes, and workshops offered by the Civic Garden Center.

Frank Foster Library
2115 West Eighth Street, Price Hill
(513) 251-0202

The city of Cincinnati's Urban Appalachian Council runs this research library, which contains the largest collection of books and materials on Appalachia outside of Appalachia. It is open to the public.

Johnnie Mae Berry Library
3520 Central Parkway
(513) 569-1606

The Johnnie Mae Berry Library features the largest assortment of cookbooks in the city. Named for the wife of a former Cincinnati mayor, Johnnie Mae Berry, the library includes 25,000 volumes and 300 periodicals.

Literary Club
500 East Fourth Street
(513) 621-6589

For 151 years, a group of about a hundred book lovers has met on Monday night at this brick structure in the heart of downtown. Each meeting begins with a glass of wine, then it's on to the Reading Room (adorned with the Shakespeare motto, HERE COMES ONE WITH A PAPER). And indeed, each member must, within every two years, produce a paper on some literary topic. Members include former Scripps Howard CEO Bill Burleigh, former *Enquirer* editorial page editor Thom Gephart, and former *Post* columnist Nick Clooney. The club also counts two former presidents, Rutherford B. Hayes and William Howard Taft, among its former members. About four openings become available each year; anyone interested in joining must be sponsored by a current member.

Lloyd Library and Museum
917 Plum Street
(513) 721-3707

The works of John Uri Lloyd, a prominent Cincinnati pharmacist and author, are housed here. Lloyd wrote hundreds of articles for medical and scientific journals on the chemical properties of plants and books on pharmacology. More than 50 years after his death, the library is still a major center for scholars researching the history of pharmacology.

Lloyd also wrote in 1895 one of the world's first science fiction/fantasy novels, *Etidorhpa* (that's Aphrodite spelled backward), in which the protagonist is kidnapped and taken into the center of the earth, where he is guided through bizarre crystal forests by an eyeless humanoid. It was one of the more offbeat things ever to come out of Cincinnati and made a few folks wonder if Mr. Lloyd was sampling what he studied. But the book became a cult classic and has remained popular. An endowment from Lloyd's family keeps his legacy alive in this library, which is open to the public for research.

McGuffey Museum at Miami University
410 East Spring Street, Oxford
(513) 529-8380
Housed in the former home of William Holmes McGuffey, this is a depository of the complete works of McGuffey. That includes his influential *McGuffey Readers,* the first books read by generations of schoolchildren 100-plus years ago.

Memorial Music Library
1 Blegen Building
(513) 556-6000
The Memorial Music Library is devoted to all things relating to music composition as well as dance, electronic media, and other topics. The library holds 26,000 volumes, 7,000 periodicals, 56,000 music scores, 40,000 LPs, and 6,000 microfilms. There is a Music Listening Center.

Mercantile Library
414 Walnut Street
(513) 621-0717
This historic library in the Mercantile Library Building downtown, is a sort of book-lined home away from home for its members, says executive director Albert Pyle. You can do things here you just can't do at other libraries, such as bring your lunch and eat it as you read. (Gasp!)

The elevator to the 11th floor seems something of a time machine that transports visitors to an era and place far removed from the modern bustle of downtown Cincinnati. You can relax in a leather-and-wood book lover's paradise, replete with an extensive collection of statuary that seems to invite leisurely perusal. The library literally reeks of history, with that musty smell that can only come from an accumulation of volumes that goes back to when the library opened at this site in 1835 (some books in the rare-book collection date from well before then).

The general public is welcome to visit. Membership in the Young Men's Mercantile Library Association (also open to women, of course) costs $45 a year ($15 for students) and entitles you to borrow materials, plus you get first dibs on frequently filled-to-capacity lectures by renowned writers. Among the authors who have appeared here are Ralph Waldo Emerson, Herman Melville, Tom Wolfe, John Updike, Julia Child, and Ray Bradbury.

Hours are 9:00 A.M. to 5:30 P.M. Monday through Friday, with occasional weekend hours for lectures and concerts.

Municipal Reference Library
801 Plum Street
(513) 352-3000
This tiny library, squirreled away in Cincinnati City Hall, includes heady volumes on urban planning, architecture, and engineering. There are also copies of civil service employment exams from around the country.

Vent Haven Museum
33 West Maple Avenue, Fort Mitchell, KY
(859) 341-0461
www.venthavenmuseum.com
Certainly the region's most exhaustive collection of works regarding ventriloquism, this is also one institute of learning where you can feel comfortable being, um, a dummy.

COLLEGE LIBRARIES

Thanks to a unique arrangement through the Greater Cincinnati Library Consortium, an association of 44 local public and college libraries, you can stroll into just about any library in the region that you want—as long as you're armed with a library card from the Public Library of Cincinnati and Hamilton County. (Don't fret if you live in an adjoining county or even in Kentucky—you can still qualify for such a card.) This interchange of library access means all the literary

CLOSE-UP

Dark Deeds and Dandy Detectives

Cincinnati loves a mystery. The Queen City landscape is littered with literary murders, and at least a half-dozen nationally published mystery authors reside here or use the city as the setting for their tales.

One of the first was C. W. Grafton (father of Sue) in *The Rat Began to Gnaw the Rope.* One of the newest mystery writers on the scene is Cora Miller, an accountant who has created the character of financial planner Audrey Wilson for such Cincinnati novels as *Taxes, Death, and Trouble* and *Accrual Way to Die.* A native Cincinnatian, Miller sets her tales of accounting and murder in the fictional African-American neighborhood of Rosemont. Her heroine constantly stumbles from balance sheets to unbalanced killers, and the series is loaded with local references, from characters munching Grippo's chips to picnics at Sawyer Point. And yes, Miller has her degree in accounting from the University of Cincinnati.

You can learn a great deal about the city's foibles and felons by reading works by these writers because spread in amongst the fiction is a great deal of fact. A quick survey:

D. B. Borton—Her series of novels begins with *One for the Money* and is currently in a sixth entry, *Six Feet Under.* Her hero is Cat Caliban, a Northside grandmom who's raised three kids and has now settled down to snoop. Borton wonderfully weaves real-life Cincinnati politicos and media types into her private-eye narrative.

Jim DeBrosse—After toiling in the trenches at both the *Cincinnati Post* and the *Cincinnati Enquirer,* DeBrosse decided to turn the tables on the local papers and write a series of novels loosely based on his Cincinnati journalism experience. His fictional reporter, Rick Decker, exposes shady dealings and the foibles of the press beginning in *The Serpentine Wall* and later in *Hidden City* and *Southern Cross. Hidden City* is particularly notable for its fascinating details about Cincinnati's long-abandoned subway system.

Lynn S. Hightower—Granted, she lives just down the road in Lexington, but she chooses to set her grim police procedu-

resources of the region's universities are open to you. And we're talking more than just dusty tomes and shopworn encyclopedias—each facility boasts fascinating special collections and a focus on certain areas of interest. Here's a roundup:

Archbishop Alter Library
College of Mount St. Joseph
5701 Delhi Road, Delhi Township
(513) 244-4216

The Alter Library possesses 97,000 volumes and 650 periodicals. Also on hand are 200 videos and a substantial CD collection. Rarities include rare Bibles and other religious books.

Frank Steely Library
Northern Kentucky University, Nunn Drive, Highland Heights, KY
(859) 572-5456

rals in the Queen City. Her heroine, Sonora Blair of the Cincinnati Homicide Division, investigates the bizarre underground life of the town. Start with *Flashpoint* and move on in the series of books to *No Good Deed* and *Angel's Bidding.*

Cathie John—Actually, she is a she and a he: the husband-and-wife writing team of John and Cathie Celestri. Their murder-mystery novels feature Cincy detective Kate Cavanaugh. *Add One Dead Critic,* the first book in the series, was about the nasty murder of a nasty restaurant critic. The second culinary mystery, *Beat a Rotten Egg to the Punch,* is set at the Taste of Cincinnati food fest. The third is *Carve a Witness to Shreds.*

Jeffrey Marks—New on the Cincy mystery scene is Jeffrey Marks. Tired of all the mystery collections honoring felines, he finally convinced Ballantine to publish his *Canine Crimes* anthology. The book includes short stories by Anne Perry and Amanda Cross as well as a few tales by Marks himself, including "The Long Arm of the Paw." And yes, Marks does own a dog, a Scottish terrier named Ellery (as in Ellery Queen).

A. M. Pyle—Also known as Albert Pyle (see the listing for the Mercantile Library), he has turned out a riveting series starring detective Cesar Franck. Start with *Murder Moves In* and *Trouble Making Toys,* then graduate to *Pure Murder.*

Larry Rochelle—The former Indian Hill High and Sycamore High English teacher is the author of a new murder mystery, *Dance with the Pony,* featuring Rochelle's tennis-playing and beer-drinking protagonist, Palmer Morel.

Jonathan Valin—Valin is the honorary granddad of Cincinnati mystery novelists. His Harry Stoner novels, starting with *Lime Pit* and *Final Notice* and moving on to *Fire Lake* and *The Music Lovers,* have received national kudos and have even been turned into TV movies. Stoner is a throwback, Sam Spade–kind of detective but with some modern twists.

A footnote: the "English" mystery writer Kate Charles actually hails from Cincinnati, but it's been so long since she left, we can hardly claim her. Especially since her novels—including *Strange Children* and *Cruel Habitations*—are set across the Atlantic in the Church of England.

Steely Library is a richly historic library where you can access books and photographs on Kentucky and Appalachia. If you need to, you can purchase discs to save collected data on. This library also offers a half-million documents from federal and Kentucky state governments.

King Library
Campus of Miami University, Oxford
(513) 529-2800

King Library boasts more than one million volumes, and subscriptions to magazines and newspapers are in the thousands. Rare items include the First Folio of Shakespeare from 1623, the Third Folio (worth $700,000), and the other folios (total value at $21 million). Also in the collection: *The Book of Hours,* published in 1450 with sacred illuminations.

Langsam Library
University of Cincinnati, Martin Luther King Drive at Campus Drive
(513) 556-1424
Langsam Library is devoted to the social sciences, humanities, education, and business. A number of governmental records are on file here: the *Congressional Record,* presidential papers, government maps, and various consumer information. There's also a rare collection of Charles Dickens volumes. Within the library are a number of special areas, such as the Elliston Poetry Room, devoted to specific topics.

McDonald Memorial Library
Xavier University, 3800 Victory Parkway
(513) 745-4808
The McDonald Memorial Library is a midsize library with the heart of a large library. There are three floors with more than 350,000 volumes and 1,500 periodical titles available to the public. Other materials include microfilm/media, back issues of periodicals, audio/video materials, and other multimedia resources.

Thomas More College Library
333 Thomas More Parkway
Crestview Hills, KY
(859) 341-5800
You'll be shocked and surprised to learn that the Thomas More College Library, with more than 131,000 volumes and 570 periodicals, boasts the ultimate collection of materials relating to Thomas More. There's also a terrific collection of Kentuckiana.

WRITERS' AND BOOK GROUPS

Writing, poetry, and reading groups abound at Cincinnati's libraries, bookstores, coffeehouses, and other literary centers. (For a listing of bookstores, see the Shopping chapter; for coffeehouses, see the Restaurants chapter.) Here are a few of the larger literary groups:

Cincinnati Playwrights
Carnegie Arts Center
1028 Scott Street, Covington, KY
(859) 491-2030
This group meets every Monday night at the Carnegie and encourages local playwrights.

Cincinnati Society of Professional Journalists
1148 Main Street
(513) 479-0713
Cincinnati Society of Professional Journalists sponsors monthly public forums with newsmakers, runs writing critiques and journalism conferences, underwrites college scholarships for budding writers, and cosponsors the statewide excellence in journalism prizes.

Cincinnati Writers Project
Carnegie Arts Center, 1028 Scott Street
Covington, KY
(859) 491-2030
The Cincinnati Writers Project is generally considered the premier organization to join if you're a struggling or freelance writer, be it fiction or nonfiction. It meets monthly at the Carnegie.

National League of American Penwomen
5713-B Kugler Mill Road
No phone
The local chapter of the National League of American Penwomen welcomes writers, artists, and musicians.

Ohio Valley Romance Writers of America
20 Compton Road, Wyoming
No phone
Jacques ripped our heroine's bodice, drawing her close and . . . Well, you get the idea. These folks meet monthly at the Valleydale Civic Center and other locations.

Writers' Workshops
Arts Consortium of Cincinnati
1515 Linn Street
(513) 381-0645
The Arts Consortium holds monthly meetings to read and discuss participants' works in progress.

MEDIA

Greater Cincinnati is something of a media-mad locale. At least a half-dozen new publications have launched startups in recent years, spawning fresh competition for news, for readers, and for advertising dollars. In total the region boasts 7 daily newspapers, 30 weeklies, and 2 dozen monthlies—enough to fill home recycling bins to the brim each week. The airwaves are jammed as well, with more than 50 radio and television broadcast stations jockeying for exclusives, audiences, and a winning spot in the ratings.

The two biggest local news sources are the *Cincinnati Post* and the *Cincinnati Enquirer,* which are published under a joint operating agreement. Because of this agreement, many people think they are one and the same paper, but that is far from the truth. The agreement simply means that the two papers maintain separate editorial voices, but they save money by sharing costly business operations, including advertising, distribution, and printing. The larger *Enquirer* handles all the business-related items. Profits are shared, albeit unevenly, between the two papers. In fact, the *Post,* sadly, will join the growing list of dead evening newspapers when the agreement expires on December 31, 2007. (The *Enquirer* has given the three-year notice required by the U.S. Justice Department that it will not renew the pact.)

The biggest media brouhaha this town has ever seen came in 1998, courtesy of a feud between Chiquita Banana Co. and the *Enquirer*. Chiquita, owned by Cincinnati's wealthiest man, Carl Lindner, was the target of an *Enquirer* investigative series that badly misfired. By year's end the reporter on the series, Mike Gallagher, had been fired by his newspaper and sentenced as a felon for illegally tapping into Chiquita's corporate voice-mail system as he dug for facts. The editor of the paper, Larry Beaupre, had been canned as well. And an embarrassed publisher, Harry Whipple, had publicly renounced the series in three prominent front-page apologies, not to mention paying Lindner (who, ironically, used to own the daily himself) $14 million in a hastily arranged legal settlement. The impact on Cincinnati journalism was felt for years. First, the *Enquirer* inherited a series of new editors. Then there was the fallout on newsroom morale and ensuing staff exodus. "Welcome to the *Enquirer,*" read an unsigned Jim Borgman cartoon posted on office bulletin boards soon after the news of the public apology broke. It showed dazed reporters standing amid apocalyptic rubble. And dazed they were.

The banana scandal—it spawned a million groaner headlines: "Final A-peel." "Bitter Fruit." "Yes, We Have No Bananas." *U.S. News & World Report, Newsweek,* NPR, ABC, CNN, Reuters, *Newsday,* the AP, and Agence France-Presse all came to town to cover the story, which made the front pages of the *New York Times* and the *Wall Street Journal* on the same day. Call it our very own media banana-gate, one that, to this day, won't go away.

At least the *Enquirer* was trying to do serious investigative reporting with its Chiquita series, however botched the results. When it comes to the television landscape around here, with the notable exception of Channel 9's I-Team investigative reports, you're more likely to view gory crime coverage on the nightly newscasts. "If it bleeds, it leads" is the station managers' motto around here.

On the radio side, the face of the Cincinnati market is changing, and it looks a lot like Clear Channel Communications Inc. The Texas-based media monolith operates some 500 stations. In this market, it owns eight radio stations, including the highly popular WLW (700 AM) and

WEBN (102.7 FM). In the process of acquiring these stations, it bought out or eliminated much of its competition.

Clear Channel isn't the only national media giant in town. The E.W. Scripps Company and its spinoff broadcasting company, Scripps-Howard, are also headquartered in Greater Cincinnati and, collectively, the two own 40 daily and weekly newspapers and nine TV stations across the country, in addition to numerous cable franchises and cable channels (including HGTV and the Food Network), a newspaper syndicate, an entertainment production company, and a news service. Scripps also distributes such comic strip mainstays as *Dilbert*. That's a lot of national media influence coming out of Cincinnati.

Much of Cincinnati's electronic media presence dates from Powel Crosley, who manufactured affordable tabletop radios in the 1920s and who founded WLW radio in 1922 and WLWT-TV (Channel 5) in 1945. WLWT was the first television station to go on the air in Ohio. In its early days, WLW radio broadcast at 500,000 watts. It had to cut back to 50,000 watts, though, after complaints that it was drowning out stations from here to Cuba and that the signal was so strong people were picking it up in the metal fillings in their teeth. The station remains a clear-channel station, meaning it is the only station in the region that broadcasts at its 700 kilocycle (AM) frequency.

DAILY NEWSPAPERS

The Cincinnati Enquirer
312 Elm Street
(513) 721-2700

The morning *Enquirer* is a staple in the area; local residents are addicted to it, along with their coffee and toast.

The *Enquirer* offers a decidedly conservative editorial slant, paralleling the views of most area residents. The paper's conservative editorial nature is often offset by the more liberal work of editorial cartoonist Jim Borgman. Borgman won the paper's only Pulitzer Prize in 1991 for his humorous and well-stated editorial drawings.

In addition to Borgman's cartoon, which is a daily must-see, popular columnists include Jim Knippenberg in the "Tempo" section and Paul Daugherty in sports.

The paper sometimes struggles, though, with its position as the area's source for national and international news and its desire to also be a community paper. Even though it can't do everything, it tries. The paper added more community news with zoned news pages each day. It also added a "Weekend" entertainment guide each Friday in an attempt to better cover the local entertainment scene, with reviews of local bands and nightlife.

In 2004 the paper began publishing its own version of an alternative weekly, *CiN Weekly,* which is available at various downtown newsstands for free. While the free tabloid mimics the city alternative *CityBeat* in some respects, it is a toned-down, G-rated version that somewhat resembles the "Weekend" section available in the mainstream edition.

The *Enquirer* was first published on April 10, 1841, and was the first newspaper in the nation to publish a Sunday edition, beginning in 1848. The paper has gone through a handful of different owners through the years. In 1952 the paper's owner intended to sell the *Enquirer* to then rival *Times-Star,* but employee investments, wealthy sponsors, and bonds sold by brokers raised $7.5 million for a counteroffer and kept the paper alive as an employee-owned operation.

In 1956 Cincinnati-based E. W. Scripps Company purchased a majority interest in the *Enquirer* from the employees but never exercised control. A court order in 1971 forced Scripps, which also owned the afternoon *Post,* to divest its ownership in the *Enquirer.* Scripps eventually sold its shares to American Financial Corporation, a privately owned company controlled by Cincinnati's self-made millionaire Carl Lindner, who became the paper's publisher. Lindner kept the paper for four years before selling to Combined Communications Corporation, a diversified media company that merged with Gannett Company Inc. in 1979.

The Cincinnati Post
125 East Court Street
(513) 352-2000
The *Post* has been a Cincinnati staple since 1883 when E. W. Scripps bought control of the *Cincinnati Penny Paper* and renamed it the *Penny Post.* At that time, Cincinnati had seven English and five German newspapers. In 1956 the *Post* purchased its afternoon rival, the *Times-Star,* and made Cincinnati a two-newspaper town. The *Post* became the cornerstone for Scripps, which also owns WCPO-TV (Channel 9) in Cincinnati as well as numerous newspapers, television stations, publishing and production companies, syndicates, and cable companies nationally.

As with many afternoon papers, the *Post* has a difficult time maintaining subscription levels, which have dropped below 40,000, down by more than half from when it entered into a joint operating agreement with the *Enquirer*. And that is translating into reductions in its editorial efforts. The *Post* has been forced five times in recent years to offer buyout or early-retirement packages to its employees, resulting in the loss of veteran reporters. Add to that the no-longer-uncommon occurrence of reporters jumping over to the *Enquirer* for the sake of job security, and the effectiveness and reporting ability of the paper continue to be hurt.

The *Post* offers a more liberal editorial viewpoint than the *Enquirer* and devotes more space and effort to covering high school sports. Despite its lagging circulation and loss of staff, it often scoops the *Enquirer*. Essentially, it must provide better reporting, since the *Enquirer* controls its destiny outside of the newsroom.

Dayton Daily News
45 South Ludlow Street, Dayton
(937) 225-2000
What's that, you say? A Dayton newspaper ranked among the Cincinnati print elite? But it's hard to avoid. After all, the daily built a printing plant just a few minutes north of West Chester, with an announced intention to dominate Warren and Butler County—and perhaps Sharonville and other of the north-central suburbs soon after.

Don't underestimate the Dayton paper's challenge to the *Enquirer* and *Post* for regional dominance. This is a daily newspaper that won the prestigious Pulitzer Prize for public service (for groundbreaking coverage on the shoddy practices of military doctors nationwide). The editors have already lured popular Cincinnati columnist Mary McCarty and local mystery author Jim DeBrosse (see the Close-up in the Libraries chapter) onto their staff. And the paper's Reds coverage is generally considered superior to anything the Cincinnati dailies can offer. The *Dayton Daily News* is owned by Cox Communications, a company founded a century ago by a guy who went on to become governor of Ohio.

Hamilton Journal News
Court Street and Journal Square, Hamilton
(513) 863-8200
The *Journal News* offers some national and international news but concentrates on the news and events in Hamilton, Fairfield, and surrounding northern communities.

The Kentucky Enquirer
226 Grandview Drive, Fort Mitchell, KY
(859) 578-5555
The *Cincinnati Enquirer* began making a more concerted effort to cover the news of Northern Kentucky by opening a Northern Kentucky bureau and publishing the *Kentucky Enquirer.* The staff concentrates strictly on events south of the river and produces a separate front page and "Metro" section. As a result, the paper is making a small dent in the virtual monopoly on Kentucky news that the *Kentucky Post* once had.

CLOSE-UP

The Czar of Zany

It's 10 o'clock on a Tuesday evening at the offices of the *Cincinnati Enquirer,* and Elvis has left the building.

Well, many Elvises, actually. "Dozens and dozens of them," Jim Knippenberg is saying, as he shakes his head in disbelief. "They started lining up at 6:00 P.M. Men. Women. Even little girls in Elvis swimwear. I thought, oh yeah, this is gonna be a long night."

We're at 312 Elm—the high-rise headquarters of Cincinnati's morning newspaper, the *Enquirer*—and Knippenberg has just finished one of the most bizarre story assignments in a 30-year newspaper career that boasts no particular shortage of aberrant assignments.

To properly commemorate the 25th anniversary of the King's death, Knippenberg invited—through his "Tempo" section column—all the area's Elvi, every amateur, professional, and semipro Elvis imitator in Greater Cincinnati, to the newsroom for an all-night photo shoot: jumpsuits, blue suede shoes, slicked-back hair, and tacky gold chains at the ready.

They came, they swiveled, they conquered.

"For some reason nobody knows, one of them brought a dead bird," the writer shrugs. "At least he took it back with him. We were grateful for that."

You read the outrageous Jim Knippenberg every week. Now meet the genuine article. . . . The *Enquirer*'s celebrity columnist plays ringmaster to the wacky and bizarre carnival that is Cincinnati life.

The columnist, who grew up in Price Hill and attended Elder High, has been working at the daily since 1971, making him one of the three or four veterans in the newsroom with any sort of institutional memory. "It was the year our daughter, Michelle, was born," he recalls. "Now, she's made me a granddad."

Before launching his journalistic career, Knippenberg had taught English at Newport Catholic High School while obtaining his master's degree in—get this—educational psychology at the University of Cincinnati.

Over the years at the newspaper, he's labored as an entertainment editor, gossip writer (the old "Psst!" column), rock 'n' roll reviewer, "Ask a Stupid Question" advice columnist, "Knip's Eye View," and more.

Colleagues are asked to—anonymously, of course—describe Jim. "Knip's a wonderful, funny funny guy—but he never met a free cocktail shrimp he didn't like," says one ink-stained wretch, referring to the columnist's penchant for parties. Another scribe adds: "There are those of us in the office—our numbers are legion—who'd say to drive Jim into an absolute state of insanity, well, it could be a very short drive. Let's just say he lives *real* close to the state line."

Knippenberg, for his part, simply says his reputation for goofy insanity—earned or not—is all part of the job description. "One of the things I like most about this job is I never know from day to day what I will be covering," he observes. "The only given is that, frequently, I'm the last one in the office to find out."

As a reporter, Knippenberg also covers the amusement park beat (his favorite coaster is the Magnum at Cedar Point in Sandusky, Ohio). "One day, somebody got the idea I should ride every roller coaster in the states of Ohio, Kentucky, and Indiana—in the same week—while I was hooked up to a portable heart monitor," he says. "I had to jump off every coaster and immediately run to a public telephone and play the monitor back to the cardiologist.

"What I found out is, whenever I snuck a cigarette, he knew about it. And when the kid in front of me threw up on one ride, my heart rate *really* went up."

Known as a consummate practical joker, Knippenberg concedes he'll sometimes pass himself off as columnist David Wecker, formerly his opposite number at the competing *Cincinnati Post* for many yeaer. The jokester recalls the time a friend was meeting him at the curb outside of the *Enquirer* high-rise on Elm Street. "I jump into his blue BMW, the engine running. Now who would have thought there could be *two* blue BMWs, with their motors running, outside my office door at the same time? The driver, this lady, she looked at me and just started screaming. So, I just said, 'Hi, I'm David Wecker. Sorry, my mistake' and I got out of there fast."

This is Knippenberg at his finest—frank, honest, outlandish, totally out there. Is there anything, in fact, the public *doesn't* know about Jim Knippenberg? "I play the piano every evening to relax, but nobody has ever heard me. I play Mozart pieces, mostly."

"I like what I'm doing," Knippenberg says of his chosen profession. "I'm old enough to retire." He concedes there are days when he pictures himself as a retiree, living on a beach somewhere while sipping Coronas. "But, frankly, I'd go nuts."

We're walking out the door, but before we can leave, one of the columnist's loyal readers spots him and immediately trots over to shake hands, complimenting him on that particular morning's "Tempo" column. Knippenberg flashes his "ain't nothing but a hounddog" smile and accepts the praise with due modesty. "Thankyouveryverymuch." Then, he's gone.

Knippenberg has left the building.

The Kentucky Post
421 Madison Avenue, Covington, KY
(859) 292-2600
The *Kentucky Post* is a one- or two-section paper that is "wrapped" over the early edition of the *Cincinnati Post* and distributed to Northern Kentucky residents. The *Kentucky Post* covers Northern Kentucky issues in depth and dominates Northern Kentucky's news coverage, which is becoming increasingly important as more and more businesses and residents locate south of the river.

Its staff gives particular attention to the area's sporting interests, which tend to differ from those north of the river. The paper gives detailed coverage of the University of Kentucky and local high school sports, which are highly popular in Northern Kentucky.

The *Kentucky Post* is also responsible for more than half of the *Cincinnati Post*'s total circulation.

UC News-Record
Student Life Center,
University of Cincinnati main campus
(513) 556-5900
The "other daily" newspaper of Cincinnati is the student newspaper published at the University of Cincinnati. Founded in 1880 and originally a university publication, the *News-Record* is now independently operated by students and has evolved into a sizable business (advertising pays the freight; 30,000 free copies are distributed in and around the Clifton Heights campus). In addition to local news, opinion, campus sports, and entertainment, the paper subscribes to various news services (AP, Knight Ridder, etc.) and covers the world at large.

COMMUNITY NEWSPAPERS

Community Press Newspapers
4910 Para Drive
(513) 242-4300
Community Press Newspapers publishes 20 zoned newspapers that cover virtually all of Cincinnati's and Northern Kentucky's suburban communities. These weeklies ring the city on both sides of the river, and if you add up their total circulation, they can actually rival the *Enquirer* in daily readership. As you'd expect, these weeklies excel in bread-and-butter community journalism (zoning meetings, school board fracases, etc.). The papers are usually so on top of happenings in the communities that they are often one step ahead of the daily newspapers on larger suburban issues as well.

These papers—recently bought by Gannett, owner of the *Enquirer*— are the best place to find out what's happening in your particular neighborhood: road repairs, business openings or closings, area residents who did something noteworthy, and school honor rolls. The papers are also well read for their classified ads, police reports, and school lunch menus.

The papers include: *Delhi Press, Hilltop Press, Northwest Press, Price Hill Press, Western Hills Press, Bethel Journal, Clermont Community Journal, North Clermont Community Journal, Mason Community Press, Eastern Hills Journal, Forest Hills Journal, Loveland Herald, Milford Advertiser, Northeast Suburban Life, Suburban Life, Campbell County Recorder, Boone County Recorder, Kenton County Recorder,* and *Erlanger Recorder.*

Journal News Weeklies
5120 Dixie Highway, Fairfield
(513) 829-7900
Cox Ohio Publishing publishes four community weeklies: *Fairfield Echo, Oxford Press, Mason Pulse-Journal,* and *West Chester Press.*

ALTERNATIVE NEWSPAPERS

CiN Weekly
2055 Reading Road
(513) 768-6000

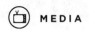

This free entertainment weekly offers thorough calendar coverage of the city's events, but it is not the true "alternative" source for news it might seem at first glance. *CiN Weekly* is owned and produced by the *Cincinnati Enquirer.*

CityBeat
811 Race Street
(513) 665-4700

CityBeat reviews the arts, movies, records, bands, nightclubs, and events, but it also offers an alternative look at the major news issues around the city. It often tackles news stories not covered by the daily and suburban papers. For instance, it revealed the Cincinnati Zoo was tacitly encouraging walrus poaching in Alaska, a story picked up nationally by *Mother Jones* magazine.

Alternative lifestyles, arts, and entertainment, though, are its staple. Its movie and music reviewers are so popular they are also heard on various radio stations. And the paper frequently cosponsors entertainment events and puts its alternative spin on them. At one event it provided on-the-spot tattoo artists and body piercers. *CityBeat* publishes a once-a-year "Dining Guide" (in April), an annual "Best of Cincinnati" issue each March, and a year-end roundup. The urban weekly also sponsors the annual Cincinnati Entertainment Awards, the city's local version of the Grammy Awards.

This free weekly paper—named "Best Weekly in Ohio" in a recent statewide journalism contest—publishes every Wednesday and can be found in sidewalk racks around downtown, Clifton, and Over-the-Rhine. It's also available at the entrance of many restaurants and bars throughout the city.

BUSINESS PUBLICATIONS

Cincinnati Business Courier
101 West Seventh Street
(513) 621-6665

The *Business Courier,* which recently celebrated its 25th anniversary, usually offers more in-depth analyses of the major business stories of the day than what is found in the business sections of the daily papers, in addition to dozens of smaller business stories that the daily papers don't have space for.

Cincy Business Magazine
30 Garfield Place, Suite 440
(513) 290-2030

Publisher Eric Harmon launched this glossy, full-color business magazine in 2003, catering to the Cincinnati CEO crowd with profiles of chief executives and other business news. Features include CEO "Passions," "Cincy Entrepreneur," behind-the-scene takes on local powerbrokers, and more. The magazine seeks to "tell the story of local business" through the personalities who run those businesses.

OTHER WEEKLY PAPERS

Cincinnati Herald
354 Hearne Avenue
(513) 961-3331

The *Herald* serves Cincinnati's African-American community with news, arts, sports, entertainment, and religion articles focusing on the city's African-American lifestyle and issues. It offers a different perspective from that of any of the area's other newspapers.

Since its purchase by Sesh Communications, the paper has turned around from early financial difficulties and is becoming a must-read for everyone, not just the African-American community.

Clermont Sun
465 East Main Street, Batavia
(513) 732-2511

The *Clermont Sun* is one of the few remaining independent small-town newspapers. The weekly covers the town of Batavia—a Clermont County burg that once was Ohio's largest gold-mining center—and its environs.

Filmed in Cincinnati

Cincinnati isn't exactly Hollywood East, but a number of major movies have been filmed here. Any Queen City video collection would have to include *Traffic*, *Little Man Tate*, and the seminal Cincy movie, Tom Cruise's *Rain Man*. Other theatrical releases shot here: *Milk Money*, *Eight Men Out*, *Fresh Horses*, *The Public Eye*, *Tango & Cash*, *Dream Catcher*, *Crocodile*, *Vamps*, *In Too Deep*, *This Train*, *April's Fool*, *People Like Us*, *The Late Last Night*, *What Angels Fear*, *The Mighty*, *Crossing Fields*, *Airborne*, *Lost in Yonkers*, *City of Hope*, *A Rage in Harlem*, and *An Innocent Man*.

The Downtowner
128 East Sixth Street
(513) 241-9906

The *Downtowner* is a free publication that focuses mostly on the positive issues, events, business news, and people of downtown, with regular feature columns mixed in. Designed with a four-color cover, the tabloid is heavy on columnists. There's a gossip column by Catherine Penny, business etiquette advice from Ann Marie Sabath, and the "Main Attraction," a helpful primer on what's new and notable at the public library, by Richard Helmes. The *Downtowner* can be picked up at a number of news racks around downtown. It is common lunchtime reading.

OUT-OF-TOWN NEWSPAPERS

Out-of-town newspapers can be found at the bookstores and news shops that you'll find listed in the Shopping chapter. Generally speaking, avid fans of statehouse news turn to the daily that's published in the state capital, the *Columbus Dispatch*. Other large newspapers that make it their business to cover the state are the *Cleveland Plain-Dealer*, which is the only Ohio newspaper that actually maintains a full-time bureau in Cincinnati, and the *Akron Beacon Journal*. For more-thorough Kentucky news than is offered in the Kentucky editions of the *Post* and *Enquirer*, consider the *Louisville Courier Journal* or the *Lexington Herald-Leader*, both of which maintain newsboxes on the downtown sidewalks.

MAGAZINES

Applause!
7710 Reading Road
(513) 961-3331

The magazine "for Cincinnati's black lifestyle" offers profiles of the area's highly prominent African Americans and features on places of special interest to the area's African-American community. This bimonthly magazine publishes special editions during the year that focus on Cincinnati's African-American business community, as well as a calendar of events.

The magazine is perhaps best known and highly respected for its annual Imagemaker Awards, which honors exceptional achievements of African Americans and names local African-American pacesetters.

Cincinnati Magazine
One Centennial Plaza
(513) 421-4300

After a couple of years of sliding subscriber interest, the city magazine has a new owner and yet another new editor. After a massive redesign, *Cincinnati Magazine* certainly looks glitzier and more colorful.

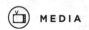

Features include a column by editor Jay Stowe, shopping advice, and our favorite, the back page's "Please?" trivia section. Each month, a unique Cincinnati person or institution is profiled; it's here that we learn that Graeter's peach flavor of ice cream is the most popular (available only in the month of July), and it's here we first read about the exploits of the late Dick Von Hoene, a Cincinnati cult classic in his persona as "the Cool Ghoul" (Von Hoene was the host of Channel 19's horror movie lineup for years).

The magazine is well known for its dining critiques and restaurant listings, including its annual "Dining Out Guide," which provides a complete list of area restaurants. (To make things easier, though, just flip back to the Restaurants chapter.) A separate "Schools Guide" provides a look at all of the area's schools and day-care facilities, and a separate "Bridal Guide" lists resources for brides. Other special sections on a variety of topics are published each month.

Inspire Cincinnati
312 Elm Street
(513) 721-2700
Inspire Cincinnati is a yupscale lifestyle magazine catering to the high-end residents of Hyde Park and its environs. Features focus on fashions, home decor, and travel.

Living Magazines
179 Fairfield Avenue, Bellevue, KY
(859) 291-1412
This company publishes seven magazines in the suburban Cincinnati and Northern Kentucky communities of Blue Ash, Hyde Park, Indian Hill, Oakwood, Wyoming, Fort Mitchell, and Fort Thomas. The magazines run wedding and engagement announcements, birth announcements, retirements, and "anything that you think might be something people would like to know and read about." Distribution of the monthlies is staggered throughout the month. Residents of the communities receive the publications free through the mail.

Njema
354 Hearne Avenue
(513) 961-3331
Njema is an African word that essentially translates to "good news." The magazine focuses on the news, social life, and entertainment of the African-American community in the Cincinnati region. The magazine is also available in Dayton, Columbus, Indianapolis, Lexington, and Louisville.

Ohio Magazine
30 Garfield Place, Suite 440
(513) 479-0713
Ohio Magazine is a must-read for anybody who travels and shops around the state or is an Ohio history and nature buff. There's a new editorial emphasis on covering southern Ohio with the opening of a Cincinnati office in 2004.

Monthly features include a handy planning calendar that lists all the festivals and museum exhibits in the state during a given month, plus profiles, first-person essays, and stories on the arts. Sports, gardening, and the environment are also regular topics.

St. Anthony Messenger
1615 Republic Street
(513) 241-5615
This century-old national magazine for Catholics is headquartered in Cincinnati. Articles focus on issues and people of the modern world, including highly controversial topics such as abortion, racism, and the sexual revolution and how they mix with Christian values and beliefs.

OTHER PUBLICATIONS

All About Kids
1077 Celestial Street
(513) 684-0501
All About Kids is a free monthly paper that deals with family issues, some of

them controversial. Psychologist Earladeen Badger publishes the paper, which is an Award of Excellence winner from Parenting Publications of America. You can pick up a copy at newsstands and local libraries.

The American Israelite
18 West Ninth Street
(513) 621-3145
A weekly paper centering around the area's Jewish community, this is the oldest English-Jewish weekly in America, established in 1854 by Isaac M. Wise.

Catholic Telegraph
100 East Eighth Street
(513) 421-3131
The Archdiocese of Cincinnati began publishing this weekly paper, which focuses on the area's Catholic community, in 1831.

Cincinnati Court Index
119 West Central Parkway
(513) 241-1450
The *Cincinnati Court Index* details Hamilton County's daily legal activities, including legal notices and scheduled trials and hearings and provides a full list of the previous day's municipal, common pleas, district, and bankruptcy court filings. The paper is directed toward the legal community and interested businesses. (You can get a single subscription to the popular Monday edition. Why is the Monday issue such a hot commodity? That's when sheriff's sales and auctions are listed.)

Cincinnati Family
895 Central Avenue, Suite 900
(513) 241-9898
Subtitled "A Complete Parenting Resource for Cincinnati Families," this free monthly magazine is crammed with helpful hints and leads. Features range from a comparison of maternity wards at Cincinnati hospitals to interviews with child experts. There's also a calendar of local kids' events. The magazine is published by local radio station WRRM-FM.

Cincinnati Woman Magazine
P.O. Box 8170, West Chester, OH 45069-8170
(513) 697-6433
This monthly publication profiles notable Cincinnati women and offers mothering advice, health and beauty tips, fashion and style articles, and shopping guides. Editor Cathy Habes has assembled some of the city's best-known writers; restaurant critic Lilia Brady, for instance, was the longtime food editor at *Cincinnati Magazine*. The publication is available free at many bookstores, restaurants, and retail outlets.

Express Cincinnati
P.O. Box 46926, Hyde Park, OH 45246-0926
(513) 771-5088
Express Cincinnati is a monthly newspaper chronicling the activities of the city's upscale social scene. Photos and articles of previous events, stories about upcoming events, columns, a calendar, and even Blue Book wedding announcements are detailed. The publication can be found at newsstands around the city and at select fund-raising events.

Kentucky Monthly
213 St. Clair Street, Frankfort, KY
(888) 329-0053
This monthly magazine serves the interests of folks living on the "south side of Cincinnati" (translated: Kentucky). Features include profiles of prominent Kentuckians, recreational opportunities in the Bluegrass state, regional news and notes, and an inserted 24-page "Visions" program guide to Kentucky public television.

Spanish Journal
P.O. Box 498787, Cincinnati, OH 45249-8787
(513) 225-8543
The *Spanish Journal* launched in 1999 to serve the estimated 50,000 Hispanics in the Greater Cincinnati area. The tabloid

newspaper, produced twice a month by publisher George Perez, runs about half its stories in English and the other half in Spanish. Free at Mexican restaurants and libraries.

StreetVibes
1506 Elm Street
(513) 421-7803
StreetVibes focuses on social justice and poverty-related news, plus a smattering of letters, poems, and essays contributed by low-income contributors. Published by the Greater Cincinnati Coalition for the Homeless, *StreetVibes* strikes an unusual arrangement with its vendors (most of whom are homeless): They hawk the monthly on the downtown streets for $1.00 per issue, and get to keep 80 cents for every paper sold. It's a win-win situation: The coalition fulfills its mission of helping street people transcend from panhandling to actually running a small business, plus the agency collects revenue from sales and advertising.

The Whistleblower
1116 Birney Lane, Anderson
(513) 232-1902
No discussion of Cincinnati print media is complete without some discussion of this faxed daily news release. Is it primarily schlock? Of course. Does it contain some germs of truth, littered among the gossip and innuendo? Most assuredly. Does it, on occasion, even break new ground? Oh, yes. Underground publisher Jim Schifrin, our own Matt Drudge, produces this rag and faxes it daily to powerbrokers and interested parties around the region. The fact that the majority of Cincinnatians never see the *Whistleblower* does nothing to belittle its force. The *Whistleblower* has influenced public policy, sent seasoned politicians running like scared rabbits, and remains—after two decades of publication—the most influential gossip sheet in the region.

TELEVISION

Major Local Stations

Newcomers to Cincinnati often have trouble understanding Cincinnati's love affair with television and its personalities. You have to understand that the relationship between viewers and TV goes back to the mid '40s here, when Powel Crosley began beaming Channel 5 out of Crosley Square downtown. Legends such as daytime talk show host Ruth Lyons, anchorman Bob Braun, funnyman Paul Dixon, and some Dayton kid named Phil Donahue are still spoken of reverently in these parts. (Lucky is the person who wrangles an invite to dine with "The Lunch Bunch," a group of old-time television stars who meet monthly to swap stories.)

While today's television landscape is nowhere near as colorful as the past's, Cincinnati does offer a wide variety of viewing options and newscasts. We've got ABC, CBS, and NBC affiliates as well as Fox and WB stations. We've got not one but two PBS stations: Channel 48 and Channel 54. With a good antenna, you can also pull in Dayton stations 2, 7, 14, 16, 22, and 45. Channels 14 and 16, both PBS stations, are also carried on cable, which means lucky cable viewers have a grand total of four different PBS channels (making Cincinnati a great spot to raise kids—all *Barney,* all the time).

That's the good news. The bad news is that these are the only stations Greater Cincinnati will *ever* have. The new PAX

i

You've just arrived in town and don't know what TV newscast to watch? A shorthand guide: Channel 5, consumer news. Channel 9, hard news. Channel 12, cutesy features. Channel 19, crime and punishment. All nightly newscasts air at 11:00 P.M., except for Channel 19, which airs at 10:00 P.M.

network, for instance, wanted to start a station here in Cincinnati but found it couldn't. Due to our proximity to other major TV markets (Dayton, Columbus, Louisville, Lexington, and even Indianapolis), all the available broadcast bandwidths are taken up. The FCC won't allow a new channel here for fear its signal would interfere with a neighboring city's existing channel.

Channel 5 WLWT
1700 Young Street
(513) 412-5000

This NBC affiliate's newscasts offer solid reportage on beats such as education and personal health but also stress a heavy emphasis on the crime du jour. Channel 5 is known as "the mayor's station." That's because two of the station's anchormen—Charlie Luken and Jerry Springer (yes, *that* Jerry Springer)—have served as mayor of Cincinnati. A third anchor, Courtis Fuller, recently ran for the office as well. Must be something in the newsroom's water.

Channel 9 WCPO
1720 Gilbert Avenue
(513) 721-9900

This ABC affiliate is generally considered the best station for hard news in town, plus it broadcasts some award-winning I-Team investigative reports. Channel 9 dominated the ratings for many years as a CBS affiliate. Nielsen numbers show Channel 9 has been the local ratings leader for early-evening news for two consecutive years and in second place for the 11:00 P.M. nightly news. Anchor Clyde Gray has been manning the desk for the better part of two decades. Other veterans include Carol Williams, John Popovich, and Chic Poppe, with Dennis Janson at the sports desk and Laure Quinlivan knocking out I-Team investigative reports.

Channel 12 WKRC
1906 Highland Avenue
(513) 763-5500

This CBS affiliate has managed to stay on top of the ratings for its 11:00 P.M. newscast for a couple of years' worth of books. Part of that ratings success is due to the stability of the anchor desk: Rob Braun and Kit Andrews have been paired for years, along with weathercaster Tim Hedrick. Braun's popularity isn't hurt by the fact he's the son of a locally famous television entertainer, Bob Braun. This is certainly the station to turn to for weather reports: Hedrick, Steve Horstmeyer, and the others who staff the "Doppler 12 Weather Center" have nearly a century of weather forecasting experience between them. The station is owned by Clear Channel, which also dominates the radio market (explaining why there are so many cross-promotions between the newscast and the company's many radio stations).

Channel 19 WXIX
635 West Seventh Street
(513) 421-1919

The Fox affiliate, "Fox 19" offers a 10:00 P.M. newscast for those who like to retire early. The news team includes Jack Atherton, Tricia Macke, and Rich Appuzzo.

Channel 48 WCET
1223 Central Avenue
(513) 381-4033

The first public television station in America (its call letters are short for Children's Educational Television), this PBS affiliate airs the predictable fare as well as reruns of *Mystery!* and Ken Burns's various documentaries. Don't miss the channel's Cincinnati Pops specials.

Channel 54 WKET
600 Cooper Road, Covington, KY
(859) 258-7000

The town's other PBS affiliate. Airs much the same as Channel 48, though the Covington station's Kentucky programming includes some terrific bluegrass and down-home music.

Channel 64 WSTR
5177 Fishwick Drive
(513) 641-4400
The WB affiliate, it's otherwise known as Star 64. Programming includes endless reruns of *Seinfeld* and other sitcoms from the '80s and '90s.

Public Access

Public access broadcasting is provided by locally based programmers (listed below) and is carried on Time Warner Cable's Channel 24. Programmers encourage community participation. Shows produced in an average week by the various programmers include "Your Civil Rights," "Basement Flava Classic," and "TV Toastmasters."

Anderson-Union Community Television, 8550 Beechmont Avenue, Suite 800, Anderson, (513) 474-3488.

Media Bridges (formerly Cincinnati Community Video), 1100 Race Street (513) 651-4171.

Waycross Community Media, 2086 Waycross Road, Forest Park, (513) 825-2429.

Intercommunity Cable Regulatory Commission, 2492 Commodity Circle, (513) 772-4272.

Norwood Community Television, 2020 Sherman Avenue, Norwood, (513) 396-5573.

Cable TV

If you have a complaint relating to your cable operation, Greater Cincinnati has outlets to help you. Cable subscribers within Cincinnati city limits can call the city's Office of Cable Communications at (513) 352-1914. Subscribers in the suburbs can call the Intercommunity Cable Regulatory Commission of Southwest Ohio at (513) 772-4272. In Northern Kentucky, call the Kenton-Boone Counties Cable Television Board at (859) 261-1300.

Former Cincinnati mayor and TV anchorman Jerry Springer is certainly the city's most notable contribution to the nation's current television landscape. Locals shudder over what bizarre aberration, manic fistfight, or deviation in the gene pool will appear next on Springer's daily syndicated talk circus. But they watch. Oh, they do watch.

Adelphia
1272 Ebenezer Road
(888) 683-1000
This company serves rural areas on the extreme western side of Greater Cincinnati, including Delhi, Miami, Whitewater, Cleves, Addyston, and North Bend.

Insight Communications
717 Madison Avenue, Covington, KY
(859) 431-0300
Insight Communications serves all of Northern Kentucky with two levels: basic (24 channels) and classic (more than 78 channels). Prices for the basic package differ depending on the location.

Time Warner Cable
11252 Cornell Park Drive, Blue Ash
(513) 469-1112
Time Warner serves Cincinnati and most of Hamilton County, offering three cable packages—basic, expanded, and standard. It is in the process of upgrading its lines from coaxial to fiber optic (digital cable), which allows for more channels. That upgrade is not available in all locations yet, though. Call to find out if your area has been upgraded. Since the far majority of Cincinnatians are served by Warner, it's worth highlighting their channel lineup: Offerings include Animal Planet, the Travel Channel, the History Channel, the Food Network, Soap Channel, Oxygen, Bravo, Sundance, Golf Channel, and Sci-Fi Channel. This, in addition to predictable fare such as HBO, Cinemax, Showtime, and the Movie Channel. Sorry, no Playboy Channel or any of its counterparts,

not in this conservative town. Warner also airs pay-per-view movies on five different channels, and there's an option to subscribe to 40 music channels (audio only).

TWC Cable of Ohio
341 City Centre Mall, Middletown
(513) 896-5455
TWC serves Butler County. It offers basic and expanded packages.

RADIO

Who listens to radio in Greater Cincinnati? About 1.6 million young people, ages 12 to 24, as well as 850,000 "older" folks, say ages 25 to 54. While Clear Channel Communications controls about half the market, there are a number of independent and mom-and-pop operations that beam out of high schools, college campuses, even a nursing home. WAKW is a particularly interesting story, an unrepentant Christian station (the traffic reporter, for instance, offers a quick prayer for accident victims). The College Hill operation is certainly the only radio station in the city with its own chapel.

We list the radio stations in order of their popularity in Cincinnati (as determined by a couple years' worth of Arbitron ratings). And no, to answer the question we know you are about to ask, there is no WKRP in Cincinnati.

WLW (700 AM)
8044 Montgomery Road, Kenwood
(513) 241-9597
Once the largest station in the country, WLW is still a formidable power here in town. Nicknamed "the Big One," the format is talk, sports, and shock radio. The programming on this Clear Channel station starts off tame in the morning with the pleasant Jim Scott, with John Phillips doing live traffic reports. Midday talk show host Mike McConnell takes on hefty political issues. Afternoon drive time is devoted to laughs and sports talk, courtesy of humorist Gary Burbank. Afternoon shock jock is Bill Cunningham. And during the season, WLW is the radio home of the Reds. WLW's history is rich: Rod Serling scribbled scripts here for a drama show that eventually evolved into *The Twilight Zone.* A freckled blonde named Doris Day got her first on-air job here. So did Rosemary Clooney, Andy Williams, Red Barber, the McGuire Sisters, Red Skelton, and Fats Waller.

i ***Turn your radio dial to 700 AM if you're seeking the latest news, traffic reports, weather alerts, and details on school closings. WLW is the town's information source when it comes to the radio airwaves. News is consistently delivered on the half hour—unless, of course, a Reds game is on the air.***

WEBN (102.7 FM)
8044 Montgomery Road, Kenwood
(513) 621-9326
This is the station every teenager in town grew up on, tuning in the morning Dawn Patrol. Programming on "the Frog" is album-oriented rock, cutting-edge comedy, and antics. Recently named Mainstream Rock Station of the Year by *Billboard* magazine, the station is perhaps known best for organizing the 'EBN Fireworks (also known as Riverfest) and for outlandish billboards.

WUBE (105.1 FM)
2060 Reading Road
(513) 699-5105
"B105" spins country music. This Infinity Broadcasting station was honored recently as the Country Music Association's large-market station of the year.

WGRR (103.5 FM)
2060 Reading Road
(513) 699-5103
"Great oldies all the time" is the motto of this Infinity Broadcasting station specializing in rock oldies from the '50s, '60s, and '70s.

WIZF (100.9 FM)
1 Centennial Plaza,
705 Central Avenue
(513) 679-6000
"The Wiz" plays urban contemporary and hip-hop. The station is a major sponsor of the Midwest Regional Black Family Reunion celebration. The station is owned by a local company, Blue Chip Broadcasting.

WRRM (98.5 FM)
895 Central Avenue
(513) 241-9898
"Warm 98" plays adult contemporary music. It's owned by Susquehanna Radio.

WMOJ (94.9 FM)
895 Central Avenue
(513) 241-9500
The "New Mojo" plays jammin' oldies from the '60s and '70s. It's owned by Susquehanna Radio.

WKRQ (101.9 FM)
2060 Reading Road
(513) 699-5102
"Q102" favors a top-40 format.

WKRC (550 AM)
8044 Montgomery Road, Kenwood
(513) 241-9597
Another Clear Channel talk radio channel.

WVMX (94.1 FM)
1906 Highland Avenue
(513) 686-8300
Clear Channel's "MIX" offers up female-friendly rock.

WOFX (92.5 FM)
8044 Montgomery Road, Kenwood
(513) 621-9326
"The Fox" is a Clear Channel property playing classic rock. Mornings are dominated by the adolescent antics of the syndicated *Bob & Tom* show. The rest of the day is devoted to rock tunes.

WCKY (1530 AM)
8044 Montgomery Road, Kenwood
(513) 421-9724
Sports is the rule of the day at this Clear Channel station.

WKFS (107.1 FM)
1906 Highland Avenue
(513) 686-8300
"The Kiss" is a Clear Channel property broadcasting in a top-40 format.

WYGY (96.5 FM)
895 Central Avenue
(513) 241-9500
"The Star" features country music, news, and traffic in the afternoon.

WAKW (93.3 FM)
6275 Collegeview Place, College Hill
(513) 542-9393
News, traffic, weather, and sports, all with a Christian twist. You gotta love their slogan: "There's nothing holy about dead air." Owner is Pillar of Fire Inc.

WCIN (1480 AM)
3540 Reading Road
(513) 281-7180
Classic R&B, talk radio, and religious shows are the staple of this station, which recently celebrated its 50th anniversary. WCIN, in fact, is the nation's second-oldest R&B station. The station is required listening in the African-American community—and beyond. The owner is John Thomas.

WDBZ (1230 AM)
1 Centennial Plaza, 705 Central Avenue
(513) 679-6000
Blue Chip Broadcasting recently launched the area's first all-talk radio station aimed at the African-American community. And WDBZ ("the Buzz of Cincinnati") has certainly maintained the buzz, especially during the city's racial tensions of 2001. Lincoln Ware was hired away from his longtime job at WCIN to become program director,

joined at the new station by Edna Howell-Parish, veteran news director at WIZF, and WLW talk show producer Jeri Toliver.

WHKO (99.1 FM)
1414 Wilmington Avenue, Dayton
(937) 259-2111
This Dayton station, playing "New Country," is consistently among Cincinnati's top 20 in the Arbitrons. The owner is Cox Ohio, publisher of the *Dayton Daily News*.

WAQZ (97.3 FM)
2060 Reading Road
(513) 699-5959
The station plays alternative rock. Owner is Infinity Broadcasting.

Public/Volunteer Radio

They don't top the Arbitrons, but Cincinnati has a thriving public and all-volunteer radio scene.

WAIF (88.3 FM)
1434 McMillan Street
(513) 961-8900
This all-volunteer station offers an eclectic array of programming, from world music to ethnic.

WGUC (90.9 FM)
1223 Central Parkway
(513) 241-8282
Classical music and NPR are the hallmarks of this, the former University of Cincinnati station (now an independent nonprofit).

WMKV (89.3 FM)
11100 Springfield Pike, Springdale
(513) 782-2427
This unusual station broadcasts from a nursing home in Springdale and counts many of the region's senior citizens as loyal audience members. Programming includes big band music as well as talk shows revolving around elder health and aging topics and programs hosted by such local notables as singer Mary Ellen Tanner, *Cincinnati Post* topics-on-aging columnist Alice Hornbaker, and editorials by Charlie Murdock.

WMUB (88.5 FM)
810 Oak Street, Miami University, Oxford
(513) 529-5885
WMUB is one place where you go for big-band music around here.

WNKU (89.7 FM)
Northern Kentucky University,
Highland Heights, KY
(859) 572-6500
"Your Natural Alternative" is the town's source for Celtic, acoustic folk, and bluegrass, as well as airing NPR and local public affairs. Particularly popular are Kathy Costello's Sunday afternoon Celtic bash and Katie Laur's Sunday bluegrass show.

WOBO (88.7 FM)
4156 Half-Acre Road,
Williamsburg Township
(513) 724-3939
Country, big bands, and ethnic dominate this all-volunteer station. Don Littman is the big-band man (Thursday and Saturday), and country men include Steve Doggett (Monday nights).

WVXU (91.7 FM)
1648 Herald Avenue
(513) 745-3780
This station features news, nostalgia shows (*The Shadow*), "intelligent talk radio," and jazz. Weekdays feature public radio talk and information shows. Mornings feature Cincinnati notables such as celebrity chef Jimmy Gherardi's *Everybody's Cooking*.

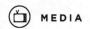

Other Stations

WCNW (1560 AM) Christian
WCVG (1320 AM) Gospel
WFCJ (93.7 FM) Inspirational
WHSS (89.5 FM) Voice of the Hamilton City School District, plus alternative music
WIOK (107.5 FM) Southern gospel
WJVS (88.3 FM) Voice of the Great Oaks Joint Vocational School District, plus adult contemporary
WJCY (90.1 FM) Contemporary Christian
WLHS (89.9 FM) Adult contemporary rock (Broadcasts from offices in Lakota High School in West Chester)
WLMH (89.1 FM) Voice of the Little Miami Local School District and rock
WMOH (1450 AM) Sports
WNKR (106.5 FM) Country mix
WNLT (104.3 FM) Contemporary Christian
WNOP (740 AM) Roman Catholic programming as part of the Archdiocese of Cincinnati
WOXY (97.7 FM) Alternative Rock
WRBI (103.9 FM) Country
WSCH (99.3 FM) Country
WTSJ (1050 AM) Christian

WORSHIP

Religion can literally be found on almost every corner of Cincinnati: The city has more than 1,000 churches, synagogues, temples, chapels, mosques, and other meeting places for various denominations.

The places of worship are some of the most interesting and historic buildings in our community. The crown jewel is probably the Cathedral Basilica of the Assumption in Covington, Kentucky. (See the close-up in this chapter.)

But there are many other historically and architecturally significant buildings, especially in the older parts of Greater Cincinnati such as Over-the-Rhine, Covington, and downtown. Then there also are some newer noteworthy architectural additions such as the Islamic Mosque in West Chester.

It would be impractical to write about all 1,000 houses of worship, so we provide you with an overview of part of the religious scene. However, if you're looking for a specific church or place of worship, check the Yellow Pages for listings of churches or, for specific times of worship, check the Saturday religion pages of the *Cincinnati Post* and the *Cincinnati Enquirer*.

A study by *Cincinnati Magazine* in 1995 showed that the No. 1 denomination in Greater Cincinnati was Roman Catholic. Baptist was a distant second, while Presbyterian and Methodist were third and fourth, respectively. Other religions in the top 10 were Church of God, Church of Christ, Jewish, Lutheran, Episcopal, and the United Church of Christ.

In 2006 *Cincy Business Magazine* listed the biggest congregations in the area as Good Shepherd in Symmes Township and St James in White Oak. Seven of the top-10 congregations sizewise were Roman Catholic.

Crossroads Community Church in Oakley is No. 6 on the list. It is the largest Protestant church in Ohio and one of the 100 largest in America. Some 5,500 people attend services each weekend at the church, housed in a former home improvement warehouse store. Other large Protestant churches include the Vineyard as well as congregations that meet in at least two renovated movie theaters, one in West Chester and one in Milford.

There are other superlatives at area houses of worship.

The smallest worship facility in the world is Monte Casino, on the grounds of Thomas More College in Crestview Hills, Kentucky. The chapel was used for prayer by monks working in the vineyards. The vineyards are gone now, and the chapel is near the entrance to the college, where it is more of an attraction these days. It is rarely used, because it can only accommodate a few people at a time.

The only replica of the tomb of Jesus in the United States, which includes trees and plants mentioned in the Bible, is in Covington's Garden of Hope.

The first Jewish cemetery west of the Allegheny Mountains is located in the West End.

Greater Cincinnati has been the home of many noted theologians. The Rev. Lyman Beecher headed the Lane Theological Seminary for 18 years, beginning in 1832. Although the most powerful preacher of his day, the Rev. Mr. Beecher was eventually surpassed in recognition by his daughter, Harriet Beecher Stowe, who used her experiences in Cincinnati to help write *Uncle Tom's Cabin*. Isaac M. Wise founded the Reform Judaism in America movement after coming to Cincinnati in 1854 and founded Hebrew Union College here. Joseph L. Bernardin, who later became a cardinal in the Catholic church, was named archbishop of the Cincinnati diocese in 1972.

There are several groups that promote ecumenism in Greater Cincinnati. The Northern Kentucky Interfaith Commission has existed for 30 years and provides a number of programs in Northern Kentucky including Exodus Jail Ministry and the chapel at the Northern Kentucky/Cincinnati International Airport.

In Cincinnati there are two organizations where ecumenically, various churches work together. The Metropolitan Area Religious Coalition of Cincinnati was created to bring people together during the race riots of the 1960s. Today it works with 16 local denominations on social issues in metropolitan Cincinnati in order to influence political decisions.

The second organization is the Council of Christian Communions, which has a jail ministry and sponsors the Weekday School of Religion at various schools.

On occasion, though, religious leaders also will get together for political reasons. Several ministers from the area's predominately African-American churches have formed a coalition known as the Black Ministers Conference. The conference has become an influential political entity within the city, regularly voicing an opinion on issues affecting the city's African-American community.

But the mixing of church and state doesn't stop there. Each holiday season, religion seems to dominate the news, which may not be too surprising except when the Ku Klux Klan and American Civil Liberties Union get involved. Several years ago, the Jewish Federation began erecting a large menorah on Fountain Square to celebrate Hanukkah. Offended, a local chapter of the KKK decided that because the menorah was in a public place, a giant wooden cross should be erected as well, and the KKK should be the ones allowed to build it. The battle over the legality of the idea raged between the KKK and the city, eventually ending up in the courts, where the KKK, with the ACLU's help, won the right to put up a cross. However, the Cincinnati city council voted to only allow "government use" for Fountain Square from mid-November to early January, effectively keeping the cross off the square during the holidays.

More recently, there has been some controversy about the Ten Commandments. In Adams County, monuments with the Ten Commandments were placed at four high schools in the Ohio county. A lawsuit was filed on behalf of one resident with the support of the American Civil Liberties Union. They were removed in 2003, but the case is under appeal.

On a more peaceful note, every Good Friday more than 10,000 Catholics from the area and from other states walk the 200-plus steps up a steep hillside to Immaculata Church in Mount Adams, pausing on each step to pray a bead of the rosary. This ritual has been going on for 138 years. And on occasion huge masses of people gather in suburban Norwood at the Our Lady of the Holy Spirit Center, where sightings of the Virgin Mary have been reported.

THE CATHOLIC COMMUNITY

The Greater Cincinnati area has a sizable Catholic community (222 parishes in 2006), which includes Roman and Anglican Catholics. Cincinnati became the eighth diocese in the United States, established by Pope Pius VII in 1821. As of 2006, the archdiocese included 500,000 parishioners.

In addition to those mentioned above, many of the area's Catholic churches are quite interesting. Downtown's St. Xavier church is on the National Register of Historic Places. The church was built in 1860 but burned on Good Friday 1882, only to be rebuilt. Xavier University and St. Xavier High School both had their beginnings as part of the church.

Old St. Mary's Church is the oldest Catholic church in Cincinnati and is a National Historic Site. Built in 1842 by German immigrants in Over-the-Rhine, the church features Bavarian-style stained-glass windows and offers Latin, German, and English Masses. Several churches also

CLOSE-UP

Houses of Worship Offer Food for the Soul, Feast for the Eyes

Many of the worship facilities in the Cincinnati area aren't just prayerful—they also are full of history and art.

From Old St. Mary's Church in Over-the-Rhine, which has remains of a martyr from Rome, to the Cathedral Basilica of the Assumption in Covington, Kentucky, with its Italian tile mosaics and paintings of Frank Duveneck, these buildings hold a wealth of artifacts and a record of the past.

Each has its own style. Old St. Mary's is simple because it was hand built by the early German settlers of Cincinnati. St. Peter in Chains Cathedral is in a Greek revival style. Elements of Christ Church Cathedral, an Episcopal church, are reminiscent of a church from Great Britain.

There is a treasure trove of historic churches in Greater Cincinnati that are very popular places for tourists and residents to visit, says Jo Ann Rice, a docent with the Heritage Program. "They're so popular because of the art, the history, and the architecture."

Many of the older houses of worship in Cincinnati still standing are in the Over-the-Rhine area. Old St. Mary's was built in 1842 and was soon followed by several other churches, including Philippus United Church of Christ and St. Francis Seraph.

Many of the city's early worship facilities were built near the river and have since been torn down to make room for development downtown, says Mike Crusham, a docent with the Cincinnati Historical Society who gives tours at St. Mary's. "[Cincinnati] was known as the city of steeples for a while." This was before taller buildings took over downtown, he says.

Many of the historic churches still in operation today are Catholic churches. Father Stanley Neiheisel, pastor of the Holy Cross Immaculata Church in Mount Adams, says the Catholic churches got many of the prime spots in the city because many of the early settlers in the city were Catholic. But there are other denominations that date from the middle of the 19th century.

Isaac Wise Temple was started in 1865. The Plum Street landmark is no longer used as the main temple for the Jewish people of Cincinnati, but it remains in use today on a limited basis. Its two steeples are still very much a part of the downtown landscape. A $2 million restoration was completed in 1995. The church was named after the founder of Reform Judaism and of Hebrew Union College.

The cornerstone for Old St. Mary's Church was laid in 1841 by German Catholics in the Over-the-Rhine area. It was built with trees from the nearby Pendleton Woods; they were carved by the men of the church, while the women baked the bricks for the structure in their home ovens, Crusham says.

The church's relics include the bones of a martyr and many items from other churches in the area that have closed, Crusham says. "It's a garage-sale, hand-me-down church," he says jokingly. The church's original items include the first clock tower in the city and stained-glass windows from Bavaria. The church still has Mass in German, Latin, and English.

St. Francis Seraph Church, 1615 Vine Street, was built in 1859. The corner it is on was the site of one of the first one-room churches in Cincinnati, built in 1818, Crusham says. The church is now run by the Franciscan friars who also operate various other ministries on the corner in Over-the-Rhine, including a soup kitchen and *St. Anthony Messenger,* a national Catholic magazine.

In the basement of the church are still the old gravestones from the Irish cemetery that was on the site before the church was built.

Erected in 1891, Philippus United Church of Christ has a dozen stained-glass windows depicting scenes from the Bible. Instead of a cross at the top of its steeple, a hand perpetually points upward, says Virginia Larberg, a Bridgetown resident who is the church's historian. "It's Philippus pointing the way." Philippus is located at Race and McMicken.

St. Peter in Chains Cathedral is the home of the archbishop of Cincinnati and was built in 1841 in Greek revival style. Its art reflects that and includes many statues and figures as well as the stations of the cross by artist Carl Zimmerman, a mosaic designed in Germany in Byzantine style.

Christ Church Cathedral congregation was founded in 1817, but the original structure no longer exists. The current building was constructed in 1951. However, the congregation preserved the Gothic-style Centennial Chapel that was built to celebrate the church's 100th anniversary in 1917. It looks like a chapel you could see in England. In the main cathedral are most of the stained-glass windows from the earlier church building finished in 1835.

Holy Cross Immaculata Church in Mount Adams also was one of the early churches in Cincinnati. Although it was built after many of the downtown and Over-the-Rhine churches, its history dates from 1859. It is probably one of the more popular churches in the area, especially on Good Friday, when about 10,000 people walk the steps up to the church while praying on each step.

Stanley Neiheisel, the pastor of the church, says there are 85 steps on the upper part near the church. But if you start on Columbia Parkway, there are an additional 150 steps to go up.

The church was built by Archbishop John B. Purcell, who encountered a bad storm on a return voyage from Rome. He prayed and told God that if he survived the storm, he would build a church on the highest point in Cincinnati, Neiheisel says. Immaculata is that church.

Inside the church are murals by Johann Schmitt, a local artist who also started the Art Academy of Cincinnati. Passionist priests ran the church from 1873 to 1996, but it is now back in the hands of the archdiocese. It is one of the many Catholic churches in Cincinnati that have art dedicated to Mary.

Northern Kentucky also has some historically interesting churches. Mother of God Church on West Sixth Street in Covington was built by the German community in 1841. The church is in an Italian Renaissance style, with stained-glass windows imported from Germany in 1890 and five murals created by parishioner Johann Schmitt, some of whose works are in the Vatican.

Trinity Episcopal Church on Madison

Continued

Avenue in Covington was built in the late 19th century, but the church community has been in Covington since the 1840s. The current building has more than a dozen stained-glass windows. It is well known for its "Midday Musical Menu," which offers workers in Covington music and lunch once a month.

But the crown jewel of religious facilities has to be the Cathedral Basilica of the Assumption, 1140 Madison Avenue in Covington, Kentucky. It is a masterpiece of architecture and art. It was renovated recently to restore the murals and clean the mosaics and stained-glass windows.

The cathedral claims to have the largest stained-glass window in the world. Its facade is patterned after Notre Dame in Paris, complete with gargoyles. Inside, there are paintings by Frank Duveneck, Italian mosaics for the stations of the cross, and three pipe organs. The Cathedral Concert series makes use of the three organs with concerts on Sunday afternoon once a month from October through April.

Many of the churches offer tours by appointment or after Sunday services. The Christ Church Cathedral on East Fourth Street downtown offers tours after the 10:00 A.M. service, as does the Cathedral Basilica of the Assumption. Many others offer tours by appointment including Philippus and Old St. Mary's. Other churches, such as Mother of God, St. Peter in Chains, and Christ Church Cathedral, are open on weekdays.

offer traditional Latin services including Sacred Heart in Camp Washington, which is part of the archdiocese. Two other Catholic churches (not part of the archdiocese) that offer Latin Mass are Immaculate Conception in Norwood and St. Gertrude the Great in Sharonville.

St. Peter in Chains cathedral downtown became the second permanent cathedral in the country when it was built in 1845. It now holds regular worship sessions—including one in which the service is signed for the hearing impaired—and all the liturgical functions of the archdiocese.

Many of the churches along the Ohio River participated in the Underground Railroad. One example is Bethel Baptist Church, which dates from 1799. Its facility built in 1853 served as a hiding place for slaves escaping to the North through the Underground Railroad. The church is located on Ohio Highway 125.

The Archdiocese of Cincinnati also has its own Roman Catholic seminary and graduate school of theology on the east side of Cincinnati.

The Athenaeum of Ohio also is the home of the Chapel of St. Gregory the Great, which has a number of special events throughout the year, including vespers and concerts that are open to the public. The Athenaeum Chorale (a semi-professional chorus) presents the events, which include "Advent Lessons and Carols" each December.

CINCINNATI'S JEWISH HERITAGE

Rockdale Temple was the first Jewish congregation west of the Allegheny Mountains, chartered on January 8, 1830. The temple, which was previously on Rockdale Avenue, is now at Ronald Reagan Highway and Ridge Road.

In 1846 German-born Jews, unhappy with the English-born Jews at Rockdale

Temple, established a new congregation, B'nai Yeshurun. They brought in Isaac M. Wise in 1854 to lead the congregation, which later became the foundation of the Reform Judaism in America movement. The congregation began constructing its own temple in 1866, after a two-year delay due to the Civil War. Now named after Isaac Wise, who led the congregation until his death in 1900, the temple is still the main sanctuary of the congregation. Members split worship services between this temple and the one in Amberley Village, also named after Wise.

The interior of the main temple, which is illuminated by 1,100 lightbulbs, is stenciled with Hebrew inscriptions in color and gilt. When the temple underwent a $2 million restoration in 1995, more than 65 colors and 135 different stencils were used to paint the interior. During the renovation, a prayer book and newspaper dated 1890 were found behind a wall. All of the pews and sanctuary furniture are original to the building, including an 1866 pipe organ. The temple is a National Historic Landmark.

Isaac Wise also founded the first rabbinic school in America, Hebrew Union College, in Cincinnati in 1876. The college now has additional campuses in New York, Los Angeles, and Jerusalem. The Cincinnati campus includes an extensive museum of Jewish art, history, and culture. HUC continues to make contributions to the Jewish religion: It graduated the first woman rabbi in 1972, and its scholars are leading the way in piecing together and translating fragments of the Dead Sea Scrolls.

Greater Cincinnati now has 23 synagogues. The Jewish Federation of Cincinnati includes the Cincinnati Board of Rabbis and the Rabbinical Council of Cincinnati.

A PLACE FOR EVERYONE

Regardless of your religious affiliation, you will most likely find a house of worship in the Greater Cincinnati area.

There are now about 250 local Baptist churches in the Cincinnati area, with much of the growth in Northern Kentucky. The Hebron Baptist Church opened a $3.7 million facility in 2006 and has more than 250 members.

The Columbia Baptist Church was the first Protestant church west of the Alleghenies, organized on January 20, 1790. The Columbia Baptist Cemetery, across from Lunken Airport, holds the remains of area pioneers, including Maj. Benjamin J. Stites, who led the first group of settlers to the area (they established homesteads in what is now the Columbia-Tusculum neighborhood). Union Baptist Church is the second-oldest predominantly African-American congregation in the state.

The area has 25 Episcopal churches, including Christ Church Cathedral, which was erected in 1835. The Boar's Head and Yule Log Festival, one of the oldest continuing festivals of the Christmas season, has been held here since 1940. (See the Annual Events chapter.)

Methodist denominations include Free Methodist and United Methodist. Milford United Methodist Church was founded in 1797, followed by Armstrong Chapel Church in 1798. For 120 years Armstrong Chapel was the only church in Indian Hill. The Korean Madisonville United Methodist Church offers services in both Korean and English.

Presbyterians founded Covenant-First Presbyterian Church in 1790. Lyman Beecher, one of the best-known preachers in the country in his day, served at the church. The Korean Presbyterian Church has a Korean School for its parishioners.

Among the area's 40 Lutheran churches is Concordia Lutheran Church, which still offers services in German.

Although many Quakers stayed in the eastern part of the state, three congregations made their way here, including the Friends Meeting, which was established in 1813, making it one of the oldest congregations in the area.

Six Mormon churches are spread throughout the area, including Cincinnati Stake Center in Fort Mitchell, Kentucky, and Cincinnati North Stake Center in Sycamore.

Hyde Park United Methodist Church does the most weddings in Greater Cincinnati each year—125, according to a study done by Cincinnati Magazine. *It's mostly due to the very popular Sunday Night Singles group that the church sponsors for singles of all religions and ages.*

The large Islamic mosque built in 1995 in West Chester serves the 3,000 to 5,000 Muslims in southwestern Ohio. Although Buddhists comprise a small segment of the population, their needs are met at the Yoseikan Zen Buddhist Center in Covington, Kentucky.

In addition to those mentioned above, many other religions and denominations are represented in the Greater Cincinnati area. There are also churches that offer services in Chinese, Latin, Spanish, Arabic, and sign language for the deaf.

RELIGIOUS ATTRACTIONS

Cathedral Basilica of the Assumption
1140 Madison Avenue, Covington, KY
(859) 431-2060
This masterpiece of architecture and art has just been completely renovated. The eight-month, $4.7 million project restored the murals and cleaned the mosaics and stained-glass windows. The cathedral's largest stained-glass window is 67 feet tall and 24 feet wide. It depicts two scenes with Mary because the cathedral's original name was St. Mary's. It also has an angel stepping on the devil. Tours are available after 10:00 A.M. Mass each Sunday. The church is open to visitors daily from 10:00 A.M. to 4:00 P.M.

Garden of Hope
699 Edgecliff Drive, Covington, KY
(859) 491-1777
The Garden of Hope is a replica of the tomb of Jesus. A pastor from Covington saw the original tomb in the Middle East and decided to build a replica for the people in the United States to experience the same magic. It is a peaceful garden full of artifacts from the area where Jesus lived as well as a statue of Jesus preaching the Sermon on the Mount. There also is a replica of a Spanish Mission church from California and a carpenter's shop similar to what Jesus may have worked in with his father. Many weddings are performed in the garden these days, and tours also are available. Admission is free and the garden is open from dawn to dusk.

Isaac M. Wise Temple
8329 Ridge Road
(513) 793-2556
This large temple actually has two locations. The Historic Plum Street Temple in downtown Cincinnati was dedicated in 1866. It is considered the main sanctuary of the congregation and is the choice of many families when selecting the setting for life cycle ceremonies. A major restoration of Plum Street Temple was completed in 1995 at a cost of $2 million. The Wise Center in Amberley Village, located on 30 wooded acres, is contemporary in design and houses the Religious School, a 260-seat sanctuary, social hall, and rabbinic and administrative offices. This facility was dedicated in 1976. A major addition, which increased the size of the building by 50 percent, was rededicated in 1996.

Skirball Museum
3101 Clifton Avenue
(513) 221-1875
The Skirball Museum in Clifton follows the life of the Jewish people in Greater Cincinnati. On the campus of Hebrew Union College on Clifton Avenue, the museum also teaches about Jewish traditions and the Holocaust. Besides artifacts from the early Jewish settlers in the tristate, the museum carries religious and artistic pieces as well as historically significant information.

The museum is open 11:00 A.M. to 4:00 P.M. Monday through Thursday and noon to 5:00 P.M. on Sunday. Closed on Friday and Saturday and on Jewish and national holidays. Admission is free.

INDEX

C

X

Y

Z

ABOUT THE AUTHORS

FELIX WINTERNITZ

Felix has lived in Greater Cincinnati for more than two decades. The Texas native attended Temple University and quickly moved from reporting stints at midsize dailies in Wilmington, Delaware; Savannah, Georgia; and Rochester, New York, to deputy features editor and entertainment editor at the *Cincinnati Enquirer.* Then, for six years, he worked as editorial director at *Cincinnati Magazine.*

He currently serves as senior editor at *Ohio Magazine* and *Long Weekend* magazine as well as editor of a sister publication, *Cincy Business* magazine. He also teaches a "Cincinnati 101" course on the city for the University of Cincinnati's Communiversity. Felix is a past president of the Queen City Society of Professional Journalists and continues to sit on the board of directors.

Felix's articles have appeared in *USA Weekend, Aloft Inflight Magazine, Quill Magazine, Writer's Digest, Panoramic Ohio, Cincinnati CityBeat, Xavier Magazine, Dayton Daily News, Hamilton Journal News, Cincinnati Business Courier, Community Press,* and numerous newspapers across the nation. He lives with his wife, *Cincinnati Post* reporter Connie Yeager, and their daughters Katie and Abby, in Anderson, just a few paces from the Cincinnati city line.

SACHA DeVROOMEN BELLMAN

A native of the Netherlands, Sacha moved to Willliamstown, Kentucky, at age 14. She studied journalism at the University of Kentucky. After a short stint at the *News Enterprise* in Elizabethtown, Kentucky, Sacha moved back to Greater Cincinnati to edit the *Eastern Hills Journal* and *Suburban Life Press* for *Community Press.* She worked for six years at the *Kentucky Post* and worked part-time as the editor of the *Equine Edition* and *In Your Prime.* She is currently a visiting instructor of journalism and adviser to the student newspaper at Miami University in Oxford, Ohio, and a freelance writer.

Sacha has won awards for her work from the Kentucky Press Association, Society of Professional Journalists, Scripps-Howard, Community Press, and Landmark Community Newspapers Inc. She lives with her husband, Tom Bellman, and their two sons, Brett and Alex, in Colerain Township.